Organization Theory and Design

SECOND EDITION

Organization Theory and Design

Richard L. Daft
Texas A&M University

WEST PUBLISHING COMPANY
St. Paul   New York   Los Angeles   San Francisco

Copy editing: Rosalie Koskenmaki
Artwork: Brenda Booth
Composition: Parkwood Composition Services, Inc.
Cover photo: R. Hamilton Smith/Frozen Images

Library of Congress Cataloging-in-Publication Data

Daft, Richard L.
    Organization theory and design.

    Includes bibliographies and index.
    1. Organization.   I. Title.
HD31.D135   1986   658.4   85-20256
ISBN 0-314-93170-8

To Kathy

Contents

PART III   ORGANIZATION STRUCTURE AND DESIGN

Chapter 5   **Organization Bureaucracy, Size, and Life Cycle 172**

PART V   MANAGING DYNAMIC PROCESSES

Chapter 9   **Decision-Making Processes 345**

Chapter 10

Chapter 13   **Organizational Learning and Renewal 519**

Preface

"Does organization theory have to be so theoretical?" "How will this stuff help me as a manager?" "Organization theory is boring." Comments like these from students motivated the first edition of this book, which tried to dispel the perception that organization theory is abstract, theoretical, and dull. This second edition is written for the same purpose—to describe the usefulness, interest, and applicability of organization theory concepts. Organization theory is intriguing, rich, and helpful. Organization theory frameworks have been developed from contact with real organizations. The concepts can help students and managers explain their organizational world and solve pressing problems. This book is written for the student, teacher, or manager who wants not only to understand organization theory, but to understand organizations and to function effectively within them.

Special Features Many students do not have organizational experience, especially at the middle and upper organizational levels where O.T. is most applicable. To reach students, a textbook in organization theory has to explain concepts in a simple and clear fashion, and provide real-world illustrations. Several features have been adopted in this book to achieve this outcome.

1. Over 95 case illustrations provide a real-world anchor, and most of these cases are new to this edition. Each chapter begins with an introductory case to pull the reader into the material. Several industry and government cases are used within each chapter to illustrate key concepts and frameworks. Additional examples are sprinkled throughout chapter discussions.
2. Each chapter ends with one or more cases for analysis. The new end-of-chapter cases are longer and more problem oriented than the first edition. Organization theory concepts are best and most powerful when applied to live organizational problems. This text takes full advantage of organization theory's ability to relate to the real world.
3. The book includes the most up to date organization theory concepts. The first edition included all topic areas that were in the domain of organization theory. To make the book even more current and relevant to students, new theoretical frameworks have been added to this edition. For example, the *population ecology model* has been added to the environment chapter; the *competing values model* has been added to the effectiveness chapter; *service technology concepts* have been added to the technology chapter; material on

new venture management has been added to the innovation chapter; new material on *management control systems* and *electronic information processing* has been added to the information and control chapter; *escalating commitment* has been added to the decision making chapter; the topic of *corporate culture* has been expanded and updated; the value of organization theory for *strategy implementation* has been described in the top management chapter; and the final chapter has been revised to incorporate the most recent thinking on *organizational learning and revitalization.*

4. Each chapter is organized into a logical framework. Many O.T. books treat material in sequential fashion, such as, "Here's view A, here's view B, here's view C," and so on. This book shows how the views mesh together. Several chapters conclude with a single contingency framework that organizes the major ideas into a single scheme.

5. Each chapter sticks to the essential point. The student is not introduced to the confusing theoretical and empirical squabbles that occur among organizational researchers. Most research areas point to a major trend, which is reported here. The essential point is then applied to real organizational situations.

6. Several pedagogical devices are used to enhance student involvement in the material. "A Look Inside. . ." introduces the chapter from an organizational perspective. "In Practice" illustrates theoretical concepts in organizational settings. Frequent figures and tables are used to help students visualize the material. "Summary and Interpretation" tells students which points are important, and what the points mean in the context of organization theory. "Guides to Action" tell students how to use material to analyze cases and manage organizations.

7. The book has been extensively tested on students. Feedback from students has been used in the revision. The combination of organization theory concepts and case examples is designed to meet student learning needs, and students have responded very favorably.

Acknowledgments   Textbook writing is a team enterprise. The second edition has integrated ideas and hard work from a number of people to whom I am very grateful. Reviewers made an important contribution. They were critical and blunt about things that didn't work well, and they offered many suggestions that were included in each chapter. I thank each of the following reviewers for their significant contribution to this text.

Robert Allison
Wayne State University

Thomas Keon
University of Missouri-Columbia

John Goodwin
Concordia University

Jean McGuire
University of Massachusetts

Royston Greenwood
University of Alberta

William Verespy
Sacred Heart University

Durward Hofler
Northeastern Illinois University

Edith Zober
Iowa State University.

A number of users of the first edition sent me suggestions to use in the second edition. The suggestions were excellent and I was able to include most of them. I want to thank the following people for their valuable ideas.

Peggy Anderson
University of Wisconsin-Whitewater

David B. Hoffman
Northern Michigan University

Judy Babcock
Rhode Island College

William J. Ickinger
Tulane University

George C. Davis
Jacksonville State University

Stuart M. Klein
Cleveland State University

Dennis Duchon
University of Cincinnati

Hugh Lena
Providence College

Cecilia Falbe
Baruch College

Udo Staber
University of New Brunswick

Behshid Farsad
Niagara University

Timothy V. Stearns
University of Wisconsin-Madison

Joseph Forest
Georgia State University

William D. Todor
The Ohio State University

Elizabeth Frederick
Oakland University

(Reverend) David T. Tyson, C.S.C.
University of Notre Dame.

I continue to owe a special debt to Don Hellriegel and John Slocum. Their valuable suggestions on the first edition continue to be evident in the second edition. Don gave me detailed suggestions for several chapters, granted me liberal use of his personal library, and offered many ideas for both teaching and writing about organization theory. John helped me acquire a few basic skills for textbook writing, and I continue to find them invaluable. John also provided several theoretical ideas and case illustrations that continue to be applicable in the revision. The book has many shortcomings, but it is much better than it would have been without Don and John's help.

I want to extend special appreciation to Phyllis Washburn. The revision was undertaken under impossible conditions. The amount of typing was great, exhibits were many, and deadlines were short. Yet the chapters were typed on time, every time, and without errors. Phyllis was cheerful and helpful during the entire project, and worked hard on a variety of things that gave me more time to write. It's still hard to believe we made it. Thanks, Phyl!

Several colleagues and students at Texas A&M also contributed to this book. Bob Albanese, Barry Baysinger, Ricky Griffin, Bob Hoskisson, Gareth Jones, George Rice, Jim Skivington, Kristen Skivington, David Van Fleet, Dick Woodman and Carl Zeithaml all provided intellectual stimulation and commiseration. Both were needed and appreciated. Several classes of students used the first edition without complaint and gave me feedback on what they liked and didn't like.

The editors at West also deserve special mention. Richard Fenton got the original project started, and Esther Craig has kept it moving. They both were wonderfully helpful and supportive. David Farr and Beth Wickum, production editors, provided several valuable suggestions. I appreciate their help on this text.

Administrators also played a role in this project. Lyle Schoenfeldt, Department Head, and Bill Mobley, Dean, maintained an almost perfect scholarly atmosphere here at Texas A&M. They also provided resources as needed. I also want to thank Richard Hand, who was Dean at Queen's during my formative years. His early guidance enabled me to grow and flourish in organization theory.

There is another kind of support that was crucial to the successful completion of this book. This book was written during evenings, weekends, holidays, and vacations. My wife Kathy and daughters Danielle and Amy learned what it was like to be without a husband and father. Kathy made a special contribution by supporting this book when all of us were sick of it. Kathy's love and encouragement were absolutely essential. Friday and Saturday evenings were kept free, and we made the most of them. Without Kathy's support, the book would not have been written. For that reason the book is dedicated, with love and affection, to her.

R.L.D.

Organization Theory and Design

PART ONE

Introduction to Organizations

■ *CHAPTER ONE*
Organizations and Organization Theory

Organizations and Organization Theory

CHAPTER TOPICS

- ■ **What Is An Organization?**
  Definition
- ■ **Organizations as Systems**
  Open Systems
  Organizational Subsystems
  Social Systems
- ■ **Dimensions of Organization**
  Structural Dimensions
  Contextual Dimensions
- ■ **What Is Organization Theory?**
  Models
  Contingency
  Levels of Analysis
- ■ **What Organization Theory Can Do**
- ■ **Framework for the Book**
  Major Themes
  Plan of the Book
  Plan of Each Chapter
- ■ **Summary and Interpretation**

JOSEPH SCHLITZ BREWING COMPANY

In the fall of 1976, the cloudy liquid from 10,000,000 bottles and cans of the beer that made Milwaukee famous flowed into the sewer systems of Memphis and Tampa. For months, bulldozers rocked back and forth catatonically in the yards of Joseph Schlitz Brewing Company's facilities in those two cities, destroying the defective product of a brewery gone haywire.

"It was absolutely demoralizing," remembers a Memphis plant worker who observed the secret burial. The bottles and cans crushed by the bulldozers contained hazy or "flaky" beer that had been recalled from taverns and stores across much of the country, lest it poison the loyalty of yet more faithful Schlitz drinkers. "You spend all that time and effort trying to make the best beer you can, and then you have to watch, day in and day out, as it's bulldozed under. We were literally crying in our beer."

During the years since, many thousands of persons associated with Schlitz—stockholders, employees, wholesalers—have shared this worker's sadness as they helplessly watched fortunes, businesses, and careers tumble along with the stature of the once-great company. Consider:

■ Since that fateful period in the mid-1970s, volume sales have plummeted about 40%, dropping the brewer from a strong second place in the industry (behind Anheuser-Busch) to a tie for fourth. The flagship Schlitz brand, which for most of the twenty-five years following Prohibition was the country's best-selling beer, now trails far behind six other brands, having lost almost six of every ten customers it had in 1974.
■ The value of Schlitz stock nosedived from about $69 a share to a low of $5, with investors suffering paper losses in excess of $1.7 billion in the process.
■ Independent wholesalers, angry and impatient with the company, turned their energies to other brands to fill their trucks and stay in business, making long-term prospects for a Schlitz turnaround that much more difficult.[1]

Schlitz's deterioration is a classic story of organizational failure. In the '50s, '60s, and early '70s, Schlitz experienced rapid growth and large profits. Then, suddenly, Schlitz was fighting to stay out of the grave. Schlitz suffered from an image so tarnished that many people were embarrassed to be seen drinking the beer.[2]

How could the number-one brewery collapse so dramatically? How could its management take the largest and richest brewery and ruin its reputation and future prospects? The answer is that Schlitz's situation is the consequence of several organizational mistakes, which began about fifteen years ago.

History When prohibition was repealed in the 1930s, each brewery had to start from scratch. Under the direction of Erwin C. Uihlein, the Joseph Schlitz Brewing Company pulled into the industry lead in 1947. Schlitz held the lead for ten years, but was not aggressive and did not take advantage of its position. One executive described Schlitz as "a big lion dozing in the sun" during these years.[3] A more aggressive Anheuser-Busch took over the industry lead in 1957

Loss of the industry lead jolted Schlitz's top management into taking action. A management shake-up followed. Erwin Uihlein became chairman, and his nephew Robert Uihlein became president (both were major stockholders and members of the founding family). They brought in Fred Haviland from Anheuser-Busch to take over marketing. They switched advertising agencies in 1961. These changes led to a series of innovations during the 1960s. The "pop top" can was introduced. So were the company's successful new products—Old Milwaukee and Schlitz Malt Liquor. Schlitz also imprinted American culture with its advertising slogans: "You only go around once in life so you have to grab for all the gusto you can." "Go for it, go for the gusto." "When you're out of Schlitz, you're out of beer."

Their First Mistake　In the late 1960s, Schlitz had abundant cash, and management decided to acquire other companies. Top management hoped diversification would provide stability and long-run protection against fluctuations in the beer business. Without careful investigation, the vice-president in charge of finance pumped $100 million into several ventures, most of which were unprofitable. He was promptly fired. A new financial expert was brought in to sort out the chaotic diversification effort. Several of the early acquisitions were sold, but new big-time acquisitions were never completed. Only a small vinegar and jug-wine producer and a grain farm were acquired. Schlitz had a chance to get Lowenbrau, a German-based beer, but lost out to Miller. Paul Masson was passed up because of the high price.

The diversification effort failed because family interests owned most of the stock. The family had power. After the early diversification mistakes, the family would not risk the loss of short-run dividends for long-run stability. The long-term prospects of Joseph Schlitz Brewing Company would thus rest entirely on its ability to make and sell beer.

Real Trouble Begins　Early in 1973, Robert Uihlein was moved up to chairman. For various reasons, the position of president and chief executive officer was not filled for about eighteen months. This is when the real trouble began. Schlitz started to drift because, as Jacques Neher said in his analysis of the company, "no one was minding the store." [5]

Individual departments began working independently of each other. Changes were made in the product without anyone consulting with marketing. Price increases were ordered by the financial department despite warnings from marketing that consumers would not pay them. Schlitz was reorganized into a straight functional structure. The brand management group was disbanded because marketing was no longer receiving priority. The brand management group had been responsible for coordination across departments, which was rapidly being replaced by conflict across departments.

A more insidious and dangerous change was also taking place. Gradually, perhaps without realizing it, Schlitz changed its strategic emphasis from marketing to cost reduction. The dominant group of managers was becoming concerned with production efficiency rather than with advertising, with cost reduction rather than with increased sales and customer allegiance. The bottom line was emphasized at the expense of the company's product and image. Non-marketing people, such as a finance expert and an attorney, were making operating decisions. Schlitz had once become the largest brewer in the country through sound marketing knowledge and principles. Now key decisions were shaped by people who had never sold a case of beer.[6]

The cost-reduction strategy led to two innovations, both in production rather than in new products. The more significant innovation was accelerated batch fermentation, which shortened the fermentation process from twelve days to four. The potential savings were enormous, because beer quality remained high. Anheuser-Busch retaliated with a rumor that Schlitz was brewing "green beer." The less significant innovation was the decision to cheapen the beer. Cheaper ingredients were used because the operating managers believed consumers couldn't tell the difference. Whether the green-beer rumor affected consumers or whether they could actually taste a difference, Schlitz drinkers began to defect from the flagship brand.

The Last Straw   Two additional events crippled the company. In 1976, nervous about a pending government requirement to list ingredients on cans of beer, the company dropped an enzyme and added a stabilizer called Chillgarde.[7] Unknown to the company, the stabilizer reacted with another ingredient and caused tiny flakes to appear in the beer after a short time on the shelf. The flakes looked bad and were not discovered until thousands of cases had been sold. The company shifted ingredients to correct the mistake, and this caused the beer to go flat. The result was a complete disaster. "Thousands of Schlitz drinkers who came upon the unappealing (but perfectly safe) beer were making their last purchase of Schlitz."[8] That year Schlitz physically buried 10,000,000 bottles and cans of beer.

The second event was Robert Uihlein's illness. He entered the hospital, learned he had acute leukemia, and was dead two weeks later. The organization was in chaos. Not a single marketing expert was left in the top management group. As one marketing staffer saw it, "It was amateur night at the zoo."[9]

Schlitz was now in a tailspin. Consumers couldn't leave Schlitz beer fast enough. Schlitz's image was severely damaged. In 1977, total corporate sales dropped into third place below Miller Brewing Company. Schlitz replaced managers and reinstalled the brand management group, but nothing helped.[10] By 1980, third place in corporate sales was lost to Pabst, and the Schlitz brand fell into seventh place.

The Present   Schlitz was now an acquisition target of other companies because of its low stock price. In 1982, Stroh Brewing Company purchased a controlling interest of Schlitz stock. Stroh gambled it could turn Schlitz around and at the same time enhance its own national competitive position.[11] The Joseph Schlitz Brewing Company could not rebound from its errors. Without help the company couldn't regain its competitive edge. The flagship brand still has a poor image, although recent advertising campaigns have halted the downward trend. One campaign is directed toward blue-collar people with the theme: "Here's to the guys who are making America great from the guys who make a great American beer—Schlitz." The latest campaign shows J. R. Ewing (Larry Hagman) from the T.V. show *Dallas* buying a Schlitz brewery because he loves the beer. This campaign also resurrects the magic of the gusto image with the line: "The gusto is back." These campaigns are concentrated in the Southeast, Southwest, and Midwest regions where the brand has suffered, but a few loyal followers remain.[12] Schlitz's products are still being sold and may once again prosper in the years to come. But an independent Joseph Schlitz Brewing Company exists no more.[13]

Welcome to the real world of organization theory. The rise and fall of the Joseph Schlitz Brewing Company illustrates organization theory in action. Schlitz managers were deeply involved in organization theory each day of their working lives. But they never realized it. Schlitz managers didn't understand how the organization related to the environment, or how it should function internally. We can't claim that formal training in organization theory would have prevented Schlitz's troubles. But familiarity with organization theory would have enabled the managers to understand their situation, and to analyze and diagnose what was happening to them. Organization theory enables us to explain what happened to Schlitz. Organization theory also helps us predict what will happen in the future, so we can manage our organizations more effectively. Each of the topics to be covered in this book is illustrated in the Schlitz case. Consider, for example:

Schlitz's lack of effort to ensure consumer satisfaction, and the alienation of instrumental organizations, such as distributors and wholesalers, are issues affecting the organization's environment. To survive and prosper, organizations must both respond to and control elements in the external environment. These issues are discussed in chapter 2.

Profit goals dominated at Schlitz during the early 1970s, to the detriment of such goals as product quality, diversification, and corporate image. Management was unable to balance multiple goals and was not sensitive to multiple indicators of corporate effectiveness over the long term. They were oriented toward short-term profit. These are issues of goals and effectiveness, the topics discussed in chapter 3.

As Schlitz grew and developed, it never took advantage of its size. In the early years, it was a lion dozing in the sun. In later years, Schlitz did not develop into a mature corporation, with impersonal administrative procedures and bureaucratic efficiencies. The family stayed involved too long. Moreover, the shift to a straight functional structure from a brand-management concept led to coordination problems between departments. Finance and production made decisions to suit their own narrow interests. The organization structure did not reflect task requirements, interdependencies between departments, or a market orientation. These are issues of organization size, structure, and design, which are discussed in chapters 4, 5, and 6.

Companies must change. Schlitz was innovative in the 1960s, when the pop top can and new brands were unusually successful. The production innovations in the 1970s were a disaster. These are issues of innovation and change. Techniques for managing change are described in chapter 7.

Information and control systems at Schlitz were not designed or used properly. Good information about the environment and internal problems was not available. Control was not used to achieve corporate targets. Information and control systems are discussed in chapter 8.

Decision-making at Schlitz was uneven. Several top-level decisions at Schlitz had no rationale. Cheapening the beer and changing ingredients without adequate testing hurt Schlitz badly in the marketplace. Managers were not paying attention to problems, were not following the progress of their solutions, and were not learning from trial and error. These are the types of decision-making issues covered in chapter 9.

The family with dominant ownership used their influence to direct the organization toward their short-run interest rather than toward long-run health and prosperity. Managers were removed when the family felt it necessary. These are issues of power and politics in organizations, topics of chapter 10.

Within the organization, conflicting points of view emerged. Mechanisms to decrease conflict between departments in order to improve overall corporate performance were not in place. This is an issue of intergroup conflict. Techniques for managing conflict are described in chapter 11.

Schlitz shifted from a market orientation to a concern for production efficiency to achieve profit goals. The misinterpretation of the external environment and internal corporate strengths was the biggest single error Schlitz executives made. These are issues of corporate strategy, which is the concern of top management in corporations. The top management domain is explored in chapter 12.

As part of Stroh Brewing Company, Schlitz is now struggling to renew itself. Stroh's managers have to undertake a massive turnaround by helping Schlitz learn what it takes to succeed in the marketplace. Techniques for organizational learning and renewal are covered in chapter 13.

The Joseph Schlitz Brewing Company illustrates all the topics covered in this book. Of course, organization theory is not limited to Schlitz, nor even to business corporations. Every organization, every manager in every organization, is involved in organization theory. Organization theory applies to elementary schools, universities, welfare agencies, not-for-profit foundations, symphony orchestras, local employment agencies, myriad government departments, and the YMCA. Organization theory draws lessons from these organizations and makes those lessons available to students and managers of organizations. The story of the Joseph Schlitz Brewing Company is important because it demonstrates that large organizations are vulnerable, that lessons are not learned automatically, that organizations are only as strong as their decision-makers. Organization theory provides the tools to make Schlitz, or any other organization, more effective.

Purpose of This Chapter

The purpose of this chapter is to explore the nature of organizations and organization theory. Organization theory has developed from the systematic study of organizations by scholars. Systematic research often seems formal and academic, but concepts are obtained from living, ongoing organizations. Organization theory can be very practical, as illustrated in the Schlitz case. It helps people understand, diagnose, and respond to organizational needs and problems. The next section begins with a formal definition of organization, and explores introductory concepts for describing and analyzing organizations. Then the scope and nature of organization theory is discussed more fully. We consider what organization theory can and cannot do, its usefulness, and how organization theory models can help people manage complex organizations. The chapter closes with a brief overview of the important themes to be covered in this book.

WHAT IS AN ORGANIZATION?

Organizations are hard to see. We see outcroppings, such as a tall building, or a can of beer, or a friendly employee. But the whole organization is vague and abstract, and may be scattered among several locations. We know organizations are there because they touch us every day. Indeed, they are so common we take them for granted. We hardly notice that we are born in a hospital, have our birth records registered in a government agency, are educated in schools and universities, are raised on food produced on corporate farms, are treated by doctors engaged in a joint practice, buy a house built by a construction company and sold by a real-estate agency, borrow money from a bank, turn to police and fire departments when trouble erupts, use moving companies to change jobs, receive an array of benefits from government agencies, spend forty hours a week working in an organization, and are even laid to rest by a church and undertaker.[14]

Definition

Organizations as diverse as a church, a local hospital, and the Joseph Schlitz Brewing Company have characteristics in common. The definition that we will use to describe organizations in this book is: **organizations** are social entities that are goal-directed, deliberately structured activity systems with an identifiable boundary.[15] There are four key elements in this definition:

1. *Social Entities.* Organizations are composed of people and groups of people. The building block of a social system is the human being. People interact with each other to perform essential functions in organizations.

2. *Goal-Directed.* Organizations exist for a purpose. An organization and its members are trying to achieve an end. Participants may have goals different from the organization, and the organization may have several goals. But organizations exist for one or more purposes without which they would cease to exist.

3. *Deliberately Structured Activity System.* Activity system means that organizations use knowledge to perform work activities. Organizational tasks are deliberately subdivided into separate departments and sets of activities. The subdivision is intended to achieve efficiencies in the work process. The deliberate structure is also characterized by mechanisms to coordinate and direct separate groups and departments.

4. *Identifiable Boundary.* The boundary identifies which elements are inside and which are outside the organization. Membership is distinct. Members normally have some commitment or contract to contribute to the organization in return for money, prestige, or other gain. The organization exchanges resources with the environment, but it must maintain itself as an entity distinct from the environment. A visible boundary is a necessary characteristic of organizing. When random pieces of scrap metal are organized they become a machine distinct from other machines. When sounds are organized they become a song that is distinct from other noise. When people are organized into a company to accomplish a goal, they become a social entity distinct from other companies. To exist, an organization must have a definable boundary.

ORGANIZATIONS AS SYSTEMS

Open Systems

One of the significant developments in the study of organizations was the distinction between closed and open systems.[16] A **closed system** does not depend on its environment; it is autonomous, enclosed, and sealed off from the outside world. It has all the energy it needs, and can function without the consumption of external resources. Early studies looked at internal workings of organizations to understand and explain organizational design and behavior. Early management concepts, including scientific management, leadership style, and industrial engineering, were closed system approaches. They focused on activities inside the organization. These approaches took the environment for granted and assumed the organization could be made more effective through internal design. The management of a closed system would be quite easy. The environment would be stable, predictable, and would not cause problems. The primary management issue would be to run things efficiently. The closed system approach to organizations is not really incorrect, but it is not complete.

An **open system** must interact with the environment to survive; it both consumes resources and exports resources to the environment. It cannot seal itself off. It must continuously change and adapt to the environment. Open systems can be enormously complex. Internal efficiency is just one issue, and is sometimes a minor issue. The organization has to find and obtain needed resources, interpret and act on environmental changes, dispose of outputs, and control and coordinate internal activities in the face of environmental disturbances and uncertainty. Even large corporations such as General Motors are vulnerable to the environment. Every system that must interact with the environment to survive is an open system. The human being is an open system. So is planet earth, the city of New York, and the Joseph Schlitz Brewing Company. Indeed, one problem at Schlitz was that top managers may have forgotten they were part of an open system. They concentrated on internal efficiency rather than on relationships with customers and other organizations in the environment.

To understand the whole organization, it should be viewed as a system. A **system** is a set of interrelated elements that acquires inputs from the environment, transforms them, and discharges outputs to the external environment. The need for inputs and outputs reflects the dependency on the environment. Interrelated elements mean that people and departments depend upon one another and must work together.

Exhibit 1.1 illustrates an open system. Inputs to an organization system include employees, raw materials and other physical resources, information, and financial resources. The transformation process changes these inputs into something of value that can be exported back to the environment. Outputs of the system include specific products and services for customers and clients. Outputs may also include employee satisfaction, pollution, and other byproducts of the transformation process.

Organizational Subsystems

An organization system is composed of several subsystems. The specific functions required for organization survival are performed by departments

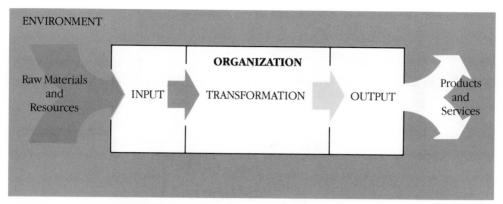

EXHIBIT 1.1. An Open System.

that act as subsystems. Each subsystem is a system in its own right, because it has a boundary and obtains inputs from other departments and transforms them into outputs for use by the remainder of the organization. Organizational subsystems perform five essential functions: production, boundary spanning, maintenance, adaptation, and management.[17] These subsystems are illustrated in Exhibit 1.2.

Production   The production subsystem produces the product and service outputs of the organization. This is where the primary transformation takes place. This subsystem is the production department in a manufacturing firm, the teachers and classes in a university, and the medical activities in a hospital. In the Joseph Schlitz Brewing Company, the production subsystem is that part of the company that actually manufactures the beer. The remaining subsystems are organized around the production subsystem.

Boundary spanning   Boundary subsystems handle transactions at organizational boundaries. They control the boundary and are responsible for exchanges with the environment. On the input side, boundary subsystems acquire needed supplies and materials. On the output side, they create demand and deliver outputs. Boundary subsystems work directly with the external environment. At Schlitz, boundary subsystems included marketing on the output side and purchasing on the input side.

Maintenance   The maintenance subsystem is responsible for the smooth operation and upkeep of the organization. Maintenance includes cleaning and painting of buildings and the maintenance of machines. Maintenance activities also try to meet human needs, such as morale, compensation, and physical comfort. Maintenance functions in a corporation like Schlitz include departments such as personnel, the employee cafeteria, and the janitorial staff.

Adaptation   The adaptive subsystem is responsible for organizational change. The adaptive subsystem scans the environment for problems, opportunities, and technological developments. It is responsible for creating innovations

ENVIRONMENT

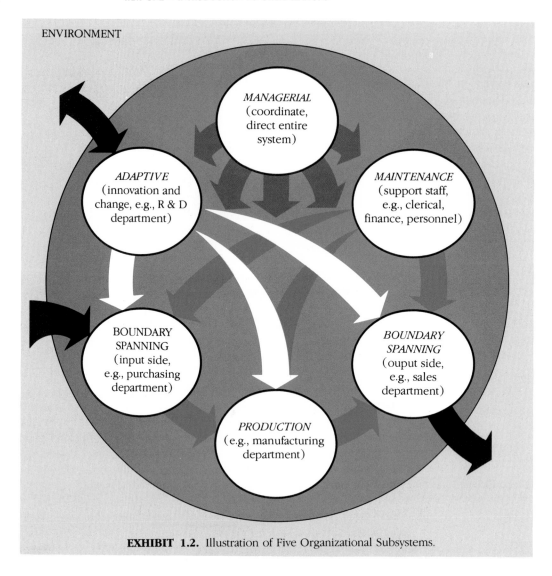

EXHIBIT 1.2. Illustration of Five Organizational Subsystems.

and for helping the organization change and adapt. At Schlitz, engineering, research, and the marketing research departments were responsible for the adaptive function.

Management Management is a distinct subsystem, responsible for directing the other subsystems of the organization. Management provides direction, strategy, goals, and policies for the entire organization. Management also coordinates other subsystems and resolves conflicts between departments. The managerial subsystem is also responsible for developing organization structure and directing tasks within each subsystem. At Schlitz, the management subsystem consisted of the chairman, president, vice-presidents, and the managers of functional departments.

The arrows in Exhibit 1.2 show how the five subsystems are intercon-nected, and indicate the extent to which an organization is an open system. In ongoing organizations, several departments may interact with the envi-ronment. Moreover, subsystem functions may overlap. Departments often have multiple roles. Marketing is primarily a boundary spanner, but may also sense problems or opportunities for innovation. Managers coordinate and direct the entire system, but they are also involved in maintenance, boundary spanning, and adaptation. People and resources in one subsystem overlap and perform other functions in organizations.

Social Systems

We have described human organizations as systems, and some of the char-acteristics we have identified apply to other systems as well. A thermostat is a system, and so is a houseplant, and a human being. Two things distinguish human organizations from these other systems. First, human beings are the basic building block, so organizations are social systems rather than machine or biological systems. Second, human organizations are incredibly complex, far more complex than other types of systems.

Kenneth Boulding analyzed many types of systems and concluded that they can be arranged in order from simple to complex.[18] Four levels of system complexity are illustrated in Exhibit 1.3. The simplest system is the framework, such as an atom, a bridge, or a building. Frameworks sometimes include movement among elements in a predictable manner, such as a clock or the solar system. Control systems are the second level of complexity. These systems are self-regulating. Thermostats and many types of machine systems, such as an assembly line or oil refinery, are control systems. The third level of complexity is biological systems, which are living, self-maintaining

EXHIBIT 1.3. Scale of System Complexity.

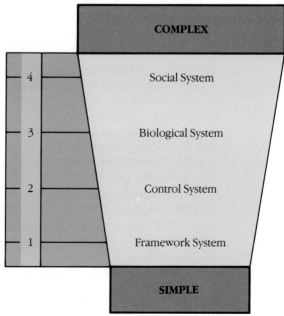

Source: Based on Kenneth E. Boulding, "General Systems Theory: The Skeleton of Science," *Management Science* 2 (1965):197–207.

systems. Plant and animal systems are far more complex than either control systems or frameworks. These systems exchange resources with the environment and can adapt on their own to changes in the environment. Many subsystems also make up each biological system.

The social system is the most complex system of all, and is at level 4. The social system incorporates forms of complexity beyond machine and biological systems.[19] The sources of this complexity are characteristics found only in human groups: norms and values appear and are intangible and hard to detect; cultural dimensions such as music and art appear; system elements (humans) display self-awareness; the structure of elements and roles continuously changes; and information is processed through abstract forms of language, symbols, and meaning systems.

Organization managers must be sensitive to the complex nature of the social systems if they are to understand and cope with their organizations.[20] Companies are open systems that must interact continuously with the environment, and they have subsystems to perform specific functions. These systems are also complex because of social characteristics. A number of factors interact so that it is impossible to completely understand and predict future behavior. Organizational dimensions interact so that changing one element may affect the whole system. A single cause does not have a single effect. Organizational systems can be difficult to manage because many important dimensions are intangible, a large number of factors can influence any situation, and external conditions change. If managers oversimplify organizational issues, mistakes can be made, as in the following incident at Alcan.

IN PRACTICE 1.1

Alcan Aluminum Ltd. (Canada)

Canada's Alcan and the U.S.'s Alcoa are rivals to be the largest aluminum company in the world. Alcan has a strong desire to be number one despite high energy costs, volatile aluminum prices, and the rise of third world producers that create environmental changes for the industry. Alcan has decided to purchase a major aluminum plant in the United States, has embarked on an energy drive in Quebec to improve profits, and is investing heavily in research and development to find more uses for aluminum.

Alcan also takes pride in its employees. Worker motivation and job satisfaction have high priority. Personnel innovations have been introduced in plants around the world to improve the quality of life for Alcan workers. Most of these innovations have succeeded, but one change in the Kingston, Ontario, plant produced an unusual outcome.

A personnel specialist proposed that time clocks be removed from the shop floor. With only limited discussion, the personnel manager agreed that time clocks were demeaning to the workers, and that all workers should be put on straight salary. Approximately 1,000 workers were affected, and for the first few weeks all of them enjoyed the new freedom. But after a few months, several problems emerged. A few workers began to show up late, or leave early, or stay away too long at lunch. Less than 5% of the workers were involved, but the problem had to be managed. People who worked a full shift found it unfair for other workers to receive full pay.

Supervisors had no previous experience with timekeeping or attendance, and now had new demands placed upon them. Supervisors had to observe and record when the workers came and left. They were also responsible for confronting workers who were late, which required interpersonal skills that many supervisors had not developed. The workers resented the reprimands, which led to a less supportive relationship between themselves and their supervisors. After just a few months, Alcan found it necessary to reduce the supervisors' span of control. Supervisors were unable to manage as many people because of the additional responsibilities. Moreover, pay was no longer docked when workers were late because they were on salary. Punishment was a letter written for the worker's file, which required yet more time and additional skills from supervisors. Workers did not want permanent letters in their files, so they filed grievances with the union. As grievances were passed up the hierarchy, both union officials and upper-level managers spent more time handling these disputes, which left less time for other management activities.

As Alcan discovered, the simple time clock was connected to many parts of the organization. The time clock influenced worker tardiness and absenteeism, closeness of supervision, whether supervisors had a coercive or supportive relationship with workers, interpersonal skills, forms of punishment and discipline, span of control, number of grievances, the relationship between union and management, and even the overall work climate in the Kingston plant. About eighteen months after the time clocks were removed, a personnel specialist concluded, after talking with several workers, that "nobody minded punching the time clocks anyway." [21]

Alcan is a large, complex social system. The personnel department is part of the maintenance subsystem at Alcan. Removing the time clocks at the Kingston plant led to unexpected outcomes for two reasons. First, personnel specialists assumed they understood worker values and attitudes. These are intangible dimensions of social systems, and differ from one part of the organization to another. Based perhaps upon their own values, personnel specialists assumed that workers found time clocks demeaning, when in fact they did not. Careful investigation is required to accurately assess employee attitudes. Second, the personnel department assumed that one cause had one effect, that removing time clocks would cause greater worker satisfaction. Single cause-effect logic may apply to simple framework or machine systems, but not to human organizations. Time clocks were interconnected with many other dimensions in the organization. Their removal eventually influenced such things as organization structure, worker climate, union-management relations, and supervisor roles. While it is hard to anticipate every outcome of an organizational change, managers should realize that unanticipated outcomes can occur, and plan for them. It can be a mistake to assume that an organization is similar to simpler systems.

DIMENSIONS OF ORGANIZATION

Organizations are open systems, within which the functions of production, maintenance, boundary spanning, adaptation, and management are performed. The systems view pertains to dynamic, ongoing activities within organizations. The next step is to look at dimensions that characterize and describe specific traits of organizations.

Organizational dimensions fall into two types—structure and context. **Structural dimensions** pertain to internal characteristics of organization. **Contextual dimensions** characterize the whole organization, and include size, technology, and environment. Structural dimensions are important because they provide labels to describe organizational differences. They are static dimensions, like the physical and personality characteristics of people, and they provide a basis for measuring and comparing organizations. Contextual dimensions are important because they describe the organizational setting and influence the structural dimensions. Both structural and contextual dimensions are necessary to evaluate and understand organizations.[22] Key structural and contextual dimensions are listed in Exhibit 1.4.

Structural Dimensions

1. **Formalization** pertains to the amount of written documentation in the organization. Documentation includes procedures, job descriptions, regulations, and policy manuals. These written documents describe behavior and activities. Formalization is often measured by simply counting the number of pages of documentation within the organization. Large universities, for example, tend to be high on formalization because they have several volumes of written rules for such things as registration, drop and add, student associations, dormitory governance, financial assistance, and even the use of bulletin boards. A small, family-owned business, in contrast, may have almost no written rules and would be considered informal.

2. **Specialization** is the degree to which organizational tasks are subdivided into separate jobs. If specialization is extensive, each employee performs only a narrow range of tasks. If specialization is low, employees perform a wide range of tasks in their jobs. Specialization is sometimes referred to as the **division of labor.**

3. **Standardization** is the extent to which similar work activities are performed in a uniform manner. In a highly standardized organization, work content is described in detail, so similar work is performed the same way across departments or locations.

4. **Hierarchy of authority** describes who reports to whom and the span of control for each manager. The hierarchy is depicted by the vertical lines on an organization chart as illustrated in Exhibit 1.5. The hierarchy is related to **span of control**—the number of employees reporting to a supervisor.

EXHIBIT 1.4. Structural and Contextual Dimensions of Organizations.

Structural	Contextual
1. Formalization	1. Size
2. Specialization	2. Technology
3. Standardization	3. Environment
4. Hierarchy of Authority	4. Goals
5. Centralization	
6. Complexity	
7. Professionalism	
8. Personnel Configuration	

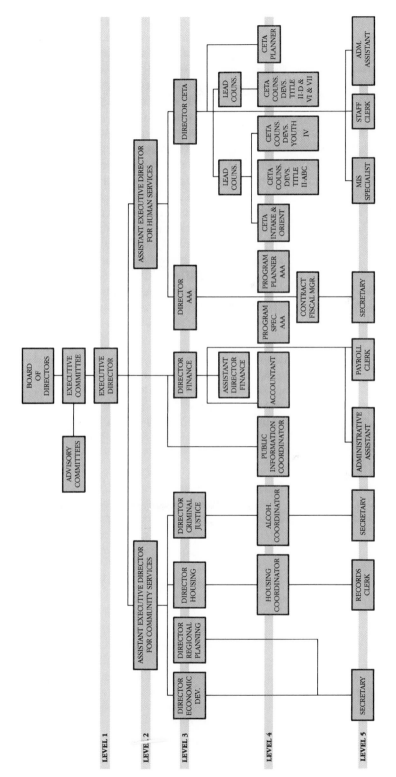

EXHIBIT 1.5. Organization Chart Illustrating the Hierarchy of Authority and the Structural Complexity for a Community Job Training Program.

When spans of control are narrow, the hierarchy tends to be tall. When spans of control are wide, the hierarchy of authority will be shorter.

5. **Complexity** refers to the number of activities or subsystems within the organization. Complexity can be measured along three dimensions—vertical, horizontal, and spatial. Vertical complexity is the number of levels in the hierarchy. Horizontal complexity is the number of job titles or departments existing horizontally across the organization. Spatial complexity is the number of geographical locations. The organization in Exhibit 1.5 has a vertical complexity of five levels. The horizontal complexity can be calculated as either thirty-four job titles or seven major departments. Spatial complexity is low because the organization is located in one place.

6. **Centralization** refers to the hierarchical level that has authority to make a decision. When decisions are delegated to lower organizational levels, the organization is decentralized. When decision-making is kept at the top level, it is centralized. Organizational decisions that can be centralized include equipment purchases, goals, choosing suppliers, setting prices, and deciding marketing territories.[23]

7. **Professionalism** is the level of formal education and training of employees. Professionalism is considered high when employees require long periods of training to be job holders in the organization. Professionalism is generally measured as the average number of years of education of employees, which could be as high as twenty in a medical practice and less than ten in a construction company.

8. **Personnel configuration** refers to the deployment of people to various functions and departments. Personnel configuration is measured by ratios such as the administrative ratio, the clerical ratio, the professional staff ratio, or the ratio of indirect to direct labor employees. A configuration ratio is measured by dividing the number of employees in a classification by the total number of organizational employees.

Contextual Dimensions

1. **Size** is the organization's magnitude as reflected in the number of people in the organization. Since organizations are social systems, size is measured by the count of employees. Other measures such as total sales or total assets also reflect magnitude, but do not indicate the size of the human part of the social system.

2. **Organizational technology** is the nature of the task in the production subsystem, and includes the actions, knowledge, and techniques used to change inputs into outputs. An assembly line, a college classroom, and an oil refinery are technologies, although they differ from one another.

3. The **environment** includes all elements outside the boundary of the organization. Key elements include the industry, government, customers, suppliers, and the financial community. Many environmental elements that affect the organization are other organizations.

4. The organization's primary **goals** define the unique purpose that sets it apart from other organizations. Goals are sometimes written down as an enduring statement of company intent. The goal statement defines the scope of operations, and the desired relationship with employees and clients. Goals are influenced by ownership, which are the stockholders in a business firm, members of a union organization, the parent company of a subsidiary, or the central government for a state agency.

The twelve dimensions above represent variables that can be diagnosed and analyzed for any organization. They provide a basis for measurement and analysis of characteristics that cannot be seen by the casual observer, and they reveal significant information about the organization. Consider, for example, the dimensions of W. L. Gore & Associates compared to Wal-Mart and a welfare agency.

IN PRACTICE 1.2

W. L. Gore & Associates

When Jack Dougherty began work at W. L. Gore & Associates, Inc., he reported to Bill Gore, the company's founder, to receive his first assignment. Gore told him, "Why don't you find something you'd like to do." Dougherty was shocked at the informality, but quickly recovered and began interrogating various managers about their activities. He was attracted to a new product called Gore-tex, a membrane that was waterproof but breathable when bonded to fabric. The next morning he came to work dressed in jeans and began helping feed fabric into the maw of a large laminator. Five years later, Dougherty was responsible for marketing and advertising in the fabrics group.

Bill Gore runs an organization without official titles, orders, or bosses. People are expected to find a place where they can contribute and to manage themselves. The company has some 2,000 associates (not employees) in twenty plants. The product lines are wire and cable, medical, Gore-tex fabrics, Gore-tex fibers, and industrial filter bags. The plants are kept small to maintain a family atmosphere. Several employees are assigned to develop new products, but the administrative structure is lean. Good human relations is a more important goal to management than internal efficiency, and it works. New plants are being built almost as fast as Bill Gore can obtain financing.

Contrast that approach to Wal-Mart where efficiency is the goal. Regional discount retailers such as Wal-Mart achieve their competitive edge through internal cost efficiency. A standard formula is used to build each store, with uniform displays and merchandise. Wal-Mart has over 500 stores, and the administrative expenses are the least of any chain. The distribution system is a marvel of efficiency. Goods can be delivered to any store in less than two days after an order is placed. Stores are controlled from the top, but store managers are also given some freedom to adapt to local conditions. Performance is high and employees are satisfied because the pay is good and over half of them share in corporate profits.

An even greater contrast is the situation in the welfare office at Newark, New Jersey. The office is small, but workers are overwhelmed with rules. One employee pointed to a four-inch stack of memos about recent rule changes resulting from Congress rewriting the laws concerning food stamp distribution. Employees don't have time to read the memos, much less learn the new rules. Applicants have to fill out four-page forms without a single mistake or food stamps will be delayed for weeks. Along with the rules, the number of applicants has also been increasing because of the recent recession. Most office employees have been thrown into serving clients and there is little staff to do typing and filing. Employees are frustrated and so are welfare applicants. Fights break out occasionally. One employee commented, "We're lucky we don't have a riot." [24]

Several structural and contextual dimensions of Gore & Associates, Wal-Mart, and the welfare agency are illustrated in Exhibit 1.6. Gore & Associates is a medium-sized manufacturing organization that ranks very low with respect to formalization, standardization, and centralization. A number of employees are assigned to non-workflow activities to do the research and development needed to stay abreast of developments in the fiber industry. Wal-Mart is much more formalized, standardized, and centralized. Efficiency is more important than new products, so most activities are guided by standard regulations. The percentage of non-workflow personnel is kept to a minimum. The welfare agency, in contrast to the other organizations, reflects its status as a small part of a large government bureaucracy. The agency is overwhelmed with rules and standard ways of doing things. Rules are dictated from the top. Most employees are currently doing workflow activities, although in normal times a substantial number of people are devoted to administration and clerical support.

Structural and contextual dimensions thus can tell us a lot about an organization and differences among organizations. Organization dimensions will be examined in more detail in later chapters to determine the appropriate level of each dimension needed to perform effectively in each organizational setting.

EXHIBIT 1.6. Example Characteristics of Three Organizations.

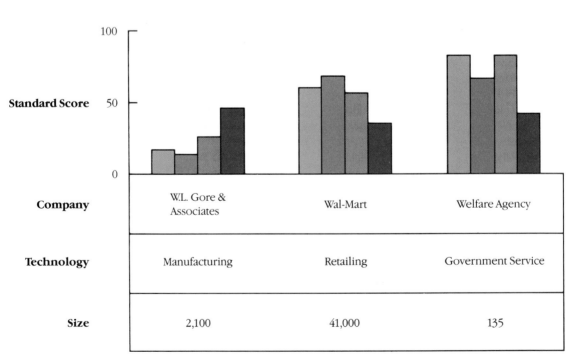

WHAT IS ORGANIZATION THEORY?

Organization theory is not a body of knowledge. Organization theory is not a collection of facts. Organization theory is a way of thinking about organizations. Organization theory is a way to see and analyze organizations more accurately and deeply than one otherwise could. The way to see and think about organizations is based upon patterns and regularities in organizational design and behavior. Organization scholars search for these regularities, define them, measure them, and make them available to the rest of us. The facts from the research are not as important as the general patterns and insights into organizational functioning.

Medical doctors are said to memorize the details of thousands of chemicals and drugs by the time they graduate from medical school. Engineers and physicists have precise formulas to calculate with incredible accuracy the stress tolerance of a piece of metal or the amount of force required to lift a satellite into orbit. Accumulation of facts and precise equations are not part of organization theory. The physical and biological sciences have a well-defined body of knowledge, and study often involves learning facts and formulas. Social systems, as we have already discussed, are more ambiguous and complex than physical and biological systems. Organization theory thus works with less precise relationships. A student of organization theory can acquire a vocabulary to describe organizational dimensions, and learn the patterns and regularities that explain relationships among those dimensions. Those relationships provide the basis for understanding organizational phenomena, diagnosing and analyzing problems, and responding with well-formulated solutions.

Models

One technique for understanding organizational relationships is the use of models. A **model** is a simplified representation of reality. A model is simplified because it never captures reality in its full complexity. A model describes a few important dimensions. Many types of models can be used to represent reality. In a mathematical model, dimensions are represented by abstract numbers, and relationships among dimensions can be computed mathematically. Physical models provide a physical representation of reality. For the movie "Raiders of the Lost Ark," a small-scale physical model was constructed for every set. The models were used to diagnose potential filming problems before the real sets were constructed. Verbal models are a verbal description of reality. An example of a verbal model is the description of twelve dimensions of organizations in the previous section. Schematic models are pictorial representations. A map is a schematic model of a geographical territory, and a wiring diagram is a model of a television set. Exhibit 1.2 was a schematic model of an organization as a system with five subsystems.

Throughout this book, we are going to be looking at organizations through the use of models. These models may contain several variables, or as few as two. **Variables** are organizational characteristics that can be measured and that vary in magnitude across organizations. A simple model may indicate that the variables of organizational size and standardization are positively related. That model would help a person understand and predict that large organizations require greater rules to ensure standard behavior for a large number of people. Even two-variable models can be important if they describe key relationships. When a larger number of variables are involved, as they often are in organizations, the model will be more complicated. Each chapter in this book reports models that can be used to understand important organizational patterns and processes.

Contingency

Organizations are not all alike. A great many problems in organizations stem from the assumption that all organizations can be treated as similar.[25] A consultant may recommend the same management by objectives (MBO) system for a manufacturing firm that was successful in a school system. Or a central government agency may impose similar rules on a welfare agency and a worker's compensation office. Or a conglomerate may take over a chain of restaurants and impose the same organizational charts and financial systems that are used in a banking division. These approaches assume that organizations behave according to universal principles, which is not the case.

Contingency means that one thing depends upon another thing, or that one characteristic depends upon another characteristic. What works in one setting may not work in another setting. There are no universal principles that apply to every organization. There is no one best way. Contingency theory means "it depends." The most efficient organization structure may be contingent upon the organization's size and technology. The MBO system may be contingent upon the professional level of employees. Organization charts and financial systems may depend upon the organization's past experience, ownership, environment, and technology. Big mistakes are made when organization contingencies are ignored or not understood, as in the case of the Joseph Schlitz Brewing Company. When the non-marketing executives gained influence, they were able to swing the profit strategy toward internal cost reduction and away from sales and advertising. The financial vice-president assumed that cost reduction was a universal principle, and that it would work at Schlitz. Strategy, however, is a contingency variable. Strategy depends upon the nature of the organization. Cost reduction to achieve profits is appropriate in a manufacturing firm that produces a standardized product in a consumer market. The organization must build and maintain a favorable image to win customer loyalty to its product line. The failure to appreciate this important contingency was a major reason for Schlitz's downfall.

Most research in organization theory is a search for contingencies. Investigators try to understand the relationships among variables so they can recommend which strategies and structures are appropriate in each situation. Because organizations are open systems, one important contingency is the environment. Organization theorists attempt to determine which organization characteristics allow firms to deal effectively with different kinds and rates of environmental change. Other important contingencies are organization size and technology. Since there is no single best way for firms to organize in all situations, the recurring question in organization theory is: What kind of organization does it take to deal with different environments, technologies, or sizes? The answers have great significance for present-day managers.[26]

Levels of Analysis

One of the confusing and sometimes perplexing aspects of organization theory is level of analysis. In systems theory, each system is composed of subsystems. Systems are nested within systems and one level of analysis has to be chosen as the primary focus. Four levels of analysis normally characterize organizations, as illustrated in Exhibit 1.7. The individual human being is the basic building block of organizations. The human being is to the organization what a cell is to a biological system. The next higher system level is the group or department. These are collections of individuals who work together to perform group tasks. The next level of analysis is the organization itself. An organization is a collection of groups or departments that combine into the total organization. Organizations themselves can be grouped together into the next higher level of analysis, which is the community. Other organizations in the community make up an important part of an organization's environment.

The concept of systems nested within systems can be extended beyond the four levels in Exhibit 1.7. The individual person is composed of subsystems (e.g., circulatory, respiratory), which are composed of organs (heart, lungs), which in turn are composed of cells, and the cells themselves are made up of smaller pieces of matter. Likewise, at higher levels of analysis, communities can be aggregated into a society, societies can be aggregated into the world, the world can be combined with other worlds to form our solar system, solar systems combine to form galaxies, and galaxies combine to form the universe.

Within this range of systems, organization theory focuses on the organizational level of analysis. In the study of social systems, the most powerful sources of causal explanation are the social system itself, and those systems one level above and below. To explain the organization, we should look not only at its characteristics, but also at the characteristics of the environment and of the departments and groups that make up the organization. Additional

EXHIBIT 1.7. Levels of Analysis in Organizations.

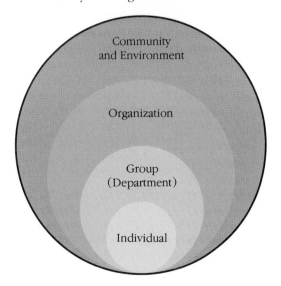

explanation may be derived by going to levels farther out, such as down to the individual or up to the solar system, but the impact of levels far removed tends to be less powerful. The focus of this book is to understand organizations by examining their specific characteristics, the nature and relationships among groups that make up the organization, and the collection of organizations that make up the environment.

But what about individuals? Are they included in organization theory? Individuals are the building blocks of social systems, and their role in organizations is important. Individuals do the behaving, make the decisions, and otherwise provide the energy that makes organizations go.

The answer is that organization theory does consider the behavior of individuals, but in the aggregate. People are important, but are not the focus of analysis in organization theory. Organization theory is a macro examination of organizations because it analyzes the whole organization as a unit. Organization theory is distinct from organizational behavior. **Organizational behavior** is the micro approach to organizations because it focuses on the individuals within organizations as the relevant unit of analysis. Organizational behavior examines concepts such as motivation, leadership style, and personality, and is concerned with cognitive and emotional differences among people within organizations. **Organization theory** is concerned with people aggregated into departments and organizations, and with the differences in structure and behavior of the organization level of analysis. Organization theory is the sociology of organizations, while organizational behavior is the psychology of organizations. Psychology concentrates on the individual person, while sociology concentrates on the social system.

Organization theory can also be characterized as the situation of organization participants. Organizational behavior is concerned with the *person,* organization theory with the person's *situation.* The dilemma between these levels of analysis is illustrated by the unusual shift of executives from Best Western to Quality Inn. Both the individual and the situation explained corporate success.

IN PRACTICE 1.3

Best Western International Inc.

Ronald A. Evans is doing fine as the new president of Best Western International. He is a conservative executive who will delegate responsibility, watch budgets, and facilitate slow, controlled growth. His style is democratic, and he is quick to respond to the wishes of motel operators.

Executives at Best Western are pleased with the change, which occurred when Robert T. Hazard, Jr. resigned. Hazard was a strong-minded leader who forced rapid motel expansion from 1974 to 1980. The chain increased from 800 to 2,597 hotels, and Hazard seemed involved in everything down to picking out the color of tablecloths. The installation of expensive new programs, such as a super sophisticated reservation system, didn't pay off. The disaffection between Hazard and hotel affiliates became irreparable.

The curious thing is that Hazard left Best Western to become chief executive at Quality Inns International Inc. Observers indicate he is doing well. Quality Inns had just finished a period of cost cutting and decline in order to survive, and is now ready for an ambitious building program. Hazard plans to increase the number of franchise units from 345 to 750 in about two years, will refurbish many of the hotels, and will revamp the computerized reservation system. Every one of Hazard's initiatives has been received enthusiastically by the board of directors.

Why is Evans doing so well at Best Western and Hazard so well at Quality Inns? After all, Hazard had to leave Best Western. The answer lies partly with the person, and partly with the situation. In the early years of Hazard's tenure at Best Western, the organization was ready for growth. Best Western needed to take advantage of the trend toward motor hotels and strong, top-down leadership was the way to succeed. But as Best Western matured, the situation demanded a different style. Maintaining orderly growth and a profitable operation became more urgent than rapid growth. Thus the democratic style of Evans suited the new situation at Best Western.

The same is true at Quality Inns. Quality Inns came through a period of decline to avoid bankruptcy, and is now ready to dive into a rapid growth period. An autocratic leader who pushes new ideas is the right leader in this situation. Quality Inns needs to move forward or lose its share of the market.[27]

The executive shuffle between Best Western and Quality Inns illustrates the importance of the situation. Hazard's leadership style was appropriate when it fit a high-growth situation. Other leadership styles were better for a situation of carefully controlled growth. Contingencies like the environment and the need for growth had significant impact on company profitability. The situation, not just leadership style, influenced performance.

WHAT ORGANIZATION THEORY CAN DO

Why study organizations? Most people who study organization theory belong to one of two groups—those who are managers or potential managers, and those who will not be managers. For the second group, the reason is to appreciate and understand more about the world around you. Nearly everyone works in an organization. Organization theory will provide an appreciation and understanding of what is happening in the organization. Organizations are a major part of our environment. They affect us enormously. By studying organizations you will know more about that environment, just as you would by studying geography, astronomy, or music.

For people who are or will be managers, organization theory provides significant insight and understanding to help you become better managers. As in the case of the Joseph Schlitz Brewing Company, many managers learn organization theory by trial and error. At Schlitz, the managers did not understand the situation they were in or the contingencies to which they should respond. Organization theory identifies variables and provides models so that managers know how to diagnose and explain what is happening around them, and thus can organize for greater effectiveness.

The study of organization theory is similar to the study of botany. People who do not work with trees find it enjoyable and enlightening to be able to identify and describe trees around them, know their history, their relevant differences, and the role trees play in ecology systems. For a manager at Weyerhauser, however, who is responsible for cutting trees in a forest, the value of botany is much more applied. Botany enables the manager to identify and label trees, and to make decisions about which trees to cut and which to ignore. The manager understands how many and what types of trees to cut down based upon needs for certain kinds of wood, and understands contingency relationships, such as between tree size and wood volume, age and wood quality, or tree type and wood density.

In a very real sense, organization theory can make a manager more competent and more influential. Understanding how and why organizations act lets managers know how to react. The study of organizations enables people to see and understand things that other people cannot see and understand. When managers use organization theory concepts, their organizations do better. Consider Richard Cyert, who is both an organization theorist and president of Carnegie-Mellon University.

IN PRACTICE 1.4
Carnegie-Mellon University

As the number of students entering colleges declines and as state and federal funding for education is cut back, many universities are starting to act like business corporations. Top administrators are adopting management techniques to run their organizations. A leading example is Richard Cyert at Carnegie-Mellon University. Carnegie-Mellon began a serious planning process in the early 1980s. Planners look carefully at competition, the marketplace, available resources, quality of employees, size, and what the students want. In a competitive environment, a university cannot be all things, and Richard Cyert has emphasized "comparative advantage" at Carnegie. By allocating resources to only a few departments that have exceptional strengths, Carnegie-Mellon has seen several departments catapult into national prominence. Student applicants are also up by 15%, despite the national decline in college applications.

Richard Cyert's background in organization theory has helped in other ways: "My work in organization theory has helped me understand the behavior of people and departments in a university. It became clear, for example, that our budget procedures were almost guaranteed to lead to deficits, for we started the process by soliciting from each budget unit the amount of money it expected to need in the coming year. Organization theory suggests that expected needs would be inflated, and that it would be difficult politically to reduce the initial estimates significantly. So I decided to reverse the procedure, starting with income estimates and allocating a specific amount of income to each unit based on university priorities."

Other universities use organizational planning as needed to fit their own situations. The University of Miami used it to overcome an image problem associated with race riots and the flood of Cuban refugees that discouraged applicants. The undergraduate degree program in education will be dropped, and additional money will be allocated to the Rosenstiel School of Marine & Atmospheric Sciences and to the School of Music. Stanford uses environmental analysis and planning procedures to reduce the gap between income and expenses. Planning enables them to cut expenses and still provide quality *education. The value of organization theory to universities, says Richard Cyert, is that "Organization theory helps put the problem in perspective. . . ."* [28]

The experience at Carnegie-Mellon, University of Miami, and Stanford show the positive side of what organization theory can do in the areas of environmental analysis, budgeting, goal conflict, and relationships among departments. Organization theory also covers many additional topics that will be discussed in this book. The next section provides an overview of these topic areas.

FRAMEWORK FOR THE BOOK

Major Themes

Three themes will appear throughout this book. One theme is the conflict between the ideal of a rational organization and the reality of a social organization. The second theme is whether managers should exert loose versus tight control. The third theme is management level because many organization theory topics pertain to upper-management levels.

Rational versus social system pressures   The **rational approach** to organizations strives for logic and order. This approach assumes the organizational world is stable and predictable. In this view, the manager's job is to arrange efficient work relationships and let the organization run as a machine. Managers try to organize as a closed system. Cost-benefit analysis and economic logic are the bases upon which decisions should be made. The manager's role is to push the organization toward maximum efficiency and rationality. The organization should be characterized by order rather than by disorder, as one early rational theorist wrote:

> For social order to prevail in a concern there must, in accordance with the definition, be an appointed place for every employee and every employee must be in his appointed place. Perfect order requires, further, that the place be suitable for the employee and the employee for the place.[29]

The **social system approach** assumes that organizations cannot achieve perfect order. Organizations may not even come close. Complex human organizations can be chaotic, irrational, and disorderly. As an open system, the organization responds to environmental turbulence, uncertainty, internal changes, technological developments, and shifts in consumer demand. Disagreement and conflict emerge. Organizational decisions may be based on power and politics. All these pressures work against order and tend to create disorder.

Management is in the middle of this conflict. Managers must balance the need for both rational and social organization, for order and disorder, for internal efficiency and external adaptation if the organization is to perform effectively. The pressures are illustrated in Exhibit 1.8. If the organization is managed too rationally, it may achieve remarkable efficiencies, but will not be adaptive, will not respond to the environment, and may not meet the needs of its employees. If the organization responds too freely to uncertainty

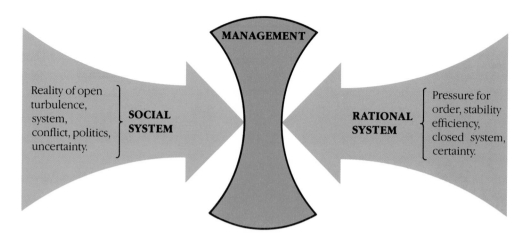

EXHIBIT 1.8. Conflicting Pressures from Both Rational and Social System Characteristics.

and external changes, anarchy could result. The organization would not achieve sufficient economies and efficiencies to survive.

Loose versus tight control   A basic assumption underlying organization theory is the need for managers to control the organization. In the face of disruptive social system pressures, the question becomes whether managers should accept loose control or strive for tight control over the organization. The answer is that management control is contingent upon factors in the organization's context. Some organizations have uncertain environments, nonroutine technologies, and are vulnerable to disruptive, social system influences. Other organizations have certain environments, routine technologies, and can be controlled much more tightly.

The terms and images associated with loose versus tight control are summarized in Exhibit 1.9. These terms appear throughout the book, but they come back to the same underlying theme—should organizational control be loose or tight? Tight control is typically associated with mechanistic internal processes, stable environment, a routine technology, large size, and goals of efficiency. Tight control is also associated with functional organizational structure, bureaucratic control mechanisms, formalized communications, stability, cooperation, and a rational, systems analysis approach to decision-making. Organizations that use loose control have organic, free-flowing internal processes, and typically exist in an uncertain environment, have a nonroutine technology, are smaller, and have goals that emphasize external effectiveness. Management tools associated with loose control include matrix structure, clan control, face-to-face decision-making, frequent change, conflict, and decision trial and error.

These concepts will be discussed in separate chapters of the book, but in ongoing organizations they often are related. An organization in an uncertain environment may also have a nonroutine technology, be oriented toward effectiveness, and use a matrix structure. Another organization might have a stable environment, a routine technology, bureaucratic control processes, and efficiency goals. The important point is that both types of control are correct, depending on the organizational situation. The discussion in

EXHIBIT 1.9. Topics Associated with Loose versus Tight Organizational Control.

Topic	Tight Control	Loose Control
Dominant Internal Process:	Mechanistic	Organic
Environment:	Certain	Uncertain
Technology:	Routine	Nonroutine
Size:	Large	Small
Goals:	Efficiency	Effectiveness
Structure:	Functional, Centralized	Matrix, Decentralized
Control Mechanism:	Bureaucratic	Clan
Communication:	Formal Information System	Face-to-Face
Innovation:	Infrequent	Frequent
Interdepartment Relationships:	Cooperation	Conflict
Decision-Making:	Rational Analysis	Trial and Error

each chapter will identify the appropriate setting and methods for the extent of control by managers.

Managerial level The third theme that appears in the book is managerial level. Organizations are usually divided into top, middle, and lower management. These levels are called the institutional level, managerial level, and operational level.[30] These three levels are illustrated in Exhibit 1.10. **Institutional level** managers are responsible for the entire organization. At this level, managers are concerned with goal-setting (e.g., profit, market share), strategy, interpreting the external environment, and how the organization can cope with the external environment. The institutional level is the domain of top management, and is described in the chapters on size, technology, and organization structure.

The **managerial level** pertains to major departments within the organization. The marketing department and research departments are examples. Managers at this level are concerned with the behavior of an entire department, and how the department relates to the rest of the organization. The managerial level is described in the material on work-unit technology, power and politics, intergroup conflict, and information and control systems.

The **operational level** is at the bottom of the organization. This level pertains to the supervision of employees who operate machines, type letters, teach classes, sell goods, and schedule work. The operational level is concerned with supervisors and individual employees.

This text focuses on the point of view of middle- and top-level managers. They are at the managerial and institutional levels in organizations. They have impact on the total organization. Several chapters treat the organization as a whole and cover techniques and strategies for managing the entire system. The level of major departments is also covered, along with techniques and strategies for management at this level. In many ways, the two levels are similar, but there are also important differences, which are explored in the chapters ahead.

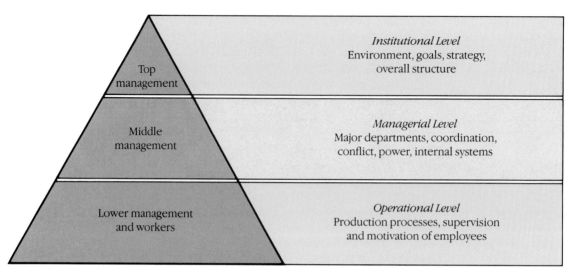

EXHIBIT 1.10. Institutional, Managerial, Operational Levels of Management.

**Plan of
the Book**

The topics within the field of organization theory are interrelated. Chapters are presented so that major ideas unfold in logical sequence. The framework that guides the organization of the book is shown in Exhibit 1.11. Part I introduces the basic idea of organizations as social systems and the nature of organization theory. This discussion provides the groundwork for Part II, which is about the external environment and goals and effectiveness. Organizations are open systems that exist for a purpose. The nature of the environment and the achievement of that purpose are the topics of Part II.

Part III describes how the organization is structured from the institutional viewpoint. Organization design is related to factors such as organizational technology and size. This section concludes with a chapter that explains how to design organization charts and reporting relationships for product, functional, and matrix structures.

Parts IV and V look inside the organization. Part IV describes how structure can be designed to influence internal processes such as innovation and change, and information and control. Part V shifts to dynamic behavioral processes that exist within and between major organizational departments. The management of intergroup conflict, decision-making, and power and politics are covered there.

In the concluding section, Part VI returns to the institutional level and considers the special role of top managers in organizations. In many ways, top managers are involved in all the issues discussed in Parts I to V plus have responsibility for corporate strategy and culture. The overall role of top management and its effect on the organization are examined. The final chapter incorporates recent topics of concern to top management as reflected in books like *In Search of Excellence* and *Theory Z* that explain how organizations learn and renew themselves. Human resources are used to attain higher levels of productivity. Organizations must learn, and they learn through employees at both the management and operational levels.

Plan of Each Chapter

Each chapter begins with an organizational case to illustrate the topic to be covered. Theoretical concepts are introduced and explained in the body of the chapter. Several IN PRACTICE sections are included in each chapter to

EXHIBIT 1.11. Framework for the Book.

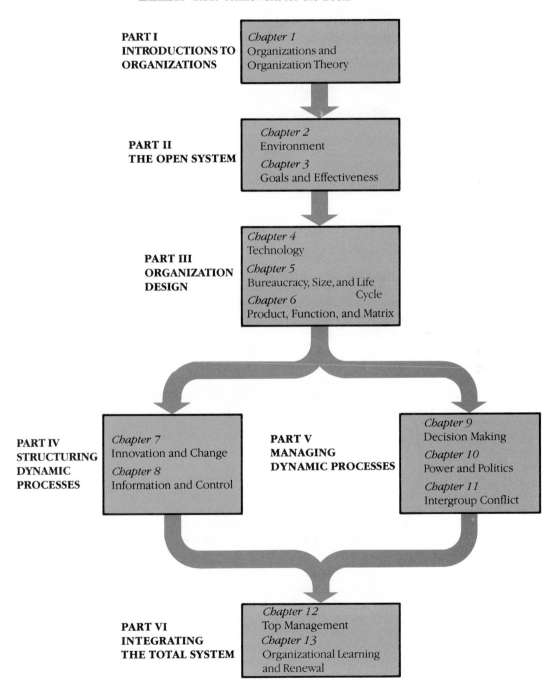

PART I
INTRODUCTIONS TO
ORGANIZATIONS

Chapter 1
Organizations and
Organization Theory

PART II
THE OPEN SYSTEM

Chapter 2
Environment
Chapter 3
Goals and Effectiveness

PART III
ORGANIZATION
DESIGN

Chapter 4
Technology
Chapter 5
Bureaucracy, Size, and Life Cycle
Chapter 6
Product, Function, and Matrix

PART IV
STRUCTURING
DYNAMIC
PROCESSES

Chapter 7
Innovation and Change
Chapter 8
Information and Control

PART V
MANAGING
DYNAMIC PROCESSES

Chapter 9
Decision Making
Chapter 10
Power and Politics
Chapter 11
Intergroup Conflict

PART VI
INTEGRATING
THE TOTAL SYSTEM

Chapter 12
Top Management
Chapter 13
Organizational Learning
and Renewal

illustrate the concepts and show how they apply to real organizations. Each chapter closes with a Summary and Interpretation and a Guides to Action section. Summary and Interpretation reviews and interprets important theoretical concepts. Guides to Action highlight key points for use in designing and managing organizations.

SUMMARY AND INTERPRETATION

The single most important idea in this chapter is that organizations are systems. They are open systems, which must adapt to the environment to survive. As social systems, organizations differ from other types of lower-level systems. Organizations are more complex and ambiguous. Thus the organization is a unique management situation, and concepts developed for simpler mechanical systems do not apply.

The focus of analysis for organization theory is not individual people, but the organization itself. Relevant concepts include the dimensions of organization structure and context. The dimensions of formalization, specialization, standardization, hierarchy of authority, centralization, complexity, professionalism, configuration, size, technology, goals and environment provide labels for measuring and analyzing organizations. These dimensions vary widely from organization to organization. Subsequent chapters provide frameworks for analyzing organizations with these concepts.

Another important idea is the difference between organization theory and disciplines in the physical and biological sciences. The usefulness of organization theory is not in the memorization of facts or in the application of precise formulas. Organization theory provides a set of concepts and models that inform the way a person thinks about organizations. Many of these concepts and models are not obvious and will not be learned through trial and error. Organization theory describes the patterns and relationships among organizational dimensions. If a manager understands important characteristics, other dimensions and behaviors can be predicted. Organization theory enables managers to understand their organizational situation, which is the first step toward effective management and control.

Finally, organization theory consists of certain themes or dilemmas that will appear throughout the book. One is the conflict between social system and rational system pressures. Managers try to balance this conflict by providing sufficient rationality to control and direct the organization. Organizational control may be loose or tight depending on organizational characteristics. In many settings tight control is appropriate, while in other settings loose control is preferred. Loose vs. tight control issues will be discussed in several chapters. Finally, most concepts pertain to the top- and middle-management levels of the organization. Topics are concerned with these levels more than with the operational level of supervision, motivation of employees, and production processes.

KEY CONCEPTS

closed system
contextual dimensions
contingency
goals
institutional level
levels of analysis
loose control
managerial level
model
open system

operational level
organization
organizational subsystems
rational approach
social system approach
social system complexity
structural dimensions
tight control
variable

DISCUSSION QUESTIONS

1. What is the definition of organization? Briefly explain each part of the definition.

2. What is the difference between an open and closed system? Can you give an example of a closed system?

3. What are the five subsystems in organizations? If an organization had to go without one system, which one could it give up and survive the longest? Explain.

4. Why are human organizations considered more complex than other types of systems? What is the implication of this complexity for managers?

5. What is the difference between formalization, specialization, and standardization? Do you think an organization high on one of these three dimensions would also be high on the others? Discuss.

6. What is the difference between vertical and horizontal complexity?

7. What might be the reasons for prescribing rules in detail? Is this helpful or harmful to the organization? To employees?

8. Discuss the meaning of the following statement: Organization theory is not a collection of facts; organization theory is a way of thinking about organizations.

9. What does contingency mean? What are the implications of contingency theories for organization theory?

10. What levels of analysis are typically studied in organization theory? How would this contrast with the level of analysis studied in a course in organization behavior? A course in sociology?

11. What is the value of organization theory for nonmanagers? For managers?

12. Early management theorists believed that organizations should strive to be logical and rational, with a place for everything and everything in its place. Do you agree with that approach to the management of organizations? Discuss.

13. How do the institutional, managerial, and operational levels in an organization's hierarchy differ? Which of these hierarchical levels are most relevant to organization theory?

GUIDES TO ACTION

As an organization manager:

1. Do not ignore the external environment or protect the organization from it. Exchange resources with the environment in order to survive and prosper. Because the environment is unpredictable, do not expect to achieve complete order and rationality within the organization. Strive for a balance between order and flexibility.

2. Assign people and departments to perform the subsystem functions of production, boundary spanning, maintenance, adaptation, and management. Do not endanger the organization's survival and effectiveness by overlooking these functions.

3. Think of the organization as an entity distinct from the individuals who work in it. Describe the organization according to its level of size, formalization, decentralization, complexity, specialization, professionalism, personnel configuration, and the like. Use these characteristics to analyze the organization and to compare it to other organizations

4. Be cautious when applying something that works in one situation to another situation. All organizational systems are not the same. Use organization theory to identify the correct structure, goals, strategy, and loose versus tight control for each organization.

5. Make yourself a competent, influential manager by using the frameworks and models that organization theory provides to interpret and understand the organization around you. Use organization theory to understand and handle such things as intergroup conflict, power and politics, organization structure, environmental change, and organizational goals. Organization theory can help you see and understand things that other people miss.

Consider these guides when analyzing the following case.

CASES FOR ANALYSIS

IN BROKEN IMAGES

Peter Vaill of George Washington University uses poetry to describe how courses in organizations differ from courses in other fields.[31] The following poem is one he uses to help students think about the correct mental set for approaching material on the behavior of organizations.

In Broken Images
by
ROBERT GRAVES

He is quick, thinking in clear images;
I am slow, thinking in broken images.

He becomes dull, trusting to his clear images;
I become sharp, mistrusting my broken images.

Trusting his images, he assumes their relevance;
Mistrusting my images, I question their relevance.

Assuming their relevance, he assumes the fact;
Questioning their relevance, I question the fact.

When the fact fails him he questions his senses;
When the fact fails me, I approve my senses.

He continues quick and dull in his clear images;
I continue slow and sharp in my broken images.

He in a new confusion of his understanding;
I in a new understanding of my confusion.[32]

Questions

1. Robert Graves's poem implies that facts are less important than senses. Is that true for organization theory? For a course in statistics? In finance?
2. Do the images in this poem correspond to the rational versus social systems approach to organizations? Explain.
3. The poem seems to value broken images, confusion, mistrust of facts, and the act of questioning. Is that an appropriate point of view for managers in organizations? For university students? Discuss.

PIERCE COUNTY*

Pierce County, the second largest county in the state of Washington, is located in west central Washington. It contains 1,676 square miles of land and 279 square miles of water. The county includes extremely varied topography, ranging from sea level to the 14,410-foot summit of Mt. Rainier. The present population is approximately 420,000 of which about 205,000, or 49%, reside in the eighteen incorporated towns and cities within the county. These towns and cities range in size from South Prairie with a population of 210 to Tacoma, the third largest city in the state, with a population of about 157,000. There are approximately 215,000 persons, or 51% of the county's population, who live in the unincorporated areas of the county.

Pierce County has a strong economic base; the three dominant forces are wood products, aerospace, and military support. The lumber and wood products industry has become much more sophisticated with plywood and paper production assuming greater importance. Aerospace activity, mainly related to Boeing, is currently strong as a result of a substantial backlog of commercial aircraft orders. Military support activity has fluctuated, although it is currently quite strong with indications of continued strength. The county is served by three major transcontinental railroads, excellent highways, modern airport facilities, and one of the finest deep water ports in the world, and is well situated for continued residential, commercial, and industrial growth. Several urban centers have developed throughout the county and a

* This case was prepared by Professor Davis W. Carvey at Pacific Lutheran University, Tacoma, WA. Preparation of this case was made possible by a grant from the Univar Corporation. Copyright © 1980. Reprinted with permission.

continued and steady population growth is anticipated in all areas of the county, which will exert a considerable impact on the need for governmental services to ensure orderly development in the future.

Pierce County is governed by a board of three commissioners elected, one each, from three commissioner districts. A number of other county officials, each with his/her own staff, are also elected, as mandated by the Washington State Constitution and subsequent statutes, including: the sheriff, clerk, treasurer, prosecuting attorney, and judges of superior courts (by state constitution), and the auditor, assessor, and coroner (by statute). The present county organization consists of approximately 1,200 employees, of which about 450 work under the county engineer in the department of public works. The overall organization is structured such that approximately forty department and/or other budget heads, some of whom don't even appear on the formal organization chart, report directly to the board of county commissioners. [See Exhibit 1.12.]

At least some of the hodgepodge nature of the present organizational structure can be attributed to the rapid growth of both federal and state programs impinging upon county government and services. Frequently, in order to obtain monies channeled through these programs, the county has had to establish a separate administrative unit to apply for funds and then administer that particular program. Many of these programs also result in overlapping responsibilities and relationships with a variety of other programs, governmental (federal, state, and local) units, and numerous planning and advisory groups. The result has been a growing bureaucracy consisting of many semiautonomous "fiefdoms" reporting to the commissioners. This system has been subject to increasing citizen criticism in recent years as more and more county residents become disenchanted with what they apparently consider to be an inadequate governmental response to their problems.

An attempt was made by the commissioners during the early 1970s to regain effective control over the county government organization by grouping the numerous individual programs into several major departments, each to be headed by a single administrator reporting directly to the commissioners. Unfortunately, even though a tentative organization structure was mapped out, the commissioners were never able to agree upon the operational details of the arrangement, and the idea was dropped.

Citizen criticism of Pierce County government in general, and of individual commissioners from time to time, continued to mount during the next few years. During this period a substantial and growing pressure for change developed, eventually culminating in a 1976 freeholder election to determine whether a "board of freeholders" (that is, a group of fifteen county residents) should be elected for the purpose of studying various forms of government and framing a charter for Pierce County (which would then be put to a vote, for approval or rejection). The most vocal support for the charter plan came from a group called Citizens for a Freeholder Election, chaired by attorney Robert Deutscher. This group conducted a year-long campaign to have the freeholder plan approved. The major opposition came from civic affairs leader Virginia Shackelford and the Factual Information on Freeholder Elections Committee, which she headed. The Pierce County Central Labor Council

EXHIBIT 1.12. Pierce County Government Organization.

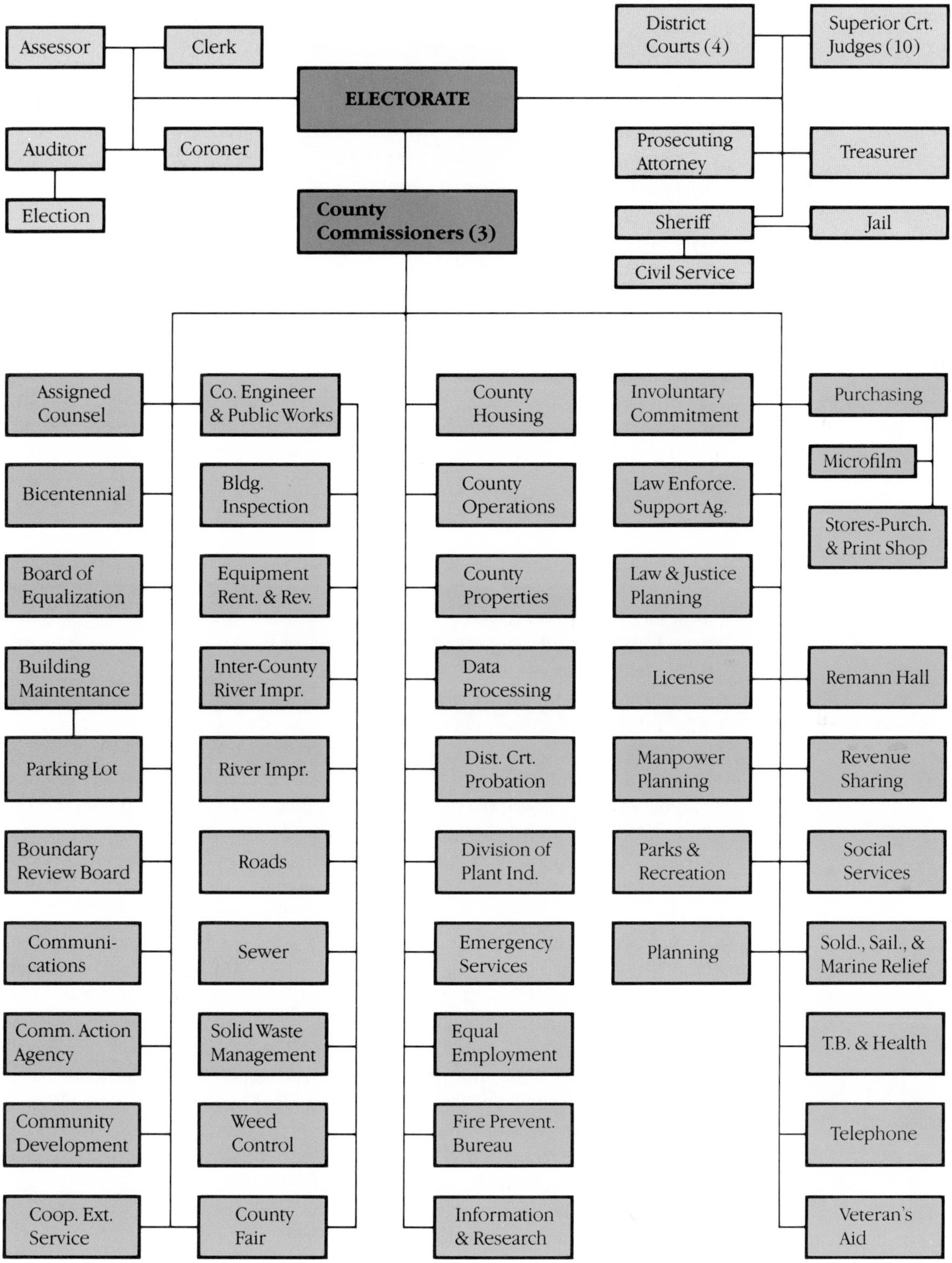

also came out strongly against the plan. The main arguments in favor of the freeholder plan seemed to be:

a. Need to eliminate the present system of political patronage in favor of a more systematic and fair means of hiring qualified county personnel.
b. Need to separate the legislative (that is, policy-making) from the administrative responsibilities that now rest largely with the commissioners.
c. Need to minimize external control by state agencies and the legislature, for example, over land use and zoning.
d. Need to consolidate a number of offices currently run by elected officials, for example, the auditor and clerk; the sheriff and coroner; and the assessor and treasurer.

Arguments against the freeholder plan were:

a. It would probably result in a strong executive council form of county government similar to that of King County (encompasses Seattle and is the most populous county in the state) and become less accessible to the people.
b. The cost of implementing the study and a new form of government would be excessive.
c. A new form of government is simply not needed.

The 1976 election showed that the citizens of Pierce County did want a change, although, judging from the election results, not as drastic a change as some had hoped. On the one hand, the freeholder proposition was defeated, capturing approximately 48 percent of the vote. On the other hand, the single commissioner up for reelection, two-term incumbent George Sheridan, was soundly beaten by state senator Joe Stortini. There was considerable post-election speculation as to why the voters turned down the freeholder plan; many knowledgeable observers attributed the loss to a combination of three factors: (a) voters didn't like the idea; (b) they were afraid of what might happen; or, (c) too many voters simply didn't understand the issue. Mr. Stortini, however, suggested that the voters were convinced that meaningful changes were possible within the framework of the present county governmental system, and that his own antiincumbent campaign may have contributed to the freeholder drive's defeat.

One of the Commissioner Stortini's first acts after being sworn in was to begin following through on his major reform campaign promises by announcing the appointment of two citizen task forces. One group was to be charged with designing a centralized personnel system, while the other would focus on developing a plan for restructuring the organization (both plans to be implemented within the present commissioner system framework). This action immediately drew the wrath of the local League of Women Voters. The *Tacoma News Tribune* article in Exhibit 1.13 gives an indication of the political climate faced by the new commissioner and his recently appointed task forces. Mr. Stortini, in spite of this early hostility to his methods, went ahead with his task force program. He presented each group with its formal charge at separate meetings during the early part of January (shown in Exhibit 1.14).

The Task Force on Reorganization soon found that the actual workings of the existing organization were so complex and yet so uncoordinated that it was difficult to get complete information concerning each county program in a reasonable length of time. Thus, after several meetings, they decided to proceed using the information already gathered and summarized in the preliminary matrix (shown in Exhibit 1.15), as a starting point from which to begin developing a meaningful organizational structure.

You have just been appointed as an advisory member on the Task Force on County Reorganization. Specifically, you have been asked to draft a pre-

EXHIBIT 1.13. Stortini Quickly Draws League's Ire.

By Barbara Anderson
TNT County Writer

The president of the local League of Women Voters took County Commissioner Joe Stortini to task this morning—even before his first meeting as a county commissioner.

Thelmagene Collings said she was bitterly disappointed that Stortini, who only took office this morning, did not consult the League for recommendations before naming members of two task forces to deal with county-government problems.

One group will try to develop a centralized personnel system for the county and the other will attempt to make plans for a reorganization of county government.

"He has talked about openness in government," Mrs. Collings said. "Yet his first act—these appointments—certainly were not done in the open.

"It's kind of like a slap in the face to a good-government group."

After being sworn in as county commissioner this morning by Superior Court Judge Waldo Stone, Stortini named these citizens to the two task forces:

*Personnel: Everett Foster, assistant budget director of Pierce County, chairman; Bruce Alexander, the county's contract-compliance officer; Dr. Paul Anton, associate professor of business administration at the University of Puget Sound; Robert Brewer, credit and insurance manager at Nalley's, Inc.; Sigmund Cook, the county's equal-employment officer; Les Crowe, the county's director of manpower planning; Dorothy Gannon, director of personnel at Tacoma General Hospital; and Elwin Hart, director of the county's law and justice committee.

*Reorganization: Jim Taylor, Pierce County coordinator, chairman; Dr. Davis Carvey, associate professor of business administration at Pacific Lutheran University; Tim Keely, chairman of the division of business and economics at Tacoma Community College; Keith McGoffin, attorney; Tom Raquer, community-development planner for the county; Les Rea, county purchasing agent; William Thornton, director of county public works; and Inez Weir, president of Weir's Corp.

Stortini defended the task forces, saying they are made up of people who are working in or are knowledgeable in the personnel or government fields.

"They have experience in making the necessary changes" he said, suggesting the experience was needed as he wanted recommendations from the groups in 30 to 40 days.

"When I was looking for people to appoint, I did not ask what clubs or groups they belonged to," he explained. "I asked for dedication and experience in the two fields.

"I would like to think these groups which are disappointed or are not a part of the task forces, rather than criticize, would work hand-in-hand with us for better government in Pierce County."

He said all task-force meetings will be open to the public. Meeting dates have not yet been scheduled.

Mrs. Collings said the League would begin monitoring the new Board of County Commissioners today.

Source: *Tacoma News Tribune,* January 10, 1977.

liminary organizational chart reflecting the latest in sound management thinking. Of course, this should also include a narrative, explaining in detail the rationale used in arriving at the organizational structure you recommend. The commission will also be especially interested in your comments pertaining to the expected impact of your suggestions on meeting both the program objectives of the county and the service expectations of the public. The Task Force, Commissioner Stortini, and the League of Women Voters anxiously await your input.

Questions

1. In addition to drafting a proposed chart, analyze and discuss the contextual and structural dimensions of the Pierce County government organization.

2. What are rational versus social system forces acting on the County Commissioners? Will these forces result in loose or tight control? Explain.

EXHIBIT 1.14. Task Force of County Reorganization.

Definition of Goals:

The primary goal of the Task Force on Reorganization will be the economizing of that portion of County government which is administratively accountable to the County Commissioners. The economizing of County government can be accomplished by the following:

1. The elimination of functions that have outlived either their political or administrative usefulness as a result of the recent election.
2. The consolidation of departments that are now either overlapping in function, or a duplication of effort.
3. The subordination of departments now operating independently when their goal would be more appropriately reorganized as a function of another department.

If the major goal of this task force is the economizing of County government, it should be achieved without the downgrading of either the effectiveness or the efficiency of the current level of service delivery. This is a delicate area for none of the three standards of measurement (economy, efficiency, effectiveness) can be substantially changed without affecting the other two. If the goal then is to economize without reducing the effectiveness or the efficiency of the delivery of services, then the basic assumption of the task force will be that there is a misuse of resources that increases neither the effectiveness or efficiency or service delivery; but instead, because of this misuse, indirectly impairs the potential level of service delivery. In short, we want to cut the fat out of the ham without ruining the meat.

Area of Study:

I believe the area of study should include the perceived goals of all departments directly accountable to the County Commissioners, inclusive of the operations of the County Commissioners themselves. By defining, articulating and studying individual department goals, similarities should emerge that will dictate appropriate recommendations for consolidation, elimination and the transformation of what was a goal to merely a function within another department.

EXHIBIT 1.15. Task Force for the Development of a Centralized Personnel System.

Definition of Goals:

The goals of this task force should be the development of a centralized personnel system that effectively incorporates the advantages of both a patronage system and a civil service system, while minimizing their obvious disadvantages.

The major advantage of a civil service system is found in the placing of individuals into positions commensurate with their abilities and needed by the government. This is, of course, a result of the development of job descriptions, classification methods, recruiting methods, and other characteristics of a personnel system. The major disadvantage of a civil service system is getting the work force to move in line with the needs of policy implementation, either through wrong action or nonaction. This is a consequence of the severing of accountability lines between the executive (Commissioners) and the work force.

I believe a centralized personnel system can be developed that will incorporate the advantages of accountability in policy implementation and the recruiting of qualified personnel for needed County positions. Politics will be a secondary factor to the primary needs of the County.

To reach this balance, the following must be existent in the personnel system:

1. The personnel director will be directly accountable to the Commissioners. This will ensure accountability in hiring and firing of all personnel.
2. All department heads will remain directly accountable to the Commissioners, while employees will be accountable to department heads. This will help in the development of a chain of command and increase accountability.

Areas of Study:

1. Present hiring practices to determine changes that must be made to develop uniformity in classification and pay.
2. Study of all positions in the County to determine whether they are productive toward individual department goals.
3. Development of standard job descriptions, outside of staff positions for elected officials.

EXHIBIT 1.16 Design of Task Force.

The most critical element in achieving the goals of reorganizing for economy and developing a centralized personnel system will be the composition of the two committees themselves. I believe the composition of the members of both committees should be homogeneous in outlook, so they may be able to reach agreement, but heterogeneous in background so that they can make distinctive contributions toward final recommendations. In short, the goals should be explicit and agreed upon at the beginning. Room for individual variation can take place within the means that are to be used to reach the defined goals.

Because of the strong similarities between the two committees, I believe that they should work concurrently, but independently. It would make little sense for the personnel committee to be reviewing the personnel practices of a given department that has been marked for consolidation or elimination by a Reorganization Task Force. I would propose that one consolidation or elimination by a Reorganization Task Force. I would propose that one individual be named coordinator for both committees.. The duties would be to set the direction the committees are to take, coordinate relevant activities and make assignments of members concerning public administration and the present political environment. I believe the committee structure could resemble the following:

COUNTY COMMISSIONERS

Task Force Coordinator

Task Force on Personnel — Task Force on Reorganization

7 members — 7 members

EXHIBIT 1.17. Department Responsibilities

The primary responsibility of each department shown on the Pierce County Government Organization Chart (Exhibit 1.12) is described below. The approximate number of full-time employees is shown in parentheses after the name of the department. A few departments not on the organizational chart are also described.

Assigned Counsel (9)
Defense services for those without legal counsel.

Bicentennial (0)
Dissolved at the end of 1976.

Annex Manager (17)
Maintenance, security and fire protection for the County Annex (a large suburban county office building).

Board of Equalization (7)
Property assessment and appeals hearings.

Tax Title Properties (1)
Inventory and disposition of tax title properties (i.e., properties owned by the county as a result of tax defaults).

Leases (1)
Negotiate and prepare county lease agreements.

Building Maintenance (45)
Maintenance of County-City Building (downtown Tacoma office building) operations and grounds (excluding gardens).

Community Action Agency (34)
Services for low-income residents.

Community Development (3)
Plan, administer and evaluate programs using federal community development monies.

Cooperative Extension Service (11)
Continuing adult education; primarily agricultural/farming related.

County Fair (1)
Responsible for yearly county fair; primarily with parks and recreation manpower.

Building Inspection (21)
Issue permits and perform building inspections.

Equipment Rental and Revolving (28)
Equipment purchase and maintenance (primarily county road department related).

Inter-County River Improvement (6)
Care and maintenance of rivers crossing County boundaries.

River Improvement (13)
Care and maintenance of rivers flowing only within the County.

County-City Parking (1)
Parking at the County-City building.

Boundary Review Board (2)
Activities related to annexations; expanding water, sewer or fire districts; and dissolution of special purpose districts.

Disability Board (1)
Disability, retirement and leave applications submitted by police officers and fire fighters of Pierce County (except the City of Tacoma).

County Coordinator (1)
Coordinate with the U.S. Corps of Engineers concerning permits for projects in navigable waters.

Overall Economic Development Program Committee (1)
Review and prioritization of public works projects to be submitted for federal funding.

Communications (5)
Technical operation and maintenance of all county communications systems (except telephone). Coordinate communications of surrounding fire districts, small town police, etc.

District Court Probation (10)
Pre-sentence reports, probation and parole services for Pierce County District Courts.

Division of Plant Industries (0)
Agricultural inspection services funded by the State.

Emergency Services (2)
Develop and execute plans to be used during emergencies.

Fire Prevention Bureau (15)
Fire inspections and related enforcement.

Information and Research (2)
Research, analysis and report preparation.

Involuntary Commitment (6)
Actions related to arranging care and/or hospitalization for the mentally ill.

Law Enforcement Support Agency (43)
Answer Pierce County emergency telephone number; and police dispatching for the Pierce County Sheriff and the Tacoma Police Department.

EXHIBIT 1.17. Department Responsibilities *(continued)*

Roads (236)
Road construction and maintenance.

Sewers (7)
Design and supervise sewer system construction.

Solid Waste Management (31)
Refuse disposal.

Weed Control (2)
Weed control (primarily toxic weeds along County roads).

Safety Engineer (2)
Job-related accident prevention.

County Housing (2)
Inventorying and planning for housing needs in unincorporated Pierce County.

County Operations (7)
Maintenance of buildings other than the County-City Building.

County Properties (6)
Maintain county buildings' grounds.

Data Processing (0)
Now contracted out.

Social Services (9)
Contract with outside agencies for social services.

Soldiers, Sailors and Marine Relief (0)
Part of veteran's aid.

T.B. and Health (0)
Tax money budgeted to the State for T.B. hospital facilities.

Telephone (5)
Telephone services (i.e., primarily switchboard operation).

Law and Justice Planning (6)
Crime reduction planning and improvement of the criminal justice system.

License (6)
Business and occupational licenses.

Manpower Planning (34)
Employment and training programs.

Parks and Recreation (65)
Parks and recreation.

Planning (23)
Comprehensive planning for the county; and administration of zoning and related codes.

Purchasing (6)
Purchasing supplies and equipment for County operations.

Central Stores, Print Shop and Mail Room (18)
Office supplies, printing and mail collection/distribution, respectively.

Microfilm (8)
Microfilm copying and film processing.

Remann Hall (104)
Juvenile court and related services.

Revenue Sharing (0)
Federal money budgeted through individual departments.

Veteran's Aid (4)
Veteran's emergency services.

Area Agency on Aging (7)
Services for older citizens.

Equal Employment Opportunity (3)
Implementing and monitoring effectiveness of the Pierce County Affirmative Action plan.

NOTES

1. Jacques Neher, "What Went Wrong," *Advertising Age,* April 13, 1981, p. 61.

2. Mark Schulz, Mike Agar, and Jim Grubert, "The Rise and Fall of Schlitz: A Case Analysis," unpublished manuscript, Texas A&M University, November, 1981, p. 1.

3. Neher, "What Went Wrong," p. 62.

4. Schulz, Agar, and Grubert, "Rise and Fall of Schlitz," p. 1.

5. Neher, "What Went Wrong," p. 64.

6. "Schlitz Puts Top Marketing Men on Leave; Cites Probes," *Advertising Age,* August 30, 1976, p. 2.

7. Jacques Neher, "Lost at Sea," *Advertising Age,* April 20, 1981, p. 49.

8. Ibid.

9. Ibid., p. 52.

10. Christy Marshall, "Schlitz Reverts to Brand Management Structure," *Advertising Age,* July 3, 1978, p. 3.

11. "U.S. Conditionally Lets Stroh Buy Schlitz," *The Wall Street Journal,* April 19, 1982, p. 4; "Stroh's Gamble in Swallowing Schlitz," *Business Week,* April 26, 1982, pp. 31–32.

12. Arthur M. Louis, "Schlitz's Crafty Taste Test," *Fortune,* January 26, 1981, pp. 32–34; Jay McCormick, "Schlitz is back with 'Gusto' Ads," *Advertising Age,* March 28, 1983, pp. 2, 72.

13. The analysis of the Joseph Schlitz Brewing Company was inspired by Mark Schulz, Mike Agar, and Jim Grubert, "Rise and Fall of Schlitz."

14. Howard Aldrich, *Organizations and Environments* (Englewood Cliffs, NJ: Prentice-Hall, 1979), p. 3.

15. Arthur G. Bedeian, *Organizations: Theory and Analysis* (Hinsdale, IL: Dryden, 1980), p. 4; Aldrich, *Organizations and Environments,* pp. 4–6.

16. James D. Thompson, *Organizations in Action* (New York: McGraw-Hill, 1967), pp. 4–13.

17. Daniel Katz and Robert L. Kahn, *The Social Psychology of Organizations* (New York: John Wiley, 1978).

18. Kenneth E. Boulding, "General Systems Theory: The Skeleton of Science," *Management Science* 2 (1956):197–207.

19. Ibid.; Richard L. Daft, "The Evolution of Organization Analysis in *ASQ,* 1959–1979," *Administrative Science Quarterly* 25 (1980):623–635.

20. Louis R. Pondy and Ian I. Mitroff, "Beyond Open Systems Models of Organization," in Barry M. Staw, ed., *Research in Organizational Behavior* (Greenwood, CT: JAI Press, 1978), pp. 13–40; Richard L. Daft and John C. Wiginton, "Language and Organization," *Academy of Management Review* 4 (1978):179–192.

21. Personal communication from an Alcan personnel manager, and "Alcan Goes Toe to Toe with Alcoa for the No. 2 Spot in Aluminum," *Business Week,* August 27, 1984.

22. The following discussion was heavily influenced by D. S. Pugh, "The Measurement of Organization Structures: Does Context Determine Form?" *Organizational Dynamics* I (Spring, 1973):19–34; and D. S. Pugh, D. J. Hickson, C. R. Hinings, and C. Turner, "Dimensions of Organization Structure," *Administrative Science Quarterly* 13 (1968):65–91.

23. D. S. Pugh, "Measurement of Organization Structures," pp. 19–34.

24. Adapted from Lucien Rhodes, "The Un-Manager," *Inc.,* August, 1982, pp. 34–46; Howard Rudnitsky, "How Sam Walton Does It," *Forbes,* August 16, 1982, pp. 42–44; and Janet Guyan, "Food-Stamp Red Tape Raises Tension Levels in Understaffed Offices," *The Wall Street Journal,* June 27, 1984, pp. 1, 16.

25. Henry Mintzberg, "Organization Design: Fashion or Fit?" *Harvard Business Review* (January-February, 1981):103–116.

26. Bertrand Fox, "Forward," in Paul R. Lawrence and Jay W. Lorsch, *Organization and Environment* (Homewood, IL: Irwin, 1969), p. vi.

27. Adapted from "Matching Managers to a Company's Life Cycle," *Business Week,* February 23, 1981, p. 62; "Best Western: Ready to Put on the Brakes," *Business Week,* February 23, 1981, pp. 62–70; and "Quality Inns: Ready for Fast-Track Growth," *Business Week,* February 23, 1981, pp. 70–74.

28. Adapted from "How Academia is Taking a Lesson from Business," *Business Week,* August 27, 1984, pp. 58–60, and Richard M. Cyert, "Does Theory Help?" *The Wall Street Journal,* April 7, 1980, p. 18.

29. Henry Fayol, "General Principles of Management," in H. F. Merrill, ed., *Classics in Management* (New York: American Management Association, 1960), p. 236.

30. Talcott Parsons, *Structure and Process in Modern Societies* (New York: Free Press, 1960).

31. Peter D. Vaill, "Thoughts on Using Poetry in the Teaching of OB," *Exchange: The Organizational Behavior Teaching Journal* 6 (1981):50–51.

32. Robert Graves, "In Broken Images," *Collected Poems* (Garden City, NY: Anchor Books, 1966), p. 78. Used with permission.

PART TWO

The Open System

The External Environment

PACOR INC.

It is hard to imagine how Jim Sullivan lives each day with the knowledge: He is dying, and Pacor Inc., the $20 million-a-year company over which he presides, is succumbing to a legal bloodletting. The Philadelphia-based firm, which distributes and installs insulation in commercial and industrial settings, has been sued more than 1,800 times during the past five years. Sullivan, 52, now spends all his time on litigation, and Pacor earmarks approximately 20% of its annual expenses for legal expenditures, up from about 1% before the onslaught began.

Sullivan and Pacor are both victims of asbestos, a material much more dangerous than most people realized until barely a decade ago. . . . But . . . the problem transcends asbestos. Strict liability interpretations, an improved ability on the part of the scientific community to trace medical cause-and-effect, and juries that are more and more likely to look with favor upon the injured have created a climate that is increasingly fraught with risk for business, and small business in particular. While companies that handled asbestos watch their profits shrink and contemplate bankruptcy, half a dozen different industries are preparing for their decade in court.

"I guess I get bitter at times," Sullivan says. "When your company gets sued 1,800 times in five years—unfairly—and there's no end in sight, you feel bitter. And when the suits come in, pile after pile, and you know that you're just working for lawyers, it gets to you." Pacor had been averaging seventy-five new lawsuits per month, but recently the pace has picked up; on one day in mid-April, fifty arrived in the mail. "Pacor started cleaning up its operation—started to phase out of asbestos whenever it was possible—in 1969," Sullivan notes.

The trouble began in 1975, when the first lawsuit appeared on Sullivan's desk. "We had heard some suits were being filed against manufacturers," he says, "so it wasn't a complete surprise. But we had no idea what was coming. By 1977, we knew that we were into some real problems." In most of the 1,800 suits filed against Pacor to date the company is named as one of fifteen to twenty-five defendants, along with manufacturers and other firms that handled the product. In only about twenty-five cases has the company been sued by former employees.

Approximately 350 of the suits have already been settled. The final figure, which the defendants share on the basis of a percentage agreement hammered out in negotiations, has been averaging $85,000.

Not only is the company spending an inordinate amount of its income on attorneys and settlements, the gauntlet of litigation has also required extraordinary expenditures of time and energy. "It puts real pressure on your top executives," Sullivan explains. "They have to perform their regular work, and find time to answer interrogatories or write letters.

"We had to hire one girl to do nothing but make copies of complaints. We have to make eight copies of each one that comes in, and that's all she does—makes copies of complaints all day. And another girl spends about 25% of her time overseeing the first one, making sure that everything's perfect before it's sent out."[1]

Jim Sullivan and executives at other companies that handle asbestos have a problem. They have to cope with an unpredictable and seemingly hostile environment. Just a few years ago asbestos was a valuable product. But changes in medical knowledge, liability laws, public sympathy and knowledge of the harmfulness of asbestos combined to deal a severe blow to manufacturers. The magnitude of the problem is staggering. Hundreds of lawsuits from people these companies never dealt with directly are being filed.

The problem of a changing environment is not unique to Pacor. In the automobile industry, the supply of gas, government rules about mileage, consumer safety requirements, and labor unrest over wages have created difficult times for automobile manufacturers. In the computer industry, the rapid development of new products creates staggering demands for investment in research and development. In the airline industry, deregulation and periodic price wars keep the red ink flowing. International catastrophes, such as the more than 2,000 people killed by a pesticide gas leaking from a Union Carbide plant in Bhopal, India, sent waves of fear and calls for new regulation through the chemical industry. The list could go on and on. If a comprehensive list of the threats and opportunities facing major corporations were developed, the majority of these elements would originate in the external environment.

Purpose of This Chapter

This chapter is about the organization's environment. In a broad sense, the environment is infinite and includes everything outside the organization. Our analysis will consider only those aspects of the environment to which the organization is sensitive and must respond to survive. Thus our definition of **organizational environment** is all elements existing outside the boundary of the organization that have the potential to affect all or part of the organization.

The purpose of this chapter is to develop a framework for assessing environments and how organizations can respond to them. First we will identify the organizational domain and the sectors that influence the organization. Then we will explore two major environmental forces on the organization: the need for information and the need for resources. Organizations respond to these forces through structural design, planning systems, and attempts to change and control elements in the environment. Finally, we will examine a new perspective on organization-environment relationships that is described in the population ecology model.

THE ENVIRONMENTAL DOMAIN

The environment of an organization can be understood by analyzing its domain. An organization's **domain** is the environmental field of action. The domain is the set of environmental elements that the organization seeks to interact with or has to interact with to accomplish organizational goals. The environment is comprised of several **sectors,** which are subdivisions of the external environment that contain similar elements. Nine sectors can be analyzed for each organization: industry, raw materials, human resources, financial resources, the market, technology, economic conditions, government, and the larger social culture in which the organization functions. The sectors and a hypothetical organizational domain are illustrated in Exhibit 2.1.

Industry   Industry includes competitors in the same type of business. The recording industry is different from the steel industry or the broadcasting industry. Industry influences the size of the organization, amount of advertising, type of customers, and typical profit margins.

Industry concentration determines the amount of competitive uncertainty for each organization.[2] An industry with a few large companies is considered

EXHIBIT   2.1. An Organization's Environment.

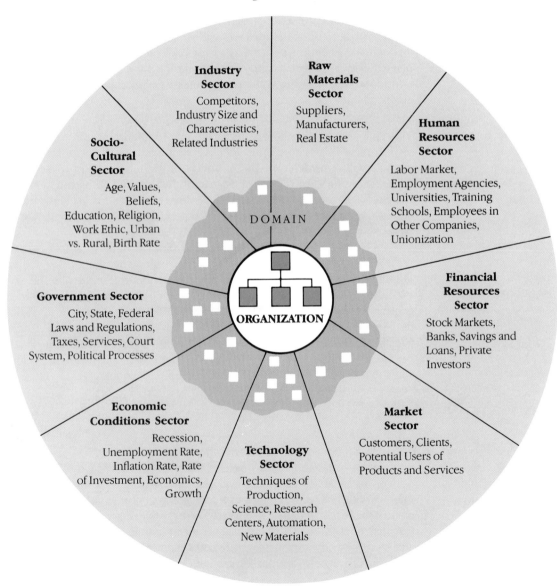

more uncertain than an industry with many small ones. The action of a large competitor has great significance for an organization. Examples of intense competitive battles are the soft drink industry where the war between Coke and Pepsi has battered the small brands, the beer industry where the increasing dominance of Anheuser-Busch and Miller have forced consolidation among other companies, and the cigarette industry where the introduction of Barclay by Brown & Williamson caused a backlash from competitors. Another industry battleground is disposable diapers, where the major rivals are Kimberly-Clark and Procter & Gamble.

IN PRACTICE 2.1
Kimberly-Clark Corp.

Kimberly-Clark has become a major player in the diaper wars. Procter & Gamble completely dominated the business with Pampers during the 1970s, but early in 1985 Pampers was down to 32% and K-C's Huggies brand was up to 24% and climbing. Kimberly-Clark beat P & G with refastenable tabs and high absorbent material.

Now Procter & Gamble is responding with a new version of Pampers that is thinner, more absorbent, better fitting, and has a waste barrier to prevent leakage. It is being test marketed in Wichita, and parents like it.

The war between Kimberly-Clark and P & G has gotten so hot that Johnson & Johnson and Scott Paper Company have been driven out of the business. But new competition is surfacing from private label brands, which are cheaper and to which merchants assign favorable shelf space because of profit margins. The war had made a big dent in Procter & Gamble's bottom line. Earnings are down, and if the new diaper business isn't an immediate success, competition will drive earnings down even further.[3]

Raw Materials Organizations must acquire raw materials from the external environment. These materials include everything from paper, pencils, and typewriters to patients for a hospital, iron ore for a steel mill, manuscripts for a publisher, or green coffee beans for a coffee distributor. Raw materials are often readily available at a low price. Companies such as Xerox, International Harvester, and Hewlett Packard may depend on as many as 5,000 suppliers. Sometimes raw material supplies are threatened or are available at high prices or not at all.

Human Resources Human resources are employees. Organizations must have a supply of trained, qualified personnel. Without an abundant supply of human resources, the organization will have a hard time producing output. At Mary Kay Cosmetics, a shortage of human resources accounts for the decline in growth and profits in recent years. Mary Kay's salesforce stands at more than 200,000 women. Growth is fueled by hiring additional women, but recruits have been scarce. Fewer women are available because the number of women working at full time jobs is increasing as the economy improves, and fewer women are at home to buy beauty products. Avon and Tupperware also face stagnant sales and declining profits because of insufficient human resources.[4]

Financial Resources   Financial resources reflect the availability of money. The stock and bond markets, banks, and insurance companies are included in this environmental sector. Interest rates also influence the availability of money. The availability of cheap money encourages an organization to grow fast. If an organization has to finance growth internally, growth slows down. Extensive borrowing also transfers some control of the company to lending agencies.

Market   Customers who acquire goods and services represent the market sector. Hospitals serve patients, schools serve students, supermarkets supply homemakers, airlines move travelers, and government agencies provide benefits to practically everyone. The market influences the organization through demand for the organization's output. If the market is shrinking, the organization must cut back or diversify into other markets. If the market expands, the organization must expand to supply customer needs or lose its standing in the industry.

Customers must be taken care of. Organizations typically try to understand and anticipate potential market changes. Mistreatment of customers, even by large, influential organizations can have disastrous results. Burroughs Corporation was sued by 129 users of its small computer systems who were not given the services promised. In the example of Schlitz described at the beginning of this book, unhappy customers left in droves to buy other brands of beer.

Technology   Technology is the use of available knowledge and techniques to produce goods and services. The complexity of the technology influences the skill level and organization size required to use the technology. New technological developments also have impact on organizations. Recent technological developments that threaten some firms are the flat LCD tube that will replace the traditional television tube, typewriters that take dictation, a new generation of zinc chloride batteries that may revolutionize automobiles and utilities, super-efficient propeller-driven airplanes, and fiber optics, computer animation, and computer imaging. Materials used in production technologies that were completely unheard of ten years ago include the ceramic turbine engine, a composite skin used in the Boeing 767 airliner, gallium arsenide lasers used in fiber optics, and the all-composite automobile body marketed by General Motors. Even in a traditional industry like meat packing, technological change can put companies out of business if they do not adapt:

> In a business where success or failure hinges on fractions of a cent profit or loss, Idle Wild Foods is just about as good as they come. If there is anyone better, It's Iowa Beef Processors, which revolutionized the way finished beef is produced. The new technology was first perfected in a huge slaughtering and processing plant IBP built at Dakota City, Nebr. in 1967, and overnight most of the competition had to acquire IBP's cost-cutting skills or get out of the business. Most of them got out.[5]

Economic Conditions   Economic conditions reflect the general economic health of the country and region where the organization operates. Unemployment rates, consumer purchasing power, interest rates, inflation, and excess production capacity are all part of external economic health. The availability of supplies, labor, and the demand for output are related to economic conditions. Economic conditions also affect government and not-for-profit organizations. High tax revenues are a direct result of economic prosperity. Contributions to the Salvation Army and the Red Cross go down during periods of economic recession, just when helping agencies experience greater demand for their services. Business leaders prefer stable economic conditions with moderate growth and prosperity. Violent economic changes restrict business investment and growth.

Government   The government includes the regulatory, legal, and political systems that surround the organization. The political system, such as capitalism versus socialism, determines the amount of freedom organizations have to pursue their own ends. In Canada and the United States, organizations operate in a capitalistic economy, but the government specifies the rules of the game through laws and regulations. The federal government influences organizations through the Occupational Safety and Health Administration, fair trade practices, subsidies for certain products and services, libel statutes that encourage or discourage lawsuits against businesses, consumer protection legislation, product safety, requirements for information and labeling, import and export restrictions, and pricing constraints. The Reagan administration's reduction of business regulation has been offset by increases in state regulation. In 1984, 250,000 bills were introduced in state government, of which 50,000 will become law. An additional 50,000 regulations were proposed, with about 35,000 adopted. These laws and regulations include everything from "lemon laws," to merger regulations and protective measures to force businesses to buy in-state.[6]

Although government regulation is necessary, many businesses find it objectionable. Some regulations have unfortunate consequences. The following case illustrates how government regulations affected a small construction company.

IN PRACTICE 2.2

Dante's Construction Company

Sole proprietor of Dante's Construction Co., employer of one carpenter and two laborers, and proud owner of a Ford pickup truck, Dante Di Gaitano, forty-nine, has lately been on the receiving end of the kind of official attention the federal government normally reserves for Fortune 500 companies.

The first intimation of trouble came in November 1978 when Di Gaitano received a letter from the Philadelphia field office of OFCCP (Office of Federal Contract Compliance Programs) admonishing him that he had failed to send in his monthly affirmative-action reports. Applicable to any federal construction contract in excess of $10,000, the one-page Form 257 requires contractors to break down the number of hours worked by craft, race, sex, and ethnicity. Figuring that most of the questions didn't really apply to him, Di Gaitano sent back forms for October and November reporting "no activity." He says he felt secure in doing so because one of his two laborers, Robert Sutton, was black: "I'd hired him because we'd worked alongside each other for many years before I went into business on my own—not because anybody in government made me do it."

Unfortunately for Di Gaitano, OFCCP was less interested in the state of his conscience than in his failure to submit any further reports. OFCCP inspector Lee Tolbert went to the Navy Yard construction site to ask Di Gaitano some questions.

Tolbert's first concern was Di Gaitano's record with blacks. Black himself, Tolbert asked to meet alone with laborer Robert Sutton to make sure he had not been harassed. No harassment, Sutton replied; in fact Di Gaitano had been buying him breakfast every morning.

Looking around the site, Tolbert inquired next about separate toilets for women. "What for, when we have no women on the site?" Di Gaitano exploded. No women, Tolbert noted on his checklist.

About five weeks later, Di Gaitano received a "deficiency citation" listing seventeen flaws in his "equal-opportunity posture." Topping the list was Di Gaitano's failure to set himself the goal of filling at least 5% of his jobs with women. Among other flaws were failures to conduct and document an out-reach program and to publicize Dante's Construction's equal-employment-opportunity policy through the news media, at staff meetings, in the company's "annual report," and in the "company newspaper."

To purge himself of these failings, Di Gaitano was invited to sign an eleven-page, seventeen-section "conciliation agreement" itemizing at least forty-three filing and reporting requirements. Some of them struck Di Gaitano as more than a little odd, like the one "to maintain records that parties and picnics have been posted and available to all employees." If he refused to sign, he could be barred from receiving federal contracts.

Though the government has locked him into a vast paper chase he still does not employ a woman. He briefly had one working for him as a laborer but admits that he was relieved when her mother called him that her daughter could not continue on the job because she had been called up for duty in the National Guard.[7]

Socio-Cultural   This sector includes the demographic characteristics and the value system within a society. Demographic characteristics include age of the population, income distribution, composition of the work force (age, sex, race), whether people live in rural or urban areas or are migrating from one area to the other, and the incidence of slums, crime, and educational facilities.

Values and norms are also important components of culture. Protest groups in the 1960s and 1970s tarnished the public image of munitions manufacturers, whose stock was divested from many foundations and university portfolios. Ralph Nader led the movement toward consumers fighting back. Corporations were portrayed as uncaring and exploitative, which encouraged lawsuits against companies such as Pacor, Inc. described at the beginning of this chapter.

Organizations have tried to adopt value changes, but some changes have been tough. The recreational use of drugs, such as among some air traffic controllers, is unacceptable to Federal Aviation Administration officials even if it is acceptable in the larger society. Many companies extended equal employment rights to gays, and now find themselves mired in unanticipated problems. Some gays are demanding full medical and other company benefits for their partners. Companies don't know how to include gay couples in social activities. The norms and values of society continue to change, so firms will be facing additional dilemmas in the future.[8]

Summary   Each of the nine sectors is made up of elements that have the potential to influence the organization. Each sector can be scanned and analyzed by the organization's managers. Perhaps three or four sectors will be especially important and should be watched closely. Moreover, the sectors in the organization's domain will affect each other, such as when economic conditions affect the market, or government policy affects financial resources. The next section introduces the concept of environmental uncertainty and explains how organizations can adapt to it.

ENVIRONMENTAL UNCERTAINTY

How does the environment influence an organization? The patterns and events in the environment can be described along six dimensions, such as whether the environment is stable versus unstable, homogeneous versus heterogeneous, concentrated versus dispersed, simple versus complex, the extent of turbulence, and the amount of resources available to support the organization.[9] These ideals boil down to two essential ways the environment influences organizations: (1) the need for information and (2) the need for resources. Some environmental conditions create a greater need to gather information and to respond to that information. Other characteristics pertain to the need for scarce material and financial resources, and the need to ensure the availability of resources. In the remainder of this section we will discuss the information perspective, which is concerned with the amount of uncertainty the environment creates for the organization. Then we will turn to the topic of resources, which is called the resource dependence model because it pertains to the dependence of the organization on the environment.

Organizations must cope with and manage uncertainty in order to be effective. **Uncertainty** means that decision-makers do not have information about environmental factors, and they have a difficult time predicting external changes. Uncertainty increases the risk of failure for organizational actions, and makes it difficult to compute costs and probabilities associated with decision alternatives. Characteristics of the environmental domain that influence uncertainty can be summarized along two dimensions: the extent to which the external domain is simple or complex, and the extent to which events are stable or unstable.[10]

Environmental complexity refers to heterogeneity, or the number of external elements that are relevant to an organization's operations.[11] In a complex environment, a large number of diverse external elements will interact with and influence the organization. In a simple environment, as few as three or four external elements influence the organization.

Universities have complex environments. Universities span a large number of technologies, and are a focal point for cultural and value changes. Government regulatory and granting agencies interact with the university, and so do a variety of professional and scientific associations, alumni, parents, foundations, legislators, community residents, international agencies, donors, corporations, and athletic teams. A large number of external elements thus make up the organization's domain, which means the university's environment is complex. On the other hand, a hardware store in a suburban community is in a simple environment. The only external elements of any real importance are the parent company (for supplies) and customers. Government regulation is minimal, and cultural change has little impact. Human resources are not a problem because the store is run by family members or part-time help.

The **stable-unstable** dimension refers to whether elements in the environment are dynamic.[12] An environmental domain is stable if it remains the same over a period of months or years. Under unstable conditions, environmental elements shift abruptly. Instability may occur when competitors react with aggressive moves and counter moves regarding advertising and new products. Sometimes specific, unpredictable events such as the poisoning of Tylenol or Union Carbide's gas leak in Bhopal, India, create an unanticipated reaction.

An example of a stable environment would be a public utility.[13] In the rural midwest, demand and supply factors for the public utility are stable. A gradual increase in demand may occur, which is easily predictable over time. Garment makers, by contrast, have experienced an unstable environment in recent years. A financial squeeze, combined with a shrinking customer base, slow retail sales, and increasing imports have driven big, well-known companies like Bobbie Brooks, Fashion Enterprises, Gallant International, Norstan, and Brookfield clothes out of business.[14]

Framework

The simple-complex and stable-unstable dimensions are combined into a framework for assessing environmental uncertainty in Exhibit 2.2. In the *simple, stable* environment uncertainty is low. There are only a few external elements to contend with and they tend to remain stable. The *complex, stable* environment represents somewhat greater uncertainty. A larger number of elements have to be scanned and analyzed in order for the organization to perform well. External elements do not change rapidly or unexpectedly in this environment.

Even greater uncertainty is felt in the *simple, unstable* environment.[15] Rapid change creates uncertainty for managers. Even though the organization has few external elements, they are hard to predict, and they react unexpectedly to organizational initiatives. The greatest uncertainty for an organization occurs in the *complex, unstable* environment. A large number of elements impinge upon the organization, and they shift frequently or react strongly to organizational initiatives. When several sectors change simultaneously, the environment becomes turbulent.[16]

A beer distributor functions in a simple, stable environment. Demand for beer changes only gradually. The distributor has an established delivery route, and supplies of beer arrive on schedule. State universities, hospitals, and insurance companies are in stable, complex environments. A large number of external elements are present but, although they change, the changes are gradual and predictable. Fashion industries are in simple, unstable environments. Organizations that manufacture and sell women's clothing, or that are involved in the toy or music industry, face shifting supply and demand. The oil industry and the airline industry face complex, unstable environments. Many external sectors are changing simultaneously. In the case of airlines, in just a few years they have been confronted with deregulation, the entry of regional airlines as a new set of competitors, dramatically increased fuel

EXHIBIT 2.2. Framework for Assessing Environmental Uncertainty.

	Simple	Complex
Stable	**Simple + Stable =** *LOW UNCERTAINTY* 1. Small number of external elements 2. Elements remain the same or change slowly Examples: Soft drink bottlers, beer distributors, container manufacturers, local utilities	**Complex + Stable =** *LOW MODERATE UNCERTAINTY* 1. Large number of external elements 2. Elements remain the same or change slowly Examples: Universities, hospitals, insurance companies
Unstable	**Simple + Unstable =** *HIGH MODERATE UNCERTAINTY* 1. Small number of external elements 2. Elements change frequently, unpredictably, and reactively Examples: Personal computers, fashion clothing, music industry, Atari, toy manufacturers	**Complex + Unstable =** *HIGH UNCERTAINTY* 1. Large number of external elements 2. Elements change frequently, unpredictably, and reactively Examples: American Airlines, oil companies, electronic firms, aerospace firms local utilities

ENVIRONMENTAL CHANGE *(vertical axis: Stable / Unstable)*

Uncertainty *(diagonal arrow)*

Simple   Complex

ENVIRONMENTAL COMPLEXITY

Source: Adapted and reprinted from "Characteristics of Perceived Environments and Perceived Environmental Uncertainty" by Robert B. Duncan, published in *Administrative Science Quarterly* 17(3) (1972):313–327 by permission of *The Administrative Science Quarterly*. Copyright © 1972 by Cornell University.

prices, price changes from competitors, shifting customer demand, an air-traffic controller strike and mass firing, and a reduction of scheduled flights.

For large, diversified organizations, one division may exist within an uncertain environment while another division exists within a relatively certain environment. The diverse and changing nature of environments are illustrated in Playboy Enterprises Inc.

IN PRACTICE 2.3

Playboy Enterprises Inc.

The first issue of *Playboy* was left undated for fear of failure. With that first issue in 1953, *Playboy* became an overnight success. By 1974, *Playboy* was considered to be the most widely read magazine among business executives. As Hugh Hefner, founder and owner, explained, "The notion behind *Playboy* was to combine things sexual and things intellectual—bring the mind and body of man together, as opposed to puritanism, whose whole thrust upon society was to separate the two . . .."[17]

Playboy overcame legal and moral objections to become firmly established in the 1960s, but went through a difficult period in the late 1970s. *Playboy* became entangled in a "pubic war" when several new sex magazines were introduced. The leading competitor was *Penthouse*, which was a raunchy imitation of *Playboy*. *Playboy* responded with the introduction of *Oui*, and with more explicit nudity and sexuality in *Playboy* photographs. The response from readers and advertisers was immediate and negative. They did not want to be associated with a raunchy magazine. By the end of the '70s, *Playboy* had returned to a fresh-scrubbed approach.

Perhaps because of the pubic war, *Playboy* was undergoing new challenges from pornography rulings. The Supreme Court allowed communities to determine their own obscenity standards, and many were harassing *Playboy*. Newsstand displays posed a problem for *Playboy*. The emergence of the moral majority caused additional litigation against *Playboy*.

The environment surrounding *Playboy* magazine has settled down and is no longer turbulent. Playboy has won most of the pornography cases and is now concentrating on developing new businesses, such as the Playboy network on cable television. This is a new field with fierce competition, both with other cable channels and with other forms of entertainment. Many changes in technology are yet to come. The Federal Communication Commission is involved, and local governments are divided about whether to accept the Playboy channels in their communities. Playboy would like to use its channel to advertise the magazine for competitive synergy. Developments in video disks and video tape, along with changing consumer tastes, new forms of competition, and possible legal backlash create uncertainty in this environmental domain.

The Playboy clubs went through a similar period of uncertainty but now experience a stable domain. The first Playboy club was opened in 1960, and the "bunny" concept proved an immediate success. The issuing of Playboy keys was also an attractive novelty. Expansion into resort hotels and gambling casinos led to enormous problems. Playboy managers did not have expertise running resorts and Playboy lost its license to operate the highly profitable

British casinos. Restrictions on advertising, loans to gamblers, and plane charters reduced Playboy's competitiveness in this domain.

The latest development at Playboy was the appointment of Hefner's daughter Christie to the presidency. Future plans call for the expansion of publishing into noncontroversial areas such as a feminist monthly magazine devoted to the young career woman. The remaining Playboy clubs will switch emphasis to franchising to allow for low investment and local control. Primary attention will be to the development of the Playboy television channel.[18]

The environment of Playboy Enterprises reflects moderate to rapid change in several sectors. The Playboy Club division is currently in the low uncertainty quadrant of Exhibit 2.2. The traditional clubs are established in their markets, and have a reliable clientele. The Playboy publishing division would be in the low-moderate uncertainty category. The environment is complex, with many suppliers, competitors, government regulations, advertisers, customers, and technology considerations. Change has been slow to moderate in these sectors during the first half of the 1980s. The cable television division would be in the high uncertainty category. The intense rivalry among competitors, new developments in technology, alternative forms of entertainment, and reluctant community acceptance all have impact on this division. The environment is both complex and unpredictable.

ADAPTING TO ENVIRONMENTAL UNCERTAINTY

Now that we see how environments differ with respect to change and complexity, the next question is: How do organizations adapt to each level of environmental uncertainty? Environmental uncertainty represents an important contingency for organization structure and internal behaviors. An organization in a certain environment will be managed and controlled differently from an organization in an uncertain environment with respect to number of positions, boundary spanning, internal coordination, the formalization of internal work activities, and future planning. Organizations need to have the right fit between internal structure and the external environment.

Positions and Departments

Structural Complexity   As the complexity in the external environment increases, so does the number of positions and departments within the organization, which increases internal complexity. The law of requisite variety says that complexity in one system is required to control complexity in another system.[19] This relationship is part of being an open system. Each sector in the external environment requires an employee or department to deal with it. The personnel department deals with unemployed people who want to work for the company. The marketing department finds customers. Procurement employees obtain raw materials from hundreds of suppliers. The finance group deals with bankers. The legal department works with the courts and government agencies.

An organization in a complex environment needs a greater number of departments and positions to help buffer the environment. James Thompson conceptualized the organization as a technical core surrounded by buffering departments.[20] **Buffering departments** help absorb uncertainty from the environment. The **technical core** performs the primary production activity of the organization, which is manufacturing and assembly in a manufacturing firm or research and teaching in a university. In order for the technical core to be efficient as possible, it should not be disturbed by external uncertainties. Specific departments are established to deal with environmental sectors and absorb the uncertainty originating from them. The goal of buffer departments is to make the technical core as nearly a closed system as possible so it can function efficiently. Examples of buffering departments are shown in Exhibit 2.3. Nonproduction departments absorb environmental uncertainty and fluctuations, thereby enabling the technical core to be efficient.

Boundary Spanning

Boundary spanning roles link and coordinate the organization with key elements in the external environment. The boundary role establishes a relationship with individuals and organizations in the environment. By carrying information back and forth between the environment and the organization,

EXHIBIT 2.3. Buffer Departments Reduce Environmental Uncertainty for the Technical Core.

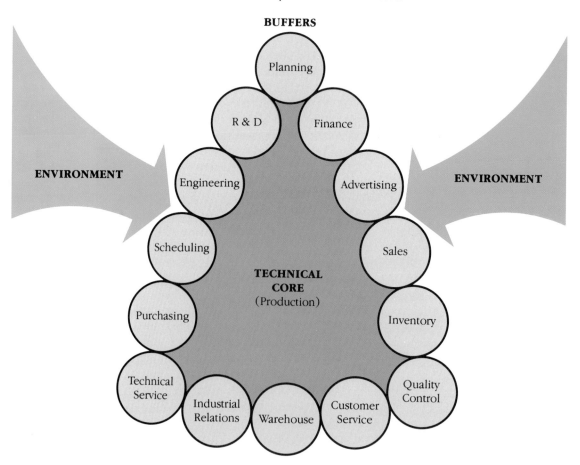

plans and activities can be coordinated and uncertainty reduced. The organization will be better equipped to adapt to the environment, and some environmental elements may be able to adapt to the needs of the organization.

Boundary spanning roles serve two purposes: (1) to detect and process information about changes in the external environment, and (2) to represent the organization to the environment.[21] Boundary roles concentrate on information, and hence serve an overlapping function with buffer departments that transfer materials, resources, services, and money between the environment and organization.

Boundary personnel scan and monitor events in the environmental domain. Market research is a boundary role that monitors trends in consumer taste. Other boundary spanners identify new technological developments, innovations, regulations, and sources of supply. Boundary spanners prevent the organization from stagnating by facilitating planning by top managers and by keeping them current about environmental changes.[22]

The boundary task of representing the organization is to send information out to the environment. This boundary role influences other people's perception of the organization. In the marketing department, advertising and sales agents represent the organization to customers. Purchasers may call suppliers and describe purchasing needs. Accounting personnel may phone the bank or customers about payment schedules. The legal department may inform lobbyists or elected officials about the organization's needs or views on political matters.

Many universities employ federal relations officers to represent them in Washington. In a given week, Ohio State University may send thirty representatives to prowl the halls of Congress and federal agencies seeking federal aid. In other organizations, the problem may be simply to scan and interpret rapidly changing and complex events in the industry sector. One such boundary spanner is the tariff department at Delta Air Lines.

IN PRACTICE 2.4
Delta Air Lines

"Seated around an L-shaped desk, a group of Delta tariff experts hash over possible counter moves to the fare changes reported by the competition overnight. 'What are the yields on those new Braniff fares again?' says Robert Coggin, Assistant Vice-President for Marketing Development. 'It's bad,' replies an associate."

Mr. Coggin is responsible for the tariff department that monitors pricing changes throughout the airline industry. On a typical day, his group may compare 5,000 industry price changes against Delta's approximately 70,000 fares. Fares are monitored intensely because pricing is the key battleground in the deregulated airline industry. The boundary spanning role is incredibly complex because Delta's fares must change with the supply and demand of customers as well as with fare changes by competitors. Shifts occur from day to day and from flight to flight from city to city. A major competitive move, such as American Airlines' decision to reduce prices on 2,400 routes, almost swamps the information-processing capacity of the tariff department.

Information starts coming to the group early in the morning when Delta computers produce up to several hundred pages of new fares listed the previous day. The tariff department also receives telexes and other information from company field offices about price changes announced in local newspapers or when a customer talks about a good deal elsewhere. Yet more information, such as the number of discounted seats a competitor is offering, is obtained when Delta agents make reservations until a competitor says only full-priced seats remain. The reservations are then cancelled.

The volume of information is so great that Delta assigns fifty computers to the task. Daily reports analyzing trends and reporting the volume of change are circulated to top executives. A recent daily report showed Eastern Airlines with 3,709 fare adjustments and United Airlines with 5,282.

Delta responds in as short as two hours if a fare change threatens its own sales. The information also helps develop competitive strategies, such as sending a tour group to help fill a competitor's plane with low-fare passengers so that the Delta plane will have full-fare seats waiting for last-minute business travelers. Smaller airlines cannot afford to scan fare changes so intensely, and may be at a competitive disadvantage. The ability to monitor all fares and respond quickly has helped Delta increase its share of the market and earn a profit during difficult times for the airline industry.[23]

Differentiation and Integration

Another response to environmental uncertainty is the amount of differentiation and integration among departments. **Organizational differentiation** is "the difference in orientations among managers in different functional departments, and the difference in formal structure among these departments."[24] When the external environment is complex and rapidly changing, organizational departments become highly specialized to handle the uncertainty in their external sector. Success in each sector requires special expertise and behavior. Employees in a research and development department have unique attitudes, values, goals, and education that distinguish them from employees in manufacturing or sales departments.

A study by Paul Lawrence and Jay Lorsch at Harvard examined three organizational departments—manufacturing, research, and sales—in ten corporations.[25] Their study found that each department evolved toward a different orientation and structure in order to effectively interact with specialized parts of the external environment. The market, scientific, and manufacturing subenvironments they identified are illustrated in Exhibit 2.4. Each department interacted with different external groups. The differences that evolved among departments within the organizations are shown in Exhibit 2.5. In order to work effectively with the scientific subenvironment, R&D had a goal of quality work, a long-time horizon (up to five years), an informal structure, and task-oriented employees. Sales was at the opposite extreme. They had a goal of customer satisfaction, were oriented toward the short term (two weeks or so), had a very formal structure, and were socially oriented.

The impact of high differentiation is that coordination between departments is difficult. More time and resources must be devoted to achieving coordination when attitudes, goals and work orientation differ so widely. **Integration** is the quality of collaboration between departments.[26] Formal integrators are often required to coordinate departments. When the envi-

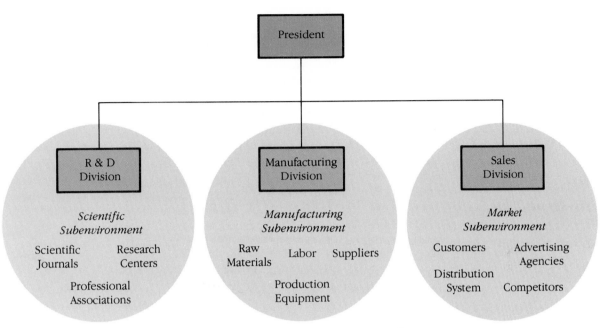

EXHIBIT 2.4. Organizational Departments Differentiate
to Meet Needs of Subenvironments.

ronment is highly uncertain, frequent changes require more information
processing to achieve coordination, so integrators become a necessary addition to the organization structure. Sometimes they are called liaison personnel, brand managers, or coordinators. As illustrated in Exhibit 2.6, organizations with highly uncertain environments and a highly differentiated
structure have about 22% of management personnel assigned to integration
activities, such as serving on committees, task forces, or in liaison roles.[27] In
organizations characterized by very simple, stable environments, almost no
managers are assigned to integration roles. The important point in Exhibit
2.6 is that as environmental uncertainty increases, so does differentiation
between departments, and hence the organization must assign a larger percentage of managers to coordinating roles.

EXHIBIT 2.5 Differences in Goals and Orientations
among Organizational Departments.

Characteristic	R & D Department	Manufacturing Department	Sales Department
Goals	New developments, quality	Efficient production	Customer satisfaction
Time Horizon	Long	Short	Short
Interpersonal Orientation	Mostly task	Task	Social
Formality of Structure	Low	High	High

Source: Adapted from Paul R. Lawrence and Jay W. Lorsch, *Organization and Environment* (Homewood,
IL: Irwin, 1969), pp. 23–39.

Another response to environmental uncertainty is the amount of formal structure and control imposed on employees. Burns and Stalker observed twenty industrial firms in England and discovered that external environment was related to internal management structure.[28] When the external environment was stable, the internal organization was characterized by rules, procedures, and a clear hierarchy of authority. Organizations were formalized. They were also centralized, with most decisions made at the top. Burns and Stalker called this a **mechanistic** organization system.

In rapidly changing environments, the internal organization was much looser, free flowing, and adaptive. Rules and regulations often were not written down, or if written down were ignored. People had to find their own way through the system to figure out what to do. The hierarchy of authority was not clear. Decision-making authority was decentralized. Burns and Stalker used the term **organic** to characterize this type of management structure.

Exhibit 2.7 summarizes the differences in organic and mechanistic systems. These systems combine several structural characteristics, including formalization, centralization, standardization, and specialization. The following case illustrates an organic organization in the electronics industry.

IN PRACTICE 2.5
Electronics Firm

[I]n the electronics industry proper . . . there is often a deliberate attempt to avoid specifying individual tasks, and to forbid any dependence on the management hierarchy as a structure of defined functions and authority. The head of one concern . . . attacked the idea of the organization chart as inapplicable in his concern and as a dangerous method of thinking about the working of industrial management. The first requirement of management, according to him, was that it should make the fullest use of the capacities of its members; any individual's job should be as little defined as possible, so that it will "shape itself" to his special abilities and initiative. . . .

. . . When the position of product engineer was created, for example, the first incumbents said they had to "find out" what they had to do, and what authority and resources they could command to do it.

In fact, this process of "finding out" about one's job proved to be unending. Their roles were continually defined and redefined. This happened through a

EXHIBIT 2.6 Environmental Uncertainty and Organizational Integrators.

		Industry	
	Plastics	Foods	Container
Environmental Uncertainty	HIGH	MODERATE	LOW
Departmental Differentiation	HIGH	MODERATE	LOW
Percent Management in Integrating Roles	22%	17%	0%

Source: Adapted from Jay W. Lorsch and Paul R. Lawrence, "Environmental Factors and Organizational Integration," *Organization Planning: Cases and Concepts* (Homewood, IL: Irwin and Dorsey, 1972), p. 45.

EXHIBIT 2.7. Mechanistic and Organic Organization Forms.

Mechanistic	Organic
1. Tasks are broken down into specialized, separate tasks.	1. Employees contribute to common task of department.
2. Tasks are rigidly defined.	2. Tasks are adjusted and redefined through employee interactions.
3. Strict hierarchy of authority and control. Many rules.	3. Less hierarchy of authority and control. Few rules.
4. Knowledge and control of tasks are centralized at top of organization.	4. Knowledge and control of tasks are located anywhere in organization
5. Communication is vertical.	5. Communication is horizontal.

Source: Adapted from Gerald Zaltman, Robert Duncan, and Jonny Holbek, *Innovations and Organizations* (New York: Wiley, 1973), p. 131.

perpetual sequence of encounters with laboratory chiefs, with design engineers, product engineers, draughtsmen, the works manager, with the foremen in charge of the production shop, with rate-fixers, buyers, and operatives. In every single case they had to determine their part and that of the others through complex, though often brief, negotiations.

"Normally," said a department manager, "management has a sort of family tree showing who is responsible for what, and what he is responsible for. It's a pity there's nothing like that here. It's rather difficult not knowing. You get an assistant to a manager who acts as though he were an assistant manager, a very different thing." Another man, a product engineer, said, "One of the troubles here is that nobody is very clear about his title or status or even his function." A foreman said that when he had first been promoted he had been told nothing of his duties and functions.[29]

The electronics firm was not managed very tightly, but Burns and Stalker concluded that the organic system was appropriate in the rapidly changing electronics industry. The "finding out" of jobs facilitated the horizontal information-sharing needed for change and adaptation. Rules, procedures, job descriptions, and centralized decisions would just get in people's way. In a rapidly changing environment, old rules seldom apply. Although managers and employees were often frustrated, they were able to coordinate changes and respond to external emergencies and crises.

Planning and Forecasting

The final organizational response to uncertainty is to increase planning and environmental forecasting. When the environment is stable, the organization can concentrate on current operational problems and day-to-day efficiency. Long-range planning and forecasting are not needed because environmental demands in the future will be the same as they are today.

Under conditions of environmental uncertainty, planning and forecasting are necessary.[30] Planning can soften the adverse impact of external shifting. A separate planning department is often established in organizations that have unstable environments. In an unpredictable, reactive environment, planners must identify relevant environmental elements, and analyze potential moves and counter moves by other organizations. Planning can be extensive and may forecast various scenarios for environmental contingencies. As time passes, plans are updated through replanning.[31] The emphasis on updated plans is consistent with the organic form of organization. Decisions are pushed down to lower organization levels where information relevant to the decision is held. There is little time for passing information to the top of the hierarchy, as would be the case in a mechanistic structure.

Texas Instruments uses an extensive planning system to anticipate and reduce the effects of environmental change. It is called the Objective, Strategies, and Tactics (OST) system. The OST planning system is unique because it ties together long-range strategic plans with short-term operational plans. Strategic decisions are made in response to anticipated environmental changes and then translated into day-to-day operational activities. OST helps Texas Instruments cope with the high level of uncertainty in the electronics industry.

FRAMEWORK FOR ENVIRONMENTAL UNCERTAINTY AND ORGANIZATIONAL RESPONSE

The ways environmental uncertainty influences organizational characteristics are summarized in Exhibit 2.8. This framework uses the environmental dimensions of change and complexity described earlier. In a simple environment, the organization structure is simple. As the environment becomes more complex, the organization needs a larger number of buffer departments and boundary spanners. When the environment is stable, internal structure and processes are mechanistic. When the environment is unstable, the organization structure is organic and less formalized and centralized. Planning also becomes more important because the organization reduces uncertainty by anticipating future changes.

The change and complexity dimensions are combined in Exhibit 2.8 and illustrate four levels of uncertainty. The low uncertainty environment is simple and stable. Organizations have few departments and a mechanistic structure. In a low-moderate environment more departments are needed along with more integrating roles to coordinate the departments. Some planning is used to analyze and predict the external domain. Environments that are high-moderate uncertainty are unstable but simple. Organization structure is organic. Planning is emphasized. The high uncertain environment is both complex and unstable, and is the most difficult environment from a management perspective. Organizations are large and have many departments, but are also organic. A large number of management personnel are assigned to coordination and integration, and the organization stresses boundary spanning, planning, and forecasting.

RESOURCE DEPENDENCE

Thus far we have described several ways in which organizations adapt to uncertainty caused by environmental change and complexity. Now we turn

	Simple	Complex
Stable	*LOW UNCERTAINTY* 1. Mechanistic structure formal, centralized 2. Few departments 3. No integrating roles 4. Operational orientation *simple stable*	*LOW MODERATE UNCERTAINTY* 1. Mechanistic structure formal, centralized 2. Many departments, boundary spanning 3. Few integrating roles 4. Some planning *Complex stable*
Unstable	*HIGH MODERATE UNCERTAINTY* 1. Organic structure informal, decentralized 2. Few departments, boundary spanning 3. Few integrating roles 4. Planning orientation *simple unstable*	*HIGH UNCERTAINTY* 1. Organic structure informal, decentralized 2. Many departments, differentiated, boundary spanning 3. Many integrating roles 4. Extensive planning, forecasting *Complex unstable.*

ENVIRONMENTAL CHANGE (vertical axis)

Simple   **Complex**

ENVIRONMENTAL COMPLEXITY

EXHIBIT 2.8. Contingency Framework for Environmental Uncertainty and Organization Structure.

to another characteristic of the organization-environment relationship, which is the need for material and financial resources. The environment is the source of scarce and valued resources essential to organizational survival. Research in this area is called the resource dependence perspective. **Resource dependence** means that organizations depend on the environment, but strive to acquire control over resources that will minimize their dependence.[32] Organizations are vulnerable if vital resources are controlled by other organizations, and hence they try to be as independent as possible. But companies also team up when needed to share costs and risk and hence reduce resource dependence and the possibility of bankruptcy.

Interorganizational Relationships

One outcome from the need to obtain scarce resources is the establishment of relationships among organizations. Organizations can reduce vulnerability and uncertainty through formal linkages to other organizations. For example, during the fuel crisis, airlines moved to control fuel supplies by establishing long-term contracts and even attempted to acquire energy suppliers and pipeline owners to get control of storage tanks and other fuel facilities. Ford, American Motors, General Motors, and Chrysler Corporation have all attempted to overcome their vulnerability in the area of small cars by establishing linkages with efficient foreign producers of small cars. The two most important reasons for establishing or breaking specific interorganizational relationships are resource exchange and government mandate.[33]

Resource Exchange   The principle reason for entering into a formal relationship with another organization is that each organization has something that the other wants. Money can be exchanged for raw materials, a position on the board can be exchanged for legal advice, or one agency can refer clients to another. Each party to the exchange see instrumental value in the exchange; each organization receives some benefit. Organizations can use the exchange relationship to achieve their respective goals. A large organization will be engaged in hundreds of exchange relationships to perform effectively. When a positive exchange is not possible, the interorganizational linkage will be broken.

Government Mandate   Some interorganizational linkages are required by law. This is frequently the case with not-for-profit organizations and government agencies. Welfare agencies in a local community are required to interact with the State Human Resources Agency, with local employment agencies, and with municipal, state, and federal departments. For-profit corporations also have to file reports, to be inspected, and in other ways develop mandated relationships. Every organization thus will have a number of interorganizational relationships that are required by law.

Organizational Set

The **organizational set** includes all organizations that have a relationship with an organization under analysis, called the focal organization. Analyzing organizational sets is one way to understand the pattern of linkages that may influence organization behavior. A partial organization set for a CETA organization is shown in Exhibit 2.9. CETA organizations were established by government mandate under the Comprehensive Employment Training Act. The goal of CETA organizations is to provide job training to underprivileged people. A typical CETA organization interacts with the local school district, employment commission, private business, the Department of Community Affairs, and the State Rehabilitation Commission. Several of these relationships are mandated and formalized, such as those with school districts that provide a class in welding or carpentry. Other relationships are informal. The CETA director frequently visits the director of the Chamber of Commerce to exchange information about which businesses are interested in hiring CETA employees.

The size of an organization's set indicates something about the relationship between the organization and the environment. When resources from the external environment are highly uncertain, an organization will develop many linkages.[34] Multiple linkages provide a measure of protection in sectors important to the organization's survival. A large set provides substitute suppliers and customers if they are needed, but also requires more interorganizational coordination and communication.[35]

Power and Dependence

Formal relationships with other organizations present a dilemma to managers. Organizations wish to have access to external resources to minimize

EXHIBIT 2.9. Organizational Set for a CETA Agency.

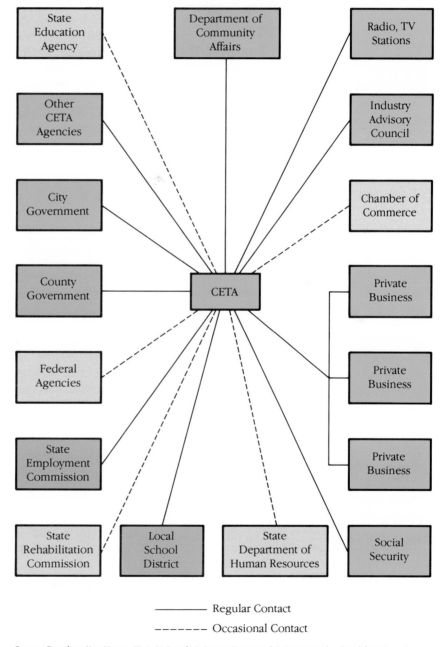

Source: Based on Ken Hogue, W. A. McIntosh, J. Steven Picou, and S. Renee Rigsby, "Model CETA and Private Sector Linkage System," Occupational Research Division, Texas A & M University, 1981.

their vulnerability. Organizations seek to reduce vulnerability with respect to resources by developing links with other organizations. Yet organizations also like to maximize their own autonomy and independence. But organizational linkages reduce the freedom of each organization to make decisions without concern for the needs and goals of other organizations. Linkages require coordination.[36] To maintain autonomy, organizations that have resources will tend not to establish new linkages. Interorganizational relationships thus represent a tradeoff between resources and autonomy. Organizations will give up independence to acquire needed resources. Dependence on resources gives power to others. Once the organization relies on others for valued resources, those organizations can influence managerial decision-making. Nowhere is this more visible than in the power of advertisers over the print and electronic media. Advertisers spend so much money, and the media rely so heavily on advertisers for resources, that advertisers sometimes can dictate media content, as in the following case.

IN PRACTICE 2.6

American Cancer Society

The American Cancer Society believes that the tobacco industry exerts a powerful influence over what is published about smoking hazards. Paul Maccabee was fired from a newspaper in Minneapolis for his coverage of the Kool Jazz Festival. Brown & Williamson Tobacco Corporation sponsored the festival, and Maccabee had inserted in his story a list of jazz greats who had died of lung cancer. Another example is Carol Wheeler's removal from the masthead of *Savvy* magazine in New York. Her published review of a book entitled *The Ladykillers: Why Smoking Is a Feminist Issue* was feared to offend tobacco-company advertisers.

The fear of the tobacco industry is based on the enormous amount of its advertising in the print media. A large company like Time or Newsweek can resist the pressure, but small publishers can't. The pressure is often unspoken, although sometimes policies are established that require editors to review articles pertaining to advertisers. It is typical for advertisers to cancel ads when a news event reflects badly on their product. At *Savvy* the editor said she failed to read Ms. Wheeler's book review before publication. After publication, the magazine felt that its tone might offend advertisers so Ms. Wheeler was removed from the masthead. *Savvy's* competitors might show the review to companies to gain their business.[37]

CONTROLLING ENVIRONMENTAL RESOURCES

In response to the need for resources, organizations try to maintain a balance between linkages with other organizations and their own independence. Organizations maintain this balance through attempts to modify, manipulate, or control other organizations.[38] The focal organization often tries to reach out and change or control elements in the environment to increase visibility to survive. Two types of strategies can be adopted to manage resources in the external environment: (1) establish favorable linkages with key elements in the environment, and (2) shape the environmental domain.[39] Techniques to accomplish each of these strategies are summarized in Exhibit 2.10.

Establishing Interorganizational Linkages

Ownership/Merger   Companies use ownership to establish linkages when they buy a part or controlling interest in another company. This gives companies a stake in one another so they cooperate in future transactions. For example, in recent years computer companies have been teaming up through stock purchases. The computer industry has become so complex that companies by themselves do not have all the resources and expertise to do everything well. Control Data has purchased substantial interest in Centronics and Source Telecomputing. IBM has invested heavily in Intel and Rolm. Western Union spent $11.5 million to acquire 25% of Vitalink. The trend toward collaboration is reshaping the industry.[40]

A greater degree of ownership is obtained through merger, which occurs when one company completely acquires another company. Merger is an effective linkage strategy, because it removes all dependence on the external element. If a source of raw material is uncertain, buying the supplier removes that uncertainty. The supplier will give priority to the parent organization. Steel companies have bought iron mines. Soft drink manufacturers have purchased bottle-makers.

Horizontal integration is a form of merger that occurs when one company acquires another company in the same line of business, such as when one computer company acquires another computer company. Vertical integration occurs when a company has been acquired that either supplies raw materials or distributes the company's products. For example, General Host acquired Hickory Farms, a retail chain, that could be an outlet for General Host's meat products. In this case, uncertainty was on the market side. Hickory Farms provided a guaranteed market for General Host's output.

Contracts, Joint Ventures   Contracts and joint ventures reduce uncertainty through a legal and binding relationship with another firm. In a joint venture, organizations share the risk and cost associated with large projects or innovations. Contracts can provide long-term security for both the supply of raw materials and consumption of output. By tying customers and suppliers to specific amounts and prices, risk is reduced. McDonald's contracts for an entire crop of russet potatoes to be certain of its supply of french fries. Lucky-

EXHIBIT 2.10. Organization Strategies for Controlling the External Environment.

Establishing Interorganizational Linkages	Controlling the Environmental Domain
1. Ownership/merger	1. Change sectors
2. Contracts, joint ventures	2. Political activity, regulation
3. Cooptation, interlocking, directorates	3. Trade associations
4. Executive recruitment	4. Illegal activities
5. Advertising, public relations	

Goldstar, a huge Korean conglomerate, uses joint ventures to stay ahead of its competitors back home. Lucky signed an agreement with Shiron Corporation to develop hepatitis vaccines and interferon, and with Dow Corning to make silicone. Altogether, Lucky-Goldstar has nineteen joint ventures, and technological agreements with fifty foreign companies.[41]

Cooptation, Interlocking Directorates   Cooptation occurs when leaders from important sectors in the environment are made part of the organization. Cooptation occurs, for example, when influential customers or suppliers are appointed to the board of directors. As a board member, they have an interest in the organization. Community leaders are also appointed to boards of directors or to organizational committees. They are introduced to the needs of the company and are more likely to include the company's interests in their decision-making.

An **interlocking directorate** is a formal linkage that occurs when a member of the board of directors of one company sits on the board of directors of another company. The individual is the link between companies and can influence policy and decision. When one individual is the link between two companies, this is typically referred to as a direct interlock. An indirect interlock occurs when a director of company A and a director of company B are both directors of company C. They have access to one another but do not have direct influence over their respective companies.[42]

Executive Recruitment   Exchanging executives also offers a method of establishing favorable linkages with external organizations. The aerospace industry each year hires retired generals and executives from the Department of Defense. These generals have personal friends in the department, so the aerospace company obtains better information about technical specifications, prices, and dates. They learn the needs of the defense department, and are able to present their case for defense contracts in a more effective way. Companies without personal contacts find it nearly impossible to get a defense contract. Having channels of influence and communication between organizations serves to reduce uncertainty and dependence for the organization.

Advertising, Public Relations   A traditional way of establishing favorable relationships is through advertising. Organizations spend large amounts of money to influence the taste of consumers. Advertising is especially important in highly competitive industries, and in industries that experience variable demand. Hospitals have begun to advertise through billboards, newspapers,, and radio commercials to promote special services and such bonuses as steak dinners and champagne. The increase in advertising has occurred because of the declining demand for health care.

Public relations is similar to advertising, except that stories often are free and aimed at public opinion. Public relations people cast the organization in a favorable light in speeches, press reports, and on television. Public relations shapes the company's image in the minds of customers, suppliers, and government officials.

In summary, organizations can use a variety of techniques to establish favorable linkages that ensure the availability of scarce resources. Linkages provide control over vulnerable environmental elements. Contracts, joint ventures, interlocking directorates, and outright ownership provide mechanisms to reduce dependency on the environment. Linkages are popular among movie companies and the newly emerging home video industry, for example, because of the high risk associated with new ventures.

IN PRACTICE 2.7

Columbia Pictures

Movie makers are suffering their own recession or worse. So they are busy working on ways to exploit cable television and other video programming for the home. But so far, the home video "revolution" has failed to deliver on its promise of a vast, rich market for the entertainment and information that movie makers are capable of packaging. Although the market is growing, it isn't growing nearly as fast or as lushly as so many people had expected. Uncertain of the shape the home TV market will take, even the richest companies are joining with others to try to guarantee a piece of the action and to spread their risks. Only one thing is certain: big money will be required to produce the programming demanded in the future.

The new alliances among film studios, television networks, and cable TV services could change the entertainment industry by blurring the distinction between makers and distributors of programs. They also could help smooth the industry's financial cycles with large alternate sources of revenue to counter two decades of stagnant box office ticket sales.

"The whole problem today is people trying to predict with certainty what can't be predicted," says Barry Dillard, chairman of Gulf and Western Industries, Inc.'s Paramount Pictures Corp. subsidiary. "There's so much technology and so little present application of it, it's absurd to try to guess which will turn into a national industry. We're in the dark." Paramount itself has quietly gone into home video distribution. It is manufacturing and marketing video cassettes of movies, and it has joined Time, Inc. and MCA, Inc. as partners in USA Network, an advertiser-supported cable channel that aims eventually at pay programming.

Columbia Pictures has organized ventures with four other companies. The most notable and controversial arrangement gives exclusive pay-TV rights on many Columbia films produced from January 1981 to mid-1984 to Home Box Office, the Time, Inc. subsidiary.

The myriad linkages among companies is sketched in Exhibit 2.11. Warner Communications Inc. has supplied home video to a joint venture with American Express Company. MCA, Inc.'s Universal Studios has arrangements with Oak Industries Inc., an operator of over-the-air pay-TV, and with the British entertainment company, Thorn EMI LTD. Even Walt Disney Productions has entered a joint venture, with the Western Electric Corp. subsidiary—to spend $100 million on producing programs for family entertainment channels over the next four years.

"Everyone wants to hedge his bets," says Dennis Forst, entertainment industry analyst for Bateman Eichler, Hill Richards Inc., the Los Angeles securities firm. "It isn't that they particularly love jumping into bed with each other, but all the alliances point out how expensive a proposition it's going to be to make it big in home video.[43]

The linkages among Columbia Pictures, Paramount, Home Box Office, and other organizations illustrate how ownership and joint ventures can be used to control resources and reduce dependency. The other major strategy companies can use to manage resource dependency is to control or redefine the external environmental domain.

Controlling Environmental Domains

In addition to establishing favorable linkages, organizations can often change the environment. There are four techniques for influencing or changing a firm's environmental domain.

EXHIBIT 2.11. Interorganizational Linkages Among Movie Makers and Home Video Companies.

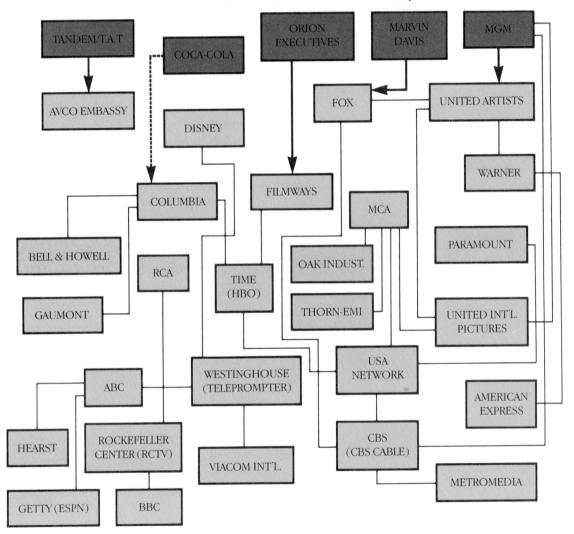

———— Ownership (Coca-Cola and Columbia deal pending)
——— Joint ventures or programming/distribution deal

Source: Stephen J. Sansweet, "Movie, TV Firms Building Alliances to Take Advantage of Home Video," *Wall Street Journal,* March 26, 1982, p. 23, with permission.

Change Domains The nine sectors described earlier in this chapter are not fixed. The organization has decided which business it is in, the market to enter, and the suppliers, banks, employees, and location to use. The current domain can be changed.[44] An organization can seek new environmental relationships and drop old ones. An organization may try to find a domain where there is little competition, no government regulation, abundant suppliers, affluent customers, and barriers to keep competitors out.

Diversification and divestment are two techniques for altering the domain. Rockwell International felt vulnerable with 63% of its revenues coming from the federal government when President Reagan and Congress needed to reduce deficits. Thus they acquired Allen Bradley to move into factory automation, which was not dependent on the government. Kaman Corporation's helicopter business collapsed in the mid-1960s, so the company diversified into other areas to obtain a much broader environmental domain.

Political Activity, Regulation Political activity includes techniques to influence government legislation and regulation. Organizations pay lobbyists to express their views to members of federal and state legislatures. Political strategy can be used to erect barriers against new competitors, and to establish rules for the game that are favorable to extant organizations. Corporations try to influence the appointment of people to agencies who are sympathetic with their needs. The value of political activity is illustrated by Bethlehem Steel's effort to roll back foreign steel imports by 15%. Assuming that domestic consumption remains the same, the average price for steel would increase about $50 a ton, and the increase in tons for Bethlehem could mean a quarter of a billion dollars of new business plus an additional half-billion dollars from higher prices on old volume. The total effect of successful political activity would amount to profits of over $9 per Bethlehem share of stock.

Trade Associations Much of the work to influence the external environment is accomplished jointly with other organizations that have similar interests. Most manufacturing companies are part of the National Association of Manufacturers, and also belong to associations relevant to their specific industry. By pooling resources, these organizations can pay people to carry out activities such as lobbying legislators, influencing new regulations, developing public relations campaigns, and blocking competition. Most organizations engage in external activity through trade associations. They work with the larger membership to change unfavorable elements in the external environment.

Illegal Activities Illegal activities represent the final technique that companies sometimes use to control their environmental domain. Certain conditions such as low profits, pressure from senior managers, or scarce environmental resources may lead managers to consider activities outside the law. Many well-known companies such as Braniff Airlines, Exxon, and Southwestern Bell have been found guilty of behavior considered unlawful. Example behaviors included payoffs to foreign governments, illegal political contributions, promotional gifts, and wire tapping. Intense competition among cement producers and in the oil business during a period of decline led to thefts and illegal kickbacks.[45] One study found that companies in industries with low demand, shortages, and strikes were more likely to be convicted for illegal activities, implying that a greater frequency of illegal acts is an attempt to cope with resource scarcity. The illegal acts included such things as price fixing, conspiracy, allocation of markets, illegal mergers, franchise violations, refusal to bargain, and illegal entry barriers.[46]

Summary Framework

The relationships illustrated in Exhibit 2.12 summarize the major themes discussed in this chapter about organization-environment relationships. The environmental domain for an organization consists of nine sectors. The amount of complexity and change influences the need for information and hence the uncertainty felt within the organization. Greater uncertainty is resolved through greater structural flexibility or through the assignment of additional departments and boundary roles. When uncertainty is low, management structures can be more mechanistic, and the number of departments and boundary roles can be fewer. The other theme pertains to the scarcity of material and financial resources. The more dependent the organization is on other organizations for these resources, the more important it is to either establish favorable linkages with these organizations or control entry into the domain. If dependence on external resources is low, the organization can maintain autonomy and does not need to establish linkages or control the external domain.

THE POPULATION PERSPECTIVE

In this final section we introduce a different perspective on organization-environment relationships. This perspective is called the **population ecology model.**[47] The important difference from other models is the focus on characteristics of organizational populations rather than on characteristics of management strategies and individual organizations. The population, not the organization, determines whether an organization survives and is successful. The population ecology model is developed from theories of natural selection in biology, and the terms "evolution," "natural selection," and "ecological" are often used to refer to the underlying behavioral processes. Theories of biological evolution try to explain why certain life forms appear and survive while others perish. Those that survive are typically best fitted to immediate environmental circumstances.

The population ecology model is concerned with organizational forms. **Organizational form** is the configuration of organizational technology, products, goals, and personnel that can be selected or rejected by the environment. Each new organization tries to find a **niche**—a domain of unique environmental resources and needs—sufficient to support it. The niche is usually small in the early stages of an organization, but may increase in size over time if the organization is successful.

In the population ecology model, luck, chance, and randomness play an important part in survival of any single firm. New products and ideas are continuously being proposed by both entrepreneurs and large organizations. When these ideas are pushed into the external environment, success or failure

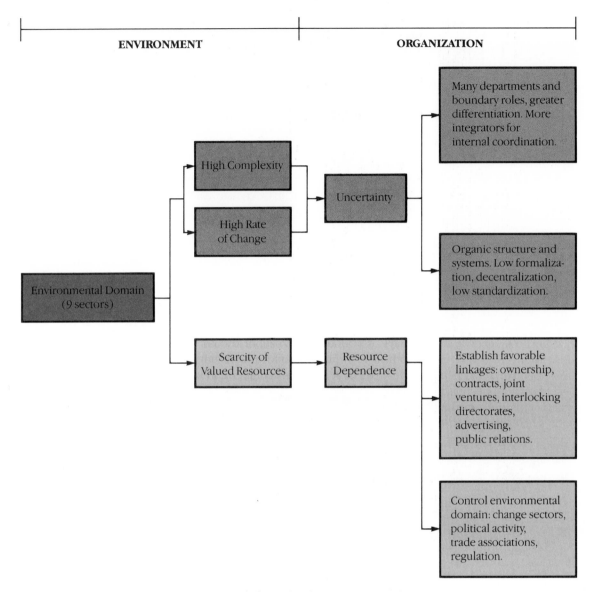

EXHIBIT 2.12. Relationship between Environmental Characteristics and Organizational Actions.

is often a matter of chance—whether external circumstances happen to support it. An idea that failed in the 1960s can be a smashing success in the 1980s because the environment is different. A person who started a small electrical contracting business in a rapidly growing community in Texas or Florida would have an excellent chance of success because of the growth and prosperity in the environment. If the same person were to start the same business in a declining community elsewhere in the United States, the chance of success would be far less. Success or failure thus is determined by characteristics of the environment more than by individual skills or strategies used by the organization.

The population ecology model assumes that new organizations are always appearing. Thus organization populations are continuously undergoing change. The process of change in the population is defined by three principles that occur in stages: variation, selection, and retention. These stages are summarized in Exhibit 2.13.

Principle of Variation   New organizational forms continuously appear in a population of organizations. They are initiated by entrepreneurs, established with venture capital by large corporations, or set up by a government seeking to provide new services. Some forms may be purposefully conceived to cope with a perceived change in the external environment. Others may be blind variations that occur by chance. Analogous to mutations in biology, these variations add to the scope and complexity of organizational forms in the environment.

Principle of Selection   Some variations will suit the external environment better than others. Some variations prove more beneficial and thus are able to acquire resources from the environment necessary to survive. Other variations fail to meet the needs of the environment and perish. When there is insufficient demand for the product and insufficient resources made available to the organization, it will be "selected out." Only a few variations are "selected in" and survive over the longer term.

Principle of Retention   Retention is the preservation and institutionalization of selected organizational forms. Certain technologies, products and personnel are valued by the environment. The preserved organizational form may diffuse through the environment and become a dominant part of the environment. Many forms of organizations are institutionalized, such as government, schools, churches, and the makers of television sets and automobiles. They are relatively permanent features in the population of organizations. But they are not permanent in the long run. The environment is always changing, and if the dominant organizational forms do not develop variations with which to adapt to external change, they will gradually diminish and perhaps perish.

Another principle that underlies the population ecology model is the **struggle for existence.** Organizations and populations are engaged in a competitive struggle over resources. Each organizational form is struggling to survive. The struggle is intense among new organizations, and both the

EXHIBIT 2.13. Elements in the Population Ecology Model of Organizations.

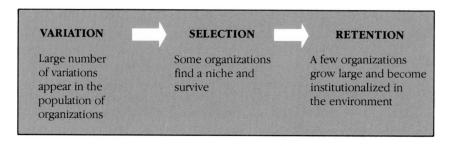

VARIATION	**SELECTION**	**RETENTION**
Large number of variations appear in the population of organizations	Some organizations find a niche and survive	A few organizations grow large and become institutionalized in the environment

birth frequency and survival frequency are related to factors in the larger environment. Factors such as size of urban area, percentage of immigrants, political turbulence, industry growth rate, and environmental variability have been factors in the launching and survival of newspapers, telecommunication firms, railroads, and even physicians.[48]

From the population ecology perspective, the environment is the important determinant of organizational success or failure. The organization must be lucky and meet an environmental need or it will be selected out. For the thousands of organizational forms initiated each year, chance environmental circumstances largely determine which survive and which perish.

The process of variation, selection, and retention leads to the establishment of new organizational forms and to changes in current organizational forms. Variations from existing ideas may emerge within an organization and lead to new products and internal changes that meet environmental needs. The population ecology model explains why change takes place both within and between organizations, why new organizational forms appear, and why many of these forms fail to survive. The following IN PRACTICE illustrates why Timex succeeded as a new form and is now struggling to survive in the competitive watch industry.

IN PRACTICE 2.8

Timex Corporation

During World War II, Timex manufactured clock-timers for artillery shells. But in 1945, the environment changed. The war was over, and there was little demand for these timing mechanisms. Timex's niche was disappearing. Top management decided to adapt the organization to the manufacture of wristwatches. Top management identified a new niche in which Timex could become established. The goal was to produce a highly accurate watch at low cost. Manufacturing techniques rather than crafts people would be used to produce the watches. Manufacturing efficiencies could be realized by using a pen-level movement instead of a jeweled movement.

The manufacturing process was successful, but marketing presented a new set of barriers. Jewelry stores would not handle Timex watches because they undercut traditional lines of watches that provided a larger profit markup. One answer was to develop a new distribution system through drugstores and supermarkets. Another answer was the strong advertising campaign that featured torture tests to show that Timex watches could "take a licking and keep on ticking." The development of Timex's niche required several years of struggle to teach and convince distributors and customers. After eight years, the entire distribution system was in place. Timex watches were distributed through some 250,000 stores. By the late 1960s, every second watch sold in the United States was a Timex.

But times change. In the early 1970s new challengers were taking the field, using the new electronic technology. The electronic era arrived by 1976, when the price of digital watches undercut Timex's mechanical watches. Timex responded with its own line of digital watches, but prices were 50% above the competition. Timex was unable to adapt. By 1982, the company was in real trouble. Operating losses were running about $130 million a year, and the number of outlets was down to about 100,000. By 1983, another new era in wristwatch variation began. Seiko sells a watch that takes your pulse. The Swiss watch industry started producing brightly colored, plastic Swatch watches in scents of banana, raspberry, or mint. Casio has a watch that will translate thirty-six phrases into four foreign languages. The watch of the future will be a personal microelectronic wrist system. The entire industry is in turmoil and no company is making money. Timex is taking a long time to get up to speed, and it may lose further ground before a shakeout in the watch industry occurs.[49]

The Timex watch manufacturing process and distribution system were organizational variations, which after a struggle were selected by the environment. A need existed in the external environment that was coupled with Timex's ability to manufacture watches at low cost. Low-cost watches are institutionalized today. The environment for watch manufacturers continues to change rapidly, however. Now variations threaten the niches of manufacturers that produce low-cost mechanical watches. If Timex is unable to keep up, they may have to move into other lines of business or be selected out by the environment.

SUMMARY AND INTERPRETATION

The single most important idea in this chapter is the overwhelming impact of the external environment on management uncertainty and organization functioning. Organizations are open social systems. They are continuously involved with hundreds of external elements. The change and complexity in environmental domains has major implications for organizational design and action. Most organizational decisions, activities, and outcomes can be traced to stimuli in the external environment.

Organizational environments differ in terms of uncertainty and resource dependence. Organizational uncertainty is the result of the stable-unstable and simple-complex dimensions of the environment. Resource dependence is the result of scarcity of the material and financial resources needed by the organization.

Organization design takes on a logical perspective when the environment is considered. Organizations try to survive and achieve efficiencies in a world characterized by uncertainty and scarcity. Specific departments and functions are created to deal with uncertainties. The organization can be conceptualized as a technical core surrounded by departments that buffer environmental uncertainty. Organizations must have information on relevant external domains, and boundary-spanning roles provide that information.

The concepts in this chapter provide specific frameworks to understand how the environment influences structure and functioning of the organization. Environmental complexity and change, for example, have specific impact on internal complexity and adaptability. Under great uncertainty, more resources are allocated to departments that will plan, deal with specific environmental elements, and integrate diverse internal activities. Moreover, when resources are scarce, the organization can establish linkages through the acquisition of ownership, contracts, joint ventures, interlocking directorates, executive recruitment, or advertising that will maintain a supply of scarce resources. Other techniques for controlling the environment include changing the domain in which the organization operates, political activity, trade associations, and perhaps illegal activities.

Two important themes in this chapter are that organizations can learn and adapt to the environment and that they can also change and control the environment. These strategies are especially true for large organizations that command many resources. They can adapt when necessary, but also neutralize or change problematic areas in the environment. The environment is not fixed. It can be influenced, and indeed should be influenced, by organizations alone or in groups.

Another important idea in this chapter is the concept of population ecology. The focus here is on an entire population of organizations, and the concepts are especially relevant to new, emerging organizations. The concepts of variation, selection, and retention suggest that the needs of the overall environment are more important for success and survival than intentional organization actions. In this view the appropriate role of management is to find a niche where products and services are desired by the larger population. The population is competitive with many organizations struggling to survive. However, even large, established organizations like Timex need to find ways to adapt to new variations and changes appearing in the environment.

KEY CONCEPTS

boundary-spanning roles	mechanistic
buffers	niche
controlling the domain	organic
differentiation	population ecology
domain	resource dependence
environment	retention
environmental change	sectors
environmental complexity	selection
integration	uncertainty
interorganizational linkages	variation
interorganizational set	

DISCUSSION QUESTIONS

1. Define organizational environment. Is it appropriate to include only those elements that actually interact with the organization?

2. Briefly describe the nine environmental sectors identified in the chapter. How does the industry sector differ from the market sector? Are any aspects of the environment not included in these sectors?

3. What is environmental uncertainty? Which has the greatest impact on uncertainty—environmental complexity or environmental change?

4. Why does environmental complexity lead to organizational complexity? Explain.

5. Is changing the organization's domain a feasible strategy for coping with a threatening environment? Explain.

6. Describe differentiation and integration. In what type of environment will differentiation and integration be greatest? Least? In which environment might differentiation occur without extensive integration?

7. Under what environmental condition is organizational planning emphasized? Under what condition is planning likely to be ignored to concentrate on day-to-day operational activities? Is planning an appropriate response to a turbulent environment?

8. What is an organic organization? A mechanistic organization? How does the environment influence organic and mechanistic structures?

9. Why do organizations become involved in interorganizational relationships? Do these relationships affect the organization's dependency on the external environment? Explain.

10. Assume you have been asked to calculate the ratio of staff employees to production employees in two organizations—one in a simple, stable environment and one in a complex, shifting environment. How would you expect these ratios to differ? Why?

11. How do the processes of variation, selection, and retention explain the evolution of a population of organizations?

12. What role does chance play in the population ecology model? If chance processes dominate, what relevance does the model have for managers?

GUIDES TO ACTION

As an organization designer:

1. Scan the external environment for threats, changes, and opportunities. Organize elements in the external environment into nine sectors for analysis: industry, market, raw materials, human resources, financial resources, technology, government, economic conditions, and cultures. Focus on sectors that may experience significant change at any time.

2. Match internal organization structure to the external environment. If the external environment is complex, make the organization structure complex. Reflect the rate of environmental change in the internal structure. Associate a stable environment with a mechanistic structure, and an unstable environment with an organic structure. If the external environment is both complex and changing, make the organization highly differentiated and organic, and have mechanisms to achieve coordination across departments.

3. Reach out and control external sectors that threaten needed resources. Influence the domain by engaging in political activity, by joining trade associations, and by establishing favorable linkages. Establish linkages through merger, contracts, joint ventures, interlocking directorates, advertising, and executive recruitment. Reduce the amount of change or threat from the external environment so that the organization will not have to change internally.

4. Adapt the organization to new variations being selected and retained in the external environment. If you are starting a new organization, find a niche

that contains a strong environmental need for the products and services you provide, and be prepared for a competitive struggle over scarce resources.

Consider these Guides when analyzing the following case.

CASE FOR ANALYSIS

PENNSYLVANIA MOVIE THEATRES, INC.*

The Corporate Perspective

Pennsylvania Movie Theatres, Inc. (PMT) is an organization of largely autonomous and previously independent theatres located throughout Pennsylvania. Several years ago, twenty-eight manager-owners of privately held operations exchanged their theatre ownerships for PMT stock and the right to continue as theatre managers with the newly formed corporation. At their first annual meeting, the managers voted to select a five-member Board of Directors from their ranks to coordinate theatre operations and to oversee all corporate activities. Further, they determined that one new director would be elected each year to fill a scheduled vacancy. Each director would serve in a part-time capacity for a four-year term at $3,000 per year.

The PMT managers believe that as a corporation they have better opportunities and capabilities than were available to them when they owned their theatres separately. Because of their system of cooperative exchange, they are better able to minimize film rental and advertising costs. They can also offer better opportunities for advancement to their assistant managers. Additionally, the corporate form enables the managers to provide support to weaker member theatres because of their collective managerial experience and collective financial strength. Taking a long-term perspective, the managers believe that this consolidation arrangement will result in more profitable operation for all theatres.

The PMT managers wish to offer their communities a safe, inexpensive, and pleasurable leisure-time activity. By satisfying these and other societal needs, they believe that they can achieve their basic corporate objectives of survival and profitability. Among other pertinent societal needs, the managers see the desire for:

1. a safe, inexpensive form of entertainment;
2. a wholesome, imaginative, and stimulating children's diversion;
3. a forum for social debate;
4. an opportunity for family activity;
5. a source for employment of local manpower;
6. an "escape" from demanding realities;
7. an opportunity for educational and cultural enhancement.

Because of their concern for satisfying these needs, the managers choose their films carefully, attempting to offer high-quality movies at the peak of their popularity. They are also concerned with appealing to an audience that includes people of all ages and descriptions. The managers see the corpo-

* This case was written by Dr. John A. Pearce, II, Professor of Management, College of Business Administration, University of South Carolina. Reprinted by permission of the author.

ration as a group of "family theatres," so they want to ensure that, with few exceptions, a family unit can attend any show at a PMT theatre without totally sacrificing the enjoyment of any single member. Since their incorporation, PMT theatres have therefore restricted their film offerings primarily to those movies rated "G" (general audience), "PG" (parental guidance suggested), and "R" (restricted to persons over 18). With rare exceptions, "X"-rated, but never "hard" pornographic, films have been shown.

The managers also want to ensure that the family can enjoy a movie in pleasant surroundings. They attempt to maintain a future-oriented perspective in supervising the daily operations of theatres as well as when selecting films to be shown. Theatre facilities are periodically renovated, and employees are well trained. All of these efforts are expended in order to provide the most comfortable of theatre experiences and to ensure continued audience patronage.

PMT gauges its corporate performance in a number of different ways, among which are ticket sales by type, show time, and movie rating; quarterly revenues; and quarterly profits. Last year, PMT's seventh in operation, the net profits of the PMT theatres dropped almost 7% from the year before, even though during the same period, the theatre industry at large had reached all-time high profit levels. Two years ago, the return on investment achieved by PMT had been 11.7%, while the industry average was 11.3%. Last year, the return on investment for PMT was down to 10.1%, while the industry average climbed to 11.8%. The industry average return on investment for the past five years was 10.9%.

In reviewing the performance of individual films shown during the past year, the PMT directors found that the few "X"-rated films they had offered far and away resulted in the greatest profit per film, followed by those rated "R." They also noted that on dates when their competitors had shown pornographic-type films, they had appeared to outdraw PMT theatres. Further, since adult ticket sales are the most profitable, the "loss" of these customers probably represented an associated loss in net income.

An Alternative

A major film distributor recently approached the PMT directors with an offer to supply them with a selection of good-quality "X"-rated and pornographic-type films for the minimum contract period of twelve months. If ordered, these films would constitute approximately one-third of the movies shown at any single theatre during the year, with the remaining two-thirds being supplied by the corporation's present distributor.

While a revised movie offering would not require any major technological changes for PMT (e.g., the present projection screens and sound systems would be adequate), there is a potentially strong psychological impact upon both the PMT employees and their audiences.

Thus, the directors realize that a large and varied set of factors needs to be taken into consideration prior to any contractual commitment to the second distributor.

One such factor is the possible consequence of a bill currently before the Pennsylvania State Legislature that would ban the showing of pornographic films within the state. Although the bill is being hotly debated, it is given only a 10% chance of being passed. The directors are also watching the upcoming gubernatorial election in the state with particular interest. One of the declared candidates is running as a "morality" candidate, and a major plank in his platform is the banning of all "X"-rated films in Pennsylvania theatres. While he is given only a 5% chance of being elected, the news media have given great attention to the "morality issues" raised by this candidate, as they have to the pending legislation.

On the other hand, the directors perceive a widespread belief among the general population that sexual explicitness in any medium has some value. They also sense growing support for the individual's right to decide what does or does not possess redeeming social value.

Another factor that the directors have considered is that as the nation's affluence increases, so does its leisure time and its demand for leisure-time activities such as movie theatre entertainment. They are uncertain, however, about the effects that current economic conditions will have upon their operations. They expect an economic recession but are unsure whether the accompanying period of "tight" money will bring more people to the theatre in lieu of more expensive forms of entertainment or, alternatively, whether all entertainment businesses will suffer.

Another consideration affecting the directors' decision is the fact that the majority of PMT theatres are in small- to medium-sized towns with an average population of 23,569 people. All of the theatres are located in downtown business districts, and all theatre fronts open onto main shopping streets. In nearly every case, however, the PMT theatres have a competitor within two city blocks. These facts concern the directors, since they believe that trends toward liberalism are relatively slow to develop in small towns and that any failure on their part would be to the immediate advantage of their competitors.

The possible impact upon price policies and theatre hours is also being considered. The average for an adult movie ticket at a PMT theatre in the past year was $2.675, while the average for PMT competitors was estimated at $2.83. Should the second contract be approved, PMT estimates that its average could rise to $2.77, reflecting the corporation's ability to increase its rates for the "X"-rated movie audiences.

Although show hours vary slightly among PMT theatres, the pattern for weekdays includes a matinee at 2:00 P.M. and two evening shows at 7:30 P.M. and 9:30 P.M.. On weekends, a late-afternoon performance at 5:30 P.M. is added. On Saturdays, the matinee is often reserved for the showing of children's films which are scheduled by the individual managers especially for this purpose. Although these films contribute no profit to the corporation— because of their low ticket prices—the managers feel that this policy develops goodwill between the theatre and the community. No change in these theatre hours is anticipated by the directors in the event that the second supplier contract is signed.

In addition to price policies (selective rate increases needed) and to theatre hours (no changes required), the directors have considered the possible effects of showing "X"-rated films on other facets of the theatres' operations, for example, media advertising and in-theatre promotion.

PMT theatres currently advertise through the radio and newspaper media. Whether or not the new contract with the supplier of the "X"-rated films is signed, these two media will continue to be used, with the expectation that neither costs nor potential audiences will change significantly.

However, if the contract is signed, some changes with in-house promotion will probably be necessary. One possible plan is that the audiences of "G"-, "PG"-, and "R"-rated movies will be exposed only to previews and billboards advertising similarly rated movies. The exception will be in the case of viewers of "X"-rated movies, who will be shown in-theatre promotions on any up-coming films, regardless of their ratings.

Concession stand operations are not expected to be affected, since on previous occasions when "X"-rated movies were shown, managers did not notice any changes in concession volume or item preference. The directors believe that the concession stand will continue to yield approximately 53¢ (gross) per customer regardless of the movie being shown.

PMT's distribution channels should be unaffected in the event that a contract with the second film supplier is approved. No additional distribution costs are expected, therefore, but some inventory control changes would be necessary. The main change would be that the two brands of film would need to be kept separate in the film depository, which would be possible through the initiation of a second numerical filing system. The PMT managers recognize the difficulties commonly associated with such a new system but feel that the required adjustments could be quickly overcome.

No attempt has yet been made to determine how nonmanagerial PMT employees would feel about an increase in the number of "X"-rated films being shown in their theatres. Of central concern is the impact that the change might have upon the employees' interest in union membership. To management's knowledge, no attempt has ever been made by its employees to bring in a union. The directors attribute this favorable situation to its employee relations effort and to the high turnover rate among its teenage employees. To date, there has been only one incident, involving a fifty-five-year-old female street booth ticket clerk who objected to "dirty films," to indicate that the employees might react negatively to any increase in "X"-rated offerings.

Consolidated Projections

After conducting the broad based assessment of the impact that offering "X"-rated and pornographic films might have upon PMT's profits, the directors reached the following projection for three years from now, assuming that the second contract is signed:

■ Likelihood of reaching or exceeding industry average   30%
■ Likelihood of equaling their own performance of last year   30%
■ Likelihood of 10% decrease in the PMT return on investment from the previous year   20%
■ Likelihood of 20% (or greater) decrease in the PMT return on investment from the previous year   20%

Overall, the directors foresee an opportunity to increase business by attracting a new segment of moviegoers. Additionally, the prospective new supplier argues that regular adult PMT customers will attend the theatre more often. Thus, the directors believe that a revised film offering could enable them to better meet the interests of an enlarged segment of the population and that, in return, these customers would help ensure PMT's long-term survival.

Should they contract with the second supplier, the directors plan to monitor the corporate performance carefully. Among their targets would be the following:

1. Adult ticket sales per movie for all but "X"-rated films should remain stable or increase slightly.
2. Children's ticket sales should remain stable or increase slightly.
3. Adult ticket sales per movie on "X"-rated films should exceed adult ticket sales per movie for films of any other rating.
4. Quarterly profits, adjusted for seasonal variations, should reflect an upward trend.

In the event that any of these targets is not being met, it would signal a need to reassess the wisdom of the revised film offering.

Although the PMT directors have the responsibility of proposing corporate strategy, the success of the strategy rests upon the commitment of the managers in carrying it out. The question arises for the directors as to the extent to which the managers would give the films of the second supplier a "real chance." Although, or since, a manager's bonus reflects the degree of profit of his theatre, he may be reluctant to fully implement a new strategy regardless of the directors' judgment. A recent straw vote of managers to the question "Do you favor an increased offering of 'X'-rated and pornographic-type films?" showed twelve in favor, five against, and eleven undecided.

In two months, the annual stockholders' meeting will take place. The managers all anticipate that the main order of business will be a discussion of the directors' proposal regarding a contract with the second distributor.

Questions

1. Analyze the environment of PMT with respect to sectors, uncertainty and resources. How compatible is the environment with PMT's goals, strengths, and structure?

2. Should PMT sign a contract with the second film distributor? Why? What other strategies might PMT adopt to succeed in its environment? Explain.

NOTES

1. Craig R. Waters, "The Private War of James Sullivan," *Inc.*, July, 1982:41–46. Used with permission.

2. Jeffrey Pfeffer and Gerald R. Salancik, *The External Control of Organizations: A Resource Dependent Perspective* (New York: Harper & Row, 1978), p. 138.

3. John Bussey, "P & G's New Disposable Diaper Intensifies Marketing Battle With Kimberly-Clark," *The Wall Street Journal*, January 4, 1985, p. 13.

4. Dean Rotbart and Laurie P. Cohen, "The Party at Mary Kay Isn't Quite So Lively As Recruiting Falls Off," *The Wall Street Journal*, October 23, 1983, pp. 1–25.

5. James Cook, "Nothing But the Best," *Forbes*, September 28, 1981, p. 157.

6. "State Regulators Rush in Where Washington No Longer Treads," *Business Week,* September 19, 1983, pp. 124–131.

7. Herman Nickel, "Dante in the Federal Inferno," *Fortune,* June 2, 1980, pp. 78–83. © 1980 Time, Inc. All rights reserved.

8. Albert R. Karr, "Air-Traffic Controllers' Abuse of Drugs Alarms Many in the Profession," *The Wall Street Journal,* May 27, 1983, pp. 1–12; "Job Rights for Gays: The Price Tag Gets Higher," *Business Week,* November 26, 1984, pp. 135–137.

9. Howard E. Aldrich, *Organizations and Environments* (Englewood Cliffs, NJ: Prentice-Hall, 1979); Fred E. Emery and Eric L. Trist, "The Causal Texture of Organizational Environments," *Human Relations* 18 (1965):21–32.

10. Robert B. Duncan, "Characteristics of Organizational Environment and Perceived Environmental Uncertainty," *Administrative Science Quarterly* 17 (1972):313–327; Gregory G. Dess and Donald W. Beard, "Dimensions of Organizational Task Environments," *Administrative Science Quarterly* 29 (1984):52–73.

11. Ray Jurkovich, "A Core Typology of Organizational Environments," *Administrative Science Quarterly* 19 (1974):380–394.

12. Ibid.; Dess and Beard, "Dimensions of Organizational Task Environments."

13. J. A. Litterer, *The Analysis of Organizations,* 2nd ed. (New York: Wiley, 1973), p. 335.

14. "Garment Makers Wear Black," *Business Week,* September 27, 1982, pp. 91–92.

15. Rosalie L. Tung, "Dimensions of Organizational Environments: An Exploratory Study of Their Impact on Organization Structure," *Academy of Management Journal* 22 (1979):672–693.

16. Joseph E. McCann and John Selsky, "Hyperturbulence and the Emergence of Type 5 Environments," *Academy of Management Review* 9 (1984):460–470.

17. Ranse Crain, "A Conversation with Hugh Hefner," *Advertising Age,* July 21, 1975, pp. 25–26, 28–32.

18. Inspired by and adapted from Kristen M. Dahlen, Sandra Hart, and Joanne Williams, "Breeding the Bunny: Playboy Enterprises, Inc.: A Case Analysis," unpublished manuscript, Texas A&M University, 1982; Sandra Salmans, "Profits Again at a Shrunken Playboy," *New York Times,* March 25, 1984, pp. F1, 24.

19. Ross W. Ashby, *An Introduction to Cybernetics* (New York: Wiley, Science Edition, 1956).

20. James D. Thompson, *Organizations in Action* (New York: McGraw-Hill, 1967), pp. 20–21.

21. David B. Jemison, "The Importance of Boundary Spanning Roles in Strategic Decision-Making," *Journal of Management Studies* 21 (1984):131–152; Howard Aldrich and Diane Herker, "Boundary Spanning Roles and Organization Structure," *Academy of Management Review* 2 (1977):217–239.

22. Ibid.

23. Adapted from John Koten, "In Airlines' Rate War, Small Daily Skirmishes Often Decide Winners," *The Wall Street Journal,* August 24, 1984, pp. 1, 8.

24. Jay W. Lorsch, "Introduction to the Structural Design of Organizations," in Gene W. Dalton, Paul R. Lawrence, and Jay W. Lorsch, eds., *Organization Structure and Design* (Homewood, IL: Irwin and Dorsey, 1970), p. 5.

25. Paul R. Lawrence and Jay W. Lorsch, *Organization and Environment* (Homewood, IL: Irwin, 1969).

26. Lorsch, "Introduction to Structural Design," p. 7.

27. Jay W. Lorsch and Paul R. Lawrence, "Environmental Factors and Organizational Integration," in J. W. Lorsch and Paul R. Lawrence, eds., *Organizational Planning: Cases and Concepts* (Homewood, IL: Irwin and Dorsey, 1972), p. 45.

28. Tom Burns and G. M. Stalker, *The Management of Innovation* (London: Tavistock, 1961).

29. Ibid., pp. 92–94. Reprinted by permission.

30. Mansour Javidan, "The Impact of Environmental Uncertainty on Long-Range Planning Practices of the U.S. Savings and Loan Industry," *Strategic Management Journal* 5 (1984):381–392; Tung, "Dimensions of Organizational Environments," pp. 672–693; Thompson, *Organizations in Action.*

31. Tung, "Dimensions of Organizational Environments," pp. 672–693.

32. David Ulrich and Jay B. Barney, "Perspectives in Organizations: Resource Dependence, Efficiency, and Population," *Academy of Management Review* 9 (1984):471–481; Jeffrey Pfeffer and Gerald Salancik, *The External Control of Organizations* (New York: Harper and Row, 1978).

33. Keith G. Provan, "Technology and Interorganizational Activity As Predictors of Client Referrals," *Academy of Management Journal* 27 (1984):811–829; David A. Whetten and Thomas K. Leung, "The Instrumental Value of Interorganizational Relations: Antecedents and Consequences of Linkage Formation," *Academy of Management Journal* 22 (1979):325–344.

34. Paul M. Hirsch, "Processing Fads and Fashions: An Organization-Set Analysis of Cultural Industry Systems," *American Journal of Sociology* 72 (1972):639–659.

35. Steven K. Paulson, "Causal Analysis of Interorganizational Relations: An Axiomatic Theory Revised," *Administrative Science Quarterly* 19 (1974):319–337; Andrew H. Van de Ven, "On the Nature, Formation and Maintenance of Relations Among Organizations," *Academy of Management Review* 1 (1976):24–36; Whetten and Leung, "Instrumental Value of Interorganizational Relations."

36. Andrew H. Van de Ven and Gordon Walker, "The Dynamics of Interorganizational Coordination," *Administrative Science Quarterly* 29 (1984):598–621; Huseyin Leblebici and Gerald R. Salancik, "Stability in Interorganizational Exchanges: Rulemaking Processes of the Chicago Board of Trade," *Administrative Science Quarterly,* 27 (1982):227–242.

37. Adapted from Janet Guyon, "Do Publications Avoid Anti-Cigarette Stories to Protect Ad Dollars?" *The Wall Street Journal,* November 22, 1982, pp. 1, 16.

38. Judith A. Babcock, *Organizational Responses to Resource Scarcity and Munificence: Adaptation and Modification in Colleges Within a University,* doctoral dissertation, The Pennsylvania State University, 1981.

39. This discussion is based on Jeffrey Pfeffer, "Beyond Management and the Worker: The Institutional Function of Management," *Academy of Management Review* 1 (April, 1976):36–46; and Kotter, "Managing External Dependence," pp. 87–92.

40. "Reshaping the Computer Industry," *Business Week,* July 16, 1984, pp. 84–98.

41. "Lucky-Goldstar: Using Joint Ventures to Spring Ahead in the High-Tech Race," *Business Week,* July 9, 1984, pp. 102–103.

42. Donald Palmer, "Broken Ties: Interlocking Directorates and Intercorporate Coordination," *Administrative Science Quarterly* 28 (1983):40–55; F. David Shoorman, Max H. Bazerman, and Robert S. Atkin, "Interlocking Directorates: A Strategy for Reducing Environmental Uncertainty," *Academy of Management Review* 6 (1981):243–251; Ronald S. Burt, *Toward a Structural Theory of Action* (New York: Academic Press, 1982).

43. "Movie, TV Firms Building Alliances to Take Advantage of Home Video," *The Wall Street Journal,* March 26, 1982, p. 23. Used with permission.

44. Kotter, "Managing External Dependence."

45. Bryan Burrough, "Oil-Field Investigators Say Fraud Flourishes from Wells to Offices," *The Wall Street Journal,* January 15, 1985, pp. 1, 20; Irwin Ross, "How Lawless Are Big Companies?" *Fortune,* December 1, 1980, p. 57–64.

46. Barry M. Staw and Eugene Szwajkowski, "The Scarcity-Munificence Component of Organizational Environments and the Commission of Illegal Acts," *Administrative Science Quarterly* 20 (1975):345–354.

47. Howard Aldrich, Bill McKelvey, and Dave Ulrich, "Design Strategy from the Population Perspective," *Journal of Management* 10 (1984):67–86; Howard E. Aldrich and Jeffrey Pfeffer, "Environments of Organizations," *Annual Review of Sociology,*

vol. 2 (Palo Alto, CA: Annual Reviews Inc., 1976):79–105; Howard E. Aldrich, *Organizations and Environments* (Englewood Cliffs, NJ: Prentice-Hall, 1979); Michael Hannan and John Freeman, "The Population Ecology of Organizations," *American Journal of Sociology* 82 (1977): 929–964.

48. Jacques Delacroix and Glenn R. Carroll, "Organizational Foundings: An Ecological Study of the Newspaper Industries of Argentina and Ireland," *Administrative Science Quarterly* 28 (1983):274–291; Johannes M. Pennings, "Organizational Birth Frequencies: An Empirical Investigation," *Administrative Science Quarterly* 27 (1982):120–144; David Marple, "Technological Innovation and Organizational Survival: A Population Ecology Study of Nineteenth-Century American Railroads," *The Sociological Quarterly* 23 (1982):107–116; Thomas G. Rundall and John O. McClain, "Environmental Selection and Physician Supply," *American Journal of Sociology* 87 (1982):1090–1112.

49. Adapted from Myron Magnet, "Timex Takes the Torture Test," *Fortune,* June 27, 1983, pp. 112–119; Charles E. Summer, *Strategic Behavior in Business and Government* (Boston: Little-Brown, 1980); "A Last-Minute Comeback for Swiss Watch Makers," *Business Week,* November 26, 1984, pp. 139–142.

CHAPTER THREE

Goals and Effectiveness

RALSTON PURINA COMPANY

William P. Stiritz, President of the $5-billion Ralston Purina agribusiness giant, learned a lesson in the early 1960s that shapes his approach to business today.

In the early days, he was a brand manager at Pillsbury. Another bright young brand manager figured out a way to drive up sales of angel food cake mix. Prices were cut 20% in the Denver area. Volume doubled. The brand manager persuaded Pillsbury to extend the price-cutting strategy nationwide. Then competitors responded with price cuts of their own. As a result, Pillsbury's profits plunged. The brand manager was fired.

The lesson Mr. Stiritz learned was to maintain profit margins, even if market share is sacrificed. "The end isn't just selling goods," Mr. Stiritz stresses, but rather to "earn an adequate return. That goal sometimes gets lost." [1]

The goal of adequate profit margins is being applied to each of Ralston's divisions. The division that sells Chicken of the Sea tuna, for example, has 30% of the market but has been only marginally profitable. The industry requires huge amounts of capital and discounts to retailers. Mr. Stiritz is moving to increase the division's profitability by eliminating its marketing structure, which will save several million dollars. Tuna will be sold through another division. Mr. Stiritz believes that running with marginal profits is a poor way to do business.

The board of directors appointed Mr. Stiritz president because they approve of his philosophy. He came to their attention during an intense domestic pet-food war that began in 1977. As vice-president, he was confronted with four major competitors spending more than $100 million to introduce new dog-food products.

Pet food is the largest source of Ralston's profits. The company had more than 40% of the dog and cat food market. Instead of lowering prices to protect market share, Mr. Stiritz decided to hold prices stable and step up product development and advertising.

Market share dropped several points but profits held up. Competitors found that the pet-food market was not an easy payday. Ralston's market share quickly recovered. The directors admired his coolness. Instead of panicking when market share dropped, he stuck to the goals he considered most important for Ralston.

Stiritz's goals are a stark contrast to those of his predecessor, R. Hal Dean. Dean's primary goal was rapid growth, which was accomplished through a series of acquisitions, including the Jack-in-the-Box fast-food chain and the St. Louis Blues hockey team. The rapid growth and flamboyant deal-making often was accomplished at the expense of profits. Stiritz has redirected Ralston toward cutting back to achieve high profits from core businesses.

Under Stiritz's guidance, Ralston Purina is also concerned for employees and the community. The company recently completed a transformation of the area surrounding its St. Louis headquarters from a slum into a well-manicured community. The community now has new homes, rehabilitated town houses, apartments for the elderly, churches, and light industrial facilities.

Why invest in real estate? Ralston Purina believes that attractive, safe surroundings attract the very best employees. It also makes the existing land and buildings more valuable real estate assets. The investment will not show up in profit margins, but employees at the St. Louis headquarters are delighted. A textbook example of the worst type of urban decay is now an attractive community where several employees reside.[2]

An **organizational goal** is a desired state of affairs that the organization attempts to realize.[3] The desired state of affairs at Ralston Purina is composed of several elements. First, William Stiritz and other top managers want to make a solid profit, which seems to be the primary goal. They also want to sell goods. They want to maintain a reasonable market share. Managers are also concerned with attracting quality employees and maintaining an attractive community around Ralston's St. Louis headquarters. Moreover, Ralston has both long- and short-term goals. Ralston will sacrifice profits in one period to gain larger profits later on. They will also invest in nonmarketing activities, such as real estate, to secure stability in its valued labor force. Other outcomes, such as growth, providing an adequate return to investors, and customer loyalty, may also be goals at Ralston.

What can we learn about goals from the Ralston case? First, a large organization like Ralston has many goals. Second, these goals are in competition with one another. The goal of high profits may hurt the goal of market share. The goal of being in an attractive community may work against the goal of profits. Third, managers decide upon goals. Goals are not fixed. Goals are value judgments, and different managers have different goals. Fourth, some goals are the means to achieve other goals. Goals are linked together. The immediate goal of introducing a new product may lead to the attainment of the long-term goal of high profits.

Purpose of This Chapter

The purpose of this chapter is to explore the issues of organizational goals and effectiveness. We want to understand the types of goals that organizations pursue, and the importance of these goals to organizational performance. Organizations are goal-attainment devices. Organizations are tools that owners and managers use to achieve certain ends. The clear statement of an organizational goal is extremely important for communicating the organization's purpose to employees and to external groups.

In order to manage organizations well, managers need a clear sense of organizational goals, and of how to measure the effectiveness of organizational efforts. The first part of this chapter explores the types of goals used within organizations and the process by which goals are chosen. The latter part of the chapter evaluates the relative strengths and weaknesses of the more popular approaches for measuring effectiveness.

ORGANIZATIONAL GOALS

Importance of Goals

Why should we care about organizational goals? Two reasons. First, goals represent the reason for an organization's existence. An organization is a goal-attainment device. Without some purpose, there is no need for the organization. Goals summarize and articulate that purpose.

The second reason for studying goals is that the management process of identifying goals and carrying them out provides several benefits for the organization. The presence of goals provides legitimacy for the organization, direction and motivation of employees, decision guidelines, criteria of performance, and reduction of uncertainty.

Legitimacy　For corporations, legitimacy is granted in a legal charter. Corporations are given the right to produce goods and services for a profit. Not-for-profit organizations are also granted legal rights to incarcerate prisoners, provide welfare services, or to perform the myriad activities of local and federal government.

Just as important as the legal charter, the stated goals of the organization provide a symbol of legitimacy to external constituencies. Goals describe the purpose of the organization so people know what it stands for and will accept its existence. Goals also legitimize the organization for employees. Employees join and become committed to an organization when they identify with the organization's stated goals. Goals serve to legitimize the organization by signaling to both internal and external groups what the organization stands for.

One task of management is to establish the legitimacy of the organization's output. For economic organizations, if the product is viewed as legitimate it will be purchased and the firm can make a profit. Organizations in the tobacco industry, for example, voice the legitimacy of cigarettes, but at the same time have diversified so that they do not depend upon the acceptance of cigarettes for their organization's prosperity.

Not-for-profit organizations and government agencies must maintain the goodwill of external groups such as legislators, taxpayers, and users in order to survive. In recent years, the role of welfare departments has been questioned by taxpayers, and hence many departments are receiving fewer funds.

Employee Direction and Motivation　Goals give a sense of direction to organization participants. The stated end toward which an organization is striving tells employees what they are working toward. Goals help motivate participants, especially if they help select the goals. At 3M, for example, the overall goal that "25% of sales should come from products developed in the past five years" is widely accepted and pursued by employees. All employees work toward innovation. Employee motivation can sometimes be in a negative direction as well. American Express pressured its subsidiaries to meet the goal of a 36th straight year of earnings increases. To comply, Fireman's Fund managers used doubtful accounting practices to inflate earnings. When discovered, American Express's profits and image plummeted.[4]

Decision Guidelines　The goals of an organization also act as guidelines for employee decision-making. Organizational goals are a set of constraints on individual behavior and decisions.[5] By directing employees toward certain outcomes, goals also tell employees what to avoid. Goals help define the correct decisions concerning organization structure, innovation, employee welfare, and growth. When Owens-Illinois Inc., the glass container manufacturer, established the goal of reducing volume to improve profits, internal decisions were redirected. Owens-Illinois had been a volume-oriented company and would run marginal plants just to maintain volume. The new goals of increased profits provided guidelines that led to the closing of these marginal plants. Similarly, when regional managers at Ralston understood that the primary goal was to make a reasonable profit, they could adopt behavior that enhanced this goal rather than attempting to penetrate new markets with price-cutting efforts.

Reduce Uncertainty   The process of goal-setting and reaching agreement about specific goals reduces uncertainty for organization participants. This is especially true for senior managers. The desired future state of the organization may involve diverse and conflicting opinions. Goal-setting enables management to discuss options and to settle upon the goals that are most important and should take priority. Once goals are established, there is a sense of relief and accomplishment. Uncertainty is reduced for the entire organization:

> Goal-setting is attempted as a psychological means for reducing uncertainty, and when participants succeed in stating and agreeing on goals, it symbolizes a reduction in uncertainty. It is, in this case, an agreement, usually tacit, on a prediction: "This is what can be made to work out. . . ."[6]

Criteria of Performance   Goals provide a standard for assessment.[7] The level of organization performance, whether in terms of profits, units produced, or number of complaints, needs a basis for evaluation. Is a profit of 10% on sales good enough? The answer lies in goals. Goals reflect past experience and describe the desired state for the future. If the profit goal is 8%, then a 10% return is excellent. When Owens-Illinois shifted from volume to profit goals, profits increased by 30%. This occurred during the period when two competitors reported profit declines of 61% and 76%. Profit became the criteria of performance rather than production volume as during previous years.[8]

Types of Goals

Many types of goals exist in an organization, and each type performs a different function. One of the major distinctions is between the officially stated goals of the organization and the goals that it actually pursues.

Official Goals   **Official goals** are the formally defined outcomes that the organization states it is trying to achieve. Official goals describe the organization's mission, what it should be doing, the reason it exists, and the values that underlie its existence.[9]

Official goals are normally written down in a policy manual or in the annual report. They are also emphasized in public addresses by top officials of the organization. Upon close analysis, official goals may appear abstract and vague. They describe a value system for the organization, so they are not specific or measurable. Official goals serve the purpose of legitimizing the organization. Official goal or mission statements are designed to appeal to public opinion. They signal the purpose of the organization to important constituencies. Official goals are also the goals that employees identify with as they become committed to the organization. The following IN PRACTICE illustrates the enduring mission as reflected in official goal statements of Hewlett-Packard and a high school district.

IN PRACTICE 3.1

Hewlett-Packard

Early in 1984, the touchscreen HP 150, Hewlett-Packard's first major entry in the personal computer business, failed in the marketplace. The company that had years of prosperity based on engineering excellence could not keep pace with rapid changes in the small computer market. The setback hurt, but has not changed the enduring goals of Hewlett-Packard. The current needs of the marketplace, and the year-to-year fluctuations in the environment, do not change the basic mission. Hewlett-Packard exists to accomplish several ends, which are summarized in Exhibit 3.1. These ends pertain to serving customers, growth, taking care of people, creativity, corporate citizenship, and profits. These goals communicate HP values to customers and employees alike.

Not-for-profit organizations have official goals also. An example of goals developed for a high school district is also illustrated in Exhibit 3.1. These goals are founded on the belief in a democratic way of life and the intrinsic worth of every student. Individuals must be given the opportunity for maximum development of their capabilities through education. Administrators and teachers within the district are committed to encouraging students to become thinking, feeling, creative, healthy, communicating, contributing members of society. The official goals are used to direct efforts toward providing each student with high-quality instruction.

The official goals for both organizations provide enduring statements that are not affected by events in the short run. The school district may suffer from increases in students that strain its resources, or from enrollment decline because of population migration. Hewlett-Packard suffered temporary reverses in the personal computer market. But official goals do not pertain to month-to-month or year-to-year performance. Official goals set the premise and provide the overall framework within which employees function, and they tell people outside the organization what it stands for. Incidentally, by the end of 1984, Hewlett-Packard had brought out three additional new products in the personal computer market, and they caused quite a stir. By sticking to its overall goals of innovation and customer satisfaction, Hewlett-Packard learned how to succeed in this new market.[10]

Operative Goals

Now we turn to the concept of operative goals. **Operative goals** designate the ends sought through the actual operating procedures of the organization and tell us what the organization is actually trying to do.[11] Operative goals describe desired operational activities and are often concerned with the short run. Operative goals are intended to be the means through which official goals are accomplished.

Operative goals typically pertain to the primary tasks an organization must perform.[12] Primary tasks are similar to the subsystem activities identified in chapter one. These subsystems pertain to management, boundary spanning, maintenance, adaptation, and production. Management is concerned with performance goals for the overall organization, such as profit and growth. Boundary spanning goals pertain to the acquisition of resources and the marketing of outputs. Maintenance goals pertain to employee development. Adaptation goals pertain to innovation and change. Production goals pertain

EXHIBIT 3.1. Official Goals for Hewlett-Packard and a High School District.

Hewlett-Packard	High School District
1. To achieve sufficient profit to finance our company growth and to provide the resources we need to achieve our other corporate objectives.	1. To develop intellectual curiosity, a love of learning, and skills in communication and basic subjects.
2. To provide products and services of the greatest possible value to our customers, thereby gaining and holding their respect and loyalty.	2. To develop the ability to cope with problems and to seek solutions through effective use of knowledge, and the application of both logical and creative problem-solving techniques.
3. To enter new fields only when the ideas we have, together with our technical, manufacturing, and marketing skills, assure that we can make a needed and profitable contribution to the field.	3. To develop the capacity for self-direction and self-discipline by fostering a sense of self-worth and an awareness of one's ability to influence one's own destiny.
4. To let our growth be limited only by our profits and our ability to develop and produce technical products that satisfy real customer needs.	4. To impart a sense of historical perspective, and appreciation of the heritage of humankind and an understanding of the rights and responsibilities of citizenship that will encourage a respect for the rights of others.
5. To help our own people share in the company's success, which they make possible: to provide job security based on their performance, to recognize their individual achievements, and to help them gain a sense of satisfaction and accomplishment from their work.	5. To develop the ability for the expression of ideas and emotions through participation in creative and cultural activities.
6. To foster initiative and creativity by allowing the individual great freedom of action in attaining well-defined objectives.	6. To become aware of career opportunities and develop skills to pursue an occupation and/or continued education.
7. To honor our obligations to society by being an economic, intellectual, and social asset to each nation and each community in which we operate.	7. To acquire an understanding of personal hygiene, nutrition, and physical exercises, develop wholesome attitudes toward competition, and learn lifetime physical skills essential to the maintenance of personal health.
	8. To develop knowledge about and a positive attitude toward the structure and processes of the American Free Enterprise System.

to efficiency. Specific goals for each primary task are important because they provide direction for the day-to-day decisions and activities within departments. Each type of goal and the purpose it serves are summarized in Exhibit 3.2.

Overall Performance Goals Managers are responsible for overall performance. **Profitability** reflects the overall performance of for-profit organizations. Profitability may be expressed in terms of net income, earnings per share, or return on investment. Other overall goals are growth and output volume. Growth pertains to increases in sales or profits over time. Volume pertains to total sales or the amount of products or services delivered. Not-for-profit organizations do not have overall goals of profitability, but they do have goals that attempt to specify the delivery of services to the public within specified budget expense levels. Growth and volume goals also may be indicators of overall performance in not-for-profit organizations.

EXHIBIT 3.2. Goal Type and Purpose.

Type	Purpose
OFFICIAL GOALS	Legitimacy
OPERATIVE GOALS:	Employee Direction and Motivation
Overall Performance (profit, volume, growth)	Decision Guidelines
	Reduction of Uncertainty
Resources	Standard of Performance
Market	
Employee Development	
Innovation	
Productivity	

Resources   Resource goals pertain to the acquisition of needed material and financial resources from the environment. Resource goals may involve the acquisition of financing for the construction of new plants, finding less expensive sources for raw materials, or hiring top quality employees. Resource goals are typically executed by departments on the input side of the organizational transformation process. Purchasing, personnel, and finance departments help achieve these goals.

Market   Market goals relate to the output side of the transformation process and define the market share or market standing desired by the organization. Market goals may involve the introduction of new products, the desired sales volume, or market share. Market goals are the responsibility of marketing, sales, and advertising departments. An example of a market goal is the desire by Bausch & Lomb to capture at least 50% of every segment of the contact lens market. Managers at Bausch & Lomb give high priority to maintaining market leadership in the industry.[13] Bausch & Lomb is willing to cut prices and reduce profits in order to maintain dominance in the industry.

Employee Development   Employee development pertains to the training, promotion, safety, and growth of employees. It includes both managers and workers. Organizations frequently specify goals for employee quality and development, including the maintenance of positive attitudes and the effective conduct of their respective jobs.

Innovation   Innovation goals pertain to internal flexibility and readiness to adapt to unexpected changes in the environment. Innovation goals are often defined with respect to the development of specific new services, products, or production processes. As we saw in the previous chapter, the environment is continuously changing and the organization must adapt or fall behind. Innovation goals typically are the responsibility of engineering and R&D departments. Bausch & Lomb successfully pursued an innovation goal of developing soft contact lenses. Gillette has the innovation goal of introducing a new shaving system that will supercede the Actra razor system.

Productivity   Productivity goals concern the amount of output achieved from available resources. Productivity goals typically describe the amount of resource inputs required to reach desired outputs. Organizations try to be efficient, and productivity goals are stated in terms of "cost for a unit of production," "units produced per employee," or "resource cost per employee."

Operative goals represent the primary tasks of the organization and are the means through which the organization attains its official goals. Operative goals are more explicit and measurable than official goals. For example, the official goal at Chase Manhattan Bank is to become the number one service quality bank in the world. But to achieve this goal, a number of operative goals were put into place, including: (1) develop a worldwide network of branch banks; (2) implement a sophisticated foreign exchange system; (3) offer a good electronic funds transfer system; and (4) improve the use of human resources.[14] The respective priority given to operative goals reflects the environmental pressures and organizational needs at the time. When Datapoint Corporation was trying to achieve greater efficiency in customer service, managers adopted the operative goals of schedule, cost, and quality. Manufacturing was expected to "deliver a product to the customer on time, deliver it at minimal cost, and deliver a good quality product."[15] These operative goals helped maintain the overall company goal of continuing to have consecutive quarterly increases in net revenues, net earnings, and shipments.

MANAGING MULTIPLE AND CONFLICTING GOALS

An important point so far is that organizations have multiple goals. These goals are often in conflict with one another. Market share and profit maximization are not compatible; success in one goal may mean less success in the other. Organizations not only have multiple goals, but they are trying to achieve goals at both departmental and organizational levels in the hierarchy. There are overall performance goals for the organization itself, and another set of goals pursued by departments.

How does the organization satisfy these different goals, many of which pull in different directions? Managers typically use four techniques.

1. **Satisficing** means that organizations accept a "satisfactory" rather than a maximum level of performance.[16] By accepting satisfactory performance across several criteria, the organization can achieve several goals simultaneously. Ralston Purina tries to attain satisfactory levels of profits, market share, and new products. It doesn't maximize any of these goals. University students also satisfice. They have multiple goals, including a livable income, good grades, and social activities. Instead of maximizing income, getting straight A's, and spending large amounts of time with family and friends, which would be goal maximization, most students satisfice. They earn enough money to get through the next semester, achieve a few A's but accept some B's and

C's, and try to see the family on weekends. Organizations use a similar process to satisfice across multiple goals.

2. **Sequential attention** means that organizations attend to important goals for a period of time and then turn to other goals.[17] Sequential attention enables an organization to achieve satisfactory levels of performance on one goal before going to another goal. When an organizational crisis occurs, such as a precipitous loss in market share, reestablishing market share receives attention until satisfied. During final examinations, students put more of their energy into study, but during the summer they turn to other goals, such as earning income. Organizations do likewise, perhaps sacrificing profits this year in order to increase advertising and new product development.

3. **Preference ordering** means that top management establishes goal priorities. In the case of Ralston described at the beginning of this chapter, profitability was given priority over market share and sales volume. Giving priority to profit-making does not mean that other goals will be ignored. These other goals simply will not receive as much emphasis. For example, Daimler-Benz, the producer of Mercedes automobiles, has always emphasized quality and innovation. When hard choices have to be made, the preference is given to innovation and maintaining quality rather than to profits, market share, or efficiency. Recent innovations include a unique suspension system, dramatic improvements in fuel economy, and a smaller car that has the ride and feel of the luxury Mercedes.

4. **Goal changes** mean that goal priorities are periodically revised. Goals are not static. They are constantly being reevaluated and changed in light of new information, generally from the environment.[18] The desired state of affairs will change to reflect changes in customers, regulations, or competitor goals. Continental Illinois changed its goal from expansion at any cost to conservative lending after overextending itself and having loans go bad. Many hospitals have changed goals from emphasis on total health care to cost efficiency because the government and insurance companies are beginning to pay limited amounts for medical procedures rather than whatever the hospital charges.

Most goal changes are a response to external factors. A dramatic goal change was accomplished by the Foundation for Infantile Paralysis. This organization was committed to the goal of developing a cure for polio, and it succeeded. It no longer had a legitimate goal for its activities. Rather than disband, the organization developed a new goal: fighting birth defects and arthritis. Senior management redirected the efforts of the organization toward a new outcome.[19]

Who Defines Goals?

The final issue to understand is who determines organizational goals. Goals are value judgments. They are not fixed or given.[20] They originate with people, and the key people are managers or owners. Top managers set the direction of the organization and define the desired future state.[21] Since organizational goals reflect manager values and preferences, mistakes can be made. If the wrong goal is selected the organization suffers. Managers try to interpret the environment correctly and select appropriate goals. Sometimes this is done by individuals, sometimes by a management coalition.

Single Managers   In a few organizations, a single person may decide upon goals. In small organizations, the owner typically decides what is to be attained. Occasionally the vision of a single person dominates goal-setting in large corporations, which was the case of Rickenbacker at Eastern Airlines for many years and for McDonnell at McDonnell-Douglas. The more typical case is that goals are decided upon by a group of managers.

Coalitions   A **coalition** is an alliance among several managers who agree about organizational values and goals. Coalitions are used because agreement is not automatic. Competing goals are valued by different managers. Departments have an interest in different organizational outcomes. Managers work to overcome these differences and to build a coalition for certain goals. The term coalition describes the political nature of the goal-forming process. Substantial bargaining and compromise may take place. Through discussion and negotiation, most interest groups are able to attain some part of their goals.

Geico Insurance Company uses an annual planning meeting to build a coalition for operative goals. The president of Geico says the annual planning ritual is a combination of the Spanish Inquisition and a fraternity initiation. All key executives work together twelve to sixteen hours a day, five days a week, for three weeks. Each manager proposes a budget and goals for the next year from the front of the room while other managers try to rip the proposal to shreds. Through these annual meetings, which resemble debates, managers agree that Geico should stick to auto insurance as the major product line, that it will try to earn a 5% pretax profit, and that it will strive to be the low-cost operator in the insurance industry.[22]

Coalition building is also used to overcome goal conflicts among medical practitioners, administrators, and trustees in hospitals.[23] Trustees raise money, and want to see the hospital involved in highly visible activities that will attract donors. Physicians are concerned with the quality of health care, and want to provide the most up-to-date health-care techniques. Administrator goals are to find efficient ways to process large numbers of patients, and to decrease costs. Administrators may try to reduce the number of charity patients, even if it conflicts with the physicians' goal of delivering medical care or upsets the trustees' goal of using charity patients as a device for raising funds.

How are these differences resolved? Discussion and debate among trustees, doctors, and administrators will lead to a coalition that may give the goals a preference ordering, or treat goals sequentially. The hospital may accept "satisfactory" performance on each of the competing goals. Each goal will receive some attention, although no goal will dominate completely. A coalition will normally emerge that defines goal preferences and orderings.[24]

ORGANIZATIONAL EFFECTIVENESS

Understanding organizational goals is the first step toward understanding organizational effectiveness. Organizational goals represent the reason for the organization's existence, its purpose and mission. In this part of the chapter we explore the topic of effectiveness, and how effectiveness is measured in organizations.

Effectiveness and Efficiency

Goals were defined earlier as the desired future state of the organization. **Organizational effectiveness** is the degree to which an organization realizes its goals.[25] Effectiveness is a broad concept. It implicitly takes into consideration a range of factors both inside and outside the organization. The organization pursues multiple goals, and goals must be achieved in the face of competition, limited resources, and disagreement among managers.

Efficiency, by contrast, is a more limited concept that pertains to the internal workings of the organization. **Efficiency** is the amount of resources used to produce a unit of output.[26] Efficiency can be measured as the ratio of inputs to outputs. If one organization can achieve a given production level with fewer resources than another organization, it would be described as more efficient.[27] Sometimes efficiency leads to effectiveness. In other organizations, efficiency and effectiveness are not related. An organization may be highly efficient but fail to achieve its goals because it makes a product for which there is no demand. Likewise, an organization may achieve its goals but be inefficient. Efficiency and effectiveness represent two different approaches to organizational assessment.

Effectiveness is an important concept, but the assessment of effectiveness has proven to be one of the more intractable problems in organization theory. There has been no simple solution. Organizations are large, diverse, and fragmented. They perform many activities simultaneously. They pursue multiple goals. They generate many outcomes, some intended and some unintended. A variety of frameworks has evolved to measure performance, and each examines a different criterion of effectiveness.[28]

TRADITIONAL EFFECTIVENESS APPROACHES

The measurement of effectiveness has focused on different parts of the organization. Organizations bring resources in from the environment that are transformed into outputs delivered back into the environment, as shown in Exhibit 3.3. The **system resource approach** assesses effectiveness by observing the beginning of the process and evaluating whether the organization effectively obtains resources necessary for high performance. The **internal process approach** looks at internal activities and assesses effectiveness by indicators of internal health and efficiency. The **goal approach** to organizational effectiveness is concerned with the output side, and whether the organization achieves its goals in terms of desired levels of output.[29]

We will first examine effectiveness as evaluated by the system resource approach. Then we will turn to the internal process and goal approaches to effectiveness. In the final section of this chapter we examine contemporary approaches that integrate these perspectives and we consider goals for all organizational activities.

**System
Resource
Approach**

The system resource approach looks at the input side of the transformation process shown in Exhibit 3.3. Organizations must be successful in obtaining resource inputs and in maintaining the organizational system in order to be effective. The system resource approach is based on open-systems theory. Organizations have an exchange relationship with the external environment. Resources in the external environment are scarce and valued. Organizational effectiveness from a systems view is defined as "the ability of the organization, in either absolute or relative terms, to exploit its environment in the acquisition of scarce and valued resources."[30]

Indicators   Obtaining resources to maintain the organization system is the criterion by which organizational effectiveness is assessed. In a narrow sense, the amount of resources acquired from the environment would be the criterion of effectiveness. In a broader sense, indicators of system resource effectiveness encompass the following dimensions.

1. Bargaining position—the ability of the organization to exploit its environment in acquisition of scarce and valued resources.
2. Ability of the system decision-maker to perceive and correctly interpret the real properties of the external environment.
3. Ability of the system to use resources to produce a specified output.
4. Maintenance of internal day-to-day organizational activities.
5. Ability of the organization to respond to changes in the environment.[31]

One important reason for the development and use of the system resource approach is that it provides a unique basis of comparison. A school district and a juvenile court, for example, have different missions, so how can their

EXHIBIT 3.3. Traditional Approaches to the Measurement of Organizational Effectiveness.

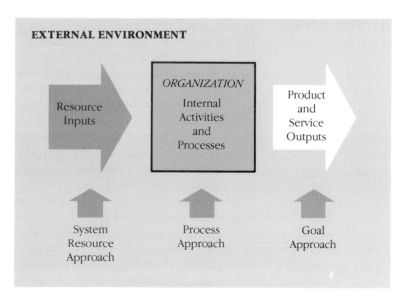

relative effectiveness be assessed? One solution is to look at their ability to acquire resources. Each organization must obtain financial and human resources, office space, and physical facilities. The ability to obtain common resources is one way to compare effectiveness, even if the organizations do not do the same thing.

The first criterion of system effectiveness is survival. Organizations that survive are more effective than those that do not. If the organization obtains sufficient inputs to stay alive, one level of effectiveness is achieved. Beyond survival, effectiveness can be assessed by the dollar value of scarce resources obtained from the environment. Organizations can be compared on the same criteria even if their outputs differ.

Evaluation   The value of the system resource approach is threefold: it takes the entire organization as a frame of reference, it considers the relationship of the organization to the external environment, and it can be used to compare organizations that have different goals. However, the system resource approach has not been used extensively to measure effectiveness. Part of the problem is that it provides a limited perspective on organizations. One study assessed public agencies in Iowa counties.[32] The agencies included the Soil Conservation Service, Extension Service, and Farmer's Home and Administration. These were different types of organizations with different missions, so the system resource approach was used to assess resource inflows. Resources such as personnel, equipment, meeting rooms, or funds received from other organizations were indicators of effectiveness. The agencies differed in the amount of resources obtained. The investigators also assessed outputs, and found that resource inflows were not correlated with attainment of output goals.

The findings from county agencies raise the question of whether acquisition of resources is as important as the utilization of these resources. Utilization is measured by looking at output goal achievement or efficiency. Moreover, exploiting a large number of resources, if they are not used, might not be considered effective. A college football team that acquires many star players would not be considered effective if the team loses its games.

The system resource approach does offer an alternative perspective on organizational effectiveness. It is especially useful when organizational mission and outputs are different because outputs cannot be used as the measure to compare effectiveness across organizations.

Internal Process Approach

In the internal process approach, effectiveness is measured as internal organizational health and efficiency. The effective organization has a smooth, well-oiled internal process. Employees are happy and satisfied. Departmental activities mesh with one another to ensure high productivity. This approach is not concerned with the external environment. The important element in effectiveness is what the organization does with the resources it has, which is reflected in internal health and efficiency.

Indicators   The best-known proponents of a process model are from the human relations approach to organizations. Writers such as Argyris, Bennis,

Likert, and Beckhard have all worked extensively with human reso
organizations and emphasize the connection between human resou... and
effectiveness.[33] Indicators of an effective organization, as seen from this viewpoint, are listed below. Each of these dimensions can be assessed by inter-
viewing organizational employees.

1. Supervisor interest and concern for workers.
2. Team spirit, group loyalty, and teamwork.
3. Confidence, trust, and communication between workers and management.
4. Decisions are made near sources of information, regardless of where these
sources are on the organizational chart.
5. Communication horizontally and vertically is undistorted. People share
relevant facts and feelings.
6. The total organization and individuals manage their work toward goals
and plans.
7. The reward system rewards managers for performance, growth, and development of subordinates, and for creating an effective working group.
8. The organization and its parts interact with each other. Conflict will occur
over projects but will be resolved in the interest of the organization.[34]

A second set of indicators of internal process effectiveness is to measure
economic efficiency. William Evan developed a method that uses quantitative
measures of efficiency.[35] He proposed that three variables could be measured:
"inputs" of resources, "transformation" of resources into outputs, and "outputs" that are delivered to consumers outside the organization.

This approach is relevant to internal processes because Evan developed
a series of ratios that measure efficiencies within organizations. The first step
is to identify the financial cost of inputs (I), transformation (T), and outputs
(O). Next, the three variables can be combined in ratios to evaluate various
aspects of organizational performance. The most popular assessment of efficiency is O/I. For business organizations, this would be return on investment. For a hospital, the O/I ratio is the number of patients/annual budget.
For a university, it is the number of students graduated divided by the resource inputs. The O/I ratio indicates overall financial efficiency for an organization.

Evaluation

The internal process approach is important because the efficient use of
resources and harmonious internal functioning is one way to measure effectiveness. The internal process approach can be used to compare organizations if outputs are not the same or are not identifiable. This approach
also controls for environmental differences to some extent so that organizational efficiency is compared on a similar basis.

The internal process approach also has shortcomings. Internal efficiency
is a very limited view of organizational effectiveness. Output and the organization's relationship with the external environment are not evaluated. Also,
evaluations of internal health and functioning are often subjective, because
many aspects of inputs and internal processes are not quantifiable. Like the
other approaches to organizational effectiveness, the internal process ap-

proach has something to offer. But managers should be aware that efficiency and internal functioning represent a limited view of organizational effectiveness.

The Goal Approach

The goal approach to effectiveness consists of identifying an organization's output goals and assessing how well it has attained those goals.[36] This is a logical approach because organizations do try to attain certain levels of output, profit, or client satisfaction. This approach measures progress toward attainment of those goals.

The important goals to consider are operative goals. Efforts to measure effectiveness have been more productive using operative goals than using official goals.[37] Operative goals reflect activities the organization is actually performing. Identifying operative goals and measuring performance, however, present several problems. In order to accurately evaluate effectiveness, issues of multiple outputs, subjective indicators, and contextual effects must be resolved.

Multiple Outcomes   Application of the goal approach is complicated by the problem of multiple goals and outcomes. Since organizations have multiple and conflicting goals, effectiveness cannot be assessed by a single indicator. High achievement on one goal may mean low achievement on another. Moreover, there are department goals as well as overall performance goals. The assessment of effectiveness has to take into consideration several goals simultaneously.

One example of multiple goals is from a survey of U.S. business corporations.[38] Their reported goals are shown in Exhibit 3.4. Twelve goals were listed as being important to these companies. These twelve goals represent outcomes that cannot be achieved simultaneously. Exhibit 3.5 contains the

EXHIBIT 3.4. Reported Goals of U.S. Corporations.

Goal	% Corporations
Profitability	89
Growth	82
Market share	66
Social responsibility	65
Employee welfare	62
Product quality and service	60
Research and development	54
Diversification	51
Efficiency	50
Financial stability	49
Resource conservation	39
Management development	35

Source: Adapted from Y. K. Shetty, "New Look at Corporate Goals," *California Management Review*, 22, No. 2 (1979):71–79.

EXHIBIT 3.5. Frequency of Evaluation Criteria in Studies of Organizational Effectiveness.

Criteria	# Mentions
Adaptability-flexibility	10
Productivity	6
Satisfaction	5
Profitability	3
Resource acquisition	3
Absence of strain	2
Control over environment	2
Development	2
Efficiency	2
Employee retention	2
Growth	2
Integration	2
Open communications	2
Survival	2
All other criteria	1

Source: Reprinted from "Problems in the Measurement of Organizational Effectiveness" by R. M. Steers, published in *Administrative Science Quarterly* 20(4) (1975): 546–558 by permission of *The Administrative Science Quarterly*. Copyright © 1975 by Cornell University Press.

fourteen indicators of effectiveness used most frequently by organizational researchers.[39] Several of these indicators, such as growth, profit, and efficiency, were goals in Exhibit 3.4. The total set of outcomes in Exhibits 3.4 and 3.5 illustrates the array of goal outcomes that organizations attempt to achieve.

One confounding aspect of multiple goals is that some goals overlap the system resource and process approaches to effectiveness. As we discussed earlier in the section on goals, operative goals pertain to the required subsystem tasks needed for success. Some of these tasks are to acquire resources and maintain an efficient, healthy internal system. Thus the goals in Exhibits 3.4 and 3.5 of diversity, resource conservation, resource acquisition, and employee retention are similar to the system resource approach. Goals of employee satisfaction, employee welfare, open communications, and efficiency pertain to the process approach. Other goals pertain to overall performance indicators such as profit and growth. Thus only a limited set of organizational goals pertain to outputs, which the goal approach attempts to measure.

A broad use of the goal approach would tend to integrate aspects of the system resource and process approaches as well. Organizations indeed have many goals and many tasks to accomplish. In order to assess performance, several indicators of goals probably have to be selected and combined. Effectiveness should not be assessed on only one dimension, because this would oversimplify the goals pursued by the organization.

Indicators   The next issue to resolve with the goal approach is how to actually identify operative goals and measure goal attainment. For business organizations, there are often objective indicators for certain goals. The stated objectives of top management and measures such as profit or market share are available in published reports. Subjective assessment is needed in business organizations for such outcomes as employee development or job satisfaction, which may be among the goals of top administrators. For nonbusiness organizations, almost no goal attainment can be measured objectively. The goals that are formally written down are official rather than operative goals. Someone has to go into the organization and learn what the goals are. Since goals are the values of top management, the best informants are members of the top-management coalitions.[40] These managers can report on the actual goals of the organization. Once goals are identified, subjective perceptions of goal achievement can be obtained if quantitative indicators are not available. The subjective nature of goals and the measure of progress toward goals is a complicating factor in the assessment of effectiveness. However, these problems can be overcome, as indicated in the following example of a juvenile court.

IN PRACTICE 3.2

Juvenile Court

Richard Hall and John Clark studied youth-related welfare organizations in twelve large cities.[41] The organizations included juvenile courts, adolescent mental-health centers, juvenile detention divisions, and school social work activities.

In order to assess goal effectiveness, the research team visited each organization. Members and employees were asked to list the five most important tasks of the organization. From these responses they developed a long list of goals. Respondents then indicated which were the key goals for the organization. The final list of goals was approved by the organization's top administrator. This procedure was quite effective for identifying operational goals. The operative goals for one organization—the juvenile court—are as follows.

1. Determine the best disposition for each child who appears before the court.
2. Protect the civil and legal rights of minors.
3. Protect the community from those youths who pose personal threats to the community.
4. Hear and justly dispose of cases before the court.
5. Cooperate with other agencies who deal with problem youths.
6. Remove children from family situations that are damaging to their welfare.
7. Foster acceptance of an individualized rehabilitative treatment philosophy by the general public and other system agencies.
8. Develop more resources and better methods of helping problem youth.[42]

These eight goals are specific and operational. These goals were then used to evaluate effectiveness by asking each employee how well the organization performed them. Objective indicators were also available for several goals.

Objective indicators provided information for such things as percentage of cases closed, proportion of recommendations accepted by other agencies, and percentage of time devoted to a given goal. A positive association was found between objective and subjective indicators of effectiveness. The identification of goals and assessment of performance through interviews with employees were useful techniques for assessing goal effectiveness in the juvenile court.

Contextual Effects   The third issue when assessing organizational effectiveness on the basis of goal achievement concerns the organizational environment and context. Some organizational settings are more conducive to high performance than others. Each organization functions in an environmental niche that is unlike any other. Resource availability, consumer demand, quality of employees, competition, and government regulations differ by industry, town, and location.

One of the most dramatic examples of contextual effects was reported in a study of pharmaceutical manufacturing firms and phonograph record companies.[43] Effectiveness was measured by profits and rates of return. Despite many similarities between the two types of companies, phonograph record manufacturers were much less profitable. The average rate of return for the record industry was about 7%. Pharmaceutical manufacturing was one of the most profitable industries in the United States, with return on investment averaging from 16.7% to 20.3%. The reasons were that factors in the general environment—pricing and distribution, patent and copyright law, and external opinion leaders—placed constraints on firms in each industry. The highest performing record company would show less return than a poor performing pharmaceutical company because of contextual factors outside management's control.

Factors outside the organization's control thus may influence goal achievement. Measuring differences in external factors can be important if the organizations have similar goals but are in different industries.[44] Another way to allow for external differences is to include measures of internal efficiency in the assessment of effectiveness. This would indicate how efficiently resources are used within the organization, regardless of environmental differences.

Evaluation   The goal approach is a logical way to assess organizational effectiveness. Effectiveness is defined as the ability of an organization to attain its goals. But the actual measurement of effectiveness is a complex problem. Organizations have many goals, so there is no single indicator of effectiveness. Some goals are subjective and have to be identified by managers within the organization. The rating of the organization's performance on some goals is also subjective and must be provided by people familiar with the organization's activities. Moreover, the attainment of goals may be influenced by factors outside the organization's control. The assessment of organizational effectiveness using the goal approach requires that the evaluator be aware of these issues and allow for them in the final evaluation of effectiveness.

CONTEMPORARY EFFECTIVENESS APPROACHES

The three approaches—goal, system resource, internal process—to organizational effectiveness described above all have something to offer and all have shortcomings. Each approach tells only part of the story. An organization may be good at exploiting resources, but may squander them and thus fail to achieve its goals. Or an organization may have excellent internal working relationships, but is going broke and will fail to survive because customers don't like the product. The conclusion from the three approaches is that there is no ultimate criterion of effectiveness. There is no single measure, no single theory, that will allow us to arrive at an unequivocal measurement of performance.

Recently, integrative approaches to organizational effectiveness have been introduced. These new approaches acknowledge that organizations do many things and have many outcomes. No single criterion of effectiveness is appropriate. Even managers in organizations that do the same thing may select different outcomes to emphasize. One college coach may emphasize winning at all costs (goal approach), while another emphasizes character building of athletes (process approach). The assessment of effectiveness to some extent has to be tailored to the goals and the situation of the organization under study.

Constituency Approach

One proposed approach that integrates diverse organizational activities focuses on organizational constituencies. A **constituency** is any group within or outside the organization that has a stake in the organization's performance. Stockholders, suppliers, employees, and owners are all constituencies, and effectiveness can be assessed by determining how satisfied each group is with the organization's performance.[45] Each constituency will have a different criterion of effectiveness because it has a different interest in the organization. Each constituency has to be surveyed to learn whether the organization performs well from its viewpoint.

Indicators The initial work on evaluating effectiveness on the basis of constituencies included ninety-seven small businesses in Texas. Seven constituencies relevant to these businesses were surveyed to determine the perception of effectiveness from each viewpoint.[46] Each constituency and the criterion of effectiveness are as follows:

Constituency	**Effectiveness Criteria**
1. Owners	Financial return
2. Employees	Work satisfaction, pay, supervision
3. Customers	Quality of goods and services
4. Creditors	Credit worthiness
5. Community	Contribution to community affairs
6. Suppliers	Satisfactory transaction
7. Government	Obedience to laws, regulations

The survey of constituencies showed that the small business found it difficult to simultaneously fulfill the demands of all groups. One business may have high employee satisfaction, but satisfaction of other groups may be lower. Nevertheless, measuring all seven constituencies provides a more accurate view of effectiveness than any single measure. Evaluating how organizations perform across each constituency offers an overall assessment of effectiveness.

Evaluation   The strength of the constituency approach is that it takes a broad view of effectiveness and examines factors in the environment as well as within the organization. The constituency approach also includes the community and the notion of social responsibility, which was not incorporated in previous models. Managers sometimes list social responsibility as a company goal, and the constituency approach incorporates that criterion of performance. The constituency approach also handles several criteria simultaneously—inputs, internal processing, outputs—and acknowledges that there is no single measure of effectiveness. The well-being of employees is just as important as achievement of the owner's goals.

The constituency approach is gaining in popularity, based on the view that effectiveness is a complex, multi-dimensional concept that has no single measure.[47] A valid approach is to evaluate organizations across several criteria that represent outcomes to relevant interest groups. If the organization performs poorly according to several interest groups, it is probably not meeting its major goals and may even be struggling to survive. One example of how constituency dissatisfaction illustrates poor performance is seen in the difficulties experienced by International Harvester.

IN PRACTICE 3.3

International Harvester

A recent headline screamed, "International Harvester's Last Chance."[48] After eighty years of steady growth, after becoming a giant among U.S. corporations, International Harvester is near the precipice of bankruptcy. On almost any scale, Harvester's performance has been terrible. Its last good profit was in 1979. Employee development has been a disaster. Antagonism from the union runs deep. Resource acquisition is difficult because no one wants to provide materials on credit—Harvester must pay cash in advance or no deal.

Harvester's woes take a heavy toll on everyone associated with the troubled firm. Employees were the first to be hit. At one time, Harvester employed more than 111,000 people. Worldwide employment is now about 50,000. Employees who remain have had their pay and benefits cut back. Employees who were laid off have not found new jobs. One who did, a 38-year-old engineer, has to commute several hundred miles weekly to his new employer. He had to take the job to survive, but will not be with his wife on their twentieth anniversary, nor be at home to celebrate his daughter's birthday party.

More than 5,000 suppliers sell Harvester glass, steel, paint, diesel engines, and tractor seats. Many of these are small- and medium-sized businesses who have been devastated because Harvester owes them money and can't pay.

The assets of Challenge Tool Company dropped 50% because of nonpayment, and if Harvester goes bankrupt so will Challenge Tool. For every person working in Challenge Tool's machine shop, four or five machines are now idle, because it has been all but impossible to replace the lost Harvester orders.

Harvester's dealers have been decimated. One hundred and five Harvester farm-equipment dealers have gone out of business. The competition for farm and truck business is brutal. Competitive dealers play on customer fears that Harvester will go bankrupt and not be able to supply service and parts over the long run.

Stockholders have also suffered with Harvester's decline. Many stockholders have seen their shares plunge from $40 to less than $4. Harvester hasn't paid a dividend for over a year. People who trusted the stability of Harvester for investment income are struggling. These people include retirees and widows of former employees. They worry about their pensions because the value of stock and dividends has eroded dramatically during recent years.

The poor performance of Harvester is felt deeply by constituents. You don't need an official measure of profit and loss, return on investment, or efficiency. Everyone who deals with the company is hurting. Ask them. They, more than anyone, hope International Harvester can take advantage of its last chance.[49]

Competing Values Approach

The competing values approach to organizational effectiveness was developed by Quinn and Rohrbaugh to integrate the diverse indicators of performance used by managers and researchers.[50] Using a comprehensive list of performance indicators, a panel of experts in organizational effectiveness rated the indicators for similarity. The analysis produced underlying dimensions of effectiveness criteria that represented competing values.

The first value dimension pertains to **organizational focus,** which is whether dominant values are internal or external to the firm. Internal focus reflects a management concern for the well-being and efficiency of employees, and external focus represents an emphasis on the well-being of the organization itself with respect to the environment. The second value dimension pertains to **organization structure,** and whether stability versus flexibility is the dominant structural consideration. Stability reflects a management value for top-down control, similar to the mechanistic model described in chapter 2. Flexibility represents a value for adaptation and change, and is similar to the organic organization structure.

The value dimensions of structure and focus are illustrated in Exhibit 3.6. The combination of dimensions provide four models of organizational effectiveness. Each model reflects a different emphasis with respect to the basic value dilemmas.

The **open systems model** reflects a combination of external focus and flexible structure. The primary goals are growth and resource acquisition. The organization accomplishes these goals through the subgoals of flexibility, readiness, and a positive external evaluation. The dominant value in this model is establishing a good relationship with the environment to acquire resources and grow. This model is similar in some ways to the system resource model described earlier.

The **rational goal model** represents the values of structural control and external focus. The primary goals are productivity, efficiency, and profit. The organization wants to achieve output goals in a controlled way. Subgoals that facilitate these outcomes are internal planning and goal setting, which are rational management tools. The rational goal model is in some way similar to the goal approach described earlier.

The **internal process model** is in the lower left section of Exhibit 3.6 and reflects the values of internal focus and structural control. The primary outcome is a stable organizational setting that maintains itself in an orderly way. Organizations that are well established in the environment and simply want to maintain their current position would fit this model. Subgoals for this model include mechanisms for efficient communication, information management, and decision-making.

The **human relations model** incorporates the values of an internal focus and a flexible structure. Here the concern is on the development of human resources. Employees are given opportunities for autonomy and development. Management works toward the subgoals of cohesion, morale, and training opportunities. Organizations adopting this model are more concerned with employees than with the environment.

The four models in Exhibit 3.6 represent opposing organizational values. Managers must decide which goal values will direct their organizations. The

EXHIBIT 3.6. Four Models of Effectiveness Values.

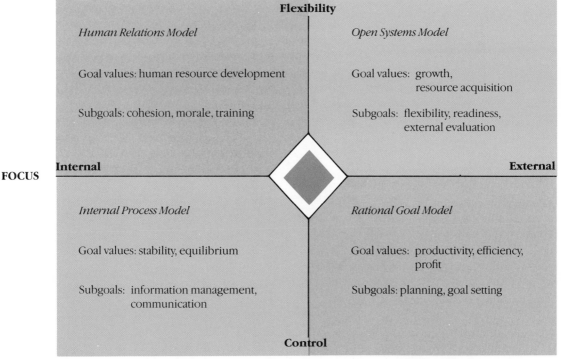

STRUCTURE

Source: Adapted from Robert E. Quinn and John Rohrbaugh, "A Spatial Model of Effectiveness Criteria: Toward a Competing Values Approach to Organizational Analysis," *Management Science,* 29 (1983): 363–377; and Robert E. Quinn and Kim Cameron, "Organizational Life Cycles and Shifting Criteria of Effectiveness: Some Preliminary Evidence," *Management Science,* 29 (1983):33–51.

way two organizations are mapped onto the four models is shown in Exhibit 3.7.[51] Organization A might be a new, young organization that is concerned with finding a niche and becoming established in the external environment. Primary emphasis is given to flexibility, innovation, the acquisition of resources from the environment, and satisfaction of external constituencies. This organization gives only moderate emphasis to human relations and to current productivity and profits. Satisfying and adapting to the environment is more important. The emphasis given to open systems values means that the internal process model is practically nonexistent. Stability and equilibrium receive little emphasis.

Organization B, in contrast, reflects an organization in which the dominant value is productivity and profits. This organization is characterized by planning and goal setting. Organization B could be a large business corporation that is well established in the environment and is now primarily concerned with successful production and profit indicators of performance. Flexibility and human resources are not major concerns. The organization prefers sta-

EXHIBIT 3.7. Effectiveness Values for Two Organizations.

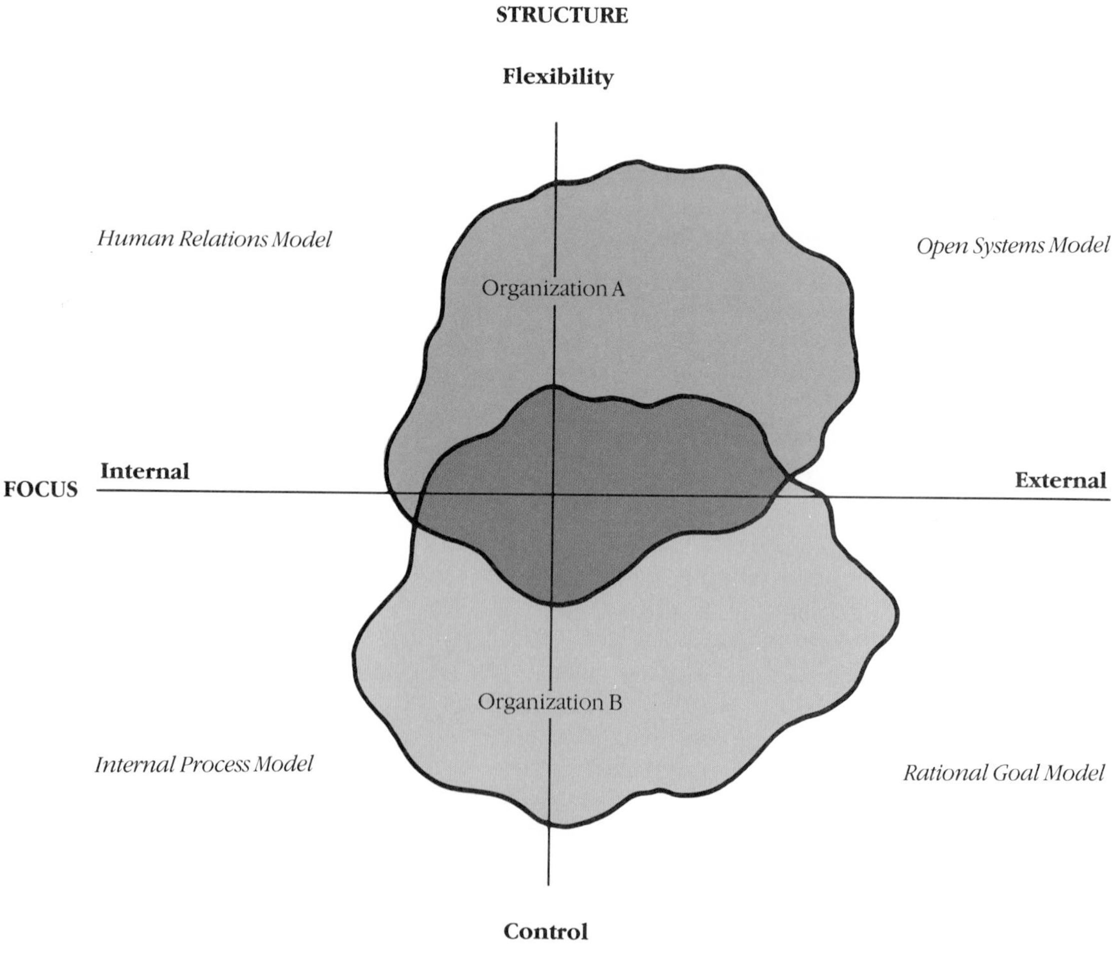

STRUCTURE

Flexibility

Human Relations Model

Organization A

Open Systems Model

FOCUS   Internal   External

Internal Process Model

Organization B

Rational Goal Model

Control

bility and equilibrium to readiness and innovation because it wants to take advantage of its established clientele.

Evaluation   The competing values model helps integrate diverse concepts of effectiveness. It incorporates the idea of output goals, resource acquisition, and the development of human resources. The model also calls attention to effectiveness criteria as values. The organization must decide which values it wishes to pursue, and this will mean that other values are excluded. A highly controlled and stable organization cannot accomplish goals of innovation and flexibility. An organization that concentrates primarily on satisfying the external environment will give less emphasis to employees. These are necessary tradeoffs in the establishment of goals and the evaluation of effectiveness. An example of a large business firm that has adopted a rather explicit set of values is Northwest Airlines.

IN PRACTICE 3.4

Northwest Airlines

When Donald Nyrop was recruited to become president of Northwest Airlines in 1954, costs were out of control. Part of Northwest's fleet was costly to operate and part had been grounded. Mr. Nyrop adopted a spartan style and invoked a value of cost-cutting and efficiency. In 1979, when Mr. Nyrop retired, these values were helping Northwest soar. The new president, Mr. Rothmeier, has now led Northwest into becoming the most efficient major airline in the industry. It ranks near the top in cost, profit, and debt ratios.

Virtually every efficiency indicator is positive. Northwest's overhead costs are about 2% of total costs, compared to 5% for major competitors. Labor costs were the lowest of major airlines at 24% of operating revenue. Revenue ton mileage per employee was 66% higher than other major airlines. Operating revenue per employee was 27% higher. Cost per available seat mile was the lowest in the industry. The efficiency has been a major reason why income is up, and Northwest was one of only a handful of profitable carriers in 1983. Stock prices have risen to a high, indicating that industry observers approve.

The stress on efficiency has not always led to good relations with employees. Mr. Nyrop was combative and would take a strike rather than give in to unreasonable demands. Northwest has also insisted on work-rule changes to increase efficiency despite union resistance. Currently employee relations are characterized by a better atmosphere. Northwest has also been making some gains in growth. Traffic is up 16% in 1983, one of the industry's best gains. Northwest has also been gradually adding new aircraft so that it has a modern fleet without the huge debt. Northwest's debt ratio was 35% below the ratio of most airlines, indicating they have sufficient resources for the future.

Mr. Rothmeier, only thirty-seven years old, will infuse new blood into the company, but he will pursue the same goals. He was personally recruited by Mr. Nyrop, and will insist on an efficient, profitable airline.[52]

The criteria of effectiveness at Northwest Airlines reflect the rational goal model. Productivity, efficiency, and profit are important. There is a secondary emphasis given to open system values, which is reflected in growth and resource acquisition. Human relations and internal processes receive less emphasis than other values. New managers could conceivably change the values, but that is not likely because of Northwest's success under this approach.

FACTORS INFLUENCING THE SELECTION OF EFFECTIVENESS CRITERIA

So far in this chapter we have examined a multitude of goals and effectiveness criteria. Traditional effectiveness approaches use resource acquisition, internal efficiency, or outputs to evaluate effectiveness. Contemporary approaches attempt to integrate these perspectives by combining the preferences of several constituencies or by mapping the organization onto a competing values framework. In this last section of the chapter, we will explore some factors that determine which criteria receive priority in a given organization. Organizations cannot maximize all criteria simultaneously, so certain forces will influence the priority given to goals and effectiveness criteria. These forces include leader influence, task and goal clarity, organizational stage of development, and environmental conditions.

Leader Influence   As we have already discussed, goals represent value judgments by managers, so top leaders have substantial influence over organizational direction. Leader preferences do make a difference in the adoption of goals and effectiveness criteria. Donald Nyrop was instrumental in establishing efficiency criteria as the dominant value at Northwest Airlines. William Stiritz of Ralston Purina was a major force in redirecting the company away from goals of growth and market share toward the goal of profitability. Jockey International Inc. provides T-shirts, longjohns, and other products to crisis areas around the world because Howard Cooley, president, thinks the corporation ought to serve a humanitarian need. Pirsh & Sons is a small fire-engine manufacturing company that chooses to stay small. Andrew Sale, president, emphasizes stability and the development of employees into crafts people rather than efficiency and profits. In each of these organizations, the leaders influence the dominant goal and effectiveness criteria.[53]

Task and Goal Clarity   Another factor is the extent to which tasks and goals are clearly defined in the organization.[54] If internal tasks are routine and well defined, the organization can measure each step in the sequence, and will tend to adopt an efficiency orientation. If internal tasks are not easily measured, then organizations will tend to adopt output or goal criteria. One example is a college basketball team. The exact process needed to create a winning team is not calculable because various coaching techniques may achieve a winner. In these cases, internal efficiency will not be valued, and the orientation will be toward goal outputs, which in this case is the number of games the team wins. Certain types of medical, research, and service organizations do not have quantifiable tasks, so they tend to use goal output criteria for effectiveness.

In a few organizations even goal outputs are hard to define. In a human service organization, such as the local YMCA, a welfare organization, or the chamber of commerce, explicit, measurable goals do not exist. When outcomes are ill-defined, organizations tend to adopt either human relations or external constituency criteria. Since there is no quantifiable test of performance, the organization will rate success by how happy clients and other constituents are with the services. Or the organization may concentrate on the development and satisfaction of internal employees as the criterion of effectiveness.

Organizations tend to prefer precise criteria of performance when available.[55] Organizations first prefer efficiency criteria, then goal outcomes, then internal process criteria, and finally criteria of social reference groups and constituencies. The latter criteria are hardest to define and the most difficult to measure, but will be used if organizations do not have well-defined goals and tasks.

Organizational Stage of Development   Stage of development also has influence on organizational goals and effectiveness criteria. Organizations typically pass through early, middle, and late stages of development. The early stage is when the organization is small and struggling to survive. The middle stage is when the organization is firmly established, and the later stage is when the organization becomes large and institutionalized in the environment.

In the early stage of development, the organization has to develop a niche in the environment and acquire sufficient resources to survive. Thus the primary goals tend to be concerned with the acquisition and efficient use of resources. Some concern is also given to positive human relations because people are the means through which the organization will succeed. There is little concern for stability or for the satisfaction of diverse constituents. An examination of the newly established New York State Department of Mental Hygiene and a study of small businesses in Texas found a primary concern for resource acquisition and efficient use of resources. Managers must acquire resources and keep the organization alive in order for it to grow and prosper.[56]

In the middle stage of development the emphasis shifts from resource acquisition to primary concern with efficiency and with achieving output goals. There is sometimes less concern for flexibility and human resources than in the early stages of development.

In the later stages of organizational development, primary goals tend to deal with outputs and with environmental relationships. The organization has become well established so resource acquisition is taken for granted. The organization becomes concerned with its role in the environment and may emphasize community and constituent satisfaction, although emphasis will continue to be given to desired outputs.

When Colonel Sanders first started selling his chicken franchises, his primary goal was to grow and obtain sufficient resources to survive and develop a surviving business. These goals dominated from 1971 to 1977 until Kentucky Fried Chicken finally became established as a thriving organization. The organization was a hit, and rapid growth caused managers to become concerned with control and efficiency. After 1977, priority was given to consolidation and enhancing internal efficiency. As the organization matured, managers also became concerned with product quality, customer service, and store image to make sure important constituencies were satisfied.[57]

Environmental Conditions Recall from the previous chapter that environments vary with respect to resource scarcity and munificence. When resources are perceived as scarce, organizational goals will take on an efficiency criterion. The organization will want to protect its share of the environment and to use declining resources efficiently and wisely. On the other hand, in a dynamic, growing, munificent environment, efficiency is less important and the dominant effectiveness criteria become output goals and growth. The organization attempts to find new markets and to develop new products.[58] Airlines, companies in the oil industry, and hospitals in recent years have experienced declines in demand and hence effectiveness criteria within the organizations have tended to emphasize efficiency. In other industries, such as personal computers or express mail delivery, rapid growth, flexibility, and high output are the dominant criteria of effectiveness.

Any or all of the above factors may influence the specific goals and effectiveness criteria used in an organization. In the analysis of an organization, leader influence, task and goal clarity, organizational stage of development, and environmental conditions all represent contingency factors that can be used to explain criteria of effectiveness.

IN PRACTICE 3.5
Montreal Psychiatric Hospital

The nurses had never witnessed anything like it. The psychiatrists were split down the middle, polarized, about how to deliver psychiatric care at Montreal. Several of the psychiatrists wanted to adopt the milieu approach to therapy that had been developed in England. Milieu therapy engaged the entire hospital environment in the therapeutic process. Patients would interact with nurses, support staff, and each other in structured group activities. Patients' idle time was converted to therapeutic encounters. Private sessions with doctors were also retained as needed.

The other psychiatrists believed in the traditional approach to therapy. Mental illness was perceived by them as a disease that must be fought by physicians. The doctor was the primary expert in the fight, and he should use drugs or other techniques to combat the illness. The physician's skill was the primary ingredient in helping the psychotic patient recover. Nonexperts should not be involved in so difficult a task.

Administrators and psychiatrists could agree on one thing: they wanted to deliver higher quality therapeutic care to both private and public patients in the Montreal area. But they could not agree on the best techniques for providing this care. The hospital staff committee (made up of twelve physicians and the directors of nursing and support staff) made policy decisions about therapeutic care. Their decisions usually reflected the consensus among medical staff. As one member described the decision-making process: "It is impossible to reduce things down to solely hard facts and rigid rules; psychiatry is not an exact science."

Dr. Macintosh, head of the hospital, was concerned with overall effectiveness. Everyone agreed that the goal of the hospital was to provide high-quality health care, but they were severely split about how to achieve it. Calculations of efficiency based upon cost-benefit analyses had little impact.

Milieu therapy was somewhat cheaper because physician time was reduced, but that had little sway on decision-makers because Montreal was a generously endowed hospital. Doctors would not use a technique just because it was cheaper or more efficient. They wanted to deliver quality care.

The dilemma was finally resolved on a temporary basis by conducting an experiment. Facilities would be made available for both types of therapy over a period of two years. Patients would be randomly assigned to each type of therapy by a subcommittee of psychiatrists representing both factions. The best test of effectiveness, they decided, was to learn which form of therapy had the more positive impact on the mental health of patients.[59]

In the psychiatric hospital, an internal efficiency goal was not used because the process of converting mentally ill people into mentally healthy people was not well defined. The primary test of effectiveness became one of achieving outcomes—which form of therapy enabled the organization to achieve its output goal of providing the best mental-health care. The output goal of quality care was also congruent with the availability of resources and the values of administrators to provide quality care. If the situation at Montreal changed so that new administrator values were present, resources were scarce, or the process of treating mentally ill patients became routine and definable, then other goal priorities might emerge.

SUMMARY AND INTERPRETATION

This chapter discussed organizational goals and ways to measure organizational effectiveness. Goals specify the mission or purpose of the organization and its desired future state. Effectiveness indicates how well the organization realizes its purpose and attains its desired future state.

Goals and effectiveness are important topics because organizations exist for a purpose. They have a specific mission or task to be accomplished. Sometimes this mission is taken for granted, because employees become involved with day-to-day activities and forget about which direction they are headed. The importance of organizational goals is that they make explicit the purpose and direction of the organization. Moreover, organizational goals are not given or fixed. They change over time, and new goals must be sequenced and given priority. Goals are a key element in organizations because they meet several needs—establishing legitimacy with external groups, reducing uncertainty, and setting standards of performance for participants. Goals must be explicit, and they must be updated. Understanding the diverse and critical roles of goals in organizations is one of the most important ideas in this chapter.

A second important idea is the complexity of measuring organizational effectiveness. There is no easy, simple, guaranteed measure that will provide an unequivocal assessment of performance. The complexity of effectiveness measurement reflects the complexity of organizations as a topic of study. Organizations do many things. They have many outcomes, and they must perform diverse activities well—from obtaining resource inputs to delivering outputs—to be successful. Traditional approaches used output goals, resource acquisition, or internal health and efficiency as the criteria of effectiveness. Contemporary approaches stress a broad-based view of effectiveness that considers multiple criteria simultaneously. Organizations can be assessed by surveying constituencies that have a stake in organizational performance, or by evaluating competing values for effectiveness. One approach may be suitable in one organization but not in another. No framework is perfect, but each offers some advantage that the others may lack.

From the point of view of managers, the goal approach to effectiveness and measures of internal efficiency are appropriate when they are available. The attainment of goals reflects the purpose of the organization, and efficiency reflects the cost of attaining those goals. Other factors such as top management preferences, the extent to which tasks and goals are clearly defined, organizational stage of development, and the scarcity of environmental resources may lead to the use of alternative effectiveness criteria. In not-for-profit organizations, where internal processes and output criteria often are not quantifiable, constituency satisfaction may be the only available indicator of effectiveness.

From the point of view of people outside the organization, such as academic investigators or government researchers, the constituency and competing values approaches to organizational effectiveness may be preferable. The constituency approach evaluates the organization's contribution to society. The competing values approach acknowledges different areas of focus (internal, external) and structure (flexible, control), and allows for managers to choose one value to emphasize.

KEY CONCEPTS

coalition	internal process approach
competing values approach	official goals
constituency approach	operative goals
effectiveness	satisficing
efficiency	sequential attention
importance of goals	system resource approach
goal	preference ordering
goal approach	

DISCUSSION QUESTIONS

1. What is the purpose of official goals in organizations? Of operational goals?

2. How do output goals differ from product goals?

3. Hurco Manufacturing Company produces high-technology machine tools. Hurco's president is a religious person, and senior management has pledged Hurco to "create products which contribute to the benefit of mankind; provide a stimulating, stable and safe working environment which fairly rewards each employee in proportion to his or her contribution of talent and effort; be an example in society as a company which serves the living God, believes

only in fair and ethical practices, recognizes its responsibility to help preserve the free enterprise system." [60] Based upon the constituency and competing values approaches, which outcomes are Hurco pursuing? Explain. Do you expect management to look also at more traditional criteria such as profits and market share? Discuss.

4. IN PRACTICE 3.2 described eight goals pursued in a juvenile organization. How is it possible for an organization to pursue this many goals simultaneously?

5. Who is responsible for goal-setting in an organization? Discuss.

6. Define effectiveness versus efficiency. Are they related in organizations?

7. Is it appropriate to use the subjective judgments of managers to identify organizational goals and measure effectiveness? Why?

8. You have been asked to evaluate the effectiveness of the police department in a medium-sized community. Where would you begin and how would you proceed? What effectiveness approach would you prefer?

9. What are the advantages and disadvantages of the system resource approach versus the goal approach for measuring organizational effectiveness?

10. What are the similarities and differences between assessing effectiveness on the basis of competing values versus constituencies? Explain.

11. A noted organization theorist once said, "Organizational effectiveness can be whatever top management defines it to be." Discuss.

12. How do situational factors such as life cycle, environment, and task or goal clarity influence the adoption of specific goals or values by management? Are these situational factors more important than top manager preferences? Discuss.

GUIDES TO ACTION

As an organization manager:

1. Establish and communicate organizational goals. Communicate official goals in order to provide a statement of the organization to external constituents. Communicate operational goals to provide internal direction, guidelines, and standards of performance for employees.

2. Sort out the many competing goals of an organization and establish priorities. Identify the area in which the organization truly wants to succeed. Achieve multiple goals through the processes of satisficing, sequential attention, priority setting, and goal changing.

3. Do not set goals alone. Discuss goals widely with other managers, and develop a coalition that agrees on which goals to emphasize.

4. Assess the effectiveness of the organization. Use the goal approach, internal process approach, and system resource approach to obtain specific pictures of effectiveness. Assess constituency satisfaction or competing values to obtain a broader picture of effectiveness.

5. Evaluate organizational factors during the adoption of goals and effectiveness criteria. The organizational stage of development, environmental conditions, clarity of tasks and outputs, and top leader preferences all influence preferred outcomes. Effectiveness criteria should find the right fit be-

tween organizational factors and environmental needs and opportunities. Once the goals and effectiveness criteria have been clearly articulated they can be used to assess performance.

Consider these Guides when analyzing the following case.

CASE FOR ANALYSIS

THE PARADOXICAL TWINS: ACME AND OMEGA ELECTRONICS*

PART I

In 1965, Technological Products of Erie, Pa., was bought out by a Cleveland manufacturer. The Cleveland firm had no interest in the electronics division of Technological Products and subsequently sold to different investors two plants that manufactured printed circuit boards. One of the plants, located in nearby Waterford, Pa., was renamed Acme Electronics and the other plant, within the city limits of Erie, was renamed Omega Electronics, Inc. Acme retained its original management and upgraded its general manager to president. Omega hired a new president, who had been a director of a large electronics research laboratory, and upgraded several of the existing personnel within the plant. Acme and Omega often competed for the same contracts. As subcontractors, both firms benefited from the electronics boom of the early 1970s and both looked forward to future growth and expansion. Acme had annual sales of $10 million and employed 550 people. Omega had annual sales of $8 million and employed 480 people. Acme regularly achieved greater net profits, much to the chagrin of Omega's management.

Inside Acme

The president of Acme, John Tyler, credited his firm's greater effectiveness to his manager's abilities to run a "tight ship." He explained that he had retained the basic structure developed by Technological Products because it was most efficient for high volume manufacture of printed circuits and their subsequent assembly. Tyler was confident that had the demand not been so great, its competitor would not have survived. "In fact," he said, "we have been able to beat Omega regularly for the most profitable contracts thereby increasing our profit." Acme had detailed organization charts and job descriptions. Tyler believed that everyone should have clear responsibilities and narrowly defined jobs, which would lead to efficient performance and high company profits. People were generally satisfied with their work at Acme; however, some of the managers voiced the desire to have a little more latitude in their jobs.

Inside Omega

Omega's president, Jim Rawls, did not believe in organization charts. He felt that his organization had departments similar to Acme's, but he thought the

* Adapted from John F. Veiga, "The Paradoxical Twins: Acme and Omega Electronics," in John F. Veiga and John N. Yanouzas, *The Dynamics of Organization Theory* (St. Paul, MN: West, 1979), pp. 132–138.

plant was small enough that things such as organization charts just put artificial barriers between specialists who should be working together. Written memos were not allowed, since, as Jim expressed it, "The plant is small enough that if people want to communicate they can just drop by and talk things over." The head of the mechanical engineering department said, "Jim spends too much of his time and mine making sure everyone understands what we're doing and listening to suggestions." Rawls was concerned with employee satisfaction and wanted everyone to feel part of the organization. The top management team reflected Rawls' attitudes. They also believed that employees should be familiar with activities throughout the organization so that cooperation between departments would be increased. A newer member of the industrial engineering department said, "When I first got here, I wasn't sure what I was supposed to do. One day I worked with some mechanical engineers and the next day I helped the shipping department design some packing cartons. The first months on the job were hectic but at least I got a real feel for what makes Omega tick."

Questions

1. *What are the goals at Acme? At Omega?*
2. *Who chooses these goals?*
3. *Do these goals reflect different values concerning organizational focus and structure?*

PART II

In 1976, integrated circuits began to cut deeply into the demand for printed circuit boards. The integrated circuits (I.C.) or "chips" were the first step into micro-miniaturization in the electronics industry. Because the manufacturing process for I.C.'s was a closely guarded secret, both Acme and Omega realized the potential threat to their futures and both began to seek new customers aggressively. In July 1976, one of the major photocopy manufacturers was looking for a subcontractor to assemble the memory unit for their new experimental copier. The projected contract for the job was estimated to be $5 to $7 million in annual sales. Both Acme and Omega were geographically close to this manufacturer and both had submitted highly competitive bids for the production of one hundred prototypes. Acme's bid was slightly lower than Omega's; however, both firms were asked to produce one hundred units. The photocopy manufacturer told both firms that speed was critical because their president had boasted to other manufacturers that they would have a finished copier available by Christmas. This boast, much to the designer's dismay, required pressure on all subcontractors to begin prototype production before final design of the copier was complete. This meant that Acme and Omega would have at most two weeks to produce the prototypes or delay the final copier production.

Questions

1. *Which firm do you think will produce the best results? Why?*

PART III

Inside Acme

As soon as John Tyler was given the blueprints (Monday, July 11, 1976), he sent a memo to the purchasing department requesting them to move forward on the purchase of all necessary materials. At the same time, he sent the blueprints to the drafting department and asked that they prepare manufacturing prints. The industrial engineering department was told to begin methods design work for use by the production department supervisors. Tyler also sent a memo to all department heads and executives indicating the critical time constraints of this job and how he expected that everyone would perform as efficiently as they had in the past.

The departments had little contact with one another for several days, and each seemed to work at its own speed. Each department also encountered problems. Purchasing could not acquire all the parts on time. Industrial engineering had difficulty arranging an efficient assembly sequence. Mechanical engineering did not take the deadline seriously, and parceled its work to vendors so the engineers could work on other jobs scheduled previously. Tyler made it a point to stay in touch with the photocopy manufacturer to let them know things were progressing and to learn of any new developments. He traditionally worked to keep important clients happy. Tyler telephoned someone at the photocopy company at least twice a week and got to know the head designer quite well.

On July 15, Mr. Tyler learned that mechanical engineering was way behind in its development work, and he "hit the roof." To make matters worse, purchasing did not obtain all the parts so the industrial engineers decided to assemble the product with one part missing, which would be inserted at the last minute. On Thursday, July 21, the final units were being assembled, although the process was delayed several times. On Friday, July 22, the last units were finished while John Tyler paced around the plant. Late that afternoon, Tyler received a phone call from the head designer of the photocopy manufacturer who told Tyler that he had received a call on Wednesday from Jim Rawls of Omega. He explained that Rawls' workers had found an error in the design of the connector table and taken corrective action on their prototypes. He told Tyler that he checked out the design error and that Omega was right. Tyler, a bit overwhelmed by this information, told the designer that he had all the memory units ready for shipment and that as soon as they received the missing component, on Monday or Tuesday, they would be able to deliver the final units. The designer explained that the design error would be rectified in a new blueprint he was sending over by messenger and that he would hold Acme to the Tuesday delivery date.

When the blueprint arrived, Tyler called in the production supervisor to assess the damage. The alterations in the design would call for total disassembly and the unsoldering of several connections. Tyler told the supervisor to put extra people on the alterations first thing Monday morning and to try to finish the job by Tuesday. Late Tuesday afternoon the alterations were finished and the missing components were delivered. Wednesday morning, the production supervisor discovered that the units would have to be torn apart again to install the missing component. When John Tyler was told this, he again "hit the roof." He called industrial engineering and asked if they could help out. The production supervisor and the methods engineer couldn't agree on how to install the component. John Tyler settled the argument by ordering that all units be taken apart again and the missing component installed. He told shipping to prepare cartons for delivery on Friday afternoon.

On Friday, July 29, fifty prototypes were shipped from Acme without final inspection. John Tyler was concerned about his firm's reputation so he waived the final inspection after he personally tested one unit and found it operational. On Tuesday, August 2, Acme shipped the last fifty units.

Inside Omega

Jim Rawls called a meeting on Friday, July 8, that included department heads to tell them about the potential contract they were to receive. He told them that as soon as he received the blueprints, work could begin. On Monday, July 11, the prints arrived and again the department heads met to discuss the project. At the end of the meeting, drafting had agreed to prepare manufacturing prints while industrial engineering and production would begin methods design.

Two problems arose within Omega that were similar to those at Acme. Certain ordered parts could not be delivered on time. The assembly sequence was difficult to engineer. The departments proposed ideas to help one another, however, and department heads and key employees had daily meetings to discuss progress. The head of electrical engineering knew of a Japanese source for the components that could not be purchased from normal suppliers. Most problems were solved by Saturday, July 16.

On Monday, July 18, a methods engineer and the production supervisor formulated the assembly plans and production was set to begin on Tuesday morning. On Monday afternoon, people from mechanical engineering, electrical engineering, production, and industrial engineering got together to produce a prototype just to ensure that there would be no snags in production. While they were building the unit, they discovered an error in the connector cable design. All the engineers agreed, after checking and rechecking the blueprints, that the cable was erroneously designed. People from mechanical engineering and electrical engineering spent Monday night redesigning the cable and on Tuesday morning the drafting department finalized the changes in the manufacturing prints. On Tuesday morning, Jim Rawls was a bit apprehensive about the design changes and decided to get formal approval. Rawls received word on Wednesday from the head designer at the photocopier firm that they could proceed with the design changes as discussed on the phone. On Friday, July 22, the final units were inspected by quality control and were then shipped.

Questions

1. Which organization was more effective at developing the prototype and meeting the deadlines? Was their level of effectiveness due to the goals chosen by top management?
2. Predict which organization will get the final contract. Why?

PART IV

Ten of Acme's final memory units were defective while all Omega's units passed the photocopier firm's tests. The photocopier firm was disappointed with Acme's delivery delay, and incurred further delays in repairing the defective Acme units. However, rather than give the entire contract to one firm, the final contract was split between Acme and Omega with two directives added: (1) maintain zero defects and (2) reduce final cost. In 1977, through extensive cost-cutting efforts, Acme reduced its unit cost by 20% and was ultimately awarded the total contract.

Questions

1. How can Acme's success be explained? Did Acme's goals seem more appropriate? Did constituent satisfaction play a role?
2. Overall, who was more effective, Acme or Omega? Explain.

NOTES

1. David T. Garino, "New Ralston Chief Says He'll Sacrifice Sales to Keep Company's Profit Margins High," *Wall Street Journal,* July 2, 1981, p. 21.

2. Ibid.; "Ralston Purina: Dumping Products That Lead it Away from Checkerboard Square," *Business Week,* January 31, 1983, pp. 63–64; "Ralston's Urban Commitment," *Dun's Business Month,* January, 1982, pp. 98–100.

3. Amitai Etzioni, *Modern Organizations* (Englewood Cliffs, NJ: Prentice-Hall, 1964), p. 6.

4. Carol J. Loomis, "How Fireman's Fund Singed American Express," *Fortune,* January 9, 1984, pp. 80–81.

5. Herbert A. Simon, "On the Concept of Organizational Goal," *Administrative Science Quarterly* 9 (1964):1–22.

6. Donald N. Michael, *On Learning to Plan—and Planning to Learn* (San Francisco: Jossey-Bass, 1973), p. 149.

7. James D. Thompson, *Organizations in Action* (New York: McGraw-Hill, 1967), pp. 83–98.

8. "Owens-Illinois: Giving Up Market Share to Improve Profits," *Business Week,* May 11, 1981, pp. 81–82.

9. Charles Perrow, "The Analysis of Goals in Complex Organizations," *American Sociological Review* 26 (1961):854–866.

10. Adapted from Bill Saporito, "Hewlett-Packard Discovers Marketing," *Fortune,* October 1, 1984, pp. 51–56; Y. K. Shatty, "New Look at Corporate Goals," *California Management Review,* 22, No. 2 (1979):71–79; policy manual from a Texas high school district.

11. Perrow, "Analysis of Goals."

12. Johannes U. Stoelwinder and Martin P. Charns, "The Task Field Model of Organization Analysis and Design," *Human Relations* 34 (1981):743–762; Anthony Raia, *Managing by Objectives* (Glenview, IL: Scott-Foresman, 1974).

13. "Bausch & Lomb: Hardball Pricing Helps It to Regain Its Grip in Contact Lenses," *Business Week,* July 16, 1984, pp. 78–80.

14. Steven Adams, Wade Foster, Dennis Heiner, and Arnie Lunding, "Report on Chase Manhattan Bank," unpublished manuscript, Texas A&M University, 1982.

15. Richard Crone, Bruce Snow, and Ricky Waclawcayk, "Datapoint Corporation," unpublished manuscript, Texas A&M University, 1981.

16. James G. March and Herbert A. Simon, *Organizations* (New York: Wiley, 1958); Richard M. Cyert and James G. March, *A Behavioral Theory of the Firm* (Englewood Cliffs, NJ: Prentice-Hall, 1963); Thompson, *Organizations in Action.*

17. Cyert and March, *Behavioral Theory of the Firm,* p. 118.

18. Etzioni, *Modern Organizations.*

19. David L. Sills, *The Volunteers* (New York: The Free Press, 1957).

20. Simon, "On the Concept of Organizational Goal," pp. 1–22.

21. Perrow, *Organizational Analysis.*

22. Stratford P. Sherman, "Muddling to Victory at Geico," *Fortune,* September 5, 1983, pp. 66–80.

23. Perrow, "Analysis of Goals," pp. 859–864.

24. Cyert and March, *Behavioral Theory of the Firm,* pp. 114–127.

25. Etzioni, *Modern Organizations,* p. 8.

26. Ibid.; Gary D. Sandefur, "Efficiency in Social Service Organizations," *Administration & Society,* 14 (1983):449–468.

27. Richard M. Steers, *Organizational Effectiveness: A Behavioral View* (Santa Monica, CA: Goodyear, 1977), p. 51.

28. Karl E. Weick and Richard L. Daft, "The Effectiveness of Interpretation Systems," in Kim S. Cameron and David A. Whetten, eds., *Organizational Effectiveness: A Comparison of Multiple Models* (New York: Academic Press, 1982).

29. Steven Strasser, J. D. Eveland, Gaylord Cummins, O. Lynn Deniston, and John H. Romani, "Conceptualizing the Goal and Systems Models of Organizational Effectiveness—Implications for Comparative Evaluation Research," *Journal of Management Studies,* 18 (1981):321–340.

30. Ephraim Yuchtman and Stanley E. Seashore, "A System Resource Approach to Organizational Effectiveness," *Administrative Science Quarterly* 12 (1967):377–395.

31. J. Barton Cunningham, "A Systems-Resource Approach for Evaluating Organizational Effectiveness," *Human Relations* 31 (1978):631–656.

32. Joseph J. Molnar and David C. Rogers, "Organizational Effectiveness: An Empirical Comparison of the Goal and System Resource Approaches," *The Sociological Quarterly* 17 (1976):401–413.

33. Chris Argyris, *Integrating the Individual and the Organization* (New York: Wiley, 1964); Warren G. Bennis, *Changing Organizations* (New York: McGraw-Hill, 1966); Rensis Likert, *The Human Organization* (New York: McGraw-Hill, 1967); Richard Beckhard, *Organization Development: Strategies and Models* (Reading, MA: Addison-Wesley, 1969).

34. J. Barton Cunningham, "Approaches to the Evaluation of Organizational Effectiveness," *Academy of Management Review* 2 (1977):463–474; Beckhard, *Organization Development.*

35. William M. Evan, "Organization Theory and Organizational Effectiveness: An Exploratory Analysis," *Organization and Administrative Sciences* 7 (1976):15–28.

36. James L. Price, "The Study of Organizational Effectiveness," *The Sociological Quarterly* 13 (1972):3–15.

37. Richard H. Hall and John P. Clark, "An Ineffective Effectiveness Study and Some Suggestions for Future Research," *The Sociological Quarterly* 21 (1980): 119–134; Price, "Study of Organizational Effectiveness"; Perrow, "Analysis of Goals."

38. George W. England, "Organizational Goals and Expected Behaviors in American Managers," *Academy of Management Journal* 10 (1967):107–117.

39. Richard M. Steers, "Problems in the Measurement of Organizational Effectiveness," *Administrative Science Quarterly* 20 (1975):546–558.

40. Johannes M. Pennings and Paul S. Goodman, "Toward a Workable Framework," in Paul S. Goodman, Johannes M. Pennings, et al., *New Perspectives on Organizational Effectiveness* (San Francisco: Jossey-Bass, 1979), p. 152.

41. Hall and Clark, "An Ineffective Effectiveness Study," p. 39.

42. Ibid., pp. 129–130.

43. Paul M. Hirsch, "Organizational Effectiveness and the Institutional Environment," *Administrative Science Quarterly* 20 (1975):327–344.

44. Michael T. Hannan and John Freeman, "Obstacles to Comparative Studies," in Goodman, Pennings, et al., *New Perspectives,* pp. 106–131.

45. Terry Connolly, Edward J. Conlon, and Stuart Jay Deutsch, "Organizational Effectiveness: A Multiple-Constituency Approach," *Academy of Management Review* 5 (1980):211–217; Michael Keely, "A Social-Justice Approach to Organizational Evaluation," *Administrative Science Quarterly* 23 (1978):272–292.

46. Frank Friedlander and Hal Pickle, "Components of Effectiveness in Small Organizations," *Administrative Science Quarterly* 13 (1968):289–304.

47. Kim S. Cameron, "The Effectiveness of Ineffectiveness," in Barry M. Staw and L. L. Cummings (eds.), *Research in Organizational Behavior* (Greenwich, CT: JAI Press, 1984), pp. 235–286; Rosabeth Moss Kanter and Derick Brinkerhoff, "Organizational Performance: Recent Developments in Measurement," *Annual Review of Sociology,* 7 (1981):321–349.

48. Geoffrey Colvin, "International Harvester's Last Chance," *Fortune,* April 19, 1982, pp. 102–107.

49. Adapted from Meg Cox, "Harvester's Woes Take a Heavy Toll on Those Serving Troubled Firm," *The Wall Street Journal,* May 21, 1982, pp. 1, 12; "Can Don Lennox Save Harvester?" *Business Week,* August 15, 1983, pp. 80–84; and Jabby Lowe, Greg Millsap, and Bill Breedlove, "International Harvester," unpublished manuscript, Texas A&M University, 1982.

50. Robert E. Quinn and John Rohrbaugh, "A Spatial Model of Effectiveness Criteria: Towards a Competing Values Approach to Organizational Analysis," *Management Science,* 29 (1983):363–377.

51. Robert E. Quinn and Kim Cameron, "Organizational Life Cycles and Shifting Criteria of Effectiveness: Some Preliminary Evidence," *Management Science* 29 (1983): 33–51.

52. Harlan S. Byrne, "At Northwest Airlines, Emphasis on Keeping Costs Low Pays Off," *The Wall Street Journal,* October 31, 1983, pp. 1, 22; "Cost Control Champ," *Barron's,* April 23, 1984, p. 54.

53. Thomas J. Lueck, "One Less Word for a Time of Crisis: Jockey Gives Underwear to Needy," *The Wall Street Journal,* April 27, 1982, p. 33; Susan E. Currier, "After Eighty-One Years, Pirsh & Sons Proves that Quality Pays," *Inc.,* August, 1981, pp. 65–66.

54. James D. Thompson, *Organizations in Action* (New York: McGraw-Hill, 1967).

55. Ibid.

56. Quinn and Cameron, "Organizational Life Cycles," pp. 33–51; Frank Hoy and Don Hellriegel, "The Kilmann and Herden Model of Organizational Effectiveness Criteria for Small Business Managers," *Academy of Management Journal,* 25 (1982):308–322.

57. Martha Elzen, Eric Klasson, Michele Mahon, and Sow-Num Pang, "Kentucky Fried Chicken: Application in Organizational Theory and Design," unpublished manuscript, Texas A&M University, 1982.

58. Raymond E. Miles and Charles C. Snow, *Organizational Strategy, Structure, and Process* (New York: McGraw-Hill, 1978).

59. This case was inspired by Danny Miller, "Davidson Psychiatric Hospital," distributed by the Intercollegiate Case Clearing House, Soldier's Field, Boston, MA 02136, 1976.

60. John Halbrooks, "Making Money Isn't the Religion at Hurco," *Inc.,* April 1981, pp. 104–110.

Organization Design

CHAPTER FOUR
Organizational Technology

INTERNAL REVENUE SERVICE

Every year, the Internal Revenue Service Center in Austin hires about 2,000 additional workers to process the truckloads of tax returns that arrive during the peak season, from January through April. In the unit for which I worked, the sole requirement for the job is to pass the GS Level 2 or 3 Civil Service examination, which tests one's ability to read, alphabetize, and solve rudimentary arithmetic problems.

We were told that we would be doing "extraction," which is officialese for opening the mail. We visited the enormous room where we would be working, which was furnished with row after row of specially designed desks called Tingle tables, so named for their inventor, James Tingle. There were about 120 of the Tingle tables in all. Five stacks of sorting bins, three bins to a stack, lined the outer edge of each tabletop; the work space left in the middle was barely large enough to open a return on. A small, elbow-high ledge, made to hold a box of mail, jutted out on the table's left-hand side. In the middle of the room sat the managers and work leaders, decidedly the upper echelon, watching over the rest of the workers from their executive desks.

That day we learned the procedures we would be following as we worked. Once we had removed the contents from an envelope, our next task would be to identify the type of return. In 1983 there were nine major classifications: 1040, 1040A, 1040EZ, 1040ES, 1120, 1065, 1041, the 940 family, and tax-return correspondence. All other forms were to be lumped together in a "miscellaneous" category.

Each type of return had its own rules. 1040's were considered business returns if an amount was written on line 12 or line 19; unsigned 1040's and 1040's without a W-2 form called for special handling; past-due 940's and 940's that had a remittance but not an IRS computer-generated label went to miscellaneous. The extractor had to compare the amount of any payment with the amount owed; if the two numbers differed, the return was sorted as a partial-payment return, even if the sender had overpaid. From moment to moment we would determine, for example, whether the 1040 return in hand was a 1040 business with-remit full-paid, a 1040 business with-remit partial-paid, a 1040 business non-remit, or a 1040 non-business.

It was a rare return that came in with its various parts stapled in the proper order. Often the taxpayer, in his eagerness to explain some problem, stapled a letter to the front of the return. Our job was to remove the letter immediately, place it in back of the return along with anything else that had come in the envelope (most commonly cartoons and prayers), and restaple the bundle in the upper left-hand corner. No one would look at the letter again unless the computer kicked out the return for some error. W-2's were also stapled to the return, front and center.

In addition to concentrating on our stapling and sorting, we had to ensure that all pre-1982 returns were kept separate from the 1982 ones, that envelopes belonging to prior years' returns were not discarded, that certain business returns were stamped "Received," and that all remittances in excess of $10,000 were put on a pole to our right for immediate pickup.

We are expected to extract, process, and sort at least five returns per minute, or three hundred per hour, on the average. Altogether, 250,000 pieces of mail were pushed through the two shifts of extractors during that April peak. As we labored, work leaders paced up and down the rows exhorting us to work faster.

Each week we received a computer printout called an individual performance record, which listed our error percentage rate and our standing within the unit. . . . We had started with the lowest rating for service-center efficiency throughout the nation (number ten) and had raised ourselves to number three. Soon an invitation was circulated to a we-survived-the-peak-of-'83 party, hosted by two women in the unit.[1]

Technology is the knowledge, tools, techniques, and actions used to transform organizational inputs into outputs.[2] Technology is the organization's transformation process, and includes machinery, employee education and skill, and work procedures used in that transformation process. Martha Ebersole's description of the extraction department above was about a technology. The input consisted of mailed-in tax returns, and the output was tax returns properly sorted, stapled, and bundled. The transformation process consisted of opening, sorting, unstapling, stapling, and bundling of tax returns.

Technologies cover an enormous range of activities. One organization might write stories for television shows. Others might produce cardboard boxes, design blueprints for building construction, or manufacture specialized fluids (muds) used for drilling oil wells. Technology also includes cancer research, coaching a football team, and fighting a war. All forms of technology begin with raw materials of some type (e.g., steel castings in a valve manufacturing plant, students in a university). Employees take action on the raw material to make a change in it (e.g., steel castings are machined, students are taught), which transforms the raw material into the output of the organization (e.g., control valves ready for shipment to oil refineries, knowledgeable university graduates).

Technology can be analyzed at both organizational and departmental levels. In terms of the systems theory described in chapter 1, the organization-level technology is the transformation process that takes place in the production subsystem. Organizational technology produces the principal products or services of the organization. In a cotton mill, the technology is the process of breaking the cotton bale, cleaning, carding, spinning, and then weaving the cotton into sheets and pillowcases for sale to consumers. Other organization-level technologies would include the transformation of crude oil into gasoline, the manufacture of chemicals, and the assembly of automobiles.

In today's large, complex organizations, different technologies are used in different parts of the organization. Each department transforms inputs into outputs. Research and development transforms ideas into new products. Marketing transforms inventory into sales. In the Internal Revenue Service, the tax returns are passed from the extractions department to the deposits department, the returns analysis department, and finally to data processing. Each tax form is handled by at least four departments that make up the overall production process. Technology can be analyzed at the department level as well as at the organization level of analysis.

The activity of an individual employee is called a **task.** Opening a tax return or throwing a bale of cotton into the breaking machine are tasks. Individual tasks combine into department level and organization-level technologies as illustrated in Exhibit 4.1. Raw materials flow into and through the organization's production process in a logical sequence, and work activities are performed with a variety of tools, techniques, or machines.

Purpose of This Chapter

The purpose of this chapter is to explore the nature of organizational technologies and the relationship between technology and organization structure. Chapter 2 described how the environment influences the organization design. The question addressed in this chapter is: How should organization structure be designed to accommodate and facilitate internal work flow? An analogy is the structure of a building. The building's structural design reflects the

EXHIBIT 4.1. Transformation Process for the Internal Revenue Service.

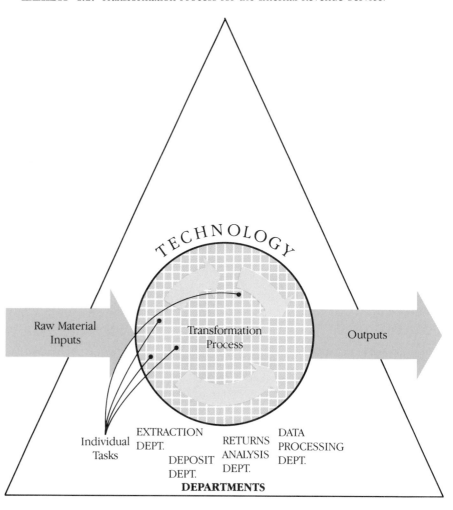

need to buffer and control the environment. But it also reflects the nature of the workflow performed within the building.

Technologies vary so widely that definitions and analyses sometimes reflect different parts of the transformation process. Technology might be assessed by examining the raw materials flowing into the organization,[3] the variability of work activities,[4] the degree of mechanization in the transformation process,[5] the use of mechanical aides,[6] the extent to which one task depends upon another in the work flow,[7] and the number of new product outputs.[8] The focus on different parts of the transformation process can be confusing, so it is best to remember that each model deals with some part of the input-transformation-output process. It is the general nature of the transformation process at either the organization or department level that is important to organization structure.

The next section describes organization-level technology and the ways in which manufacturing technology influences overall structure and design. We will also discuss recent work on service technology, and explore how organizational structure differs for the production of services rather than products. Then we will turn to technology at the department level. Departments within a single organization may have wide variation in structure.

ORGANIZATION-LEVEL TECHNOLOGY

Manufacturing Firms

South Essex Study The first and most influential study of manufacturing technology was conducted by Joan Woodward, a British industrial sociologist. Her research began as a field study of management principles in south Essex. The prevailing management wisdom at the time (1950s) was contained in what was known as universal principles of management. These principles were "one best way" prescriptions that effective organizations were expected to adopt. Each manager should have a span of control of six subordinates, each organization should have a similar structure, and so on. Scientists often question established principles, so Woodward surveyed 100 manufacturing firms firsthand to learn how they were organized.[9] She and her research team visited each firm, interviewed managers, examined company records, and observed the manufacturing operations. Her data included a wide range of structural characteristics (span of control, levels of management, management and clerical ratios, worker skill level). Her data also included dimensions of management style (written versus verbal communications, use of rewards) and the type of manufacturing process. Data that reflected commercial success of the firm were also obtained.

Analysis Initially, her data made no sense. Firms varied widely on such things as span of control, number of hierarchical levels, administrative ratio, and amount of verbal communications. No support was given to the "one best way" principles of management. Her challenge was to determine whether the organization structures reflected random choices of managers or whether previously undiscovered factors could explain the unexpected differences that were observed.

Reanalysis Woodward developed a scale and organized the firms according to technical complexity of the manufacturing process. **Technical complexity** represents the extent of mechanization and predictability of the manufacturing process. High technical complexity means that most of the work is performed by machines and is very predictable. Low technical complexity means that workers play a larger role in the production process. Woodward's scale of technical complexity originally had ten categories as summarized in Exhibit 4.2. These categories were further consolidated into three basic technology groups.

Group I: Small-Batch and Unit Production. These firms tend to be job-shop operations that manufacture and assemble small orders to meet specific needs of customers. Custom work is the norm. This technology relies heavily on the human operator; it is thus not highly mechanized, and predictability of outcome is low. Examples include many types of made-to-order manufactured products, such as specialized construction equipment, custom electronic equipment, and custom clothing.

Group II: Large-Batch and Mass Production. This manufacturing process is characterized by long production runs of standardized parts. Output often goes into inventory from which orders are filled because customers do not

EXHIBIT 4.2. Woodward's Classification of 100 British Firms According to Their System of Production.

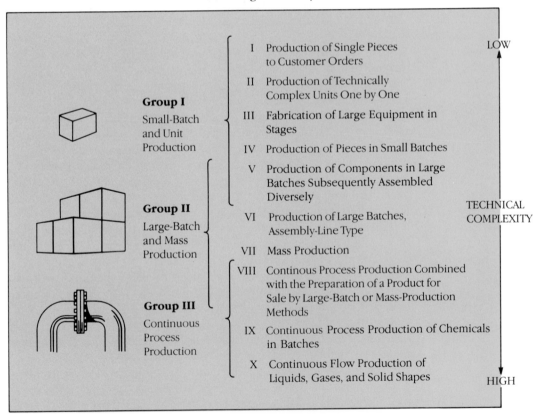

Source: J. Woodward, *Management and Technology* (London: Her Majesty's Stationery Office, 1958). Reproduced with the permission of her Britannic Majesty's Stationery Office.

have special needs. Examples include most assembly lines, such as for automobiles or trailer homes. An integrated cotton mill is also an example of a mass production technology.

Group III: Continuous-Process Production. In this technology, the entire process is mechanized. There is no starting and stopping. This represents mechanization and standardization one step beyond an assembly line. The organization has high control over the process, and outcomes are highly predictable. Examples would include chemical plants, oil refining, liquor production, and nuclear power plants.

Using this classification of technology, Woodward's data fell into place. A few of her key findings are given in Exhibit 4.3. Number of management levels and manager/total personnel ratio, for example, show definite increases as technical complexity increases from unit production to continuous process. This indicates that greater management intensity is needed to manage complex technology. Direct/indirect labor ratio decreases with technical complexity, because more indirect workers are required to support and maintain the complex machinery. Other characteristics, such as span of control, formalized procedures, and centralization are high for mass-production technology but low for other technologies because the work is standardized. Unit production and continuous process technologies require highly skilled workers to run the machines and verbal communication to adapt to changing conditions. Mass production is standardized and routinized so few exceptions occur, little verbal communication is needed, and employees are less skilled.

Overall, the management system in both unit-production and continuous-process technology are characterized as organic. They are more free-flowing and adaptive, with fewer procedures and less standardization. Mass production, however, is mechanistic, with standardized jobs and formalized procedures. Woodward's discovery about technology thus provided substantial new insight into the causes of organization structure. In Joan Woodward's own words, "Different technologies impose different kinds of demands on individuals and organizations, and those demands had to be met through an appropriate structure."[10]

Technology and Performance Another portion of Woodward's study examined the success of the firms along dimensions such as profitability, market share, stock price, and reputation. As indicated in chapter 3, the measurement of effectiveness is not simple or precise, but she was able to rank firms on a scale of commercial success according to whether they displayed above-average performance, average performance, or below-average performance.

Woodward compared the structure-technology relationship to commercial success, and discovered that successful firms tended to be those that had complementary structures and technologies. An important conclusion is that many of the organizational characteristics of the successful firms were near the average of their production category, as shown in Exhibit 4.3. Below-average firms tended to depart from the structural characteristics for their technology type. Another important conclusion was that structural characteristics could be interpreted as clustering into organic and mechanistic management systems. Successful small-batch and continuous-process orga-

EXHIBIT 4.3. Relationship between Technical Complexity
and Structural Characteristics.

Structural Characteristic	TECHNOLOGY		
	Unit Production	Mass Production	Continuous Process
Number of management levels	3	4	6
Supervisor span of control	23	48	15
Direct labor/indirect labor ratio	9:1	4:1	1:1
Manager/total personnel ratio	Low	Medium	High
Number "skilled" workers	High	Low	High
Formalized procedures	Low	High	Low
Centralization	Low	High	Low
Amount of verbal communication	High	Low	High
Amount of written communication	Low	High	Low
Overall structure	Organic	Mechanistic	Organic

Source: Joan Woodward, *Industrial Organization: Theory and Practice* (London: Oxford University Press, 1965), with permission.

nizations had organic structures, and successful mass-production organizations had mechanistic structures.

Other Studies   Two studies in the United States have reaffirmed Woodward's findings. A direct replication of Woodward's research was conducted on fifty-five firms in the Minneapolis-St. Paul area.[11] Most of the structural dimensions showed a similar relationship to technology. The large majority of small-batch and continuous-process firms had organic management systems, and the large majority of mass-production organizations had mechanistic systems. As in the Woodward study, those firms that had the appropriate structure for the technology tended to experience higher performance levels.

The other major study investigated the relationship between technology and structure in forty-three industrial organizations.[12] This study evaluated the amount of change taking place within a given form of technology, which is similar to Woodward's concept of technical complexity. Frequent changes take place in small-batch technologies, and only a few in continuous-process technologies. The findings support the relationship between manufacturing technology and organizational structure. For example, when product changes were frequent (similar to Woodward's small batch), organization structure was more organic. More change was associated with a fewer number of separate subunits, fewer levels of authority, smaller management ratios, and less formalization of structure.

Conclusion   The important conclusion from the research into manufacturing firms is that production technology has a systematic relationship with structure and management characteristics. Woodward's discovery was extremely important to the development of organization theory. Her findings spelled the beginning of the end for the universal principles of management, and opened up the new horizon called contingency theory. Such things as organizational structure, management style, and commercial success are all contingent upon factors such as production technology.

IN PRACTICE 4.1

Three Mile Island

Managers at the Three Mile Island nuclear plant requested permission to start reactor Unit One, which had been shut down since the accident that disabled Unit Two in 1979. Corporate management had a new president, a new board, new staff experts, and believed they could win a license from the Nuclear Regulatory Commission. After the NRC inspection, corporate managers were stunned. Inspectors found some valves open that should have been closed, equipment tests that weren't done right, and procedures that weren't followed correctly. The NRC levied a $40,000 fine and indicated that Unit One did not have sufficient management capacity nor organization of sufficient quality to manage the nuclear power plant. No license was granted.

The Three Mile Island decision reflects a shifting concern of the Nuclear Regulatory Commission. They no longer concentrate on gauges and valves. The NRC evaluates management competence and structure, and often suggests that executives aren't doing their jobs. The marriage between traditional management structures and nuclear technology is imperfect. The president of the Atomic Industrial Forum says, "Nuclear power requires about ten times the management intensity that a coal plant does." The best management resources need to be allocated to the nuclear entities. A nuclear plant is not just another boiler unit, and when managers learn that lesson, NRC's approval will follow.

The chairman of Georgia Power Company emphasizes that, "The world of a utility executive that has a nuclear-power plant is different from one who doesn't, and if he doesn't understand that, he's in trouble." The NRC is recommending that utilities hire outside consultants to help shape up their management systems to fit nuclear requirements.

One solution developed by the Carolina Power & Light Company was to put all nuclear activities under one senior manager. Nuclear became a separate entity, and additional management intensity and support staff were allocated to help manage that division.

The problem in the nuclear industry is that skills vary widely among companies. A company with a single nuclear plant gets into trouble when it uses the same management systems adopted from other plants. Nuclear plants are ultracomplex, and when managers treat one as just another boiler, they get in over their heads.

One solution the industry is considering is to adopt standardized management practices found in other countries that manage nuclear plants from a central state agency. Utilities could join together in a consortium, and provide a core of staff specialists who could work with all nuclear plants to achieve the right organizational structure. Another idea is to organize nuclear plants into a dozen regional companies with central management. The most probable solution is that each company will have to learn for itself that the management of nuclear plants requires different skills and systems from traditional plants. This may take a long time, and could lead to more failures, but centralized state control is not the American way.[13]

The nuclear power plant would be classified as a continuous-process technology, and is extremely complex. Highly skilled employees are required. A high percentage of staff support and maintenance personnel are needed to maintain the automated equipment. Greater management intensity is required to ensure close supervision and provide backup expertise in a crisis. The one deviation from Woodward's model is high use of standard procedures in a continuous-process technology. The cost of failure in human terms is so great in the nuclear power industry that many procedures evolve to tightly control work activities. Rigid procedures combined with highly skilled employees ensure an adequate response to an emergency.

MANUFACTURING VERSUS SERVICE TECHNOLOGY

The next stage of technology research examined service as well as manufacturing firms. A research team from the University of Aston in Birmingham, England, surveyed a wide range of organizations to develop a scale for classifying technologies.[14] The inclusion of both manufacturing and nonmanufacturing organizations meant they had to develop a scale of technology different from Woodward's. The Aston team identified three characteristics of technology that seemed pertinent to workflow operations across organizations.

1. *Automation of Equipment.* This represents the amount of activity performed by machines in self-acting capacities versus the amount of activity performed by humans.
2. *Workflow Rigidity.* This represents the extent to which operational knowledge, skills, and equipment are rigid rather than adaptable in their uses. A single-purpose machine would be considered rigid. A semiskilled employee would be adaptable to several uses. Workflow rigidity also reflects the extent to which the sequence of operations is tightly interconnected and unalterable.
3. *Specificity of Evaluation.* This characteristic refers to the extent that workflow activity can be evaluated using precise, quantitative measurements as opposed to the use of nonquantitative, personal opinions of managers.

These three technology characteristics are fairly similar to Woodward's concept of technology. Automation of equipment and workflow rigidity overlap Woodward's notion of increasing complexity and mechanization. The contribution of the Aston group is that they extended these concepts to include nonmanufacturing firms.

The Aston group visited and interviewed participants in fifty-two organizations to gather data about technology and structural characteristics. Their first discovery regarding technology was that the three technology variables were highly associated with each other. So they created a single technology variable called **workflow integration** that adds together the characteristics of automation of equipment, workflow rigidity, and specificity of evaluation. Exhibit 4.4 shows firms from their study and the workflow integration score for each firm. A higher score in Exhibit 4.4 means that the firm's technology is characterized by greater automation of equipment, greater rigidity of workflow, and more precise measurement of operations. The workflow integration scores in Exhibit 4.4 assume a scale of twenty-one points, based on seven points each for the three measures contained in workflow integration.

One important finding from Exhibit 4.4 is the difference between manufacturing and service firms. Manufacturing firms tend to have higher scores than service firms. Service technologies are characterized by less automation, less rigidity, and less precise measurements than manufacturing technologies.

The comparison of structural and management characteristics with technology across the fifty-two organizations in the Aston research indicated that structure was indeed related to technology. They found that as the workflow integration increased, so did bureaucratic characteristics. More specifically, the extent of specialization, overall standardization of procedures, and decentralization of authority all increased with workflow integration, and the supervisory ratio was smaller.[15] These findings reinforce the Woodward research that structure varies with technology, and they also indicate that the technology and organization structure in service may differ in a systematic way from manufacturing firms.

Structure Centered on the Production Workflow Further analysis of the Aston group's data led to the additional conclusion that technology is

EXHIBIT 4.4. Examples of Workflow Integration Scores for a Sample of Manufacturing and Service Firms.

Workflow Integration Score	Organization Description	Organization Type Manufacturing	Service
17	Vehicle manufacturer	✓	
16	Food manufacturer	✓	
15	Packaging manufacturer	✓	
14	Metal-goods manufacturer	✓	
13	Commercial-vehicle manufacturer	✓	
12	Vehicle-tire manufacturer	✓	
11	Printer	✓	
10	Local authority water department		✓
9	Nonferrous metal processor	✓	
8	Toy manufacturer	✓	
7	Local authority civil engineering department		✓
6	Insurance company		✓
5	Research division		✓
4	Savings bank		✓
3	Chain of shoe-repair stores		✓
2	Department stores		✓
1	Chain of retail stores		✓

Source: David J. Hickson, D. S. Pugh, and D. C. Pheysey, "Operations Technology and Organization Structure: An Empirical Reappraisal," *Administrative Science Quarterly* 14 (1969):385, with permission.

only one factor influencing structure, and it may be less important than other variables, especially size. Size was introduced in chapter 1, and the influence of environment on structure was discussed in chapter 2.

An important idea introduced by the Aston group was that production technology has its primary effect on those structural variables centered on the workflow.[16] For example, Woodward's firms were small in size, hence technology could be expected to have a strong effect because managers and structural dimensions were located closer to the production workflow. In large, diverse organizations, size, ownership, or environment may be more important to structural design because upper-management activities are several levels removed from the production workflow. Thus when organizations are small, the overall structure will be more heavily influenced by technology. In addition, technology will have a strong effect in small departments because personnel in small departments are located close to the workflow in that department. Thus the impact of technology on structure will depend on the size of the organization and will typically have major impact on activities located close to the production workflow.

SERVICE FIRMS

One finding from the Aston group research was that firms they classified as service tended to have lower scores on workflow integration than firms they classified as manufacturing. Subsequent research has focused more carefully on the unique dimensions of service versus manufacturing technologies. The definition of service technology includes the following two elements.[17]

1. *Simultaneous Production and Consumption.* In a service organization, the customer and employee interact to provide the service output. Employees within the technical core of the service organization interact directly and frequently with customers. Customers thus are engaged in the production process, and service employees can be viewed as "mini-factories" that produce the output during customer interactions. Manufacturing firms, in contrast, are characterized by separation of customers and technical employees, so that no direct interactions occur.

2. *Intangibility.* The output of a service firm is intangible. A service is abstract and cannot be stored in inventory. The service often consists of information or knowledge in contrast to a tangible, physical product provided by manufacturing firms. Manufactured products are produced at one point and time and can be sold at another point and time.

Examples of service versus manufacturing technology are given in Exhibit 4.5. Soft drinks, automobiles, and packaged foods are the output of manufacturing technologies because they are tangible products and can be made separate from the customer. Service technology includes such things as consulting, teaching, transportation, and the delivery of health care. These are intangible and are consumed when produced for the customer.

The characteristics of service versus manufacturing come in varying amounts so that some organizations produce both. A real estate firm, a brokerage

EXHIBIT 4.5. Examples of Service vs. Manufacturing Technology.

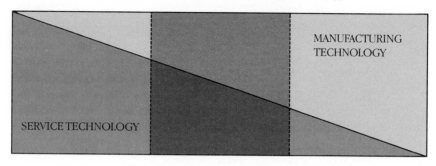

Service	Product and Service	Product
Airlines	Fast Foods Outlets	Soft Drinks
Hotels	Banks	Steel
Consulting	Post Office	Automobiles
Teaching	Cosmetics	Mining
Health Clinic	Real Estate	Food Processing
Law Firm	Stockbroker	

house, banks, and fast-food outlets provide both a product and service. They provide information or convenience along with a tangible output. All organizations can be classified as variations along a continuum that includes both manufacturing and service characteristics.

Service Firm Structure   The feature of service technologies that has distinctive influence on organizational structure and control systems is the need for technical core employees to be close to the customer.[18] The amount of customer contact required between organization and client influences both the configuration of the organization and internal characteristics. The differences between service and product organizations necessitated by amount of customer contact are summarized in Exhibit 4.6.

The impact of customer contact on organizational configuration is reflected in the use of boundary roles and structural disaggregation.[19] Boundary roles are used extensively in manufacturing firms to handle customers and to reduce uncertainty and disruptions for the technical core. Boundary roles are less suited to service firms because the customer must interact directly with technical employees. The service is intangible and cannot be stored. Information is exchanged through direct customer interactions. The technical core employees must deal with greater customer variety and unpredictability than in manufacturing firms. The service firm is often disaggregated into small units that can be located close to customers. Stockbrokers, doctors' clinics, fast-food franchises, consulting firms, and banks disperse their facilities into regional and local offices. Employees are located where customers can interact directly with them. Manufacturing firms, on the other hand, tend to aggregate operations in a single area that has raw materials and an available workforce. The manufacturing firm can take advantage of economies derived from expensive machinery and long production runs. The service firm deals in information and intangible outcomes, and does not need to be large. The

EXHIBIT 4.6. Configuration and Structural Characteristics of Service vs. Product Organizations.

	Service	Product & Service	Product
CONFIGURATION			
1. Boundary Roles	Few	Some	Many
2. Geographical Dispersion	Yes	Some	No
STRUCTURE			
1. Technical Employee Professionalization	High	Moderate	Low
2. Skill Emphasis	Interpersonal	Technical & Interpersonal	Technical
3. Centralized Decision-Making	No	Some	Yes
4. Formalization	Low	Medium	High

greatest economies are achieved through disaggregation and location close to the customer.

Internal organization characteristics used to direct and control the organization are also influenced by the nature of service technology. For one thing, the professionalism of technical employees needs to be higher. They have to have enough knowledge and awareness to handle customer problems rather than to perform a single, mechanical task. The skills needed for service employees include social and interpersonal skills as well as technical skills.[20] Service firms must be able to handle employees and provide customer satisfaction. Because of professionalism and structural dispersion, decision-making tends to be decentralized in service firms and formalization tends to be low. Employees located in the regional and local outlets of the service firm make decisions and react on their own to the customer. Employees often have more autonomy and will be regulated by fewer rules and standard procedures than lower level technical employees in a manufacturing firm.

Understanding the nature of service technology enables managers to adopt an appropriate structure that is often quite different from the structure for a product-based or manufacturing technology. Merrill Lynch provides a mix of products and services to customers, and has prospered through its emphasis on the service side of the business. Changing times, however, may require a new approach to service delivery.

IN PRACTICE 4.2

Merrill Lynch & Co.

Merrill Lynch is the largest and most prosperous securities broker in the industry. It has been an innovation leader, and has maintained market share despite withering competition. Merrill Lynch must now contend with Sears Roebuck, American Express, Citicorp, and dozens of discount brokers located at local banks. Merrill Lynch's strength has enabled it to maintain market share, but profits are in decline. Costs are too high.

Merrill Lynch prospered for years on a service philosophy. Each broker had a special bond with customers. Customers were wed to the personal relationship with each broker, not to the company. This strategy worked because Merrill Lynch emphasized the research background and special information the broker could offer the customer. But in this setting the individual broker receives a high percentage of the commission, and is hard to control. If the brokers are unhappy, they can leave and take customers with them.

Under deregulation and increasing competition, Merrill Lynch must cut costs. To do so means emphasizing products more and services less. Merrill Lynch wants to become a one-stop financial supermarket, where employees can select from numerous products, including savings, insurance, lending services, and financial instruments. The one-stop philosophy will also appeal to new customers, including retirees, women, and young professionals who desire services other than the purchases of stocks and bonds.

The change to a product emphasis has been difficult. The broker is to be converted into a financial advisor with a less intimate relationship with customers. The customer will also work with a network of salaried professionals who specialize in lending, tax matters, and insurance. These professionals are in service departments, who can handle walk-in traffic and small accounts. Brokers, however, resist this shift because they see it as taking away their sales.

One way to resolve the conflict with brokers is to segment the market. The key customers are the top 15% who provide 90% of revenues. They can be given personal service. The rest of the clientele can take advantage of one-stop shopping. The professionals need not be as knowledgeable nor develop so close a relationship to sell these new products.

Another problem with changing from personal services to more emphasis on products is the lack of central control over the brokers. Executives in New York developed new products such as new bond funds or limited partnerships, but they have to have the cooperation of brokers to sell them. Executives spend most of their time servicing important clients, and may not listen to what New York is trying to say. Many securities dealers find that decision authority rests with brokers in local offices.

The other major strategy of dealers is to stay close to customers. Brokers are expanding branch offices at a furious pace. "The more good distribution points you have, the better are your chances of picking up all the marbles," said a senior vice-president at Prudential.

The securities industry is changing. It is still a service industry, but the intense service orientation is not cost efficient. Brokerage houses like Merrill Lynch are struggling to cope with changes in the market and industry. Roger Birk, chairman of Merrill Lynch, said it best: "Who ever said it would be easy? This is a tough-business—a very difficult business to manage." [21]

Merrill Lynch executives are learning to live with changes in a service technology. To maintain their business they still need a strong service component, including the location of offices close to customers, professional personnel, and interpersonal as well as technical skills.

DEPARTMENTAL TECHNOLOGY

We have been discussing the effect of manufacturing and service technologies at the organization level of analysis. In this section we shift to the department level of analysis. Each department in an organization has a transformation process that consists of a distinct technology. Chrysler Motors has departments for engineering, R&D, personnel, manufacturing, quality control, finance, and dozens of other functions. In this section we will analyze the nature of departmental technology and its relationship with departmental structure.

The framework that has had the greatest impact on our understanding of departmental technologies was developed by Charles Perrow.[22] His model has been useful for a broad range of technologies, which made it ideal for research into diverse departmental activities.

Variety

Perrow specified two dimensions of departmental activities that were relevant to organizational structure and process. The first is number of exceptions in the work. This refers to task variety, which is the frequency of unexpected and novel events that occur in the conversion process. When individuals encounter a large number of unexpected situations, with frequent problems, variety is considered high. When there are few problems, and when day-to-day job requirements are repetitious, technology contains little variety. Variety in departments can range from the repetition of a single act, such as on an assembly line, to work that is a series of unrelated problems or projects.

Analyzability

The second dimension of technology concerns the analyzability of work activities. When the conversion process is analyzable, the work can be reduced to mechanical steps, and participants can follow an objective, computational procedure to solve problems. Problem solution may involve the use of standard procedures such as instructions and manuals, or technical knowledge such as in a textbook or handbook. On the other hand, some work is not analyzable. When problems arise, it is difficult to identify the correct solution. There is no store of techniques or procedures to tell a person exactly what to do. Employees rely on accumulated experience, intuition, and judgment. The final solution to a problem is often the result of wisdom and experience, and not the result of standard procedures. Quality-control departments at Blue Bell Creameries and Heineken Brewery have unanalyzable technologies. Inspectors taste each batch of product to identify the mix of ingredients and to see whether it fits within acceptable flavor limits. These quality-control tasks require years of experience and practice. Standard procedures will not tell a person how to do this task.

Framework

The two dimensions of technology and examples of departmental activities on Perrow's framework are shown in Exhibit 4.7. The dimensions of variety and analyzability form the basis for four major categories of technology—routine, craft, engineering, and nonroutine.

Routine   Routine technologies are characterized by little task variety and the use of objective computational procedures. The tasks are formalized and standardized. Examples include an automobile assembly line and bank tellers.

Craft   Craft technologies are characterized by a fairly stable stream of activities, but the conversion process is not analyzable or well understood. Tasks require extensive training and experience because employees respond to intangible factors on the basis of wisdom, intuition, and experience. Glassmakers at Corning's glass plant in upstate New York are an example. It takes twenty years to reach the highest skill level.

Engineering Engineering technologies tend to be complex because there is substantial variety in the tasks performed. But the various activities are usually handled on the basis of established formulas, procedures, and techniques. Employees normally refer to a well-developed body of knowledge to handle problems. Engineering and accounting tasks usually fall in this category.

Nonroutine Nonroutine technologies have high task variety, and the conversion process is not analyzable or well understood. In nonroutine technologies, a great deal of effort is devoted to analyzing problems and activities. Several equally acceptable options typically can be found. Experience and technical knowledge are used to solve problems and perform the work. Basic research, strategic planning, and other work that involves new projects and unexpected problems are nonroutine.

Routine vs. Nonroutine Exhibit 4.7 also illustrates that variety and analyzability can be combined into a single dimension of technology. The dimension is called routine versus nonroutine technology, and is the diagonal line in Exhibit 4.7. The analyzability and variety dimensions are often correlated in departments, meaning that technologies high in variety tend to be low in analyzability, and technologies low in variety tend to be analyzable. Departments can be analyzed along a single dimension of routine versus nonroutine that combines both analyzability and variety, which is a useful shorthand measure for analzying departmental technology.

EXHIBIT 4.7. Framework for Department Technologies.

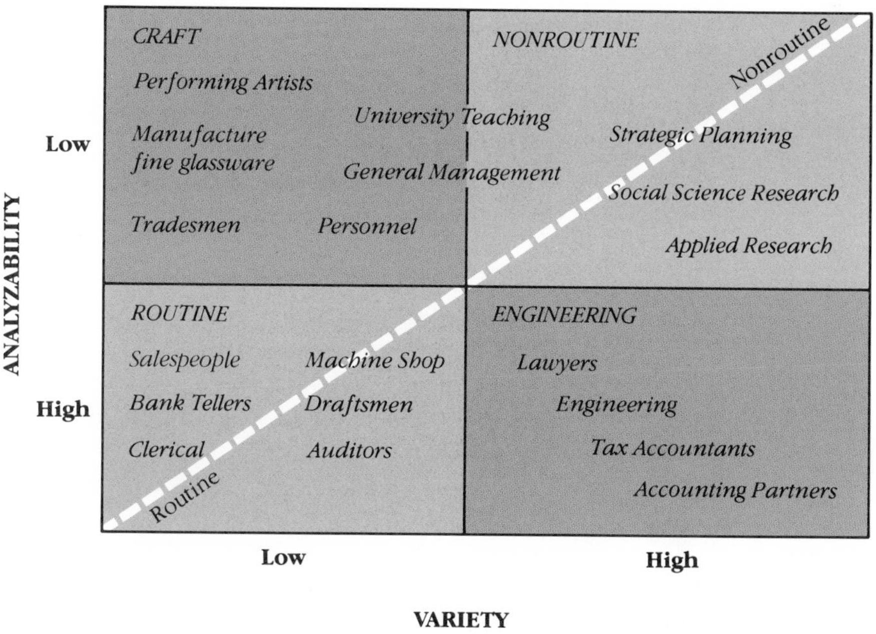

Source: Adapted with permission from Richard Daft and Norman Mcintosh, "A New Approach to Design and Use of Management Information," *California Management Review* 21 (1978): 82–92. Copyright © 1978 by the Regents of the University of California. Reprinted by permission of the Regents.

IN PRACTICE 4.3

Extraction Department

What type of technology does the extraction department described at the beginning of this chapter have, and is it different from the data-processing department to which the tax returns are sent? Organization researchers have tried various techniques for measuring technology, such as having experts assign departments to specific categories and asking employees to describe their activities on questionnaires. Questionnaire scales have been the most successful approach. The two questionnaire scales below have psychometric validity and can be used to measure department technology.[23] Employees normally circle a number from one to seven in response to each question.

Variety

1. How many of these tasks are the same from day-to-day?
2. To what extent would you say your work is routine?
3. People in this unit do about the same job in the same way most of the time.
4. Basically, unit members perform repetitive activities in doing their jobs.
5. How repetitious are your duties?

Analyzability

1. To what extent is there a clearly known way to do the major types of work you normally encounter?
2. To what extent is there a clearly defined body of knowledge or subject matter that can guide you in doing your work?
3. To what extent is there an understandable sequence of steps that can be followed in doing your work?
4. To do your work, to what extent can you actually rely on established procedures and practices?
5. To what extent is there an understandable sequence of steps that can be followed in carrying out your work?

Answers for the extraction department would suggest that the work is of low to moderate variety. The tasks are pretty much the same from day to day although there is modest variety in the types of tax returns received. The work is also analyzable because there is an exact way to handle each type of tax return. An established procedure guides almost every activity. Thus the extraction department would go into the "routine" quadrant in Exhibit 4.7.

The data-processing department would probably have greater variety. The work would be somewhat more complex with less repetition when all duties within the department are considered. Data processing would be analyzable because there would be a body of knowledge and procedures to guide the work. Thus the data-processing department would tend to be located in the "engineering" quadrant of Perrow's framework.

DEPARTMENT DESIGN

Department technology tends to be associated with a cluster of other department characteristics, such as the qualification of employees, formalization, and pattern of communication. Definite patterns do exist in the relationship between work unit technology and other characteristics, just as we saw for manufacturing and service technologies above. Key relationships between technology and other dimensions of departments are described below.

Organic versus Mechanistic   The single most persistent pattern is that routine technologies are characterized by mechanistic structure and processes and nonroutine technologies by organic structure and processes. Traditional rules and tightly centralized management apply to routine units. When work is nonroutine, department administration is characterized as more organic and free flowing. Differences in management systems are very visible and can be observed by simply walking through different departments, such as production versus research and development. Atmosphere, dress, work habits, and autonomy all seem related to technology. In the R&D lab at Datapoint Corporation, employees wear T-shirts and sandals, may wear a beard, and ride to work on motorcycles. In the production department, employees wear more traditional dress, including shoes, shirts, and short haircuts, which reflects the more structured nature of the work.[24]

Professional Qualifications of Staff   Staff in routine technologies typically require little education or experience, which is congruent with repetitious work activities. In work units with greater variety, staff are more qualified, and often have formal training in technical schools or universities. Training for craft activities, which are less analyzable, is more likely to be through job experience. Nonroutine activities require both formal education and job experience.[25]

Formalization   Routine technology is characterized by extensive standardization, division of labor into small tasks, and formalization. Rules and procedures apply to most activities. For tasks that are nonroutine, the structure is less formal and less standardized. When variety is high, for example, fewer activities are covered by formal procedures.[26]

Span of Control   Span of control is the number of employees who report to a single manager or supervisor. Span of control is normally influenced by task complexity and employee professionalism. The more complex and nonroutine the task, the more problems arise in which the supervisor becomes involved. The span of control should be smaller for complex tasks because supervisor and subordinate must interact frequently. Highly professional employees, however, do not require close supervision. They have expert knowledge and internal standards of performance, so the span of control can be larger.

Sometimes nonroutine tasks have highly professional employees. The net effect is that the span of control is usually smaller as the work becomes nonroutine. The frequency of problems is so great that interaction is required even when employees are highly professional. The largest spans of control usually appear in routine departments.[27]

Decentralization   In routine technologies most decision-making is centralized to management.[28] In engineering technologies, employees with technical training tend to acquire moderate decision authority because technical knowledge is important to task accomplishment. Production employees who have long experience obtain decision authority in craft technologies, because they know how to respond to problems. Decentralization to employees is greatest in nonroutine settings, where many decisions are made by employees.

Communication   Communication activity and frequency increases as task variety increases.[29] Frequent problems require more information-sharing to solve problems and ensure proper completion of activities. The direction of communication is typically horizontal in nonroutine work units and vertical in routine work units.[30] The form of communication varies by task analyzability.[31] When tasks are highly analyzable, statistical and written forms of communication (memos, reports, rules, and procedures) are frequent. When tasks are less analyzable, information typically is conveyed face-to-face, over the telephone, or in group meetings.

Coordination and Control   Coordination mechanisms reflect a pattern similar to communication activities. In nonroutine technologies, lower-level employees participate in decisions and activities as a result of group meetings and horizontal processes. In routine departments, vertical processes dominate. Supervisors use their greater influence and rules and procedures to make decisions and control activities.[32]

Goal Emphasis   In routine technologies, activities are standardized and routinized and the emphasis is on efficiency and quantity of output. In other technologies, reliability and quality of output are more important than quantity and efficiency.[33]

Conclusion   The relationship between technology and other department characteristics is summarized in Exhibit 4.8. There are two important points reflected in Exhibit 4.8. First, departments do differ from one another and can be categorized according to workflow technology.[34] Second, structural and management processes differ based on departmental technology. Managers should design their departments so that requirements based on technology can be met. Design problems are most visible when the design is clearly inconsistent with technology. One study, for example, found that when structure and communication characteristics did not reflect technology, departments tended to be less effective.[35] Employees could not communicate with the frequency needed to solve problems. Well-intentioned managers

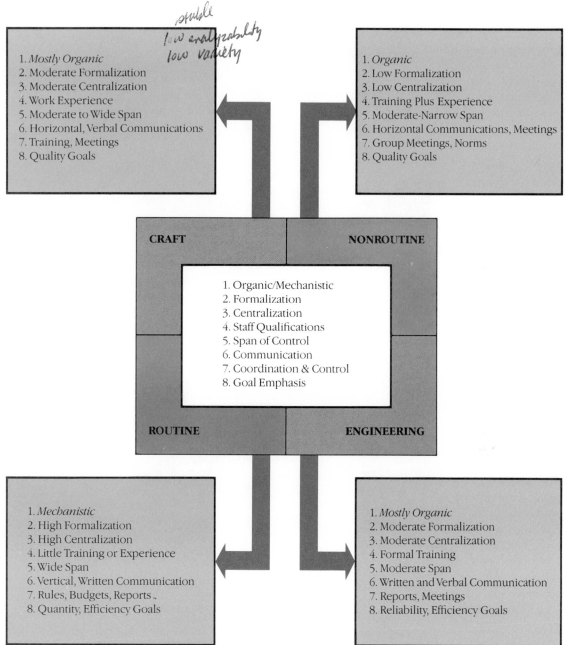

stable
low analyzability
low variety

CRAFT

1. *Mostly Organic*
2. Moderate Formalization
3. Moderate Centralization
4. Work Experience
5. Moderate to Wide Span
6. Horizontal, Verbal Communications
7. Training, Meetings
8. Quality Goals

NONROUTINE

1. *Organic*
2. Low Formalization
3. Low Centralization
4. Training Plus Experience
5. Moderate-Narrow Span
6. Horizontal Communications, Meetings
7. Group Meetings, Norms
8. Quality Goals

1. Organic/Mechanistic
2. Formalization
3. Centralization
4. Staff Qualifications
5. Span of Control
6. Communication
7. Coordination & Control
8. Goal Emphasis

ROUTINE

ENGINEERING

1. *Mechanistic*
2. High Formalization
3. High Centralization
4. Little Training or Experience
5. Wide Span
6. Vertical, Written Communication
7. Rules, Budgets, Reports
8. Quantity, Efficiency Goals

1. *Mostly Organic*
2. Moderate Formalization
3. Moderate Centralization
4. Formal Training
5. Moderate Span
6. Written and Verbal Communication
7. Reports, Meetings
8. Reliability, Efficiency Goals

EXHIBIT 4.8. Relationship of Department Technology to Structural and Management Characteristics.

who impose a tight, mechanistic structure on nonroutine activities are working against the requirements of the technology.

A new, small organization is like a single department. The relationships in Exhibit 4.8 are illustrated in the case of cabinet makers at Maxwell Brothers. Cabinet making is a craft technology.

IN PRACTICE 4.4

Maxwell Bros., Cabinet Makers

Bill Maxwell has been president of Maxwell Brothers, Cabinet Makers, for thirteen years. He was bored with his job as a college teacher and found that making fine, hand-crafted furniture was more exciting. "I enjoyed teaching, but I simply wasn't excited about it," he says. "I would get up at 5:00 each day to make furniture before going to class, and decided I should be doing this full time." He purchased a small building and workshop with his retirement savings, and started producing furniture full time. His brother, Bob, left a career as a high school teacher to join him seven years ago, and is vice-president of the company. Bob handles administration, and Bill's responsibility is furniture production.

The firm now has twenty-one top-flight cabinet makers. One of the biggest problems is getting the right people. Employees need motivation because it takes a long time to become a skilled cabinet maker. They begin with a one-year apprenticeship, during which they master fundamentals such as gluing, sanding, and assembling furniture.

"The first year is tedious, but it takes experience to learn these skills," says Bill. A single step in the construction of a Maxwell Brothers ladderback chair may take days to learn. A beginner will require a full day just to split the wood for two posts and four rungs for a chair's back. A skilled worker can do each post and rung in about three minutes.

Bob Maxwell says one problem is that people wish to become furniture designers after a couple of years. He has to make it crystal clear to new employees that they are hired to execute existing patterns for at least five years. Design requires the ability to put emotion into the work, achieving an intangible "feel" that makes the customer say, "That's exactly what I had in mind." The first challenge is to produce furniture that is technically correct, and perhaps only one in five cabinet makers attains the ability to design furniture with a feel that will satisfy customers.

Employees are evaluated on the ability to turn out high-quality furniture. "We want each piece suitable for a museum," claims Bill. There are certain procedures to follow, but cabinet makers can deviate so long as the final product is good.

The biggest management challenge facing Bob is to get and keep good people so the company can grow. People have to love furniture making, but they also have to be treated right. They won't tolerate supervision that is too close, or systems and procedures that are too constraining. One of the employees was absolutely amazed after beginning his job compared to previous work in a manufacturing plant. In the earlier job he could not go to the bathroom without permission, and there were rules and paperwork for everything. "Here we have some procedures, but things are fairly informal. We can't be too strict," says Bill. As cabinet makers acquire more skill they are given more discretion. "The thing we really pay attention to is whether they turn out high-quality furniture." [36]

TECHNOLOGICAL INTERDEPENDENCE

So far in this chapter we have explored how organization level and department level technologies influence structural design. The final characteristic of technology that influences structure is called interdependence. **Interdependence** means the extent to which employees or departments depend upon each other for resources or materials to accomplish their tasks. Low interdependence means that departments can do their work independently of each other and have little need for interaction, consultation, or exchange of materials. High interdependence means that departments must constantly exchange resources. James Thompson defined three types of interdependence that influence organization structure.[37]

Pooled Interdependence   Pooled is the lowest form of interdependence among departments. Work does not flow between units. Each department is part of the organization and contributes to the common good of the organization, but works independently. McDonald's stores or branch banks are examples of pooled interdependence. An outlet in Chicago does not need to interact with an outlet in Urbana. The connection between branches is that they share financial resources from a common pool, and the success of each branch contributes to the success of the organization.

Thompson proposed that pooled interdependence would exist in firms with what he called a mediating technology. A **mediating technology** provides products or services that mediate or link clients from the external environment, and in doing so each department can work independently. Banks, brokerage firms, and real estate offices all mediate between buyers and sellers, but the offices work independently within the organization.

The management implications associated with pooled interdependence are quite simple. Thompson argued that managers should use rules and procedures to standardize across departments. Each department should use the same procedures and financial statements so their outcomes can be measured and pooled. Very little day-to-day coordination is required among units.

Sequential Interdependence   When interdependence is of serial form, with parts produced in one department becoming inputs to another department, then the interdependence is called sequential. The first department must perform correctly in order for the second department to perform correctly. This is a higher level of interdependence than pooled, because departments exchange resources and depend upon others to perform well. Sequential interdependence occurs in what Thompson called **long-linked technology,** which "refers to the combination in one organization of successive stages of production; each stage of production uses as its inputs the production of the preceding stage and produces inputs for the following stage."[38] Large organizations that use assembly-line production, such as in the automobile industry, use long-linked technologies and are characterized by sequential interdependence.

The management requirements of sequential interdependence are more demanding than for pooled interdependence. Coordination among the linked plants or departments is required. Since the interdependence implies a one-way flow of materials, extensive planning and scheduling are generally needed. Plant B needs to know what to expect from Plant A so both can perform effectively. Some day-to-day communication among plants is also needed to ensure that problems and exceptions to plans are handled satisfactorily.

Reciprocal Interdependence   The highest level of interdependence is reciprocal. This exists when the output of operation A is the input to operation B, and the output of operation B is the input back again to operation A. The output of departments influences one another in reciprocal fashion. Reciprocal interdependence tends to occur in organizations with what Thompson called **intensive technologies,** which provide a variety of products or services in combination to a client. Hospitals are an excellent example because they provide coordinated services to patients. A patient may move back and forth between X-ray, surgery, and physical therapy as needed to be cured. A university is another example—a wide variety of disciplines and support services are provided in a coordinated way to students.

Management requirements are greatest in the case of reciprocal interdependence. The structure must allow for frequent communication and adjustment. Extensive planning is required, but plans will not anticipate or solve all problems. Continuous interaction and mutual adjustment are required. Managers are heavily involved in face-to-face coordination and decision-making. Reciprocal interdependence is the most complex interdependence for organizations to handle.

Structural Priority   Since decision-making, communication, and coordination problems are greatest for reciprocal interdependence, it should receive priority in organization structure. Activities that are reciprocally interdependent should be grouped close together in the organization so they have easy access to one another for mutual adjustment. These units should report to the same person on the organization chart and be physically close so coordination costs can be minimized. Poor coordination will result in poor performance for the organization. If the reciprocally interdependent units cannot be located close together, the organization should design additional mechanisms for coordination, such as daily meetings between departments.

The next priority is given to sequential interdependencies, and finally to pooled interdependencies. If no reciprocal interdependencies exist within the organization, sequential interdependencies take priority and should be located together. This strategy of organizing keeps the communication channels short where coordination is most critical to organizational success. The types of interdependencies and their implications for communication, coordination, and structure are summarized in Exhibit 4.9.

The impact of interdependency on coordination methods was investigated for 197 departments in a large state employment security agency.[39] The investigators found strong support for the relationship between interdependency and coordination. The relationship between workflow interdepend-

Form of Independence	Demands on Communication, Decision-Making	Type of Coordination	Priority in Structural Grouping
Pooled 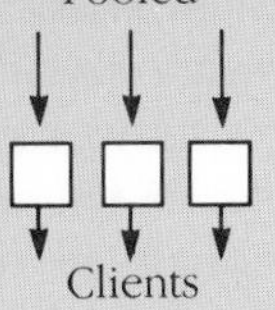 Clients	Low	Standardization, Rules, Procedures	Low
Sequential 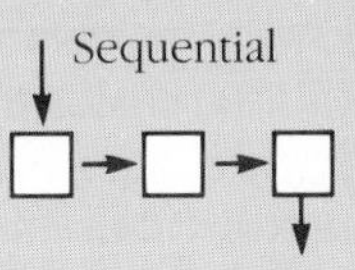 Client	Medium	Plans, Schedules	Medium
Reciprocal 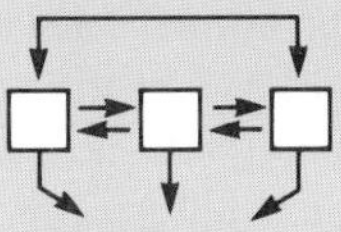 Client	High	Mutual Adjustment, Group Meetings	High

EXHIBIT 4.9. Thompson's Classification of Interdependence and Management Implications.

ence and types of coordination used within the departments in the employment agency is illustrated in Exhibit 4.10. Lesser task interdependence was handled by rules (standardization) and plans, and greater interdependence was handled by face-to-face meetings and other forms of mutual adjustment. As a general rule, low interdependence can be handled through standardization and programmed procedures, while high levels of interdependence require a nonprogrammed response through group meetings and mutual adjustment.[40]

When organization structure does not facilitate coordination of technological interdependencies, performance problems often appear. NCR solved its problems by reorganizing the structure to give priority to reciprocal interdependencies.

IN PRACTICE 4.5

NCR

NCR (Formerly National Cash Register Co.) is an electronics and computer manufacturing company. Revenues in 1983 were about $3.7 billion. In 1979 NCR perceived itself in trouble because it was not able to innovate. Electronics and computers are fast moving industries, and competitors were first into the marketplace. NCR people had good ideas, but ideas were not translated into products. One executive vice-president lamented, "The product-development group was not yielding products that hit the market as squarely as desired or as timely as the market required."

With the use of consultants, NCR studied the problem. The path of a new idea was analyzed from its initial idea to its implementation. Following this path, the consultants discovered major impediments. The development, production, and marketing of products took place in three separate divisions. Development thus might be a false start because the product could not be manufactured or did not fit the market. A new product requires simultaneous coordination among all relevant departments, so the structure was inhibiting the free flow of information.

To solve the problem NCR broke up its traditional organization structure. The new structure created a series of stand-alone units. A unit may have from 500 to 1,000 people, its own general manager, finance department, personnel department, research and development group, and manufacturing. The divisions are fully operational and can act on their own. All people and skills needed to develop a new product are located within the division.

The new structure created initial problems for managers. Suddenly managers in the units were expected to run things themselves. The expectation that innovation decisions be made within the units and that managers coordinate their own problems took some getting used to. Before long the reorganization took hold, and the results have been impressive. One new product is the self-service terminal for gas stations that uses a charge-card slot so customers can charge purchases easily. Another division designed and installed a self-service ski-lift terminal. The structure gave NCR just what it

EXHIBIT 4.10. Primary Means to Achieve Coordination for Different Levels of Task Interdependence.

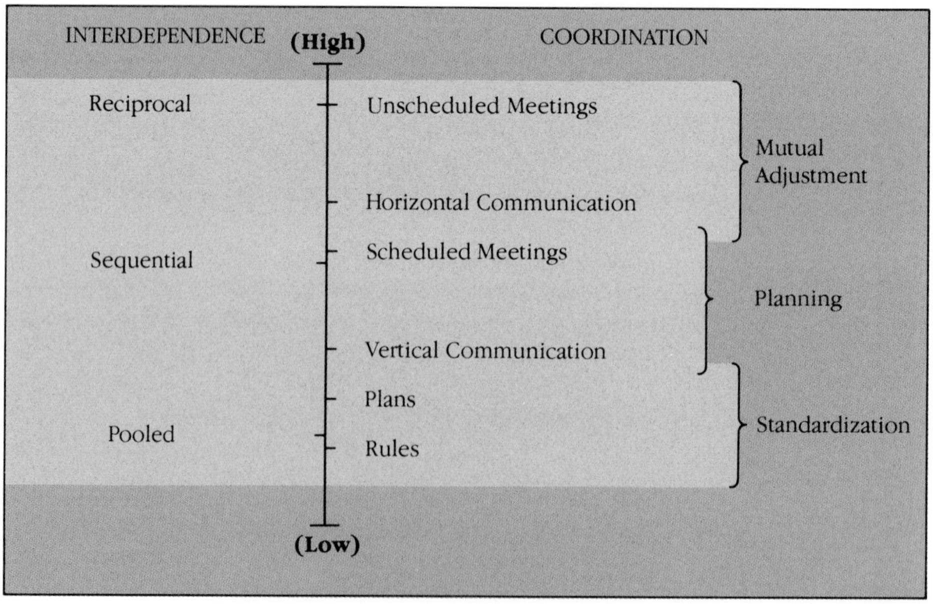

Source: Adapted from Andrew H. Van de Ven, Andre Delbecq, and Richard Koenig, "Determinants of Communication Modes Within Organizations," *American Sociological Review* 41 (1976):330.

wanted because 50% of this division's revenues came from products it did not sell the year before.[41]

HOW IMPORTANT IS TECHNOLOGY?

The discovery of technology as a relevant variable in the design of organization structure began with Woodward's findings from manufacturing firms. The notion that technology had a compelling influence on structure quickly took hold, and became known as the "technological imperative." The Aston studies did not support the notion of technology as an "imperative" because other variables, such as size or the environment, also influenced structure. Technology appeared to have greatest influence in small organizations or in specific departments of large organizations.

A substantial amount of additional research was undertaken over the next several years to sort out the relationship of technology to structure in a variety of organizational settings.[42] John Child gathered data on eighty-two British business organizations using the same variable and procedures as the Aston group.[43] Other studies followed. Pradip Khandwalla mailed questionnaires to presidents of seventy-nine American manufacturing firms.[44] Peter Blau and others compared technology and size to several structural dimensions in 110 manufacturing organizations in New Jersey.[45]

Most of this research revealed a similar pattern. In large organizations, technology has a selective relationship with structure.[46] Organization-level technologies tend to be related to organizational-level structural variables, and departmental technologies tend to be related to departmental structures.[47]

It is appropriate to conclude that technology should be considered in the design of structure at both organization and department levels. However organization structure in giant corporations is the result of many influences. The exact structure and design will reflect the influence of technology, size, environment, and goals. The effect of technology is greater when a firm is small and for structural characteristics (e.g., supervisor span of control) that are close to the workflow. The effect of technology is also greater at the department level.

Is Technology Fixed?

Another aspect of the technological imperative is whether technology is fixed and hence the structure has to be designed to fit it, or whether technology can be altered by managers so that other structures are appropriate. Several theorists have argued that technology is not fixed, but is the result of the interpretation and choice of managers.[48] In other words, managers define the technology, and managers can make mistakes. Consider the following case.

IN PRACTICE 4.6

Reform School

Street, Vinter, and Perrow described two very different structures for what appeared to be the same technology—changing delinquent boys into nondelinquent boys.[49] In Institution A, delinquent boys were handled with rigid regulation and discipline. They were constantly watched, marched about, and taught to say "Yes sir" and "No sir," and they were frequently counted and inspected. The boys had to ask permission for small requests, such as going to the bathroom. There were strict rules for all behavior. They were not allowed to talk during meals. Punishment for rule infractions was frequently physical, such as paddling in front of other boys. Runaways had their heads shaved, and they were sentenced to a diet of bread and water and put in isolation. This style for working with delinquent boys was compatible with the managers' beliefs about the transformation process. They believed that boys were delinquent because they lacked respect and obedience, and that respect and obedience could be taught through rigid regulation and discipline. Delinquent boys were all the same and the task was highly analyzable. Organization members perceived they knew exactly how to straighten the boys out. The structure and management style could be characterized as centralized and mechanistic, and were perfectly suited to a routine technology.

Institution B approached the task quite differently. Delinquents were free to talk at mealtime, and they frequently griped about the food. The boys were permitted to horse around at bedtime, and they were allowed to resolve many of their own problems with the other boys, so that quarrels would occasionally erupt. Rules and regulations were minimized. Supervision was also minimal. There were few sanctions for misbehavior. Treats might be withdrawn, but some infractions were not punished at all. Once again, this style of handling delinquent boys was compatible with the perception of the task. Members believed that the delinquents' problems were psychological. Staff members saw each delinquent as unique. They had to learn about each boy in detail, and necessary changes could be brought about only through understanding, empathy, and a permissive environment. Each boy was considered different and the task of rehabilitation was not analyzable. Thus a highly organic management approach was developed to fit this nonroutine technology.

In each of the institutions, the management structure fit the technology as perceived by organization managers. The issue is whether the technology was indeed routine or nonroutine. Most people would agree that the technology for rehabilitating delinquent boys should be considered nonroutine. One reason for different interpretations is that treating delinquent boys is a service technology. The service is intangible so managers have leeway in designing a structure. In manufacturing organizations, technologies consist of machines and a fixed production process so there is less leeway for differences in interpretation.

SUMMARY AND INTERPRETATION

This chapter has reviewed several frameworks and key research findings on the topic of organizational technology. The potential importance of technology as a factor in organizational structure was discovered during the 1960s. During the 1970s, a flurry of research activity was undertaken to understand more precisely the relationship of various technology dimensions to other characteristics of organization. In the 1980s, the number of technology studies is declining somewhat. Technology is understood quite well, and no new technology frameworks have been developed, although service technologies are receiving more attention.

There are four ideas in the technology literature that stand out as especially important. The first is Woodward's research into manufacturing technology. Her work is a model for organizational research. Woodward explored the validity of established principles, and was willing to modify her thinking based upon what she learned from her data. She went into organizations and collected large amounts of practical data, including administrative ratio, hierarchical levels, span of control, direct/indirect labor ratio, formalization, centralization, and the use of verbal and written communication. Her findings are so clear and informative that managers without training in organization theory can use them. Managers can analyze how their own organizations compare on the same dimensions of management structure.

The second important idea is that service technologies differ in a systematic way from manufacturing technologies. Service technologies are characterized by intangible outcomes and clients are involved directly in the production process. Service firms do not have the fixed, machine-based technologies that appear in manufacturing organizations. Service technologies are becoming an increasingly large percentage of organizations in Canada and the United States, so understanding how to design and manage these technologies is important.

The third significant idea is Perrow's framework applied to department technologies. Understanding the variety and analyzability of a technology tells us about the management style, structure, and process that should characterize that department. For people who do not wish to use these two dimensions separately, the notion of routine versus nonroutine work can be very informative. Department technology is an important idea because applying the wrong management system to a department will result in dissatisfaction and reduced efficiency.

The fourth important idea is interdependence. The extent to which departments depend on each other for materials, information, or other resources determines the amount of coordination required between them. As interdependence increases, demands on the organization for coordination increase. Interdependence is thus an important basis for determining organizational design. The concept of interdependence will appear again in later chapters to explain organization structure and manager behavior.

The general pattern in the technology research is that when technologies are routine, analyzable, independent, and well-defined then tighter management control is used. This control is reflected in the use of mechanistic structures, written communication, centralized decision-making, and formalized procedures. When the underlying workflow is characterized as high variety, nonroutine, interdependent, and complex, then the appropriate management structure emphasizes less control. The structure would be more organic, with face-to-face communication and coordination, decentralized decision-making, and fewer procedures.

KEY CONCEPTS

analyzability

automation of equipment

continuous process

craft technology

engineering technology

intensive technology

interdependence

large-batch technology

long-linked technology

mediating technology

nonroutine technology

pooled interdependence

reciprocal interdependence

routine technology

sequential interdependence

service technology

small batch

specificity of evaluation

task

technical complexity

technological imperative

technology

variety

workflow integration

workflow rigidity

DISCUSSION QUESTIONS

1. Where would your university department be located on Perrow's technology framework? Try to look for the underlying variety and analyzability characteristics when making your assessment. Would a department devoted exclusively to teaching be put in a different quadrant from a department devoted exclusively to research?

2. Explain Thompson's levels of interdependence. Identify an example of each level of interdependence in the university setting. What kinds of co-ordination mechanisms should management develop to handle each level of interdependence?

3. Describe Woodward's classification of organizational technologies. Explain why each of the three technology groups is related to organization structure and management processes.

4. What does it mean to say that technology has influence on structure that is centered on the workflow?

5. What was the relationship Woodward discovered between supervisor span of control and technological complexity? Would this be called a linear or curvilinear relationship? Are there factors other than technology (e.g., educational level of employees) that might account for this relationship?

6. Manufacturing versus service firms tend to be located on opposite ends of the Aston group's technology continuum (Exhibit 4.4). What does this mean with respect to workflow integration? Can you explain this difference using the definition of service technology?

7. Edna Peterson retired from the Air Force as a colonel in charge of the finance section of an air base in New Mexico. Financial work in the military involves large amounts of routine matters and paperwork, and Edna gradually developed a philosophy of management that was fairly mechanistic. She believed that all important decisions should be made by administrators, that elaborate rules and procedures should be developed and followed, and that subordinates should have little discretion and be tightly controlled. After retiring, Edna obtained a job as administrator of a small hospital in Texas.

In this administrative capacity she had to deal extensively with physicians and other professional groups (nurses, technicians) within the hospital. This hospital also had the only twenty-four-hour emergency room in the area. What do you think will happen when Edna applies her management philosophy to the hospital setting? Will she be successful? Should her management style be contingent upon the type of work the organization performs?

8. A top executive claimed that top-level management is a "craft" technology because the work contains intangibles such as handling personnel, interpreting the environment, and coping with unusual situations that have to be learned through experience. If this is true, is it appropriate to teach management in a business school? Does teaching management from a textbook assume that the manager's job is analyzable, and hence that formal training rather than experience is more important?

9. In which quadrant of Perrow's framework would a mass-production technology be placed? Where would small-batch and continuous-process technologies be placed? Why? Would Perrow's framework lead to the same recommendation about organic versus mechanistic structures that Woodward made?

10. Compare and contrast Perrow's technology framework with the concept of service technology. Where would service technologies tend to appear in the Perrow framework?

GUIDES TO ACTION

As an organization manager:

1. Relate organization structure to technology. Technology has its greatest impact in small organizations and individual departments. Use the two dimensions of variety and analyzability to discover whether the work in a department is routine or nonroutine. If the work in a department is routine, use a mechanistic structure and process. If the work in a department is nonroutine, use an organic management process. Exhibit 4.8 illustrates this relationship between department technology and organization structure.

2. Use the categories developed by Woodward to diagnose whether the primary production activities in a major manufacturing unit are small batch, mass production, or continuous process. Use an organic structure with small-batch or continuous-process technologies. Use a mechanistic structure with mass-production technologies.

3. Use the concept of service technology to evaluate the production process in nonmanufacturing firms. Service technologies are intangible and must be located close to the customer. Hence service organizations may have an organization structure with fewer boundary roles, greater geographical dispersion, decentralization, professional employees in the technical core, and generally less control than in manufacturing organizations.

4. Evaluate the interdependencies between organizational departments. Use the general rule that as interdependencies increase, mechanisms for coordination must also increase.

5. Analyze actual conditions or circumstances throughout an organization

using technology. As an example let us analyze a greeting card company (Exhibit 4.11) that produces about ten million cards a year with five hundred designs. Department technologies as well as interdependencies between departments should be considered in the design of an appropriate organization structure. Thus in the marketing department illustrated in Exhibit 4.11 forecasting is nonroutine, and should have an organic structure. Interdependence with other units is sequential, so they would send written reports to other departments as a result of their studies into future trends. The sales and advertising departments have craft characteristics, and they are highly interdependent with one another. Amount of sales influences advertising strategy and vice versa. Mechanisms are needed for continuous mutual adjustment, so frequent meetings would be required.

The shop activity in manufacturing is small batch, and should have the management system described by Woodward (organic, small number of levels, medium span of control, little indirect labor, small administrative ratio). Shipping is very routine, and should have a mechanistic structure. The interdependence between manufacturing and shipping is sequential because

EXHIBIT 4.11. Examples of Departments and Interdependencies in a Greeting Card Company.

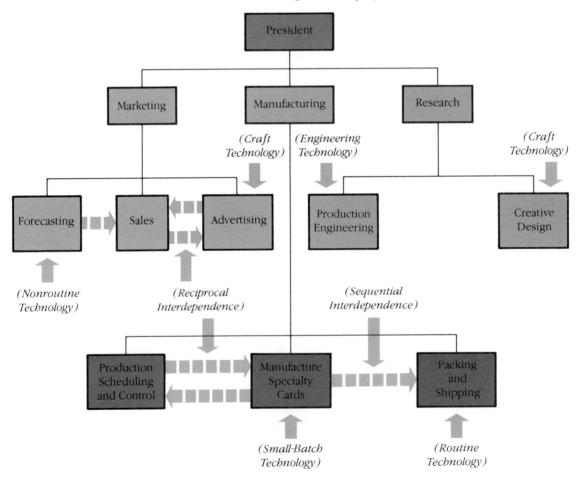

materials move in one direction to shipping. Planning would be a satisfactory way to coordinate these two units.

Production scheduling is reciprocally interdependent with manufacturing. Scheduling decides the flow of work through the manufacturing process. Any completed job or delay is an input back to scheduling, which may change the scheduling of other orders. Mutual adjustment is required between the scheduling and manufacturing departments. Production schedulers will go out on the shop floor and talk directly to supervisors.

Production research is an engineering technology, and creative design is a craft technology. Engineering personnel would have more formal education, while creative personnel would rely on experience and intuition for their work. The interdependence between the two departments is low, so employees would not need regular meetings. An occasional exchange of technical information would be all that is required. Each of these departments provides services to other parts of the organization, however, so for specific projects they would need regular meetings and horizontal communication to coordinate with users.

Consider these Guides when analyzing the following case.

CASE FOR ANALYSIS

OLSON'S LOCKER PLANT*

Olson's Locker plant is located in Grand Island, Nebraska, a city of about 50,000 people. The locker plant was started in 1952 by Herb Olson when he came out of early retirement. He had been co-owner and manager with his wife of a successful downtown hotel and restaurant until she died. He sold the business in 1950 at the age of forty. Two years later he decided to buy a small locker plant as a way to keep busy and increase his knowledge of the meat business.

For the first two years, all work was completed by Mr. Olson and an assistant who helped with the butchering. His clients were people who wished to have a hog or steer butchered, cut, and wrapped to order. The plant also had a small counter and meatcase in the front from which Mr. Olson sold meat to walk-in customers.

Olson's reputation for selling good meat at a fair price quickly spread. The business grew steadily. After ten years he had twenty-two employees, and after twenty-five years he employs seventy people. The locker plant still does custom orders, but 70% of its business in 1978 is supplying meat to independent grocery stores, restaurants, and small markets in central Nebraska. Beef products account for 60% of the volume, pork the other 40%. The locker plant now handles about 35,000 lbs. of meat a day.

* This case is based on materials from Horace Thornton and J. F. Gracey, *Textbook of Meat Hygiene,* 6th ed. (London: Bailliere Tindall, 1974), pp. 517–522; John R. Romans and P. Thomas Ziegler, *The Meat We Eat* (Danville, IL: The Interstate Printers and Publishers, 1977), pp. 94–102; "Pioneer Company (A) and (B)," in Gene W. Dalton, Paul R. Lawrence, and Jay W. Lorsch, eds. *Organization Structure and Design* (Homewood, IL: Irwin and Dorsey, 1970), pp. 165–199; "Automated Beef Boning: First Step Toward a Totally Robotic System?" *Chilton's Food Engineering* 56 (February 1984):170.

PLANT AND EQUIPMENT

As the volume of business increased, the locker plant became more mechanized. The plant is located in a single-story building with 7,000 square feet of work space. The building is divided into two parts. One side is used to kill and dress animals. The other side is used to cut and prepare finished meats for delivery to customers.

Mechanization has developed to the point where carcasses are now transported through the plant entirely by hooks and overhead rails. Workers use mechanical tools for several operations, such as power saws for splitting carcasses and a hydraulic winch to pull the skin from the carcass.

Employees range in age from eighteen to sixty-two. Workers on the shop floor are considered semiskilled and paid an hourly wage. The company is not unionized. Turnover is low. Many employees have been with the company several years. Most do not have formal education beyond high school.

ORGANIZATION

The approximate organization structure for Olson's Locker Plant is shown in Exhibit 4.12. Herb Olson is owner and president. The management team includes a treasurer, sales manager, industrial engineer, plant superintendent and his assistant, and a personnel director. The treasurer keeps the financial records and also helps with the purchase of pigs and cattle. The sales manager has two salespeople reporting to him. The sales manager and one sales representative handle outside sales. The other salesperson handles sales over the counter. The industrial engineer just hired a new assistant to help with job measurement activities. All workers involved in the conversion of live

EXHIBIT 4.12. Organization Chart for Olson's Locker Plant.

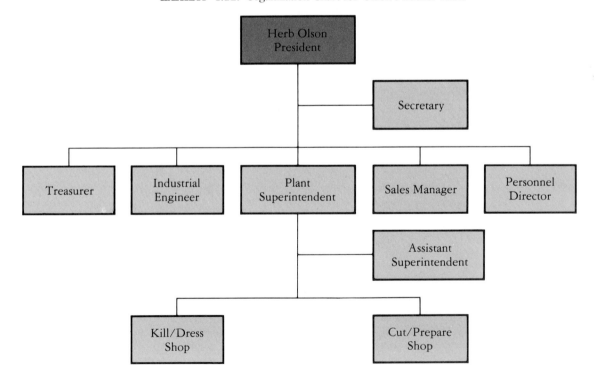

animals to packaged meat report to the plant superintendent. The assistant superintendent assists with management of the plant and is in charge when the superintendent is absent.

The managers meet every Thursday evening to review their respective activities and to share information. This meeting is used to coordinate activities and to discuss solutions to unexpected problems. The management team is beginning to think that the organization needs to tighten up. A loosely run organization has been successful, but they are feeling the need to adopt more systematic procedures. The personnel director has been asked to establish written policies on matters such as hiring, firing, benefits, absences, and promotions. The personnel director has also requested permission to hire an additional person. The industrial engineer is also helping to systematize jobs and the workflow. The management team is quite satisfied with organization structure, but they sometimes wonder if they could be organized differently to improve efficiency.

THE PORK CONVERSION PROCESS

The process for converting live pigs into bacon and ham normally requires fourteen operations. The dressing sequence begins by stunning the pig electrically. A rear limb is shackled, and the pig is elevated to an overhead rail where it is stuck and bled. The carcass is then dipped mechanically into a scalding tank for up to five minutes, where the hair is loosened. After scalding, pigs are moved mechanically to the dehairing area where the carcasses are scraped clean. The scraping process is partly accomplished by hand. After dehairing, the carcass is transferred to the singeing area. Singeing darkens the meat's outer edge and produces skin that has good leather quality. The carcass is then eviscerated. Next the carcass is skinned and the head is removed. Finally, the carcass is split in half with a handheld electric saw. At this point the carcass is inspected for disease and sent to the chilling room.

Pig halves are taken from the chilling room as needed by the meat-cutting operation. In this area, meat is thawed, cut into hams, bellies, and shoulders, injected with brine, boned, smoked, packed for sale or shipment, and rechilled.

A more detailed description of selected steps in the pork conversion process follows.

Skinning

Skinning is next to the last operation in the butchering and dressing process. The pig carcass hangs from the overhead rail, and the lower end is anchored by a hook in the jaw cavity to secure the carcass. The skin is cut open down the back of the front legs, down the back of the back legs, and down the middle of the belly. The legs are skinned out by hand with a sharp knife. An employee also loosens a fold of skin about three inches wide along each side of the belly cut. The knife should be used carefully and kept tight against the skin at all times. The fat is soft and easily cut. Gashes made by uncontrolled strokes of the knife do considerable damage to hams and bacons that are to be cured. A mechanical winch is then hooked to a fold of skin behind the neck, and it pulls the skin upward in a rapid motion, peeling it from the carcass. The carcass is then washed and moved to the next work station for splitting.

Brine Injection

Brine injection is the third procedure in the meat-cutting operation. After warming the carcass and cutting it into hams and shoulders, brine is injected into the meat. The purpose of the brine injection is to introduce a solution of salt, sugar, and nitrates into the meat. The salt acts as a preservative while the nitrates are used to retain the reddish color of the meat. The brine is injected by hand using a series of injection needles that are connected to a pumping machine. The brine ensures a more uniform cure and reduces the curing time to two or three days. Bellies are injected twice, once in the morning and again in the evening.

The injection requires modest skill. Operators are responsible to see that the quantity of solution does not exceed the limit set by federal law. They must also see that the brine is injected uniformly throughout the meat, and see that the needles are inserted into the arteries. The rate and pressure of the brine injection is controlled by the pumping machine.

Smoking

All pork products at Olson's Locker Plant are smoked during the conversion process. The purpose of smoking is to cook the raw meat and thus convert it to an edible product. The combination of heat and smoke causes a significant reduction in surface bacteria, so it is an important health item. Smoking also imparts a smoky flavor to the meat, which makes it more appealing to the customer. Smoking in the locker plant takes place in a separate smokehouse, which is actually an insulated room in which steam and smoke are introduced through a system of pipes. The smoke flavor is caused by the insertion of hickory, maple, and mahogany shavings in the fire that produces smoke. The minimum temperature for smoking a product can vary widely, depending upon the time available. Smoking at Olson's Locker Plant usually takes place at about 130° F. and lasts two days.

Smokehouse operators are responsible for deciding when a product is properly cooked. The final decision rests on the operator's judgment and is based on touch and appearance. Temperature, humidity, and other weather factors influence the required smoking time. There are many devices for measuring smokehouse conditions, but the final decision is based on personal experience and judgment.

Boning

The boning operation consists of trimming excess fat and cutting out the bones from hams and shoulders. Five employees are assigned to this task. They work around a large rectangular table. Boning the meat typically takes three times as long as trimming the fat and is the most difficult task. The workers along the boning platform are considered to be among the most skilled in the plant. Great dexterity is required to trim the fat and remove the bone with a minimum of waste. It takes a new person at least six months to gain proficiency in this task. Eight different methods of trimming and boning have to be learned to handle the various cuts of meat. Each ham within any category can present specific problems, depending upon size and the amount of fat and skin remnants. An experienced operator can tell immediately whether a ham will be difficult to work with. The criteria for assigning people to the boning operation are two years of experience working with meat and excellent manual dexterity.

OTHER TASKS

Industrial Engineering

In 1976, Mr. Olson hired an industrial engineer to improve internal efficiency. The industrial engineer works to establish production standards to control costs. He is also involved with production planning. The work includes studying the production operation throughout the plant, time and motion studies of each task, and suggesting new work procedures. The industrial engineer is also responsible for evaluating new equipment with respect to cost and labor savings. A monthly labor analysis report is also prepared for Olson and the plant superintendent.

The industrial engineering function encompasses several activities that require an engineering background. The industrial engineer's most important task is to develop production standards that measure productivity. Accurate production standards also help management schedule the flow of meat through the plant.

Purchasing and Selling

Herb Olson spends most of his time purchasing live animals and making sales to area stores. The company has two people making outside sales, but many buyers want to deal directly with Mr. Olson.

Livestock purchasing is tricky because there is no organized commodity market for meat in the area. Meat prices in the major centers (Omaha) fluctuate daily. Seventy percent of the cost of the finished product is the value of the livestock, so purchase price directly influences profit margins. Mr. Olson usually talks daily with meat brokers, local farmers, sale barns, and other sources of price information. He also negotiates directly with area farmers to buy livestock at a fixed price to reduce the risk for both sides. These purchases require Mr. Olson to visit farms and inspect the pigs.

Purchasing decisions are made quickly and informally. Formal confirmation is usually by letter, but the meat is often already shipped. Buyer and seller have to trust each other. Extensive experience is required to handle the purchase of livestock. Carcasses are also purchased from area slaughtering plants to handle unusual fluctuations in the demand for cut meat.

Mr. Olson stays in telephone contact with many buyers of his company's meat products. He visits stores on the way to visiting farms for the purchase of pigs and cattle. His salespeople also spend time telephoning and calling on local store buyers. An inside salesperson handles the sales paper work, and sells meat to customers over the counter. Mr. Olson stresses to the salesforce that they are to provide service to the customer no matter what the cost. He believes that as long as the company strives for perfection and customer satisfaction, the company will continue to grow and prosper.

Mr. Olson told an interviewer, "The most difficult part of my job is forecasting meat prices in the future. About 70% of the time I can predict whether prices will increase or decrease and make purchase contracts accordingly."

Order Assembly

The last step in the production sequence is the assembly of customer orders. Three people perform this operation. They assemble items from finished stock, move them to the packing area, check the assembled order against the customer's order, and arrange for shipment.

THE FUTURE

Mr. Olson is concerned about the future of his meat packing business. Farmers have cut back the number of cattle and hogs raised. Many farmers went bankrupt during 1984 and 1985 because of deflated land values and declining international demand for grain. Mr. Olson is afraid that if his plant does not become more efficient, it may decline and go out of business. He spends most of his time buying, rather than planning or learning about new technology. He asked the industrial engineer to inquire about automated equipment that could replace the unskilled human resources currently used. One such system is the "Beef-A-Matic," which was demonstrated at a meat packers convention in Chicago. With it, two people can produce forty forequarters and fifty hindquarters per hour. Increased mechanization seems attractive and may help reduce costs. But Mr. Olson wonders whether it would have any impact on the way the organization is currently designed and his management style.

Questions

1. How would you classify Olson's Locker Plant in the Woodward, Thompson, and Aston group frameworks? Explain.
2. Do the different tasks in the organization reflect different types of department technologies as described by Perrow? How would you classify them?
3. What structure and management characteristics would you recommend for Olson's Locker Plant? What impact will mechanization have? Discuss.

NOTES

1. Martha Ebersole, "I Opened Tax Returns for the IRS," *Texas Monthly,* April 1984, pp. 158–160, 209–214. Used with permission.

2. Charles Perrow, "A Framework for the Comparative Analysis of Organizations," *American Sociological Review* 32 (1967):194–208; Denise M. Rosseau, "Assessment of Technology in Organizations: Closed versus Open Systems Approaches," *Academy of Management Review* 4 (1979):531–542.

3. Linda Argote, "Input Uncertainty and Organizational Coordination in Hospital Emergency Units," *Administrative Science Quarterly,* 27 (1982):420–434; Charles Perrow, *Organizational Analysis: A Sociological Approach* (Belmont, CA: Wadsworth, 1970); William Rushing, "Hardness of Material As Related to the Division of Labor in Manufacturing Industries," *Administrative Science Quarterly* 13 (1968):229–245.

4. Lawrence B. Mohr, "Organizational Technology and Organization Structure," *Administrative Science Quarterly* 16 (1971):444–459; David Hickson, Derek Pugh, and Diana Pheysey, "Operations Technology and Organization Structure: An Empirical Reappraisal," *Administrative Science Quarterly* 14 (1969):378–397.

5. Joan Woodward, *Industrial Organization: Theory and Practice* (London: Oxford University Press, 1965); and *Management and Technology* (London: Her Majesty's Stationary Office, 1958).

6. Pradip Khandwalla, "Mass Output Orientation of Operations Technology and Organization Structure," *Administrative Science Quarterly* 19 (1974):74–97.

7. Hickson, Pugh, and Pheysey, "Operations Technology and Organization Structure"; James D. Thompson, *Organizations in Action* (New York: McGraw-Hill, 1967).

8. Edward Harvey, "Technology and the Structure of Organizations," *American Sociological Review* 33 (1968):241–259.

9. This discussion is based on Woodward, *Industrial Organizations* and *Management and Technology.*

10. Woodward, *Industrial Organizations,* p. vi.

11. William L. Zwerman, *New Perspectives on Organizational Theory* (Westport, CN: Greenwood Publishing Co., 1970).

12. Harvey, "Technology and the Structure of Organizations," pp. 241–259.

13. Adapted from Arlen J. Large, "Federal Agency Prods Nuclear-Plant Officials to Raise Performance," *The Wall Street Journal,* May 10, 1984, pp. 1, 22.

14. Hickson, Pugh, and Pheysey, "Operations Technology and Organization Structure,"; Derek Pugh, David Hickson, and C. Turner, "The Context of Organization Structure," *Administrative Science Quarterly* 14 (1969):91–114.

15. Derek Pugh, David Hickson, and C. Turner, "Dimensions of Organization Structure," *Administrative Science Quarterly* 8 (1968):289–315.

16. Hickson, Pugh, and Pheysey, "Operations Technology and Organization Structure."

17. Peter K. Mills and Newton Margulies, "Toward a Core Typology of Service Organizations," *Academy of Management Review* 5 (1980):255–265; Peter K. Mills and Dennis J. Moberg, "Perspectives on the Technology of Service Operations," *Academy of Management Review* 7 (1982):467–478; G. Lynn Shostack, "Breaking Free from Product Marketing," *Journal of Marketing* (April 1977):73–80.

18. Richard B. Chase and David A. Tansik, "The Customer Contact Model for Organization Design," *Management Science* 29 (1983):1037–1050.

19. Ibid.

20. Gregory B. Northcraft and Richard B. Chase, "Managing Service Demand at the Point of Delivery," *Academy of Management Review* 10 (1985):66–75.

21. "Merrill Lynch's Big Dilemma," *Business Week,* January 16, 1984, pp. 60–67; "Merrill Lynch's Market Research Campaign to Determine Customer Composition and Needs," *The New York Times,* June 12, 1984, pp. F31.

22. Perrow, "Framework for Comparative Analysis," pp. 194–208, and *Organizational Analysis.*

23. Michael Withey, Richard L. Daft, and William C. Cooper, "Measures of Perrow's Work Unit Technology: An Empirical Assessment and a New Scale," *Academy of Management Journal* 25 (1983):45–63.

24. Richard Cone, Bruce Snow, and Ricky Waclawcayk, "Datapoint Corporation," Texas A&M University, unpublished manuscript, 1981.

25. Patrick E. Connor, *Organizations: Theory and Design* (Chicago: Science Research Associates, 1980); Richard L. Daft and Norman B. Macintosh, "A Tentative Exploration into Amount and Equivocality of Information Processing in Organizational Work Units," *Administrative Science Quarterly* 26 (1981):207–224.

26. Charles A. Glisson, "Dependence of Technological Routinization on Structural Variables in Human Service Organizations," *Administrative Science Quarterly* 23 (1978):383–395; Jerald Hage and Michael Aiken, "Routine Technology, Social Structure and Organizational Goals," *Administrative Science Quarterly* 14 (1969):368–379.

27. Gerald D. Bell, "The Influence of Technological Components of Work upon Management Control," *Academy of Management Journal* 8 (1965):127–132; Peter M. Blau and Richard A. Schoenherr, *The Structure of Organizations* (New York: Basic Books, 1971).

28. A. J. Grimes and S. M. Kline, "The Technological Imperative: The Relative Impact of Task Unit, Modal Technology, and Hierarchy on Structure," *Academy of Management Journal* 16 (1973):583–597; Lawrence G. Hrebiniak, "Job Technologies, Supervision and Work Group Structure," *Administrative Science Quarterly* 19 (1974):395–410; Jeffrey Pfeffer, *Organizational Design* (Arlington Heights, IL: AHM, 1978), ch. 1.

29. W. Alan Randolph, "Matching Technology and the Design of Organization Units," *California Management Review,* 22–23, No. 4 (1980–81):39–48; Daft and Macintosh, "Tentative Exploration into Amount and Equivocality of Information Processing"; Michael L. Tushman, "Work Characteristics and Subunit Communication Structure: A Contingency Analysis," *Administrative Science Quarterly* 24 (1979):82–98.

30. Andrew H. Van de Ven and Diane L. Ferry, *Measuring and Assessing Organizations* (New York: Wiley, 1980); Randolph, "Matching Technology and the Design of Organization Units."

31. Richard L. Daft and Robert H. Lengel, "Information Richness: A New Approach to Managerial Behavior and Organization Design," in Barry Staw and Larry L. Cummings, eds., *Research in Organizational Behavior,* vol. 6 (Greenwich, CT: JAI Press, 1984), pp 191–233; Richard L. Daft and Norman B. Macintosh, "A New Approach to Design and Use of Management Information," *California Management Review* 21 (1978):82–92; Daft and Macintosh, "Tentative Exploration in Amount and Equivocality of Information Processing"; W. Alan Randolph, "Organizational Technology and the Media and Purpose Dimensions of Organizational Communication," *Journal of Business Research* 6 (1978):237–259.

32. Linda Argote, "Input Uncertainty and Organizational Coordination in Hospital Emergency Units," *Administrative Science Quarterly,* 27 (1982):420–434; Andrew H. Van de Ven and Andre Delbecq, "A Task Contingent Model of Work Unit Structure," *Administrative Science Quarterly* 19 (1974):183–197.

33. Perrow, *Organizational Analysis,* p. 81.

34. Peggy Leatt and Rodney Schneck, "Criteria for Grouping Nursing Subunits in Hospitals," *Academy of Management Journal* 27 (1984):150–165.

35. Michael L. Tushman, "Technological Communication in R&D Laboratories: The Impact of Project Work Characteristics," *Academy of Management Journal* 21 (1978):624–645.

36. Sheila M. Ebby, "When Ambition Comes Out of the Woodwork," *Inc.,* September 1982, pp. 41–44; Rick Mastelli, "Green Woodworking," *Fine Woodworking* 33 (March/April, 1982):50–56; Charles Perish, "Getting the Right Feel," *Fine Woodworking* 35 (July/August, 1982):78.

37. James Thompson, *Organizations in Action* (New York: McGraw-Hill, 1967).

38. Thompson, *Organizations in Action,* p. 40.

39. Andrew H. Van de Ven, Andre Delbecq, and Richard Koenig, "Determinants of Coordination Modes within Organizations," *American Sociological Review* 41 (1976):322–338.

40. Linda Argote, "Input Uncertainty and Organizational Coordination in Hospital Emergency Units."

41. Adapted from Eugene Linden, "Let a Thousand Flowers Bloom," *Inc.,* April 1984, pp. 64–76.

42. Donald Gerwin, "Relationships Between Structure and Technology," in Paul C. Nystrom and William H. Starbuck, *Handbook of Organizational Design,* vol. 2 (London: Oxford University Press, 1981), pp. 3–38; Louis W. Fry, "Technology-Structure Research: Three Critical Issues," *Academy of Management Journal* 25 (1982):532–552.

43. John Child, "Organization Structure and Strategies of Control: A Replication of the Aston Study," *Administrative Science Quarterly* 17 (1972):163–177; John Child, "Predicting and Understanding Organization Structure," *Administrative Science Quarterly* 18 (1973):168–185; John Child and Roger Mansfield, "Technology, Size and Organization Structure," *Sociology* 6 (1972):369–392.

44. Khandwalla, "Mass Output Orientation."

45. Peter Blau, C. M. Falbe, W. McKinley, and P. K. Tracy, "Technology and Organization in Manufacturing," *Administrative Science Quarterly* 21 (1976):20–40.

46. Richard C. Reimann, "Dimensions of Organizational Technology and Structure," *Human Relations* 30 (1977):545–566.

47. Richard C. Reimann, "Organization Structure and Technology in Manufacturing: System Versus Workflow Level Perspectives," *Academy of Management Journal* 23 (1980):61–77.

48. Randolph H. Bobbitt, Jr., and Jeffrey D. Ford, "Decision Maker Choice As a Determinant of Organizational Structure," *Academy of Management Review* 5 (1980):13–23; John R. Montanari, "Managerial Discretion: An Expanded Model of Organization Choices," *Academy of Management Review* 3 (1978):231–241; Pfeffer, *Organizational Design;* Rousseau, "Assessment of Technology in Organizations."

49. David Street, Robert Vinter, and Charles Perrow, *Organization for Treatment* (New York: The Free Press, 1966), pp. 155–158.

Organization Bureaucracy, Size, and Life Cycle

A LOOK INSIDE

DEPARTMENT OF MOTOR VEHICLES

In March of 1905 Charles D. Spreckels, of San Francisco, registered the first automobile in California, presumably becoming the last person in the history of the state who did not have to stand in line to do so.

Today, the California DMV is like the world's biggest title company. It employs about 8,000 people at its Sacramento headquarters and 152 field offices and oversees the registration of twenty million vehicles and sixteen million licensed drivers.

"We are the motor vehicle state," said DMV spokesman George Farnham. "It's sheer numbers. We have all kinds of problems just relating to the numbers."

The people who comprise those numbers have all kinds of problems relating to the DMV, particularly in heavily urban DMV field offices such as San Francisco's at 1377 Fell St. People take off half-days of work to go to the DMV for business transactions. They bring long novels and longer faces. There is no such thing as dash in and out of the DMV.

"We have people who throw things at us from time to time in frustration," said George Treco, manager of the Carmichael DMV field office. Last month it was a guy slamming his motorcycle helmet down and denting the counter. Last year it was a particularly disgruntled driver who waited until the Carmichael office closed and then drove his truck through the front door.

"Everybody has some kind of story like that," Treco said.

Just under 4,000 people work in DMV headquarters, and twenty years of service is commonplace among employees. . . . Quinten Peters manages some 900 employees of the vehicle registration section of the DMV's division of registration.

"I was in private industry for fourteen years and I've been with the department for twenty-two years," Peters said. "On the whole, this operation is run as businesslike as possible. It continues to look for ways to cut corners economically but still give a quality product. It is hard for anyone to visualize the amount of paper that must be shuffled in an operation of this size, daily."

The vast amount of that paper is a result of approximately 30,000 applications for registration or renewal each day. Peters said almost 85% of these applications come off without a hitch.

"But the other 15% . . . ." Peters shook his head at the thought.

Almost anything can cause a 3 × 5 computerized card to "kick out," as DMV employees put it. This invariably adds another two or three weeks to the process. Errors in filling out a registration application or renewal are one cause. An unclear machine stamp on the ownership certificate is another.

Often people move and don't tell the DMV, and unlike other mail, DMV mail isn't forwarded by the post office; it goes straight back to Sacramento. Or people let parking tickets pile up, and sooner or later their local municipality asks DMV to hold up on the registration of their vehicle. Often people move to California and try to register a vehicle without a smog certificate or without a legitimate bill of sale for the automobile.

"It's amazing what people will bring in as a bill of sale," said Farnham.[1]

The Department of Motor Vehicles illustrates some of the problems of managing an organization of large size. The organization attempts to stan-

173

dardize and routinize its procedures, and many people have to wait in line. If clients don't follow the correct procedures, they may have to come back again and again. Managers are trying to do a good job and provide services efficiently, but the staggering volume of vehicles and licensed drivers leads to an impersonal bureaucracy.

During the twentieth century, large, bureaucratic organizations have become widespread, and over the last thirty years bureaucracy has been a major topic of study in organizational sociology.[2] Today, most large organizations have some bureaucratic characteristics. They provide us with abundant goods and services, and they surprise us with astonishing feats—astronauts to the moon, thousands of airline flights daily without an accident—that are testimony to their effectiveness. On the other hand, bureaucracy is also accused of many sins, including inefficiency, irresponsibility, and the creation of demeaning, routinized work that alienates both employees and the people the organization tries to serve.[3]

Purpose of This Chapter

The purpose of this chapter is to explore the nature of bureaucracy and its role in the design and control of today's large organizations. In the preceding chapters we discussed how the contextual variables of technology, environment, and goals influence organizational design and functioning. In this chapter we will examine another contextual variable: organization size. In the next section the concept of bureaucracy is defined, and the historical need for bureaucracy as a means to control large organizations is discussed. Then the relationship between bureaucratic characteristics and organization size is explored. The connection between the stage in an organization's life cycle and bureaucratic characteristics is also analyzed. Finally, the economic and social outcomes of bureaucratic organizations are weighed. By the end of this chapter, students should understand the nature of bureaucracy, its strengths and weaknesses, and when to use bureaucratic characteristics to make an organization effective.

BUREAUCRACY

Something over one hundred years ago, large organizations like the ones we know today did not exist. Prior to 1850, organizations were limited to what a few family members could run, and only the most simple administrative structure was needed. A few types of organizations, such as manufacturing and railroads, had sufficient demand to encourage growth, but owners did not have the skills or systems to control large organizations. Managers did not want anything larger than what they could personally oversee. The preferred size of railroads, for example, was about fifty miles in length. Larger railroads were inefficient, as Daniel McCallum, general superintendent of the Erie Railroad, noted in 1855:

> A superintendent of a road fifty miles in length can give its business his personal attention ... and any system however imperfect may under such circumstances prove comparatively successful. In the government of a road five hundred miles in length a very different state exists. Any system which may be applicable to the business ... of a short road would be found entirely inadequate to the wants

of a large one; and I am fully convinced that in the want of a system . . . properly adapted and vigilantly enforced, lies the true secret of their (the large roads) failure; and that this disparity of cost per mile in operating long and short roads, is not produced by a difference in length, but is in proportion to the perfection of the system adopted.[4]

The skills and control systems needed to manage large-scale organizations simply were not available in 1855, so organizations could be more efficient by staying small. But organizations did experience pressures for growth, and gradually they developed systems and structures needed to control larger size. Max Weber, a sociologist who studied government organizations in Europe, developed a framework of administrative characteristics that would make large organizations rational and efficient.[5] Weber wanted to understand how organizations could be designed to play a positive role in the larger society.

The question Weber asked was: What form of organization would serve the increasingly industrialized society he observed in Europe at the turn of the century? His answer was "bureaucracy." Weber proposed a set of bureaucratic characteristics that would ensure efficient organizational functioning in both government and business settings. Bureaucracies, as Weber envisioned them, would facilitate the allocation of scarce resources in an increasingly complex society. He identified the following seven characteristics that could be found in bureaucratic organizations.

1. "A continuous organization of official functions bound by rules." [6] Rules and standard operating procedures enable organizational activities to be performed in a predictable, routine manner. Organization personnel thus could depend upon each other, and clients could depend upon the organization for reliable service.

2. "A specified sphere of competence." [7] Specific duties should be divided among people in a clear division of labor, and the job holder should be given the necessary authority to do those duties.

3. "The organization of offices follows the principle of hierarchy; that is, each lower office is under the control and supervision of a higher one." [8] This is what we now call the hierarchy of authority, or chain of command.

4. "Only a person who has demonstrated an adequate technical training is qualified to be a member of the administrative staff . . . and hence only such persons are eligible for appointment to official positions." [9] Technical competence was the basis by which people were hired and assigned to jobs within the organization. Friendship, family ties, and favoritism were not the basis for hiring or promoting people in a bureaucracy.

5. "Members of the administrative staff should be completely separated from ownership of the means of production or administration." [10] Weber felt that separation of ownership maintained the impersonal aspects of organization that were important to production efficiency.

6. "There is a complete absence of appropriation of his official position by the incumbent." [11] Individuals do not take over the rights or property of the office. Weber wanted the conduct of the office to be completely objective and oriented to relevant tasks rather than to serving the personal needs of employees.

7. "Administrative acts, decisions, and rules are formulated and recorded in writing." [12] Recordkeeping provided an organizational memory, and written documents provided continuity over time. Written documents also made up part of the functions and knowledge base for specific jobs.

Ideal Type for Control   Today, many of Weber's dimensions seem to be stating the obvious. The organizations we see all around us have rules, a division of labor, written documents, and a hierarchy of authority. The important point is that these bureaucratic dimensions provide an impersonal means to control organizations. They provide a mechanism to ensure qualified employees, supervision, and predictable outcomes. Rational control was the fundamental idea for this new form of organization.

Another point is that Weber was describing an ideal type of organization. If Weber's ideas were adopted literally—e.g., everything was written down—the organization would bog down under the weight of its own paper. But bureaucracy represented many advantages over organizational forms used prior to industrialization, and even today in many nonindustrialized countries. These other forms of organization were based upon favoritism, social status, family connections, personal friends, or some type of feudalism. Graft was also a problem. Office holders would benefit from their position by selling organization services for personal profit. These activities were extremely inefficient and were not in society's interest. By comparison, the logical and rational form of organization described in Weber's ideal model had great potential. Work would be conducted efficiently, and employees would not squander valuable resources.

Bases of Authority   The ability of an organization to function efficiently depends upon the authority structure. Proper authority provides managers with the control needed to make the bureaucratic form of organization work. Weber argued that legitimate, rational authority was preferred over other types of control (e.g., payoffs, favoritism) as the basis for internal decisions and activities. Within the larger society, however, Weber identified three types of authority that could explain the creation and control of a large organization. [13]

1. **Rational-legal authority** is based on employees' beliefs in the legality of rules, the division of labor, and the right of those elevated to authority to issue commands. Rational legal authority is the basis for both creation and control of most government organizations.
2. **Traditional authority** is the belief in traditions and the legitimacy of the status of people exercising authority through those traditions. Traditional authority is the basis for control for monarchies and churches.
3. **Charismatic authority** is based upon devotion to the exemplary character or heroism of an individual person and the order defined by him or her. Revolutionary military organizations are often based on the leader's charisma.

The management of organizations with bureaucratic characteristics requires rational-legal authority. A religious or a military organization may exist because of tradition or leader's special charisma, but rational-legal authority should govern internal work activities and decision-making.

The important outcome of Weber's work is his specification of organizational characteristics that provide rational control in the pursuit of an organization's goals. Exhibit 5.1 summarizes the seven dimensions of bureaucracy and the three types of authority envisioned by Weber. The bureaucratic model has the potential for objectivity and impersonality in the hiring, firing, and promotion processes. Technical competence is preferable to family ties or social status as the basis for holding a position. Rules and the division of labor promote efficiency. Rational-legal authority enables the implementation and use of bureaucracy. Nonbureaucratic forms of organization seemed wasteful and inefficient compared to Weber's model.

The term "bureaucracy" has come to have a negative connotation because of its association with red tape, rigid rules, and standardization. But bureaucratic characteristics, as envisioned by Weber, represent important control mechanisms that enable efficient organizational functioning. Too much bureaucracy can be a problem, but moderate amounts can be very effective, as in the case of McDonald's.

IN PRACTICE 5.1

McDonald's

McDonald's Corporation has experienced a Cinderella story of growth and profits. McDonald's is a giant, selling billions of hamburgers. In spite of its huge size, McDonald's success is based on product consistency and uniformity. A person buying a McDonald's hamburger will receive the same product whether it is purchased in College Station, Texas, or College Park, Maryland. A customer can also expect the same level of quality from one purchase to the next at the local McDonald's store. To achieve this uniformity, each store must be stamped from the same mold. The McDonald's mold was designed and maintained through the use of an extensive bureaucracy. McDonald's has taken advantage of size and bureaucracy without succumbing to organizational rigidity or employee dissatisfaction.

EXHIBIT 5.1. Weber's Dimensions of Bureaucracy and
Bases of Organizational Authority.

Bureaucracy	Legitimate Bases of Authority
1. Rules and procedures	1. Rational-legal
2. Specialization and division of labor	2. Traditional
3. Hierarchy of authority	3. Charismatic
4. Technically qualified personnel	
5. Position and incumbent are separate	
6. Impersonality	
7. Written communications and records	

Rules and regulations are the gospel at McDonald's. The company's operating bible has 385 pages describing the most minute activities in each outlet. The manual prescribes that certain equipment—cigarette, candy, and pinball machines—is not permitted in the stores. It also prescribes strict standards for personal grooming. Men must keep their hair short and their shoes black and highly polished. Women are expected to wear hair nets and to use only very light makeup. The store manager is even provided with a maintenance reminder for each day of the year, such as "Lubricate and adjust potato-peeler belt."

McDonald's has a passion for standardization of products and work activities. The basic hamburger patty must be a machine-cut, 1.6-ounce chunk of pure beef—no lungs, hearts, cereal, soybean, or other fillers—with no more than 19% fat content. Hamburger buns must have 13.3% sugar in them. French fries are kept under the light for only seven minutes. A flashing light cues the cook to the exact moment to flip the hamburger patties. Specially designed scoops determine the precise number of fries to fit in each pouch. The standardization of work reduces discretion of employees, but provides uniformity and consistency of products for consumers.

McDonald's uses its well-defined hierarchy. Field service managers visit each store regularly. An inspector will observe each store for three days, timing the counter and drive-through operations, and checking cooking procedures. Grades of A through F are given for cleanliness, quality, and service. If low grades are received, the inspector will come back unannounced and check again. If problems persist, the franchise may be taken away from the owner.

Each store has a refined division of labor and qualified personnel. Assistant managers are assigned to cover each shift, and crew leaders are responsible for specific periods, such as breakfast or lunch. Cooks and waitresses know exactly what to do. Trainers teach new employees the exact procedure for greeting customers and taking orders. Hostesses are assigned the task of helping young children and old people, and they coordinate birthday parties and make sure customers are comfortable.[14]

McDonald's is a living example of Weber's bureaucracy. Rational-legal authority is the basis for McDonald's design. In this giant organization, bureaucratic structure is an important reason for an excellent record of performance and growth.

ORGANIZATION SIZE AND BUREAUCRACY

Most large organizations like McDonald's have bureaucratic characteristics such as rules, division of labor, and a clear hierarchy of authority. One question of interest to both organization managers and scholars is the impact of organization size. As the managers of railroads discovered in the 1850s, size is an important contextual variable that can influence structural design. For example, should the organization become more bureaucratic as it grows larger? In what size organizations are bureaucratic characteristics most appropriate?

Over one hundred studies have attempted to answer these questions.[15] Most of these studies indicate that large organizations are different from small organizations along several dimensions of bureaucratic structure.

Formalization

Formalization, as described in chapter 1, refers to rules, procedures, and written documentation such as policy manuals and job descriptions. The evidence supports the conclusion that large organizations are more formalized. The reason is that large organizations rely on rules, procedures, and paperwork to achieve standardization and control across the large number of employees and departments. Top management can use personal observation to control a small organization. In large firms like McDonald's, formalization of procedures allows top administrators to extend their reach through impersonal means of control. Rules take the place of personal surveillance.[16] Managers can use new rules to change employee behavior, as in the case of sexual discrimination.

Until a few years ago, most companies did not have official policies on sexual harassment. Now, almost all large companies are updating policy manuals. General Motors, General Electric, Bank of America, IBM, GTE, and numerous city, state, and federal agencies are acting to curb harassment in their organizations.

Most policies spell out no-no's. American Telephone & Telegraph Company's policy says employees can be fired for "repeated, offensive flirtations" or for using "sexually degrading words" to describe someone. The U.S. Army goes even further. It recently ordered an end to soldiers' cat calls, whistles, terms such as "honey" or "baby" around women, and the wearing of T-shirts imprinted with sexual language.[17]

In the cases of AT&T and the U.S. Army, which are huge organizations, formalization is used to specify behavior down to very small details. Management uses rules and policies to achieve an acceptable standard of behavior across a large number of people.

Decentralization

Decentralization refers to the level of hierarchy that has authority to make decisions. In centralized organizations, decisions tend to be made at the top. In decentralized organizations, similar decisions would be made at a lower level. The research on organization size indicates that large organizations (e.g., IBM, Burroughs) permit greater decentralization.[18] The explanation is that large organizations have longer chains of command and a greater number of people and departments. Decisions simply cannot be passed to the top of the hierarchy, or senior managers would be overloaded. President Roger Smith of giant General Motors pushes decisions as far down the hierarchy as he can, otherwise GM's response would be too slow. Greater formalization in a large organization like General Motors facilitates decentralization of routine decisions because rules define boundaries so that decisions can be made at a lower level without loss of control.

Complexity

As discussed in chapter 1, complexity refers to both the number of levels in the hierarchy (vertical complexity) and the number of departments or jobs (horizontal complexity). Large organizations show a definite pattern of greater complexity.[19] The explanation for the relationship between size and complexity is straightforward. First, the need for additional specialties occurs more often in large organizations. For example, a study of new departments reported that new administrative departments were often created in response to problems of large size.[20] A planning department was established in a large organization because a greater need for planning arose after a certain size was reached.

Second, a large organization can add a new specialty at a much smaller proportional expense than can a small organization. Hiring two new planners to work in a new planning department is a trivial expense in an organization with a $100,000,000 budget, but will be a substantial expense when the budget is $100,000 or so. Third, as departments within the organization grow in size, pressure to subdivide arises. Departments eventually get so large that managers cannot control them effectively. At this point, subgroups will lobby to be subdivided into separate departments.[21]

Finally, vertical complexity is needed to maintain control over a large number of people. As the number of employees increases, additional levels of hierarchy keep spans of control from becoming too large. In both vertical and horizontal directions, then, large organizations are vastly more complex than small organizations.

The characteristics of formalization, decentralization, and complexity can be seen in one of the most efficient large corporations in the United States and Canada, often called the "Brown Giant" for the color of packages it delivers.

IN PRACTICE 5.2

United Parcel Service

United Parcel Service has taken on the United States Post Office at its own game, and won. UPS specializes in the delivery of small packages. It can deliver a package anywhere in the United States for about $3. UPS sees itself in price competition with the Post Office so it sets prices below Post Office rates. Unlike the Post Office, UPS pays taxes on real estate, income, and fuel, and cannot subsidize packages with revenue from first-class letters. UPS still makes an excellent profit.

Why has the Brown Giant been so successful? There are several reasons, but two important ones are automation and bureaucracy. Automation is visible in the 100 mechanized hubs that can sort 40,000 packages per hour. A new center will sort 60,000 packages per hour. UPS handles 8,000,000 packages a day. UPS is so efficient that it can send a truck to pick up packages from a home or business, deliver packages door-to-door in two days, and still make money.

Many efficiencies are realized through adoption of the bureaucratic model of organization. UPS is bound up in rules and regulations. There are safety rules for drivers, loaders, clerks, and managers. Strict dress codes are enforced— no beards, hair cannot touch the collar, no sideburns, mustaches must be trimmed evenly and cannot go below the corner of the mouth, etc. Rules specify the cleanliness of buildings and property. All 60,000 UPS delivery trucks must be washed inside and out at the end of every day. Each manager is given bound copies of policy books with the expectation of regular use.

Jobs are broken down into a complex division of labor. UPS plants consist of specialized drivers, loaders, clerks, washers, sorters, and maintenance personnel. The hierarchy of authority is clearly defined and has eight levels, extending from a washer at the local UPS plant up to the president of the national organization.

Technical qualification is the criterion for hiring and promotion. The UPS policy book says, "A leader does not have to remind others of authority by use of a title. Knowledge, performance, and capacity should be adequate evidence of position and leadership." Favoritism is forbidden.

UPS thrives on written records. Daily worksheets that specify performance goals and work output are kept on every employee and department. Operating costs and production runs are recorded and compared to competitors'. Daily employee quotas and achievements are accumulated on a weekly and monthly basis. Computer systems have been installed to facilitate the recordkeeping process. Delivery routes are closely timed, and if drivers cannot meet the expected times, a supervisor will go around with them until they get it right.

Within the bureaucratic structure, decisions are pushed as low as possible. A few days before Christmas, 1983, a UPS regional manager learned that a flatcar with two UPS trailers had been left on a siding in the middle of Illinois. The regional manager paid for a high-speed diesel to run the flatcar into Chicago. Then he ordered two Boeing 727s diverted to Chicago to deliver the contents to their destinations in Florida and Louisiana in time for Christmas. The manager neither asked permission nor even informed UPS headquarters of his action until weeks later.[22]

UPS illustrates how bureaucratic characteristics increase with large size. Written records, formalization, complexity, and decentralization enable the Brown Giant to be managed efficiently. UPS is so productive and dependable that it dominates the small-package delivery market, with more business than even the U.S. Postal Service.

Personnel Configuration

The next characteristic of bureaucracy is the personnel configuration among administrative, clerical, and professional support staff. The most frequently studied configuration variable is the administrative ratio. In 1957, C. Northcote Parkinson published *Parkinson's Law,* which argued that work expands to fill the time available for its completion. Parkinson argued that administrators were motivated to add more administrators for a variety of reasons, including the enhancement of their own status through empire-building. Parkinson used his argument to make fun of the British Admiralty. During a fourteen-year period from 1914 to 1928, the officer corps increased by 78%, although the total navy personnel decreased by 32% and the number of warships in use decreased by approximately 68%. Parkinson's book made large organizations seem very inefficient, and provided the impetus for scholars to survey organizations to learn whether cumbersome administrative ratios were widespread.

In the years since Parkinson's book, the administrative ratio has been studied in school systems, churches, hospitals, employment agencies, and other business and voluntary organizations.[23] Two clear patterns have emerged.

The first pattern is that the ratio of top administration to total employment is actually smaller in large organizations.[24] This is the opposite of Parkinson's argument, and indicates that organizations may experience administrative economies as they grow larger. Large organizations have large departments, more regulations, and a greater division of labor. These mechanisms require less supervision from the top. Increasing bureaucratization is a substitute for personal supervision from the administrators. The ratio of top administrators to workers thus is actually smaller in large organizations.

The second pattern concerns other personnel support components. Recent studies have subdivided support personnel into subclassifications such as clerical, maintenance, and professional staff.[25] These support groups tend to increase in proportion to organization size. The clerical ratio increases in size because of the greater communication (memos, letters) and paperwork requirements (policy manuals, job descriptions) in large organizations. Plant maintenance also increases with organization size, and so do professional staff support groups.[26] The increase in these specialties is explained by the division of labor. In a small organization, an individual may be a "jack of all trades." In a large organization, people spend full time on support activities, so production employees are more efficient.

Exhibit 5.2 illustrates administrative and support ratios for small and large school districts. As districts increased in size, the administrative ratio declined from about 9% to 7% of total employment. Other support groups increased, such as clerical (3% to 8%), building maintenance (6% to 13%), and professional staff (8% to 15%), and were a much larger percentage of employment in large districts. The net effect for teachers is that they declined from 74% of employees in the smallest district to 57% in the largest district.

Total support personnel, including administrative, clerical, and maintenance groups, represent total administrative overhead. Professional staff (counselors) and teachers are assigned to the educational task. As shown in Exhibit 5.2 (dashed line), all education-related staff decreased from 82% to 72% of employees from small to large districts. For support personnel, the finding was the opposite. All support personnel increased from 18% to 28% of employees when comparing small and large school districts.[27]

The literature on personnel configuration thus both contradicts and supports intuitive ideas about administrative overhead. Top administrators do not increase their own number disproportionately in large organizations; in fact, they decrease as a percentage of total employment. Top administrators do not build empires as proposed by Parkinson. However, the idea that proportionately greater administrative overhead is required in large organizations is supported. People in clerical and maintenance departments increase at a faster rate than people who work in the technical core of the organization.

RELATIONSHIPS AMONG
BUREAUCRATIC DIMENSIONS

The above discussion indicates that large organizations are different from small organizations. Students can observe these differences in their own

EXHIBIT 5.2. Percentage of Personnel Allocated to Teaching and Support Activities.

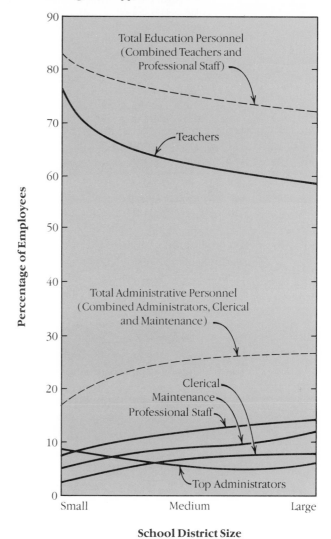

School District Size

Source: Richard L. Daft and Selwyn W. Becker, "District Size and the Deployment of Personnel Resources," *The Alberta Journal of Educational Research* 24 (1978): 181, with permission.

university. Students at large state universities have had lots of experience with bureaucratic structure. Often they have to wait in line to register or see an advisor, and they have to wade through all kinds of red tape to enroll in class or graduate. Certain forms have to be filled out in certain ways. These students have experienced the "run around" to get a task accomplished or to obtain information. Because of extreme specialization, they have to search through the bureaucracy until they find just the right person to help them.

Procedures in small colleges are quite different. Students might have many things handled on a casual basis. A request might be granted without ever being written down. Red tape is nonexistent. University employees have

EXHIBIT 5.3. Relationship between Size and Other Organization Characteristics.

Greater organization size is associated with:
1. Increased number of management levels (vertical complexity).
2. Greater number of jobs and departments (horizontal complexity).
3. Increased specialization of skills and functions.
4. Greater formalization.
5. Greater decentralization.
6. Smaller percentage of top administrators.
7. Greater percentage of technical and professional support staff.
8. Greater percentage of clerical and maintenance support staff.
9. Greater amount of written communications and documentation.

experience with a variety of tasks and are able to help students with a number of problems.

The differences between small and large organizations are summarized in Exhibit 5.3. Larger organizations have many characteristics that distinguish them from small organizations: more rules and regulations; more paperwork, written communication, and documentation; greater specialization; more decentralization and delegation; a lower percentage of people devoted to administration; and a larger percentage of people allocated to clerical, maintenance, and professional support staff.

An important additional point is that size does not cause these other variables by itself. As organizations increase in size, bureaucratic characteristics tend to influence each other as well as being influenced by size.[28] Exhibit 5.4 illustrates several relationships among bureaucratic variables. This figure shows that an increase in size has direct impact on division of labor and hierarchy of authority (complexity). Division of labor requires greater supervision and coordination to ensure that separate parts of the organization work together. The multilevel hierarchy of authority leads to greater decentralization because people at the top become overloaded. Decentralization, in turn, increases formalization, which is a substitute for personal supervision and helps provide uniformity and standardization across the organization. The increased division of labor also leads to greater support staff because staff jobs are now separate from the technical core. Formalization and decentralization reduce the need for top administrators. Rules take the place of personal surveillance, and middle managers take over some decision-making. Size is thus a major cause of organizational bureaucracy, but in a rather complex way: Bureaucratic characteristics also influence each other so that large organizations become more bureaucratic along several dimensions.

The important point about the interplay among characteristics as illustrated in Exhibit 5.4 is that bureaucracy enables managers to coordinate and control large organizations. These characteristics reinforce one another so that senior managers can direct thousands of employees. Sometimes, however, the bureaucracy becomes too great and begins to cause disadvantages, which is what happened at Sears.

IN PRACTICE 5.3

Sears, Roebuck and Co.

During most of its ninety-two-year history, Sears has been the envy of the retail industry. It built stores in excellent suburban locations, and found in-

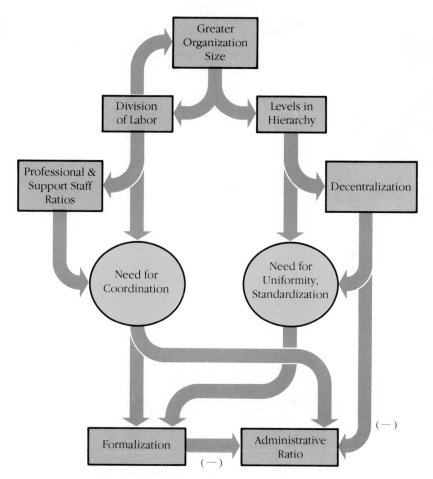

EXHIBIT 5.4. Negative and Positive Relationships among Size and Selected Elements of Bureaucratic Structure.

novative products to sell at low cost. Sears brought novel product lines (Allstate Insurance, optometrists) into its stores, and has been consistently profitable.

But no one envied Sears in 1980. Sears became known as a high-cost operator. With its huge size and cumbersome cost structure, Sears needed a 50% markup to make a profit on items when competitors needed a markup of only 35%. Its huge size got the better of Sears. Top management had to gain control over the layers of managers and the huge support staffs that have grown up in an empire of 900 stores, 12,000 suppliers, and 400,000 employees.

Sears reached the size where it could no longer compete on price with smaller retail chains. Sears tried to be efficient, and had excellent internal systems, such as for inventory control. But overhead expenses were eating them up. Sears had the highest cost in the business. Overhead and administrative expenses siphon off 29.9% of Sears' sales dollar (on $25 billion sales). By comparison, K-Mart has 23% overhead expenses ($14 billion sales) and Walmart 15.3% ($1.6 billion sales). Specialty and lower-priced discount stores took away a portion of Sears' clientele.

Sears' top management seemed tired, and needed to weed out at least $100 million a year in overhead expenses to be competitive in a low-cost market. New management and a reorganization began to have an impact about 1984. A stripped-down corporate staff gave greater autonomy to operating units. Executives from various units meet regularly to coordinate plans. Every merchandise line has been reviewed. Stores have been remodeled and better ways of arranging merchandise used. Brand-name merchandise, including Levi's jeans and Adidas athletic shoes, have been added to attract middle-class customers back into the stores. The net effect is a substantial increase in Sears' average sale. Management has gotten a huge bureaucracy back on track, and new growth and profits are expected to come from new ventures into investment advice, mortgage origination, help in selling a home, and communications.[29]

Sears is a giant corporation. Its structure reflects bureaucratic characteristics, including large costs for administrative overhead. Top management realized that Sears was intrinsically different from smaller retail chains. Sears no longer can compete on the basis of low overhead costs or a flexible structure. Sears will do best in competition for new and affluent retail customers.

ORGANIZATIONAL LIFE CYCLE

So far in this chapter we have explored the relationship between organization size and bureaucratic structural characteristics. Size is an important contextual variable that can help managers understand the appropriate configuration of personnel, formalization, decentralization, and complexity. In this section we turn to a related topic—organizational growth through the life cycle. Most organizations try to grow, and over a large number of years organizations pass through different stages of development, each one associated with unique management problems and structural characteristics.

Pressures for Growth

Why do organizations grow? Why should they grow? A few investigators have tried to understand the gradual growth and evolutionary processes that take place within an organization. This type of research traces the organization's development over time. The evidence indicates many reasons why organizations grow. The following reasons are most important.

Organizational Self-Realization Self-realization refers to managers' beliefs that the organization should carry out new functions, make progress, and become a complete unit.[30] Customers may want a complete service or product line from a single company. Managers also feel pressure to face and conquer new challenges. Those are the reasons for growth at Campbell Taggart.

Campbell Taggart, Inc. bakes bread. They bake a lot of it, and are the second largest producer in the country (after Wonder Bread). The demand for white bread is no longer growing. Top management wants to grow larger and round out the line with related products. Over the last few years, Campbell Taggart moved into dinner and sweet rolls, and have begun producing a high-quality, high-priced line of pastries, cookies, and cakes. They have also started baking for ethnic tastes. The major ethnic line is bread for Spanish tastes in the Southwest. The Earth Grain bread line was added to satisfy demand for natural foods. Executives now feel that Campbell Taggart is a well-rounded company, and has the strength for continued success.[31]

Executive Mobility A record of growth is often necessary to attract and keep quality managers. A growing organization offers greater prestige and better salaries than a stagnating one. Growing organizations are an exciting place to work. There are many challenges and opportunities for advancement when the number of employees is expanding. If an organization were stable or declining, the best executives would be unsatisfied and go elsewhere.[32]

Economic Factors Organizational growth has many financial benefits. Costs can be reduced because economies of scale in manufacturing or production are possible. Revenues can be increased, especially if greater size gives the organization additional power in the marketplace. Growth enables the organization to reduce resource dependence on the environment, which was discussed in chapter 2. Growth through vertical integration or acquisition of other firms can ensure stability, long life, and high profits for the organization.[33]

Survival Survival may be the most important reason to grow. A survey of executives found that, "If firms do not expand, they contract; they cannot stand still." [34] Competitors develop new products and try to increase their share of the market at the expense of your organization. To be stable, to relax, or to accept decline may begin the ultimate demise of the organization. The administrator of a hospital said that he could not restrict growth. If the hospital turned away patients for any reason, they would feel unwanted and go elsewhere. If patients went elsewhere, the hospital would be in severe trouble. Hospital administrators thus have to increase facilities sufficient to meet the demand for their services.

Hence, there are many motives for growth. Growth is a goal for most organizations. But the process of growth is not easy. Organizations have growing pains. Growth is associated with a series of crises that must be met and solved if growth is to continue.

Stages of Life Cycle

A useful way to think about organizational growth and change is provided by the concept of a life cycle.[35] Organizations are born, grow older, and eventually die. Organization structure, leadership style, and administrative systems follow a predictable pattern through stages in the life cycle. Stages are sequential in nature, and follow a natural progression. Recent work on organizational life cycle suggests that four major stages characterize organizational development.[36] Each stage has a specific "need" or problem to be solved that propels the organization into the next stage of development.

These stages are illustrated in Exhibit 5.5, along with the problems associated with the transition to the next stage.

1. *Entrepreneurial Stage* The organization is born, and the emphasis is on creating a product and surviving in the marketplace. The founders are entrepreneurs, and they devote full energies to the technical activities of production and marketing. The organization is informal and nonbureaucratic. The hours of work are long. Control is based on the owner's personal supervision. Growth is from a creative new product or service. Apple Computer was in the entrepreneurial stage when it was created by Steven Jobs and Stephen Wozniak in Wozniak's parents' garage. New software companies like Microsoft are in the entrepreneurial stage today.

Need for Leadership: As the organization starts to grow, the larger number of employees causes problems. The creative, technically oriented owners have to deal with management issues, but they prefer to be involved with making or selling the product. The organization may enter a crisis because the founders are not skilled or interested in management activities. The owners may restrict growth. If the organization continues to grow, it may flounder. A strong manager is needed who can introduce

EXHIBIT 5.5. Organizational Life Cycle.

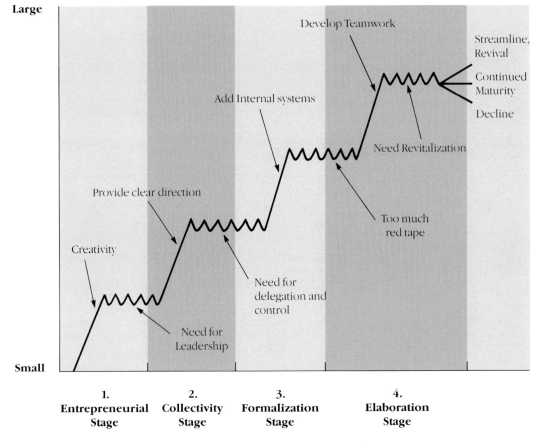

STAGE OF DEVELOPMENT

Source: Adapted from Robert E. Quinn and Kim Cameron, "Organizational Life Cycles and Some Shifting Criteria of Effectiveness: Some Preliminary Evidence," *Management Science* 29 (1983): 33–51; and Larry E. Greiner, "Evolution and Revolutions as Organizations Grow," *Harvard Business Review* 50 (July–August, 1972): 37–46.

management techniques. A. C. Markkula was brought in to run Apple Computer as it began to grow because neither Jobs nor Wozniak was a top-flight manager.

2. Collectivity Stage   If the leadership crisis is resolved, strong leadership is obtained and the organization begins to develop clear goals and direction. Departments are established along with a hierarchy of authority, job assignments, and a beginning division of labor. Employees identify with the mission of the organization, and spend long hours helping the organization succeed. Members feel part of a collective, and communication and control are mostly informal although a few formal systems begin to appear. Apple Computer was in the collectivity stage during the rapid growth years from 1978 to 1981. Employees threw themselves into the business as the major product line was established and over 2,000 dealers were signed on.

Need for Delegation with Control: If the new management has been successful, lower-level employees gradually find themselves restricted by the strong leadership. Lower-level managers begin to acquire confidence in their own functional areas and want more discretion. An autonomy crisis occurs when top managers, who were successful by strong leadership and vision, do not want to give up responsibility. Top managers want to make sure that all parts of the organization are coordinated and pulling together. The organization needs to find mechanisms to coordinate and control departments without direct supervision from the top.

3. Formalization Stage   The next stage involves the installation and use of control and information systems. Communication is less frequent and more formal. New employee specialists may be added. Top management becomes concerned with top management issues such as strategy and planning, and leaves the operation of the firm to lower-level management. Staff personnel and specialists may be hired to review company-wide programs. Product groups or other decentralized units may be formed to improve coordination. Incentive systems, based upon profits, may be implemented to ensure that managers work toward what is best for the overall company. The new coordination and control systems, when effective, enable the organization to continue growing by establishing linkage mechanisms between top management and field units. Apple Computer is in the formalization stage today.

Too Much Red Tape: At this point in the organization's development, the proliferation of systems and programs may begin to strangle middle-level executives. The organization seems over-bureaucratized. Middle management may resent the intrusion of staff people. Innovation may be restricted. The organization seems too large and complex to be managed through formal programs.

4. Elaboration Stage   The solution to the red-tape crisis is a new sense of collaboration and teamwork. Throughout the organization managers develop skills for confronting problems and working together. Bureaucracy may have reached its limit. Social control and self-discipline reduce the need for additional formal controls. Managers learn to work within the bureaucracy without adding to it. In order to achieve collaboration, teams may be formed across functions or divisions of the company. Formal systems may be simplified and partially replaced by manager conferences and task forces. Sears Roebuck, described in IN PRACTICE 5.3, is in the elaboration stage of its life cycle.

> **Need for Revitalization:** After the organization reaches maturity, it may enter periods of temporary decline.[37] Need for renewal may occur every ten to twenty years. The organization becomes out of alignment with the environment, or perhaps becomes slow moving and overbureaucratized, and must go through a stage of streamlining and innovation. Top managers often are replaced during this period. In recent years, Ford and General Motors have gone through a period of turnaround and revitalization that required employee layoffs, shrinkage, and streamlining. Sears Roebuck went through a stage of revitalization and turnaround in the early 1980s. Organizations that fail to revitalize themselves may level off as a mature organization or even go into steady decline, as indicated in the final stage in Exhibit 5.5.

Organizations that do not successfully resolve the problems associated with transitions through life cycle stages are restricted in their growth or may fail entirely. From within the organization, the problems and crises are very real, as illustrated by Bill Sauey of Flambeau Corporation. He provided strong leadership for his corporation, but almost failed to get through the need for greater delegation and formal control.

IN PRACTICE 5.4
Flambeau Corp.

"I was killing myself trying to manage 500 employees spread out in five plants around the country, running three shifts a day," says Bill Sauey, sitting in an office cluttered with plastic toys, housewares, sporting goods, and industrial parts. "After twenty-five years of keeping everything under my control, I decided there had to be a better way."

The better way Sauey found was to chop his company, Flambeau Corp., into pieces and turn over control of the pieces to a group of independent general managers. Before Sauey made the change at the beginning of 1979, Flambeau was highly centralized. The company, which manufactures plastic products, had grown steadily to $24 million with Sauey running the whole show. But as Flambeau got larger and larger, the pressure to continue that growth became too much for one man to handle. Today, Sauey presides over a company with six independent divisions under six managers—and sales have jumped to $35 million.

Sauey started Flambeau Corp. in 1947. From that point on, he guided Flambeau singlehandedly. By 1965, it had reached $10 million in sales. Sauey signed all the checks, bought all the plant equipment, interviewed all potential employees, and played a role in developing and selling all Flambeau's products. The company was a testament to his persistence and his conviction that he could solve any business problem. So he continued to manage the company in his own tightly controlled way even though there were signs that this style wasn't working so well anymore. . . .

"I didn't want to decentralize authority," says Sauey, "because I thought I'd lose the ability to get my message across and get the job done effectively." Sauey continued to make all important budgetary, sales, marketing, and production decisions for both the Georgia and Wichita plants, and he couldn't find a manager who wanted to work under those conditions.

It was the sheer weight of details Sauey wanted to keep under his control that finally led to an uncharacteristic decision—he gave up control over one part of the company. This happened in 1977 when Flambeau acquired Vlchek Plastics Co. in Middlefield, Ohio. In the past, Sauey had always merged acquisitions into the central organization. "But I didn't this time," he says, "because I was so busy with the rest of the company—which by now had 500 employees working in five plants—that I knew if I brought it into our system I'd screw it up."

Two things happened. Vlchek's sales began doubling annually, and for once, Sauey didn't feel insecure about his lack of direct control. "I was really surprised at how little I worried about what went on at Vlchek," he says, his voice still registering amazement.

Unlike the early days, Sauey couldn't just work harder to make things go; he was already overworked and tired, and he was feeling the pressure of trying to hold the company together while the forces of growth were pulling things apart.

"I was sitting at home one night after a frantic day at work, and I made up my mind. I just said to myself, 'By god, I've got to do it.'"

Things moved very fast after that. Sauey wrote up a reorganization manual that spelled out how he was going to decentralize Flambeau and give authority to general managers who would report to him but have the freedom to run their division as they saw fit. It had taken him seven years, though, to decide that it was fundamental to Flambeau's growth.[38]

The Bill Sauey example illustrates how difficult it is for a strong owner/ manager to let go and delegate after having been solely responsible for building a successful organization. But refusing to adapt to the structural needs of the organization as it entered a new stage of development would create a genuine crisis, which could have caused the stagnation of Flambeau Corp.

Organizational Characteristics during the Life Cycle

As organizations evolve through the four stages of the life cycle, changes take place in structure, control systems, innovation, and goals. The organizational characteristics associated with each stage are summarized in Exhibit 5.6.

Entrepreneurial Initially, the organization is small, nonbureaucratic, and a one-person show. The top manager provides the structure and control system. Organizational energy is devoted toward survival and the production of a single product or service.

EXHIBIT 5.6 Organization Characteristics during Four Stages of Life Cycle.

	I Entrepreneurial	II Collectivity	III Formalization	IV Elaboration
	Nonbureaucratic	Prebureaucratic	Bureaucratic	Very Bureaucratic
Characteristic				
Structure	Informal, one-person show	Mostly informal, some procedures	Formal procedures, division of labor, add new specialties	Teams work within bureaucracy
Products/Services	Single product/service	Major product, with variations	Line of products/services	Multiple lines
Reward and Control Systems	Personal, paternalistic	Personal, contribution to success	Impersonal, formalized systems	Extensive, tailored to product and department
Innovation	By owner/manager	Employees and managers	Separate innovation group	Institutionalized R&D
Goal	Survival	Growth	Reputation, stability, expand market	Uniqueness, complete organization
Top Management Style	Individualistic, entrepreneurial	Charismatic, gives direction	Delegation with control	Participation, team approach

Source: Adapted from Larry E. Greiner, "Evolution and Revolution as Organizations Grow," *Harvard Business Review,* 50 (July-August, 1972):37–46; and G. L. Lippitt and W. H. Schmidt, "Crises in a Developing Organization," *Harvard Business Review,* 45 (Nov.-Dec., 1967): 102–112; B. R. Scott, "The Industrial State: Old Myths and New Realities," *Harvard Business Review,* 51 (March-April, 1973):133–148; Robert E. Quinn and Kim Cameron, "Organizational Life Cycles and Shifting Criteria of Effectiveness," *Management Science,* 29 (1983):33–51.

Collectivity   This is the organization's youth. Growth is rapid, and employees are excited and committed to the organization's mission. The structure is still mostly informal, although some procedures are emerging. The strong, charismatic leader provides direction and goals for the organization.

Formalization   At this point the organization is entering midlife. Bureaucratic characteristics emerge. The organization adds staff support groups, formalizes procedures, and establishes a clear division of labor. Top management has to delegate, but also implements formal control systems. The organization may develop complementary products to offer a complete product line.

Elaboration   The mature organization is large and bureaucratic, with extensive control systems, rules, and procedures. Organization managers attempt to develop a team orientation within the bureaucracy and prevent further bureaucratization. Top managers are concerned with establishing a complete organization. Organizational stature and reputation are important. Innovation is institutionalized through an R&D department. Management may be frustrated with the bureaucracy, and may try to streamline it.

ORGANIZATIONAL DECLINE

A topic of increasing concern in recent years has been the management of organizational decline. Although organizational growth and stages of development are important, an increasing number of organizations have experienced periods of decline. Unexpected decline may occur at any stage during the organization's life cycle.

One of the realities facing today's organizations is that continuous growth and expansion may not be possible. All around us we see evidence that some organizations are having to stop growing. Many are declining. Schools have had decreasing enrollments, churches have closed their doors, municipal services have been curtailed, and certain industries, such as automotive, have laid off record numbers of employees in response to recession.[39]

The term **decline** is normally used to "denote a cutback in the size of an organization's workforce, profits, budget, or clients." [40] Decline may occur because an organization's command over environmental resources has been reduced (e.g., smaller share of market) or because the environment itself has become poorer (e.g., erosion of a city's tax base). A key management issue in these circumstances is to understand the reasons for downturn and to reduce the crisis within the organization.

Why Decline?   The following reasons explain why organizations decline:

1. **Organizational Atrophy.** Atrophy occurs when organizations grow older, become inefficient, and lose muscle tone. The organization gets used to success and no longer has a sharp edge. Responses are slow and competitors dominate the market.

2. **Vulnerability.** Vulnerability reflects the inability of the organization to prosper in its environment. Often this happens because the organization is small and has not become fully established. It is vulnerable to changes in consumer tastes or in the economic health of the larger society. Legitimacy may also cause vulnerability if the organization produces something not valued by the mainstream of society. A loss of legitimacy has hurt manufacturers of cigarettes and unsafe toys. Vulnerable organizations typically need to redefine the environmental domain to enter new industries and markets.

3. **Environmental Entropy.** This refers to the reduced capacity of the environment to support the organization; external resources are simply insufficient. The organization probably has to either scale down operations or redefine its domain. This is the circumstance faced by organizations in a stagnating economy. The external resource base is no longer growing, so organizations have to divide up a stable or shrinking pie. Organizations in this context will inevitably decline.[41]

Managing the Effects of Decline   Decline represents a change, perhaps a change that the organization doesn't want, but nevertheless a change that has to be managed. Two organizational factors frequently associated with decline management are recentralization and reallocation.

1. **Recentralization.** Decline decisions have to be made at the top. Top managers must reclaim authority to make the difficult decisions associated with decline. Employees may have to be laid off, pay may be cut, resources redirected, and some departments eliminated. These decisions engender enormous disagreement and debate, and without central authority the cutbacks needed for survival cannot be implemented.

2. **Reallocation.** The scarce and valued resources remaining within the organization must be reallocated for maximum effect. Perhaps the organi-

zation has one area of product strength, so resources will have to take away from declining products to enable the growing product line to prosper. Staff personnel may have to be laid off to provide additional resources for research and development, manufacturing, or advertising. The decline circumstance should be associated with sufficient budgetary flexibility that resources can be reallocated to where they will do the most good. Departments and employees typically fight the loss of resources, so central management authority is needed to implement these changes.[42]

Organizational decline is typically a time of great stress for managers and workers. Morale is low and conflicts surface. There are positive ways for organizations to manage decline.[43] The most positive approach is to simply embrace the change and try to make the best of it. Harm is minimized, and the best is made of a potentially negative situation. If people understand and are informed of the need for decline, resources can be allocated in a way to minimize the negative effects. Strategies such as selectively selling or eliminating entire plants or product lines are appropriate, because the organization can redefine its domain without eliminating employees in every department.[44]

In all cases of decline, managers should be prepared for conflict. The most serious and difficult aspect of decline is the difference of opinion and fear of loss within the organization. Resource cutbacks sharply increase conflict and force people into win-lose situations.[45]

Finally, decline increases the rate of administrative change to which management must respond.[46] Innovations adopted in response to decline should be designed to increase efficiency and make better use of scarce resources. Some city governments have rescheduled janitors to work during the day in order to save the light bill from working at night.[47] The size of police cars has been reduced, and one city even used taxi-style Checker sedans as police cruisers to save money. Managers are able to moderate the negative effect of decline by encouraging an innovative climate.

IN PRACTICE 5.5

Acme-Cleveland Corp.

Acme-Cleveland Corporation found red ink splashed on its profit and loss statement in 1980, and the future looked uncertain. B. Charles Ames, the new chief executive, quickly took charge. He decided there were too many people in the corporate structure, and believed the organization would operate more efficiently with fewer people who were given broader responsibility. Despite the earnings plunge, Acme-Cleveland's administrative overhead remained constant. During the good years, Acme-Cleveland became overloaded with corporate and staff support personnel. President Ames knew that unless costs could be cut, profits would be eroded even further. He decided to perform radical surgery. The first cuts were amputations at the corporate level of the entire departments of advertising, promotion, and market research. Acme-Cleveland also made selective cuts, including corporate accountants, computer programmers, and many assistant managers in manufacturing, research, sales, and finance. The company sold two corporate aircraft, slashed its corporate advertising program, and dispensed with its $8 million centralized computer system.

Nearly 900 persons were dismissed. It is estimated that $15.3 million was saved just by reducing white-collar personnel. Another $2.7 million was saved by eliminating the corporate advertising, promotion, and market research people.

Some of these savings were invested in other areas. Ames created twenty new product-manager positions at the division level. These people could help division managers scrutinize costs and markets, and coordinate product lines. He also hired a marketing manager, a controller, and two product market managers for the national Acme division. Cleveland Twist Drill Division, which makes cutting tools, also received additional people.

Ames' philosophy is to cut too much rather than too little. People can always be hired back but additional cuts in the near future are especially difficult.

The most difficult part for employees is the uncertainty. They are uncertain about whether they will be fired, and they are uncertain about new jobs and careers. Employees feel disappointment, anger, depression, and emptiness. Many resist. Some employees respond with lawsuits, which creates a hostile climate. Others fight internally, or simply raise a ruckus. Managers who perform surgery also experience stress. "You have to be tough-minded to make it stick," said one manager. "If you have doubts, you either fail to make the decision or you regret it afterward." [48]

B. Charles Ames both recentralized authority and reallocated resources during the decline at Acme-Cleveland. The result was a streamlined, efficient organization that went on to improved profits and growth.

SIZE, BUREAUCRACY, AND PERFORMANCE

So far in this chapter we have discussed the relationship between size and bureaucratic characteristics, and the changes in bureaucratic structure as the organization progresses through the life cycle. This discussion has assumed that bureaucracy is necessary to maintain management control. Yet bureaucracy is often criticized. It may seem good for the organization, but it also entangles employees and clients in red tape, routinizes jobs, and inhibits innovation. In this final section of the chapter we want to examine more carefully the pros and cons associated with bureaucratic characteristics. First we will look at the relationship of bureaucracy to economic performance, and then to its impact on other constituencies.

Economic Performance

The first question is whether bureaucratic characteristics are associated with profit and other indicators of economic performance. John Child surveyed business corporations in England.[49] He measured their bureaucratic characteristics and their size. We would expect bureaucracy to be associated with high performance in large corporations because bureaucracy is needed for coordination and control. Child's findings are summarized in Exhibit 5.7.

The sloped lines indicate that as organizations grow larger, higher performance is indeed related to degree of bureaucracy. Corporations that stay informal do less well if they are large. Among small organizations (less than 2,000 employees), the high-performing companies were less bureaucratized. This evidence supports a positive relationship among size, bureaucracy, and performance.

Criticisms of Bureaucracy

Child's analysis of bureaucracy and performance was concerned with profit and other economic indicators. Organizational effectiveness as discussed in chapter 3 includes many dimensions, such as employee satisfaction and organizational adaptability. Large, bureaucratic organizations have come under criticism along noneconomic dimensions of performance. Bureaucratic organizations, with their rules, paperwork and impersonality, are often seen as a problem for society, not as a solution. Specific criticisms usually pertain to employee dissatisfaction, resistance to change, and poor system management. A summary of these criticisms, as well as arguments in defense of bureaucracy, are given in Exhibit 5.8 on page 198.

Employee Satisfaction   One of the most compelling arguments against bureaucracy is that extensive rules, standardization, and specialization stifle spontaneity, freedom, and the opportunity for challenging work. Bureaucracy does not take advantage of human potential. Bureaucracy does not allow for personal growth. Employees are dehumanized, and the result is job dissatisfaction and alienation.[50]

Bureaucracies are sometimes guilty of creating work that is not challenging. In many cases, however, bureaucracy also has advantages for employees. Rules and regulations reduce uncertainty and protect employees from management whims and arbitrary decisions. Regulations are a two-edged sword, and employees can invoke rules for their own protection.[51] The absence of rules can cause as many problems as too many rules. Furthermore, the bureaucratic division of labor into specialized tasks enables

EXHIBIT 5.7. Size of Organization, Bureaucracy, and Performance.

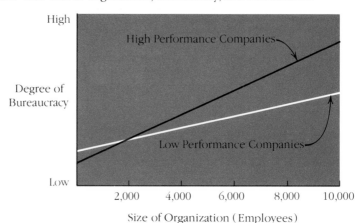

Source: Adapted from John Child, "Managerial and Organizational Factors Associated with Company Performance—Part II. A Contingency Analysis," *Journal of Management Studies* 12 (1975): 12–27.

employees to acquire skills and technical competence needed for successful performance and career development.[52]

Change   The second criticism is that bureaucratic characteristics act as a barrier to performance. The world is changing rapidly, and bureaucracies are unable to keep up. Bureaucratic characteristics promote rigidity, lack of response, and poor adaptation.[53]

Again, there is merit to this argument, especially in the case of rapidly changing environments. The defense of bureaucracy is that it provides uniformity and predictability of behavior within the organization. Sometimes innovation may be slow, but in return the organization gains efficient and reliable performance. In addition, the security and tenure associated with bureaucracy may encourage some risk-taking.[54] Bureaucracy is best suited to stable and moderately changing environments.

Management   Large bureaucracies seem unmanageable. They are incredibly complex. No single person can comprehend them. One department may not know what other departments are doing. Coordination and control from a central source are difficult. Top managers must rely on staff experts and support personnel who themselves may not comprehend more than a small piece of the total system.[55]

Proponents of bureaucracy argue that the complexity of the system, far from being a disadvantage, is the true strength of bureaucracy. Individuals have limited cognitive ability. The division of labor in organizations enables bureaucracies to achieve outcomes far beyond the comprehension and ability of individual managers.[56] Moreover, bureaucratic characteristics hold the system together. Rules, hierarchy of authority, and division of labor are mechanisms that enable managers to coordinate and control the entire system.

WHEN TO BE NONBUREAUCRATIC

The discussion of pros and cons indicates that bureaucratic characteristics have both advantages and disadvantages. The lesson is that bureaucracy should be used in the right situation and in the correct amount. Too little bureaucracy will provide insufficient coordination and control. Too much bureaucracy will stifle employees and inhibit change. Thus performance is not automatically increased by becoming more bureaucratic. Situations in which managers should consciously try to minimize bureaucracy include: when organizations are small, when employees are highly professional, when the environment is unstable, and when the technology is nonroutine.

Small Size   The theme throughout this chapter has been that bureaucratic characteristics are associated with large size. Small organizations should be nonbureaucratic. Organizations in the early stages of development should be informal and have minimum rules and paperwork. Managers can control the organization through personal supervision and face-to-face interaction with employees. Adding bureaucracy would waste employees' time. As Child's

EXHIBIT 5.8. Criticism and Defense of Bureaucracy.

Criticism	Defense
Employee Satisfaction	
Rules stifle spontaneity and restrict freedom. Rules reduce discretion.	Rules reduce uncertainty and capriciousness, and protect employees. Absence of rules causes more problems than too many rules.
Small jobs do not challenge people, and alienation results.	Specialization often enables in-depth skill acquisition and opportunity for professionalism.
Change	
Bureaucracy causes rigidity, slow response, and lack of innovation.	Bureaucracy guarantees uniform behavior and responses. Security and tenure encourage risk-taking.
Management	
Bureaucracies are too complex. No one can comprehend them.	Strength of bureaucracy is that it overcomes cognitive limits of individuals. Can perform tasks far too complex for individuals.
Control and coordination of system is difficult.	Bureaucratic structure (rules, hierarchy of authority, etc.) provides control and coordination.

study of the relationship between size and performance indicated, small organizations were more effective when they were less bureaucratic.

Professional Employees   Professionalization was defined in chapter 1 as the length of formal training and experience of employees. Through extensive training, professionals are socialized toward high standards of performance. They have extensive knowledge and are able to work without close supervision or extensive rules and regulations. In recent years, large numbers of young professionals have joined organizations. It is common to see departments of attorneys, researchers, or doctors at General Motors, K-Mart, and other organizations.

The mixing of professionals and bureaucracy causes a conflict because professionals desire freedom from bureaucratic rules and authority. Studies of professionals show that formalization and professionalization do the same thing—organize and regularize behavior of the members of the organization.[57] The experience, training, and socialization of professionals act as a substitute for bureaucracy. Professionals respond better in departments that have fewer rules and regulations. A research and development group, for instance, should have fewer hierarchical levels, fewer rules, and a more collegial atmosphere than other departments in the organization. By debureaucratizing professional departments, the needs of professionals can be met while maintaining the advantage of bureaucratic structure for the overall organization. When the entire organization is made up of professionals, such as in a consulting firm or a medical practice, managers should consciously downplay bureaucratic characteristics.

Unstable Environment   The discussion of external environments in chapter 2 indicated that the rate of environmental change influenced internal organization characteristics. Under conditions of rapid change, organizations are more organic. When the organization must be free flowing and flexible, extensive bureaucracy is inappropriate. When environments are more stable, the efficiencies of bureaucratic structure can be realized, as at companies like McDonald's and United Parcel Service. When an organization must change frequently and rapidly, the absence of bureaucracy will promote better performance.

Nonroutine Technology   The discussion of technology in the previous chapter indicated that certain technologies are characterized by complexity and unpredictability. Only routine, simple technologies work best under a highly bureaucratic structure. In research organizations where the underlying technology is poorly understood and constantly changing, fewer bureaucratic procedures are appropriate. In a strategic planning department, for example, employees must cope with ill-defined issues, and need the free flow of face-to-face information and less hierarchical control.

The value of bureaucratic structure, then, is that it be applied in the correct situation and in the correct amount. When organizations are large, when the environment is stable, when technology is routine, or when employees are not professional, bureaucratic structure provides a powerful means of coordination and control. In the following case, the absence of bureaucracy caused a terrible problem, and increasing bureaucratic characteristics provided stabilization and control for a runaway organization.

IN PRACTICE 5.6
Human Resources Administration

In late 1971, New York City's welfare operation was totally out of control and heading for sure fiscal disaster. In October there were 1,255,000 individuals receiving a total of about $1.3 billion in welfare assistance and another $1.2 billion in medical assistance; six out of every seven applicants were accepted. Quality control studies revealed that one-third of all recipients were receiving the wrong amount of money and 15% were probably ineligible for any assistance. Approximately $150 million in taxpayer funds was being misappropriated through fraud, error, and mismanagement. Welfare rolls were climbing at the disastrous rate of 10,000 persons a month; costs were increasing at the rate of $120 million per year.

Field operations were in a state of absolute and perpetual chaos. Welfare centers closed their doors routinely at 10:00 or 11:00 o'clock in the morning, unable to handle the crush of desperate recipients. Acts of violence against welfare workers were commonplace, and police measures to protect them proved inadequate. Each of the city's forty-four welfare centers had a unique layout with a different client flow; each seemed equally senseless. Over 165,000 critical transactions were backlogged, including $27 million in cases that were supposed to have been closed. Employee productivity was below 40%.

The application procedures and processing system could best be described as irrational, negligent, and chaotic. A person merely had to sign a name to an application form to receive welfare, then be recertified annually by signing a statement that nothing had changed. Over $8 million was lost in duplicate check frauds—when recipients cashed their checks, fraudulently claimed to have lost them, and then received replacements in addition.

Management was virtually nonexistent. Over one-third of the employees exceeded their allotted lateness limit, at a cost of $1.3 million a year to the city. The average employee took eleven and one-half of his twelve days of sick leave, with disproportionate concentrations around holidays and weekends. Absenteeism cost the city another $7.5 million per year. Although misconduct was prevalent, the agency terminated only nineteen employees for flagrant abuses.

On staff, there were no industrial engineers, less than twenty professional systems analysts, and few professional managers. In short, the system was out of control and the existing organization lacked the capability to bring it back in check.

In late 1971, faced with the appropriate political and fiscal climate and a consultant's in-depth report on welfare operations, Mayor Lindsay resolved to overhaul the welfare system and bring the caseload under control. To accomplish this, the mayor brought in a new management team, authorized the expenditure of $10 million a year for professional staff and computer support, and gave the effort full political backing. . . .

The project management group was the pivotal unit in the overhaul strategy. . . .

At the end of the first year, the project management staff had successfully identified and documented the system's problems, publicized "horror stories," and made appropriate recommendations. Many new systems had been implemented, special operations like "photo ID" had been completed, a comprehensive overhaul plan had been scheduled, and certain line managers had been "spun off" to run new programs.

At the end of eighteen months, the following major results had been obtained:

- The $5.5 million duplicate-check problem was solved by referring over 1,900 cases to the District Attorney for prosecution and by recouping funds from the fraudulent individuals.
- Backlogs in the processing of cases were reduced from 165,000 to 50,000, employee productivity increased by 16%. At welfare centers, the lines of waiting clients disappeared and directors regained control of their centers.

The bottom-line result of the overhaul has been a dramatic reversal in welfare expenditures. Whereas in 1971 the welfare rolls were growing at the rate of 10,000 persons a month, in 1972 this growth was arrested; the rolls remained fixed at 1,275,000 persons. In November of that year, the rolls began to decline steadily at an average rate of about 9,000 persons per month. This trend should continue through the end of 1973. The bottom line of the overall effort is a $230 million annual cost turnaround for the City of New York.[58]

The initial design of the Human Resources Administration was all wrong. It was not sufficiently bureaucratized. The organization was large, the technology was routine, and the environment was stable. Welfare employees were not highly professional. As the organization adopted specialized staff groups, and developed new rules, systems, and procedures, managers were able to gain control over what had been a monster. The Human Resources Administration is now efficient and providing better service to recipients.

SUMMARY AND INTERPRETATION

The material covered in this chapter contains several important ideas about organizations. One of the most important is that Weber's model of bureaucracy has been found to make sense. Bureaucratic characteristics such as rules, division of labor, written records, hierarchy of authority, and impersonal procedures become important as organizations grow large and complex. Bureaucracy is a logical form of organizing that lets firms use resources efficiently. The need for greater bureaucracy in large organizations means that an informal personal climate cannot be maintained as size increases.

Parkinson's notion that administrators build empires is not found in the majority of organizations. Greater support is required from clerical, maintenance, and other technical staff specialists in large organizations. This is a logical outcome of employee specialization and the division of labor. By dividing up tasks, each subgroup can become more efficient.

Organizations evolve through distinct stages as they grow and mature. Organization structure, internal systems, and management issues are different for each stage of development. Growth causes many stresses and strains. There are crises and revolutions along the way toward large size. The same is true for decline. The crises for management are intense.[59] We don't yet know very much about decline, but bureaucratic characteristics do not seem to reverse themselves toward less bureaucracy when organizations get smaller. Recentralization of authority, redeployment of resources, conflict, and cutbacks are important issues in the declining organization.

Finally, bureaucracy has advantages, but it also has shortcomings. The dilemma of how much bureaucracy to have has not been completely resolved. Bureaucracy is not appropriate in small, professional, or rapidly changing organizations. From the point of view of management, some bureaucratic characteristics are essential if the organization is to be efficient as it grows larger. In the final analysis, bureaucracy is and will continue to be the dominant form of organization in industrial societies. As a tool of humankind, bureaucratic structures have enabled us to master complex tasks and produce a volume of goods and services never before equaled in our history. In actual use, however, bureaucracies do not live up to the ideal expectations of Weber. Paperwork, routine jobs, and silly rules sometimes get to all of us. But for the most large organizations, bureaucracy seems to be the best bet. Bureaucracy may get even better as researchers and managers find ways to make them more satisfying for employees and more useful to clients while maintaining the efficiencies that bureaucratic structures provide.[60]

KEY CONCEPTS

bureaucracy
charismatic authority
collectivity stage
complexity
bureaucracy and performance
decentralization
decline
elaboration stage
entrepreneurial stage
formalization

formalization stage
life cycle
managing decline
Parkinson's law
personnel configuration
rational-legal authority
reasons for growth
traditional authority
when to be nonbureaucratic

DISCUSSION QUESTIONS

1. Describe the three bases of authority identified by Weber. Is it possible for each of these types of authority to function within departments in an organization?

2. What are the negative consequences of bureaucracy for employees? From society's point of view, is the efficiency and productivity of large organizations sufficiently important that we can sacrifice some employee satisfaction?

3. How would you define size? What problems can you identify with using number of employees as a measure of size?

4. The manager of a medium-sized manufacturing plant once said, "We can't compete on price with the small organizations because they have lower overhead costs." Based upon the discussion in this chapter, would you agree or disagree with that manager? Why?

5. Why do large organizations tend to be more formalized?

6. If you were the manager of a department of college professors, how might you structure the department differently than if you were managing a department of bookkeepers? Why?

7. Assume you are the manager of an organization that is experiencing decline. What problems should you be prepared to cope with?

8. Apply the concept of life cycle to an organization with which you are familiar, such as a university, *Playboy* Enterprises, or a local business. What stage is the organization now in? How did the organization handle or pass through its life cycle crises?

9. Discuss the advantages and disadvantages of rules and regulations.

10. Should a "no-growth" philosophy of management be taught in business schools? Is a no-growth philosophy more realistic for today's economic conditions?

GUIDES TO ACTION

As an organization designer:

1. Introduce greater bureaucratization to an organization as it increases in size. As it becomes necessary, add more rules and regulations, greater written

documentation, increased job specialization, a longer chain of command, greater impersonality, the criterion of technical competence in hiring and promotion, the subdivision of the organization into a larger number of departments, and decentralization. Increase the efficiency of a large organization by increasing the bureaucratic dimensions of structure as the organization grows.

2. With the growth of organization, decrease the percentage of top administrators and increase the percentage of support personnel. Large support ratios do not necessarily reflect inefficiency, but reflect the division of labor and greater organizational need for written communication, documentation, and technical support.

3. Do not increase bureaucracy when the organization is small, when employees are highly professional, or when the environment is rapidly changing, or when the technology is complex and nonroutine.

4. Grow when possible. With growth you can provide opportunities for employee advancement and greater profitability and effectiveness. Apply new management systems and structural configurations at each stage of the organization's development. Interpret the needs of the organization and respond with the management and internal systems that will carry the organization through to the next stage of development.

5. When an organization is in decline, recentralize authority, mediate intense conflicts among departments that do not want to give up resources, make difficult decisions about reductions in people and products/services, and promote innovations and changes that can effectively use limited resources and reduce the negative consequences of decline.

Consider these Guides when analyzing the following case and when answering the questions listed after the case.

CASE FOR ANALYSIS

HOUSTON OIL AND MINERALS CORP.*

PART I

Houston Oil and Minerals Corp. is an independent oil company. Oil exploration and production are its primary businesses. Like other small independent oil companies, HOM has kept overhead lower than the majors, and can move quickly when an opportunity presents itself.

Houston Oil's chairman and president, Joseph C. Walter, Jr., has very firm ideas about organization structure. He wants to maintain a "swashbuckling" approach to exploration. This means a minimum of bosses and a maximum of autonomy for geologists exploring in the field. "As far as possible I try to run the place with no bosses at all." Of course, every organization has to have bosses, and along with five other managers, Walter supervises the work of fifty-three geologists and geophysicists. The small number of bosses partly

* This case was based on "Houston Oil's Freehand Approach to Growth," *Business Week,* June 13, 1977, pp. 97–99; Todd A. Cohen, "We grew so big so fast . . ." *Forbes,* December 8, 1980, pp. 90–92; Alexander Stuart, "Why an Oil-Patch Legend Joined Tenneco," *Fortune,* January 12, 1981, pp. 48–52; George Getschow, "Loss of Expert Talent Impedes Oil Finding by New Tenneco Unit," *Wall Street Journal,* February 9, 1982, pp. 1, 23.

explains the low overhead. Houston Oil spends an average of $2.50 to find a barrel of oil, compared to $5 for the industry as a whole.

The company increased its growth to 500 employees in 1977, and continued to add new ones. The development budget is similar to the budgets of many major oil companies, where several layers of management are involved. These layers of management are not present in Houston Oil. Avoiding layers of management is difficult, but Walter says, "The only way I know how to do it is to push decision-making down as far as it can go." This gives geologists almost complete autonomy over how to spend the budgeted resources.

Formal committees are avoided at Houston Oil. Ad hoc task forces are used to solve problems that involve more than one department. The company does have a weekly meeting of officers, but their goal is to suppress formalized procedures in order to retain flexibility.

Questions

1. How would you rate (high or low) the formalization, centralization, administration ratio, and professionalism at Houston Oil and Minerals Corp.?

2. Will the company be able to maintain its informality as it grows larger? Is the amount of bureaucracy appropriate to the level of professionalism? Explain.

3. Predict whether the informal "swashbuckling" approach to management will lead to successful performance.

PART II

Houston Oil and Minerals Corp. developed an astonishing performance record. Houston Oil's geologists seemed to be able to pick successful drilling sites at will. Earnings increased eight-fold during a period (1970–1976) in which domestic oil and gas production fell 15%. From 1973 to 1980, the price of its stock jumped almost 5,000%. Revenues spurted from $1.5 million in 1970 to over $400 million in 1980.

One reason for this success was the absence of bureaucracy. The freewheeling approach to structure enabled Houston Oil to assemble an excellent team of exploration geologists (called explorationists in the trade). The head of exploration for another oil company said, "They manage to attract some of the more inventive geologists who feel straight-jacketed in the environment of a large corporation. It's the opposite extreme in other independents. The top guy calls all of the shots. Joe [Walter] turns his geologists loose."

Houston Oil in just a few years became an oil-patch legend. Houston Oil grew so big, so fast, that it also became overextended financially. Huge Tenneco Corp. was searching for ways to increase its reserves and new discoveries. Late in1980, Tenneco purchased Houston Oil. Tenneco can provide the financial resources for increased oil exploration around the world. Houston Oil and Minerals Corp., the oil-patch legend, is now part of a giant corporation.

Questions

1. Will Houston Oil be able to maintain its nonbureaucratic structure as part of a giant corporation?

2. Do you think Houston Oil would be better off with some of the efficiencies of bureaucratic structure? Discuss.

3. Will the professional explorationists be happy under the umbrella of a large corporation? Predict whether they will stay or leave the company.

PART III

Within a few months after the merger, 34% of Houston Oil's management and 25% of its explorationists quit. Within a year, nearly all the managers and over half its explorationists were gone. People are still leaving.

Tenneco anticipated a problem and offered lucrative salary increases and other financial inducements to Houston Oil's personnel. But it just didn't work. The professionals were entrepreneurial types who could not stand the constraints of a rigid bureaucracy. Tenneco responded by proposing a smaller corporate division with greater autonomy. But Tenneco still had a long chain of command, and emphasized things like budgeting and forecasting. It also generated an avalanche of paperwork, which Houston Oil staffers couldn't tolerate. Tenneco couldn't treat the Houston Oil division too differently from other divisions, or it would have problems of equity across the entire corporation. Some standardization was essential.

One staff member complained that it took eight weeks to get a work order approved to move a telephone. Previously, he could spend $50,000 on his own. Now he doesn't have the authority to approve a box of pencils.

The hemorrhaging of Houston Oil's staff is causing problems for Tenneco. Tenneco picked up 1.4 million acres of unexplored land, but the people who did the preliminary evaluation of the property are gone. Tenneco has to start from scratch in reevaluating the acreage—a slow process. Oil and gas leases on about 60,000 acres are beginning to expire. Tenneco is either going to have to farm out leases to other oil companies or give them up. Without professional staff, they can't evaluate and drill on time.[61]

Questions

1. How can the dramatic turnaround at Houston Oil be explained? Would it ever be possible to mix independent-minded explorationists with an organizational bureaucracy? Explain.

2. What would you recommend to large corporations like Tenneco, Mobil, Getty Oil, and Standard Oil to help them retain their first-rate exploration professionals?

3. Was the Houston Oil experience similar in any way to life cycle changes? Explain.

NOTES

1. Stephanie Salter, "Life in the Slow Lane at the DMV," *The San Francisco Examiner,* September 5, 1982. Copyright © 1982 *The San Francisco Examiner.* Used with permission.

2. Reinhard Bendix, "Bureaucracy," *International Encyclopedia of the Social Sciences* (New York: The Free Press, 1977); Charles Perrow, *Complex Organizations: A Critical Essay* (Glenview, IL: Scott, Foresman, 1979), p. 4.

3. Perrow, *Complex Organizations,* ch. 1.

4. Alfred Chandler, *Strategy and Structure: Chapters in the History of the American Industrial Enterprise* (Cambridge, MA: MIT Press, 1962), p. 21.

5. Max Weber, *The Theory of Social and Economic Organizations,* translated by A. M. Henderson and T. Parsons (New York: Free Press, 1947).

6. Ibid., p. 330.

7. Ibid.

8. Ibid., p. 331.

9. Ibid.

10. Ibid.

11. Ibid., p. 332.

12. Ibid.

13. Ibid., pp. 328–340.

14. A. Lucas, "As American as McDonald's Hamburger on the Fourth of July," *New York Times Magazine,* July 4, 1971; Melinda Culver, Lisa Mewis, and John Vaughn, "McDonald's Case Study," unpublished manuscript, Texas A&M University, 1981.

15. John R. Kimberly, "Organizational Size and the Structuralist Perspective: A Review, Critique, and Proposal," *Administrative Science Quarterly* (1976):571–597; Richard L. Daft and Selwyn W. Becker, "Managerial, Institutional, and Technical Influences on Administration: A Longitudinal Analysis," *Social Forces* 59 (1980):392–413.

16. Cheng-Kuang Hsu, Robert M. Marsh, and Hiroshi Mannari, "An Examination of the Determinants of Organizational Structure," *American Journal of Sociology,* 88 (1983):975–996; Guy Geeraerts, "The Effect of Ownership on the Organization Structure in Small Firms," *Administrative Science Quarterly,* 29 (1984):232–237; Bernard Reimann, "On the Dimensions of Bureaucratic Structure: An Empirical Reappraisal," *Administrative Science Quarterly* 18 (1973):462–476; Richard H. Hall, "The Concept of Bureaucracy: An Empirical Assessment," *American Journal of Sociology* 69 (1963): 32–40; William A. Rushing, "Organizational Rules and Surveillance: A Proposition in Comparative Organizational Analysis" *Administrative Science Quarterly* 10 (1966): 423–443.

17. Joanne S. Lublin, "Employers Act to Curb Sex Harassing on Job; Lawsuits, Fines Feared," *Wall Street Journal,* April 24, 1981, p. 1; "Sexual Harassment Lands Companies in Court," *Business Week,* October 1, 1979, pp. 120–122.

18. Jerald Hage and Michael Aiken, "Relationship of Centralization to Other Structural Properties," *Administrative Science Quarterly* 12 (1967):72–91.

19. Guy Geeraerts, "The Effect of Ownership on the Organization Structure in Small Firms"; Hsu, Marsh, and Mannari, "An Examination of the Determinants of Organizational Structure"; Robert Dewar and Jerald Hage, "Size, Technology, Complexity, and Structural Differentiation: Toward a Theoretical Synthesis," *Administrative Science Quarterly* 23 (1978):111–136.

20. Richard L. Daft and Patricia J. Bradshaw, "The Process of Horizontal Differentiation: Two Models," *Administrative Science Quarterly* 25 (1980):441–456.

21. Peter M. Blau, *The Organization of Academic Work* (New York: Wiley Interscience, 1973).

22. Kathy Goode, Betty Hahn, and Cindy Seibert, "United Parcel Service: The Brown Giant," unpublished manuscript, Texas A&M University, 1981; "Behind the UPS Mystique: Puritanism Activity," *Business Week,* June 6, 1983, pp. 66–73.

23. Jeffrey D. Ford and John W. Slocum, Jr., "Size, Technology, Environment and the Structure of Organizations," *Academy of Management Review* 2 (1977):561–575; John D. Kasarda, "The Structural Implications of Social System Size: A Three-Level Analysis," *American Sociological Review* 39 (1974):19–28.

24. Spyros K. Lioukas and Demitris A. Xerokostas, "Size and Administrative Intensity in Organizational Divisions," *Management Science,* 28 (1982):854–868; Peter M. Blau, "Interdependence and Hierarchy in Organizations," *Social Science Research* 1 (1972): 1–24; Peter M. Blau and R. A. Schoenherr, *The Structure of Organizations* (New York: Basic Books, 1971); A. Hawley, W. Boland, and M. Boland, "Population Size and Administration in Institutions of Higher Education," *American Sociological Review* 30 (1965):252–255; Richard L. Daft, "System Influence on Organization Decision-Making: The Case of Resource Allocation," *Academy of Management Journal* 21 (1978): 6–22; B. P. Indik, "The Relationship Between Organization Size and the Supervisory Ratio," *Administrative Science Quarterly* 9 (1964):301–312.

25. T. F. James, "The Administrative Component in Complex Organizations," *The Sociological Quarterly* 13 (1972):533–539; Daft, "System Influence on Organizational

Decision-Making"; E. A. Holdaway and E. A. Blowers, "Administrative Ratios and Organization Size: A Longitudinal Examination," *American Sociological Review* 36 (1971):278–286; John Child, "Parkinson's Progress: Accounting for the Number of Specialists in Organizations," *Administrative Science Quarterly* 18 (1973):328–348.

26. Child, "Parkinson's Progress"; Daft, "System Influence on Resource Allocation."

27. Richard L. Daft and Selwyn Becker, "School District Size and the Deployment of Personnel Resources," *The Alberta Journal of Educational Research* 24 (1978): 173–187.

28. Peter M. Blau, "A Formal Theory of Differentiation in Organizations," *American Sociological Review* 35 (1970):201–218.

29. Adapted from Steve Weiner and Frank E. James, "Sears, A Powerhouse in Many Fields Now, Looks into New Ones," *Wall Street Journal,* February 10, 1984, pp. 1–10; "Can Sears Come Back," *Dun's Review,* February 1979, pp. 68–70; "How Sears Became a High Cost Operator," *Business Week,* February 16, 1981, pp. 52–57; Jeremy Main, "K-Mart's Plan to Be Born Again," *Fortune,* September 21, 1981, pp. 78–85.

30. William H. Starbuck, "Organizational Growth and Development," in James G. March, ed., *Handbook of Organizations* (New York: Rand McNally, 1965), pp. 451–522.

31. Ann M. Morrison, "A Big Baker That Won't Live By Bread Alone," *Fortune,* September 7, 1981, pp. 70–76.

32. Starbuck, "Organizational Growth and Development"; Child, *Organizations,* ch. 7.

33. Starbuck, ibid.; John Child and Alfred Keiser, "Development of Organizations Over Time," in Paul C. Nystrom and William H. Starbuck, eds., *Handbook of Organizational Design,* vol. 1 (New York: Oxford University Press, 1981), pp. 28–64.

34. W. H. Newman and J. P. Logan, *Management of Expanding Enterprises* (Columbia: Columbia University Press, 1955); Starbuck, "Organizational Growth and Development."

35. John R. Kimberly, Robert H. Miles, and associates, *The Organizational Life Cycle* (San Francisco, CA: Jossey-Bass, 1980); Ichak Adices, "Organizational Passages—Diagnosing and Treating Lifecycle Problems of Organizations," *Organizational Dynamics* (Summer 1979):3–25.

36. Larry E. Greiner, "Evolution and Revolution as Organizations Grow," *Harvard Business Review* 50 (July-August, 1972):37–46; Robert E. Quinn and Kim Cameron, "Organizational Life Cycles and Shifting Criteria of Effectiveness: Some Preliminary Evidence," *Management Science,* 29 (1983):33–51.

37. David A Whetten, "Sources, Responses, and Effects of Organizational Decline," in John R. Kimberly and Robert H. Miles, eds., *The Organizational Life Cycle* (San Francisco: Jossey-Bass, 1980), pp. 342–374.

38. From David DeLong, "They All Said Bill Sauey Couldn't Let Go," *Inc.,* May 1981, pp. 89–91. With special permission of author David DeLong.

39. David A. Whetten, "Sources, Responses, and Effects of Organizational Decline," and "Organizational Decline: A Neglected Topic in Organizational Science," *Academy of Management Review* 5 (1980):577–588.

40. Whetten, "Sources, Responses, and Effects of Organizational Decline," p. 345.

41. Ibid.; Kim Cameron and Raymond Zammuto, "Matching Managerial Strategies to Conditions of Decline," *Human Resource Management,* 22 (1983):359–375.

42. Charles H. Levine, Irene S. Rubin, and George G. Wolohojian, "Managing Organizational Retrenchment," *Administration & Society,* 14 (1982):101–136.

43. Whetten, "Sources, Responses, and Effects of Organizational Decline."

44. Kathryn Rudie Harrigan, "Strategy Formulation in Declining Industries," *Academy of Management Review* 5 (1980):599–604.

45. C. H. Levine, "Organizational Decline and Cut Back Management," *Public Administration Review* 38 (1970):316–325.

46. Whetten, "Sources, Responses, and Effects of Organizational Decline."

47. Brooks Jackson, "Janitors Work Days and Cops Ride Bikes to Save Tax Dollars," *Wall Street Journal,* May 1, 1981.

48. Roger Ricklefs, "Some Colleges Drop Whole Departments to Meet Fiscal Crunch," *The Wall Street Journal,* September 11, 1981, p. 1, 17; "A New Target: Reducing Staff and Levels," *Business Week,* December 21, 1981, pp. 69–73; Carol Hymowitz, "Fear of Unemployment Takes Emotional Toll at White-Collar Levels," *The Wall Street Journal,* July 19, 1982, pp. 1, 10.

49. John Child, *Organizations* (New York: Harper and Row, 1977), ch. 7.

50. Chris Argyris, *Personality and Organizations* (New York: Harper, 1956); Warren G. Bennis, *Changing Organizations* (New York: McGraw-Hill, 1966).

51. Perrow, *Complex Organizations,* ch. 1.

52. Peter M. Blau, *The Dynamics of Bureaucracy* (Chicago: University of Chicago Press, 1973).

53. Victor Thompson, "Bureaucracy and Innovation," *Administrative Science Quarterly* 10 (1965):1–20.

54. Blau, *Dynamics of Bureaucracy.*

55. Dwayne S. Elgin and Robert A. Bushnell, "The Limits to Complexity: Are Bureaucracies Becoming Unmanageable?" *The Futurist,* December, 1977, pp. 337–349.

56. James March and Herbert Simon, *Organizations* (New York: Wiley, 1958), ch. 1.

57. Richard H. Hall, *Organizations: Structure and Process* (Englewood Cliffs, NJ: Prentice-Hall, 1977), p. 170.

58. Adapted from Kenneth L. Harris, "Organizing to Overhaul a Mess." Copyright © 1975 by the Regents of the University of California. Reprinted from *California Management Review,* vol. XVII, no. 3, pp. 40–49, by permission of the Regents.

59. Whetten, "Sources, Responses, and Effects of Organizational Decline"; Jeffrey D. Ford, "The Occurrence of Structural Hysteresis in Declining Organizations," *Academy of Management Review* 5 (1980):589–598.

60. "Special Report: The New Industrial Relations," *Business Week,* May 11, 1981, pp. 85–98; Larry L. Cummings and Chris J. Berger, "Organization Structure: How Does It Influence Attitudes and Performance?" *Organizational Dynamics,* Autumn 1976, pp. 34–39.

Functional, Product, and Matrix Structures

THOMAS NATIONAL GROUP

When I began the Thomas National Group, in 1968, I was determined to delegate authority. So I set up a management structure under which our managers reported to our vice-presidents, and our vice-presidents reported to an executive vice-president. The executive vice-president reported to the president, and the president then reported to me, the chairman.

All I had to do was sit back in my ivory tower and feel like a monarch whose kingdom is being run by others.

There's a right way and a wrong way to delegate authority, and in my company the vertical chain of command was definitely the wrong way. For the first seven years of our company's growth, the vertical system worked pretty well. Between 1968 and 1975 growth was slow. It took us that long to reach $2.8 million in sales. But the advent of minicomputers made the services of data processing bureaus less necessary, and by the mid-'70s we began looking for a field in which to specialize. We developed a software program to help administer profit-sharing/thrift plans and another for processing of medical and dental claims.

The first of these, ImpleFacts, took off like a rocket. Eli Lilly, Polaroid, Xerox, Chemical Bank, and Colgate-Palmolive were among our first customers. Our sales have grown dramatically; they were over $8 million in the year that ended in February 1981.

But along with the growth came problems, and by the time our first program was ready for the market back in 1975, our people were overworked, cash flow was a headache, turnover was too high, and about 10% of our orders were being delayed.

The vertical management structure didn't allow us to deal efficiently with those problems. It didn't grant the vice-presidents enough authority or responsibility for their departments' successes or failures. No one was responsible for finding out what was causing delays, cash problems, or high turnover. And under the strict chain of command, I was inaccessible to everyone but the president, so I couldn't find out what was causing the problems, either.

It took me several years to create the horizontal management structure that I finally implemented in mid-1979. . . .

Under our new structure, eight vice-presidents . . . report directly to me. Job descriptions were completely rewritten to maximize each vice-president's talents. The vice-presidents of systems and operations were given full responsibility for profit and loss and for daily operations including scheduling. Each of them knows that when there's a delay, I'll be in his or her office asking why.

The problems that led me to restructure the company have also been taken care of. Before we changed, about 10% of our orders were delayed. Since mid-1979, less than 1% are delayed—and never for long. They're rarely delayed because everything's too visible. . . . Our accounts receivable have been reduced from an average of fifty-six days outstanding to an average of forty-three days.[1]

Thomas Barrea, chairman of the Thomas National Group, sensed things weren't working correctly with what he called the vertical structure. The vertical structure provided a clear chain of command, but information didn't always get to the top and responsibility for performance was not always clear. A horizontal structure was created by putting each vice-president in charge of a specific type of data processing service, and giving the vice-presidents full responsibility for scheduling, marketing, programming, and overall performance. The new structure still uses vertical lines of authority, but encourages horizontal communication at lower levels to improve responsiveness and performance.

The balance between vertical control and horizontal coordination is a dilemma that most organizations face at one time or another. Managers may realize things aren't going very well, so they reorganize. The appropriate structure is found through a process of trial and error, and reorganization may be needed every few years as the organization's situation changes.

Purpose of This Chapter

The general concept of organization structure has been discussed in previous chapters. Structural characteristics include such things as the number of departments in an organization, span of control, and the extent to which the organization is formalized and centralized. The purpose of this chapter is to consolidate the ideas about structure to show how structure appears on the organization chart. This chapter focuses on the design of the overall organization to achieve the correct amount of vertical control along with horizontal devices to coordinate organizational departments.

The star in Exhibit 6.1 illustrates that structure is related to environment, goals, technology, and size, each of which was discussed in a previous chapter. Environment can be stable or unstable, certain or uncertain. Goals can reflect management's desire for internal efficiency, or for adaptation to external markets. Technologies can be routine or nonroutine, and the interdependence among departments may be high or low. Size may be large or small. Each of these factors is associated with the correct structural design. Environment, technology, goals, and size may also influence one another, as illustrated by the connecting lines in Exhibit 6.1. As each form of structure is discussed, the appropriate situation with respect to environment, goals, technology, and size will be identified.

The material on structure is presented in the following sequence. First, structure is defined, and the causes of structure are reviewed. Second, designing the organization chart to identify tasks and reporting relationships is covered. Third, after the basic concept of an organization chart is understood, vertical and horizontal linkages are explored. Organizations use a variety of linking mechanisms to coordinate each part of the organization into a coherent whole. Fourth, strategies for grouping organizational activities into functional, product, and hybrid structures will be discussed. Finally, the matrix, which is a unique structure designed to meet special circumstances, will be analyzed. By the end of this chapter, students will understand the type of problem Thomas Barrea faced with his data-processing organization, and the reasons why he changed structure to correct it.

DEFINITION OF STRUCTURE

Organization structure is reflected in the organization chart. The organization chart is the visible representation for a whole set of underlying activities and

EXHIBIT 6.1. Organization Contextual Variables That Influence Structure.

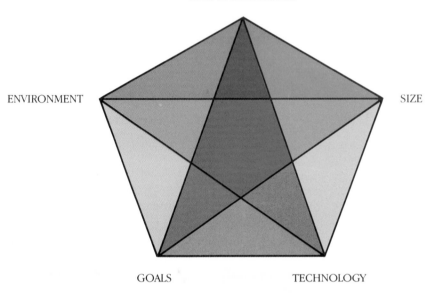

Source: Adapted from Jay R. Galbraith, *Organization Design* (Reading, MA: Addison-Wesley, 1977), ch. 1.

processes in an organization. The four key components in the definition of organization structure are:

1. Organization structure describes the allocation of tasks and responsibilities to individuals and departments throughout the organization.
2. Organization structure designates formal reporting relationships, including the number of levels in the hierarchy and the span of control of managers and supervisors.
3. Organization structure identifies the grouping together of individuals into departments and the grouping of departments into the total organization.
4. Organization structure includes the design of systems to ensure effective communication, coordination, and integration of effort in both vertical and horizontal directions.[2]

The first three elements of structure in the above definition are the organization's "framework."[3] They are the static elements of structure that are visible on the organization chart. The fourth element pertains to the pattern of "interactions" among organizational employees. These systems represent the dynamic characteristics of structure. An ideal organization structure not only draws the framework of hierarchical relationships, but encourages employees to interact in a way that provides information and coordination where and when it is needed. The framework or static characteristic of structure often defines vertical relationships. The interaction or dynamic characteristic of structure often defines horizontal communications. In the next section we will briefly describe how to allocate responsibility and designate formal reporting relationships, which are framework issues. This will be followed by a discussion of mechanisms to achieve coordination across departments and hierarchical levels.

TASKS, REPORTING RELATIONSHIPS, AND GROUPING

An ideal organization chart provides employees with information about their place in the organization, their relationship to others, their tasks and responsibilities, and to whom they report. Exhibit 6.2 is the organization chart for a printing company in Southern California. Each management title is listed on the chart along with the job titles of people who report to each manager. This organization chart illustrates reporting relationships, tasks, and groupings.

Reporting Relationships The reporting relationships in the hierarchy of authority are represented by the vertical lines in Exhibit 6.2. The lines show who reports to whom and identify the responsibility domain for each manager and supervisor. In a large organization like Standard Oil, 100 or more charts would be required to identify all reporting relationships.

Task and Responsibility Allocation The organization chart for the printing company in Exhibit 6.2 provides information about tasks and responsibilities. As the organization grows, managers must specify which tasks are required to produce the organization's product or service. These tasks are the responsibility of specific individuals and departments. Job titles and lines of authority indicate responsibility for task performance. Tasks and responsibilities are also defined in job descriptions, policy manuals, or rules and procedures.

Grouping Employees in the printing company are grouped together by function, which means that employees who do similar tasks are grouped together and report to a common supervisor. Each employee involved in the making of printing plates reports to the platemaking supervisor. Each production supervisor reports to the vice-president and general manager who is in charge of all printing activities. The administrative functions of bookkeeping, typing, and purchasing all report to the office manager.

Employees can be grouped in ways other than by function. Sometimes employees from several departments will be grouped together under a common supervisor to work on a specific project or product. Employees from separate departments may also be grouped together to serve a single geographic area or customer. The functional grouping as illustrated in Exhibit 6.2 is common, and can usually be observed at some level in most organizations.

Grouping is important because employees within a defined group have a common supervisor, share common resources, are jointly responsible for performance, and tend to identify and collaborate with one another.[4] Grouping thus ensures unity of effort within groups. The negative outcome is that coordination is difficult across groups. Departmental boundaries inhibit communication. Each major group may pursue different goals and performance criteria, and may be reluctant to coordinate activities. Thus the grouping that an organization chooses will facilitate interactions among certain employees but reduce interactions among other employees. Organizations may include additional systems or mechanisms to facilitate desired communication and coordination across departmental boundaries.

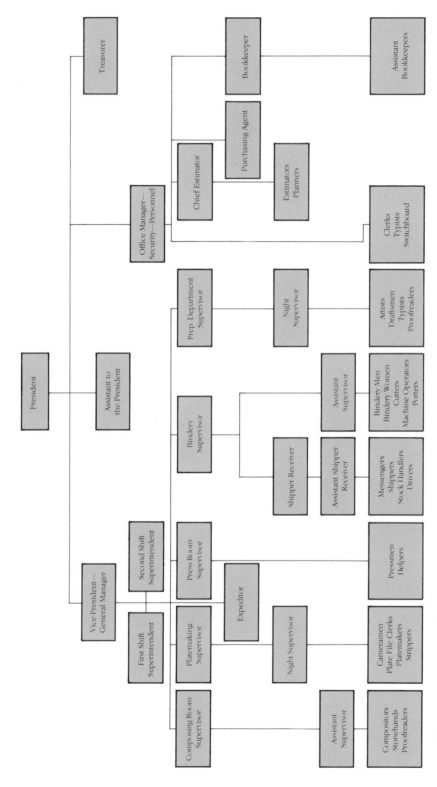

EXHIBIT 6.2. Organization Chart for a Printing Company.

Each organization develops its own system of organization charts and backup documents to allocate tasks and responsibilities, identify reporting relationships, and organize people into groups and departments. This documentation is part of the formalized paperwork of the organization, and emphasizes vertical relationships. These structural elements are often supplemented with committees, information systems, and coordinators who provide information and coordination in a horizontal direction.

The following case illustrates an organization chart and supporting documentation used to define tasks, responsibilities, and the hierarchy of authority.

IN PRACTICE 6.1

Oilfield Service Company

Oilfield Service Company is a $300-million company that markets equipment and support services for oil-drilling rigs worldwide. Oilfield Service is based in New Orleans and has about 4,000 employees. Products include drilling bits, seismic and logging equipment, valves, and drilling lubricants. As a marketing company, most goods are purchased from other suppliers. Oilfield provides engineering expertise and service at the wellhead to make sales.

The organization chart for the senior management at Oilfield Services is shown in Exhibit 6.3a. The company is large so organization charts for the areas reporting to each vice-president and general manager are developed separately. The chart in Exhibit 6.3a indicates the reporting relationships among senior management, and includes the name of each executive.

Exhibit 6.3b shows a responsibility chart developed for the Marketing and Sales Division at Oilfield Services. This chart specifies the tasks that people within each department are expected to perform. For example, marketing analysis is expected to do market evaluations, monitor and audit sales by area and affiliate, collect data on the competition, and analyze customer requirements.

Oilfield Services also provides position descriptions for each executive. An example of a position description for the Vice-President for Marketing and Sales is given in 6.3c. Responsibility charts, position descriptions, and organization charts were developed by the personnel department. Oilfield Services has a complete set of documents that specify the position in the hierarchy and task responsibilities of each employee.

VERTICAL AND HORIZONTAL STRUCTURAL LINKAGES

Once the organization charts have been developed to describe tasks, responsibilities, and reporting relationships within the organization, structural mechanisms must be designed to link together employees, departments, and hierarchical levels. The organization chart provides the framework of the organization, and additional devices provide needed interactions. **Linkage** is defined as the extent of coordination between organizational elements. Employees located at various departments and levels are physically separated;

EXHIBIT 6.3. Organization Chart and Documentation for Oilfield Services Co.

a. Organization Chart for Senior Management.

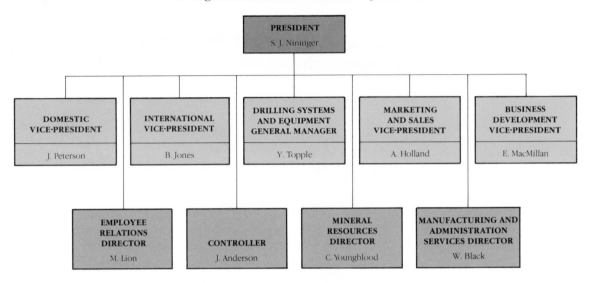

b. Departmental Responsibility Chart.

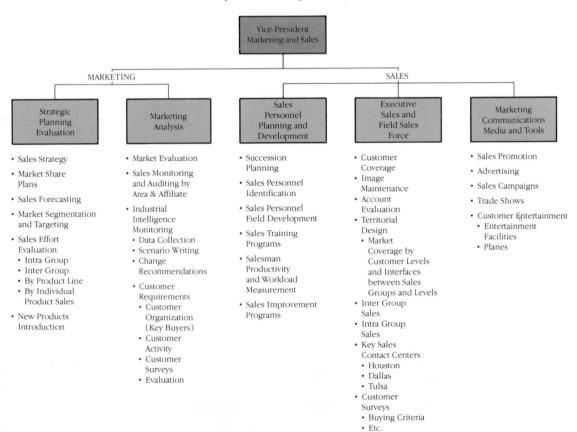

EXHIBIT 6.3 *(continued)*
c. Position Description

POSITION TITLE: Vice President Marketing and Sales
REPORTS TO: Group President
MAJOR AREAS OF RESPONSIBILITY:

Marketing Responsibility

Strategic planning and evaluation of the marketing effort.

Marketing analysis evaluation and monitoring of sales organization. Industrial intelligence, and customer requirements.

Critical sales interface between marketing and other Oilfield Service departments.

Sales Responsibilities

Sales personnel planning, development, productivity.

Executive sales and field sales force, customer coverage and territorial design. Image maintenance, account evaluation, and customer surveys.

Marketing communications, advertising, sales campaigns, trade shows, and customer entertainment.

they may not see or interact with each other on a regular basis. Yet structural linkages must be in place to ensure adequate coordination and integration of effort.

Vertical linkages are used to coordinate activities between the top and bottom of the organization. Employees at lower levels should carry out activities consistent with top-level goals. People at the top of the organization must be informed about activities and accomplishments at the lower levels. **Horizontal linkage** is used to coordinate horizontally across the organization. Without horizontal linkages, decisions and activities in the marketing department could undercut the finance or production departments. Horizontal linkage ensures that the right and left hands of the organization know what the other is doing.

The essence of linkage is control, coordination, and communication. Vertical linkage facilitates communication, but with a strong element of control. The communication is used to enable top managers to learn about and direct organizational activities. Horizontal linkage is used for coordination, but one group does not have control over another. Departments are at the similar hierarchical level and coordinate activities so that overall organization performance is enhanced.

**Vertical Linkage
Requirements**

The contextual variables in the Exhibit 6.1 star influence the amount of vertical linkage in the organization. When an organization is large and complex, the vertical hierarchy is longer and there are a larger number of departments that must be linked into the organizational whole. Environmental stability and technological routineness are also associated with greater use of vertical linkage mechanisms. Work activities are predictable, and vertical linkages provide communication and control for the organization. As uncertainty from the environment or technology increases, the use of vertical linkages in mechanisms may increase somewhat, but the dominant form of coordination will shift to horizontal coordination. Goals of internal efficiency are also associated with greater vertical linkage. During periods of resource scarcity or decline, managers closely monitor internal activities. Greater linkage enables tighter control of activities and enables changes to be coordinated up and down the hierarchy.

Vertical Linkage Devices

Organizations may use any of a variety of structural devices to achieve vertical linkage. These structural devices include hierarchical referral, rules and procedures, plans and schedules, adding positions or levels to the hierarchy, and formal management information systems.[5] When organization needs for vertical coordination and control are great, more linkage mechanisms will be used.

Hierarchy   The first vertical device is the hierarchy or chain of command. If a problem arises that employees don't know how to solve, they refer it up to the next level in the hierarchy. When a cashier in a grocery store encounters an unusual situation, the correct response is to refer it to the assistant manager. When the problem is solved, the answer is passed back down to the cashier. In hierarchical referral, the lines of the organization chart act as communication channels. Information is passed up or down the hierarchy to achieve linkage.

In a new, small organization, supervisor referral is the dominant form of vertical coordination. Whenever people have problems, they refer them to the owner/manager. As the organization becomes larger and more complex, the owner/manager may be overwhelmed with information, and yet may not know about key events because the hierarchy is overloaded. In the Thomas National Group described at the beginning of this chapter, the vertical hierarchy worked for a while, but then did not provide sufficient information to the chairman. Passing information up and down the hierarchy cannot be the sole means of vertical coordination, so other mechanisms are also used by organizations.

Rules and Procedures   The next linkage device is the use of rules and procedures. To the extent that problems and decisions are repetitious, a procedure can be established so that employees know how to respond without communicating directly with their manager. Rules and procedures standardize tasks and thus eliminate the need to process information up and down the hierarchy. Rules and procedures link upper- and lower-level employees so that many decisions can be made at lower levels. Rules and procedures enable the cashier and manager in a grocery store to be coordinated without actually communicating about every cash transaction.

Planning and Scheduling   Another device for achieving vertical linkage is planning and scheduling. The most widely used plan is the budget. By establishing carefully designed budget plans and schedules, employees at lower levels can be left on their own to perform activities within their resource allotment. Plans take into consideration the goals of top management and the needs of other departments. Scheduling enables managers to keep track of employee and departmental progress without communicating up and down the hierarchy on a day-to-day basis. If a problem occurs so that the plan or schedule will not be met, managers can then communicate by hierarchical referral to correct it.

Add Levels or Positions to Hierarchy   When many problems occur, planning and hierarchical referral may overload managers. In growing organizations or organizations experiencing high uncertainty, additional vertical linkage mechanisms may be required. One technique is to add positions to the hierarchy. In some cases, an assistant-to will be assigned to help an overloaded manager. Normally used at the top of the hierarchy where several lines of authority converge, the assistant-to acts in place of the executive and may attend meetings or establish plans in the executive's place.

As the organization grows, additional levels or positions in the direct line of authority may be added, which reduces the span of control and provides closer communication and control. One position can be subdivided into two positions, which report to the same supervisor. Responsibilities are divided between the two positions. The addition of positions provides a sufficient number of managers to handle problems and make decisions relevant to vertical responsibilities.

Vertical Information Systems   Vertical information systems are another strategy for providing vertical linkages. Vertical information systems include the periodic reports, written information, and computer-based data summaries that are distributed to managers. The purpose of information systems is to make information processing up and down the hierarchy more reliable and efficient than face-to-face communication. Vertical information systems increase the capacity to process information. Vertical information systems, for example, may reduce the need to add new positions to the hierarchy. Many corporations computerize the information system. Computerized vertical information systems summarize data and compare actual performance on a weekly or even daily basis. These periodic reports link top management to activities at lower levels.

Summary   Structural mechanisms that can be used to achieve vertical linkage are summarized in Exhibit 6.4. These structural mechanisms represent alternatives managers can use in designing an organization. Once the organization chart specifies the tasks and responsibilities for each employee and department, a means of achieving vertical integration is required. Depending upon the amount of coordination needed in the organization, several of the linkage mechanisms in Exhibit 6.4 may be used.

IN PRACTICE 6.2

Atlas Manufacturing Company

Atlas Manufacturing Company manufactures electrical and mechanical parts for home appliances. They also have a small division that specializes in heating elements. Most products are sold directly to appliance manufacturers.

The manufacturing facilities are located in Ohio, with regional sales offices located in New York and Northern California. The organization chart, including proposed additions for the future, is given in Exhibit 6.5. Atlas Manufacturing uses several vertical linkage mechanisms to achieve coordination.

The Manufacturing General Manager established rules for materials that can be acquired in the purchasing department. Each purchasing agent has a dollar limit for certain categories of raw material and equipment. Exceptionally large or nonstandard purchases are referred up to the Manufacturing General

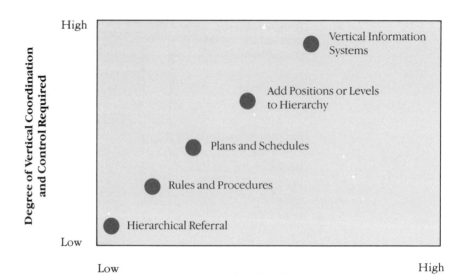

EXHIBIT 6.4. Ladder of Mechanisms for Vertical Linkage and Control.

Manager. Plans and schedules are also used at Atlas. The Manufacturing General Manager works with the production department to establish specific targets, and sufficient resources are allocated to meet the plan. Forty units will be delivered to assembly each Monday. Purchasing also uses plans to specify the number of parts that have to be ordered for the manufacturing process. Whenever a problem occurs, it is passed up the hierarchy. Rules and planning provide coordination for most day-to-day activities.

Rapid growth at Atlas caused the president to ask the personnel department to propose new organization charts. Both the president and executive vice-president are overloaded. The personnel department proposed the addition of an assistant to help the president. The assistant-to could stand in for the president for certain meetings. Another proposal was to divide the executive vice-president position into three vice-president positions. The two new vice-president positions are indicated by dotted lines in Exhibit 6.5. One vice-president would be in charge of industrial relations and marketing. Another would be in charge of research and finance. The current vice-president would have responsibility for manufacturing.

The addition of vice-presidents may be postponed because the data-processing department developed an on-line system for use by senior executives. The on-line computer system records each order received by the company, and follows its progress through manufacturing. As each stage is completed, the result is signaled to the computer. Each morning senior executives receive a report on the number of orders that are behind schedule and the progress of urgent orders. Each executive has a computer terminal and can request information on any order for which they receive an inquiry. The information provided by the computer replaces the need for direct contact with managers at lower levels. The linkage between upper and lower levels is improved because the flow of vertical information is more efficient.

Horizontal Linkage Requirements

The four contextual factors of environmental uncertainty, technological interdependence, goals, and size normally determine the amount of horizontal coordination required between departments. As uncertainty increases, the

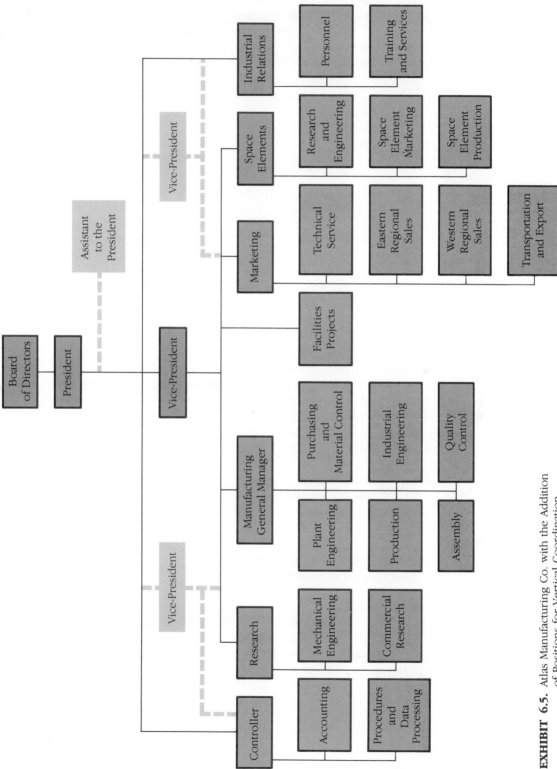

EXHIBIT 6.5. Atlas Manufacturing Co. with the Addition of Positions for Vertical Coordination.

need for information processing and horizontal coordination increases to cope with environmental change and unpredictability. As defined in the chapter on technology, the three levels of interdependence are pooled, sequential, and reciprocal. Higher interdependence between departments requires greater coordination. Horizontal linkage devices should be implemented between departments that are interdependent. Moreover, large organizations, which have many departments, typically need more horizontal linkage than small organizations to keep activities coordinated.

Organizational goals reflect what the organization is trying to achieve, and often indicate where linkage is needed. In a firm like Datapoint that manufactures electronic computers, the goal is to be innovative. Horizontal linkages are needed between the research department and other departments, because research is responsible for innovation. Linkage with marketing provides information to R&D about customer requirements and competitor activities. Linkage of R&D with production provides information about production and cost limitations that may restrict new products.

In an organization producing cardboard boxes, the goal may be to provide quick delivery at reasonable prices. Coordination thus is needed between production and sales. These two departments must be closely linked to coordinate new orders with current production runs. Orders are accepted only if they can be delivered in time to satisfy customers without destroying the efficiency of production. The research department is relatively unimportant in this type of company, and is not tightly linked to other departments.

Horizontal Linkage Mechanisms

Each of the following devices is a structural alternative that can improve horizontal coordination and information flow.[6] Each device enables people to exchange information. Horizontal linkage mechanisms are often not drawn on the organization chart, but they are an important part of organization structure.

Paperwork—Memos, Reports   One form of horizontal linkage is simply to exchange paperwork about a problem or decision or to put other departments on a mailing list so they will be informed about activities. Other departments may be sent copies of correspondence or have reports forwarded to them. Linkage through paperwork normally provides a low level of coordination and does not permit joint decisions to be made or a large volume of information to be processed.

Direct Contact   A somewhat higher level of horizontal linkage is direct contact between managers affected by a problem. Companies like Hewlett-Packard and Digital Equipment Corporation encourage managers to communicate directly with one another across departmental boundaries whenever possible. A possible disadvantage of direct contact is that top managers may not know about certain problems, or lower managers may resolve a problem in a way that is not in the interest of the overall organization.

Liaison Role   Creating a special liaison role is the next alternative. Liaison roles often exist between engineering and manufacturing departments because engineering has to develop and test products to fit the limitations of manufacturing facilities. A computer department or transportation department may assign a liaison person to work with other departments around the organization that use their services. A liaison person is located in one department but has the responsibility for communicating and achieving coordination with another department. These people normally deal with the other department as part of their full-time job.

Task Forces   Direct contact and liaison roles usually link two departments. When linkage involves several departments, a more complex linkage device is required. A task force is a temporary committee composed of representatives from each department affected by a problem. Each member represents the interest of a department and can carry information from the meeting back to their respective departments.

Task forces are an effective horizontal linkage device for temporary issues. Task forces are used in book publishing companies to coordinate the editing, production, advertising, and distribution of a special book. Business firms use task forces to study the possibility of acquiring a subsidiary and how to integrate the subsidiary into the corporation after it is purchased. Business colleges use task forces to coordinate the redesign of MBA and undergraduate curricula. The task force brings together people who can resolve the needs of each department with respect to coursework requirements, course sequences, and number of credit hours required. Task forces solve problems by direct horizontal coordination and reduce the information load on the vertical hierarchy. Task forces are created by upper-level managers to accomplish needed coordination and then are disbanded after the problem is solved.

Full-Time Integrator   A stronger horizontal linkage device is to create a full-time position or department solely for the purpose of coordination. A full-time integrator frequently has a title such as product manager, project manager, program manager, or brand manager. Unlike the liaison role described earlier, the integrator does not report to one of the functional departments being coordinated. The integrator is located outside the departments and has the responsibility of coordinating between several departments.

Sometimes an integrator will work alone and be responsible for coordination across departments. The brand manager for Planters Peanuts, for example, coordinates the sales, distribution, and advertising for that product. The MBA director at a business college is also an integrator. The director has the responsibility to coordinate scheduling, class content, classroom allocation, and testing periods across the functional departments of accounting, finance, management, statistics, and marketing. The MBA director works with professors in each department to see that teaching techniques and course content fit together into a coherent program for students in the program.

The integrator can also be responsible for an entire project. An example of the organization chart to illustrate full-time project coordinators is shown in Exhibit 6.6. The project managers are drawn to the side to indicate their separation from other departments. The dashed lines indicate project members assigned to the project. Project A for example, has a financial accountant assigned to the project to keep track of costs and budgets. The engineering

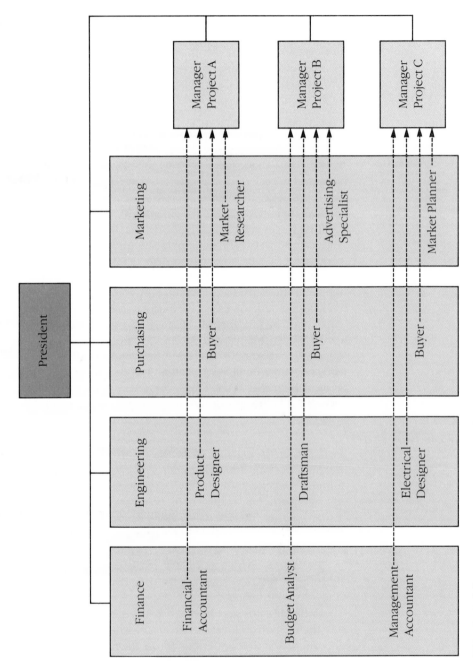

EXHIBIT 6.6. Project Manager Location in the Structure.

member provides design advice, and purchasing and manufacturing members represent their areas. The project director is responsible for the entire project. The project director sees that the project is completed on time, makes a profit, or achieves other project goals. The dashed lines in Exhibit 6.6 indicate that project directors do not have formal authority over team members with respect to giving pay raises, or hiring and firing. Formal authority rests with the managers of the functional departments.

Integrating roles requires special skills. Integrators in most companies have a lot of responsibility but little authority. The integrator has to use expertise and persuasion to achieve coordination. The integrator spans the boundary between departments, and must be able to get people together, maintain their trust, confront problems, and resolve conflicts and disputes in the interest of the organization.[7] The integrator must be forceful in order to achieve coordination, but must stop short of alienating people in the line departments. Some organizations have several integrators working simultaneously, as at General Mills.

IN PRACTICE 6.3

General Mills

"When General Mills completed a ten-story tower at its suburban Minneapolis headquarters last summer, the company discovered that not all the telephones could be installed at once. 'Hook up the product managers' first,' the senior executive ordered. The business can't run without them.' "[8]

General Mills assigns a product manager to each of the more than twenty-five products in its line, including Cheerios, Wheaties, Bisquick, Softasilk Cake Mix, Stir-n-Frost Icing, Hamburger Helper, and Gold Medal Flour. Brand managers are also assigned to develop new products, name them, and test them in the marketplace.

At General Mills, product managers have the responsibility of business managers—setting marketing goals and plotting strategies to achieve those goals. The annual cycle begins with a three-month planning process. The status of the products and key issues are analyzed. Research data on the brand and its competition for several years are analyzed. A sales forecast, an itemized list of costs to meet the forecast, and advertising, pricing, and competitive tactics are laid out. The plan must be approved by the marketing director and the division general manager. Product managers are responsible for the product's profit. They get involved in any area that affects profit, which can include manufacturing productivity, ingredient substitution, competitive advertising, and commodity pricing.

Product managers at General Mills act as if they are running their own businesses. They are responsible and accountable for product success, but they have no authority. Product management is management by persuasion. If the product manager for Cocoa Puffs needs special support from the salesforce and additional output from the plant for a big advertising campaign, she has to sell the idea to people who report to managers in charge of sales and manufacturing. Product managers work laterally across the organization rather than within the vertical structure. When the product manager for Crispy Wheats 'n Raisins decides the product needs different packaging, a new recipe, a more focused commercial, or new ingredients, he must convince the support groups to pay attention to his brand. The product manager can also expect to work with the procurement department, a controller, and the research lab at some point during the year.

A good product manager is vibrant, challenging, and a little abrasive. A good product manager gets things done without the aid of formal authority. The General Mills product managers are in their early thirties, and they have responsibilities as big as their ambitions. The young product manager for Crispy Wheats 'n Raisins was given responsibility for a $10 million introductory budget for the new product. The money was spent on a combination of direct mailing of trial packages and TV ads.[9]

The product managers at General Mills are full-time integrators. They integrate marketing, manufacturing, purchasing, research, and other functions relevant to their product line. They provide horizontal linkages within the company by persuading diverse groups to focus on the needs of their products. General Mills has been very profitable in a highly competitive industry, and an important reason is the role played by product managers.

Teams   Permanent committees and project teams tend to be the strongest horizontal linkage mechanism. Teams are permanent task forces, and are often used in conjunction with a full-time integrator. When activities between departments require strong coordination over a long period of time, a team is often the solution.

Special project teams are used when organizations have a large-scale project, such as a major innovation or new product line. A new product may require extensive coordination between research, sales, marketing research, manufacturing, and engineering for several years. The Inland Division of General Motors used teams to help the division respond to annual model changes. Teams of up to seventy-five members are responsible for Inland's product lines, which include steering wheels and padded dash boards. The teams help managers break down barriers across departments. Quality control inspectors, for example, previously were not concerned about production problems or engineering difficulties. By meeting with other managers as part of a team, everyone works to resolve any problem with the product line.[10]

The Rodney Hunt Company develops, manufactures, and markets heavy industrial equipment and uses teams to coordinate each product line across the manufacturing, engineering, and marketing departments. These teams are illustrated by the dashed lines and shaded areas in Exhibit 6.7. Members from each team meet first thing each day as needed to resolve problems concerning customer needs, backlogs, engineering changes, scheduling conflicts, and any other problem with the product line.

A more intense use of teams was adopted by Florida Power & Light Company to build nuclear power plants. Permanent teams were combined with full-time team leaders (integrators) to achieve remarkable coordination.

IN PRACTICE 6.4

Florida Power & Light Co.

Building a nuclear power plant takes ten to twelve years. Some take as long as fifteen years, and the costs are enormous. But the long delays did not

EXHIBIT 6.7 Teams Used for Horizontal Coordination at Rodney Hunt Company.

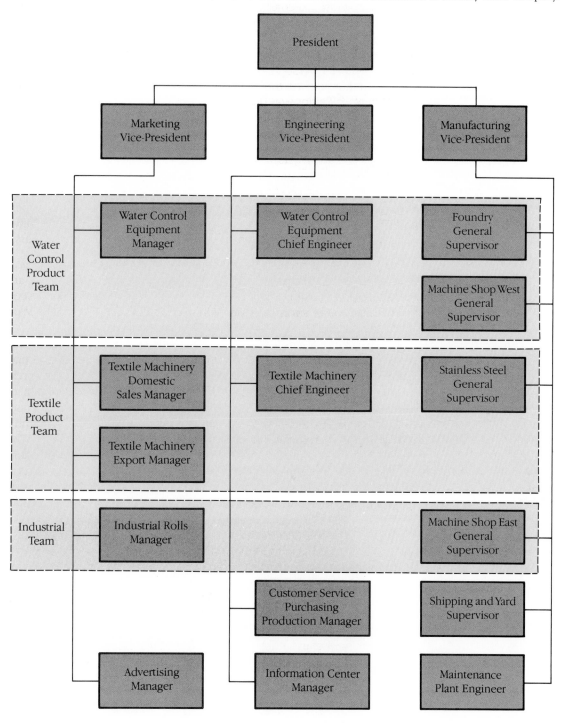

Source: Adapted from Joseph J. Famularo, *Organizational Planning Manual: Charts, Descriptions, Policies,* rev. ed. (New York: AMACOM, a division of American Management Association, 1971), p. 125.

happen when Florida Power built St. Lucie No. 2, which went into commercial operations only six years after construction started. The credit goes to Bill Derrickson, manager of the project, who overcame a hurricane, two strikes, and hundreds of federally required design changes. His solution was to develop fifteen teams to handle critical parts of the project. Each team was headed by what Derrickson called a "mother," because, he says, "If you want something to happen, it has to have a mother." One such team presided over a computerized list of 25,000 tasks needed to finish the plant. The mother was Steve Reuwer, and daily team meetings were intense. Anyone who couldn't answer questions was asked to leave and return with the answer. Supervisors who fell behind either quit or were replaced. Mr. Reuwer's job was to keep the pressure on.

The teams were able to assimilate and coordinate design changes, and were responsible for developing innovative construction techniques. A "slip-forming" technique was developed for pouring concrete around the clock, finishing the three-foot-thick, 190-foot-tall concrete shell in just seventeen days compared to a year for other power companies. The teams also worked face-to-face with government regulators and suppliers to get things done on schedule.

The use of teams by Florida Power to handle urgent problems was so as fifteen years, and the costs are enormous. But the long delays did not happen when Florida Power built St. Lucie No. 2, which went into commercial operations only six years after construction started. The credit goes to Bill Derrickson, manager of the project, who overcame a hurricane, two strikes, and hundreds of federally required design changes. His solution was to develop fifteen teams to handle critical parts of the project. Each team was headed by what Derrickson called a "mother," because, he says, "If you want something to happen, it has to have a mother." One such team presided over a computerized list of 25,000 tasks needed to finish the plant. The mother was Steve Reuwer, and daily team meetings were intense. Anyone who

EXHIBIT 6.8. Ladder of Mechanisms for Horizontal Linkage and Coordination.

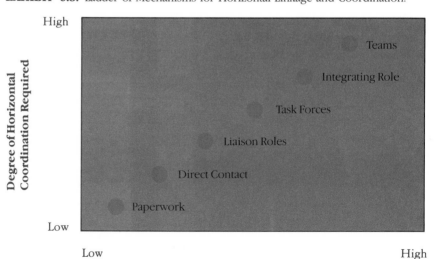

Information Capacity of Linkage Mechanism

couldn't answer questions was asked to leave and return with the answer. Supervisors who fell behind either quit or were replaced. Mr. Reuwer's job was to keep the pressure on.

REALIGNING LINKAGES WITH SELF-CONTAINED UNITS

Vertical linkages tend to be the primary linkages in organizations because they have the force of formal authority and they reinforce the departmental grouping in the organization. Horizontal linkages are secondary in the sense that they overlay the vertical structure, and designate responsibility for coordination but without formal authority. In addition, the vertical and horizontal linkage mechanisms complement one another to achieve coordination in the organization. Rules, procedures, planning, and scheduling along the vertical structure indirectly help managers coordinate horizontally across departments. The horizontal mechanisms of direct contact, task forces, and integrating roles reduce the need for communication up and down the hierarchy. The use of linkage mechanisms in one direction influences the need for linkage mechanisms in the other direction.

A problem faced by many medium-sized and large organizations is that they have excellent vertical linkages, but coordination across functional departments is poor. As organizations progress through the life cycle, they may develop several product lines and reach several markets. Coordination vertically within marketing, engineering, and manufacturing may be excellent, but the differences between marketing, engineering, and manufacturing for each product are not integrated. Even the use of task forces, teams, or full-time integrators may not provide sufficient linkage to achieve the goals for each product.

Another alternative is for organizations to reorganize into smaller, self-contained units.[12] This type of reorganization is illustrated in Exhibit 6.9. The organization is literally redesigned into separate product groups, and each group contains the functional departments that have to be coordinated. This reorganization occurs when product goals and interdependencies cannot be met within a functional structure using horizontal linkage devices.

Structural self-containment changes departmental grouping. Departments and functions that must work closely together are grouped together on the organization chart. This realigns the vertical and horizontal linkage devices. By locating different tasks together under a common manager, face-to-face coordination, planning, and hierarchical referral can be used to achieve coordination across marketing, research, and manufacturing. This reorganization gives product managers vertical authority, which is the primary linkage device. Each function needed to produce a product is now linked directly with the product manager.

Reorganization does not do away with the need for horizontal coordination. It simply realigns departmental grouping to engage vertical linkage mechanisms for each product line. After reorganization, horizontal coordination will still be needed across product groups. Top management may

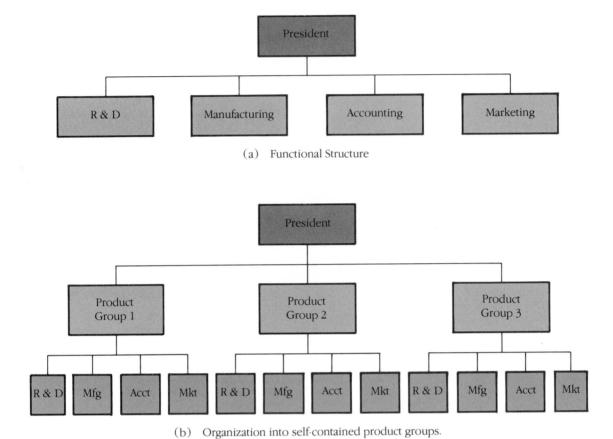

(a)   Functional Structure

(b)   Organization into self-contained product groups.

EXHIBIT 6.9. Reorganization from Functional Structure to Self-Contained Units.

establish an engineering task force, for example, to encourage weekly contact between engineers for each product line. Developments in one engineering group can be used by engineers in other product lines. Engineering task forces are used by General Motors to coordinate the engineering and design of cars in each automobile division. The effectiveness of GM's coordination is reflected in the similarity of automobile design for each division, and GM's ability to interchange standard parts. In addition, standard rules and procedures for accounting, finance, and personnel must be adhered to by all product groups. The shift to self-contained units thus does not eliminate horizontal coordination, but simply gives primary emphasis to coordination within each product line.

In the next section we will examine in more detail the advantages and disadvantages of functional versus product structural grouping, and identify when each structure should be used. We will also examine two variations of these structures called hybrid and matrix. From among these structural alternatives, managers can select the right configuration to accomplish the goals of their organization.

FUNCTIONAL STRUCTURE

The two basic organization forms are function and product (self-contained units). The issue of whether organizational departments should be grouped by function or in self-contained units is a major dilemma for organizations. Many large organizations have switched back and forth and still are not sure which design should be used. At this time, about 75% of large corporations are in some form of self-contained units.[13]

In a functional organization structure, activities are grouped together by common function from the bottom to the top of the organization. All engineers are located in the engineering department and the vice-president of engineering is responsible for all engineering activities. The same is true in marketing, research and development, and manufacturing.

The distinctive feature of **functional structure** is that people and activities are grouped by resources. Each functional department provides resources (e.g., engineering, marketing) to the overall production process of the organization. Examples of purely functional organization structure were Atlas Manufacturing Company (Exhibit 6.5) and the Rodney Hunt Corporation (Exhibit 6.7).

The functional form of organization is best when the organization context stresses functional specialization, efficiency, and quality. Recall from the discussion of differentiation and integration in chapter 2 that employees in each department adopt similar values, goals, and orientations. Similarity encourages collaboration, efficiency, and quality within the function, but makes coordination and cooperation with other departments more difficult. Even with task forces and integrators, the allegiance of employees will be toward the goals of their functions rather than toward cooperation with other departments.

Exhibit 6.10 summarizes the organizational context and internal characteristics typically associated with the functional structure. The functional structure is most effective when the environment is stable, and when the technology is relatively routine with low interdependence across functional departments. Organizational goals pertain to internal efficiency and technical specialization. Size is small to medium. Each of these characteristics is associated with low need for horizontal coordination. The stable environment, routine technology, internal efficiency, and small size mean the organization can be controlled and coordinated primarily through vertical linkage mechanisms. Within the organization, employees are committed to achieving the operative goals of their respective functional departments. Planning and budgeting is by function and reflects the cost of resources used in each department. Formal authority and influence within the organization rests with upper managers in the functional departments.

One strength of the functional structure is that it promotes economy of scale within functions. Economy of scale means that all employees are located in the same place and can share facilities. Producing all products in a single plant, for example, enables the plant to acquire the latest machinery. Constructing only one facility instead of separate facilities for each product line reduces duplication and waste. The functional structure also promotes in-

EXHIBIT 6.10. Summary of Functional Organization Characteristics.

CONTEXT ⬠
Structure: Functional
Environment: Low uncertainty, stable
Technology: Routine, low interdependence
Size: Small to medium
Goals: Internal efficiency, technical specialization and quality

INTERNAL SYSTEMS
Operative goals: Functional goal emphasis
Planning and budgeting: Cost basis—budget, statistical reports
Formal authority: Functional managers

STRENGTHS
1. Economies of scale within functions
2. In-depth skill development
3. Able to accomplish functional goals
4. Best in small- to medium-size organizations
5. Best when only one or a few products

WEAKNESSES
1. Slow response time to environmental changes
2. Decisions may pile on top, hierarchy overload
3. Poor interunit coordination
4. Less innovation
5. Restricted view of organization goals

Source: Adapted from Robert Duncan, "What Is the Right Organization Structure? Decision Tree Analysis Provides the Answer," *Organizational Dynamics,* Winter 1979 (New York: AMACOM, a division of American Management Associations, 1979), p. 429.

depth skill development of employees. Employees are exposed to a range of functional activities within their own department. The functional form of structure is best for small to medium-sized organizations when there is only one or a few products produced.[14]

The weakness of the functional structure is the slow response to environmental changes that require coordination across departments. The vertical structure described at the beginning of this chapter for the Thomas National Group was an example of a functional structure that provided insufficient coordination. If the environment is changing or the technology is nonroutine and interdependent, the vertical hierarchy becomes overloaded. Decisions pile up and top managers do not respond fast enough. Other disadvantages of the functional structure are that innovation is slow because of poor co-ordination, and each employee has a restricted view of overall goals.

IN PRACTICE 6.5

Blue Bell Creameries, Inc.

In an unmistakable country voice, the old timer on the radio told the story about the good times in rural Texas. Within seconds he had taken listeners out of their bumper-to-bumper Houston world and placed them gently in Brenham, with its rolling hills, the country fair, and the time the town got its first traffic light.

"You know," he says, "that's how Blue Bell Ice Cream is. Old fashioned, uncomplicated, homemade good." He pauses. "It's all made in that little creamery in Brenham."

That little creamery isn't little anymore, but the desire for first quality home-made ice cream is stronger than when Blue Bell started in 1907. Blue Bell today employs over 600 employees and will sell over $70 million of ice cream. Each week the creamery consumes the output of 9,600 cows and several truckloads of peanuts, pecans, eggs, cane sugar, fresh fruit, and real Nabisco Oreo cookies (which are ground into Cookies 'N Cream Ice Cream).

The company cannot meet the demand for Blue Bell Ice Cream. It doesn't even try. People outside selected counties in the state of Texas and Louisiana cannot buy Blue Bell. It is not even distributed throughout Texas, its home state. The reason is the company's unwavering dedication to product quality. Management refuses to expand into regions that cannot be adequately serviced, or to grow so fast that they can't adequately train employees in the art of making ice cream. The goal of Blue Bell Creameries is a quality product. The managers will not undertake any activity that will endanger that quality. Customers expect quality, and they know they will receive it.

Customer loyalty pays off for Blue Bell. A recent survey found that fifty-eight cents of every ice cream dollar spent in Houston went to Blue Bell.

The approximate organization structure of Blue Bell is shown in Exhibit 6.11. The major departments are sales, quality control, production, maintenance, and distribution. There is also an accounting department and a small research and development group. Product changes are infrequent because the orientation is toward tried and true products. The environment is stable. The customer base is well established. The only change has been the increase in demand for Blue Bell Ice Cream.

Blue Bell's quality control department tests all incoming ingredients to ensure that only the best products go into their ice cream. Quality control also tests all ice cream products made by Blue Bell. Every single batch is tested. Percent butterfat is measured along with acidity and alkalinity. Of course, the most important quality control test is taste. Blue Bell employs workers whose only job is to taste the ice cream. After years of experience they can spot the slightest deviation from expected quality. It's no wonder that Blue Bell has successfully maintained the image of a small-town creamery making home-made ice cream.[15]

The functional organization structure is just right for Blue Bell Creameries. The primary goal is specialization for product quality. Employees are oriented toward the goals and values of their respective departments, which add up to quality ice cream. Functional experience and training is required, which is possible when employees are grouped together on a functional basis. Blue Bell has chosen to stay medium-sized and to produce only ice cream products.

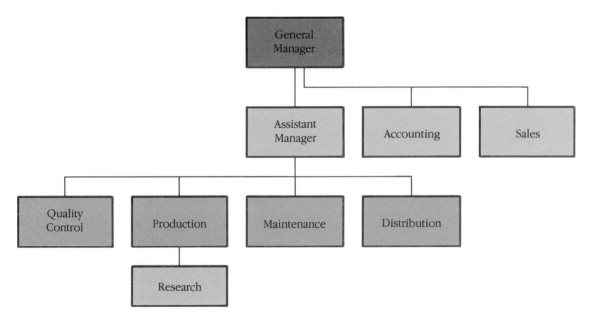

EXHIBIT 6.11. Approximate Organization Structure for Blue Bell Creameries, Inc.

The functional structure provides the coordination needed for this organization.

PRODUCT STRUCTURE

The term "product structure" is used here as the generic term for what is sometimes called a "divisional structure" or "self-contained units." Divisions can be organized according to individual products, product groups, services, regions, markets, customers, or major programs. The term used to describe the organization structure for any of these classifications will be product structure.

The distinctive feature of **product structure** is that grouping is based on organizational outputs. For each product output, all necessary resources such as manufacturing, research and development, and marketing are grouped within the department structure. Coordination across functions within each product unit is maximized. The product structure promotes flexibility and adaptability within each of the organization's product lines.

The product structure fits the context summarized in Table 6.12.[16] The product form of structure is excellent for achieving coordination across functional departments. When the environment is uncertain, when the technology is nonroutine and reflects interdependence across departments, and when the goals are external effectiveness and adaptation, then a product structure is appropriate. Large size is also associated with product structure

EXHIBIT 6.12. Summary of Product Organization Characteristics.

CONTEXT

Structure: Product
Environment: Moderate to high uncertainty, changing
Technology: Nonroutine, high interdependence
Size: Large
Goals: External effectiveness, adaptation, client satisfaction

INTERNAL SYSTEMS
Operative goals: Product line emphasis
Planning and budgeting: Profit center basis—cost and income
Formal authority: Product managers

STRENGTHS
1. Suited to fast change in unstable environment
2. Client satisfaction because product responsibility and contact points are clear
3. High coordination across functions
4. Units adapt to differences in products, regions, clients
5. Best in large organizations
6. Best when several products

WEAKNESSES
1. Lose economies of scale in functional departments
2. Poor functional coordination across product lines
3. Lose in-depth competence and technical specialization
4. Integration and standardization across product lines is difficult

Source: Adapted from Robert Duncan, "What Is the Right Organization Structure? Decision Tree Analysis Provides the Answer," *Organizational Dynamics,* Winter 1979 (New York: AMACOM, a division of American Management Associations, 1979), p. 431.

because the coordination problem is simplified. A huge, complex organization is subdivided into a series of smaller organizations for better control and coordination.

Since the self-contained units are often quite small, employees identify with the product line rather than with their own function. Budgeting and planning are on a profit basis, because each product line can be run as a separate business with both costs and income calculated. Managers with influence are those who head product divisions.

The product structure has several strengths. It is suited to fast change in an unstable environment, and provides high product visibility. Since each product is a separate division, clients are able to contact the right division and achieve satisfaction. Coordination across functions is excellent. Each product can adapt to requirements of individual customers or regions. The product structure typically works best in large organizations that have multiple products or services and enough personnel to staff separate functional units.

One disadvantage is that the organization loses economies of scale. Instead of fifty research engineers sharing a common facility in a functional structure, ten engineers may be assigned to each of five product divisions. The critical mass required for in-depth research is lost, and physical facilities have to be duplicated for each product line. Another problem is that product lines become separate from each other, and coordination across product lines can be difficult. Companies such as Hewlett-Packard, Xerox, and Digital Equipment have a large number of divisions and have had real problems with coordination. The software division may produce programs that are incompatible with personal or business computers sold by other divisions. Customers are frustrated when a sales representative from one division is unaware of developments in other divisions. Task forces and other devices are needed to coordinate across divisions. A lack of technical specialization is also a problem in a product structure. Employees identify with the product line rather than with a functional specialty. R&D personnel, for example, tend to do applied research to benefit the product line rather than basic research to benefit the entire organization.

One company that reorganized from a functional to a product structure was Sun Petroleum Products Company. The reorganization into four divisions enabled greater coordination and innovation within product lines to meet the needs of each market.

IN PRACTICE 6.6
Sun Petroleum Products Company

Sun Petroleum Products Company (SPPC) had sales of approximately $7 billion in 1980, and a workforce of 5,400 people. The refineries produced about 500,000 barrels of product per day. The six refineries manufactured fuels, lubricants, and chemicals that Sun's salesforce could market.

Until 1980, SPPC was organized by function, as illustrated in Exhibit 6.13. Each functional head reported directly to the president or the vice-president of operations. The marketing and manufacturing vice-presidents had substantial authority, and experienced occasional disagreement about changes needed as markets changed. The president began to wonder whether a new structure would enable better response to market conditions. A study revealed that the company should be more responsive to markets and environmental changes. It recommended a reorganization into three major product lines of fuels, lubricants, and chemicals. Each product line served a different market and required a different strategy, structure, and management style.

The new organization structure is illustrated in Exhibit 6.14 on page 238. Each product line vice-president was now in charge of both marketing and manufacturing so greater coordination was achieved to respond to market conditions. Planning, supply, and distribution were also incorporated in the product structure. A fourth vice-president, in charge of the refinery facilities, worked to attain close coordination with the three major product lines. The initial effort of managers was focused on realigning working relationships to fit the new structure. Once accomplished, the structure was just right for SPPC's context, which included large size, moderate environmental change, interdependence among departments, and goals of adaptation.[17]

Variations of Self-Contained Units

Other forms of self-contained units are called divisional structures and geographic structures. These are similar to product structure because required functions are brought together as needed to produce organizational outputs. Large conglomerates use a divisional structure in which all activities asso-

EXHIBIT 6.13. Sun Petroleum Products Company's Functional Organization.

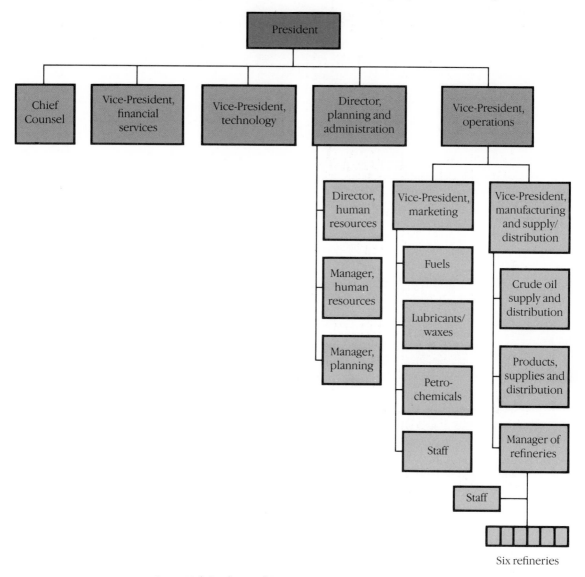

Source: Linda S. Ackerman, "Transition Management: An In-Depth Look at Managing Complex Change," *Organizational Dynamics* (Summer 1982):46–66. Used with permission.

ciated with major divisions or subsidiaries exist under a divisional general manager. Sometimes subsidiaries are independent of the parent company.

Sometimes structure reflects geography. A large corporation that distributes products nationally often cannot coordinate all regions from a central location. Each region of the country has distinct tastes, needs, and facilities that require coordination. An important form of self-contained unit is the division of the organization by geography. Each geographical unit includes all functions required to produce and market products in that region. For multi-national corporations, self-contained units are created for different

EXHIBIT 6.14. Sun Petroleum Products Company's Product Line Organization.

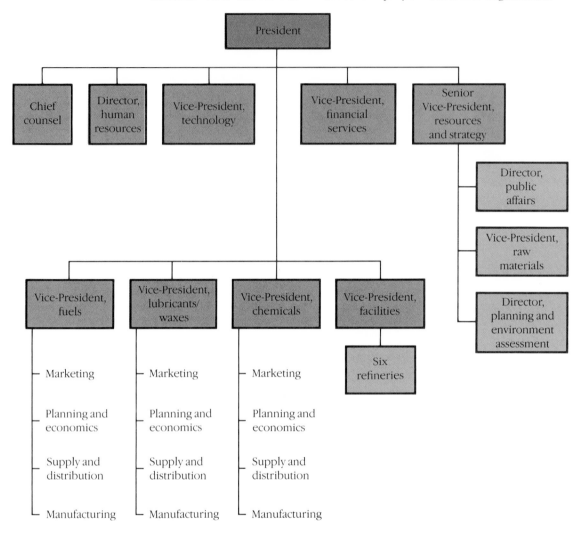

Source: Linda S. Ackerman, "Transition Management: An In-Depth Look at Managing Complex Change," *Organizational Dynamics* (Summer 1982):46–66. Used with permission.

countries and parts of the world. A geographical structure for a Canadian retail department store chain is described in Exhibit 6.15 on page 239. Customers in Quebec are physically smaller, use a different language, and have different tastes than customers in Ontario or the Maritimes. The regional structure groups together the functions that can serve each region's needs.

The strengths and weaknesses of a geographical or division structure are similar to the product organization characteristics listed in Exhibit 6.12. The organization can adapt to specific needs of its own region, and employees identify with regional goals rather than with national goals. Horizontal coordination within region is emphasized rather than vertical linkages to the national office.

HYBRID STRUCTURE

The logic of either the functional or the product grouping underlies virtually all organization structures. As a practical matter, however, most structures in the real world do not exist in pure form. Most corporations do not have either a pure product structure or a pure functional structure. One important type of structure that combines characteristics of both is called the hybrid structure.

When a corporation grows large and has several products or markets, it typically is organized into self-contained units of some type. Functions that are important to each product or market are decentralized to the self-contained

EXHIBIT 6.15. Geographical Structure for a Canadian Retail Chain.

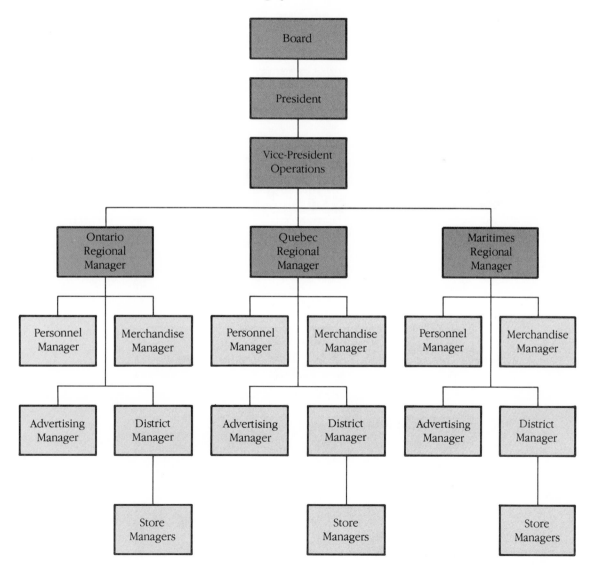

units. However, some functions are also centralized and located at head-quarters. Headquarters' functions are relatively stable and require economies of scale and in-depth specialization. By combining characteristics of both functional and product structures, corporations can take advantage of both forms of structure and avoid some of the weaknesses.

An example of a hybrid structure used at Levi Strauss is shown in Exhibit 6.16. There are eight product divisions. Each division contains its own manufacturing and marketing facilities, and engages in some product development work. These divisions are organized into three product groups. Jeanswear is the largest and most profitable division and produces straight-leg and boot jeans, corduroy blazers and shirts. The Youthwear division markets Girlswear, Activewear, and attire for toddlers. The Resistol division is the world's largest source of western and dress hats. These divisions reflect the product structure at Levi Strauss.

EXHIBIT 6.16. Partial Organization Chart for Levi Strauss USA.

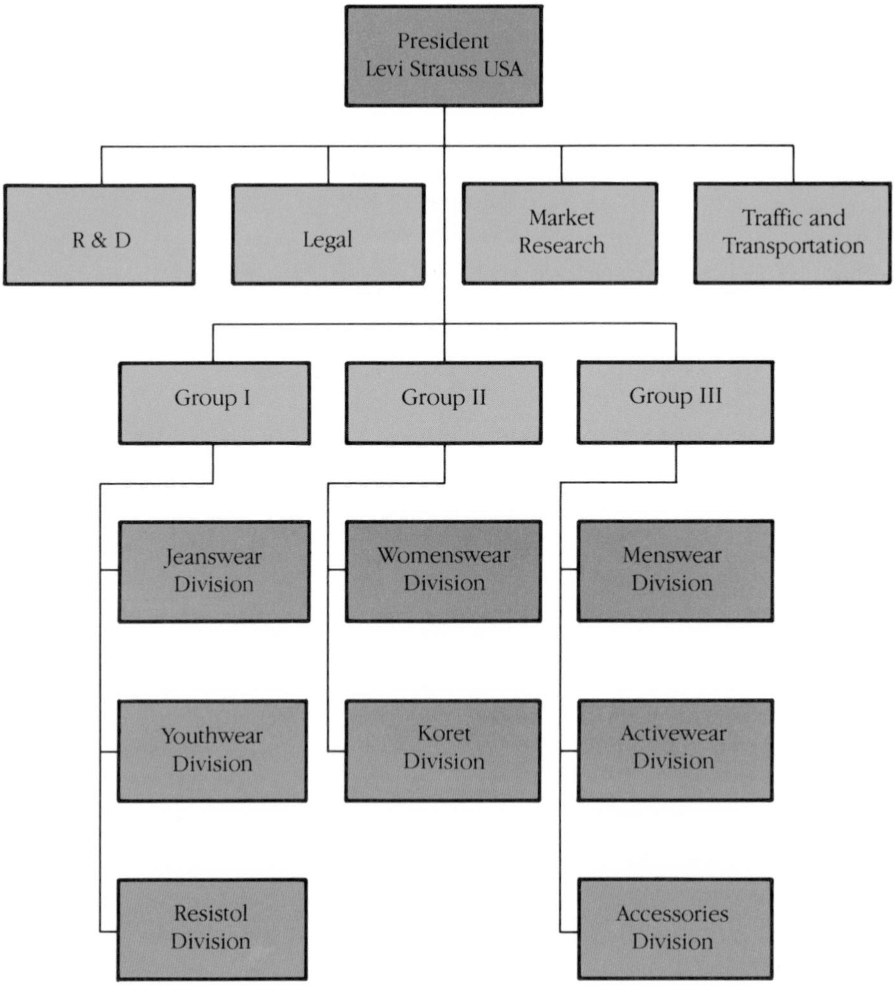

The functional part of the structure is reflected in the corporate functions that are centralized at headquarters to serve the entire corporation. The legal department handles trademark infringements and counterfeits of Levi products. Levi Strauss is normally involved in over fifty trademark cases at a given time. Fighting patent infringement applies to all divisions and can be centralized at the corporate level.

Research and Development and Market Research also provide services for all divisions. Over one thousand patents have been granted to the company. Research facilities are enormously expensive, and it would not be efficient to duplicate them for each product division. The corporate traffic and transportation office coordinates shipments within the United States. The corporate office handles negotiations with regulatory agencies and major shippers to obtain best prices for all divisions. This department also provides a trucking fleet, made up of ninety drivers and two hundred trailers that serve all product divisions.[18]

The final structure adopted by Sun Petroleum Products Company in Exhibit 6.14 was primarily a product structure, but retained a few central functional departments. Many companies group departments along product lines where close coordination is needed, and leave other departments in a functional structure to gain economies of scale and other benefits.

One weakness of the hybrid structure is administrative overhead. Some organizations experience a buildup of corporate staffs to oversee divisions. Some corporate functions duplicate activities undertaken within product divisions. If uncontrolled, administrative overhead can increase as headquarters' staff grows large. Decisions then become more centralized and the organization loses the ability for product divisions to respond quickly to market changes. An associated weakness is the conflict between corporate and divisional personnel. Headquarter functions typically do not have line authority over divisional activities. Division managers may resent headquarter intrusions, and headquarters' managers may resent the desire of divisions to go their own way. Headquarter executives often do not understand the unique needs of the individual divisions that are trying to satisfy different markets.

Strengths and Weaknesses

The hybrid structure typically appears in a context similar to product structure but with modification. Hybrid structures tend to be used in an uncertain environment because product divisions are designed for innovation and external effectiveness. Technologies may be both routine and nonroutine, and interdependencies exist across some functions as illustrated in product groupings. Size is typically large to have sufficient resources for duplication of resources across product divisions. The organization has goals of client satisfaction and innovation, as well as goals of efficiency with respect to functional departments.

As summarized in Exhibit 6.17, a major strength of the hybrid structure is that it enables the organization to pursue adaptability and effectiveness within the product divisions simultaneously with efficiency in the functional departments. Thus the organization can attain the best of both worlds. The structure also provides alignment between product division and corporate goals. The product groupings provide effective coordination within divisions, and the central functional departments provide coordination across divisions.

EXHIBIT 6.17. Summary of Hybrid Organization Characteristics.

CONTEXT ⬠

Structure: Hybrid

Environment: Moderate to high uncertainty, changing customer demands

Technology: Routine or nonroutine, with interdependencies across both
        functions and product lines

Size: Large

Goals: External effectiveness and adaptation plus efficiency within some
        functions

INTERNAL SYSTEMS

Operative goals: Product line emphasis, some functional emphasis

Planning and budgeting: Profit center basis for divisions; cost basis for
        central functions

Formal authority: Product managers; coordination responsibility with
        functional managers

STRENGTHS

1. Organization can achieve adaptability and coordination in some areas and
   efficiency in others
2. Better alignment between corporate level and division level goals
3. Achieves coordination both within and between product lines

WEAKNESSES

1. Potential for excessive administrative overhead
2. Conflict between division and corporate departments

Despite the strengths and weaknesses, the hybrid structure is often preferred to either the pure functional or pure product structure. It overcomes many of the weaknesses of these other structures, and provides some advantages of both.

MATRIX STRUCTURE

Most organizations find that some variation of either the functional or product structure provides the best reporting relationships and horizontal linkages to achieve organizational goals. The hybrid structure organizes part of the organization along product lines and part of the organization along functional lines to gain the advantages of both. In a few situations, however, organizations face a special dilemma. They need an organization chart that gives priority to both functional activities and product lines simultaneously. The organization needs both technological expertise within functions and horizontal coordination by product line for the same departments. One sector of the environment may require technological expertise, and another sector may require innovation within each product line. In addition, the uncertainty and rate of change in the external environment may be great so that continuous information-processing and coordination in both vertical and horizontal directions are necessary within the organization.

The matrix organization structure may be the answer when organizations find that neither the functional, product, nor hybrid structure combined with horizontal linkage mechanisms will work. The unique characteristic of the matrix organization is that both product and functional structures are implemented simultaneously in each department, as shown in Exhibit 6.18.

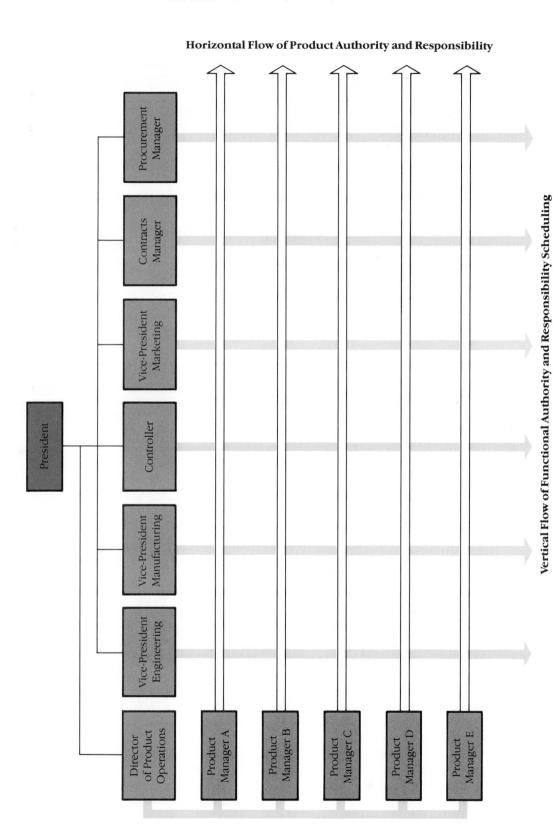

EXHIBIT 6.18. Dual Authority Structure in a Matrix Organization.

Rather than divide the organization into separate parts as in the hybrid structure, each department simultaneously reports to both product and functional managers. The product managers and functional managers have equal authority within the organization, and employees report to both of them. The matrix structure is similar to the use of full-time integrators or product managers described earlier in this chapter, except that in the matrix structure the product managers are given formal authority equal to that of the functional managers.

Conditions for the Matrix

The dual hierarchy may seem an unusual way to design an organization, but the matrix is the correct structure when the following conditions are met.[19]

Condition 1. Environmental pressure is for two or more critical outputs, such as for technical quality (functional organization) and frequent new products (product organization). This dual pressure means that a balance of power is required within the organization, and that a dual-authority structure is needed to reflect the environmental pressures.

Condition 2. The environmental domain of the organization is both complex and uncertain. Frequent external changes and high interdependence between departments require effective linkages in both vertical and horizontal directions.

Condition 3. Economy of scale in the use of internal resources is needed. The organization is typically medium-sized and has a moderate number of product lines. It feels pressure for the shared and flexible use of people and equipment. For example, the organization is not large enough to have sufficient engineers to assign them full-time to separate product lines, so engineers are allocated temporarily to several products depending upon environmental demand.

Under these three conditions, neither the functional, product, nor hybrid structure is sufficient, even when horizontal coordinating devices are implemented. The vertical and horizontal lines of authority must be given equal recognition. A dual-authority structure is thereby created so the balance of power between them is equal.

An example of a matrix organization is shown in Exhibit 6.19. The matrix organization chart can be drawn in a diamond shape to indicate the equality of the two authority structures. The organization in Exhibit 6.19 is a clothing manufacturer. It has three product lines that represent different markets and customers. As a medium-sized organization, it must effectively use the functions of manufacturing, design, and marketing. The manufacturing, design, and marketing departments require in-depth expertise and sufficient people to perform effectively. If functional departments are subdivided as in a pure product structure, the critical mass and efficiencies of scale within each function would be lost.

The unique aspect of matrix structure as reflected in Exhibit 6.19 is that some employees have two bosses, which violates the classic principles of management. The manager of the shoe manufacturing plant reports to the vice-president for manufacturing and to the director of the footwear product line. The plant manager will be subjected to conflicting pressures. The manufacturing vice-president will push for manufacturing quality, uniformity, and efficiency. The product director will be concerned with customer satisfaction and a timely response to fashion changes, even if it means losing efficiency

EXHIBIT 6.19. Example of a Matrix Design for a Clothing Manufacturer.

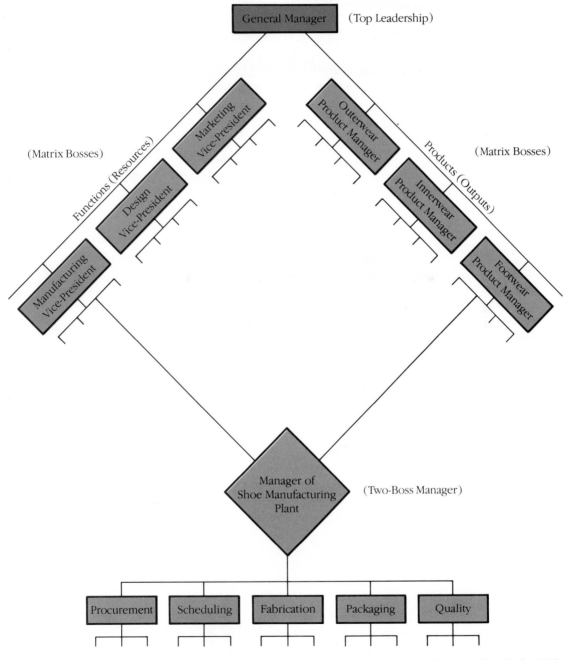

Source: Adapted from Stanley M. Davis and Paul R. Lawrence, *Matrix* (Reading, MA: Addison-Wesley, 1977), p. 22.

or quality in production. Each person who reports to two bosses is caught in a conflict, and is the person who performs the job of integration within the organization. Whenever conflicts arise, the manager and both bosses have to resolve the conflict. People in a matrix spend a great deal of time in meetings. The conflict built into the matrix forces discussion and coordination in both vertical and horizontal directions to resolve issues that pertain to both functions and products.

A common misperception about the matrix is that most employees report to two bosses, which is not the case. Although layered or multiple matrices do exist in theory,[20] they are rare in practice. Normally, the matrix is at the top of the organization, or at the top of the specific division that has adopted a matrix, as illustrated in Exhibit 6.20. If a research department adopts a matrix, for example, the research director is at the top of the matrix, and both functional and product directors report to him or her.

Key Matrix Roles

Working within a matrix structure is difficult for most managers because it requires a new set of skills compared to a single authority structure. In order for the matrix to succeed, managers in key roles have specific responsibilities. The key roles are top leadership, matrix bosses, and the two-boss managers, as indicated in Exhibit 6.19.[21]

Top Leader   The top leader is the head of both command structures. The primary responsibility for this person is to maintain a power balance between the functional and product managers. If either side of the matrix dominates, the organization will gradually evolve into either a functional or product form, and the benefits of the matrix will be lost. Top leaders must also be willing to delegate decisions and encourage direct contact and group problem-solving at levels beneath them, which will encourage information sharing and coordination.

Matrix Boss   The problem for matrix bosses is that they do not have complete control over their subordinates. Matrix bosses must work with each

EXHIBIT 6.20. Dual-Authority Structure is Typically at the Top of the Organization.

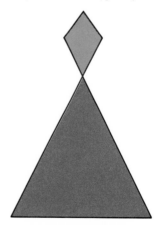

Source: Stanley M. Davis and Paul R. Lawrence, *Matrix* (Reading, MA: Addison-Wesley, 1977), p. 24.

other to delineate activities over which they are responsible. The functional manager's responsibilities pertain to functional expertise, rules, and standards. The product manager is responsible for coordinating the business whole. This person has the authority over subordinates for activities that achieve product goals. Matrix bosses must be willing to confront one another on disagreements and conflicts. They must also collaborate on such things as performance reviews, promotion, and salary increases, since subordinates report to both of them. These activities require a great deal of time, communication, patience, and skill at working with people, which are all part of matrix management.

Two-Boss Managers   The two-boss manager often experiences anxiety and stress. Conflicting demands are imposed by the matrix bosses. Demands from the functional manager and from the product manager may be legitimate, but in direct contradiction. The two-boss manager must confront senior managers on conflicting demands, and reach joint decisions with them. Two-boss managers must maintain effective relationships with both managers, even though they may occasionally feel that their own interests are not being met. Two-boss managers also need a dual loyalty to both their function and their product.

Strengths and Weaknesses

The matrix structure is best when environmental uncertainty is high and when goals reflect a dual requirement, such as for both product and function. The dual authority structure facilitates communication and coordination to cope with rapid environmental change and enables an equal balance between product and functional bosses. The matrix is also good for nonroutine technologies that have interdependencies both within and across functions. The matrix is an organic structure that facilitates discussion and adaptation to unexpected problems. The matrix structure tends to work best in organizations of moderate size with a few product lines. The matrix is not needed for only a single product line, and too many product lines make it difficult to coordinate both directions at once. Strengths and weaknesses are summarized in Exhibit 6.21.[22]

Internal systems reflect the dual organization structure. Two-boss employees are aware of and adopt subgoals for both their function and product. Dual planning and budgeting systems should be designed, one for the functional hierarchy and one for the product line hierarchy. Power and influence are shared equally by functional and product heads.

The strength of the matrix is that it enables the organization to meet dual demands from the environment. Resources can be flexibly allocated across different products, and the organization can adapt to changing external requirements. It also provides an opportunity for employees to acquire either functional or general management skills depending on their interests. The matrix structure works best in a medium-sized organization that has a moderate number of products.

One disadvantage of the matrix is that some employees experience dual authority, which is frustrating and confusing. They have to have excellent interpersonal and conflict-resolution skills, which may require specialized training in human relations. The matrix also forces managers to spend a

EXHIBIT 6.21. Summary of Matrix Organization Characteristics.

CONTEXT
Structure: Matrix
Environment: High uncertainty
Technology: Nonroutine, many interdependencies
Size: Moderate, a few product lines
Goals: Dual—product innovation and technical specialization

INTERNAL SYSTEMS
Operative goals: Equal product and function emphasis
Planning and budgeting: Dual systems—by function and by product line
Formal authority: Joint between functional and product heads

STRENGTHS
1. Achieves coordination necessary to meet dual demands from environment
2. Flexible use of human resources across products
3. Suited to complex decisions and frequent changes in unstable environment
4. Provides opportunity for functional and integration skill development
5. Best in medium-size organizations with multiple products

WEAKNESSES
1. Participants experience dual authority, which can be frustrating and confusing
2. Participants need good interpersonal skills; extensive training required
3. Time consuming—frequent meetings and conflict-resolution sessions
4. Will not work unless participants understand it and adopt collegial rather than vertical-type relationships
5. Requires dual pressure from environment to maintain power balance

Source: Adapted from Robert Duncan, "What Is the Right Organization Structure? Decision Tree Analysis Provides the Answer," *Organizational Dynamics,* Winter 1979 (New York: AMACOM, a division of American Management Associations, 1979), p. 429.

great deal of time in meetings. If managers do not adapt to the information and power-sharing required by the matrix, it will not work. They must collaborate with one another rather than rely on vertical authority in decision-making.

IN PRACTICE 6.7

Pittsburgh Steel Company

As far back as anyone can remember, the steel industry in the United States was stable and certain. If steel manufacturers could produce quality steel at a reasonable price, it would be sold. The U.S. market was growing steadily, and everything that could be made was sold. No more. Inflation, the national economic downturn, reduced consumption of autos, and competition from steelmakers in Germany and Japan have forever changed the steel industry. Today steelmakers have shifted to specialized steel products. They must market aggressively, make efficient use of internal resources, and adapt to rapid-fire changes.

Pittsburgh Steel employs 2,500 people, makes 300,000 tons of steel a year, and is 170 years old. For 160 of those years the functional structure represented in Exhibit 6.22 worked fine. As the environment became more turbulent and competitive, Pittsburgh Steel managers discovered they were not keeping up.

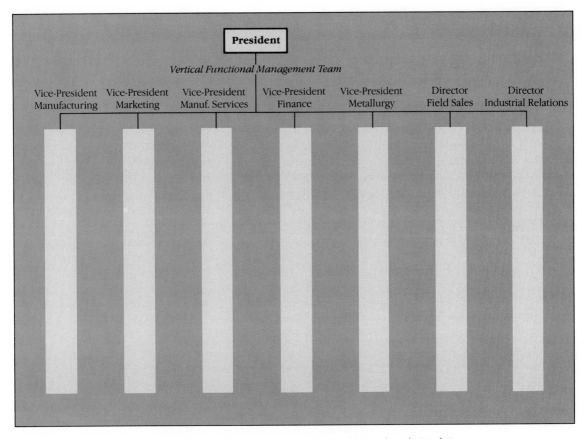

EXHIBIT 6.22. Functional Structure for Pittsburgh Steel Co.

Fifty percent of Pittsburgh's orders were behind schedule. Profits were eroded by labor, material, and energy cost increases. Market share declined.

In consultation with outside experts, the president of Pittsburgh Steel saw that the company had to walk a tightrope. Pittsburgh Steel had to specialize in a few high value added products tailored for separate markets, while maintaining economies of scale and sophisticated technology within functional departments. The dual pressure led to an unusual solution for a steel company—a matrix structure.

Pittsburgh Steel had four product lines—open-die forgings, ring-mill products, wheels and axles, and steel-making. A business manager was given responsibility and authority for each line. Department heads in each of the functional departments now reported to business managers as well as to their respective functional vice-presidents. The business managers had clearly defined responsibility, which included preparing a business plan for each product line, and developing targets for production costs, product inventory, shipping inventory, and gross profit. They were given authority to meet those targets and to make their lines profitable. Functional vice-presidents were responsible for technical decisions relating to their function. Functional managers were expected to stay abreast of the latest techniques in their areas and to keep personnel trained in new technologies that could apply to product lines. With 20,000 recipes for specialty steels, and with several hundred new recipes ordered each month, functional personnel had to stay current. Two functional departments, field sales and industrial relations, were not included in the matrix because they worked independently. The final design was a hybrid structure, with both matrix and functional responsibilities, as illustrated in Exhibit 6.23.

Implementation of the matrix was slow. Middle managers were confused. Meetings to coordinate across functional departments seemed to be held every day. One manager said, "How can we have time for our normal responsibilities and still have meetings all the time? These procedures are disturbing everything we've always done."

After about a year of training by external consultants, Pittsburgh Steel is on track. Ninety percent of the orders are now delivered on time. Market share has recovered. Both productivity and profitability are increasing steadily, despite continued foreign competition. The managers thrive on matrix involvement. Meetings to coordinate product and functional decisions have provided a growth experience. Middle managers now want to include younger managers in the matrix discussions as training for future management responsibility.[23]

Pittsburgh Steel Company illustrates the correct use of a matrix structure. The dual pressure to maintain technology economies of scale and to develop sophisticated new products gave equal emphasis to the functional and product hierarchies. Through continuous meetings for coordination, Pittsburgh Steel achieves both economies of scale and flexibility.

All kinds of organizations have experimented with the matrix, including consulting firms, hospitals, banks, insurance companies, government, and many types of industrial firms.[24] Although widely adopted, the matrix is not a cure-all for structural problems. Many organizations have found that the matrix is difficult to install and maintain. When the matrix fails, it is usually because one side of the authority structure dominates, or employees have not learned to work in a collaborative relationship. In these organizations, a single authority structure with horizontal linkage mechanisms is better than a matrix.[25]

SYMPTOMS OF STRUCTURAL DEFICIENCY

Each form of structure—functional, product, hybrid, matrix—represents an important tool that can help managers make an organization more effective depending on the demands of its larger context. Senior managers periodically evaluate organization structure to determine whether it is appropriate to changing organization needs. Many organizations try one organization structure, then reorganize to another structure in an effort to find the right fit between internal reporting relationships and the needs of the external environment. As a general rule, when organization structure is out of alignment with organization needs, one or more of the following symptoms appear.[26]

Decision-Making Is Delayed or Lacking in Quality Decision-makers may be overloaded because the hierarchy funnels too many problems and

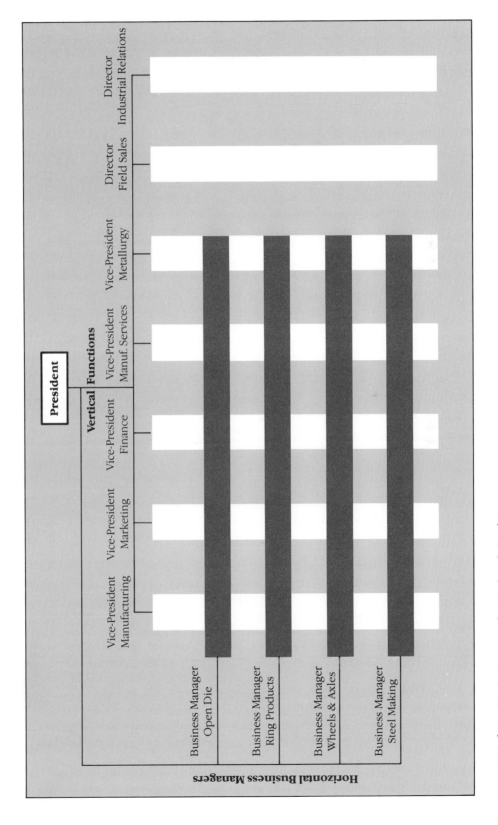

EXHIBIT 6.23. Matrix Structure for Pittsburgh Steel Co.

decisions to them. Delegation to lower levels may be insufficient. Another problem is that information may not reach the correct people. Linkages in either the vertical or horizontal direction may be inadequate to ensure decision quality. Finally, decision-makers may be too segmented. The organization structure may not integrate diverse perspectives into the decision-making process.

The Organization Does Not Respond Innovatively to a Changing Environment   One important reason for lack of innovation is that departments are not coordinated horizontally. The identification of customer needs by the marketing department and the identification of technological developments in the research department must be coordinated. Organization structure also has to specify departmental responsibilities that include environmental scanning and innovation.

Too Much Conflict Is Evident   Organization structure should allow conflicting goals to combine into a single set of objectives for the organization. When people act at cross purposes or are under pressure to achieve departmental goals at the expense of organizational goals, the structure is often at fault. Horizontal linkage mechanisms are not adequate. Vertical breakdowns occur when people at the operational level who see changing contingencies cannot feed information into the planning and objective setting at upper levels.

SUMMARY AND INTERPRETATION

Organization structure must accomplish two things for the organization: (1) provide a framework of tasks, responsibilities, reporting relationships, and groupings and (2) provide mechanisms for linking and coordinating organizational elements into a coherent whole. The framework is reflected on the organization chart. Linking the organization into a coherent whole requires the use of information systems and linkage devices in addition to the organization chart.

The single most important idea in this chapter is to understand how to manage the need for vertical and horizontal linkage mechanisms in organizations. Early organization theorists stressed vertical design, and relied upon vertical linkages such as the hierarchy, planning, and new positions to provide integration. While vertical linkages are a powerful means of coordination, they are not sufficient for most organizations in today's complex and rapidly changing world. In recent years, attention has been focused on the need for horizontal coordination through task forces, teams, and coordinators. Organization charts often show horizontal lines (dotted) to describe expected interactions as well as vertical lines of authority.

The best organization structure achieves the correct balance between vertical and horizontal coordination processes. Vertical structure and formal authority are stronger than horizontal relationships. The choice between functional, product, and hybrid structures determines vertical priority, and hence where coordination and integration will be greatest. Horizontal linkage mechanisms complement the vertical dimension to achieve the integration of departments and levels into an organizational whole. The matrix organization implements an equal balance between the vertical and horizontal dimensions of structure.

Finally, an organization chart is only so many lines and boxes on a piece of paper. A new organization structure will not necessarily solve an organization's problems. The organization chart simply reflects what people should do and what their responsibilities are. The purpose of the organization chart is to encourage and direct employees into activities and coordination processes that enable the organization to achieve its goals. The organization chart provides the structure, but employees provide the behavior. The chart is a guideline to encourage people to work together, but management must implement the structure and carry it out.

KEY CONCEPTS

functional structure	self-contained units
grouping	structure
horizontal linkage	symptoms of structural
hybrid structure	deficiency
integrator	task force
liaison role	team
matrix boss	top leader
matrix structure	two-boss manager
product structure	vertical information system
	vertical linkages

DISCUSSION QUESTIONS

1. What is the definition of organization structure? Does organization structure appear on the organization chart? Explain.

2. How do rules and plans help an organization achieve vertical integration?

3. When is a functional structure preferable to a product structure?

4. Large corporations tend to use hybrid structures. Why?

5. How does organizational context influence the choice of structure? Are some contextual variables more important than others? Discuss.

6. What is the difference between a task force and a team? Between liaison role and integrating role? Which of these provides the greatest amount of horizontal coordination?

7. What conditions usually have to be present before an organization should adopt a matrix structure? Could a matrix structure be used in a business college? Explain.

8. The manager of a consumer products firm said, "We use the brand manager position to train future executives." Do you think the brand manager position is a good training ground? Discuss.

9. In a matrix organization, how do the role requirements of the top manager differ from the role requirements of the matrix bosses?

10. An organizational consultant argued that, "The matrix structure is intermediate between the functional and product structures, and combines the advantages of both." Do you disagree or agree with this statement? Why?

GUIDES TO ACTION

As an organization designer:

1. Develop organization charts that describe the allocation of tasks and responsibilities, vertical reporting relationships, the grouping of individuals into departments, as well as supplementary documentation such as responsibility charts and position descriptions. Provide sufficient documentation so that all persons within the organization know their tasks, responsibilities, to whom they report, and how they fit into the total organization picture.

2. Provide vertical and horizontal linkages to integrate diverse departments into a coherent whole. Greater linkage is required in a large, complex organization in an uncertain environment than in a small organization and stable environment. Achieve vertical linkage through hierarchy referral, rules and procedures, planning and scheduling, adding levels to the hierarchy, and vertical information systems. Achieve horizontal linkage through paperwork, direct contact, liaison roles, task forces, and full-time integrators.

3. Choose between functional or product (self-contained units) structures when designing overall organization structure. Use a functional structure in a small or medium-sized organization that has a stable environment. Use a product structure in a large organization that has multiple product lines, and when you wish to give priority to product goals and to coordination across functions.

4. Implement hybrid structures, when needed, in large corporations by dividing the organization into self-contained product groups and assigning each function needed for the product line to the product division. If a function serves the entire organization rather than a specific product line, structure that function as a central functional department. Use a hybrid structure to gain the advantages of both functional and product design while eliminating some of the disadvantages.

5. Consider a matrix structure in certain organization settings if neither the product nor the functional structure meets coordination needs. For best results with a matrix structure, use it in a medium-sized organization with a small number of products or outputs that has a changing environment, and which needs to give equal priority to both products and functions because of dual pressures from the environment. Do not use the matrix structure unless there is truly a need for a dual hierarchy and employees are well trained in its purpose and operation.

6. Consider a structural reorganization whenever the symptoms of structural deficiency are observed. Use organization structure to solve the problems of poor quality decision-making, slow response to the external environment, and too much conflict between departments.

Consider these Guides when analyzing the following case.

CASE FOR ANALYSIS

AQUARIUS ADVERTISING AGENCY*

The Aquarius Advertising Agency is a middle-sized firm that offered two basic professional services to its clients: (1) customized plans for the content of an advertising campaign, e.g., slogans, layouts, and (2) complete plans for media such as radio, TV, newspapers, billboards, magazines, etc. Additional services included aid in marketing and distribution of products, and marketing research to test advertising effectiveness.

Its activities were organized in a traditional manner. The formal organization is shown in Exhibit 6.24. Each of the departments includes similar functions. Each client account was coordinated by an account executive who acted as a liaison between the client and the various specialists on the professional staff of the Operations and Marketing Divisions. The number of direct communications and contacts between clients and Aquarius specialists, clients and account executives, and Aquarius specialists and account executives is indicated in Exhibit 6.25. These sociometric data were gathered by a consultant who conducted a study of the patterns of formal and informal communication. Each intersecting cell of Aquarius personnel and the clients contains an index of the direct contacts between them.

Although an account executive was designated to be the liaison between the client and specialists within the agency, communications frequently occurred directly between clients and specialists and bypassed the account executive. These direct contacts involved a wide range of interactions such as meetings, telephone calls, letters, etc. A large number of direct communications occurred between agency specialists and their counterparts in the client organization. For example, an art specialist working as one member of a team on a particular client account would often be contacted directly by the client's in-house art specialist, and agency research personnel had direct communication with research people of the client firm. Also, some of the unstructured contacts often led to more formal meetings with clients in which agency personnel made presentations, interpreted and defended agency policy, and committed the agency to certain courses of action.

Both a hierarchical and professional system operated within the departments of the Operations and Marketing Divisions. Each department was organized hierarchically with a director, an assistant director, and several levels of authority. Professional communications were widespread and mainly concerned with sharing knowledge and techniques, technical evaluation of work, and development of professional interests. Control in each professional department was exercised mainly through control of promotions and supervision of work done by subordinates. Many account executives, however, felt the need for more influence and one commented:

> Creativity and art. That's all I hear around hear. It is hard as hell to effectively manage six or seven hot shots who claim they have to do their own thing. Each

---

* Adapted from John F. Veiga and John N. Yanouzas, "Aquarius Advertising Agency," in John F. Veiga and John N. Yanouzas, *The Dynamics of Organization Theory* (St. Paul, MN: West, 1984), pp. 212–217, with permission.

EXHIBIT 6.24. Aquarius Advertising Agency Organization Chart.

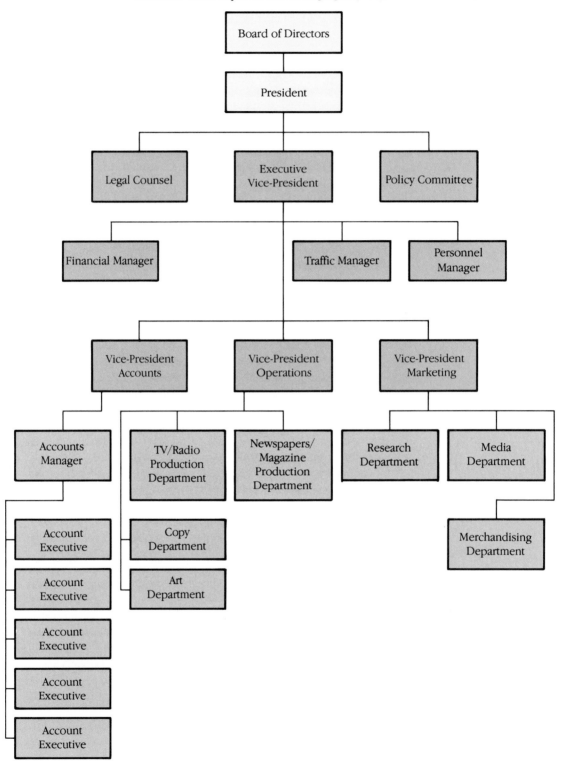

of them tries to sell his or her idea to the client and most of the time I don't know what has happened until a week later. If I were a despot I would make all of them check with me first to get approval. Things would sure change arond here.

The need for reorganization was made more acute by the changes in the environment. Within a short period of time, there was a rapid turnover in the major accounts handled by the agency. It was typical for advertising agencies to gain or lose clients quickly, often with no advance warning as

EXHIBIT 6.25. Sociometric Index of Contacts of Aquarius Personnel and Clients.

	Clients	Account Manager	Account Executives	TV/Radio Specialists	Newspaper/Magazine Specialists	Copy Specialists	Art Specialists	Merchandising Specialists	Media Specialists	Research Specialists	Traffic
Clients	X	F	F	N	N	O	O	O	O	O	N
Account Manager		X	F	N	N	N	N	N	N	N	N
Account Executives			X	F	F	F	F	F	F	F	F
TV/Radio Specialists				X	N	O	O	N	N	O	N
Newspaper/Magazine Specialists					X	O	O	N	O	O	N
Copy Specialists						X	N	O	O	O	N
Art Specialists							X	O	O	O	N
Merchandising Specialists								X	F	F	N
Media Specialists									X	F	N
Research Specialists										X	N
Traffic											X

F = Frequent—daily
O = Occasional—once or twice per project
N = None

consumer behavior and lifestyle changes emerged and product innovations occurred.

An agency reorganization was one of the solutions proposed by top management to increase flexibility in this subtle and unpredictable environment. The reorganization was aimed at reducing the agency's response time to environmental changes and increasing cooperation and communications among specialists from different departments. The top managers are not sure what type of reorganization is appropriate. They would like your help analyzing their context and current structure, and welcome your advice on proposing a new structure.

Questions

1. Analyze Aquarius with respect to the five contextual variables in Exhibit 6.1. How would you describe the structure, environment, goals technology, size and structure for Aquarius?

2. Design an organization structure that takes into consideration the contextural variables and the information flows in Exhibit 6.25.

3. Would a matrix structure be feasible for Aquarius? Why?

NOTES

1. Thomas Barrea, "I Unchained My Chain of Command," *Inc.,* October 1981, pp. 129–130.

2. John Child, *Organization* (New York: Harper & Row, 1977); p. 10.

3. Stuart Ranson, Bob Hinings, and Royston Greenwood, "The Structuring of Organizational Structures," *Administrative Science Quarterly,* 25 (1980): 1–17; Hugh Willmott, "The Structuring of Organizational Structure: A Note," *Administrative Science Quarterly,* 26 (1981):470–474.

4. Henry Mintzberg, *The Structuring of Organizations* (Englewood Cliffs, NJ: Prentice-Hall, 1979).

5. This discussion is based on Jay R. Galbraith, *Designing Complex Organizations* (Reading, MA: Addison-Wesley, 1973) and *Organization Design* (Reading, MA: Addison-Wesley, 1977), pp. 81–127.

6. This discussion is based on Galbraith, *Designing Complex Organizations.*

7. Paul R. Lawrence and Jay W. Lorsch, "New Managerial Job: The Integrator," *Harvard Business Review* (November–December, 1967):142–151.

8. Ann M. Morrison, "The General Mills Brand of Managers," *Fortune,* January 12, pp. 99–107.

9. Ibid.; Daniel Rosenheim, "The Metamorphosis of General Mills," *Houston Chronicle,* April 1, 1982, section 3, p. 4.

10. "GM's Test of Participation," *Business Week,* February 23, 1976, pp. 88–90.

11. Ron Winslow, "Utility Cuts Red Tape, Builds Nuclear Plant Almost on Schedule," *The Wall Street Journal,* February 22, 1984, pp. 1, 18.

12. Galbraith, *Designing Complex Organizations.*

13. Richard T. Rumelt, *Strategy, Structure, and Economic Performance* (Cambridge: Harvard University Press, 1974), p. 111.

14. This discussion is based upon Robert Duncan, "What is the Right Organization Structure?" *Organizational Dynamics,* (Winter, 1979):59–80; W. Alan Randolph and Gregory G. Dess, "The Congruence Perspective of Organization Design: A Conceptual Model and Multivariate Research Approach," *Academy of Management Review,* 9 (1984):114–127.

15. David Abdalla, J. Doehring, and Ann Windhager, "Blue Bell Creameries, Inc.: Case and Analysis," unpublished manuscript, Texas A&M University, 1981; Jorjanna Price, "Creamery Churns Its Ice Cream into Cool Millions," *Parade,* February 21, 1982, pp. 18–22.

16. This discussion is based upon Duncan, "What Is the Right Organizational Structure?"

17. Adapted from Linda S. Ackerman, "Transition Management: An In-Depth Look at Managing Complex Change," *Organizational Dynamics* (Summer 1982):46–66.

18. Sheri Aldridge, Jeff Jenkins, and Barry Jones, "Levi Strauss & Company," unpublished manuscript, Texas A&M University, 1981; "It's Back to Basics for Levi's," *Business Week,* March 8, 1982; pp. 77–78.

19. Stanley M. Davis and Paul R. Lawrence, *Matrix* (Reading, MA: Addison-Wesley, 1977), pp. 11–24.

20. Harry E. Peywell, "Engineering Management in a Multiple (Second- and Third-Level) Matrix Organization," *IEEE Transactions on Engineering Management* 26 (1979):51–55.

21. Davis and Lawrence, *Matrix,* pp. 46–52.

22. This discussion is based upon Duncan, "What Is the Right Organization Structure?"

23. This case was inspired by John E. Fogerty, "Integrative Management at Standard Steel," unpublished manuscript, Latrobe, Pennsylvania, 1980; Bill Saporito, "Allegheny Ludlum Has Steel Figured Out," *Fortune,* June 25, 1984:40–44; John M. Starrels, "Steel's Stiff Competition," *Wall Street Journal,* July 9, 1982, p. 12; "The Worldwide Steel Industry: Reshaping to Survive," *Business Week,* August 20, 1984, pp. 150–154.

24. Davis and Lawrence, *Matrix,* pp. 155–180.

25. This discussion is based upon Jay R. Galbraith, "Matrix Organization Designs: How to Combine Functional and Project Forms," *Business Horizons* 14 (1971): 29–40.

26. This discussion is based upon Child, *Organization,* ch. 1.

Structuring Dynamic Processes

Innovation and Change

FEDERAL EXPRESS

As the originator of the world's first overnight package delivery service, Santa Claus can only marvel at what Federal Express Corp. has wrought. It begins around midnight every weekday just across the main runway of Memphis' International Airport at a cavernous U-shaped building aptly called Super Hub. While Memphis sleeps, some sixty planes in their distinctively garish colors of purple, white, and orange land at fifteen separate bays to discharge upwards of 120,000 letters, parcels, and boxes bound for any of 13,500 U.S. communities.

As digital clocks blink the nightly countdown, 1,000 bustling workers shepherd the packages through the electronically controlled maze of belts, conveyors, diverters, and chutes, and bundle the sorted, weighed, zipcoded parcels aboard the already refueled aircraft, which speedily take off for some 100 distant distribution points. It's all done in four hours. By dawn, the Super Hub is all but deserted and deathly quiet; not a package is seen.

In eight years, Federal Express has not only zoomed from imminent bankruptcy to one of the nation's fastest growing and most profitable companies, it has also become something of a corporate legend. . . . What makes Federal Express work so effectively is its ability to stay ahead of its increasingly feverish competition with technological innovations and new services. In 1981 alone, it began operating at the expanded Super Hub, which cost $60 million and doubled capacity overnight; neared completion of its own $2.7 million pilot-training center; bolstered its in-house fleet with the delivery of two DC-10s and the purchase (for a reported $300 million) of fifteen new all-cargo Boeing 727-200Fs; extended service to twenty-nine additional cities, from Anchorage to San Juan; installed an optical-scanning tracking system that allows customers to get a fix on the location of their packages at any given time; and began testing fuel-economic diesel delivery vans with an eye toward converting its 2,500-van fleet to all-diesel by decade's end.

In June, moreover, Federal Express brashly inaugurated its Overnight Letter, a new service in which customers can dispatch correspondence weighing two ounces (about eleven pages) for next-morning delivery at a cost of $9.50. The letter service puts Federal in direct competition with the U.S. Postal Service's Express Mail—which, in turn, was a response to Federal's package service.

In a management style that Smith describes as "disciplined, participative and eclectic," every Federal Express employee is encouraged to come up with new ideas. Some 150 of the company's 800 managerial personnel are called "directors" of their particular segment, and every manager keys his or her operation to Federal's annual business plan, which sets the goals and objectives for the following two years. . . . One project that has gone from blue-sky to drawing board is a computerized image-enhancement device that allows pilots to "see" through fog and fly in poor conditions. If approved by the Federal Aviation Agency, Federal Express plans to not only use it in its own planes but market it commercially.[1]

Little wonder that Federal Express has been called "the creative courier." The organization is filled with creative energy. The most recent idea is ZapMail, which is delivered within four hours on the same day. What makes Federal

Express so innovative? Stiff competition is one reason, and another is the innovation goals and values espoused by top managers. Organization structure has also created a climate in which employees can suggest hundreds of ideas annually. Federal Express has found the right configuration to stay ahead of the competition.

But innovation is not limited to Federal Express. Every organization must cope with change in order to survive. Organizations are open systems. They cannot buffer themselves from environmental instability. Organizations must respond to internal and external pressures for change. The unprecedented pace of change in recent years prompted one writer to describe change as a fire storm that continues to gather force.[2] Most people agree that one thing organizations can be sure of is that things will not remain the same.

Many visible and tangible changes are in the technological domain. New discoveries and inventions quickly replace standard ways of doing things. The pace of technology change is revealed in the fact that the parents of today's college students grew up without cable television, crease-resistant clothing, personal computers, jet aircraft, detergents, video disks, electronic games, and talking checkout machines in supermarkets.

Purpose of This Chapter

The purpose of this chapter is to explore how organizations change, and how managers direct the change process. The idea of change appeared in chapter 2 on the environment, in chapter 5 on bureaucratic characteristics, and in chapter 6 concerning functional versus product structures. Certain environments precipitate a greater need for change within organizations, and the organization structure can be designed to facilitate either stability or change. The appropriate organization structure and internal systems to achieve desired types and amount of change is the topic of this chapter.

The next section defines the sequence of steps associated with successful change. Then four types of change—technology, product, administrative, human resource—are analyzed. The organization structure and management approach for handling each type of change is covered. Management techniques for influencing both the initiation and implementation of change are also covered. By the end of this chapter, students should be able to address the following questions: What type of organization structure is associated with each type of change? Should changes be imposed from the top down or from the bottom up? When should employees participate in the change process? But before dealing with these issues, let's determine what change is.

ELEMENTS IN THE CHANGE PROCESS

Organizational change is the adoption of a new idea or behavior by an organization.[3] **Organizational innovation,** in contrast, is the adoption of an idea or behavior that is new to the organization's industry, market, or general environment.[4] An organization that innovates is distinguished from an organization that changes by the extent to which the organization is a leader with respect to new products and production processes. For purposes of this chapter, however, the terms innovation and change will be used interchangeably because the process within organizations tends to be identical whether the change is early or late with respect to other organizations in the environment.

In order for the new idea or behavior to be adopted, a series of activities has to be completed. If one of these elements is missing, the change process will fail.[5]

1. **Need.** A need for change occurs when managers are dissatisfied with current performance. A perceived problem exists in the form of a gap between actual performance and desired performance. Organizational goals are not being met. Dissatisfaction may arise when managers learn that customers are complaining about product quality, or when a competitor develops a technology to manufacture goods more cheaply. Dissatisfaction is necessary to unfreeze managers from the current way of doing things so they will adopt new behaviors.

2. **Idea.** An idea is a new way of doing things. The idea may be a model, concept, or plan that can be implemented by the organization. The idea may be a new machine, a new product, or a new technique for managing employees. Normally an idea has to be matched to a need before it will be adopted. The idea should have the potential to reduce the dissatisfaction felt by managers about performance. The transistor, open classrooms in high school education, assembly lines, and personal computers were at one time somebody's idea.

3. **Proposal.** A proposal occurs when someone within the organization requests the adoption of a new behavior, idea, or technique. For many changes, employees provide a formal, written proposal with supporting documentation. For other changes, the proposal may be handled by an informal memo or request. The proposal is important because it crystallizes the idea and shows how it will solve a problem and improve performance. The proposal gives the organization the opportunity to decide if it wants to try the change.

4. **Decision to adopt.** A decision occurs when the organization makes a choice to adopt the proposed change. For a large change, the decision might require the signing of a legal document by the board of directors. For a small change, the decision might be informal approval by a supervisor to try a modification, such as in the assembly sequence.

5. **Implementation.** Implementation occurs when organization members actually use the new idea, technique, or behavior. Materials may have to be acquired, and workers trained to make sure that the change is in place. Implementation is a very important step because without it previous steps are to no avail. Implementation of change is often the most difficult part of the change process. Until people use it, no change has actually taken place.

6. **Resources.** Human energy and activity are required to bring about change. Change requires time and resources. Change does not happen on its own. Employees have to perceive both a need and the idea to meet that need. Someone must develop a proposal and provide the time and effort to implement it. Managers often take it upon themselves to champion a change. Sometimes they delegate the responsibility to a specific employees. Committees and task forces as described in chapter 6 are also effective ways to focus resources on a change. Organizations do not have enough time and

human resources to do everything. For a change to be successfully proposed and implemented, resources must be allocated to it.

Exhibit 7.1 indicates the sequence in which the change elements occur. Three points about Exhibit 7.1 are especially important. First, many needs for change and ideas originate in the external environment. Environments are never perfectly stable, so the organization must adapt. Organization boundary spanning units will discover problems to be solved and ideas that may improve performance. Second, needs and ideas are listed simultaneously at the beginning of the change sequence. Either may occur first. Sometimes a problem arises that precipitates search procedures to uncover an appropriate solution. Sometimes employees learn about a new idea and realize that it may be a more efficient way to do things. Many organizations adopted the digital computer, for example, because it seemed like a good way to improve efficiency. The search for a polio vaccine, on the other hand, was stimulated by a severe need. Either the need or the idea may occur first, but for the change to be accomplished, each of the steps in Exhibit 7.1 must be completed. Third, organizations differ in the frequency with which they adopt changes. An occasional change versus continuous change has great impact on the appropriate organization structure and design. Frito-Lay, for example, makes a point of organizing to facilitate frequent changes.

IN PRACTICE 7.1

Frito-Lay Inc.

When twenty managers at Frito-Lay sit around nibbling thick, white tortilla chips, there must be a reason. Small tortilla-chip makers have been hurting

EXHIBIT 7.1. Typical Sequence in Ingredients of Successful Change.

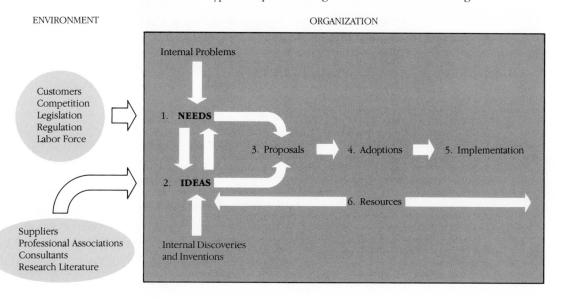

two Frito brands, Doritos and Tostitos. The twenty managers are nibbling a new Frito brand called Sabritas which they hope will counter the competition.

The managers are a committee that will decide the fate of the new product and whether test marketing can begin. Decisions have to be made about whether the chips should be white as marketing wants or yellow because manufacturing plants now use yellow corn, and whether the bag should have a twist tie around the top, which is more expensive but is used by competitors.

Committees like this are an important part of Frito-Lay. New products are essential to keeping its lead in the industry. Hundreds of suggestions are screened by managers each year. Many products are developed to meet specific competitive threats. Other products are dreamed up by researchers simply in the hope of selling more snacks. The screening process is tough, and only a few ideas are finally adopted. Successful ideas make it through the test kitchen, consumer taste testing, naming, package design, planning, manufacturing, and test marketing. Any of these tests can kill the product.

Frito-Lay has tried carrot chips and plantain chips. Plantain is a banana-like tropical fruit. "We couldn't even sell plantain chips in Miami," said Brad Todd, the marketing director for new products.

But successful products win big. Ruffles, Doritos, and Tostitos testify to that. Frito-Lay introduced Ruffles potato chips with the ridged texture in 1960. They sell at the rate of $425 million a year.

Two new chip contenders are Ta-Tos and O'Grady's. Ta-Tos are "super-crispy wavy," and O'Grady's are "extra-thick and crunchy." The names were selected after searching dictionaries and asking consumers what they thought of in response to the names. Manufacturing may be a problem because of unexpected little things. The cutting machines used to make O'Grady's won't accept potatoes longer than four inches, so the company would have to buy bigger cutters or sort its potatoes to produce O'Grady's on a large scale. Ta-Tos are soaked in a brine that may corrode the machinery.

If these problems are solved, then advertising and test marketing begin. Test marketing is the big hurdle. If a new product doesn't sell over $50 million a year, forget it. These sales have to come from money that would have been spent on competitor's products. This means that Ta-Tos and O'Grady's probably will not both make it to national marketing. The marketing people are convinced there is an extra-crispy market segment, but they will have to see if it has sufficient purchasing power, and whether it will be served by super-crispy wavy, or extra-thick and crunchy.[6]

Each of the six required change elements occurred at Frito-Lay. The competition from other chip manufacturers as well as internal ideas triggered the innovation process. Many proposals were generated, although only a few ideas were adopted and implemented. Frito-Lay is a continuous innovator, and hence devoted many resources to the change process. Special departments were established for making, testing, advertising and marketing new products, and committees with broad representation were involved in the decision process. But the allocation of so many resources paid off, because Frito-Lay continues to be the leader in the industry.

TYPES OF CHANGE

The four types of change that take place in organizations are technology, product, administrative, and human resource, as shown in Exhibit 7.2. Organization structure often facilitates one type of change more than others. In a rapidly changing industry like toys, an organization will have to introduce frequent new products. In a highly competitive environment, changes in the production process may be needed to squeeze out increased efficiency. Government organizations often have to make administrative changes in policies and procedures. Managing the six change elements described earlier and designing the correct organization structure depends upon the type of change needed by the organization.

Technology changes pertain to the organization's production process. These changes are designed to make the transformation process more efficient or to produce greater volume. Changes in technology involve the techniques for making products or services. For example, the heap leaching process for extracting gold from ore is a technology innovation that enables more efficient production of gold. In a university, technology changes are changes in techniques for teaching courses. Swearingen Aviation redesigned the assembly sequence for manufacturing light aircraft, which was a change in technology. Many supermarkets have adopted laser-scanning checkout systems, which are a change in the production process of a grocery store. Technology changes include work methods, equipment, and workflow.

Product changes pertain to the product or service outputs of the organization. New products include small adaptations of existing products, or entirely new product lines. New products are normally designed to increase the market share or to develop new markets, customers, or clients. New products often involve new technology and hence are often tied to technology change. Ta-Tos and O'Grady's are new products developed by Frito-Lay. The Saturn automobile developed by General Motors is a product change. A new

EXHIBIT 7.2. Four Types of Change in Organizations.

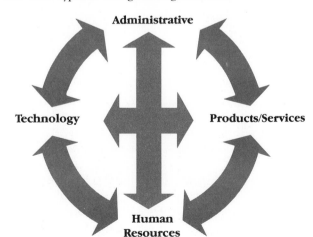

product in a university would be to offer non-credit evening courses for adults in the community.

Administrative changes pertain to the administrative domain in the organization. The administrative domain involves the supervision and management of the organization. Administrative changes include changes in organization structure, goals, policies, reward systems, labor relations, linkage devices, management information and control systems, and accounting and budgeting systems. In a university, administrative change would include a new merit pay plan, or a new promotion system. The adoption of a matrix structure by Pittsburgh Steel Company in the previous chapter was an administrative change.

Human resource changes refer to changes in the attitudes, skills, expectations, beliefs, abilities, style, and behavior of employees. An organization may wish to upgrade the leadership ability of key managers. This would be a human resource change. Other changes include improvements in communication, problem-solving, and planning skills of managers. Increased technical skills for production employees would be a human resource change. Overcoming a personal problem, such as alcoholism, is too. Human resource change is distinct from other types of changes because the primary focus is on the skill or style of employees rather than on technology, products, or administrative structure.

The arrows in Exhibit 7.2 indicate that the types of change are interdependent. A new product may require changes in the production technology. Or a change in administrative policy may require new employee attitudes and skills. Although changes affect each other, most changes can be classified as either technology, administrative, human resources, or product, depending upon the primary target. In many large organizations, all four types of change may be occurring simultaneously, as illustrated in the following example of General Telephone and Electronics Corporation.

IN PRACTICE 7.2

GTE

General Telephone and Electronics Corporation is now the largest independent telephone operating system in the United States. GTE employs almost 200,000 persons and is the thirtieth largest industrial and utility corporation. GTE is responsible for nineteen operating companies that provide communication services ranging from home phone service to highly complex data services for industry and national defense. Telephone markets have become increasingly dynamic, competitive, and technology-based. GTE has taken organizational steps to be innovative and to take advantage of opportunities created by a changing environment.

Key changes from recent years are summarized in Exhibit 7.3. New products produced by GTE companies include the GTD-5 Electronic Automatic Exchange, which offers computer-based switching systems tailored to business customers' specific needs. The Flip Phone has proved to be a popular item for home telephone users. Telemail is a nationwide electronic mail service that provides instantaneous delivery of messages anywhere in the U.S. The Micro-Fone is a credit-authorization terminal used by businesses to provide quick credit checks at the point of sale. Other new products include halogen sealed-beam headlamps for automobiles that offer greatly increased life span and that are now standard on Ford cars. GTE has also developed microprocessor control systems. The control system can sense temperature, time, position, and switch closure for automotive manufacturing and facility air conditioning applications.

Changes in technology are increasing the efficiency and scope of GTE activity. One need is for greater intercity communications capacity. Fiberoptics uses light inside extremely fine glass wires to transmit communications more efficiently than metal wires. Laser switching and transmissions systems have also been developed to increase transmission efficiency. GTE uses satellites to achieve a more efficient worldwide transmission system. Within GTE offices, many departments are adopting word processors and other labor-saving devices in day-to-day operations.

Administrative changes at GTE include new equal opportunity programs. All employees are evaluated on the basis of qualification rather than on race, religion, sex, national origin, or age. Policies of affirmative action, which seek to employ minorities, women, handicapped individuals, and disabled veterans,

EXHIBIT 7.3. Examples of Changes at General Telephone and Electronics Corp.

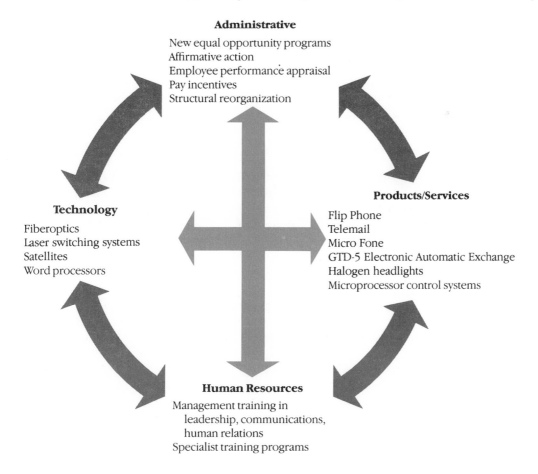

Administrative
New equal opportunity programs
Affirmative action
Employee performance appraisal
Pay incentives
Structural reorganization

Technology
Fiberoptics
Laser switching systems
Satellites
Word processors

Products/Services
Flip Phone
Telemail
Micro Fone
GTD-5 Electronic Automatic Exchange
Halogen headlights
Microprocessor control systems

Human Resources
Management training in
    leadership, communications,
    human relations
Specialist training programs

have also been established. GTE also implemented a pay-incentive system, and has periodically reorganized as necessary to maintain structural efficiency.

Programs for human resources focus on training opportunities. GTE recently finished a multimillion-dollar advanced management training center that will be used for workshops, seminars, and training sessions. Managers will receive training in leadership, communication, and human relations skills. Problem-solving and decision-making skills are also developed through formal training programs. Other programs focus on training of technical specialists so that employees in all activities can advance in their professional occupation.[7]

Under the GTE corporate umbrella are changes in products, technology, administration, and human resources. Most organizations at one point or another will make changes in each of these areas. The following sections describe the types of structures and management policies that are appropriate for regular changes of each type.

TECHNOLOGY CHANGE

As described in chapter 2, Burns and Stalker proposed two types of organization systems—the organic and the mechanistic.[8] The organic organization is typically associated with change, and is considered a better organizational form for adaptation to a shifting environment. The innovative organization is characterized by flexibility, decentralization, and the absence of rules and regulations. Mechanistic structures are believed to inhibit innovation. Mechanistic structures are fine for large organizations in a stable environment. But when organizations have to be innovative, they should be smaller and more organic.[9]

The flexibility of the organic organization is attributed to its ability to create and introduce new ideas into the organization.[10] Organic organizations encourage a bottom-up innovation process. Ideas bubble up from middle- and lower-level employees because they have the freedom to propose things and to experiment. At McDonald's, for example, a test kitchen and other facilities develop ideas. But the major source of ideas is people in the field, not people at headquarters. The inspiration for McSnack, a small McDonald's for shopping malls, came from the Minneapolis region. A manager wanted to open a restaurant in an area that didn't have space for a burger grill. The idea for McStop, a McDonald's version of a truck stop, evolved from managers in restaurants on interstate highways. Chicken McNuggets was an exception because it came from headquarters. A six-member team produced the McNugget in six months once it had the idea. The point is that everyone feels free to propose new ideas at McDonald's, which keeps the innovation juices flowing.[11]

The Ambidextrous Model

Organic characteristics represent a powerful way to promote internal innovation. Recent thinking has refined the idea of organic versus mechanistic structures with respect to innovation creation versus innovation implementation. For example, sometimes an organic structure generates innovative ideas but is not the best structure for securing implementation.[12] In other words, the initiation and the implementation of change are two distinct processes. Organic characteristics such as professional employees, decentralization, and low formalization are excellent for initiating ideas and proposals. But these same conditions often make it hard to implement change because employees do not have to comply. They can ignore the innovation because of decentralization and a generally loose structure.

How does the organization solve the dilemma? Robert Duncan suggested that organizations must be **ambidextrous**—they must incorporate structures that are appropriate to both the initiation and implementation of innovation.[13] The organization should behave in an organic way when the situation calls for the initiation of new ideas, and in a mechanistic way when implementation is required. The differences in structure for initiation and implementation are summarized in Exhibit 7.4. Organic characteristics of less formalization, employee professionalism, and decentralization encourage the initiation of ideas. Mechanistic characteristics, such as greater formalization and centralization, provide a stronger authority structure for the implementation of new ideas. The challenge is for organizations to create both organic and mechanistic conditions, which can be difficult. Techniques typically used for this are to switch structures, create separate departments, create venture teams, and encourage idea champions.

Switching Structures   Switching structures means that the organization can change between organic and mechanistic structure depending on the need for initiation or implementation. For example, the manager of a computer department might create free-flowing, organic conditions with brainstorming discussions during the early stages of developing a new computer project. Uncertainty is high and the free flow of ideas is essential. Once the project idea is developed, the department can revert to a more mechanistic structure to accomplish the more routine work.[14] Another example of switching structures is a small auto parts manufacturing plant that faced severe financial losses. Managers created organic conditions by shutting the plant down for a day. They emphasized the severity of the financial situation and asked for ideas to improve performance and increase efficiency. Mixed groups of employees and managers were formed and spent the rest of the day talking about the plant. Problems were identified and solutions were suggested. The

EXHIBIT 7.4.   Structural Characteristics That Influence Initiation and Implementation of Change in the Ambidextrous Model.

Structural Characteristic	DESIRED AMOUNT FOR THE CHANGE PROCESS	
	Initiation	Implementation
Formalization	Low	High
Centralization	Low	High
Professionalism	High	Low
Organic Structure	High	Low
Mechanistic Structure	Low	High

next day, the plant switched back to running things on a mechanistic basis. But the switch to an organic structure for idea generation proved to be effective.

Innovation Departments   In larger organizations, the initiation and implementation of innovation are often divided between departments.[15] Staff departments such as research and development, engineering, operations research, and systems analysis are involved in the initiation of changes for adoption in other departments. Departments that initiate change are organically structured to facilitate generation of new ideas and techniques. Departments that use these innovations tend to be mechanistically structured, which is more suitable for implementation. Implementation often requires a single focus, formal authority, and employee compliance, which are typical of mechanistic organizations. Exhibit 7.5 indicates how one department is responsible for initiation and how another department implements the innovation. The dual tasks of initiation and implementation thus are achieved through division of labor. The initiating department must establish a working relationship with using departments so that the innovations meet a genuine need in the user department.

Venture Teams   Venture teams are the most recent technique used to give free reign to creativity within organizations. Venture teams are often created as a separate division and given a separate location and facilities so they are not constrained by organizational procedures. Dow Chemical created an innovation department that has virtually total license to establish new-venture projects for any department in the company. Convergent Technologies uses the term "strike force" for the separate team that will develop a new computer. The team is cut loose to set up its own company and pursue members' ideas. The venture groups are kept small so they have autonomy and so that no bureaucracy emerges. Ideas at 3M Company are often developed within small groups that grow to become large divisions if the idea is successful.

To a giant corporation like IBM, use of separate groups is essential to free creative people from the bureaucracy. IBM has started fourteen of what they call independent business units since 1981. Each unit is a tiny company-within-a-company that explores areas of customized software, robots, and electrocardiographs. IBM's biggest success—the personal computer—was built by a new venture group. The wild success of the PC established the venture department as the way IBM thinks about innovation.[16]

Idea Champions   The concept of idea champion goes by a variety of names, including advocate, entrepreneur, intrepreneur, or change agent. Idea champions provide the time and energy to make things happen. Idea champions fight to overcome natural resistance to change and to convince others of the merit of a new idea. For example, when Texas Instruments reviewed fifty successful and unsuccessful technical projects, one fascinating finding emerged. Every failure was characterized by the absence of a volunteer champion. There was no one who passionately believed in the idea, who pushed the idea through all the necessary obstacles to make it work. Texas

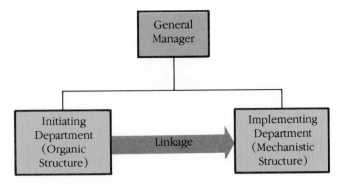

EXHIBIT 7.5. Division of Labor between Departments to Achieve Changes in Technology.

Instruments took the finding so seriously that the number one criterion for approving new technical projects is the presence of a zealous champion.[17]

The idea champion is associated with other means for generating technological innovations. The use of venture groups and separate innovation departments helps create a climate in which idea champions flourish. A company like McDonald's, although large and somewhat bureaucratic, has strong values that encourage the proposal of new ideas from the bottom. Companies encourage idea champions by providing freedom and slack time to creative people. Companies like IBM and General Electric overlook informal teams that develop new technologies without company approval. Known at General Electric as "bootlegging," the unauthorized research often pays big dividends. As one IBM executive says, "We wink at it. It pays off. It's just amazing what a handful of dedicated people can do when they are really turned on."[18]

Idea champions often come in two types.[19] The **technical champion** is the idea generator, the creator, the inventor, who develops the idea and is devoted to it. This person understands the technology. The **manager champion** acts as a sponsor to promote the idea within the organization. The manager champion sees the potential application, and has the prestige and authority to get a fair hearing and to allocate resources to it. Technical and manager champions often work together because the technical ideas will have a greater chance of success if a manager can be found to sponsor it. In other situations the champions work independently. The technical champion may push the idea all the way through to completion. This happened when an enterprising research engineer at Canadian National Railway developed a "positive traction control" device to prevent slippage on diesel locomotive drive wheels. Slippage when starting can ruin a diesel engine, and the engineer pushed the idea through to its acceptance and limited manufacture for use on Canadian National locomotives. When Steve Wozniak in 1975 tried to sell his boss at Hewlett-Packard on the idea of hooking a microcomputer to a television set, no one would listen. The idea champion was not encouraged so he quit and started his own company with Steven Jobs. The result was Apple Computer. Apple Computer certainly doesn't make the same mistake today, and has created an environment in which venture groups combined with idea champions produce many innovations.

IN PRACTICE 7.3

Apple Computer

Perhaps the most famous innovation in recent years was the Macintosh Personal Computer developed by Apple. It didn't happen by accident. Apple was being assaulted by IBM and other competitors, and needed a victory. The Macintosh dream belonged to Steven Jobs, who sponsored the whole idea. He created a separate team to develop the thing called Macintosh. He gave the group its motto: "It's better to be a pirate than to join the Navy." The group was supposed to swoop down fast, steal the best, and leave the rest. Since Jobs was chairman of the board, he had enough clout to raid anything needed from within Apple. The team was motivated to extraordinary efforts. Forty people were working 100-hour weeks. Their lives were devoted to the Macintosh.

A complete unknown, Burrell Smith, became the idea generator who pushed and pushed until the miniaturization required to achieve the Macintosh design was accomplished. Smith was working in the service department when he helped Bill Atkinson, a senior member of the Macintosh team, develop and test printouts. Burrell had an almost mystical affinity with circuitry, so Atkinson got Burrell onto the Mac design team. Burrell Smith began bubbling with electronic designs. He doesn't talk about his own achievements, but he attacks problems with evangelical fervor. As Smith honed his design for a new microprocessor, he moved more and more to the exceedingly difficult medium of Programmed Array Logic for support circuitry. When he approached the point of perfection, he threw the design away and started again. Each design got smaller, until on his fourth try it was small enough. He had packed 70% of Lisa's functions onto a single board smaller than a sheet of paper. The single board has about twice as much power as all the electronics in the IBM personal computer. The commitment of Steve Jobs to the Macintosh concept, and of Burrell Smith to reach new perfection in circuitry enabled the Macintosh to become a reality.[20]

Apple illustrates how a separate venture group and the use of idea champions leads to technological innovation. When companies need to innovate, they can facilitate bottom-up idea flow, separate departments, new venture groups, and the use of champions. Companies may use any or all of these in combination depending on the amount of technological change required. Of course companies in stable industries need not encourage frequent innovation. The responsibility of management is to find the right fit between the organization's need for technological innovation and the appropriate structure and internal processes.

NEW PRODUCTS

Many of the concepts described above are relevant to the creation of new products that involve new technology. But in many ways new products are a special case of innovation because they are used by customers outside the organization. Since new products are designed for sale in the environment, uncertainty about the suitability and success of the innovation is very high.

**New Product
Success Rate**

Research has explored the uncertainty associated with the development and sale of new products.[21] One survey examined two hundred projects in nineteen chemical, drug, electronics, and petroleum laboratories to learn about success rates. To be successful, the new product had to pass three stages of development—technical completion, commercialization, and market success. The findings about success rates are given in Exhibit 7.6.

On the average, only 57% of all projects undertaken in the R&D laboratories achieved technical objectives. All technical problems were solved and the projects had the opportunity of moving on to production. Only 55% of the projects that came out of R&D went to full-scale production and marketing. The remaining projects were rejected because production cost estimates or test market results were unfavorable. Thus, of all projects that were started, only about one-third (31%) were fully marketed and commercialized.

Finally, of the new products that were commercialized, only 38% achieved an economic return. The other 62% did not earn sufficient returns to cover the cost of development and production. The products that achieved economic success represented only 12% of all projects originally undertaken. The odds are only about one in eight that the development of a new product will return a profit to the company. New product development is thus very risky.

**Reasons for
New Product
Success**

The next question to be answered by research was: Why are some products more successful than others? Further studies indicated that innovation success was related to the collaboration between technical and marketing departments. Successful new products seemed to be technologically sound but also carefully tailored to customer needs. A study called Project SAPPHO examined seventeen pairs of new product innovations, with one success and one failure in each pair, and concluded the following:[22]

1. Successful innovators had a much better understanding of customer needs and paid much more attention to marketing.
2. Successful innovators made more effective use of outside technology and outside advice, even though they did more work in-house.
3. Responsible individuals in the successful innovations were usually more senior and had greater authority than their counterparts who failed.

EXHIBIT 7.6. Probability of New Product Success.

	Probability
Technical completion (technical objectives achieved)	.57
Commercialization (full-scale marketing)	
● Given technical completion	.55
● Given project is begun	.31
Market success (earns economic returns)	
● Given commercialization	.38
● Given project is begun	.12

Source: Adapted from Edwin Mansfield et al., *Research and Innovation in Modern Corporations* (New York: Norton, 1971), p. 57.

Thus there is a distinct pattern of tailoring innovations to customer needs, of making effective use of technology, and of having influential idea champions support the project. These ideas taken together indicate that the effective design for new product innovation is associated with horizontal linkage across departments.

Horizontal Linkage Model

The organization design for achieving new product innovation involves three components: departmental specialization, boundary spanning, and horizontal linkages. These components are similar to the differentiation and integration ideas in chapter 2 and the linkage mechanisms in chapter 6. Exhibit 7.7 illustrates these components in the horizontal linkage model.

Specialization   This means that research personnel and marketing personnel are highly competent at their own tasks. These two departments are differentiated from each other and have attitudes, goals, and structures appropriate for their specialized functions.

Boundary Spanning   This means that each department involved with new products has excellent linkage with relevant sectors in the external environment. R&D personnel are linked to professional associations and colleagues in other R&D departments. They are aware of recent scientific developments. They can apply new developments to new product design. Marketing personnel are closely linked to customer needs. They listen to what customers have to say, and analyze competitor products and suggestions by distributors. Marketing personnel conduct periodic surveys to gather market-related information, and attend association meetings to learn about developments in the market. Boundary spanning by both the research and marketing departments is important if the organization is to launch new products successfully.

Horizontal Linkages   This means that technical and market people share ideas and information. Research people inform marketing of new technical developments to learn whether the developments are applicable to customers. Marketing people provide customer complaints and information to R&D to use in the design of new products. If linkage between departments

EXHIBIT 7.7. Horizontal Linkage Model for New Product Innovations.

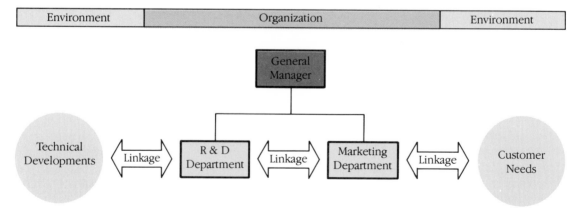

is good, the decision to develop a new product is a joint decision. Joint problem-solving will be used to resolve conflicts and problems during both development and commercialization.

In high tech companies where new products are necessary for survival, R&D people may participate in market planning that uses face-to-face, in-person interaction. During the course of innovation, marketing and R&D people talk almost daily. Marketing people are also encouraged to attend R&D planning sessions.[23] If marketing and R&D don't cooperate, innovation success is unlikely, as happened with one new product at Convergent Technologies.

IN PRACTICE 7.4

Convergent Technologies Inc.

Workslate, the Convergent portable computer, received accolades when introduced in 1983. The sophisticated machine took only one year to develop and was one of the hits of the National Computer Conference. It was featured on the cover of American Express Travel Related Services Co.'s 1980 Christmas catalog. It became the most successful product in the catalog and Convergent planned to ship 200,000 units in 1984.

By late 1984, Workslate was no more. In moving to high production, manufacturing problems appeared that were caused by hasty design. The product flew straight from engineering to manufacturing without sufficient discussion and coordination. Marketing people were under tremendous pressure to ship the product. Several months after production began, Convergent was supposed to be building one Workslate every hour. Instead, it took ten hours.

The manufacturing problems were the first sign of insufficient horizontal linkage. Marketing had not done any consumer research. They just assumed the market would consume whatever Convergent manufactured. This reflected top management's reluctance to spend money on sales and marketing because they were oriented toward developing new technology. Managers believed that if the underlying technology was sophisticated and of high quality, the product would sell itself. Overall, the marketing effort was simply not up to the needs of the product.

Convergent finally got the production process up to speed by March of 1984, but by then the market had cooled. Many orders were cancelled. It was a sad experience for everyone. The last rites were administered over Workslate in July of 1984 when the company wrote off $15 million. It didn't hurt the overall performance of Convergent badly, but senior managers learned an important lesson in how not to innovate.[24]

ADMINISTRATIVE CHANGE

So far our discussion has pertained to new production processes and products, which are based in the technology of the organization. The expertise for innovation lies within the technical core and professional staff groups such as research and engineering. Successful innovation is associated with horizontal and bottom-up innovation processes. Now we turn to administrative changes. Administrative change is the responsibility of upper managers in organizations. The overall process of administrative innovation is typically different from the process for innovations in technology or new products.

The Dual-Core Model

Administrative changes pertain to the design and structure of the organization itself, including control systems, information systems, the hierarchy of authority, and departmental grouping. Research into administrative change suggests two things. First, administrative changes occur less frequently than technical changes.[25] Administrative developments do not occur as often as changes in technology or products. Second, administrative changes occur in response to different environmental sectors and follow a different internal process than technology-based changes.[26] The dual-core model of organizational change identifies the processes associated with administrative change.[27]

Many small- and medium-sized organizations—schools, hospitals, city governments, welfare agencies, government bureaucracies, and many business firms—can be conceptualized as having dual cores, a technical core and an administrative core. Each core has its own employees, goals, problems, tasks, and environmental domain. Innovation can originate in either core. The concept of dual cores is illustrated in Exhibit 7.8.

The administrative core is above the technical core in the hierarchy, and each core has different responsibilities and vested interests. The responsibility of the administrative core includes the structure, control, and coordination of the organization itself, as well as the environmental sectors of government, financial resources, economic conditions, and human resources. The technical core is concerned with the transformation of raw materials

EXHIBIT 7.8. Administrative and Technical Activities in the Dual-Core Model.

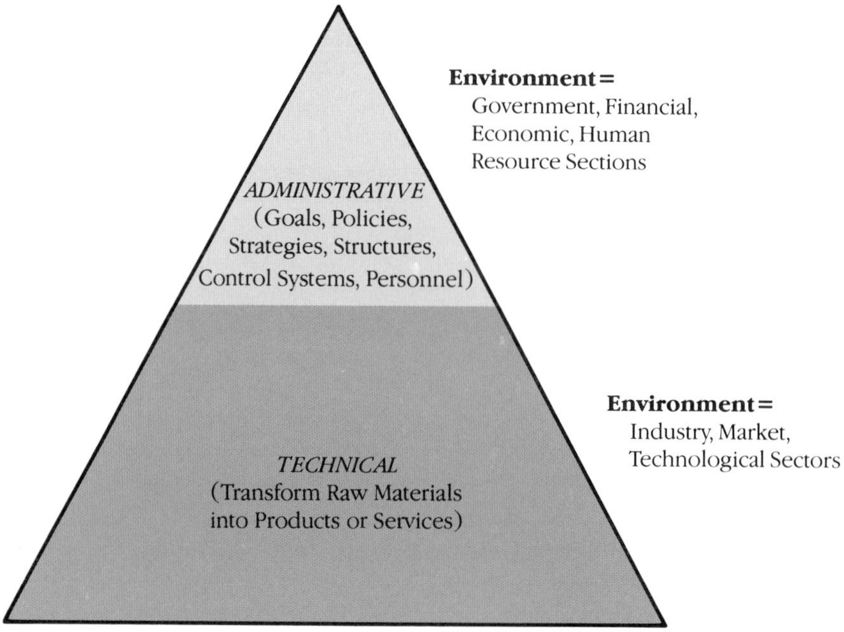

Environment =
Government, Financial, Economic, Human Resource Sections

ADMINISTRATIVE
(Goals, Policies, Strategies, Structures, Control Systems, Personnel)

Environment =
Industry, Market, Technological Sectors

TECHNICAL
(Transform Raw Materials into Products or Services)

into organizational products and services, and the important environmental sectors are customers and competitors.[28]

The findings from the research comparing administrative and technical change finds that a mechanistic organization structure is appropriate for frequent administrative changes, including changes in goals, policies, strategies, control systems, and personnel.[29] For example, administrative change is important in many government organizations that are bureaucratically structured. Low professionalism, high centralization, and high formalization facilitate the top-down implementation process that is used for administrative and structural changes. The very top levels of the organization, where ideas originate, is organic to facilitate the initiation of ideas. The middle and lower levels are mechanistic to facilitate the top-down implementation process. The mechanistic structure facilitates top-down change in response to changes in the government, financial, or legal sectors that require new internal policies, procedures, or structural arrangements. The mechanistic structure for administrative change contrasts with the use of an organic structure when changes in organizational technology or products are important to the organization.

The structural characteristics associated with administrative versus technical change are summarized in Exhibit 7.9. Technical change is facilitated by a bottom-up process and an organic structure. Organizations that must frequently adopt administrative changes tend to use a top-down process and a mechanistic structure. In tightly structured mechanistic organizations, innovations are initiated at the top and implementation is downward.

The point of the dual-core model is that when organizations must adopt frequent administrative changes, a mechanistic structure at the middle and lower levels is appropriate. This may seem to disagree with other findings about organic structure, but is consistent with the ambidextrous model. The top level of the organization is organic to facilitate the creation of administrative change, and the lower levels are mechanistic to facilitate the implementation of those changes. Many organizations do not adopt administrative innovations frequently, but when they are needed, the top-down process seems to work. For example, research into civil service reform found that the implementation of administrative innovation was extremely difficult in organizations that had an organic technical core. The professional-level em-

EXHIBIT 7.9 Dual-Core Model of Organization Change.

Organizational Characteristics	Type of Innovation	
	Technology	Administrative
Direction of Change	Bottom-Up	Top-Down
Structural Characteristic		
Formalization	Low	High
Centralization	Low	High
Professionalism	High	Low
Best Organizational Form for Change	Organic	Mechanistic

ployees with decentralized authority could resist civil service changes. By contrast, organizations that were considered more bureaucratic in the sense of high formalization, centralization, and employees who were less professional adopted the administrative changes readily.[30]

The top-down innovation process also is appropriate during periods of organizational decline or crisis. In times of an emergency, power is recentralized to the top of the organization, and changes are implemented through formal rules and procedures. A crisis may require new policies, structure, or handling of human resources, which are in the administrative domain.

One of the unresolved dilemmas is whether organizations can be structured to adopt frequent technical and administrative changes at the same time. Recent research suggests that some high-performing organizations adopt a greater number of both administrative and technical innovations than lower-performing organizations.[31] The argument is that the adoption of administrative innovations triggers the adoption of certain technical innovations. The best balance between administrative and technical innovation for specific environmental needs has yet to be determined. The dual-core model implies the organization can be structured to encourage one type of innovation or the other, but not both. For example, when the environmental pressures on Fairfield High School District shifted to require greater administrative innovation, the internal structure was changed from organic to mechanistic, and technical innovation declined.

IN PRACTICE 7.5

Fairfield High School District

Fairfield High School District was one of the most innovative districts in Cook County, Illinois. The district was decentralized to give teachers freedom and autonomy to try new ideas. Educational innovations were adopted quickly. The freedom of teachers to try new ideas encouraged them to propose changes, and administrators went along. Administrators found that teachers were happy and motivated when they had their freedom to experiment with new educational technology.

Suddenly the environment changed. The district was running a deficit. High salaries for teachers combined with high inflation for other costs were outstripping revenues. Taxpayers did not want additional tax increases. Three new board members were elected, who in turn hired a new superintendent. The new superintendent was an expert in administrative controls. His first job was to install a program, planning, and budgeting system (PPBS) in the district. The environment created a need for a new type of innovation to gain control over expenditures, give greater accountability, and provide greater value for dollars spent. These were issues of administration rather than educational technology. During the first few months the new superintendent centralized virtually all decision-making. The PPBS system reinforced the centralized decision-making. New rules and procedures were installed because any new educational program had to be cost analyzed. Approval would be contingent upon cost efficiency. Teachers no longer had professional autonomy to try new educational techniques on their own. Most innovations adopted in the district were administrative, and designed to obtain greater control over teachers.

Teachers did not like the new system, but had no choice. The new structure was mechanistic, and virtually closed down innovations in educational technology.

However, under the new system the district was very innovative in the administrative domain. It was the first district in the state to implement PPBS and other administrative procedures. The centralized structure enabled the top-down initiation and implementation of administrative changes. The same school district, during two different time periods using different structural forms, was innovative in different ways. The difference was precipitated by the environment. Technological innovation in the earlier period was a response to community demand for the district to be educationally current and up-to-date. Administrative innovation in the later period was a response to environmental demand for greater economy, reduced revenues, and cost efficiency.[32]

HUMAN RESOURCE CHANGE

The target of human resource change includes the values, attitudes, and skills of individual employees. Senior managers, for instance, may sense the need for upgrading employee ability. Human resource change programs are provided internally through training departments or through use of outside experts in organizational development.

Skill Development

Most large organizations establish training departments as the primary mechanism for upgrading employee skills. Skill development typically includes technical skills such as machine maintenance, machine operation, budgets, finance, drafting, engineering, and personnel procedures. Training departments also focus on management and leadership skills to help employees make the transition into management and to help current managers become better managers. Training departments use teaching techniques similar to those used in schools and universities. Formal classes may be held that include lectures, films, videotapes, and perhaps programmed instruction. Other methods of training include case studies, role playing, and business games. Business games simulate the organizational world of the employee, and provide an opportunity to make decisions and practice skills in the classroom where mistakes are not costly to the organization.

When training departments cannot meet employee training needs, organizations send employees to other organizations for a variety of seminars and courses. The American Management Association, consulting firms, universities, and junior colleges offer specialized courses for management and technical employees. Management courses include topics such as supervisory skills, communication, motivation, leadership, bargaining, and time management. Many small- and medium-sized companies do not have a training department, and rely on off-the-job seminars and programs to improve skills of their human resources.

Organizational Development

Organizational development (OD) has evolved as a separate field in the behavioral sciences that is devoted to a special kind of organizational change.

A primary focus of organizational development is people change. **Organizational development** uses knowledge and techniques from the behavioral sciences to improve organizational and employee climate, values, health, functioning, and well-being.[33] The goal of organizational development is to improve organizational performance by creating a positive human resource climate in which employees can be better performers. Organization development attempts to break down traditional authoritarian organizational habits to encourage power sharing, decentralization of decision-making, openness, and trust.[34] Individual growth and interpersonal competence within the organization are important targets of OD.[35] Organizational development attempts to improve the quality of life of organizational members and in so doing also improve organizational effectiveness. In terms of the goal and effectiveness models described in chapter 3, organizational development places high value on internal processes and human relationships.

The spirit of what OD tries to accomplish was illustrated in Honeywell's attempt to adopt a more participative management style. Honeywell had traditionally been a very authoritarian organization, but top management believed that engaging all employees more fully in the organization would be more productive.

> Many organizations today want to break out of the beat-'em-up school of management and move toward a more participative management style. But like abused children who grow up to become abusive parents, managers raised in a less enlightened manner may have difficulty operating under a new set of rules.
>
> At Honeywell, we have been working to change from what I call the Patton style of management to a more collaborative way of operating. We are still in the midst of this process. The way we manage people is still less than perfect. But now our employees can have a real share of the action rather than feeling blocked or frustrated by a rigid bureaucracy. And the results, both in quantifiable terms of productivity improvement and in less measurable terms of work climate and quality of innovation, have been extremely positive.[36]

The implementation of Honeywell's new way of managing was not easy. Managers and employees had to learn to think in a different way with respect to relationships with one another. Honeywell invoked the newer set of values by establishing the following management principles to guide the human resource change.

1. Productivity is a responsibility shared by management and the employee.
2. Broadened employee participation in decision-making will be fostered.
3. Team work, mutual respect, and a sense of ownership will be promoted at all levels of the division.
4. A positive climate for career growth will be supported throughout the division.
5. Work life and personal life have interacting needs that will be recognized.

Honeywell thus tried to create a higher quality of working life and participation for employees. Managers were no longer supposed to think of employees simply as instruments of production, but as whole people. This new approach would be satisfying to employees and the return to Honeywell would be improved ideas and productive use of human resources.

OD Intervention   Organizational development can take place at either the group or organizational level. Target groups are defined broadly to include all people who have working relationships. At Honeywell, autonomous divisions were the level of analysis for the organizational development efforts. The important thing is for senior management in the organization to see the need for OD, and to provide enthusiastic support for the change. Without a perceived need and a willingness to change, implementation of new values and behavior patterns is nearly impossible. Organization-wide techniques may include surveys and interviews to determine the extent of human resource problems. The implementation of new skills may occur in one department or division at a time. Three techniques used by many organizations for improving human resources are survey feedback, team building, and quality circles.

Survey Feedback   Organizational personnel are surveyed via questionnaires about their job satisfaction, attitudes, performance, leader behavior, climate, and quality of work relationships. A consultant then meets with the respective groups to discuss questionnaire results, to identify problem areas, and to discuss strategies for improvement.[37]

Team-Building   Team-development activities promote the idea that people who have working relationships can be trained to work as a team. Team-building improves employee performance both as team leaders and team members. Participants learn to build good relationships with other team members, to engage in joint problem-solving, and to reduce interpersonal friction. Improved communication, creativity, decision-making, and team performance typically result.[38] Team-building activities are useful for members of task forces, teams, and new product development groups.

Quality Circles   Quality circles are one of the most recent devices used to engage employee creativity and participation. A quality circle is a group of from six to twelve volunteer employees from the same work area. They meet regularly to discuss and solve problems affecting the common work activity. Members generally identify problems and then recommend solutions for quality and productivity improvements. In some companies, members receive training in team building, problem solving, and statistical quality control to enable the group to function more effectively. Often a facilitator is present at group meetings to help guide the discussion. Circles meet for about four hours a month on company time. The groups do not focus on personal gripes and problems. The circle objectives are quality improvement, productivity enhancement, and employee participation. The quality circle concept is spreading rapidly. A survey in 1982 showed that 44% of all companies with more than 500 employees had quality circle programs. Honeywell uses quality circles, and so do IBM, Westinghouse, Digital Equipment, and Xerox.[39]

Any major organizational development implementation requires resources and commitment on the part of the organization. Outside consultants who are experts in organizational development often provide guidance. Outside experts are important if the organization does not have its own OD staff. Implementation typically requires the cooperation of employees and their senior managers. An example of one large-scale approach to organizational development is the U.S. Navy.

IN PRACTICE 7.6
United States Navy

The Navy began to feel the need for improved human resource management in the early 1970s. Working conditions needed to be more attractive because military service was now voluntary. Several pilot steps were undertaken, and the organizational development program was ultimately called human resource management (HRM). Five HRM centers were established throughout the world. A typical HRM center might have several six-person teams who act as consultants to fleet commanders. They are located at the home ports of the fleet so that programs can be conducted while ships are in port.

A ship's crew is the level of intervention. The approach relies heavily on survey feedback techniques. The step-by-step sequence of training activities is given in Exhibit 7.10. After the cooperation of the commanding officer is obtained, the survey is administered to all crew members. The survey contains eighty-eight questions that cover five areas—work climate, supervisory leadership, peer leadership, work group processes, and work outcomes. The commanding officer decides how much participation is desired. The optional activities listed in Exhibit 7.10 are ones the CO can eliminate. A survey is conducted of all crews, but the feedback to individual work groups is optional. Many crews do complete the process, however, and find the results beneficial because leadership and work group problems are identified, and consultants work with crews to improve working relationships.

The overall impact of the human resource management program has been positive. One survey indicated that 75% of the commanding officers had a positive attitude toward involvement in the program. Another study of twenty ships and two carrier air groups found re-enlistment rates were positively related to survey findings. Disciplinary rates and indicators of operational readiness were also correlated with human resource efforts. The Navy's approach is probably the largest in the world because it involves thousands of people annually. It works because commanders are not required to participate against their will. The many crews that do participate are motivated to improve performance and receive the benefits.[40]

Relationship to Other Types of Change

Team-building and other OD training activities are often used to facilitate other types of innovation within an organization. The relationship between a research department charged with initiating change and a marketing department have to be positive in order for a new product to succeed. OD change activities such as team building can break down barriers and improve the quality of collaboration so that the organization adapts more easily to changes in the external environment. OD interventions are also used to support major administrative changes. When Ebasco Services, a nuclear power plant construction company, went to a matrix structure, trouble erupted. Organizational development training techniques were used to diagnose the trouble and to help employees adopt human relations skills needed to make the matrix work. OD helped defuse the conflicts. Now people work together much better within the sometimes confusing matrix hierarchy.[41]

STRATEGIES FOR MANAGING CHANGE

We began this chapter by looking at six ingredients—need, idea, proposal, decision, implementation, resources—that have to be present for any change to succeed. Then we discussed four types of change, and the organization structure and processes associated with frequent adoption of each type.

EXHIBIT 7.10. The Navy's Human Resource Management Cycle.

Time Phasing	Time to Conduct	Step Activity
Weeks 1 and 2	1½ days	1. Initial meetings between commanding officer (CO) and consultants
Week 2	½ day	2. Data-gathering planning meetings ■ will interview be conducted? what questions? ■ are additional survey questions desired? ■ schedule the survey administration
Week 3	1 hour per person	3. Survey administration (mandatory) ■ to all hands
Week 4	as required	4. Conduct interviews (optional)
Week 5	1 day	5. Return survey results to CO ■ brief printout format, terms ■ study and analysis
Weeks 6–7	½ day per working group	6. Survey feedback to work groups (optional) ■ familiarization with data ■ source of perceptions? ■ supervisory self-knowledge ■ possible solutions/recommendations for action
Weeks 8–9	½ day	7. Action-planning meeting (optional) ■ develop plans for human resource availability week: OD, equal opportunity, alcohol, drug abuse, and overseas diplomacy
Week 10	1–3 days per group	8. Human resource workshops (optional) ■ vertical slice of ship or intact work group ■ modular training packages (standardized series of lectures, films, and exercises on such topics as motivation, communications, MBO, leadership, and race relations)
	2 days	9. Command action-planning workshop (optional) ■ selected members of crew normally (CO participates part-time) ■ CO approves plan (a command action-plan is mandatory)
Week 11	indefinite	10. Action phase ■ implement action-plans
Weeks 25–30	½ day	11. Follow-up by consultant ■ determine effect of human resource activities through interviews and discussions ■ meet with CO
Weeks 11–104	as negotiated	12. Follow-on activities (optional) ■ survey re-administered ■ conduct additional workshops

Source: D. D. Umstot, "Organization development technology and the military: A surprising merger?" *Academy of Management Review,* 1980, 5, p. 194. Reprinted with permission.

In this final section we focus on a set of specific techniques that frequently help managers implement change. These strategies and techniques have been gleaned from a variety of change experiences to improve the probability of initiating and implementing any type of change successfully. These ideas are summarized in Exhibit 7.11.

1. **Diagnose a true need for change.** A careful diagnosis of the existing situation is necessary to determine the extent of the problem. If the people who are affected by the change do not perceive a genuine problem, the change process should stop right there. For new products, customers should feel a need. For other types of change, the need will be felt by people within the organization. A perceived performance gap is necessary to unfreeze users and make them willing to invest the time and energy to adopt new techniques and procedures.[42]

2. **Find an idea that fits the need.** Finding the right idea often involves search procedures—talking with other managers, assigning a task force to investigate the problem, sending out a request to suppliers, or asking someone within the organization to create a solution. The creation of a solution requires organic conditions. People must have the freedom to think about and explore new options. A few organizations, such as General Motors, have created positions called corporate thinkers. These individuals have no deadlines and no day-to-day responsibilities. They think about social trends, economics, politics, television, and whatever else may be relevant to solving problems. The ultimate creative insight often provides a unique solution to a management problem.

3. **Engage top management goals and support.** Successful change requires the support of top management. Top managers should articulate clear innovation goals so employees will know they are expected to initiate and adopt new ideas. For a single large change, such as a structural reorganization, the president and vice-presidents must give their blessing and support. For smaller changes, the support of influential managers in the relevant departments is required. The lack of top management support is one of the most frequent causes of implementation failure. If top management has other goals and priorities, the change may be swept aside.[43]

EXHIBIT 7.11. Strategies for Managing Change.

1. Diagnose a true need for change.
2. Find an idea that fits the need.
3. Engage management goals and support.
4. Design change for incremental implementation.
5. Plan to overcome resistance to change.
   a. Alignment with needs and goals of users.
   b. Communication and education.
   c. Participation and involvement.
   d. Forcing and coercion.
6. Establish change teams.
7. Foster idea champions.

4. **Design the change for incremental implementation.** Design of the change itself can increase the likelihood of adoption and implementation. The prospects for success are improved when the change can be broken into subparts and each part adopted sequentially. Users who see success at the first stage of implementation then throw full support behind the rest of the change program. An incremental approach also reduces the cost of failure. If it's a bad idea, only a few resources are lost. Whenever possible, the implementation of a new change should start small.[44]

5. **Plan to overcome resistance to change.** The most difficult part of any change is implementation. Many good ideas that are approved are never used because they are never implemented. Managers failed to anticipate or prepare for resistance to change by consumers, employees, or other managers. No matter how impressive the performance characteristics of an innovation, its implementation will conflict with some interests and jeopardize some alliances in the organization. To increase the chance of successful implementation, management must acknowledge the conflict, threats, and potential losses perceived by employees.[45] Proposed changes often appear awkward and inefficient to people who are supposed to use them. Employees may be uncertain about the impact on their own job and careers and thus resist implementation. Several strategies can be used by managers to overcome the resistance problem:

a. **Alignment with needs and goals of users.** The best strategy for overcoming resistance is to make sure that change meets a real need. Employees in R&D or other staff departments often come up with great ideas that solve nonexistent problems. This happens because initiators fail to consult with people who use the change. A major cause of resistance is that the change does not appear to meet a need or improve performance.[46]

Resistance can be frustrating for managers, but moderate resistance to change is good for the organization. If users believe that the change has no value, or if top management does not support it, the interest of the organization is probably not served by the change. Resistance to change provides a moderate barrier to avoid frivolous or fad changes, or change for the sake of change. The process of overcoming resistance to change normally requires that the change be good for the organization.

b. **Communication and education.** Communication can inform users about the need for change and about the consequences of the proposed change. Educational efforts prevent false rumors, misunderstanding, and resentment. Open communication often gives management an opportunity to explain what steps will be taken to ensure that the change will have no adverse consequences for employees.[47] A common mistake for managers is to assume that other people understand the change. Management should provide far more information and education than they think is necessary to be sure that users are properly informed.

c. **Participation and involvement.** Early and extensive participation in the change should be part of implementation strategy. Participation gives those involved a sense of control over the change activity. They understand it better, and they become committed to successful implementation. Involvement in a change should normally begin in the initiation stage so that ideas and proposals from users can be incorporated in the change design. The participation strategy was so successful at BF Goodrich's Oaks, Pennsylvania Power Plant that managers repeated the strategy in four other plants. They successfully implemented a new maintenance management system in all plants in about two years by letting employees be heavily involved in the implementation process.[48]

d. **Forcing and coercion.** Sometimes managers have to resort to more extreme techniques. Resistance is overcome by threatening employees with loss of jobs, promotion possibilities, or by firing or transferring them. Management power is used to overwhelm resistance. In most cases this approach is not advisable because it leaves people angry at change managers, and the change may be sabotaged. This technique may be needed when speed is essential, such as when the organization faces a crisis. It may also be required for needed administrative changes that flow from the top down in an otherwise organic organization. The change initiators must have formal authority and control over rewards and punishments.[49]

6. **Establish change teams.** Throughout this chapter we've discussed the need for resources and energy to make change happen. Separate innovation departments, new venture groups, or an ad hoc team or task force are ways to focus energy for both initiation and implementation. A separate department may have the freedom to create a new technology or new product. Separate departments or task forces can also be created to help with implementation. They can be responsible to see that all implementation activities are completed. The task force can be responsible for communication, involvement of users, training, and other activities needed for change. Change teams provide the resource focus needed to make things happen.

7. **Foster idea champions.** One of the most effective weapons in change battles is the idea champion. The most effective champion is a volunteer champion who is deeply committed to the change idea. The idea champion sees that all technical activities are correct and complete. An additional champion, such as a manager sponsor, may also be needed to move the idea through to implementation. Managers become involved because they are enthusiastic and committed to the idea, although they did not help create it. Technical and managerial champions help create novel ideas and overcome resistance to change. Idea champions often break the rules and push ahead even when others are non-believing. But the enthusiasm pays off.[50]

Sometimes several strategies work simultaneously to facilitate implementation. Consider the development of the "Polishing Pen" at Chesebrough-Ponds.

IN PRACTICE 7.7

Chesebrough-Ponds Inc.

John D. Cunningham got the idea one day when "a chap walked into the lab with a big marking pen." Cunningham saw it and said, "That could be a nail polish!" The outcome was the polishing pen, the first really new innovation in cosmetics in ten years. The idea looked easy, but implementation seemed impossible at times.

Executives at Chesebrough's Lab in Trumbell, Connecticut, encouraged employees to quit working on assigned projects every Friday at noon. The rest of the day was devoted to experimental work of their own choosing. This created an atmosphere in which employees were free to experiment. Every Friday afternoon, Cunningham worked on the challenge of getting nail polish to go through a marking pen. Usually the polish was too thick, or so thin that it had too little color. Solving the problems became a religion. Everyone told Cunningham it wouldn't work so he was determined to prove them wrong.

One problem was the use of gold and silver pigments, which were too thick to pass through the sponge-like reservoir. An ink-flow controller was developed, but that didn't always work either. Cunningham attacked the size of enamel particles to attain higher pigment with less viscosity. Fortunately, researchers elsewhere at Chesebrough were developing a method for grinding pigments into particles. Another company, Pilot Pen Co., also helped solve the problem of using gold and silver pigments in marking pens.

After several months, things started to come together, and Cunningham built a prototype. It worked. Marketers ran the product by consumers, who wanted it. Chesebrough then assigned a team for implementation. Team members came from manufacturing, development, packaging, and marketing. The pen was on the market in 1984, and the reception was good. It's still too early to tell whether it will be a big success, but something else has happened that is important. A whole series of ideas for new products have been engendered within Chesebrough Ponds. The use of free time on Fridays, the creation of the implementation team, Cunningham's role of idea champion have shown other people in Chesebrough how to innovate. Even if the pen fails, Chesebrough will ultimately succeed in the innovation business.[51]

SUMMARY AND INTERPRETATION

Organizations face a dilemma. They prefer to accomplish their day-to-day activities in a predictable, routine manner. The fewer changes undertaken, the more predictable and efficient the organization can become. But the external environment is changing. Innovation and change are required in order to adapt to the changes taking place in the environment. Change, not stability, is the natural order of things. Organizations need to achieve some degree of both stability and change, to facilitate both routinization and novelty. This is the dilemma they have to resolve.

The models and ideas described in this chapter can be thought of as solutions to this dilemma. Organizations handle the stability-change dilemma depending on the amount and type of innovation required. The organic organization is suitable when frequent technical innovations are required. The organic organization is oriented toward change rather than toward stability. Mechanistic organizations are oriented toward technological stability and efficiency. Organizations thus resolve the technology stability-change dilemma by structuring in a mechanistic way wherever possible to obtain efficiency, and by structuring in an organic way when the organization needs new ideas and frequent changes. Another approach is to create a separate department charged with developing and initiating new ideas. In this way, the organization can provide an inflow of new ideas for adaptation, yet increase efficiency through routinization and stability in parts of the organization. The ambidextrous, dual-core, and horizontal linkage models each describe how to design the overall organization to achieve specific types of change.

Another important idea from this chapter is the notion that bureaucracies can be innovative. Bureaucracies have been widely criticized for discouraging innovation and change. Bureaucracy errs on the side of stability because rules and regulations prevent change. The point from this chapter is that a bureaucratic structure is appropriate when the technical products or services are relatively stable and do not require frequent change. Bureaucracies are suited to change in the administrative domain. Government bureaucracies, for example, can adapt very quickly to new regulations or policies. The power balance favors administration, and the mechanistic structure provides a useful instrument for carrying out administrative changes in a top-down fashion.

This brings us to another dilemma: the underlying philosophy of organization theory versus the philosophy of organizational development. Organization theory takes an organizational point of view. It seeks to find the best organizational design contingent upon a variety of organizational factors. For many organizations, the best design may involve a mechanistic structure, routine work, and standardization. Organizational development, however, reflects a concern for humans within the organization. Organizational development changes are designed to make organizations more satisfying places to work by reducing autocratic processes.

The values underlying organizational development favor organic organizations. In the organization development view, workers should have freedom to participate in decisions, to do interesting work, and to initiate ideas. Both organizational development specialists and organization theorists are concerned with organizational effectiveness, but they seem to advocate different ways of achieving it. In organization theory, effectiveness is achieved by tailoring the organization to technological and environmental needs. In organizational development, the organization should be tailored to challenge the higher-level abilities and needs of organization participants.

The final point to consider is that of venture groups and idea champions, because these roles are relatively new to the literature.[52] Creating separate venture groups or teams has turned out to be a powerful form of innovation for companies like IBM, Digital Equipment, Apple Computer, and 3M. The separation of the innovation group from the constraints of the larger corporation fosters creativity, commitment, and innovation. The complete separation of responsibility for a specific new idea is costly in terms of people and resources, but produces enormous dividends. Moreover, creating an organization climate in which idea champions flower provides an abundant supply of new ideas. Idea champions often act on their own, in addition to the duties of their job. They are scattered around the organization, and take it upon themselves to interpret needs and develop solutions. Initiation takes a large amount of time and faith. Idea champions push ahead even when others disbelieve. Idea champions are tremendously valuable to the organization because they provide the organization with an opportunity to change and improve.

KEY CONCEPTS

administrative change
ambidextrous model
change process
dual-core model
horizontal linkage model
human resource change
idea champions
organizational change
organizational development
organizational innovation

overcoming resistance to
    change
product change
quality circles
strategies for managing
    change
switching structures
team building
technology change
venture teams

DISCUSSION QUESTIONS

1. Name the four primary types of change. How do they differ from each other? Do they influence each other?

2. How are organic characteristics related to changes in technology? To administrative changes?

3. Describe the dual-core model. How does administrative change normally differ from technology change? Discuss.

4. When organizations free key employees from routine work in order to develop new ideas, how are they coping with the dilemma of needing both stability and change? Discuss.

5. Why do organizations experience resistance to change? What steps can managers take to overcome this resistance?

6. "Bureaucracies are not innovative." Discuss.

7. A noted organization theorist said, "Pressure for change originates in the environment; pressure for stability originates within the organization." Do you agree? Discuss.

8. Do the underlying values of organizational development and organization theory differ? Is there any way to accommodate both sets of values in organizational design?

9. What are the six elements required for successful change to be completed? Which element do you think managers are most likely to overlook when they are involved in a change project? Discuss.

10. "Resistance to change is good for the organization because it keeps frivolous and unimportant ideas from being adopted." Do you agree or disagree with this statement? Why?

11. Briefly describe the ambidextrous model. How do organizations meet the need for simultaneous organic and mechanistic characteristics?

12. What organizational traits have been found to be associated with successful new product introduction?

13. The manager of R&D for a drug company said that only 5% of their new projects ever achieve market success. He also said that the industry average is 10% and wondered how his organization might increase its success rate. If you were acting as a consultant, what advice would you give him concerning organization structure?

GUIDES TO ACTION

As an organization designer:

1. Facilitate frequent changes in internal technology by adopting an organic organizational structure. Give technical personnel freedom to analyze problems and develop solutions for technological problems, or create a separate organically structured department or venture group to conceive and propose new ideas.

2. Facilitate administrative change of policies, goals, performance evaluation systems, and organization structure by adopting a mechanistic structure. Use a mechanistic structure when the organization needs to adopt frequent administrative changes in a top-down fashion.

3. Establish a separate training department or work with organization development consultants when changes in the attitudes, values, or skills of people are required. Use organizational development consultants for large-scale people changes.

4. Encourage marketing and research departments to develop linkages to each other and to their environments when new products are needed.

5. Make sure that every change undertaken has a definite need, idea, proposal, decision, implementation strategy, and resources. Avoid failure by not proceeding until each element is accounted for.

6. Use additional techniques to achieve successful implementation if necessary. Additional techniques include obtaining top management support, implementing the change in a series of steps, assigning an idea champion, and overcoming resistance to change by actively communicating with users and encouraging their participation.

Consider these Guides when analyzing the following cases and when answering the questions listed after each case.

CASES FOR ANALYSIS

WARD METAL PRODUCTS LTD. (Quebec)*

Ward Metal Products Ltd. was a large manufacturer of light- and medium-weight metal products such as metal frames, vestibule intercom panels, assorted metal containers, boxes, and cabinets. Its primary customers were contractors and hardware wholesalers. From rather modest beginnings in 1925, the company had steadily expanded, with few exceptions, and by 1966 it enjoyed a large volume of sales in eastern Canada. The company was located in Montreal, Quebec, where approximately three hundred persons were employed.

---

*Prepared by Professor P. E. Pitsiladis, April 1968, Sir George Williams University, Montreal. Use or reproduction of any portion of this case is prohibited, except with written permission. Reprinted by permission. The case was prepared as the basis for class discussion rather than to illustrate either effective or ineffective handling of administrative situations.

THE WARD FAMILY AND EMPLOYEE RELATIONS

Over the years the ownership and senior managerial control of the company had remained in the hands of the Ward family. Dexter Ward, the founder and president, had become wealthy as a result of his activity and investment in this company and elsewhere. Largely through their aggressive support of and involvement in civic projects and welfare drives, Dexter Ward and other members of the family had become well known to both the French- and English-speaking segments of Montreal's population.

Nearly two-thirds of the company's personnel worked in the production department. A large majority of the jobs in this area were held by French Canadians, many of whom had considerable seniority with the company. Service history records of fifteen and twenty years were quite common. The French Canadian employees in the production department seemed especially to cherish the freedom they enjoyed under their French Canadian supervisors.

STUDY OF OPERATIONS

In 1966 Mr. Donald Chapman, general manager of the Ward company, conducted a review of all the firm's operations. The company had been facing keener price competition since 1963; although sales had continued at their higher level, profits had begun to drop off noticeably because of reduced margins. The president and other senior company officials had become most anxious to improve the profitability of the company, but they were unsure as to how this might be done. Mr. Chapman, who had joined the company some ten years earlier, concluded as a result of the study that cost and procedural controls throughout the organization were lacking. He also believed that the rapid growth of the company since the end of the Second World War had created a need for additional specialized staff personnel in accounting, marketing, and related areas. Accordingly, he made it generally known that if the company was to maintain its market position and improve its profits, some of the organizational "vacuums" would have to be filled.

ORGANIZATION AND PROCEDURAL CHANGES

In the early part of 1967, Mr. Chapman appointed Jack Sillman as the first comptroller and manager of the company's new administrative services department. As a chartered accountant, Sillman had previously served as a chief officer in the revenue department of the provincial government. According to organizational plans, the administrative services department was to include, as a start, all the existing accounting functions such as accounts payable and accounts receivable. The primary function of the department was to tighten up controls throughout the company, but more particularly in "those areas where the potential for new economies was greatest."

In addition to the accounting functions, two new sections would eventually be established within the administrative services department. First, a budgeting section would be needed to install and administer a more sophisticated companywide budgeting program. Budgeting, as it had existed up until that time, was informal and for the most part consisted simply of each department manager submitting an annual estimate of expenditures for the coming year to the company treasurer for approval. Secondly, a systems section would be needed to conduct a procedures program involving the study and write-up of interdepartmental administrative practices.

IMPLEMENTATION OF NEW PROGRAM

By the summer of 1967 both section heads had been appointed. George Finch, the new supervisor of the budgeting section, was to devote his time to developing the framework and details of the budgetary control program. Charles Bond, formerly a branch manager of a systems service organization, was to begin, as supervisor of the systems section, the study and write-up of interdepartmental procedures.

George Finch in the meantime had worked out what he thought would be an acceptable budgetary control program. After Sillman had examined and approved the new program, Finch suggested that a meeting be arranged with the other department managers at which time they could outline the new program.

The meeting that followed was attended by the staff of the administrative services department and all of the departmental managers except "Rollie" Cloutier, manager of production. Chapman and other senior management officials had previously declined to attend, indicating that they preferred not to "interfere." Sillman was surprised by Cloutier's absence, however, inasmuch as he had been assured by Cloutier that the date and time of the meeting were perfectly acceptable. Finch described the new budgetary program to those present; no major objections were raised, but the reception was hardly more than lukewarm. Nonetheless, the department managers did agree to Sillman's suggestion that a task force be established to assist Finch in implementing the program and working out any of the problems that might arise. The task force was to consist of department representatives to be appointed by each of the managers.

INTERDEPARTMENTAL DIFFICULTIES

In the months that followed, Sillman kept receiving unfavorable progress reports from both Finch and Bond. Bond complained:

> My boys can't seem to make any headway in their procedure work; the biggest problem is the production department; those people never have the time for us. Whenever we do manage to nail them down to a time and a place, they don't bother to show up anyway. We are generally left standing around sucking our thumbs. To top it all off, we've found that those procedure instructions which we have managed to issue over your signature are being ignored by the production people altogether. I'm fed up with the whole thing. So are the boys. We're not getting the support of the management and the people we are supposed to be working with won't cooperate.

From the reports he received and from his own personal feelings on the matter, Sillman believed that the situation had become acute. However, as a start, he thought that a heart-to-heart talk with Rollie Cloutier might be helpful. Early one morning Sillman called Cloutier and suggested they get together to discuss the situation. "There is no point in it, Jack," Cloutier replied, "I may just as well be sincere. We are busy people here in production and we do not have a lot of time to play around. Our problems are a helluva lot more complicated than anything you'll find in bookkeeping. We'll work with you but it will have to be in our spare time."

Sillman decided to refer the entire matter to Chapman, the general manager.

Questions

1. *What type of change was initiated at Ward Metal Products? What model of change describes the attempted change process? Would the model predict successful change in this organization? Discuss.*

2. *Analyze the implementation techniques used in the case. What recommendations would you make to help implement the proposed changes? To facilitate the implementation of future changes?*

DATA GENERAL CORPORATION*

What motivates a company to abandon its tradition in order to develop a radically new machine? Edson D. de Castro, president of Data General Corp., has at least one answer. When a company is doing well, he says, few managers ponder change. It is when the company is confronted with "the dismal prospect of failure," he says, that attention finally is riveted on the need to do things differently.

De Castro speaks from experience. Data General's new line of desktop personal computers resulted from changes in the company's product-development process that were forced by the bald failure of its first entry in this category of computers. That machine, called the Enterprise, was two years late, had limited software, and was overpriced at its June 1981 debut. As one computer store owner recalls, "It was hopelessly out of step with the market." A mere 1,200 units were sold as Data General was mowed down by such challengers as Apple Computer Inc. Development of the Enterprise involved a series of classic mistakes, admits de Castro: "There was simply a lack of the focused business development needed to pull the project off."

The magnitude of the error worsened by the day as demand for the desktop machines continued to swell. Such computers are easy for the novice to use and, for $20,000 and much less, pack the power of computers costing up to $60,000. Projections now predict sales of $25.9 million, or one-third of worldwide computer sales, by 1987.

WAVE OF THE FUTURE

Yet Data General, along with most other minicomputer and mainframe computer makers, misjudged the requirements of making machines for this market and got in late. With the exception of International Business Machines Corp., they did not cope well with a different semiconductor technology geared to the smaller machines, failed to rethink distribution channels to reach mass-market buyers, and did not design for lower-cost manufacturing.

Minicomputer and mainframe companies "have realized that the microcomputer and the personal computer are the wave of the future, a huge and key strategic market," says Williams H. Gates, chairman of Microsoft Corp., a microcomputer-software vendor. But the problem, he says, is that they "are viewing it as another option in the product line, and are not giving it the resources it needs or treating it as a whole new business."

Data General has attempted to correct those misjudgments. In 1981 it formally abandoned an effort to salvage the Enterprise and recognized that the machines it wanted to develop constituted a new business and not just extensions of other product lines. To underscore that new stance, Data General took a cue from IBM—which created an independent development team

* "How A Flop Gave Birth to a New Machine," *Business Week,* August 1, 1983, pp. 77–78. Used with permission.

for its Personal Computer—and set up a separate business unit, physically removed from corporate units that might distract it.

GROUP EFFORT

"We wanted to recognize that the [product] family was more than just another computer. It was an entirely different box," says Data General's Donald L. McDougall, director of the Technical Products Business Division and marketing manager for the project. "If the engineers had had their minicomputer friends around them, they wouldn't have been radical enough." By contrast, engineers who worked on the Enterprise were not given such a clear mandate; they were expected to carry on their regular duties designing microcircuits.

Says Robert J. Conrads, a principal at management consultants McKinsey & Co.: "If an existing division is worried about several products, then [the new priority] will be lost among them. It becomes one of the items on an agenda of 14 things that top management wants done. It is pretty obvious what is going to happen." This time around, says McDougall, Data General gave the project the trappings it needed. "More than for any other product, marketing, engineering, manufacturing, and service worked together on this one," he says.

The shift is reflected in staffing. The engineers selected for the "Box 6" project, as it was code-named, "had to be young, with no preconceived notion of how computers should be built," says McDougall. "They don't know what can't be done," he says. On the other hand, experienced management was chosen partly as a means of ensuring top management time and attention for the 14-month project. And experienced hands were tapped to troubleshoot. "They knew how to get [circuit] boards from North Carolina," he says, "or semiconductors from Sunnyvale," the California town that is home to the company's proprietary semiconductor facility.

Another striking difference is evident in market research. For the Enterprise, Data General "talked to its favorite New England computer vendors and called it market research," says one former manager on that job. "There was very little listening to the marketplace."

Not so this time. In a two-pronged attack, Data General set about to determine both what potential customers really wanted in a desktop computer and what the market then offered. It had its engineers spend hour after hour in a roomful of the most successful systems on the market so that "they could take them apart and understand how competitors did it," says Robert C. Miller, senior vice-president. Others interviewed potential customers. And formal market research was studied. Using an Arthur D. Little Inc. analysis of what people looked for in desktop computers, Data General found that no competitor offered a computer that could perform using either of the two most popular operating systems, called MS–DOS and CP/M. So Data General built this dual capability into its new machines. "It cost very little to cover the competitive advantage of having both," says Miller.

To an unusual degree for Data General, marketing considerations were allowed to influence design, sometimes over engineers' objections. At one point a struggle broke out between marketing and engineering over Data General's special office automation software package, called CEO. The original plan called for building the software into only the two most expensive of the four machines, which range in price from about $3,000 to $20,000.

Marketing wanted the software on all machines, because no competitor offered anything comparable. "Our big fear was that the low-end box would get too much in it and the price would go up," says Miller. The dilemma was laid at the engineers' door, and they managed to design a single chip to carry the software as a $400 option.

POWER TRANSFER

Another debate broke out over how to transfer Data General's powerful and sophisticated minicomputer operating systems, called AOS, onto the desktop units in a simple form that neophyte computer users could handle. Engineering proposed twenty-six diskettes that the user would have to load onto the system. "Marketing said that was too many," says McDougall. Engineering finally squeezed the entire system into six diskettes, and observers say their analysis is that Data General, alone among minicomputer makers, has truly transferred the power of its minicomputer systems to the desktop.

Although the particulars differ, the special focus Data General turned on its desktop development effort is something of a sequel to a prior performance. In 1978 the company awoke late to the progress of archrival Digital Equipment Corp. in moving into more advanced minicomputers. Then, in an intensive drive, Data General produced the highly successful Eagle—a drama made legendary by the book *Soul of a New Machine.*

Data General can only hope it caught itself soon enough this time, too. Habits are hard to break. Says Microsoft's Gates, "It takes very bright management to figure out which strengths are applicable to a new business. There is a desire to draw on old strengths."

Questions

1. Are the lessons learned at Data General consistent with the Horizontal Linkage Model? Explain. Are other change ideas also illustrated in the above case? Discuss.

2. Do you predict success or failure for future product innovations at Data General? Should top managers expect occasional or even frequent new product failures, despite what they have learned? Discuss.

NOTES

1. "Federal Express: The Creative Courier," *Dun's Business Month,* December 1981, pp. 68–69. Used with permission.

2. Alvin Toffler, *Future Shock* (New York: Random House, 1970), p. 11.

3. John L. Pierce and Andre L. Delbecq, "Organization Structure, Individual Attitudes and Innovation," *Academy of Management Review* 2 (1977):27–37; Michael Aiken and Jerald Hage, "The Organic Organization and Innovation," *Sociology* 5 (1971):63–82.

4. Richard L. Daft, "Bureaucratic versus Nonbureaucratic Structure in the Process of Innovation and Change," in Samuel B. Bacharach, ed., *Perspectives in Organizational Sociology: Theory and Research* (Greenwich, CT, JAI Press, 1982), pp. 129–166.

5. Ibid.

6. Janet Guyon, "The Public Doesn't Get a Better Potato Chip without a Bit of Pain," *The Wall Street Journal,* March 25, 1983, pp. 1, 12; "Frito-Lay Introduces Sabritas Corn Tortilla Chips," *Advertising Age,* December 5, 1983, p. 5.

7. Beth Falconer, Carol Stevens, Mark Richardson, and Brian Bartels, "GTE: A Case Analysis," unpublished manuscript, Texas A&M University, 1981.

8. Tom Burns and G. M. Stalker, *The Management of Innovation* (London: Tavistock Publications, 1961).

9. Kim Linsu, "Organizational Innovation and Structure," *Journal of Business Research,* 8 (1980):225–245.

10. Aiken and Hage, "Organic Organization and Innovation"; Warren G. Bennis, *Changing Organizations* (New York: McGraw-Hill, 1966); Victor A. Thompson, "Bureaucracy and Innovation," *Administrative Science Quarterly* 10 (1964):1–20.

11. Jo Williams, "McDonald's Refuses to Plateau," *Fortune,* November 12, 1984, pp. 34–40.

12. James Q. Wilson, "Innovation in Organization: Notes Toward a Theory," in James D. Thompson, ed., *Approaches to Organizational Design* (Pittsburgh: University of Pittsburgh Press, 1966), pp. 193–218.

13. Robert B. Duncan, "The Ambidextrous Organization: Designing Dual Structures for Innovation," in Ralph H. Killman, Louis R. Pondy, and Dennis Slevin, eds., *The Management of Organization* (New York: North-Holland, 1976), vol. 1, pp. 167–188.

14. Edward F. McDonough III and Richard Leifer, "Using Simultaneous Structures to Cope with Uncertainty," *Academy of Management Journal,* 26 (1983):727–735.

15. Judith R. Blau and William McKinley, "Ideas, Complexity, and Innovation," *Administrative Science Quarterly* 24 (1979):200–219.

16. William F. Fallwell, "Dow Gears up for Research Boom in 1980s," *Chemical & Engineering News,* November 24, 1980, pp. 10–13; Erik Larson and Carrie Dolan, "Large Computer Firms Sprout Little Divisions for Good, Fast Work," *The Wall Street Journal,* August 19, 1983, pp. 1, 11; "How the PC Project Changed the Way IBM Thinks," *Business Week,* October 3, 1983, pp. 86–90.

17. Thomas J. Peters and Robert H. Waterman, Jr., *In Search of Excellence* (New York: Harper & Row, 1982).

18. Ibid., p. 205.

19. Jay R. Galbraith, "Designing the Innovating Organization," *Organizational Dynamics* (Winter 1982):5–25; Marsha Sinatar, "Entrepreneurs, Chaos, and Creativity—Can Creative People Really Survive Large Company Structure?" *Sloan Management Review* (Winter 1985):57–62.

20. Charles Rubin, "Macintosh: Apple's Powerful New Computer," *Personal Computing,* February 1984, pp. 56–86, 199.

21. Edwin Mansfield, J. Rapoport, J. Schnee, S. Wagner, and M. Hamburger, *Research and Innovation in Modern Corporations* (New York: Norton, 1971).

22. Ibid.; Science Policy Research Unit, University of Sussex, *Success and Failure in Industrial Innovation* (London: Centre for the Study of Industrial Innovation, 1972); Jay W. Lorsch and Paul R. Lawrence, "Organizing for Product Innovation," *Harvard Business Review* 43 (January–February, 1965):109–122.

23. William L. Shanklin and John K. Ryans, Jr., "Organizing for High-Tech Marketing," *Harvard Business Review* (November–December, 1984):164–171.

24. Adapted from "Two Lessons in Failure from Silicon Valley," *Business Week,* September 10, 1984, pp. 78–83.

25. Fariborz Damanpour and William M. Evan, "Organizational Innovation and Performance: The Problem of 'Organizational Lag,'" *Administrative Science Quarterly,* 29 (1984):392–409; David J. Teece, "The Diffusion of an Administrative Innovation," *Management Science,* 26 (1980):464–470.

26. John R. Kimberly and Michael J. Evaniski, "Organizational Innovation: The Influence of Individual, Organizational and Contextual Factors on Hospital Adoption of Technological and Administrative Innovation," *Academy of Management Journal* 24 (1981):689–713; Michael K. Moch and Edward V. Morse, "Size, Centralization and Organizational Adoption of Innovations," *American Sociological Review* 42 (1977): 716–725; Mary L. Fennell, "Synergy, Influence, and Information in the Adoption of Administrative Innovation," *Academy of Management Journal,* 27 (1984):113–129.

27. Richard L. Daft, "A Dual-Core Model of Organizational Innovation," *Academy of Management Journal* 21 (1978):193–210.

28. Daft, "Bureaucratic versus Nonbureaucratic Structure"; Robert W. Zmud, "Diffusion of Modern Software Practices: Influence of Centralization and Formalization," *Management Science,* 28 (1982):1421–1431.

29. Daft, "A Dual-Core Model of Organizational Innovation"; Robert W. Zmud, "Diffusion of Modern Software Practices: Influence of Centralization and Formalization," *Management Science,* 28 (1982):1421–1431.

30. Gregory H. Gaertner, Karen N. Gaertner, and David M. Akinnusi, "Environment, Strategy, and the Implementation of Administrative Change: The Case of Civil Service Reform," *Academy of Management Journal,* 27 (1984):525–543.

31. Damanpour and Evan, "Organizational Innovation and Performance."

32. Richard L. Daft and Selwyn Becker, *Innovation in Organizations: Innovation Adoption in School Organizations* (New York: Elsevier, 1978), pp. 124–126.

33. Richard Beckhard, *Organization Development: Strategies and Models* (Reading, MA: Addison-Wesley, 1969), p. 9.

34. Dennis D. Umstot, "Organization Development Technology and the Military: A Surprising Merger?" *Academy of Management Review,* 5 (1980):189–201.

35. W. Warner Burke and Warren H. Schmidt, "Management and Organizational Development," *Personnel Administration* 34 (1971):44–56.

36. Richard J. Boyle, "Wrestling with Jellyfish," *Harvard Business Review* (January–February 1984):74–83.

37. David A. Nadler, *Feedback and Organizational Development: Using Data-Based Methods* (Reading, MA: Addison-Wesley, 1977), pp. 5–8.

38. Wendell L. French and Cecil H. Bell, Jr., *Organization Development* (Englewood Cliffs, NJ: Prentice-Hall, 1978), pp. 117–129.

39. Edward E. Lawler III and Susan A. Mohrman, "Quality Circles after the Fad," *Harvard Business Review* (January–February 1985):65–71.

40. Dennis D. Umstot, "Organizational Development, Technology and the Military: A Surprising Merger," *Academy of Management Review,* 5 (1980):189–201.

41. "How Ebasco Makes the Matrix Method Work," *Business Week,* June 15, 1981, pp. 126–131.

42. Michael Aiken, Samuel B. Bacharach, and Lawrence J. French, "Organizational Structure, Work Process and Proposal-Making in Administrative Bureaucracies," *Academy of Management Journal* 23 (1980):631–652; Gerald Zaltman, Robert Duncan, and Jonny Holbek, *Innovations and Organizations* (New York: John Wiley & Sons, 1973), pp. 55–58.

43. Daft and Becker, *Innovation and Organizations;* John P. Kotter and Leonard A. Schlesinger, "Choosing Strategies for Change," *Harvard Business Review* 57 (1979): 106–114; Beckhard, *Organization Development.*

44. Everett M. Rogers and Floyd Shoemaker, *Communication of Innovations: A Cross Cultural Approach,* 2nd ed. (New York: Free Press, 1971); Stratford P. Sherman, "Eight Big Masters of Innovation," *Fortune,* October 15, 1984, pp. 66–84.

45. Mary Snepenger, "Implementing Change," unpublished manuscript, Texas A&M University, 1980.

46. Ibid.

47. Kotter and Schlesinger, "Choosing Strategies for Change."

48. Arthur E. Wallach, "System Changes Begin in the Training Department," *Personnel Journal* 58 (1979):846–848, 872; Paul R. Lawrence, "How to Deal with Resistance to Change," *Harvard Business Review* 47 (January–February, 1969):4–12, 166–176.

49. Kotter and Schlesinger, "Choosing Strategies for Change."

50. Richard L. Daft and Patricia J. Bradshaw, "The Process of Horizontal Differentiation: Two Models," *Administrative Science Quarterly* 25 (1980):441–456; Alok K. Chakrabrati, "The Role of Champion in Product Innovation," *California Management Review* 17 (1974):58–62.

51. "How Chesebrough-Ponds Put Nail Polish in a Pen," *Business Week,* October 8, 1984, pp. 196–200.

52. Daft and Bradshaw, "Process of Horizontal Differentiation"; Paul Jervis, "Innovation and Technology Transfer—The Roles and Characteristics of Individuals," *IEEE Transactions on Engineering Management* 22 (1974):19–26; Robert A. Burgelman, "A Process Model of Internal Corporate Venturing in the Diversified Major Firms," *Administrative Science Quarterly,* 28 (1983):223–224.

Information and Control

S. I. NEWHOUSE AND SONS

S. I. Newhouse and Sons is one of the largest publishing enterprises in the United States. The publishing empire includes three types of business—newspapers (twenty-nine, including the *Newark Star-Ledger* and the *Cleveland Plain Dealer*); magazines (several, including *Vogue, House and Garden* and *The New Yorker*); and broadcasting (four radio stations, six television stations, and twenty cable TV systems). The company is family-owned, yet *Business Week* estimated that the enterprise ranked number one in profits and number three in sales among companies in the communication media.[1]

The senior Newhouse, called S. I., died in 1979. He started his empire at the age of seventeen, and stayed active until the end. S. I. adopted a rather unorthodox management style for the communication industry, which is carried on by his sons. He shunned elaborate management control systems, and cared little for elaborate planning and budgeting. He was not even sure how many people were on the payroll (approximately 15,000). Relatives occupied a large number of management positions. One son was in charge of broadcasting, another was in charge of magazines. The two sons now jointly run the publishing empire. At one time, sixty-four relatives and in-laws were on the payroll, although a smaller number are now involved in management. A younger generation is coming along, who will be taught S. I. Newhouse's rule: "The ties that matter are the ties to each other."[2] All Newhouse descendents get together annually for a Thanksgiving feast.

The sons worked for their father for more than twenty-eight years, and have been carefully trained to take over the business. As one son explained, "We are essentially a nonbureaucratic, decentralized, highly autonomous organization, with each unit acting very much on its own initiative, but with personal or indirect contact with the various members of the family."[3] The Newhouses make frequent plant visits and then write memos to one another. Most reporting is informal. The family group also communicates frequently by telephone and in meetings. Major decisions are reached by consensus after much give and take. There is constant discussion between the various companies and the family group. Everyone in the family group knows what is going on at all times.

The newspaper and broadcast business operate in different environments. The newspaper industry is rapidly changing. Costs for newsprint, equipment, and labor have increased dramatically. Unions present many problems and often resist attempts to upgrade technologies. Most of the Newhouse newspapers have converted to cold-type composition, automated mail rooms, offset presses, and other new techniques. The success of each newspaper depends upon meeting area needs, which vary greatly by community. The family does not try to dictate editorial positions or management style for specific newspapers. Each paper is an autonomous business unit.

The broadcasting industry is more uniform and stable. Radio and television stations tend to use standard formats (e.g., network programming or top-forty music). Technological change is minimal. Broadcast media play a small role in local communities. Broadcast policies are less tailored to local conditions.

The newspaper part of the business is decentralized, and control is maintained through a single monthly report that is distributed to key family members. The report covers net profits, advertising lineage, circulation, and a few additional items such as labor costs.

In the broadcasting arm, the control system is centralized and bureaucratic. Budgets and statistical reports are compiled and reviewed frequently. The president of the broadcast division keeps close tabs on day-to-day performance of individual stations.

The Newhouse chain has enjoyed consistent growth and solid profits. Other newspaper chains have copied the Newhouse approach by reducing administrative controls on local newspapers. The sons and other family members have now taken over complete operation of the Newhouse business. They have no plans to change the management control philosophy.[4]

The managers at S. I. Newhouse and Sons illustrate the use of information. They exchange memos, attend meetings, make telephone calls, and read a variety of reports. They spend a lot of time processing information, and they use several channels, ranging from written documents to face-to-face meetings.

The Newhouse case also suggests that the design and the use of information support systems depends upon organization contingencies. The father disliked extensive planning and budgeting systems that are typically used for organizational control. A small amount of control information characterizes the newspaper business because the environment is changing, and uncertainty is great. Only a few key information cues are needed. The broadcasting business is quite different. The technology and environment are stable. Managers are concerned with frequent reports and check performance on a day-to-day basis.

Definitions

Information is that which alters understanding.[5] Information is not tangible or measurable. People represent what they know by pictures, symbols, verbal statements, and mental images. A change in the mental image is the result of information. A variety of cues, including verbal language, touch, personal observation, or computer printouts, convey information if the receiver's understanding is changed. Information provides insight and is perceived as useful by the receiver.

Data are the input and output of a communication channel. Data are tangible and can be counted. Data include the number of words, telephone calls, letters, or pages of computer printout sent or received. Data do not become information unless people use it to improve their understanding.

The distinction between information and data is important. Managers want information, not data. Organizations try to provide information rather than data to managers. Most managers are overloaded with data in the form of reports, printouts, and procedures. Managers want information they can use to interpret the situation around them and make decisions.

This chapter deals extensively with two major purposes of information—information for task accomplishment and information for control. **Task information** conveys knowledge and techniques for accomplishing managerial tasks. Task information is used to perform work, solve problems, and make decisions. Task information at S. I. Newhouse was conveyed through memos and in frequent meetings among managers. Many organizations use management information systems to provide information to managers and employees. A **management information system** (MIS) is the structured use of procedures and machines, often computer based, to provide internal and external data to aid managers in their tasks. Management information systems typically rely on a **data base,** which is the repository of the organization's raw data and programs. A related concept is **decision support system** (DSS), which is an MIS designed exclusively to support management decision-making. New forms of technology enable the manager to interact directly with the data base to ask questions and get responses. Personal computers and automated offices represent decision-support systems that enable managers to use organizational data bases for personal decision making.

Control information pertains to the performance of employees, departments, or the organization itself. **Management control systems** are the formal planning, data gathering, and transmission systems that provide management with information about organizational performance.[6] Control information includes information about targets, activity measurement, and feedback. At S. I. Newhouse, control information was included in the monthly report from each newspaper, or in the frequent reports from radio and TV stations to upper management.

Purpose of This Chapter

Information is important because nearly every activity in organizations involves information-processing. Managers spend 80% of their time actively exchanging information.[7] Information helps hold the organization together. The linkage mechanisms described in chapter 6 are designed to process information. In addition, organizations design formal information and control systems to provide managers with relevant data for decision-making and evaluation. To perform their jobs, managers must attend meetings, send and receive reports, evaluate performance, read printouts, talk on the telephone, and disseminate instructions—all of which require information processing.

The purpose of this chapter is to examine the design and use of information support in organizations. The next section looks at frameworks that describe information requirements for different tasks, and shows how to provide relevant information to departments performing those tasks. Then the topic of control systems is explored. The design of control systems is contingent upon both the need for control information by upper management and the stability of technology and environment. The last part of the chapter analyzes the impact on organizations of the revolution taking place in information technology. By the end of this chapter, students should understand organizational requirements for both task-related and control information, and how to meet those requirements through the design of organization structure and information systems.

TASK-RELATED INFORMATION

Manager behavior represents an information dilemma. Organizations can use technology to provide a large volume of precise, logical data to managers, yet managers often seem to prefer to communicate through social, informal, face-to-face discussions with others.[8] Moreover, managers seem to need a lot of information in some situations, but less information in others. Thus the question to be resolved in understanding task-related information is: how much and what type of information should be provided to managers to handle their departmental or organizational responsibilities?

Information Amount

The first design consideration is the amount of information needed by employees to perform their tasks. **Information amount** is the volume of data about organizational activities that is gathered and interpreted by organization participants.[9] Amount of information is important because employees—especially managers—work under conditions of uncertainty. They do not have complete understanding of the external environment or of the problems occurring within the organization. **Uncertainty** is the absence of information, so when uncertainty is high, a greater amount of information has to be acquired.[10] When uncertainty is high, the organization must encourage information-processing in the form of meetings, reports, procedures, etc., to meet the greater need for task information. When the organization does not experience uncertainty, the amount of information processed will be less.

Exhibit 8.1 indicates organizational characteristics that increase uncertainty and hence the amount of information processed by managers within the organization. The factors that influence the amount of uncertainty include nonroutine technology, organization size, environmental change, and interdependence between departments.[11] When tasks are nonroutine and interdependent, the amount of information processed is greater to understand and solve frequent problems. Organization size influences information be-

EXHIBIT 8.1. Sources of Uncertainty and Amount of Information Processed.

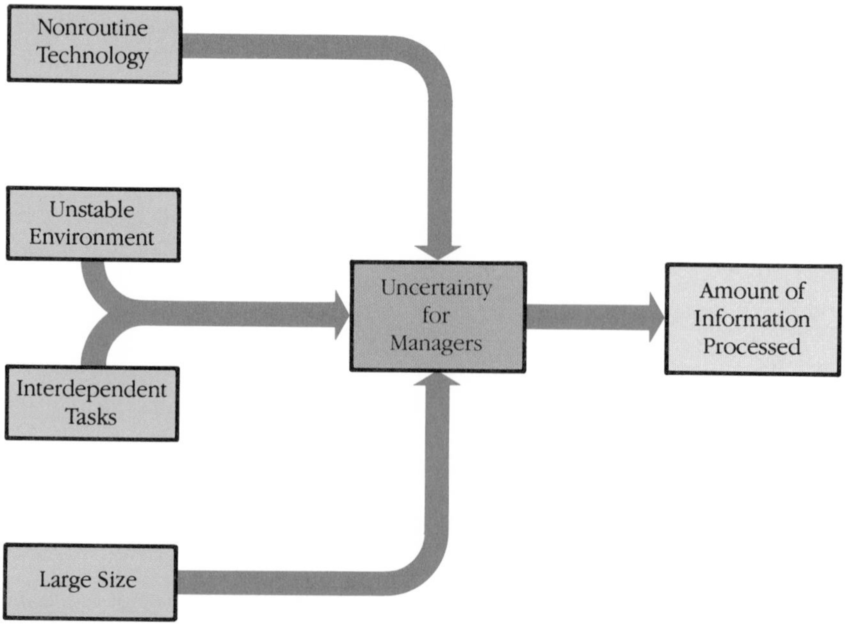

Source: Adapted from Michael L. Tushman and David A. Nadler, "Information Processing as an Integrating Concept in Organizational Design," *Academy of Management Review* 3 (1978): 613–624.

cause a larger number of people and departments have to be coordinated. Frequent changes in the environment induce uncertainty, which requires more information gathering. Changes occur when a client cancels an order, when another department changes its production schedule, when a supplier delays delivery by nine weeks, or when R&D cannot modify a product within cost estimates. These events create uncertainty for managers who then have to acquire information. They must interpret what happened and decide how to respond with a course of action.

Information Richness

The other important information design variable is information richness. **Richness** pertains to the information-carrying capacity of data.[12] Some data are highly informative for recipients while other cues provide little understanding. Information richness is related to the medium or channel through which it is communicated. Some media are richer because they provide richer information to managers. A scale of information media is presented in Exhibit 8.2. Face-to-face is the richest medium because it conveys several information cues simultaneously, including the spoken message, body language, and facial expression. Face-to-face also provides immediate feedback so that understanding can be checked and misinterpretations corrected. The richness of face-to-face communication was illustrated in a study that found 93% of meaning conveyed was by tone of voice and facial expression.[13]

EXHIBIT 8.2. Information Richness and Medium of Information Transfer.

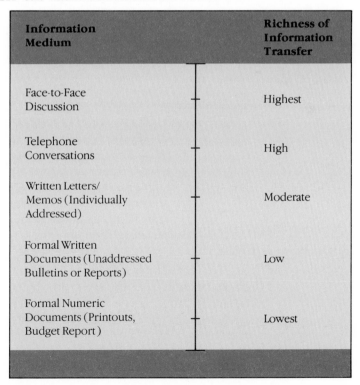

Information Medium	Richness of Information Transfer
Face-to-Face Discussion	Highest
Telephone Conversations	High
Written Letters/ Memos (Individually Addressed)	Moderate
Formal Written Documents (Unaddressed Bulletins or Reports)	Low
Formal Numeric Documents (Printouts, Budget Report)	Lowest

Source: Adapted from Richard L. Daft and Robert H. Lengel, "Information Richness: A New Approach to Managerial Behavior and Organization Design," in Barry Staw and Larry L. Cummings, eds., *Research in Organizational Behavior*, vol. 6 (Greenwich, CT: JAI Press, 1984), pp. 191–233.

The telephone is somewhat less rich than face-to-face. Immediate feedback is possible, but the visual cues are removed. Written communications are less rich still, because feedback is slow and only the information that is written down is transmitted. The least rich information is conveyed through numerical reports. Numbers tend to be used to describe simple, quantifiable aspects of organization.

Information richness is important because it relates to the ambiguity of management problems, as illustrated in Exhibit 8.3. Many issues that confront managers are not clear or well defined. When a managerial problem is ambiguous and unanalyzable, the factors surrounding it cannot be analyzed and understood in clear fashion. The manager has to acquire significant understanding in order to diagnose the situation and respond appropriately. Rich media, such as face-to-face, provide multiple cues and feedback that enable the manager to define what happened quickly, and develop a response. If the manager relies on media of low richness, such as a written report or a numerical document, the data may be late and may oversimplify the problem. The intangible, emotional, and difficult elements associated with unanalyzable problems can be conveyed only through rich media.

On the other hand, when a problem is simple, a less rich medium is preferable. For sending routine cost figures to a subordinate, for example, a written statement allows the content to be transmitted uncluttered by other cues. In a face-to-face meeting, nonverbal cues may disagree with the simple message and cause confusion and misunderstanding in the receiver. The relationship in Exhibit 8.3 indicates that unanalyzable and unclear problems require richer information. Analyzable, well-understood tasks can be interpreted and solved with less rich information.

Many executives try to achieve a balance of oral and written media. Patrick Foley, president of Hyatt Hotels, relies on memos and financial figures to evaluate hotel performance, but uses face-to-face meetings for diagnosing employee morale or planning future strategies. He schedules regular gripe sessions with employees at hotels to obtain rich information. The chief executives at Marriott Hotels, Tandem Computers, Markem Corporation, Apple Computer, and Syntex Corporation all find ways to have direct contact with employees and customers. Thus they receive information in both the right amount and richness for their own planning and decision-making.[14]

DESIGNING DEPARTMENTAL INFORMATION SUPPORT

A framework for applying information concepts to organizations is given in Exhibit 8.4. This framework is based upon Perrow's concept of department technology that was discussed in chapter 4. Technology represents the pattern of problems and tasks performed in different parts of the organization. Exhibit 8.4 identifies the two relationships that determine information requirements based upon the type of departmental task performed.

1. When task variety is high, problems are frequent and unpredictable. Uncertainty is greater, so the amount of information needed will also be greater.

EXHIBIT 8.3. Unanalyzable Problems and Richness of Information Processed.

Employees spend more time processing information, and they need access to larger data bases. When variety is low, the amount of information processed is less.[15] For example, the many problems associated with basic research require vastly greater amounts of information than do routine technical and drafting activities.[16]

2. When tasks are unanalyzable, and hence lead to ambiguous problems, employees need rich information.[17] Face-to-face discussions and telephone conversations transmit multiple information cues in a short time. Managers can also use feedback to quickly interpret the complexity of a problem and work toward a solution. When tasks are simple, managers will use less rich media. The underlying problem is clear, so only simple, written information is needed. For example, managers in finance departments rely heavily on written documents as a source of information, while general managers rely more heavily on human (face-to-face) sources.[18] Finance work tends to be more routine and better understood than general management, where many problems are unique and hard to analyze.

The implication of these relationships is reflected in the framework in Exhibit 8.4. Organization structure and information support systems should be designed to provide department managers and employees with the appropriate amount and richness of information. **Routine** activities have few problems. When problems do arise they are fairly well understood. An available store of knowledge, procedures, and data can be assembled to handle these problems. The amount of information can be small and directed toward a limited set of clear applications. Economic order quantity (EOQ) reorder systems for inventory control is an example of information support used for a routine task.

Engineering tasks have high task variety, which increases the demand for information. Many types of problems arise so it is not possible for the amount of information to be small. Engineering type departments are characterized by large bodies of established knowledge. Managers and employees typically need access to large data bases and sophisticated decision-support systems. The huge number of engineering blueprints that support an engineering project is an example of a large data base that can be stored on a computer. So is the large data base made available to airline reservation agents. Airline travel schedules involve infinite combinations of routes (high variety), but the task is well understood. A large but low rich information base is appropriate.

Craft departments require a different form of information. Task variety is not high, but the problems are ambiguous and hard to analyze. Problems

EXHIBIT 8.4. Task Characteristics and Information-Processing Requirements.

Source: Adapted from Richard L. Daft and Norman B. Macintosh, "A New Approach to Design and Use of Management Information," *California Management Review* 21 (1978): 82–92. Copyright © 1978 by the Regents of the University of California. Reprinted by permission of the Regents.

are handled on the basis of experience and judgment. There are many intangibles, so managers need rich information. An example of a craft organization is a specialized psychiatric care unit. The process of therapeutic change is not well understood. Numeric information about costs and benefits cannot be directly related to the healing process. When psychiatrists have a problem, they discuss it face-to-face among themselves to reach a solution.

Nonroutine departments are characterized by high uncertainty. Many problems arise that are ambiguous. Large amounts of rich information have to be accessible or gathered. A great deal of effort is devoted to discussing and analyzing problems and to using information in the best way. Managers spend time in both scheduled and unscheduled meetings. For unambiguous technical problems in these departments, management information and decision-support systems are valuable. Managers may need to interact directly with data bases to ask "what if" questions. Strategic planning units and basic research departments are examples of nonroutine tasks.

Design Implications

The importance of department technology is that it determines the pattern of problems and information needs within the department. The information-support systems and organization structure should provide information to managers based upon the pattern of decisions to be made. The amount of information should be larger when tasks have many problems. Information media should provide richer information when tasks are poorly defined and unanalyzable. When the organization is designed to provide the correct amount and type of information to managers, decision processes work well. When information systems are poorly designed, problem-solving and decision processes will be ineffective, and managers may not understand why. The following case illustrates how an organization can be designed to provide the correct information for engineering tasks.

IN PRACTICE 8.1

Ingersoll Milling Machine Co.

Ingersoll Milling is an extraordinarily successful machine tool builder. Ingersoll makes large-scale custom-made machines and machining systems for special applications. For example, General Motors recently ordered a $50 million system for computer-controlled auto assembly. Ingersoll is the only company in the industry that eschews government protection. The boss at Ingersoll believes companies that can't handle foreign competition should be allowed to go under.

The company's success is due to super-sophisticated planning and information systems. Ingersoll was first in the industry to use computers. Designers draw blueprints on computer screens rather than on drafting tables. Programmers write instructions to accompany a blueprint, and the computer generates a tape with those instructions. The tape is used to control machinery that shapes the metal to build the machine. Ingersoll builds some of the most sophisticated production lines in the world, including highly computerized systems for GE and Ford.

Ingersoll's smart move was to get rid of drafting tables and everything else that could be computerized. Everyone at Ingersoll speaks the same computer language. All three U.S. divisions are linked to a common computer data base. Every department—accounting, engineering, shipping, purchasing—in each division exchanges design, product, and financial information. When an engineer designs a cutting tool, the computer generates a list of materials needed that goes to purchasing. The next step is to computerize Ingersoll's tool salesforce. They will use briefcase terminals to call in specifications from the field. The central computer will then instruct the machinery to turn out the order.

Ingersoll's computer technology is so sophisticated that other machine tool builders are barely able to compete. Boeing and other aerospace companies prefer Ingersoll because they are efficient and accurate. The specialty orders that carry big profits come Ingersoll's way. The huge but highly quantified information system is perfectly tailored to a very complicated yet analyzable task of designing sophisticated machine tool systems.[19]

Large amounts of data are appropriate when a task is well understood but is complex and has many problems. For Ingersoll, a huge amount of computer-based data were appropriate. Competitors in the machine tool industry that used seat-of-the-pants and guesswork never achieved the same efficiency. Quantitative information is not suitable for ambiguous tasks, however. Providing large amounts of quantitative information to managers of poorly defined tasks doesn't work. The reliance on quantitative information when richer information was needed almost caused the failure of a clothing manufacturer in England.

IN PRACTICE 8.2
Clothing Manufacturer

A decision-support system problem occurred in one of two clothing plants, which are called Plant X and Plant Y. Each plant manufactured innerwear (underwear, socks) and outerwear (sweaters, jackets). The demand for innerwear was stable and well understood. Each plant independently developed a large decision-support system that used economic models based upon past sales, economic conditions, and related variables to predict the future demand for innerwear. The data base for this information system was large and precise. Managers at both plants used their information system to predict sales and thereby establish production targets and schedule plant operations.

The demand for outerwear, by contrast, was extremely unstable. Styles would change, total demand would change, and no one really understood why. Uncertainty for managers was high. The causes of demand changes were hard to analyze. Information system designers in Plant X tried to resolve this problem with the same type of information system used for innerwear. Extensive data were compiled about past and present economic conditions, sales records, competitors' sales, style changes, and so forth. Econometric models were used to predict outerwear styles, total demand, and to schedule production. The result was catastrophic. The manufactured clothing did not reflect consumer tastes and went unsold.

When problems are not well understood, it is better to trust rich information, which is what Plant Y did. Only a small amount of information was used in the decisions about outerwear styles. Key decision-makers made personal contact with a few store buyers. They visited stores to see what was selling. A few buyers discussed outerwear fashions in meetings. Based upon this face-to-face information and their own experience, buyers for Plant Y decided upon styles and production volume. Forecasting the demand for outerwear was essentially a craft decision. The estimates based upon rich information were much better than the forecasts based upon economic models. Plant Y prospered while Plant X nearly failed.[20]

The clothing plants illustrate how precise information fits a well-understood task (demand for innerwear), but richer information sources are more appropriate for interpreting and deciding about tasks that are poorly understood and ambiguous (demand for outerwear).

DESIGNING INFORMATION SUPPORT BY HIERARCHICAL LEVEL

The discussion above pertains to information support for problem-solving and decision-making for departments within the organization based upon their tasks. The other dimension along which information requirements differ is hierarchical level. Managerial tasks and responsibilities between top and bottom levels differ greatly. At the lower, operational level of the organization the work environment is more certain. At the top, managers are faced with uncertainty. Many events, especially those in the environment, are ambiguous and difficult to understand. The type of information provided to top managers thus serves a different purpose and has different characteristics, as illustrated in Exhibit 8.5.

Information Purpose   The primary purpose of information at the top is to scan and interpret the environment for goal setting and strategic decisions that provide direction to the organization. The organization will have boundary spanning units as described in chapter 2 that will assist upper-level managers in the scanning process. Middle levels of the organization will do some scanning of the environment with respect to their own responsibilities. Employees at lower levels tend to do little scanning. The primary purpose of information at the lower level is operational, while the primary purpose of information at the top is to interpret the environment for goal-setting and strategy formulation.[21]

Other characteristics of information also differ by hierarchical level. At the top, sources tend to be external. Many top managers make personal contacts with customers, competitors, government agencies, and suppliers to stay abreast of external events.[22] Moreover, information at the top tends to be aggregated to show the big picture. Data precision is low, but richness is high. Managers do use some written reports, but rely extensively on face-to-face discussions for information. The time perspective is typically future-oriented to reflect the need for strategic decisions. Top managers tend to not use electronic media, although some use of decision-support systems has been reported.[23]

At the lower organization levels, information reflects the purpose of monitoring operational activities. Information sources tend to be internal, and the data is both detailed and precise. Information is of lower richness because most data come through formal and written reporting systems. In-

EXHIBIT 8.5. Information Purpose and Characteristics by Hierarchical Level.

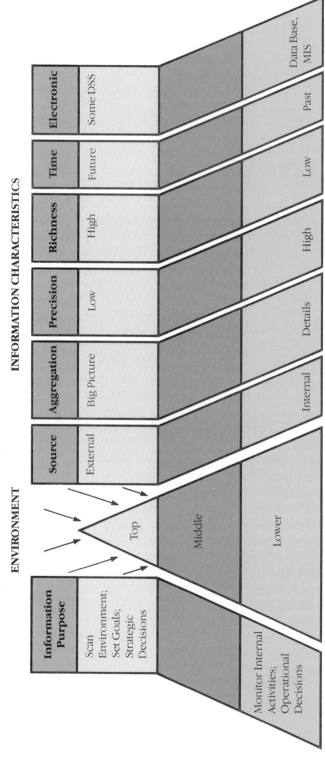

Source: Adapted from Rolland Hurtubise, *Managing Information Systems: Concepts and Tools* (West Hartford, CT: Kumarian Press, 1984), p. 57; and G. Anthony Gorry and Michael S. Scott Morton, "A Framework for Management Information Systems," *Sloan Management Review* 13 (1971):55–70.

formation is also concerned with previous performance and the recording of past activities. Electronic and computer-based information is widely used, especially for manufacturing and engineering technologies, where data bases can store the extensive knowledge needed for operational activities.

The implication for the design of information support based upon hierarchical level is that top manager information support should encourage wide information contacts rather than narrowly defined written and formal reports. On the other hand, loose, informal information at the lower hierarchical levels would also be inappropriate. Operational activities are more precise, and can be captured by detailed data reports. One of the skills required as managers move up the hierarchy is to learn to use the different sources and types of information compared to lower organizational levels. If top managers restrict their information sources to the precise, written data previously used, they will become out of touch with important events, as happened at Genesco.

IN PRACTICE 8.3

Genesco, Inc.

Genesco, Inc. operates in the uncertain and fast-moving fields of retailing and apparel. Its product lines include Bonwit Teller retail stores and Jarman Shoes. Top-management decision processes at Genesco were uncertain. Frequent decisions had to be made to keep Genesco ahead of the competition in fashion, advertising campaigns, and store locations.

Franklin Jarman took over as chief executive of Genesco in 1973. He immediately acted on his belief in strong financial controls and precise analysis. He requested extensive reports and detailed analysis for every decision. Memoranda would accumulate in files several inches thick. On one occasion, Jarman demanded a seventy-five-page report for a $44,000 store investment. The report dealt with such minor details as whether the store should have a water cooler.

Within two years, Jarman's style resulted in personal isolation. He relied on paperwork and computer printouts for information. He cancelled management breakfast meetings that brought together top executives for discussion and planning. He refused to visit the company's plants and to discuss matters with executives face-to-face. Much of his time was spent checking reports and printouts for mistakes. He argued that managing a corporation should be like flying an airplane. Watch the dials to see if the plane deviates from its course, and then nudge it back with the controls.

What Jarman didn't realize is that detailed, precise information was not reflecting conditions in the environment, or in the stores and plants throughout Genesco. His decision-making thus was inconsistent. Reports and data bases took a long time to develop, so decision-making was delayed. Indecision and missed opportunities caused trouble in a fast-moving field.

The paralysis caused by paperwork and indecision finally led to a palace revolt. Vice-presidents working under Jarman teamed with board members to oust him as chief executive officer.[24]

A major problem at Genesco was that Jarman designed the organization to provide the wrong kind of information support. In a top-management position in a fast-moving industry, information should be broad, aggregated, external, future-oriented, and rich. Formal reports and computer printouts oversimplify and fail to capture unanalyzable aspects of problems. The information provided to Jarman would have been excellent for a low-level supervisor in a stable manufacturing or utility company. But for the top executive at Genesco, the information was dead wrong, and was largely responsible for Genesco's poor performance and Franklin Jarman's removal.

ORGANIZATIONAL CONTROL

Now we turn to the topic of organizational control. Control is a major responsibility of management, and a large portion of organizational information processing pertains to control. **Organizational control** is a cycle that includes the three stages of target setting, measuring and monitoring, and feedback.[25] These three stages are illustrated in Exhibit 8.6. Target-setting involves planning and goal-setting for desired performance levels. Measuring and monitoring information indicates whether work activities are on target. Feedback information is designed to make corrections in either targets or work activities to bring them into alignment. The simple control cycle in Exhibit 8.6 is based on the cybernetic model of control. The thermostat, for example, has a control cycle in which a temperature standard is set, there is a temperature-monitoring device, and there is a mechanism for correcting the amount of heat or cooling in a home.[26]

Management Level and Control

Management control, like other forms of management information, differs by hierarchical level.[27] The three levels of hierarchy are illustrated in Exhibit 8.7. The overall control process involves both downward and upward communication. Downward communication is designed to influence work activities, inform people about the targets and plans that were established by upper management, and provide feedback to correct or reward performance. Upward communications in the form of reports, printouts, and other data are designed to help management at each level measure and monitor the performance for their responsibility center.

At the organizational level, managers are concerned with forecasting and target-setting for total organization performance. Measures of performance are aggregated to reflect performance of the organization as a whole. Managerial control pertains to specific departments such as marketing or engineering. Targets are set and information is gathered to reflect departmental activities. Supervisory control refers to the activities of individual employees. Supervisory control information is not aggregated, may be based on personal observation, and the control cycle is repeated on a frequent basis.

MAJOR CONTROL STRATEGIES

Managers at the top and middle levels of the organization can choose among three strategies for control. A framework for organizational control was pro-

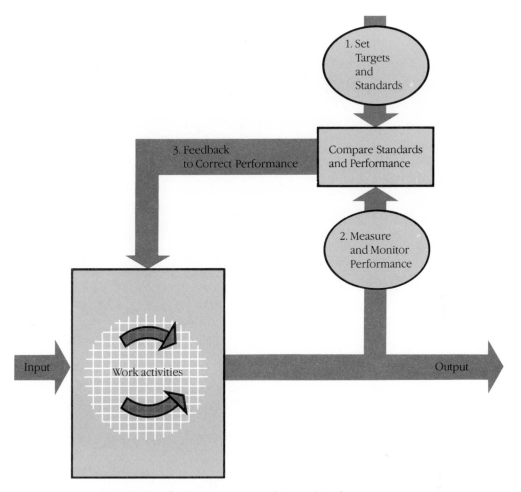

EXHIBIT 8.6. The Organizational Control Cycle.

posed by William Ouchi of UCLA. Ouchi identified three control strategies that organizations could adopt: market control, bureaucratic control, and clan control.[28] Each form of control uses different types of information. All three types may appear in an organization. The requirements for each control strategy are given in Exhibit 8.8.

Market Control

Market control occurs when price competition is used to evaluate the output and productivity of an organization. The idea of market control originated in economics.[29] A dollar price is an efficient form of control because managers can compare prices and profits to evaluate the efficiency of their corporation. Top managers nearly always use the price mechanism to evaluate performance in corporations. Corporate sales and costs are summarized in a profit-and-loss statement that can be compared to performance in previous years or to that of other corporations.

The use of market control requires that outputs be sufficiently explicit that a price can be assigned, and that competition exists. Without competition,

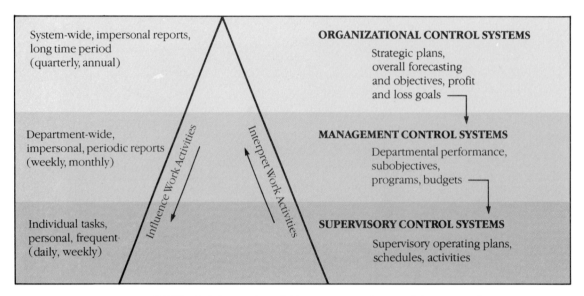

System-wide, impersonal reports, long time period (quarterly, annual)

ORGANIZATIONAL CONTROL SYSTEMS
Strategic plans, overall forecasting and objectives, profit and loss goals

Department-wide, impersonal, periodic reports (weekly, monthly)

MANAGEMENT CONTROL SYSTEMS
Departmental performance, subobjectives, programs, budgets

Individual tasks, personal, frequent (daily, weekly)

SUPERVISORY CONTROL SYSTEMS
Supervisory operating plans, schedules, activities

Influence Work Activities

Interpret Work Activities

EXHIBIT 8.7. Levels and Characteristics of Control Systems in Organizations.

the price will not be an accurate reflection of internal efficiency. A few traditionally not-for-profit organizations are turning to market control. In health care, the federal government is setting a fixed price for Medicare services rather than paying whatever the hospital charges. Efficiency is rewarded because the hospital can keep any "profit" if its cost is less than the price received.

Market control is used primarily at the level of the entire organization, but it can also be used in self-contained units. Profit centers are self-contained business divisions such as those described in chapter 6. Each division contains resource inputs needed to produce a product. Each division can be evaluated on the basis of profit or loss compared to other divisions. In the S. I. Newhouse and Sons case at the beginning of this chapter, market control was used in the newspaper business. Each newspaper was a profit center. Top managers needed only a few key profit figures to evaluate newspaper performance.

Market control is not appropriate for many organizations. It can be used only when the output of the organization can be assigned a dollar price, and when there is competition. Market control is also not appropriate for the control of functional departments within an organization. In a true market, prices are arrived at through a process of competitive bidding. Competitive bidding is an expensive and time-consuming process that is impossible to

EXHIBIT 8.8. Three Organizational Control Strategies.

Type	Requirements
Market	Prices, competition, exchange relationship
Bureaucracy	Rules, standards, hierarchy, legitimate authority
Clan	Tradition, shared values and beliefs, trust

Source: Based upon William G. Ouchi, "A Conceptual Framework for the Design of Organizational Control Mechanisms," *Management Science* 25 (1979):833–848.

achieve for the thousands of day-to-day transactions between functional departments. The organization has no means of putting an accurate price on these services, or of comparing prices to competitive services in the marketplace. Market control typically fails in functional departments, as it did in the following case.

IN PRACTICE 8.4
Bakerstown University

A private university in Bakerstown, California, organized its colleges into profit centers. The business college, engineering college, arts and science college, and graduate college all became profit centers. Each college received the tuition income from students and paid the cost for providing education to students. The university imposed tuition guidelines and academic standards, and then gave each college substantial freedom. The professional colleges, such as business and engineering, experienced a greater demand for services, and charged students a tuition premium. These colleges also paid more for resources because professors were in short supply and salaries were higher than in arts and science. Each college had to keep salaries and tuition rates at reasonable levels because other universities in the area competed for students.

After a trial period of two years, the profit center plan worked so well that top administrators decided to extend it to the centralized services provided by the university. They first examined the library, but decided that the cost of charging each college for every library transaction would be too expensive. This was not the case for computer services. Each user could be given a code that indicated the college to be billed, and all transactions could be automatically recorded by the computer. The university president decided to make the computer center a profit center. It was to become self-sufficient by selling its services to other colleges in the university.

Within three years, the colleges were in an uproar. The computer center had steadily increased the price of computer services. The teaching and research budgets of the colleges were being drained to cover the cost of computer services. The colleges joined forces and insisted that the computer center be brought back under the central administration.

A university committee met to analyze the computer situation and make a recommendation. They discovered that users of computer services were being charged a price nearly three times the actual cost to the computer center. Computer center managers used the revenue to hire additional staff and to finance their own research. They were able to increase the price because no competitive computer services were available. Each college had to buy services from the computer center or use no service at all. The price did not reflect the true value of computer services.

The university committee recommended that the computer department once again be made a part of administration and that services be provided free of charge. The colleges were in unanimous agreement. They even agreed to increase the overhead payment to the university administration to cover computer costs.

The decision by administrators at Bakerstown University to use market control for a functional department did not work because competitive services were not available. Market control is effective only when the price is set in competition with other suppliers so that it represents the true value of services provided.

Bureaucratic Control

Bureaucratic control is the use of rules, policies, hierarchy of authority, written documentation, standardization, and other bureaucratic mechanisms to standardize behavior and assess performance. Bureaucratic control uses the bureaucratic characteristics described in chapter 5 on bureaucracy. Within a large organization, thousands of transactions take place both vertically and horizontally. Rules and policies evolve through a process of trial and error to regulate this behavior. Bureaucratic control mechanisms are used when behavior and exchanges are too complex or ill-defined to be controlled with a price mechanism. An example of bureaucratic control occurred when Bakerstown University decided to make the computer center a part of administration. The provision of services to other departments was controlled by rules and policies rather than by price.

Bureaucratic control is used to some extent in almost every organization. Rules, regulations, and directives contain information about a range of behaviors. Bureaucratic mechanisms are especially valuable in not-for-profit organizations because prices and competitive markets often do not exist.

Management Control Systems At the middle-management or department level, management control systems are part of the written records and procedures that supplement overall bureaucratic control. As defined at the beginning of this chapter, **management control systems** are the formal planning, data gathering, and transmission systems that provide management with information about departmental performance. A survey of twenty Canadian and American corporations found that department managers used four management control systems.[30] The four subsystems are the operating budget, periodic statistical reports, performance appraisal system, and standard operating procedures. These four systems enable middle and upper management to both monitor and influence major departments.

The four control subsystems are listed in Exhibit 8.9. The operating budget is used to set financial targets and record costs during the year. The budget is normally determined a year in advance, and actual expenditures are compared with estimates on a monthly basis. Periodic statistical reports are used to evaluate and monitor non-financial performance. These reports are tailored to the outputs of specific departments. Performance evaluation systems are mechanisms for evaluating managers and their departments. This report is often open-ended. Managers and superiors sit down and set goals for the next year for their department and then evaluate how well previous goals were met. Standard operating procedures are traditional rules and regulations. Managers use these to correct variances and bring activities back into line.

Control System Package

One finding from research into management control systems is the way each system focuses on a different aspect of departmental performance. Each

EXHIBIT 8.9. Management Control Systems.

Subsystem	Content and Frequency
Budget	Financial, resource expenditures, monthly
Statistical Reports	Nonfinancial, outputs, weekly or monthly
Performance Appraisal	Evaluation of department managers based on department goals and performance, annually
Standard Operating Procedures	Rules and regulations, policies that prescribe correct behavior, continuous

Source: Based on Richard L. Daft and Norman B. Macintosh, "The Nature and Use of Formal Control Systems for Management Control and Strategy Implementation," *Journal of Management,* 10 (1984):43–66.

functional department transforms inputs into outputs. Each of the four control systems focuses on a different aspect of this transformation process. The management control systems thus form an overall package that provides middle managers with control information about resource inputs, process efficiency, and output.[31] The relationship of each management control system to departmental activities is illustrated in Exhibit 8.10.

The budget is used primarily to control resource input. Managers use the budget for planning the future and reducing the uncertainty about the availability of human and material resources needed to perform department tasks. Statistical reports, by contrast, are used to control outputs. These reports contain data about output volume, quality control, and other indicators that provide feedback to middle management about departmental results. The performance appraisal system and policies and procedures are directed at the control of internal processes. Performance appraisals evaluate and correct employee work activities. Standard operating procedures give explicit direction about appropriate behaviors. Managers can also use direct supervision in conjunction with performance appraisal and procedures to keep departmental work activities within desired limits.

The budget and statistical reports, which control both inputs and outputs, are associated with the cycle of target setting, monitoring of behavior, and corrective action. Thus, on a monthly basis both budget inputs and departmental outputs are monitored to ensure they are on target. The performance appraisal system involves a cycle, but target setting and feedback typically occur on an annual basis. Standard operating procedures are relatively fixed, and change only gradually as new procedures are adopted. Budgets provide resource inputs for departments, and statistical reports provide feedback about results. The performance appraisals and SOPs provide additional information for corrective action. Taken together, the control systems provide important information within the overall bureaucratic framework for the target setting, monitoring, and corrective action needed to influence departmental performance.

An example of how the four control systems mesh together is illustrated in the credit department of a department store chain in Canada.

EXHIBIT 8.10. Four Management Control Subsystems and Focus of Control.

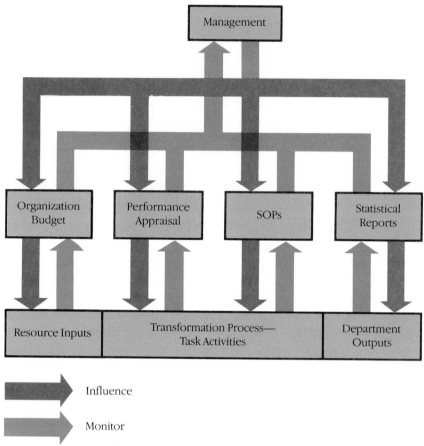

Source: Adapted from Richard L. Daft and Norman B. Macintosh, "The Nature and Use of Formal Control Systems for Management Control and Strategy Implementation," *Journal of Management* 10 (1984):43–66.

IN PRACTICE 8.5

Simpson Department Store

Simpson's is a department store chain in Canada. Like most retail organizations, each store is a profit center, and market control is used to evaluate store performance. The credit department in one of the Simpson's highest volume stores uses four management control systems to evaluate performance.

The budget consists of five pages that report budgeted versus actual expense for each month and year-to-date. The budget describes resources in three categories: (1) personnel salaries, including the salary for each employee in the department; (2) noncapital equipment, including expenditures for office machines and related equipment; and (3) day-to-day operating expenses.

The credit department made extensive use of statistical reports for measuring and monitoring weekly and monthly outputs. The statistical reporting system includes the following reports, which evaluate different aspects of output performance.

1. Comparative credit report—details of each charge account.
2. Effectiveness and efficiency report—income and payroll costs per credit account.
3. Credit sales ratio—percentage of credit sales to total store sales.
4. Delinquent accounts—analysis of delinquent accounts, including the ratio to active accounts.
5. Uncollectable accounts—analysis of uncollectable recoveries.
6. Growth report—details of credit account growth in the previous year.

The performance appraisal system at Simpson's is a simple two-page report that is filled out jointly by the credit department manager and the store manager. The credit department manager describes credit department targets for the coming year. Another meeting at the end of the year evaluates performance of the credit department. Results of this session determine pay increase, promotion, and bonus for the credit department manager.

The standard operating procedures within the credit department amount to about 700 pages. They include step-by-step procedures for such things as disciplining employees, when to refund money to a customer, and job descriptions. The manager of Simpson's department store, when discussing the overall management control system package, commented that "It seems like a lot of paper. But we need all of it for the overall picture of credit department performance and to take remedial action." [32]

| Clan Control | **Clan control** is the use of social characteristics such as values, commitment, traditions, and shared beliefs to control behavior. Organizations that use clan control require trust among employees.[33] Clan control is important when ambiguity and uncertainty are high. High uncertainty means the organization cannot put a price on its services, and rules and regulations are not able to specify appropriate behavior. People may be hired because they are committed to the organization's purpose, such as in a religious organization. New employees may be subjected to a long period of socialization to gain acceptance by colleagues. The clan mechanism is used most often in small, informal organizations because personal involvement in the purpose and activities of the organization is possible. Clan control also is used within departments where performance is difficult to measure in a systematic way. |

An example of clan control was the S. I. Newhouse case at the beginning of the chapter. S. I. Newhouse and Sons hired family members in the upper echelons of the organization. Family members trusted each other, and shared common beliefs and traditions. With clan control, S. I. Newhouse and Sons did not need as many bureaucratic controls to regulate the behavior of its executives. The same process occurred when Christie Hefner took over as president of Playboy Enterprises in 1982. Christie is Hugh Hefner's daughter, and his control over the organization is assured by having a family member in the top position.

One important use of clan control is in departments that experience high uncertainty, such as research and development. The important thing for managers is not to assume that the absence of written, bureaucratic controls means that no control is present. Clan control is invisible yet very powerful.

When clan control works, bureaucratic control is not needed, as in the following case.

IN PRACTICE 8.6
Metallic, Inc.

Metallic, Inc. is a producer of chrome finishes and specialty metals. In 1982, the new executive vice-president, Stuart Tubbs, went on record saying that he was going to get the research and development department under control. Tubbs came up through the manufacturing ranks, where lengthy budgets and statistical reports were used. Almost every activity in manufacturing was counted and evaluated on a weekly basis. The research department, by contrast, seemed loosely controlled. Performance was satisfactory, but people had freedom to do as they pleased, such as to work either during the day or evening. Stuart Tubbs was going to do something about that.

His first step was to install a detailed budget system. A budget was established for each research project. Even minor expenditures had to be budgeted. The research and development director was expected to keep each expense category on target. Statistical reports were implemented to keep track of all nonfinancial items, such as how employees spent their time and their productivity levels. Number of technical papers written, conferences attended, and use of equipment were all measured and monitored.

As the detail and intensity of the bureaucratic control system increased, satisfaction and productivity within research and development decreased. At least once a week the executive vice-president and the R&D director battled over differences between actual expenditures and budget, or over the interpretation of activity reports. After about a year the R&D director resigned. This was followed by the resignations of several key researchers.

The board of directors asked that a management consultant examine problems in R&D. She found that the control procedures were not appropriate in an R&D department characterized by fast change and uncertainty. Precise, detailed reports may work for a stable manufacturing department, but they do not capture the uncertain nature of R&D activities. Minor deviations from budget are the rule rather than the exception. A general control system used to plan future projects and to keep research output consistent with company goals would be more effective. The consultant recommended that the bureaucratic system be reduced so that the shared values and commitment of professional employees regulate behavior.

Stuart Tubbs had not recognized or understood clan control. R&D employees were socialized into professional norms and practices. Most researchers worked extra hours at night to finish projects because they were deeply committed. The lack of bureaucratic control mechanisms did not mean lack of control.

CONTINGENCY CONTROL MODEL

A question for organization designers is when to use each control strategy. A model that describes contingencies associated with market, bureaucratic, and clan control is shown in Exhibit 8.11. Each type of control often appears in the same organization, but one form of control will usually dominate at a given management level.

Bureaucratic control mechanisms are by far the most widely used control strategy. Some form of bureaucratic control combined with internal management control systems are almost always necessary. Bureaucratic control is used extensively when organizations are large, and when the environment and technology are certain, stable, and routine. Bureaucratic control is also associated with the functional structure described in chapter 6. Bureaucratic control emphasizes a vertical information and control process. Management control systems complement the bureaucratic strategy by controlling resource inputs to departments and evaluating outputs with statistical reports.

Clan control is used in the opposite circumstances. When organizations are small, and when the environment and technology are uncertain, unstable and nonroutine, then trust, tradition, and shared values are important. Clan control is best when horizontal information and control processes are needed, as they are with a matrix organization structure. Rules and budgets will be

EXHIBIT 8.11. Contingency Model for Organizational Control Strategies.

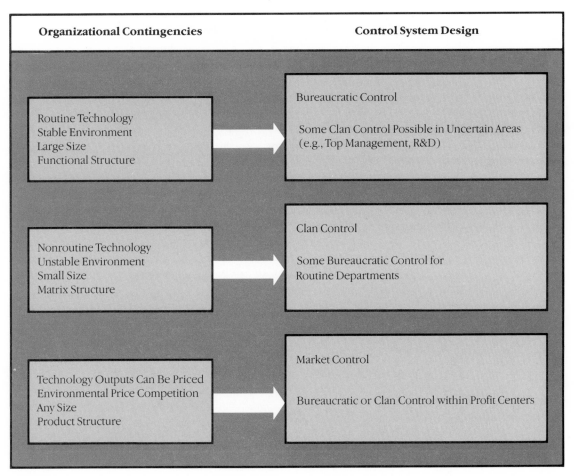

used, of course, but trust, values, and commitment will be the primary reasons for employee compliance.

Market control has limited applications. Market control is used when costs and outputs can be priced, and when a market is available for price competition. The technology must produce outputs that can be defined and priced, and competition must exist in the environment. Market control can be used in organizations of any size so long as costs can be identified and outputs are competitively priced. Market control is frequently used in self-contained divisions in a business corporation, as described in chapter 6. Each division is a profit center. When applicable, market control is efficient because performance information is summarized in a profit and loss statement.

The balance among control strategies may differ from organization to organization. The use of each strategy reflects the structure, technology and environment as well as the ability to price output. Control strategies may appear in almost any combination, so long as the control emphasis reflects the underlying needs and contingency factors of the organization. When managers emphasize the correct type of control, the outcome can be very positive, such as at Allegheny Steel.

IN PRACTICE 8.7

Allegheny Ludlum Steel Corporation

Unlike most steel companies, Allegheny Ludlum makes a profit. One reason is that chief executive Richard Simmons has installed an information system that borders on the fanatic. Simmons believes, "If you can't measure it, you can't manage it." The system counts every nickel's worth of nickel that goes into the furnace. The cost information is tourniquet-tight, which Simmons believes keeps his high volume business competitive. Steel making is complex, with thousands of recipes for specialty steels, and hundreds of new recipes monthly. Allegheny makes steel by the numbers. The information system categorizes more than fifty possible blemishes a coil can have, for example. Production managers get weekly reports allowing them to adjust controls quickly. Precise information has enabled them to improve quality by thirty percent.

Every order received at Allegheny is analyzed by size, profit margin, and the demand it makes on production time. Some orders are rejected if they are inefficient. The information system schedules production. A computer tracks the order through the system.

During the toughest years the steel industry has ever known, Allegheny Steel is riding a crest of profitability. The computer has memorized an engineering model of the production process. Scheduling, cost control, and problems are compared against the model and the managers are quickly informed. The data base is huge, but efficient. A large but number-based management control system is just right for a highly complex but analyzable organization task.[34]

Allegheny Ludlum uses both market and bureaucratic control. Outputs can be priced, and the industry is very competitive, so bottom line profit is the important criterion for company success. Moreover, internal rules, budget, and statistical reports are used ruthlessly to monitor all activities. This, too, is appropriate because the technology is well defined and measurable. Clan control is not used. There is little shared value or tradition. Cost efficiency is the dominant issue in the control strategy.

SUPERVISORY CONTROL STRATEGIES

The control strategies described so far apply to the top and middle levels of the organization where the concern is for the entire organization or major departments. Control is also an issue at the lower, operational level in organizations where supervisors must directly control employee subordinates, which is called supervisory control. **Supervisory control** focuses on the performance of individual employees. The two types of supervisory strategies available to managers are output control and behavior control.[35]

Output control is based upon written records that measure employee outputs and productivity. Output control is used when the outputs of individual workers can be easily measured. Examples are piece-rate jobs where the number of units per hour can be easily calculated. Many sales jobs can be handled with output control because measurement of performance is reflected in the number of sales, the amount of sales, or in commissions earned. Output information is communicated through written records. This control strategy is similar to the use of statistical reports described earlier, except that these reports focus on individual rather than departmental performance.

The research productivity of university professors is normally evaluated by output control. The process of creative research is not well understood, so bureaucratic procedures for researchers cannot be prescribed. The test of good research is whether the output is accepted in journals and by colleagues. Research activity is normally measured by the number and quality of publications.

Behavior control is based upon personal observation of employee behavior and procedures. Behavioral control usually takes more time than output control because it requires personal surveillance.[36] Managers observe employees at work. Behavior control is used when outputs are not easily measured. High school and college teaching is often monitored and influenced through behavior control. The outputs of teaching are the amount of student learning and how long students retain what they have learned. These outputs are enormously difficult to measure. Consequently, teachers are usually evaluated on the process or behavior they use in teaching. A high school principal may personally observe teachers to learn whether they follow accepted practices. Student evaluations are often used at the college level to provide information about classroom behavior of teachers. Teaching and research activities are thus controlled in different ways. The form of supervisory control depends on whether employee output or behavior is measurable. Many organizations incorporate a balance of output and behavioral control to provide broader evaluation for employees.[37]

COMPUTERS AND INFORMATION TECHNOLOGY

A major revolution has occurred over the last twenty-five years in technology for processing task-related and control information. Computers process millions of pieces of organizational data in a short time. Computers have vastly increased the capacity of both management information systems and management control systems.

Exhibit 8.12 gives an example of a computer-based information system developed for a marketing department. Data about the market is fed into the computer from three sources. The market research subsystem includes formal surveys and studies from a market research department. The marketing intelligence subsystem includes information from sales representatives and other people in contact with customers and competitors. The internal accounting subsystem consists of cost and performance data for product lines. After these data are fed into the computer, reports and models can be developed about market size, promotional activity, and market share. Marketing managers could never have these reports without computers because the cost and time of accumulating data would be too expensive.

Two distinct trends have occurred in the development of computer technology. During the 1960s and early 1970s, a centralized computer was adopted by many organizations. The computers were large and powerful, and located in a separate department. A more recent trend is toward decentralization of computer facilities. The development of powerful small computers enables each department in an organization to have its own information-processing capacity. More powerful central computers also enable distributed data processing, which means that computer terminals are located in each department. User departments can have access to the data bases on the large central computer.

From an organization theory perspective, new technology is important for two reasons. First, it has the potential to make information processing more efficient, and hence improve managerial decision-making and control. Second, we know from chapter 4 that organizational technology has impact on organizational structure and management behavior. Computers represent an important new technology for administration. The adoption of computer technology thus can have impact on organizational structure and design.

Computer Impact on Structure

The introduction of a new, central computer doesn't just add a computer or a computer department to the organization. It realigns power. It changes the need for certain types of jobs, employee skills, and decisions. Research into the adoption of centralized computer systems has been done on a variety of organizations, including insurance companies and newspapers.[38] In insurance companies the computers were used for processing the huge volumes of financial and statistical data. In the newspaper industry, the computer was used for word processing, typesetting, and other functions. After computers became operational, organizations changed in the followings ways.

1. *Reduced Number of Clerical Personnel.*[39] The computer replaced the need to hire clerical personnel because it absorbed the routine data-processing tasks performed by these personnel. There was also a small savings in supervisory personnel who directed clerical activities.

EXHIBIT 8.12. Management Information System for a Management Department.

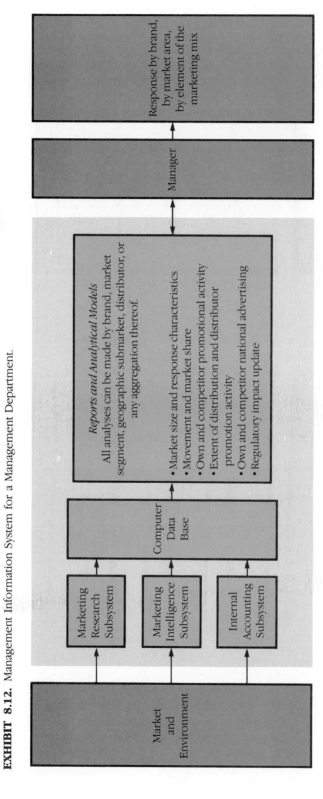

Source: Raymond McLeod, Jr., and John Rogers, "Marketing Information Systems: Uses in the *Fortune* 500," *California Management Review,* 25 (Fall, 1982):106–118. Used with permission.

2. *Increased Power and Influence for Computer Specialists.*[40] As more activities were taken over by the computer, computer personnel acquired greater control and authority over organizational activities. Line managers become more dependent on staff specialists.

3. *Greater Structural Complexity.* The computer created the need for a new department, which itself was often divided into several subdepartments. The functional form of structure seemed to make more efficient use of the computer than self-contained or product structure.[41]

4. *Decision-Making.* Findings concerning decision-making are mixed. Some organizations saw the need to involve managers from different functions in the decision-making process, which encouraged greater collaboration at lower levels. In large organizations, decentralization took place when computers were introduced, but in small organizations decisions tended to be more centralized.[42]

5. *Greater Proportion of Professional Staff.*[43] Professional staff tended to increase with the introduction of a computer. Staff were needed for computer programming and operations as well as to work with users around the organization.

Impact of Office Automation

The more recent development in computer technology has involved decentralization of information technology to departments. The technology has led to the automated office, which includes personal computers, videoconferencing, and electronic mail. Atlantic Richfield has a satellite hookup and wall-size projection screens so employees can confer with each other visually all around the country. Companies like Xerox use electronic mail to swap and file memos for executives in a minute or so. These developments are important, and just like the advent of the central computer, are having impact on the structure and design of organizations. Systematic research in this area is scarce because so few organizations have implemented office automation. However, the following trends have appeared.[44]

1. *Greater Professionalization of Staff.* The development of sophisticated information systems means that employees have to be more highly trained and professional to operate the system. For example, after North American Banking Group installed a customer service information system, the staff mix shifted from 30% professionals to 60% professionals.

2. *Reduced Number of Clerical Personnel.* Many clerical personnel are replaced by the new technology. The electronic revolution decreases the need for employees who type letters, file memos, fill out forms, and do other forms of routine clerical activity.

3. *Decreased Number of Hierarchical Levels.* In a few cases, the adoption of sophisticated technology has enabled the reduction of one or more layers of the management hierarchy. For example, Hercules, Inc., a chemical company, adopted a combination of word processing, electronic mail, videoconferencing, and other high-speed communication. The vice-president for information services found that the number of management levels between the president and plant foreman was reduced from a dozen to about seven.

4. *Greater Structural Complexity.* Although the number of hierarchical levels may shrink, the adoption of office automation increases horizontal complexity. Many organizations adopt a new department called an "information

center." This center provides expertise to managers who use the technology, and they provide training to new adopters. Experts within the center help managers develop data bases, analyze reports, and use software relevant to their own needs.

The impact of office automation and distributive data processing is similar to the impact of central computers. Employee professionalism increases, the number of clerical employees decrease, and the organization becomes more complex. Both forms of technology influence the organization.

Undesirable Side Effects

Information technology has expanded the capacity of organizations to provide decision-making and control information to managers. Yet the new technology has been a mixed blessing. In many organizations the technology has not been fully used. Managers are reluctant to work with the remote terminal in their office, or fail to use new reports in their decision-making. Problems with the new technology arise when managerial information needs are deemphasized, information systems are not flexible, and lower-level employees become dissatisfied because of overcontrol.

Hardware versus Managerial Needs   Too often information flow is defined by hardware capacity rather than by managerial needs.[45] Earlier in this chapter we saw that managers within many departments and managers near the top of the organization often deal with ambiguous problems for which they need face-to-face information. Computer hardware excels at processing quantitative, precise, and historical information. Consider, for example, the marketing information system illustrated in Exhibit 8.12. The information system could report quantified data on the number of completed sales transactions, sales calls, purchases by customers, and market share. But if market share is declining, sales managers will not understand why specific sales were lost based only on computer data. Sales managers also need to talk directly to sales people or customers. A visit to the field will provide face-to-face information that will give insight into a complicated problem.

Information System Inflexibility   Managerial activities are unstructured and constantly changing. Information, to be valuable, must change too. Yet computer information systems often fail to support management because they are not flexible enough to keep pace. Technology induces standardization and requires procedures to govern data handling into and out of the computer. Formal information systems, once in place, have a life of their own and do not adapt to the changing needs of users.[46] Changes in MIS outputs are often rejected as too costly or inefficient by the information center.

The failure to produce new reports is not the only problem. Entrenched reporting systems gradually become inaccurate and out of synchronization. The information system does not provide a feedback mechanism to correct and update report content. One management report in a welfare office was about worker recording errors that went to top management. The top division chief explained that it was of no use to him:

> I get a listing of errors, but they don't give me sufficient details. It does not identify who is doing what errors. It is just telling me frequencies of types of

error. I don't know if it is one or two workers that are doing it or if it is widespread.[47]

The statistical reporting system simply doesn't provide the correct details, nor could it be easily adapted to provide managers what they needed.

Employee Dissatisfaction   Although electronic technology increases the skill level for many employees, other employees find themselves negatively affected. The electronic technology provides a powerful means of surveillance. Employees who perform routine work throughout the organization can be wired into the information system, and hence be overwhelmed with control.[48] For example, electronic surveillance can count the number of key strokes made by a word processing employee, count the lines of copy written by a programmer, record the actions of an engineer operating a nuclear facility, and calculate the dollar value of sales per call of a catalog telephone operator.

The capacity of computer-based data processing enables the organization to monitor employees and to increase the pace and routinization of work. Supermarket checkout scanners can precisely record the pattern of behavior of each checker, which enables management to ask for increased production. American Express uses electronic monitoring techniques to monitor data-entry personnel who record account payments and the operators who answer phone queries. The monitoring system tells the average time it takes to answer a call and the time each representative spends with each caller. Standards have been set of answering the phone within ten seconds, and supervisors listen in to assess quality of the conversation.[49]

Structural Solution

The problems of hardware emphasis, system inflexibility, and employee dissatisfaction often result from organization structure as described in chapter 6. Functional departmentation is typically used to create a separate computer department with responsibilities for management information systems. When integration between the computer department and users is poor, problems are enhanced. Computer personnel are concerned with hardware efficiency, not with user needs. They are concerned with volume of reports rather than with flexibility and employee satisfaction. The goals and work orientation of computer departments are different from those of user departments. The solution to greater use of the computer resource is closer coordination with other departments.

One way to achieve coordination is through the horizontal linkage devices described in chapter 6. A liaison person can be assigned from the computer department to work with users. Stronger linkage devices involve the use of temporary task forces or permanent teams composed of both MIS experts and users. In this way the different needs can be integrated, and the changing needs of users can be fed back to the MIS department. Another solution is to decentralize the computer operation. The development of powerful small computers and distributed data processing means that user departments can have their own MIS capability. If user departments have their own employees designing information systems, the outcomes will reflect manager and employee needs rather than hardware efficiency. Decision-making by users will prevent undue electronic surveillance and rigid report formats. The computer resource can be designed on the order of self-contained units described in chapter 6, with many major departments housing their own MIS technology.

Information technology is a wonderful tool, but it can have both positive and negative effects. Middle- and upper-level managers who understand the appropriate role of MIS's in the organization can help increase the positive benefits while decreasing the negative side effects. An example of how to manage the information resource is Hanover Trust.

IN PRACTICE 8.8.

Hanover Trust Company

Deregulation of the banking industry has forced a radical change in data-processing departments to meet the need for new kinds of information. Data-processing departments previously did little but record interest rates and other data, but now are a central factor in competitive strategy.

Each bank department used to be autonomous. Savings accounts, loans, and checking accounts were handled by different managers. Recordkeeping and MIS data were gathered for each type of account. Managers in the savings section would be unaware of the extent to which customers also made loans or had checking accounts at the bank.

Under increased competition, top managers need market related information by customer. A complete profile of each customer's accounts is a valuable asset for the marketing of additional services. But this also requires flexibility in bank data processing, which is difficult. The current systems are set up and running, and have momentum. Even the managers who would benefit from the new data are reluctant to give up current reports.

Manufacturers at Hanover Trust solved the problem by picking a very senior manager to head a committee to design a new system. The standing committee integrated the interests of each department and helped generate flexibility in MIS design. Once the overall design of the information system was accepted, the next step was to create four data-processing sections, one each for wholesale banking, retail banking, securities, and internal housekeeping. Each system serves its own users, but all four are tightly integrated and can share data. New reports can be created that cut across sections as managers' needs dictate. The careful integration of sophisticated technology with user needs enables upper managers to look at customers' total needs rather than at separate accounts, while minimizing the conflict between information designers and users. The new systems are more flexible, provide data relevant to user needs, and satisfy employees.[50]

SUMMARY AND INTERPRETATION

The ideas covered in this chapter are some of the newest in organization theory. In the last few years, organization researchers have begun to develop frameworks that explain information and control processes in organizations.

The two important information dimensions are amount and richness. Determining how manager and department information needs differ along these two dimensions and how to design the organization's structure and information support systems are key problems for organizations to solve. Generally as the ambiguity of managerial tasks or departmental tasks increases, rich, personal information is required. Clear, well-defined tasks are associated with the need for precise, quantitative information. Information requirements also differ by hierarchical level, with managers at the top needing information that is rich, future-oriented, and descriptive of the external environment. Information for managers at lower levels is more precise, internal, historical, and detailed.

Organizations must also solve the problem of directing and evaluating the performance of the overall organization, its departments, and individual employees. The concepts of market, bureaucratic, clan, output, and behavior control help explain how control is exercised at each level in organizations.

Market control is used where markets can be priced and where competition exists. Clan control is associated with uncertain and rapidly changing organizational processes, and relies on commitment, tradition, and shared values for control. Bureaucratic control relies on the bureaucratic characteristics of organizations described in chapter 5, as well as on the four internal management control systems of budgets, statistical reports, standard operating procedures, and performance appraisal systems.

Exciting new developments are taking place in the technology for processing organizational information. Computers and other forms of electronic technology have helped solve the need for large amounts of data. The problem for information systems of the future is to meet managerial needs for rich information. New developments such as videoconferencing systems enable visual contact among far-flung managers. New systems may transmit face-to-face cues and provide rapid feedback to enhance the information-processing effectiveness of the organization.

The final point is that the material in this chapter builds upon concepts described in chapter 6. In chapter 6 we saw that organization structure serves to direct the flow of information. Vertical and horizontal linkage devices are used to ensure that information is passed where it is needed for problem-solving, control, and coordination. Management information and control systems are an important component of organization structure.

KEY CONCEPTS

behavior control
bureaucratic control
clan control
contingency control model
control information
control system package
data
decision support system
information
information amount
information richness
information technology
   impact on structure

management control systems
management information
   systems
management level differences
market control
organizational control
output control
information technology side
   effects
task information
uncertainty

DISCUSSION QUESTIONS

1. Define information. How does information differ from data?

2. Assume that students have two ways to inform professors about the quality of their teaching. The first way is for each student to rate the professor's teaching ability on a seven-point scale. The second way is for students to write a paragraph stating what they liked and disliked about the professor's teaching. Which of these techniques will provide the richest information to the professor? Is your answer consistent with the richness scale given in Exhibit 8.2?

3. The manager of a computer processing department told his employees: "Top managers need the same data everyone else needs, except that instead of all the details we'll aggregate it for the company as a whole." Agree or disagree with the manager's philosophy, and explain why.

4. An organization consultant argued that managers need information support that is independent of computers. Explain why you agree or disagree with his point of view.

5. In writing about types of control, William Ouchi said, "The Market is like the trout and the Clan like the salmon, each a beautiful highly specialized species which requires uncommon conditions for its survival. In comparison, the bureaucratic method of control is the catfish—clumsy, ugly, but able to live in the widest range of environments and, ultimately, the dominant species." Discuss what Ouchi meant with that analogy.

6. What type of controls do most professors use to control students—output, behavior, or both?

7. How do technology and environment influence the design of control systems?

8. What types of organizational and environmental conditions influence the amount of information-processing in organizations? Which media are used to process information?

9. Government organizations often seem more bureaucratic than for-profit organizations. Could this partly be the result of the type of control used in government organizations? Explain.

10. Discuss the following statements: "Things under tight control are better than things under loose control." "The more data managers have the better decisions they make."

11. Discuss the impact of computer technology on organizations. How can structure soften the negative effects of computer-based information and control systems?

GUIDES TO ACTION

As an organization designer:

1. Provide information support to managers and employees that reflects the frequency and type of problems with which they deal. Design both the amount and richness of information to meet the problem-solving needs of managers.

2. Implement one of the three basic choices—bureaucratic, clan, market—as the primary means of organizational control. Use bureaucratic control

when organizations are large, have a stable environment, and routine technology. Use clan control in small, uncertain departments. Use market control when outputs can be priced, and when competitive bidding is available.

3. Use management-control systems to monitor and influence department-level activities. The budget controls resources into the department and statistical reports control the product and service outcomes of the department. Performance appraisal and standard operating procedures can be used to control work activities within departments.

4. Predict and plan for changes associated with the adaptation of sophisticated information-processing and computer technology. Prepare for a shift in power between those who manage the technology and those who do not. Expect an increase in the professionalism of employees working with the technology, and a decrease in clerical personnel. Overcome the undesirable side effects of technology by integrating information services departments with user departments. Frequent meetings between MIS designers and users, or the decentralization of information services to user departments, can help the information system meet managerial needs for information, be more flexible, and enhance employee satisfaction.

Consider these Guides when analyzing the following case.

CASE FOR ANALYSIS

SUNFLOWER INCORPORATED*

Sunflower Incorporated is a large distribution company with over 5,000 employees and gross sales of over $450 million (1984). The company purchases and distributes salty snack foods and liquor to independent retail stores throughout the United States and Canada. Salty snack foods include corn chips, potato chips, cheese curls, tortilla chips, and peanuts. The U.S. and Canada are divided into twenty-two regions, each with its own central warehouse, salespeople, finance department, and purchasing department. The company distributes national as well as local brands, and packages some items under private labels. Competition in this industry is intense. The demand for liquor has been declining, and competitors like Procter & Gamble and Frito-Lay develop new snack foods to gain market share from smaller companies like Sunflower. The head office encourages each region to be autonomous because of local tastes and practices. The northeast U.S., for example, consumes a greater percentage of Canadian whisky and American bourbon, while the West consumes more light liquors such as vodka, gin, and rum. Snack foods in the Southwest are often seasoned to reflect Mexican tastes.

Early in 1985, Sunflower began using a financial reporting system that compared sales, costs, and profits across company regions. Each region was

---

* This case was inspired by "Frito-Lay May Find Itself in a Competition Crunch," *Business Week,* July 19, 1982, p. 186, and "Dashman Company," in Paul R. Lawrence and John A. Seiler, *Organizational Behavior and Administration: Cases, Concepts, and Research Findings* (Homewood, IL: Irwin and Dorsey, 1965), pp. 16–17.

a profit center, and top management was surprised to learn that profits varied widely. By 1985, the differences were so great that management decided some standardization was necessary. They believed that highly profitable regions were sometimes using lower quality items, even seconds, to boost profit margins. This practice could hurt Sunflower's image. Other regions were facing cut-throat price competition to hold market share. National distributors such as Frito-Lay, Bordens, Nabisco, Procter & Gamble (Pringles), and Standard Brands (Planters Peanuts) were pushing to increase market share by cutting prices and launching new products.

As these problems accumulated, Mr. Steelman, president of Sunflower, decided to create a new position to monitor pricing and purchasing practices. Mrs. Loretta Williams was hired from the finance department of a competing organization. Her new title was Director of Pricing and Purchasing, and she reported to the Vice-President of Finance, Mr. Langly. Langly gave Williams great latitude in organizing her job, and encouraged her to establish whatever rules and procedures were necessary. She was also encouraged to gather information from each region. Each region was notified of her appointment by an official memo sent to the twenty-two regional directors. A copy of the memo was posted on each warehouse bulletin board. The announcement was also made in the company newspaper.

After three weeks on the job, Mrs. Williams decided that pricing and purchasing decisions should be standardized across regions. As a first step, she wanted the financial executive in each region to notify her of any change in local prices of more than 3%. She also decided that all new contracts for local purchases of more than $5,000 should be cleared through her office. (Approximately 60% of items distributed in the regions were purchased in large quantities and supplied from the home office. The other 40% were purchased and distributed within the region.) Williams believed that the only way to standardize operations was for each region to notify the home office in advance of any change in prices or purchases. Williams discussed the proposed policy with Langly. He agreed, so they submitted a formal proposal to the president and board of directors, who approved the plan. The changes represented a complicated shift in policy procedures, and Sunflower was moving into the peak holiday season, so Williams wanted to implement the new procedures right away. She decided to send a telex to the financial and purchasing executives in each region notifying them for the new procedures. The change would be inserted in all policy and procedure manuals throughout Sunflower within four months.

Williams showed a draft of the telex to Langly and invited his comments. Langly said the telex was a good idea but wondered if it was sufficient. The regions handled hundreds of items, and were used to decentralize decision-making. Langly suggested that Williams ought to visit the regions and discuss purchasing and pricing policies with the executives. Williams refused, saying that the trips would be expensive and time-consuming. She had so many things to do at headquarters that a trip was impossible. Langly also suggested waiting to implement the procedures until after the annual company meeting in three months when she could meet the regional directors personally. Williams said that this would take too long, because the procedure would not take effect until after the peak sales season. She believed the procedures were needed now. The telexes went out the next day.

During the next few days, replies came in from seven regions. The managers said they were in agreement with the telex, and said they would be happy to cooperate.

Eight weeks later, Williams had not received notices from any regions about local price or purchase changes. Other executives who had visited regional warehouses indicated to her that the regions were busy as usual. Regional executives seemed to be following usual procedures for that time of year. She telephoned one of the regional managers, and discovered that he did not know who she was, and had never heard of the position called Director of Pricing and Purchasing. Besides, he said, "We have enough to worry about reaching profit goals without additional procedures from headquarters." Williams was chagrined that her position and suggested changes in procedure had no impact. She wondered whether field managers were disobedient or whether she should have used another communication strategy.

Questions

1. What type of control did the home office use to evaluate the performance of each region? What type of control did Mrs. Williams try to use to change the behavior of regional purchasing and financial managers at Sunflower? What type of control were the executives used to? Did Mr. Langly's suggestion that Williams meet the executives personally represent a different form of control? Discuss.

2. Mrs. Williams had a choice of two information media—written and face-to-face. What information medium is appropriate to communicate procedures for pricing and purchasing? Which medium is appropriate for announcing and providing authority to a new position? Why?

NOTES

1. "S. I. Newhouse and Sons: America's Most Profitable Publisher," *Business Week,* January 26, 1976, pp. 56–64; Mary Vespa and Lee Wohlfert-Winborg, "The Talk of the Town," *People,* March 25, 1985, pp. 87–88.

2. Daniel Machalaba, "Newhouse Chain Stays with Founder's Ways and with His Heirs," *Wall Street Journal,* February 12, 1982, pp. 1, 15.

3. "S. I. Newhouse and Sons," *Business Week.*

4. This case was based on "S. I. Newhouse and Sons," *Business Week,* and on Daniel Machalaba, "Newhouse Chain Stays with Founder's Ways and with His Heirs."

5. Richard L. Daft and Norman B. Macintosh, "A Tentative Exploration into the Amount and Equivocality of Information Processing in Organizational Work Units," *Administrative Science Quarterly* 26 (1981):207–224.

6. Richard L. Daft and Norman B. Macintosh, "The Nature and Use of Formal Control Systems for Management Control and Strategy Implementation," *Journal of Management,* 10 (1984):43–66.

7. Henry Mintzberg, *The Nature of Managerial Work* (New York: Harper & Row, 1972), p. 39.

8. Ibid.

9. Daft and Macintosh, "A Tentative Exploration," p. 210.

10. Jay R. Galbraith, *Organization Design* (Reading, MA: Addison-Wesley, 1977), pp. 35–36.

11. Michael L. Tushman and David A. Nadler, "Information Processing As an Integrating Concept in Organization Design," *Academy of Management Review* 3 (1978): 613–624; Samuel B. Bacharach and Michael Aiken, "Communication in Administrative Bureaucracies," *Academy of Management Journal* 20 (1977):365–377.

12. Richard L. Daft and Robert H. Lengel, "Information Richness: A New Approach to Managerial Behavior and Organization Design," in Barry Staw and Larry L. Cummings, eds., *Research in Organizational Behavior,* vol. 6 (Greenwich, CT: JAI Press), 1984, pp. 191–233; Robert H. Lengel, "Managerial Information Processing and Communication-Media Source Selection Behavior," unpublished Ph.D. dissertation, Texas A&M University, 1982.

13. A. Meherabian, *Silent Messages* (Belmont, CA: Wadsworth, 1971), p. 44.

14. Thomas F. O'Boyle and Carol Hymowitz, "More Corporate Chiefs Seek Direct Contact with Staff, Customers," *The Wall Street Journal,* February 27, 1985, pp. 1, 12; Lawrence Rout, "Hyatt Hotels' Gripe Sessions Help Chief Maintain Communications with Workers," *The Wall Street Journal,* July 15, 1981, pp. 27–33.

15. Daft and Macintosh, "A Tentative Exploration"; W. Alan Randolph, "Matching Technology and the Design of Organization Units," *California Management Review,* 22–23 (no. 4, 1980–81):39–48.

16. Michael L. Tushman, "Technical Communication in R&D Laboratories: The Impact of Project Work Characteristics," *Academy of Management Journal* 21 (1978): 624–645.

17. Daft and Macintosh, "A Tentative Exploration"; Robert H. Lengel and Richard L. Daft, "The Relationship Between Message Content and Media Selection in Managerial Communications: Some Preliminary Evidence," unpublished manuscript, Texas A&M University, 1984.

18. Warren J. Keegan, "Multi-National Scanning: A Study of Information Sources Utilized by Headquarters Executives in Multi-National Companies," *Administrative Science Quarterly* 19 (1974):411–421.

19. Michael McFadden, "The Master Builder of Mammoth Tools," *Fortune,* September 3, 1984, pp. 58–64.

20. Adapted from Richard L. Daft and Norman B. Macintosh, "A New Approach to Design and Use of Management Information," *California Management Review* 21 (1978), p. 89. Copyright © 1978 by the Regents of the University of California. Reprinted by permission of the Regents.

21. G. Anthony Gorry and Michael S. Scott Morton, "A Framework for Management Information Systems," *Sloan Management Review* 13 (1970):55–70. Richard L. Daft and Robert H. Lengel, "Information Richness: A New Approach to Managerial Behavior and Organization Design"; Richard L. Daft and Robert H. Lengel, "A Proposed Integration among Organizational Information Requirements, Media Richness, and Structural Design," *Management Science,* (1986): in press.

22. F. Aguilar, *Scanning the Business Environment* (New York: Macmillan, 1967); Richard L. Daft and Karl E. Weick, "Toward a Model of Organizations As Interpretation Systems," *Academy of Management Review,* 9 (1984):284–295.

23. George P. Huber, "Organizational Information Systems: Determinants of Their Performance and Behavior," *Management Science,* 28 (1982):138–155; J. C. Higgins and R. Finn, "The Chief Executive and His Information System," *Omega,* 5 (1977): 557–566; Michael L. Tushman and Elaine Romanelli, "Uncertainty, Social Location, and Influence in Decision Making: A Sociometric Analysis," *Management Science,* 29 (1983):12–23.

24. "What Undid Jarman: Paperwork Paralysis," *Business Week,* January 24, 1977, pp. 67–68; "Genesco Ousts Franklin Jarman as Top Officer," *Wall Street Journal,* January 4, 1977, p. 2.

25. Kenneth A. Merchant, *Control in Business Organizations* (Marshfield, MA: Pitman Publishing, 1985); William G. Ouchi, "The Relationship between Organizational Structure and Organizational Control," *Administrative Science Quarterly* 22 (1977):95–113;

John Todd, "Management Control Systems: A Key Link Between Strategy, Structure, and Employee," *Organizational Dynamics* (Spring, 1977):65–78.

26. Geert Hofstede, "The Poverty of Management Control Philosophy," *Academy of Management Review* 3 (1978):450–461.

27. Anthony Hopwood, *Accounting and Human Behavior* (London: Haymarket Publishing, 1974).

28. William G. Ouchi, "Markets, Bureaucracies, and Clans," *Administrative Science Quarterly* 25 (1980):129–141; and "A Conceptual Framework for the Design of Organizational Control Mechanisms," *Management Science* 25 (1979): 833–848.

29. Oliver A. Williamson, *Markets and Hierarchies: Analyses and Antitrust Implications* (New York: Free Press, 1975).

30. Richard L. Daft and Norman B. Macintosh, "The Nature and Use of Formal Control Systems for Management Control and Strategy Implementation," *Journal of Management,* 10 (1984):43–66.

31. Ibid.

32. Norman B. Macintosh and Richard L. Daft, "Management Control Systems and Organizational Contexts," Report to the Society of Management Accountants and National Association of Accountants, Kingston, Ontario, 1980.

33. Ouchi, "Markets, Bureaucracies, and Clans."

34. Bill Saporito, "Allegheny Ludlum Has Steel Figured Out," *Fortune,* June 25, 1984, pp. 40–44.

35. Ouchi, "Relationship Between Organizational Structure and Organizational Control"; William G. Ouchi and Mary Ann McGuire, "Organizational Control: Two Functions," *Administrative Science Quarterly* 20 (1975):559–569.

36. Peter M. Blau and W. Richard Scott, *Formal Organization* (San Francisco: Chandler Publishing Company, 1962).

37. Ouchi and McGuire, "Organizational Control."

38. Thomas L. Whisler, *The Impact of Computers on Organizations* (New York: Praeger, 1973; Nancy M. Carter, "Computerization As a Predominant Technology: Its Influence on the Structure of Newspaper Organizations," *Academy of Management Journal,* 27 (1984):247–270.

39. Ibid.

40. Elmer H. Burack and Peter F. Sorensen, Jr., "Computer Technology and Organizational Design: Toward a Contingency Model," *Organization and Administrative Science* 8 (1977):223–235.

41. B. C. Reimann, "Organization Structure and Technology in Manufacturing: System Versus Workflow Level Perspectives," *Academy of Management Journal* 23 (1980): 61–77; Whisler, *Impact of Computers on Organizations,* p. 11; Carter, "Computerization as a Predominant Technology."

42. Whisler, ibid., p. 12; Carter, ibid.

43. Reimann, "Organization Structure and Technology."

44. "Office Automation Restructures Business," *Business Week,* October 8, 1984, pp. 118–125; Peter Nulty, "How Personal Computers Change Managers' Lives," *Fortune,* September 3, 1984, pp. 38–48.

45. George P. Huber, "Organizational Information Systems: Determinants of Their Performance and Behavior," *Management Science,* 28 (1982):138–155; Ian Mitroff and Richard O. Mason, "Can We Design Systems for Managing Messes? or, Why So Many Management Information Systems Are Uninformative," *Accounting, Organizations and Society,* 8 (1983):195–203; Richard L. Daft and John C. Wiginton, "Language and Organizations," *Academy of Management Review,* 4 (1979):179–191.

46. B. Hedberg and S. Johnson, "Designing Semi-Confusing Information Systems for Organizations in Changing Environments," *Accounting, Organizations and Society,* 3 (1978):47–64.

47. David Dery, "The Bureaucratic Side of Computers: Memory, Evocation and Management Information," *Omega,* 9 (1981):25–32.

48. Richard E. Walton, "Social Choice in the Development of Advanced Information Technology," *Human Relations,* 35 (1982):1073–1084; E. E. Lawler, III, and John Grant Rhode, *Information and Control in Organizations* (Los Angeles: Goodyear, 1976).

49. "Corporate Big Brother Is Watching You," *Dun's Business Month,* January 1984, pp. 36–39.

50. Inspired by and adapted from "The Banks' Great Struggle to Master a Tangle of Data," *Business Week,* December 10, 1984, pp. 106–108.

Managing Dynamic Processes

Decision-Making Processes

MORGAN GUARANTY

Morgan Guaranty executives had been discussing the idea for several months. A majority of them were finally in agreement. A new "Morgan Guaranty Building" was needed. A lavish $250-million skyscraper would be comparable to their competitors' buildings, such as the Chase Manhattan Plaza and the Citicorp Center. It would also be a good investment, and would bring together most of the bank's New York employees who were scattered among half a dozen buildings. Morgan executives decided on it, and cast their eye on the Wall Street block next to their current building as a potential site.

Building a skyscraper in Manhattan requires an assemblage—the uncertain business of secretly buying individual properties located on the building site. Long-term leases also have to be purchased from tenants. Any seller who discovers the assemblage can hold out for a ransom price because the buyer has to obtain every parcel. Morgan's target block contained six highrises, of which the three largest were essential to the project. If any of the three was lost, the project was dead. The three critical properties were owned by some of the smartest and best-connected real estate operators in Manhattan.

James Austrian was hired to direct the assemblage. He would try to grab the three buildings before the landlords realized what was happening. Then he would have to arrange to move out sixty tenants whose leases expired after the wrecking crews were to begin their work.

The first building was purchased in two weeks for $6.8 million. Negotiations with the second owner took less than two weeks, and were handled over the phone. The price was $2.7 million. The deal for the third building was stickier, because it was owned by a limited partnership with 350 members. If the owners of the first two buildings were in the partnership, they would realize an assemblage was in progress. The cover would be blown. Austrian made a deal with the principal partner for $19 million. After "two months of sweat," [1] the contract was ratified. Neither of the other owners was part of the partnership group.

While waiting for the third building to close, Austrian began the delicate task of persuading tenants in the first two buildings to leave. Within a few months, he had reached agreement or was near agreement with every tenant. Everything was moving nicely, certainly better than expected.

Except for one minor problem. The contract for the second building could not be legally closed because of $1.7 million owed in back taxes. The city of New York had filed a foreclosure proceeding against the building. Paying off back taxes was a routine matter, so the owner offered to settle up—after all, he was going to sell for $1 million more than the taxes owed. The city of New York refused. The Koch administration had adopted a tough new policy on delinquent landlords. The city became the new owner.

This was an uncertain stage. An assemblage normally should not be revealed. However, city administrators should be thrilled at the prospect of a new skyscraper that would pump over $13 million a year into the city's treasury. So Morgan executives and Austrian decided to come clean. A veteran Morgan executive sat down with the deputy commissioner of general services. The commissioner said of course the city would sell the property to Morgan. The

Morgan executive offered $2 million. If Morgan wanted the building, the commissioner said, the price was $17 million.

The city was trying to extract an assemblage ransom! The Morgan executive was furious. That price would destroy the assemblage budget. The price was six times the price of comparable property.

Morgan's vice-chairman jumped into the negotiations. He pushed the decision up a notch or two in the city's hierarchy. The city stood firm. He called the city's price "highway robbery" and "a hold-up."

The assemblage is dead. The commissioner admitted that the building was worthless to the city, and that $17 million was too high, but said it was the negotiating price. If Morgan had wanted the building, why did they back out so quickly? One reason is that dissension within Morgan surfaced when the assemblage price increased. Several executives felt the price wasn't worth it. Morgan didn't need a new building that badly. The city believes someone will eventually build a skyscraper on that site. In the meantime, it will receive only about $1 million in property tax revenues instead of $13 million. As for Morgan Guaranty, they sold the other two buildings to a Canadian developer and made an unexpectedly handsome profit.[2]

Morgan's skyscraper decision provides several insights into decision-making. First, decision-making in the corporate world can be a messy, uncertain process. Morgan executives could not be certain that a new building would improve business, improve employee working relationships, or that the next block over was the best location. These issues were decided without complete information. Second, executives may not agree on the severity of the problem or with the proposed solution. Organizational decisions often have to focus on building agreement among key people, which is called a coalition. Morgan had the coalition, which promptly fell apart when the building's price went up. Third a big decision is not made all at once. Big problems are identified and solved through a series of small decisions, such as deciding that multiple locations are unproductive, that Morgan's image needed improving, that the assemblage should be revealed to the city, and so on. Finally, corporate decisions don't always work out. Mistakes are made. The decision plan may fall apart. Working under uncertainty, the organization may cycle through the decision process several times, reassessing whether a problem truly exists, and trying new solutions.

Definitions

Organization decision-making is formally defined as the process of identifying and solving problems. The process contains two major stages. The **problem identification** stage is where information about environmental and organizational conditions is monitored to determine if performance is satisfactory and to diagnose the cause of shortcomings. The **problem solution** stage is where alternative courses of action are considered and one alternative is selected and implemented. Morgan Guaranty's decision to build a skyscraper came unravelled in the problem-solution stage. An unexpectedly high price by the city made the decision infeasible to implement. The barrier to implementation will cause Morgan to recycle to the problem-identification stage. The original problems were that Morgan's building was less than competitive and that the internal climate could be improved by bringing employees together. A great amount of discussion and analysis will be undertaken to evaluate whether a problem truly exists and what the solution might be.

Organizational decisions vary in complexity, and can be categorized as programmed or nonprogrammed.[3] **Programmed decisions** are repetitive and well-defined, and procedures exist for resolving the problem. Programmed decisions are well-structured because criteria of performance are normally clear, good information is available about current performance, alternatives are easily specified, and there is relative certainty that the chosen alternative will be successful. Examples of programmed decisions include the decision rule for replacing office equipment, when to reimburse managers for travel expenses, or whether an applicant has sufficient qualifications for an assembly line job.

Nonprogrammed decisions are novel and poorly defined, and no procedure exists for solving them.[4] The organization has not seen the problem before, and may not know how to respond. Information about the extent of the problem is hard to obtain. Clear-cut criteria do not exist. Alternatives are fuzzy. Little certainty exists that a solution will solve the problem. Normally only one or two alternatives can be developed, so the solution will be custom-tailored to the problem. The decision to build a "Morgan Guaranty Building" was a nonprogrammed decision.

Purpose of This Chapter

Decision-making processes represent the brain and nervous system of the organization. Decision-makers monitor the external environment, interpret internal information, detect shortcomings in expected behavior and performance, analyze potential alternatives, and implement new courses of action. Decision-making is the end use of the information and control systems described in the previous chapter. Decisions are made about organization structure, innovation, goals, products, facilities, and technology. In this chapter, we will explore how organizations can and should make decisions about these issues. Decision-making by individual managers and decision-making by the organization are interconnected, so both types of decisions are considered in this chapter. At any time, an organization may be identifying problems and implementing alternatives for hundreds of decisions. Organizations somehow "muddle through" these processes.[5] Our purpose here is to analyze these processes to learn what decision-making is actually like in organizational settings.

In the next section, we examine how individual managers make decisions. Then we explore several models of organizational decision-making. These models include systems analysis, the Carnegie model, the incremental decision model, and the garbage can model. Each model is important because it is used in a different organizational situation. The final section in this chapter combines the models into a single framework that describes when and how they should be used.

MANAGER DECISION-MAKING

Rational Approach

The rational approach to individual decision-making stresses the need for systematic analysis of the problem followed by choice and implementation in a logical step-by-step sequence. The rational approach was developed to guide decision-making because many managers were observed to be unsystematic and arbitrary in their approach to organizational decisions. According to the rational approach, the decision process can be broken down into eight steps.[6]

1. *Monitor the Decision Environment.* This means monitoring internal and external information that will indicate deviations from planned or acceptable behavior. Managers will talk to colleagues and review financial statements, performance evaluations, absentee reports, industry indices, competitors' activities, and so forth.

2. *Define the Problem.* The manager responds to deviations by identifying essential details of the problem: where, when, who was involved, who was affected, and how are current activities influenced.

3. *Specify Decision Objectives.* The manager determines what performance outcomes should be achieved by a decision.

4. *Diagnose the Problem.* In this stage, the manager digs below the surface to analyze the cause of the problem. Additional data may be gathered to facilitate this diagnosis. Understanding the cause enables appropriate treatment.

5. *Develop Alternative Solutions.* Alternative courses of action that may achieve decisional objectives are identified. The manager will rely on previous experience and seek ideas and suggestions from other people.

6. *Evaluate Alternatives.* This may involve the use of statistical techniques or personal experience to assess the probability of success. The merits of each alternative are assessed as well as the probability that it will reach the desired objectives.

7. *Choose the Best Alternative.* This is the core of the decision process. Managers use their analysis of the problem, objectives, and alternatives to select a single alternative that has the best chance for success.

8. *Implement the Chosen Alternative.* The manager uses managerial, administrative, and persuasive abilities and gives directions to ensure that the decision is carried out. Monitoring activity (step 1) begins again as soon as the solution is implemented.

The first four steps in this sequence are the problem identification stage, and the next four are the problem solution stage of decision-making, as indicated in Exhibit 9.1. All eight steps will normally appear in a manager's decision, although each step may not be a distinct element. Managers may know from experience exactly what to do in a situation, so one or more steps will be minimized. The following case illustrates how the rational approach is used to make a decision about a personnel problem.

IN PRACTICE 9.1

Alberta Manufacturing

1. *Monitor the Decision Environment.* It is Monday morning, and Joe Defoe, one of Alberta's most skilled cutters, is absent again.

2. *Define the Decision Problem.* This is the sixth consecutive Monday that

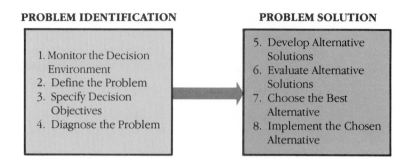

PROBLEM IDENTIFICATION

1. Monitor the Decision Environment
2. Define the Problem
3. Specify Decision Objectives
4. Diagnose the Problem

PROBLEM SOLUTION

5. Develop Alternative Solutions
6. Evaluate Alternative Solutions
7. Choose the Best Alternative
8. Implement the Chosen Alternative

EXHIBIT 9.1. Steps in the Rational Approach to Decision-Making.

Joe has been absent. Company policy forbids unexcused absenteeism and Joe has been warned about his excessive absenteeism on the last three occasions. A final warning is in order, but can be delayed if warranted.

3. *Specify Decision Objectives.* Joe should attend work regularly and establish the production and quality levels of which he is capable. The time period for solving the problem is two weeks.

4. *Diagnose the Problem.* Discreet discussions with Joe's co-workers and information gleaned from Joe indicate that Joe has a drinking problem. He apparently uses Mondays to dry out from weekend benders. Discussion with other company sources confirms that Joe is a problem drinker.

5. *Develop Alternative Solutions.* (1) Fire Joe. (2) Issue a final warning without comment. (3) Issue a warning and accuse Joe of being an alcoholic to let him know you are aware of his problem. (4) Talk with Joe to see if he will discuss his drinking. If he admits that he has a drinking problem, delay the final warning and suggest that the company will be reasonably flexible if he makes a serious attempt to seek professional aid. (5) If he does not admit he has a drinking problem, let him know that the next absence will cost him his job.

6. *Evaluate the Alternative.* The cost of training a replacement is the same for each alternative. Alternative 1 ignores cost and other criteria. Alternatives 2 and 3 do not adhere to company policy, which advocates counseling, where appropriate, to assist employees in overcoming personal problems. Alternative 4 is designed for the benefit of both Joe and the company. It might save a good employee if Joe is willing to seek assistance. Alternative 5 is primarily for the benefit of the company. Final warning might provide some initiative for Joe to admit that he has a drinking problem. If so, dismissal might be avoided, but further absences will no longer be tolerated.

7. *Choose the Best Alternative.* Joe does not admit that he has a drinking problem. Choose Alternative 5.

8. *Implement the Best Alternative.* Write up the case, and issue the final warning.[7]

Issuing the final warning to Joe Defoe was a programmable decision. The standard of expected behavior was clearly defined, information on the frequency and cause of Joe's absence was readily available, and acceptable alternatives and procedures were described. The rational procedure works well when the decision-maker has sufficient time for an orderly, thoughtful process. Moreover, Alberta Manufacturing had mechanisms in place to implement the decision, once made. When decisions are nonprogrammed, ill-defined, and piling on top of one another, the individual manager may use intuition and experience rather than rational procedures.

Bounded Rationality Approach

The point of the rational approach is that managers should try to use systematic procedures to arrive at good decisions. Yet research into managerial decision-making shows that managers are unable to follow these step-by-step procedures much of the time. The reason is that time pressure, a large number of factors affecting the decision, and the ill-defined nature of many problems make systematic analysis nearly impossible. Managers have only so much time and mental capacity, and hence cannot evaluate every goal, problem, and alternative. The attempts to be rational is bounded (limited) by the enormous complexity of many problems. There is a limit to how rational managers can be. For example, an executive in a hurry may have a choice of fifty ties on a rack, but will take the first or second tie that matches his suit. The executive doesn't carefully weigh all fifty alternatives because the short amount of time and the large number of plausible alternatives would be overwhelming. The manager simply selects the first tie that solves the problem and moves on to the next task.

Large organizational decisions are not only complex, but ambiguous too. In a study of the decision-making surrounding the Cuban missile crisis, key decision-makers in the White House knew that a problem existed, but were unable to specify desired goals and objectives. The act of making decisions led to the discovery of desired objectives and helped clarify the course of action and possible consequences.[8] Even seemingly simple decisions, such as selecting a job upon graduation from college, can quickly become so complex that a bounded rationality approach is used. Graduating students have been known to search for a job until they have two or more acceptable job offers, at which point their search activity rapidly diminishes. Hundreds of firms may be available for interviews, and two or three job offers are far short of the maximum number that would be possible.[9]

The bounded rationality approach is often associated with intuitive decision processes. Managers build up long experience with organizational issues, which provides them with a gut feeling or hunch about the correct response. Intuition does not mean that the manager is irrational. In a situation of great complexity or ambiguity, previous experience and judgment are needed to incorporate intangible elements.[10] The intuitive processes may be associated with both the problem identification and problem solution stages of a decision. A study of manager problem-finding showed that thirty of thirty-three problems were ambiguous and ill-defined.[11] Bits and scraps of unrelated information from informal sources resulted in a pattern in the manager's mind. The manager could not "prove" a problem existed, but knew intuitively that a certain area needed attention. Examples of problems discovered through the informal, intuitive process are:

1. Reorganization to exploit opportunity for multidivisional projects.
2. Changing social attitudes toward company.
3. Need for department to develop new products.

4. Address long-term growth through reorganization.
5. Effect of changing technology on sales.
6. Creation and placement of new departments.[12]

Intuitive processes are also used in the problem-solution stage. A survey found that executives frequently made decisions without explicit reference to the impact on profits or other measurable outcomes of the organization.[13] Many intangible factors, such as a person's credibility, concern for the support of other executives, fear of failure, and social attitudes influenced selection of the best alternative. These factors cannot be quantified in a systematic way, so intuition guided the choice of a solution. Managers may make a decision based upon what they sense to be right rather than upon what they can document with hard data.

A number of important decisions, some quite famous, have been based on hunch and intuition. Ray Crock felt that purchasing the McDonald name for $2.7 million was highway robbery, but knew intuitively he should pay whatever price was demanded, and he did. Donald Fisher decided on a hunch to open a store that carried every size and style of jeans that Levi made. The idea led to Gap Stores, Inc., which sells over $500 million worth of pants and other sportswear. Designer Bill Blass, who likes chocolate, used his personal taste to design luxury chocolate candies. Victor Kiam was so taken with a Remington electric razor that he bought the company. He claimed that rational analysis would not have led to that decision, and his enthusiasm for the company turned it into a highly profitable operation.[14]

An important point to remember is that the bounded rationality approach applies to nonprogrammed decisions. The novel, unclear, complex aspects of nonprogrammed decisions mean that hard data and logical procedures are not available. A study of executive decision-making found that managers simply could not use the rational approach for nonprogrammed decisions such as when to buy a CT scanner for an osteopathic hospital, or whether a city had a need for and could reasonably adopt a data-processing system.[15] Some factors simply can't be measured, analyzed, and calculated when the decision is nonprogrammed. To do so can cause mistakes because only the quantifiable factors are included in the decision process, which may over-simplify decision criteria. Executives at Paramount Pictures have learned to rely on intuition for nonprogrammed decisions, and have been highly suc-cessful.

IN PRACTICE 9.2

Paramount Pictures Corp.

When Barry Diller and Michael Eisner go to the movies, it's not for entertain-ment. They are checking audience reaction on one of their new movies. Barry Diller is chairman and Michael Eisner is president of Paramount Pictures Corp. Audience reaction has been delightfully favorable for several years.

Some of Paramount's successes have been *Indiana Jones and the Temple of Doom*, *Raiders of the Lost Ark*, *An Officer and a Gentleman*, *Trading Places*, *48 Hours*, *Flashdance*, and *Terms of Endearment*. A major reason for the string of hits has been the excellent choice of films. Paramount decision-makers have been attuned to the tastes of 18-to-24-year olds, who count most. Paramount has also gotten into other ventures, such as selling its films to Showtime. *Entertainment Tonight,* the entertainment-news TV show, has also been hugely successful.

Why has Paramount been so successful at selecting films? Diller and Eisner claim it is because they rely on gut reaction when picking films or other projects. Their tastes were shaped while executives at ABC, where they were responsible for the *Movie of the Week.* Their experience has paid off. Columbia Pictures, a Division of Coca-Cola, uses market research to identify what people want to see. "We don't use Coca-Cola type research. We think it's junk," says Eisner. He thinks about what he likes, not what the public likes. "If I ask Miss Middle America if she wants to see a movie about religion, she'll say yes. If I say, 'Do you want to see a movie about sex,' she'll say no. But she'll be lying."

Experience is so important Eisner says, because "you tend not to make the same mistakes twice." Eisner and Diller have made their share of mistakes, and they frequently disagree about the right path. They hammer out the best decision and combine their intuition through intense arguments. One bomb was *The Keep* that ran for only three weeks. *Flashdance* went the other way because no one realized it would be a smash. The experience of both successes and failures has helped Diller and Eisner develop a feel for projects the public wants. The payoff has been on the bottom line. Paramount is the only studio among the top three in film rentals every year since 1978. Paramount's earnings have gone up in each of the past four years. Their goal for the future is to do even better. If there is a screen anywhere, they want a Paramount picture to be on it.[16]

The president and chairman of Paramount realize that intangible factors are part of decision-making for selecting new films. Market research and other rational procedures can't capture everything. Trial and error combined with intuitive judgment are an important part of these difficult decisions.

Summary   Individual managers within organizations make decisions using what we have called the rational and bounded rationality approaches. Rational processes work best for programmable problems because both causes and solutions are analyzable and well-defined. The bounded rationality approach is used for nonprogrammable decisions that are complex and contain intangible decision elements. Managers often combine both rational analysis and intuition for a major decision. Ford's introduction of the Tempo involved both rational and intuitive decisions. Executives analyzed statistics to see what features were popular, they talked to consumers, and used market research surveys and panels. Executives also trusted their instincts to redesign the trunk deep enough so that sacks of groceries would stand upright, and to redesign the parking lamps in an upward curve so the car would not have a sad look.[17]

ORGANIZATIONAL DECISION-MAKING

Organizations are composed of managers who make decisions using both rational and intuitive processes. But a single manager making a decision is not representative of organization-level decision processes. Many organizational decisions involve multiple managers. Problem-identification and problem-solution involve many departments, multiple viewpoints, and even other organizations. These decisions are beyond the scope of an individual manager because the decision is so complex and is relevant to many employees. Moreover, the overall decision may be less a conscious choice than a series of small, incremental decisions. The linking together of individual decisions into a significant organizational decision is a process that must be understood and controlled by the organization. Research into organization-level decision-making has identified four models of organizational decision-making processes: the systems analysis model, the Carnegie model, the incremental decision process model, and the garbage can model.[18]

Systems Analysis Model

The systems analysis approach to organization-level decision-making is the analog to the rational approach by individual managers. Systems analysis came into being during World War II.[19] Mathematical and statistical techniques were applied to urgent, large-scale military problems that were beyond the ability of individual decision-makers. Mathematicians, physicists, and operations researchers used systems analysis to develop artillery trajectories, anti-submarine strategies, and bombing strategies such as salvoing. Consider the problem of a battleship trying to sink an enemy ship with its artillery. The enemy ship could be several miles away, and the calculation for aiming the ship's guns should consider distance, wind speed, shell size, the speed and direction of both ships, the pitch and roll of the firing ship, and curvature of the earth. Trial and error and intuition are not accurate, take far too long, and may never achieve success.

This is where systems analysis comes in. Analysts were able to identify the relevant variables involved in aiming the ship's guns, and could model them with the use of mathematical equations. Distance, speech, pitch, roll, shell size, and so on could be calculated and entered into the equations. The answer was immediate and the guns could begin firing. Factors such as pitch and roll were soon measured mechanically and fed directly into the targeting mechanism. Today, the human element is completely removed from the targeting process. Radar picks up the target and the entire sequence can proceed automatically.

Systems analysis yielded astonishing success for many military problems. This approach to decision-making diffused into corporations and business schools where techniques were studied and elaborated. Today, systems analysis is sometimes called "management science," and many corporations have departments to use these techniques. The computer department develops information systems to provide data to managers on a continuous basis. Operations research departments use sophisticated mathematical models to quantify relevant variables for problem solution. A quantitative representation of alternative solutions and the probability of each one solving the problem are developed using devices such as linear programming, Bayesian statistics, PERT charts, and other analytical devices.

Systems analysis is an excellent device for organizational decision-making when problems are analyzable and when the number of variables is beyond the ability of individual decision-makers to handle. Mathematical models can contain a thousand or more variables, each one relevant in some way to the ultimate outcome. Economic criteria can be inserted into these models so that cost-efficient methods as well as methods most likely to achieve a given goal can be identified. Management science techniques have been successfully used to find the right spot for a church camp, using multiple variables such as population, number of churches, and travel distance.[20] Other uses include decisions about test marketing the first of a new family of products, the development of a site on which a company has mineral rights, and the decision to radically alter the distribution of telecommunications services.[21] Other problems amenable to management science techniques are the efficient scheduling of air crews for commercial flights,[22] and the training of crews, as illustrated in the following case.

IN PRACTICE 9.3

Commercial Airlines

The problem involved the training of stewardesses, of whom the company employed approximately one thousand. Most of these [women] left the airline before they had given two years of service, primarily to get married. Because of the high rate of attrition, the airline had a continuous need to recruit and train additional stewardesses.

The company had set up a stewardess training school. It was capable of conducting three classes of fifty [persons] each. Actual training took five and a half weeks. An additional half-week was required for outfitting; a week was required to get them to their bases after training. This made for a total of eight weeks "lead time."

The company wanted to know how often it should run a class and how large the classes should be. On examination it became apparent that this was a familiar problem in production and inventory control. The conversion of a young woman (the raw material) into a stewardess (the finished product) by training (the production process) has associated with it an inventory carrying cost (the salary paid to excess [women] whose available time for work is not completely used), shortage costs (those associated with emergency measures of cancellations of flights arising from shortage of stewardesses), and setup costs associated with preparing the school for a class. The problem, then, was one of determining the size and frequency of "production runs" so as to minimize the sum of these costs, that is, to find the economic "lot sizes."

The appropriate mathematical analysis was applied to this familiar problem and it was solved, yielding a set of tables that the school administrator could use to conduct his operation in an optimal way. The savings indicated were impressive.[23]

Systems analysis can accurately and quickly solve problems too complicated for human processing. Systems analysis is at its best when applied to problems that are analyzable, measurable, and can be structured in a logical way, and are too vast for the human mind to comprehend.

Systems analysis has also produced many failures.[24] Part of the reason, as we discussed in the last chapter, is that quantitative data are not rich. The computer-based scanning systems of the organization provide abundant data, but only about tangible, measurable factors. Intangible, informal cues that indicate the existence of many problems have to be sensed on a more personal basis by managers.[25] The most sophisticated mathematical analyses are of no value if the important factors cannot be quantified and included in the model. Consumer "tastes," product "beauty," and the "warmth" or "feel" of an advertising campaign are qualitative dimensions. In these situations, the important role of systems analysis is to act as a supplement to manager decision-making. Quantitative results can be given to managers for discussion and interpretation to use along with their informal opinions, judgment, and intuition. The final decision will include qualitative factors as well as quantitative calculations.

The Carnegie Model

The Carnegie model of organizational decision-making is based upon the work of Richard Cyert, James March, and Herbert Simon, who were all associated with Carnegie-Mellon University.[26] Until their work, research in economics assumed that business firms made decisions as a single entity, as if all relevant information were funneled to the top decision-maker for a choice. Research by the Carnegie group indicated that organizational-level decisions involved many managers. The final choice was based upon a coalition among these managers. A **coalition** is an alliance among several managers who agree about organizational goals and problem priorities. The coalition could include managers from line departments, staff specialists, and even external groups such as powerful customers, bankers, or union representatives.

Management coalitions are needed during decision-making for two reasons. First, organizational goals often are ambiguous, and operative goals of departments often are inconsistent. When goals are ambiguous and inconsistent, problem-identification is difficult. Managers disagree about problem priorities. They must bargain about problems and build a coalition around the priority of problems to solve with limited resources. As illustrated by the Morgan Guaranty situation at the beginning of this chapter, the identification of the problem that led to the decision to build a skyscraper was based upon a consensus of senior executives. Substantial bargaining and discussion took place in the months preceding the decision to act. After the cost of the new building skyrocketed, the coalition began to fall apart because some members no longer believed the problem was important.

The second reason for coalitions is that individual managers are intendedly rational, but function with human cognitive limitations, described earlier as bounded rationality. Managers do not have the time, resources, or mental capacity to identify all dimensions and to process all information relevant to a decision. These limitations lead to coalition-building behavior. Managers talk to each other and exchange points of view to gather information and reduce uncertainty. People who have relevant information or a stake in the decision outcome are consulted. Joint decision-making will lead to a decision that is acceptable to interested parties. The solution may be modified through discussion to meet the needs of managers whose support is needed to achieve implementation.

The process of coalition-formation has several implications for organizational decision behavior. First, as discussed in chapter 2 on goals, decisions will be made to satisfice rather than to optimize problem solutions. The coalition will accept a solution that is perceived as satisfactory to all coalition members. Second, managers will be concerned with immediate problems and short-run solutions. They engage in what Cyert and March called prob-lemistic search.[27] **Problemistic search** means that managers look around in the immediate environment for a satisfactory solution to quickly resolve the problem. Managers don't expect a perfect solution when the situation is ill-defined and conflict-laden. This contrasts with the systems analysis ap-proach, which assumes that analysis can uncover every reasonable alternative. The Carnegie model says that search behavior is just sufficient to produce a satisfactory solution, and managers will normally adopt the first satisfactory solution that emerges. Third, discussion and bargaining are especially im-portant in the problem-identification stage of decision-making. Unless co-alition members perceive a problem, the problem does not exist. The joint perception of a problem is more important than any single manager's per-ception. The decision process described in the Carnegie model is summa-rized in Exhibit 9.2.

The Carnegie model points out that building agreement through a man-agerial coalition is a major part of organizational decision processes. This is especially true at upper management levels. Discussion and bargaining are time-consuming processes, so search procedures are usually simple, and the selected alternative satisfices rather than optimizes problem solution. When problems are programmed—they are clear and have been seen before— the organization will rely on previous procedures and routines. Rules and procedures prevent the need for renewed coalition-formation and political bargaining. Nonprogrammed decisions, however, require bargaining and conflict-resolution. If senior managers are unable to build a coalition about

EXHIBIT 9.2. Choice Processes in the Carnegie Model.

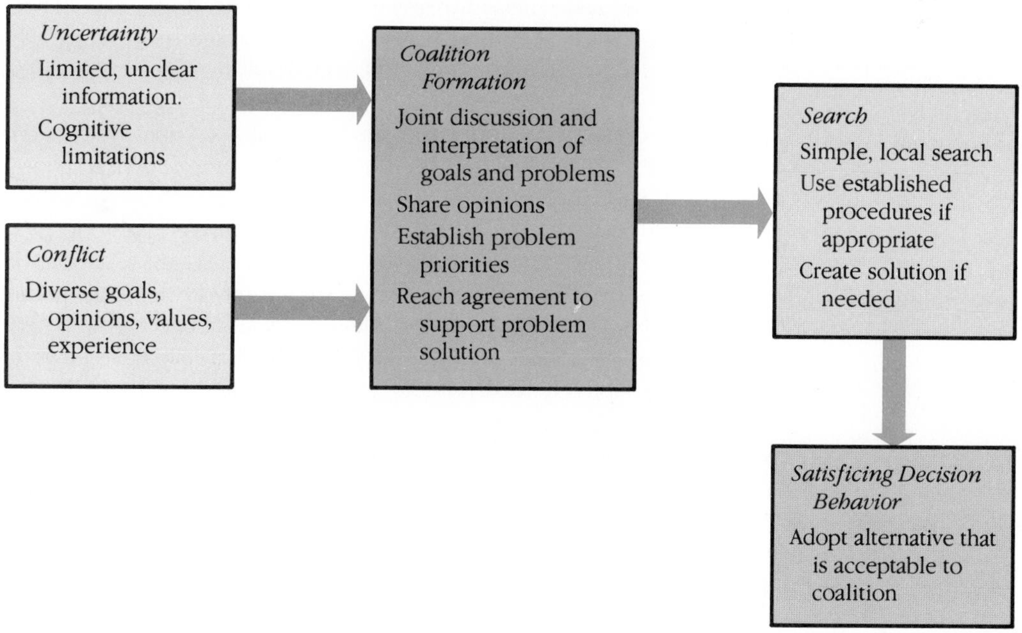

Uncertainty
Limited, unclear information.
Cognitive limitations

Conflict
Diverse goals, opinions, values, experience

Coalition Formation
Joint discussion and interpretation of goals and problems
Share opinions
Establish problem priorities
Reach agreement to support problem solution

Search
Simple, local search
Use established procedures if appropriate
Create solution if needed

Satisficing Decision Behavior
Adopt alternative that is acceptable to coalition

goals and problem priorities, the results can be a disaster, as illustrated by Arp Instruments.

IN PRACTICE 9.4

Arp Instruments, Inc.

When Alan Pearlman founded Arp Instruments in the late 1960s, it quickly became the premier manufacturer of musical synthesizers, instruments that produce electronic music. Arp provided synthesizers to the stars, including Stevie Wonder, Paul McCartney, Elton John, The Bee Gees, Kiss, and The Who. By the mid 1970s, Arp had 40% of the market, ahead of Moog synthesizers, and enjoyed preeminence in the marketplace. By 1981, Arp Instruments was dead, the victim of management disagreement and in-fighting.

Arp was shaped by three individuals: Pearlman, Chairman of the Board; Louis G. Pollock, Legal Counsel and Chairman of the Executive Committee; and David Friend, President. Each individual brought distinct goals and backgrounds to the company. Pearlman was concerned with new technology and planning, Pollock was an entrepreneur who pushed new products, and Friend was a technical and musical whiz kid. The egos and goals of the three frequently clashed. They clashed about which products to invest in, about whether the disco market would change the demand for synthesizers, and about expense budgets.

As time passed, the division among the three intensified. Each man pursued his own vision, and would align himself with whoever would support his own ideas. Pearlman became increasingly alienated from his own company. The three managers kept one another in the dark about their own plans. The problem crystallized when Arp embarked on development of a guitar synthesizer, despite an uncertain demand and having only skills accumulated on keyboard synthesizers. Friend pushed the idea and Pearlman couldn't stop it, having lost his voice at Arp. The in-fighting continued and the guitar synthesizer, called the Avatar, was marketed. The Avatar was an excellent product, but it flopped for lack of demand.

The disagreements among executives led to bitter compromises and more product failures. Lower-level managers and employees experienced chaos and conflicting signals. The company could not focus itself sufficiently to adapt to the changing music world. The lack of agreement translated into lousy management. A management consultant who also served as a director knew where the blame should rest: "It's a sin. It's a tragedy to see a beautiful little company, and two hundred jobs, go under because of bad management. . . . All three of them—honest to God—they should physically have to go to jail and serve six months for screwing up a beautiful thing like that." [28]

The point of the Carnegie model and the Arp case is that coalitions are important to performance. When managers perceive a problem or want to make a major decision, they should seek out other managers for discussion and agreement. Through this process, agreement is established about the importance of the problem and the feasibility of a desired solution.[29]

**Incremental
Decision
Process Model**

Henry Mintzberg and his associates at McGill University in Montreal approached organizational decision-making from a different perspective. They identified twenty-five decisions made in organizations, and traced the events associated with these decisions from beginning to end.[30] This research identified each step in the decision sequence. This approach to decision-making places less emphasis on the political and social factors described in the Carnegie model, but tells us more about the sequence of activities undertaken from the initial discovery of a problem to its eventual solution.

Sample decisions in Mintzberg's research included the choice of which jet aircraft to acquire for a regional airline, development of a new supper club, development of a new container terminal in a harbor, identifying a new market for a deodorant, installing a controversial new medical treatment in a hospital, and the decision to fire a star announcer.[31] The scope and importance of these decisions are revealed in the length of time taken to complete them. Most of these decisions took over a year, and one-third of them took over two years. Most of these decisions were nonprogrammed and required custom-made solutions.

One of the important discoveries from this research is that major organization choices are usually a series of small choices that combine to produce the major decision. Most organizational decisions are a series of nibbles rather than a big bite. Organizations move through several decision points and may hit barriers along the way. Mintzberg called these barriers "decision interrupts," and an interrupt may mean that the organization has to cycle back through a previous decision and try something new. Decision loops or cycles are one way the organization learns which alternatives will work. The ultimate solution may be very different from what was initially anticipated.

The pattern of decision stages discovered by Mintzberg et al. is shown in Exhibit 9.3. Each box indicates a possible step in the decision sequence. The steps take place in three major decision phases: the identification phase, the development phase, and the selection phase.

Identification Phase   The identification phase begins with _recognition_. Recognition means that one or more managers becomes aware of a problem and the need to make a decision. Recognition is usually stimulated by a problem or an opportunity. A problem exists when elements in the external environment change or when internal performance is perceived to be below standard. In the case of firing a radio announcer, comments about the announcer came from listeners, other announcers, and advertisers. Managers interpreted these cues until a pattern emerged that indicated a problem had to be dealt with.

The second step is _diagnosis,_ which is where more information is gathered if needed to define the problem situation. Diagnosis may be systematic or informal depending upon the severity of the problem. Severe problems do not have time for extensive diagnosis. The response must be immediate. Mild problems are usually diagnosed in a more systematic manner.

Development Phase   The development phase is when the response is shaped to solve the problem defined in the identification phase. The devel-

EXHIBIT 9.3. The Incremental Decision Process Model.

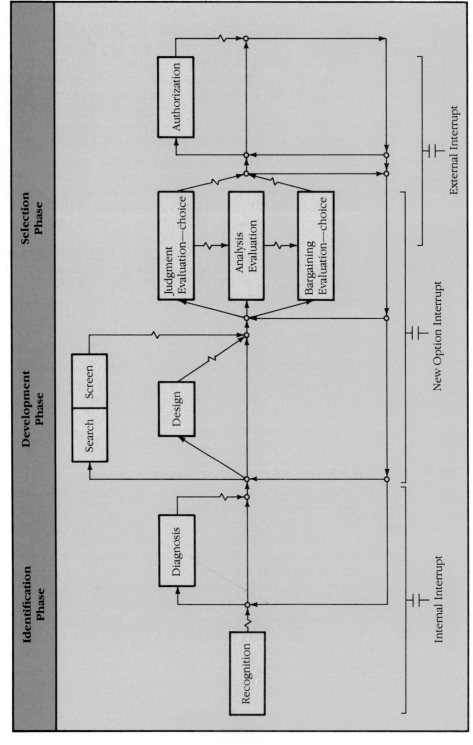

Source: Adapted and reprinted from "The Structure of Unstructured Decision Processes" by Henry Mintzberg, Duru Raisinghani, and André Théorêt published in *Administrative Science Quarterly* 21(2) (1976): 266 by permission of *The Administrative Science Quarterly.* Copyright © 1976 Cornell University.

opment of a solution takes one of two directions. First, *search* procedures may be used to seek out standard solutions and alternatives within the organization's current repertoire. Organization participants may look into their own memories, talk to other managers, or examine the formal procedures of the organization.

The second direction of search is to *design* a custom solution. This happens when the problem is novel so that previous experience has no value. Mintzberg found in these cases that key decision-makers have only a vague idea of the ideal solution. Gradually, through a trial and error process, the custom-designed alternative will emerge. Development of the solution is a groping, incremental procedure, building a solution brick by brick.

Selection Phase The selection phase is when the solution is chosen. The selection phase is not always a matter of a clear choice among alternatives. In the case of custom-made solutions, selection is not so much a choice among alternatives as an evaluation of the single alternative that seems feasible.

Evaluation and choice may be accomplished in three ways. The *judgment* form of selection is used when the final choice falls upon a single decision-maker, and the choice involves judgment based upon experience. In *analysis*, alternatives are evaluated on a more systematic basis. Mintzberg found that the majority of decisions did not involve a distinct analysis and evaluation of alternatives. *Bargaining* occurs when selection involves a group of decision-makers. Each decision-maker may have a different stake in the outcome, so conflict emerges. Discussion and bargaining occur until a coalition is formed, as in the Carnegie model described earlier.

Authorization takes place when the decision is formally accepted by the organization. The decision may be passed up the hierarchy to the responsible hierarchical level. Authorization is often routine because the expertise and knowledge rest with the lower decision-makers who identified the problem and developed the solution. A few decisions are rejected because of implications not anticipated by lower-level managers.

Dynamic Factors The lower part of the chart in Exhibit 9.3 shows lines running back toward the beginning of the decision process. These lines represent loops or cycles that take place in the decision process. Organizational decisions do not follow an orderly progression from recognition through authorization. Minor problems arise that force a loop back to an earlier stage. These are decision interrupts. If a custom-designed solution is perceived as unsatisfactory, the organization may have to go back to the very beginning and reconsider whether a problem truly exists, as happened in the Morgan Guaranty case at the beginning of this chapter. Feedback loops can be caused by problems of timing, politics, disagreement among managers, inability to identify an appropriate alternative or to implement the solution, turnover of managers, or the sudden appearance of a new alternative. When an airline made the decision to acquire jet aircraft, the board authorized the decision. But shortly thereafter, a new chief executive was brought in and he cancelled the contract. He accepted the diagnosis of the problem, but insisted upon a new search for alternatives. A foreign airline went out of business and two used aircraft became available at a bargain price. This presented an unexpected option, so the chief executive used his own judgment to authorize the purchase of the aircraft.[32]

Since most decisions take place over an extended period of time, circumstances change. Decision-making is a dynamic process that may require a number of cycles before a problem is solved. An example of the incremental process and cycling that can take place is illustrated in the decision to produce a new beer.

IN PRACTICE 9.5

Anheuser-Busch Companies, Inc.

During the last ten years, under the direction of August A. Busch, III, Anheuser-Busch has accomplished the following: introduced "Michelob Light," "Wurzburger Hoffbrau," "Anheuser-Busch Natural Light," "Budweiser Light," expanded the brewery facility, acquired a can manufacturing and malt production facility, and opened a new Busch garden theme park. These accomplishments represent major decisions, some of which took several tries to complete.

Anheuser-Busch is the beer industry leader. Executives sensed the shift toward diet consciousness and lighter foods, but did not realize it was a problem until Miller Lite was introduced. With the help of extensive advertising, Miller Lite grabbed a large percentage of this new market, and made serious inroads into Anheuser-Busch's dominance in the industry. Anheuser-Busch did not have a low-cal beer, and something had to be done quickly. Employees hurried to formulate a new product, called Anheuser-Busch Natural Light. The development of the new beer was rushed, and quality was low. Authorization came easily. Its introduction into the marketplace was a flop. The first attempt to solve the problem failed.

Executives went back to the drawing board and reanalyzed the problem. They had more information to go on from their earlier experience. A light beer was still needed, so they proceeded again into the development stage. More time was devoted to developing a custom, well though out solution. Budweiser Light was the new alternative. This new beer eventually became Bud Light, and was a success in the marketplace. The new decision was not straightforward, however. Bargaining and haggling over calorie content, taste, aging, and price had to be resolved. Authorization came in 1982 and nationwide marketing immediately followed. The second time was the charm. After a year Bud Light had 20% of the light beer market.[33]

At Anheuser-Busch, the identification phase occurred when Miller introduced Miller Lite, and Bud's market share dropped. The initial development phase was rushed, and so the authorized solution did not solve the problem. The poor sales of the beer was an interrupt, and Budweiser executives recycled back to the identification phase. The same problem existed, but more effort was devoted to custom designing a solution. Bud Light was the answer. The decision to produce a strong entry into the low calorie beer market took over two years to complete.

Incremental Process versus Carnegie Model

At the beginning of this chapter, decision-making was defined as two stages—problem identification and problem solution. The incremental process model and the Carnegie model describe organizational responses to uncertainty in each stage of decision-making. The Carnegie description of political coalitions is relevant when problem-identification is ambiguous and managers disagree. Discussion, negotiation, and coalition-building are necessary to reach agreement about problems and priorities. Once agreement is reached, the organization can move toward a solution.

The incremental process model describes the process used to reach a solution. After managers agree upon the problem, the step-by-step process is a way of trying various solutions to see what will work. When problem solution is unclear, various ideas may have to be tried to solve the problem.

The two models do not disagree with one another. They describe how organizations make decisions when either problem identification or solution is uncertain. The application of these two models to the stages in the decision process is illustrated in Exhibit 9.4. When both parts of the decision process are highly uncertain simultaneously, the organization is in an extremely difficult position. Decision processes for organizations in that situation are described in the garbage can model.

The Garbage Can Model

The garbage can model is one of the most recent and interesting descriptions of organizational decision processes.[34] The garbage can model is distinct from the models described above because it pertains to the overall "pattern" of decisions rather than to the sequence involved with a single decision. The garbage can model was developed to explain the pattern of decision-making in organizations that experience very high uncertainty. Cohen, March, and Olsen, the originators of the model, called the extremely uncertain conditions an "organized anarchy."[35] Organized anarchies do not have the normal hierarchy of authority and bureaucratic decision rules. Instead, organized anarchies have three characteristics.

1. *Problematic Preferences.* Problems, alternatives, solutions, and goals are ill-defined. Ambiguity characterizes each aspect of a decision process.
2. *Unclear, Poorly Understood Technology.* Cause and effect relationships are difficult to identify. The knowledge base that applies to decisions is not clear.

EXHIBIT 9.4. Organizational Decision Process When Either Problem Identification or Solution Is Uncertain.

PROBLEM IDENTIFICATION

When problem identification is uncertain, *Carnegie Model* applies.
Political and social process.
Build coalition, seek agreement and resolve conflict about goals and problem priorities.

PROBLEM SOLUTION

When problem solution is uncertain, *Incremental Process Model* applies.
Incremental, trial and error process.
Solve big problems in little steps.
Recycle and try again when blocked.

3. *Fluid Participation.* Organizational roles experience turnover of participants. In addition, the organization is energy-poor. Employees are busy and have only limited time to allocate to any one problem or decision. Participation in any given decision will be fluid and limited.

The organized anarchy describes organizations characterized by rapid change and a collegial, nonbureaucratic environment. No organization fits the organized anarchy circumstances all the time. Most organizations will occasionally find themselves in positions of making decisions under unclear, problematic circumstances. The garbage can model is useful for understanding some types of decisions in all organizations.

Streams of Events   The unique and important characteristic of the garbage can model is that the decision process is not a sequence of steps that begins with a problem and ends with a solution. Indeed, the problem-identification and problem-solution stages may not even be connected to each other. Ideas may be proposed as a solution when no problem is specified. Problems may exist and never generate a solution. The reason problems and solutions are not connected is that decisions are the outcome of independent streams of events within the organization. The four streams relevant to organizational decision-making are as follows:

1. *Problems.* Problems are points of dissatisfaction with current activities and performance. Problems represent a gap between desired performance and current activities. Problems are perceived to require attention. However, problems are distinct from choices and solutions. The problem may lead to a solution or it may not. Problems may not be solved when solutions are adopted.
2. *Solutions.* "A solution is somebody's product." [36] Solutions represent a flow of ideas and alternatives through the organization. Ideas may be brought into the organization by new personnel, or be invented by existing personnel. Participants may be attracted to certain ideas and push them as logical choices. Attraction to an idea may cause an employee to look for a problem to which it can be attached. Solutions exist independently of problems.
3. *Participants.* Organization participants come and go throughout the organization. People are hired, reassigned, and fired. Participants vary widely in their ideas, perception of problems, experience, values, and training. The problems and solutions recognized by one participant will differ from those recognized by another participant. Time pressures lead participants to allocate different amounts of participation to a given problem or solution.
4. *Choice Opportunities.* Choice opportunities are those occasions when an organization makes a decision. An alternative is authorized and implemented. Choice opportunities occur when contracts are signed, when people are hired, when a new product is authorized. Choice opportunities may be precipitated by events such as an urgent problem, the proposal of an idea, a supplier who wants an answer on the purchase of new equipment, or a customer who needs a new product.

The importance of the concept of independent streams is that the pattern of organizational decision-making takes on a random quality. Problems, solutions, participants, and choices are all flowing through the organization. In one sense, the organization is a large garbage can in which these streams are being stirred, as illustrated in Exhibit 9.5. When a problem, solution, participant, and choice happen to connect at one point, the problem may be solved. But it also may not be solved. The solution may not fit. A single choice opportunity can be considered a small garbage can. Any problem and solution may be connected when a choice is made. But the problem does not always relate to the solution and the solution may not solve the problem. Organizational decisions simply are not the result of the logical step-by-step sequence of events that other descriptions of decision-making imply. Organization members are intendedly rational, but events are so ill-defined and complex that decisions, problems, and solutions are independent. Four consequences of the garbage can decision process for organizational decision-making are described below.

1. *Solutions Are Proposed Even When Problems Do Not Exist.* An employee may be sold on an idea and may try to sell it to the rest of the organization. An example was the adoption of computers by many organizations during the 1960s. The computer was an exciting solution and was pushed both by computer manufacturers and systems analysts within organizations. The computer did not solve any problems in those initial applications. Indeed, some computers caused more problems than they solved.

2. *Choices Are Made without Solving Problems.* A choice may be made with the intention of solving a problem, but under conditions of high uncertainty

EXHIBIT 9.5. Illustration of Independent Streams of Events in the Garbage Can Model of Decision-Making. (P = problems; S = ideas for solutions; CO = choice opportunity; PAR = participants.)

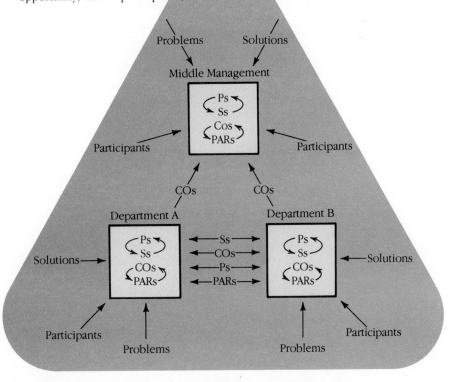

the choice may be incorrect. Moreover, many choices just seem to happen. People decide to quit, the organization's budget is cut, or a new policy bulletin is issued. These choices may be oriented toward problems but do not necessarily solve them.

3. *Problems May Persist without Being Solved.* Organization participants get used to certain problems and give up trying to solve them. Or participants may not know how to solve certain problems because the technology is unclear. A university in Canada was placed on probation by the American Association of University Professors because a professor had been denied tenure without due process. The probation was a nagging annoyance that the administrators wanted to remove. Fifteen years later, the nontenured professor died. The probation continues because the university did not acquiesce to the demands of the heirs or the Association to reevaluate the case. The university would like to solve the problem, but administrators are not sure how, and they do not have the resources to allocate to it. The probation problem persists without a solution.

4. *A Few Problems Are Solved.* The decision process does work in the aggregate. In computer simulation models of the garbage can model, important decisions were often resolved. Solutions do connect with appropriate problems and participants so that a choice is made. Of course, not all problems are resolved when choices are made, but the organization does move in the direction of problem reduction.

The effects of independent streams and the rather chaotic decision processes in the garbage can model were illustrated in the reorganization of a drama department at a major university.

IN PRACTICE 9.6
Department of Drama

The catalogue for a major university describes the faculty and program for each department. The catalogue for 1970–71 listed a "Department of Speech and Drama" with 20 faculty members and 117 courses. For 1972, the catalogue listed a "Department of Drama" with 15 faculty members and 100 courses. The change seems the result of a rational decision by university administration. But the chain of events began fifteen years earlier.

The Department was in the College of Liberal Arts, and the new dean was appointed in 1956. The Dean's goal was to stress research and to seek a national reputation. His influence led to the retirement of one full professor in public speaking, the movement of faculty in speech correction and audiology to a new department in the College of Medicine, the elimination of the undergraduate major in speech, and the resignation of a top young professor.

In 1961, the Dean left and a new Dean was hired. By this time only one senior faculty member was left in the area of speech, and three new faculty members had been appointed. The senior faculty member died, leaving a graduate program with only inexperienced assistant professors. The Dean informed the junior faculty members that they were not doing sufficient research to support a graduate program. Junior faculty members wanted to reorganize the program in speech and hire senior research faculty.

At the same time, other deans in the university were establishing a new Department of Communication Science to replace the "journalism" program. In 1963, the junior faculty from the Department of Speech and Drama left to join the new department.

In 1968, other activities were transferred away from the Department of Speech and Drama, including one associate professor who moved to the College of Education.

A new associate dean in the College of Liberal Arts was hired in 1970, who had the responsibility to review contracts in speech. On the basis of other speech departments, the associate dean recommended that the program in speech be discontinued. The recommendation was accepted, not because of the low quality of the speech faculty, but because the senior administrators were under pressure to save money in the university budget. The Dean and Provost quickly chose to eliminate speech altogether, and thus the new Department of Drama was created.[37]

The decision to eliminate the speech program was not a rational process that started with a problem and ended with a logical solution. Many events occurred by chance and were intertwined, which characterizes the garbage can model. First, a number of participants came and went in the decision process. There was turnover among deans and faculty members, and new employees brought new ideas and values to the situation. Second, the larger decision process was the result of streams of small events. Several small problems surfaced in the speech program. Several choices were made, such as increasing or decreasing the emphasis on the program, hiring and firing faculty, making transfers, and adding new administrators. These streams of events accumulated into the larger decision to eliminate the program. Third, many of the choices had little to do with problems. Letting a research-oriented faculty member leave, for example, was independent of the decision to drop the program, but eventually influenced it. Fourth, the system had more than one solution. The faculty within the speech program pushed one set of ideas and the deans pushed another set. Fifth, the ultimate decision to drop the program was made in response to a problem unrelated to the program itself, which was to save money for the university. Overall, the decision process had a random, chancy flavor characteristic of garbage can processes. But the apparent randomness did not necessarily work against the organization. An important problem was eventually resolved, although for reasons other than faculty members and the associate dean intended.

CONTINGENCY DECISION-MAKING FRAMEWORK

This chapter has covered several models of organizational decision-making, including systems analysis, the Carnegie model, the incremental decision model, and the garbage can model. We have also discussed rational and intuitive decision processes used by individual managers. Each decision model is a relatively accurate description of the actual decision process, yet they differ from each other. Systems analysis, for example, reflects a different set of decision assumptions and procedures than does the garbage can model.

One important reason for different models is that they appear in different organizational situations. The use of a model is contingent on the organization setting. Two characteristics of organizations that determine the use of decision models are (1) goal uncertainty and (2) technical uncertainty about the means to achieve those goals.[38] Analyzing organizations along these two dimensions suggests which model will be used to make decisions.

Goal Uncertainty

Goal uncertainty refers to the agreement among managers about which organizational goals to pursue. This variable ranges from complete agreement to complete disagreement. When managers agree, the goals of the organization are clear, and so are standards of performance. When managers disagree, organization direction and performance expectations are in dispute. One famous example of goal uncertainty occurred among cabinet members and presidential advisors during the Cuban missile crisis. Participants fought intensely over what goals should be pursued.[39] Another example of goal uncertainty occurred within the Penn Central Railroad after it went bankrupt. Some managers wanted to adopt the goal of being a railroad organization, and to become efficient and profitable in that activity. Other managers wanted to diversify into other businesses. Eventually a strong coalition formed in favor of diversification, and that goal was adopted.

Agreement about goals is important for the problem-identification stage of decision-making. When goals are clear and agreed upon, they provide clear standards and expectations for performance. Problems can be identified. When goals are not agreed upon, problem-identification is uncertain and more attention has to be focused on defining goals and problem priorities.

Technical Uncertainty

Technical uncertainty refers to the knowledge, understanding and agreement about how to reach organizational goals. This variable can range from complete agreement and certainty to complete disagreement and uncertainty about cause-effect relationships. An example of technical uncertainty is reflected in market strategies at 7-Up. The goal is clear and agreed upon—increase market share from 6% to 7% by 1985. But the means for achieving this increase in market share are not known or agreed upon. A few managers want to use discount pricing in supermarket outlets. Other managers believe they should increase the number of soda fountain outlets in restaurants and fast-food chains. A few other managers insist that the best approach is to increase advertising through radio and television. Managers cannot agree on what would cause an increase in market share. To date, the advertising judgment has prevailed at 7-Up. It has not worked very well, which reflects the uncertainty about means to achieve goals.

Technical uncertainty is important to the problem-solution stage of decision-making. When means are well understood, the appropriate alternatives can be identified and calculated with some degree of certainty. When means are poorly understood, rational alternatives are ill-defined and uncertain. Intuition, judgment, and trial and error become important decision criteria.

Contingency Framework

The contingency decision framework brings together the two organizational dimensions of goal and technical uncertainty. Exhibit 9.6 shows how these two variables influence the decision situation. Goals and means determine whether the problem-identification and solution stages are uncertain. Depending on the situation, the organization may have to focus on reducing uncertainty in either goals, means, or both. Low uncertainty means that rational, analytical procedures can be used. High uncertainty leads to greater use of judgment, bargaining, and other less systematic procedures.

Exhibit 9.7 describes the contingency decision framework. Each cell represents an organizational situation that is appropriate for decision-making approaches described in this chapter.

Cell 1 In cell 1 of Exhibit 9.7, rational decision procedures are used because goals are agreed upon and cause-effect relationships are well understood. Decisions are made in a computational manner. Alternatives can be identified and the best solution adopted through analysis and calculation. The rational models described earlier in this chapter, both for individual managers and for the organization, are appropriate when both goals and technical means are well understood. The identification of problems is straightforward, and the calculation of the best solution is also straightforward. When deviations occur, a logical process can be used to decide upon the solution. When a problem is large and involves many variables, systems analysis techniques are appropriate.

Cell 2 The important step here is to use bargaining and compromise to reach agreement about goals and problems. Diverse opinions about goals are present in this organization setting. One goal may be achieved at the expense of another goal. The priorities given to respective goals and the appropriate levels of performance are decided through discussion, debate, and coalition-building.

EXHIBIT 9.6. Contingency Decision Situations.

Goal Uncertainty

	Low	High

Low	*Cell 1*
	
	Problem Identification:
	  Low Uncertainty
	Problem Solution:
	  Low Uncertainty
		Cell 2
		
		Problem Identification:
		  High Uncertainty
		Problem Solution:
		  Low Uncertainty

High	*Cell 3*
	
	Problem Identification:
	  Low Uncertainty
	Problem Solution:
	  High Uncertainty
		Cell 4
		
		Problem Identification:
		  High Uncertainty
		Problem Solution:
		  High Uncertainty

Technical Uncertainty

Managers in this situation should use broad participation to reduce goal uncertainty in the decision process. Opinions should be surfaced and discussed until compromise is reached. The organization will not otherwise move forward as an integrated unit. In the case of Penn Central Railroad, the diversification strategy was eventually adopted, but only after extensive bargaining. During the Cuban missile crisis, debate finally led to the goal of establishing a blockade to prevent Russian ships from reaching Cuba.

The Carnegie model applies when there is uncertainty about organizational goals. When groups within the organization disagree, or when the organization is in conflict with relevant constituencies (government regulators, suppliers, union), bargaining and negotiation are required. The bargaining strategy is especially relevant to the problem-identification stage of the decision process. Once the bargaining and negotiation are completed, the organization will have a sense of direction and standards against which to compare performance.

Cell 3   Judgment reflects the use of manager experience and intuition to choose among decision alternatives. In a cell 3 situation, goals and standards of performance are certain, but technical alternatives are vague and uncertain. Techniques to solve the problem are ill-defined and poorly understood. When an individual manager faces this situation, intuition will be the decision guideline. The manager will rely on past experience and judgment to make the decision. Rational, analytical approaches are not effective because the alternatives cannot be identified and calculated in a logical way. Hard facts and accurate information are not available.

The incremental decision process model reflects trial and error on the part of the organization. Once the problem or crisis is identified, a sequence of small steps will eventually lead to a solution. As new problems or barriers

EXHIBIT 9.7.   Contingency Framework for Using Decision Models.

Goal Uncertainty

	Low	High

Low	*Cell 1*
	
	Manager:
	  Rational Approach,
	  Computation
	Organization:
	  Systems Analysis
		Cell 2
		
		Manager:
		  Bargaining,
		  Coalition Formation
		Organization:
		  Carnegie Model

High	*Cell 3*
	
	Manager:
	  Judgement, Trial
	  and Error
	Organization:
	  Incremental
	  Decision Model
		Cell 4
		
		Manager:
		  Inspiration,
		  Imitation
		Organization:
		  Garbage Can
		  Model

Technical Uncertainty

arise, the organization may recycle back to an earlier point. Eventually, over a period of months or years, the organization will acquire sufficient experience to solve the problem in a satisfactory way. The Anheuser-Busch effort to enter the low-calorie beer market described earlier is an example of a cell 3 situation in which the goal was certain but managers had to use trial and error to learn how to develop and distribute Bud Light.

Cell 4   Inspiration and imitation take place in cell 4 where everything seems uncertain. Goals are not certain, and means are not clear. Inspiration refers to an innovative, creative solution that is not reached by logical means. A new idea from an unexpected source may be adopted. Sometimes the organization will imitate ideas adopted by other organizations simply because managers don't know what else to do.

For a manager experiencing this high level of uncertainty, intuition and creativity are important for both the problem-identification and problem-solution stages of decision-making. Indeed, the solution may precede the problem. In a university accounting department, faculty were completely dissatisfied with their current circumstances, but could not agree upon the direction the department should go. Some faculty members wanted a greater research orientation, others wanted greater orientation toward business firms and accounting applications. The disagreement about goals was compounded because neither group was sure about the best technique for achieving their goals. The ultimate solution was inspirational on the part of the dean. An accounting research center was established with funding from big-eight accounting firms. The funding was used to finance research activities for faculty interested in basic research, and to provide contact with business firms for other faculty. The solution provided a common goal and unified people within the department to work toward that goal.

When the entire organization is characterized by continuous high uncertainty with regard to goals and technical means, the garbage can model applies. The rational decision sequence that starts with problem-identification and ends with a problem solution does not take place. Solutions will precede problems as often as problems precede solutions. In this type of organization, managers can encourage widespread discussion of problems and ideas to facilitate the opportunity for choices to be made. Choices will often not resolve problems, but choices must be made anyway. Eventually, through trial and error, the organization will solve some problems, perhaps by trying a variety of solutions. Substantial bargaining and political activity will also take place to decide upon goals and help identify relevant problems.

IN PRACTICE 9.7

Adolph Coors Co.

In 1978, Adolph Coors Co. decided to enter the big time. An extensive marketing program was undertaken to thrust Coors into the national market and to stop competitors from encroaching on its territory.

By 1982, the plan had realized only limited success. Coors made some gains, such as with its new low-calorie beer. But overall the company was still having trouble hanging onto its territory and cracking new markets. In

California, market share had slipped by a third since 1976. In 1981, net income was down and so was total volume.

Industry observers say that Coors' goal of going national was associated with problems inside the company. Managers know what they want to achieve, but haven't yet learned to be a sophisticated competitor. The company's chairman suggested that Coors is on a learning curve to find out what works and what doesn't work.

The internal problems came to a head when two key marketing executives departed in 1981. The executives disagreed about marketing strategy. There were other disagreements as well. A few executives pushed to adopt a straight-forward, national advertising campaign that would accompany price reduc-tion. Another faction believed the company should direct its advertising toward developing a positive corporate image at the national level. A consultant claims that Coors is trying to sell a little bit of beer and a little bit of image, instead of putting forward a well-focused advertising program. Yet another idea pro-posed by an external consultant was that Coors should concentrate on entering the east coast market. He suggested building a plant there. Other advisors disagree, arguing that the East is a difficult market to crack. Coors should first square things away in its own backyard.

Why all the confusion and disagreement about how Coors should pro-ceed? For years, Coors was a family-dominated corporation that didn't have to assert itself. Its original beer was so popular that people from other parts of the country would take trunkloads back home. Then Anheuser-Busch Co. and Miller Brewing Co. successfully penetrated Coors' following. Coors had to respond with bigger advertising budgets and a more aggressive marketing effort.

But the transition wasn't easy. By 1985, the trial and error learning process began to pay off. Coors had a new advertising agency, had expanded in the east coast market, redesigned the packages for both bottle and canned beer, and began to recover its market, moving past Pabst in market share.[40]

The executives at Adolph Coors Co. were certain about goals, but did not know the means to reach those goals (cell 3). Their goal was to move Coors into the national market and to increase market share, but whether this should be done through increased advertising, new advertising campaigns, east coast expansion, or new packaging was not understood. Coors' decisions reflected the incremental process model. Executives tried one strategy to see if it worked. Coors tried a strategy and then recycled and made new decisions as executives learned the marketing process better.

DECISION MISTAKES

Organizational decisions, especially when made under conditions of uncer-tainty, produce many errors. Managers cannot be certain about the correct choice. Uncertainty leads to two types of decision mistakes. One mistake is to select an alternative that does not work. The organization then abandons that choice, and tries another alternative. The other type of mistake is to persist in a course of action even when it is failing. Managers may be reluctant to admit that they were wrong, and refuse to try other choices. The first type of mistake is not really a mistake at all because it facilitates organizational learning. The second type of mistake inhibits learning, and can have overwhelmingly negative consequences for the organization.

Decision Learning In many organizational situations, managers simply cannot determine or predict which alternative will solve a problem. In these cases, intuition, judgment, and trial and error are used to find solutions. But trial and error means that some trials will not work.

The point for managers is to move ahead with the decision process despite the potential for mistakes. Information about problems may be inadequate, and alternatives may seem ill-conceived. But managers must make decisions anyway. Managers must be willing to take risks. "Chaotic action is preferable to orderly inaction." [41] Action enables the organization to learn what works and to accumulate experience. When an alternative fails to improve performance, another alternative can be tried. Only by making mistakes can managers and the organization acquire sufficient experience and knowledge to perform more effectively in the future. Robert Townsend, for example, gives the following advice:

> Admit your mistakes openly, maybe even joyfully. Encourage your associates to do likewise by commiserating with them. Never castigate. Babies learn to walk by falling down. If you beat a baby every time he falls down, he'll never care much for walking.
>
> My batting average on decisions at Avis was no better than a .333. Two out of every three decisions I made were wrong. But my mistakes were discussed openly and most of them corrected with a little help from my friends.[42]

Escalating Commitment A much more dangerous mistake is to persist in a course of action when it is failing. Research suggests that organizations often continue to invest time and money despite strong evidence and information that it is not working. Commitment actually escalates in some cases because managers throw good money after bad even when the strategy seems incorrect.[43] One explanation is that managers may block or distort negative information when they are personally responsible for negative decisions. Moreover, managers create hopes that they can turn the situation around to prove themselves correct, so they invest more time and resources in the project to make it succeed. Another reason is that consistency is valued in contemporary society. Consistent managers are considered better leaders than those who switch around from one course of action to another. Despite the fact that organizations learn in uncertain situations through trial and error, organizational norms may value consistency. A course of action will be maintained, resources will be squandered, and learning will be inhibited. Consider the millions of dollars lost when WPPSS refused to change course in the construction of a nuclear power plant.

> The epic blunder by the Washington Public Power Supply System (WPPSS—now commonly called Whoops) caused a $2.3 billion municipal bond default in 1983. WPPSS began construction of nuclear power plants to meet the increasing power needs of the Northwest in 1972. The original estimated cost for three power

plants was $3.1 billion. By 1974, cost overruns on plant construction had already amounted to nearly $1 billion, and managers saw that construction delays could lead to further escalations in costs. Moreover, managers saw evidence that the expected increases in power consumption were not going to materialize. However, WPPSS financial statements disclosed little negative information, and money was raised through bond issues to continue building the power plants. Indeed, plans for two additional nuclear power plants—for a total of five—were started and funds were raised.

The bandwagon rolled on for several years. As late as 1981, Whoops raised another $200 million in bonds for plants four and five. Then came the shocker—the cost of the entire project had soared to $23.8 billion from the estimated $8.9 billion, and analysis of power demand showed that all the plants were not needed. Ten years after the project began, and only with enormous negative public exposure and default on bonds, was the project brought to a halt.[44]

Failure to admit a mistake and adopt a new course of action is far worse than an attitude that encourages mistakes and incremental learning. Based upon what we know about decision-making from this chapter, we can expect companies to ultimately be successful in their decision-making process by adopting a gradual, incremental approach toward solutions. They will make mistakes along the way, but by moving forward they will resolve uncertainty through the trial and error process.

SUMMARY AND INTERPRETATION

The single most important idea in this chapter is that most organizational decisions are not made in a logical, rational manner. Most decisions do not begin with the careful analysis of a problem, followed by systematic analysis of alternatives, and finally implementation of a certain solution. Decision processes are characterized by conflict, coalition-building, trial and error, and mistakes. Intuition and hunch are often the criteria for choice. The decision process is disorderly, and may even seem random. In a few cases, the solution may actually drive the problem because someone likes an idea and tries to find a problem as an excuse to adopt it.

Another important idea is that individuals make decisions, but organizational decisions are not made by a single individual. Organizational decision-making is a social process. Only in rare circumstances do managers analyze problems and work through solutions by themselves. Many problems are not clear, so widespread discussion and coalition-building take place. Once goals and priorities are set, alternatives to achieve those goals can be tried. When managers do make an individual decision, it is often a small part of a larger decision process. Organizations solve big problems through a series of small steps. A single manager may initiate one step, but should be aware of the larger decision process in which it is imbedded.

The greatest amount of conflict and coalition-building occurs when goals are not understood and agreed upon. Priorities must be established to indicate which goals are most important and what problems should be solved first. If a manager attacks a problem other people do not agree with, the manager will lose support for the solution to be implemented. Thus time and activity should be spent in building a coalition in the problem-identification stage of decision-making. Once problems are identified and agreed upon, the organization can move toward solutions. Intuition and trial and error often characterize this part of the process. Under conditions of uncertainty the solution unfolds as a series of incremental trials that will gradually lead to an overall solution.

One of the most interesting descriptions of decision-making is the garbage can model. The garbage can model describes how decision processes can almost seem random. Garbage can processes may occur in most organizations some of the time. Decisions, problems, ideas, and people flow through organizations and mix together in various combinations. When a participant discovers an idea or makes a connection between a problem and a solution, the problem may be solved. But it may not, because neither the problem nor the solution was well understood. But through this process the organization gradually learns. Some problems may never be solved, but many will be, and the organization will move toward maintaining and improving its level of performance.

Finally, organizations make mistakes. The mistakes made through trial and error should be encouraged. Managers do not have perfect knowledge or information. The best alternative cannot be known in advance when uncertainty is high. By encouraging trial and error increments, organizational learning is facilitated. On the other hand, an unwillingness to change from a failing course of action can have serious negative consequences for the organization. Norms for consistency or the desire to prove one's decision correct can lead to a continued investment of time and resources in a wasted course of action.

KEY CONCEPTS

bounded rationality approach
Carnegie model
coalition
contingency decision making
    framework
decision learning
escalating commitment
garbage can model
goal uncertainty
incremental decision process
    model

nonprogrammed decisions
organizational decision
    making
problem identification
problem solution
problemistic search
programmed decisions
rational approach
systems analysis model
technical uncertainty

DISCUSSION QUESTIONS

1. A professional economist once told his class, "We assume that the firm's decisions are made by a single individual at the top of the organization. The organization is a single decision-making entity." Do you agree with the economist's view? Discuss.

2. The economist went on to say, "The individual decision-maker processes all relevant information and selects the economically rational alternative." Do you agree? Why or why not?

3. Briefly describe the eight steps in the rational approach to manager decision-making. Which steps are problem-finding and which are problem-solving?

4. When is intuition used in decision-making? Is intuition a valid decision technique? Is intuition likely to be used more often by decision-makers at the top or at the bottom of the organization?

5. For what types of organizational decisions would systems analysis be most appropriate?

6. The Carnegie model emphasizes the need for a political coalition in the decision-making process. When and why are coalitions necessary?

7. What are the three major phases in Mintzberg's incremental decision process model? Why might an organization recycle through one or more phases of the model?

8. An organization theorist once told his class, "Organizations never make big decisions. They make small decisions that eventually add up to a big decision." Explain the logic behind this statement.

9. Describe the four streams of events in the garbage can model of decision-making. Why are they considered independent?

10. How does the amount of agreement among managers about goals influence the problem-identification process in organization?

11. According to the contingency decision-making framework, what type of organizational situation is associated with the Carnegie model? The rational approach to decision-making?

12. Are there decision-making situations in which managers should be expected to make the "correct" decision? Are there situations in which decision-makers should be expected to make mistakes?

13. Why are decision errors accepted in organizations but penalized in college MBA courses that are designed to train managers?

GUIDES TO ACTION

As an organization manager:

1. Adopt decision processes to fit the organizational situation.

2. Use a rational decision approach—computation, systems analysis—when the problem situation is well understood.

3. Use a coalition-building approach when organizational goals and problem priorities are in conflict. When managers disagree about priorities or the true nature of the problem, they should discuss and seek agreement about priorities. The Carnegie model emphasizes the need for building a coalition and maintaining agreement about goals and problems.

4. Take risks and move the company ahead by increments when the problem is defined, but solutions are uncertain. Try solutions in a step-by-step manner to learn whether they work. Analytical procedures do not apply when possible solutions are unclear and uncertain.

5. Use garbage can procedures in a situation in which problems are not

clear and underlying cause-effect relationships are not known. Move the organization toward better performance by proposing new ideas, spending time working in important areas, and persisting with recommended solutions.
6. Do not persist in a course of action that is failing. Some actions will not work out if uncertainty is high, so encourage organizational learning by readily trying new alternatives. Seek information and evidence that indicates when a course of action is failing, and allocate resources to new choices rather than to unsuccessful ventures.

Consider these Guides when analyzing the following cases.

CASES FOR ANALYSIS

FORT JACKSON HIGH SCHOOL DISTRICT*

PART I

July 17, 1974. Dr. Alan Rollins, the new superintendent for the Fort Jackson School District, arrived in town to take over the new job as school superintendent. He was hired because he had impressive ideas for improving the school system. Parents and school board members had set a high priority on academic excellence.

Over the next few years, Dr. Rollins set about achieving that goal. The school built a 2,000-seat auditorium and a 450-seat fine arts theater. The percentage of students going off to college increased to 85%. The football field was covered with astro-turf, and the school produced winning teams. The school district became a magnet for the community. Professional people and corporate executives wanted to move their families to Fort Jackson to take advantage of the school system.

Dr. Rollins made occasional small mistakes when trying a new idea to improve academic excellence. They were corrected before any damage was done. Dr. Rollins was the educational expert, and the school board, parents, and teachers deferred to him.

Board members, teachers, and parents in Fort Jackson did not understand how to attain academic excellence. They were happy to turn the job over to Dr. Rollins and were pleased with the results.

PART II

June 22, 1985. Dr. Rollins is preparing to leave Fort Jackson. He resigned under pressure from school board members, parents, and teachers.

The last straw was the teachers' strike last spring. The teachers were angry about the way the school was run and about budget cutbacks. They wanted salaries increased to keep ahead of inflation. Dr. Rollins' labor relations skill was not sufficient to win over teachers who felt strongly about budget issues.

Parents were upset because the school district ran two consecutive deficits. Other taxpayers complained about tax increases and were threatening a referendum to set a maximum limit on school taxes.

Selected parental groups were also becoming more assertive. They insisted on extensive special programs for underachievers, overachievers, and

* This case was inspired by Douglas R. Sease, "School Superintendent, Once Pillar of Society Now Is Often a Target," *Wall Street Journal,* June 2, 1981, p. 1.

the handicapped. These demands came at a time when the cost of education was skyrocketing and revenues were not keeping pace.

The school board election in May demonstrated just how deeply the community was divided on the goals for the school system. Teachers, parental groups, and a taxpayer group all ran their own candidates. The three newly elected board members all disagreed with the direction Dr. Rollins was taking the school.

Board members and parents agreed that Dr. Rollins' strength was in building a first-rate academic school system. So long as there were plenty of resources to keep everyone happy, he did fine. But he was not skillful at getting to know teachers, parents, and taxpayers. The teachers would not rally behind him, and so they went on strike. Perhaps the new superintendent will do better.

The editor of the local newspaper said that the superintendent simply focused on the wrong problems. Dr. Rollins continued working toward the goal of academic excellence when other groups no longer considered that goal important. They wanted the budget under control, higher salaries, and special programs. He was unable to maintain his coalition. Said a city council member, "Without a political coalition in this school, you're out."

In talking about his dismissal afterward, Dr. Rollins was still unhappy about being fired. His decision-making style worked in previous school districts, and he couldn't see why his expertise wasn't used at Fort Jackson.

Questions

1. Analyze the Fort Jackson School District situation with respect to the contingency decision framework. Did goal or technical uncertainty change? Discuss.

2. What decision process did Dr. Rollins use? What decision process should he have used? Discuss.

RCA CORPORATION*

In April 1984, RCA Corp. officially pulled the plug on its videodisc technology, after gambling more than $580 million. RCA was a leader in television technology, and wanted VideoDisc to extend its TV product line. Videodiscs were a new way to use the television for home entertainment. As far back as 1970, market projections indicated a $1 billion consumer appetite by 1980. RCA investigated several technologies, but went with the videodisc because of its precision. RCA executives believed that the competing videocassette (VCR) technology would not overcome basic problems. Videocassette technology was not competitive unless tape recorder pickup heads could be improved. The price of VCRs back in 1970 was also enormous and executives figured costs could not come down far enough to beat videodisc players. VCRs cost $1,300 in 1977.

RCA's failure indicates how electronic devices change with blinding speed. Decision-making must be incredibly objective, and be willing to abandon technology when necessary. RCA wanted to be a leader in a new technology,

---

* "The Anatomy of RCA's Videodisc Failure," *Business Week,* April 23, 1984, pp. 89–90; "RCA: Still Another Master," *Business Week,* August 17, 1981, p. 81; Cody Jetton, Julie Mosley, and Karen Jetton, "Radio Corporation of America," unpublished manuscript, Texas A&M University, 1982.

and accepted the assumptions that VCR technology would not improve and that consumers would prefer videodiscs.

Some experts recommended that VCR technology would be better than videodiscs. VCRs could record TV programs off the air, and tapes could be reused. Discs could only play prerecorded material. But RCA didn't listen.

The Japanese improvements in VCR technology became obvious to everyone except RCA by 1977. Other competitors got out of the market or switched to VCR technology. RCA held back, pumping more money into videodiscs to get it right.

During the period of development, executive turnover was a problem as well. The chief executive's office had a revolving door. The Board of Directors went through four CEOs in six years. Edgar H. Griffiths brought some stability, but held up production until the videodisc technology was perfected—a full four years after VCRs hit the market and their prices dropped dramatically. When the videodisc player was finally launched in1981, RCA sold only half of what it projected. Sales limped along. In 1983, RCA made a final thrust, cutting prices sharply to make inroads in the market. In April 1984, the company finally threw in the towel.

The loss was massive. One consultant who specializes in technology said, "If they asked the right questions about video technology, they could have assessed their options better. As it is, the company had to make a series of heroic assumptions to ignore some of the clear evidence."

Questions

1. Analyze the decision process at RCA. Which decision model or models describe this process? Discuss.

2. How would you explain RCA's failure to abandon the Videodisc technology earlier? Is this type of mistake avoidable? Discuss.

NOTES

1. Shawn Tully, "The Block That Got Away," *Fortune,* July 13, 1981, p. 45.

2. This case was based on Tully, "The Block That Got Away," pp. 44–46; Robert Guenther, "The Real Estate World's Version of Poker: Assembling Parcels for a Big-City Project," *Wall Street Journal,* May 18, 1982, p. 37; Joanne Lipman, "Owners Who Stay Put Play a Part in Shaping the American Skyline," *The Wall Street Journal,* May 22, 1984, pp. 1, 24.

3. Herbert A. Simon, *The New Science of Management Decision* (Englewood Cliffs, NJ: Prentice-Hall, 1960), pp. 1–8.

4. Ibid.

5. Charles Lindblom, "The Science of 'Muddling Through,' " *Public Administration Review* 19 (1954):79–88.

6. Earnest R. Archer, "How to Make a Business Decision: An Analysis of Theory and Practice," *Management Review* 69 (February 1980):54–61.

7. Adapted from Earnest R. Archer, "How to Make a Business Decision: An Analysis of Theory and Practice," *Management Review,* February 1980 (New York: AMACOM, a division of American Management Associations, 1980), pp. 59–61.

8. Paul A. Anderson, "Decision Making by Objection and the Cuban Missile Crisis," *Administrative Science Quarterly,* 28 (1983):201–222.

9. Per O. Solberg, "Unprogrammed Decision Making," *Industrial Management Review* 8 (1967):19–29.

10. Thomas F. Issack, "Intuition: An Ignored Dimension of Management," *Academy of Management Review* 3 (1978):917–922.

11. Majorie A. Lyles and Ian I. Mitroff, "Organizational Problem Formulation: An Empirical Study," *Administrative Science Quarterly* 25 (1980):102–119.

12. Ibid.

13. Ross Stagner, "Corporate Decision-Making: An Empirical Study," *Journal of Applied Psychology* 53 (1969):1–13.

14. Trish H. Hall, "For a Company Chief, Where There's a Whim, There's Often a Way," *The Wall Street Journal,* October 1, 1984, pp. 1, 18; Roy Rowan, "Those Business Hunches Are More Than Blind Faith," *Fortune,* April 25, 1979, pp. 110–114.

15. Paul C. Nutt, "Types of Organizational Decision Processes," *Administrative Science Quarterly,* 29 (1984):414–450.

16. "How Paramount Keeps Turning Out Winners," *Business Week,* June 11, 1984, pp. 148–151.

17. Douglas R. Sease, "Ford Awaits the Payoff On Its 4-Year Gamble on New Compact Car," *Wall Street Journal,* May 4, 1983, pp. 1, 22.

18. Charles J. McMillan, "Qualitative Models of Organizational Decision Making," *Journal of Management Studies* 5 (1980):22–39; Paul C. Nutt, "Models for Decision Making in Organizations and Some Contextual Variables Which Stimulate Optimal Use," *Academy of Management Review* 1 (1976):84–98.

19. "Where The War Stories Begin—Some Founding Fathers Reminisce," *Interfaces,* 11 (1981):37–44; Harold J. Leavitt, William R. Dill, and Henry B. Eyring, *The Organizational World* (New York: Harcourt Brace Jovanovich, 1973), ch. 6.

20. Stephen J. Huxley, "Finding the Right Spot for a Church Camp in Spain," *Interfaces,* 12 (October 1982):108–114.

21. James E. Hodder and Henry E. Riggs, "Pitfalls in Evaluating Risky Projects," *Harvard Business Review* (January–February, 1985):128–135.

22. Edward Baker and Michael Fisher, "Computational Results for Very Large Air Crew Scheduling Problems," *Omega,* 9 (1981):613–618.

23. Russell L. Ackoff and Patrick Rivett, *A Manager's Guide to Operations Research* (New York: John Wiley, 1963), pp. 12–13. Reprinted by permission.

24. Harold J. Leavitt, "Beyond the Analytic Manager," *California Management Review* 17 (1975):5–12; C. Jackson Grayson, Jr., "Management Science and Business Practice," *Harvard Business Review* 51 (July–August, 1973):41–48.

25. Richard L. Daft and John C. Wiginton, "Language and Organization," *Academy of Management Review* 4 (1979):179–191.

26. This discussion is based on Richard M. Cyert and James G. March, *A Behavioral Theory of the Firm* (Englewood Cliffs, NJ: Prentice-Hall, 1963), and James G. March and Herbert A. Simon, *Organizations* (New York: John Wiley, 1958).

27. Cyert and March, *Behavioral Theory of the Firm,* pp. 120–122.

28. Craig R. Waters, "Raiders of the Lost Arp," *Inc.,* November 1982, pp. 39–44; Tom Richman, "What America Needs Is a Few Good Failures," *Inc.,* September 1983, pp. 63–72.

29. Lawrence G. Hrebiniak, "Top-Management Agreement and Organizational Performance," *Human Relations,* 35 (1982):1139–1158; Richard P. Nielsen, "Toward a Method for Building Consensus during Strategic Planning," *Sloan Management Review* (Summer 1981):29–40.

30. This discussion is based on Henry Mintzberg, Duru Raisinghani, and Andre Théorêt, "The Structure of 'Unstructured' Decision Processes," *Administrative Science Quarterly* 21 (1976):246–275.

31. Ibid.

32. Ibid., p. 270.

33. Harold Smith, David Wheat, and Steve Terry, "Anheuser-Busch Companies Incorporated," unpublished manuscript, Texas A&M University, 1982; "Anheuser Tries Light Beer Again," *Business Week,* June 29, 1981, pp. 136–137; David P. Garino, "If Anheuser-Busch Gets Its Way, Saying 'Bud' Won't Say It All," *The Wall Street Journal,* January 15, 1981, p. 25.

34. Michael D. Cohen, James G. March, and Johan P. Olsen, "A Garbage Can Model of Organizational Choice," *Administrative Science Quarterly* 17 (March, 1972):1–25; Michael D. Cohen and James G. March, *Leadership and Ambiguity: The American College President* (New York: McGraw-Hill, 1974).

35. Cohen, March, and Olsen, "Garbage Can Model."

36. Ibid., p. 3.

37. James G. March and Pierre J. Romelaer, "Position and Presence in the Drift of Decisions," in James G. March and Johan P. Olsen, eds., *Ambiguity and Choice in Organizations* (Bergen: Universitepsfarbaget, 1976), pp. 254–258. Reprinted by permission.

38. Adapted from James D. Thompson, *Organizations in Action* (New York: McGraw-Hill, 1967, ch. 10, and McMillan, "Qualitative Models of Organizational Decision Making," p. 25.

39. Paul A. Anderson, "Decision Making by Objection and the Cuban Missile Crisis."

40. This case is based on Lynda Schuster, "Internal Conflicts Inhibiting Coors' Move to the Big Time," *Wall Street Journal,* July 10, 1981, pp. 23, 26; "Coors' Movement to National Company Stems Market Share Decline," *Market Competitor,* June 1984, p. 17; "Coors Redesigns Bottle and Canned Beer Packages," *Modern Brewer,* October 17, 1983, p. 1; "Coors Fights for Survival Despite Expansion into New Markets," *Forbes,* October 24, 1983, p. 88.

41. Karl Weick, *The Social Psychology of Organizing,* 2nd ed. (Reading, MA: Addison-Wesley, 1979), p. 243.

42. Robert Townsend, *Up the Organization* (New York: Knopf, 1974), p. 115.

43. Barry M. Staw, "The Escalation of Commitment to a Course of Action," *Academy of Management Review,* 6 (1981):577–587, and "Knee-Deep in the Big Muddy: A Study of Escalating Commitment to a Chosen Course of Action," *Organizational Behavior and Human Performance,* 16 (1976):27–45.

44. "Whoops: How It Happened," *Dun's Business Month,* October 1983, pp. 48–57.

Power and Politics

McDONNELL DOUGLAS CORPORATION

At McDonnell Douglas Corp. there was never any doubt about who was in charge. James S. McDonnell, chairman of the board, ran the company with an iron hand for more than forty years. He was involved in everything from deciding next year's plan to discouraging executives from going out to lunch. Mr. Mac, as he was known, called the shots until he was eighty years old. In 1980, he died.

What happened next? Mr. Mac's death left a power vacuum. The betting was that an intense power struggle would occur. Two of the contenders were Mr. Mac's sons—John F. McDonnell, executive vice-president and a financial expert, and James S. McDonnell III, vice-president for marketing. Sanford N. McDonnell, Mr. Mac's nephew, was president, and some people felt he might blossom into a strong leader.

The loss of the chief executive was only one of the shocks felt by McDonnell executives. The emotional wounds of the American Airlines DC-10 crash in Chicago persisted. The company had been picked apart by the press and humiliated when the FFA removed the DC-10's Certificate of Airworthiness for more than a month. Lawsuits and expensive repairs hang over McDonnell Douglas still. So does the bribery scandal. McDonnell Douglas was accused of paying bribes to foreign airlines to purchase the DC-10. In 1981, the company pleaded guilty and paid a fine.

Poor sales of commercial airliners are a major source of uncertainty to be resolved by the new executive team. The DC-10 has petered out. McDonnell Douglas developed a new, fuel-efficient mid-range aircraft called the MD-80. Sales have been dismal, so executives took an enormous risk by allowing American Airlines to lease twenty MD-80s for five years, with the option to return them. This seemed the only way to get the MD-80 into the marketplace. Another problem is the relationship between McDonnell and Douglas. The Douglas division is responsible for commercial airliners, and has been a consistent money loser and a drain on the company's cash flow. The McDonnell side brings in three-fourths of the $4 billion revenues and provides the profit. McDonnell produces weapons for the defense department, such as the F-18, and has a reputation as an efficient, high-quality contractor.

Despite all the uncertainties, the expected power struggle never materialized. Sandy McDonnell, Mr. Mac's nephew, has been elected chairman and is chief executive officer. John McDonnell took Sandy's position as president. Jim McDonnell still holds his position as corporate vice-president for marketing. The two sons own a large block of stock, but they supported rather than fought against Sandy, who owns little stock. Sandy built up credibility in his eight years as president under Mr. Mac. Since taking over as CEO, he has promoted new executives into key positions, hired new executives from outside, and installed new board members. These moves have enabled him to consolidate his position. He has allowed more executives to become involved in decision-making. His relationship with Mr. Mac's sons is such that the power vacuum has been filled by a top management team rather than by a single individual.[1]

The McDonnell Douglas example illustrates the circumstances associated with power and political intrigue. The participants have high-level positions within the organization. Mr. Mac's death left a power vacuum, and uncertainty was high. The payoff scandal, the DC-10 crash, the need for commercial aircraft sales, and the success of the McDonnell division compared to the Douglas division all created unpredictables for top management. The only missing ingredient was disagreement. If deeply held disagreements had arisen, the formal positions, experience, and resources of Mr. Mac's nephew and two sons could have been thrown into a battle against one another to determine the future of McDonnell Douglas Corp.

Purpose of This Chapter

The purpose of this chapter is to explore power issues similar to those illustrated in the McDonnell Douglas case. We will examine sources of power in organizations, and the way power is used to attain organizational goals. Vertical and horizontal power sources are quite different, so we will discuss them separately. We will also look at politics. Politics is related to power because politics is the use of power and authority to achieve the ends of an individual or department.

The study of power and politics is a natural outgrowth of the previous chapter on decision-making. Remember that successful decision-making uses coalition building to achieve agreement among diverse interest groups. Power is also acquired through the development of coalitions among executives. The dynamic processes associated with power and politics thus will be similar in some respects to the processes associated with decision-making.

Individual versus Organizational Power

In the popular literature, power is often described as a personal characteristic. A frequent topic is how one person can influence or dominate another person.[2] Power in organizations, however, is often the result of more than individual characteristics. Organizations are large, complex systems that contain hundreds, even thousands, of people. There is an extensive division of labor. Some tasks become more important regardless of who performs them. Some positions have access to greater resources, or their place in the organization is more central. Some people have high positions of great power, other people have positions lower in the hierarchy. Horizontal power differences across the organization are less visible, but nevertheless influence organizational goals and the allocation of resources. The important power processes in organizations reflect larger organizational relationships, both horizontal and vertical. Organizational power is invested in the position, not in the person.

POWER VERSUS AUTHORITY

Power is an intangible, elusive process in organizations. Power is a force that cannot be seen, but its effects can be felt. Power is often defined as the ability of one person (or department) to influence other persons (or departments) to carry out orders,[3] or to do something they would not otherwise have done.[4] Other definitions stress that power is the ability to achieve goals or outcomes that powerholders desire.[5] The achievement of desired outcomes is an important use of organizational power, so the following definition is used here: **power** is the ability of one person or department in an organization to influence other people to bring about desired outcomes. Power is used to influence others within the organization, but with the goal of attaining desired outcomes for powerholders.

Power exists only in a relationship between two or more people, and can be exercised in either vertical or horizontal directions. The source of power derives from an exchange relationship in which one position or department provides scarce or valued resources to other departments. When one person depends on another person, a power relationship emerges in which the person with the resources has greater power.[6] When power exists in a relationship, the power holders can achieve compliance with their requests. For example, the following outcomes are indicators of power in an organization.

■ Obtain a larger increase in budget than other departments.
■ Get a hearing before top decision-makers.
■ Obtain above-average salary increases for subordinates.
■ Obtain production schedules that are favorable to your department.
■ Get items on the agenda at policy meetings.
■ Get a desirable position for a talented subordinate.[7]

The concept of formal authority is related to power, but is narrower in scope. Authority is also a force for achieving desired outcomes, but only as prescribed by the formal hierarchy and reporting relationships. Three properties that identify authority are:

1. *Authority Is Invested in Organizational Positions.* People have authority because of the positions they hold, not because of personal characteristics.
2. *Authority Is Voluntarily Accepted by Subordinates.* Subordinates comply because they perceive that position holders have a legitimate right to exercise authority.[8]
3. *Authority Flows Down the Vertical Hierarchy.*[9] Authority exists along the formal chain of command, and positions at the top of the hierarchy are invested with more formal authority than positions at the bottom.

Organizational power can be exercised in upward, downward, and horizontal directions in organizations. Formal authority is exercised only in a downward direction along the hierarchy, and is the same as vertical power. In the next section we will examine the use of vertical power down the hierarchy as well as sources of power for lower participants. Then we will examine the use of horizontal power in organizations, which is not defined by the vertical hierarchy and is determined by power relationships across departments.

VERTICAL POWER

Power Sources for Upper Management

The formal hierarchy of authority provides power and authority to top management. Top management is responsible for a great number of people and many resources, and authority is equal to those responsibilities. The chain of command converges at the top of the organization, so authority is great for top offices. The authority granted to top management to govern is reflected in both the formal organization structure and the decision authority defined by that structure.

> The design of an organization, its structure, is first and foremost the system of control and authority by which the organization is governed. In the organizational structure, decision discretion is allocated to various positions and the distribution of formal authority is established. Furthermore, by establishing the pattern of prescribed communication and reporting requirements, the structure provides some participants with more and better information and more central locations in the communication network. . . . Thus, organizational structures create formal power and authority by designating certain persons to do certain tasks and make certain decisions, and create informal power through the effect on information and communication structures within the organization. Organizational structure is a picture of the governance of the organization and a determinant of who controls and decides organizational activities.[10]

A great deal of power is allocated to senior management positions from the organizational structure. The power of top management comes from four sources—formal position, resources, control of decision premises, and network centrality.

Formal Position   Certain rights, responsibilities, and prerogatives accrue to top positions. Top managers have a great deal of responsibility, hence authority is also great. People throughout the organization accept the legitimate right of top managers to set goals, make decisions, and direct activities. So long as the position and directives are perceived as legitimate, lower-level managers will obey. People in our society accept the right of top managers to direct the organization. Most of us believe, "Those in authority have the right to expect compliance; those subject to authority have the duty to obey." [11]

Resources   Organizations allocate huge amounts of resources. Buildings are constructed, salaries are paid, and equipment and supplies are purchased. Each year new resources are allocated in the form of budgets. These resources are allocated downward from top managers. In many organizations top managers own stock, which gives them property rights over resource allocation. Top managers own the resources and hence can determine their distribution. Resources can be used to reward and punish, which are primary sources of power.[12] Resource allocation also creates a dependency relationship. Lower-level participants depend upon top managers for the financial and physical resources needed to perform their tasks. Top management can exchange resources in the form of salaries, personnel, promotion, and physical facilities for compliance with the outcomes they desire.

Control of Decision Premises   Control of decision premises means that top managers place constraints on decisions made at lower levels. In one sense, top managers make big decisions while lower-level participants make small decisions. Top management, for example, decides which goal the organization will try to achieve, such as increased market share or profits. Lower-level participants then decide how the goal is to be reached. Top management can decide such things as the products to be manufactured, from whom supplies will be purchased, and the limits on signing authority for expenditures ("No more than $5,000 for department heads"). These decisions place limits on the decisions of lower-level managers and thereby influence their behavior.[13]

An additional way to influence decision premises is through the control of information. Information flows continuously into the organization and up and down the hierarchy. By carefully controlling this information, the manager has a major source of power. Information can be released to define the decision premises for other people.

In one organization, which we will call Clark Ltd., the senior manager controlled information given to the board of directors, and thereby influenced the decision to purchase a large computer system.[14] The board of directors had formal authority to decide from which company the computer would be purchased. The management services group was asked to recommend which of six computer manufacturers should receive the order. Jim Kenny was in charge of the management services group, and Kenny disagreed with other managers about which computer to purchase. As shown in Exhibit 10.1, other managers had to go through Kenny to have their viewpoints heard by the board. Kenny shaped the decision premises of the board by discussing his preferred computer manufacturer more often than other manufacturers. His comments about other manufacturers tended to be negative. He influenced the board to select the computer he preferred by controlling information given to them.[15]

EXHIBIT 10.1. Information Flow for Computer Decision at Clark Ltd.

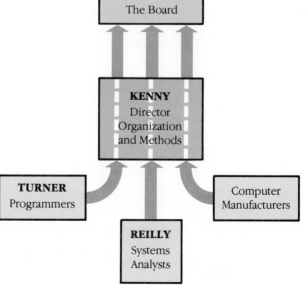

Source: Andrew M. Pettigrew, *The Politics of Organizational Decision-Making* (London: Tavistock, 1973), p. 235, with permission.

Network Centrality   Top managers are centrally located in the organization. Managers are in the center of an information network, and are in a position to know about events throughout the organization so they can coordinate the activities of others.[16] Managers often try to construct a network by placing managers whom they know in critical positions. By surrounding themselves with other managers whom they know and trust, top managers increase their power. They gain power by being well informed, having access to other people in the network, and by having multiple people dependent upon them. Managers can use their central position to build alliances and loyalty, and hence be in a position to wield substantial power in the organization.

New managers often use their formal authority in combination with resources and network development to consolidate their power. Consider the case of Gulf & Western's new chief.

IN PRACTICE 10.1

Gulf & Western Industries Inc.

Martin S. David took over as chief executive officer of Gulf & Western in 1983. His ascendancy was something of a surprise because as senior vice-president he was promoted over the president. He had a good relationship with the board of directors, who selected him as CEO over the president. Davis moved quickly to establish his control. In less than a month, he moved members of his own management team into key positions, ousted the previous president, and restructured the company. He was also establishing support among new members of the board.

The previous president, Mr. Bluhdorn, died unexpectedly, and Davis was his heir. Within hours of Mr. Bluhdorn's death, Mr. Davis was at headquarters marshalling executives, telephoning directors, and even helping make the funeral arrangements. His contacts went back to 1969 when Mr. Bluhdorn made him senior vice-president with the responsibility to be liaison with the directors. His effective performance caught their eye and was appreciated by directors. He also built management alliances as a behind-the-scenes strong man who handled things for the previous CEO.

Now that Mr. Davis is clearly calling the shots, he is moving the company in the direction he wants it to go. He sold part of the G & W's large portfolio to reduce the huge debt. He also simplified the corporate structure, centralizing the legal and purchasing departments at headquarters and creating three independent product groups. These decisions have been readily implemented because of his alliance with board members and other executives. He also plans to reshape Gulf & Western by selling some subsidiaries and acquiring new ones. He apparently has all the power and political acumen to get that job done.[17]

Power Sources for Middle Managers

The distribution of power down the hierarchy is influenced by organization design factors. Of course, top managers will have more power than middle managers, but the amount of power provided to any given position or organizational group can be built into the organization's vertical design.

The allocation of power to middle managers and staff is important, because power enables employees to be productive. Managers need sufficient power and latitude to perform their jobs well. When positions are powerless, managers may seem ineffective, and may become petty, dictatorial, and rules-minded.[18] Several factors that influence the amount of power along the hierarchy are shown in Exhibit 10.2. Power is the result of both task activities and network interactions. When the position is nonroutine, it encourages discretion, flexibility, and creativity. When the job pertains to pressing organizational problems, power is more easily accumulated. Power is also increased when the position encourages contact with high-level people, brings visibility and recognition to employees, and facilitates peer networks both inside and outside the organization.

The variables in Exhibit 10.2 can be designed into specific roles or departments. For example, funds can be allocated to a department so members can attend professional meetings, thereby increasing visibility and stature. Allowing people to approve their own decisions gives more discretion and reduces dependence on others and increases power.

The logic of designing positions for more power assumes that the organization does not have a fixed amount of power to be allocated among high-level and low-level employees. The total amount of power in an organization can be increased by designing tasks and network interactions along the hierarchy so that everyone has more influence. If the distribution of power is too heavily skewed toward the top so that others are powerless, research suggests the organization will be less effective.[19] A study by Rosabeth

EXHIBIT 10.2. Ways in Which Vertical Design Contributes to Power.

Design Factor	Generates Power When Factor Is	Generates Powerlessness When Factor Is
Task Activities:		
Rules, precedents, and established routines in the job	few	many
Task variety/flexibility	high	low
Rewards for unusual performance/ innovation	many	few
Approvals needed for nonroutine decisions	few	many
Relation of tasks to current problem areas	central	peripheral
Network Interactions:		
Physical location	central	distant
Publicity about job activities/contact with senior officials	high	low
Participation in programs, conferences, meetings	high	low
Participation in problem-solving task forces	high	low

Source: Adapted from Rosabeth Moss Kanter, "Power Failure in Management Circuits," *Harvard Business Review* 57 (July-August, 1979):65–75.

Moss Kanter showed that design factors prevented some middle managers and staff personnel from having enough power to accomplish their jobs:

> Design factors can leave an entire level of the hierarchy, such as first line supervisors, in a position of powerlessness. Their jobs may be overwhelmed with rules and precedents, and they may have little opportunity to develop an interaction network in the organization. Minority group members often have little power because management is overprotective, and thereby precludes opportunities for initiative and exposure needed for power accumulation. The same fate can befall staff specialists.
>
> As advisers behind the scenes, staff people must sell their programs and bargain for resources, but unless they get themselves entrenched in organizational power networks, they have little in the way of favors to exchange. They are not seen as useful to the primary tasks of the organization. When staff jobs consist of easily routinized administrative functions which are out of the mainstream ... and involve little innovative decision-making, [staff personnel may end up powerless].
>
> Staff people, unlike those who are being groomed for important line positions, may be hired because of a special expertise or particular background. But management rarely pays any attention to developing them into more general organizational resources. Lacking growth prospects themselves and working alone or in very small teams, they are not in a position to develop others or pass on power to them. They miss out on an important way in which power can be accumulated.[20]

Without sufficient power, middle-level people cannot be productive. Power can be built into positions and departments through the design of task activities and interaction opportunities.

Power Sources for Lower-Level Participants

Positions at the bottom of the organization have less power than positions at higher levels. Often, however, people at the bottom levels obtain power disproportionate to their positions, and are able to exert influence in an upward direction. Secretaries, maintenance people, word processors, computer programmers, and others find themselves being consulted in decisions or having great latitude and discretion in the performance of their activities. The power of lower-level employees often surprises managers. Presidents and vice-presidents of organizations frequently are not able to obtain immediate compliance for new directives. The vice-president of a university may be more reluctant to reprimand his secretary than to fire an academic department head. Why does this happen?

People at lower levels obtain power from several sources. Some of these sources are individual because they reflect the personality and style of employees. Other power sources are position-based, as indicated in Exhibit 10.3. One study found that unexpectedly high levels of power came from expertise, physical location, information, and personal effort.[21] When lower-level participants become knowledgeable and expert about certain activities, they are in a position to influence decisions. Sometimes individuals take on difficult tasks and acquire specialized knowledge, and then become indispensable to managers above them. Power accumulation is also associated with the amount of effort and interest displayed. People who have initiative and who work beyond what is expected often find themselves with influence. Physical location also helps because some locations are in the center of things. Central

EXHIBIT 10.3. Power Sources for Lower-Level Participants.

Personal Sources	Position Sources
Expertise	Physical Location
Effort	Information Flow
Persuasion	Access
Manipulation	

location lets the person be visible to key people and become part of inter-action networks. Likewise, certain positions are in the flow of organizational information. One example is the secretary to a senior executive. The secretary can control information that other people want. The secretary will be able to influence those people.

Additional personal sources of upward influence are persuasion and manipulation.[22] Persuasion is a direct appeal to upper management, and is the most frequent type of successful upward influence.[23] Manipulation means arranging information to achieve the outcome desired by the employee. Manipulation differs from persuasion because the true objective for using influence is concealed. The final source of power is a position that provides access to other important people.[24] Exposure to powerful people and the development of a relationship with them provides an important base of influence. The use of access, as well as information, effort, and other power sources, was effectively adopted by Lyndon Johnson to build power and influence when he was a university student, as described in the following case.

IN PRACTICE 10.2

Campus Politico

From the beginning at San Marcos College (later Southwestern Texas State Teachers College), [Lyndon] Johnson set out to win the friendship and respect of those people who would assist his rise within the community that composed San Marcos. Most obvious was the president of the college, Cecil Evans, whose favor would have a multiplier effect with the faculty and student body. But Johnson was not alone in the desire to have a special relationship with Evans. "I knew," Johnson said later, "there was only one way to get to know Evans and that was to work for him directly." He became special assistant to the president's personal secretary.

As special assistant, Johnson's assigned job was simply to carry messages from the president to the department heads and occasionally to other faculty members. Johnson saw that the rather limited function of messenger had possibilities for expansion; for example, encouraging recipients of the messages to transmit their own communications through him. He occupied a desk in the president's outer office, where he took it upon himself to announce the arrival of visitors. These added services evolved from a helpful convenience into an aspect of the normal process of presidential business. The messenger had become an appointments secretary, and in time, faculty members came to think of Johnson as a funnel to the president. Using a technique that was later to serve him in achieving mastery over the Congress, Johnson turned a rather insubstantial service into a process through which power was exercised. By redefining the process, he had given power to himself.

Evans eventually broadened Johnson's responsibilities to include handling his political correspondence and preparing his reports for state agencies with jurisdiction over the college and its appropriations. The student was quick to explain that his father had been a member of the state legislature (from 1905 to 1909, and from 1918 to 1925), and Lyndon had often accompanied him to Austin where he had gained some familiarity with the workings of the legislature and the personalities of its leaders. This claim might have sounded almost ludicrous had it not come from someone who already must have seemed an inordinately political creature. Soon Johnson was accompanying Evans on his trips to the state capital in Austin, and, before long, Evans came to rely upon his young apprentice for political counsel. For Johnson was clearly at home in the state legislature, whether sitting in a committee room during hearings or standing on the floor talking with representatives. He could, in later reports to Evans, capture the mood of individual legislators and the legislative body with entertaining accuracy. The older man, on whose favor Johnson depended, now relied on him, or at least found him useful.[25]

Protection against Tyranny   One of the puzzlements in organizations is that the wide disparity in power between the top and bottom of the organization is not often used to exploit employees. Top managers have great power in areas such as strategy formulation, goals, the design of structure, and environmental interpretation. However, upper-level managers are often frustrated when they try to move the organization in a new direction because employees are slow to respond. The wide differences in resources, prestige, expertise, and legitimacy should mean that top management can enforce its will upon lower-level employees, even if the outcomes are illegal or immoral. This kind of power use is seldom seen in organizations, and the question is why? There are three answers.

1. *Lower-Level Employees Have Some Power.* As discussed above, the vertical dimension of organization is not a perfect hierarchical system. Lower-level participants acquire information and expertise, and they are able to persuade and manipulate, which are sources of power. There is enough latitude at all levels in the organization that absolute control is typically not possible.

2. *There Is Safety in Groups.* The work group structure of organizations provides a built-in safeguard against top-management tyranny. Laboratory experiments have shown that power is greatest over a single individual who is isolated from other people. Organizations, however, are composed of groups. Individuals are seldom isolated. In these experiments, power was applied to individuals alone and in the presence of a group.[26] The rate of compliance dropped off dramatically when other people were present. Group members reinforced social norms so that illegal or immoral activities were blocked. Group members did not even have to talk to the person to whom power was applied. Simply having other people present who knew about the act was enough for the person to resist compliance. Employees provide support for each other and a defense against the undue use of power by people above them in the hierarchy.

3. *Whistle-Blowing.* **Whistle-blowing** occurs when organization members disclose employers' illegal, immoral, or illegitimate practices.[27] A whistle-blower may seek to stop organizational activities by going to newspaper or television reporters to obtain public support. Whistle-blowers may also use channels within the organization to obtain support for their resistance to specific organizational activities. Whistle-blowing has become a fairly widespread phenomenon in recent years, although it typically is costly to the employee. Top management may feel they are doing the correct thing, and hence may attempt to fire or sabotage the employee. For example, Helen Guercil noticed something peculiar when she went to work as a secretary to the bankruptcy court of Detroit, Michigan. She noticed one judge tended to receive the multimillion-dollar cases, typically handled by the same attorneys, and another judge received only smaller cases. She started digging for an explanation, and over a period of months discovered that one lawyer had been awarded $400,000 in bankruptcy fees from the judge trying the big cases. She also discovered evidence of special favors bought with lavish trips and expensive gifts, and special favors such as sex on the job. She blew the whistle by contacting the Chief Judge of the District Court, and by calling the Justice Department and the U.S. Courts in Washington. She experienced a lot of pressure on the job, and was eventually fired. But an investigation led to the retirement of two judges, the indictment of the chief clerk, and the conviction of the attorney who'd been awarded all the money.[28]

In summary, top managers do have power, but the difference between the top and the bottom level is not so great that top managers can give orders without constraints. In only a few incidents, such as in the Watergate scandal during the Nixon administration, can the organization be taken in a direction that people believe is improper. In those situations, power was used on isolated people who did not have the social support of others. But someone eventually blew the whistle and the improper behavior was stopped.

HORIZONTAL POWER

Horizontal power pertains to relationships across departments. All vice-presidents are usually at the same level on the organization chart. Does this mean each department has the same amount of power? No. Horizontal power processes are not defined by the formal hierarchy or the organization chart. Each department makes a unique contribution to organizational success. Some contributions are of greater value than others. Some departments will have greater say and will achieve their desired outcomes, while others will not. For example, Charles Perrow surveyed managers in fourteen industrial firms.[29] He bluntly asked, "Which department has the most power?" among four major departments: Production, Sales and Marketing, Research and Development, and Finance and Accounting. The survey results are given in Exhibit 10.4. In most firms, sales had the greatest power. In a few firms, production was also quite powerful. On average, the sales and production departments were more powerful than R&D and finance, although substantial variation existed. Differences in the amount of horizontal power clearly existed in those firms.

EXHIBIT 10.4. Ratings of Departmental Power in 14 Industrial Firms

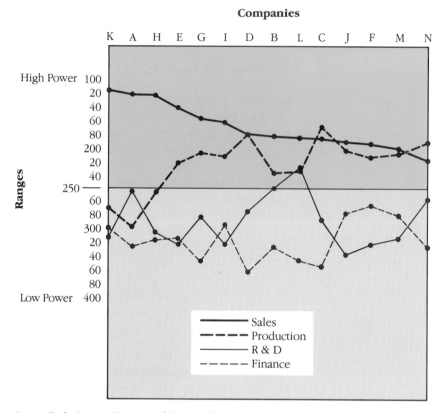

Source: Charles Perrow, "Departmental Power and Perspective in Industrial Firms," in Mayer N. Zald, ed., *Power in Organizations* (Nashville, TN: Vanderbilt University Press, 1970), p. 64, with permission.

Horizontal power is difficult to measure because power differences are not defined on the organization chart. Some initial answers that help us explain departmental power differences such as those shown in Exhibit 10.4 have been found. The theoretical concept that explains relative power is called strategic contingencies.[30] **Strategic contingencies** are those events and activities both inside and outside the organization that are essential for attaining organizational goals. Those departments that are involved with strategic contingencies for the organization tend to have greater power. Departmental activities are important when they remove problems that have strategic value for the organization. If an organization faces an intense threat from lawsuits and regulations, the legal department will gain power and influence over organizational decisions because they cope with this threat.[31] If product innovation is the key strategic issue, the power of R&D can be expected to be high.

Strategic Contingencies

Jeffrey Pfeffer and Gerald Salancik, among others, have been instrumental in conducting research on the strategic contingency theory.[32] Their findings indicate that a department rated as powerful may possess one or more of the following characteristics, which are illustrated in Exhibit 10.5.

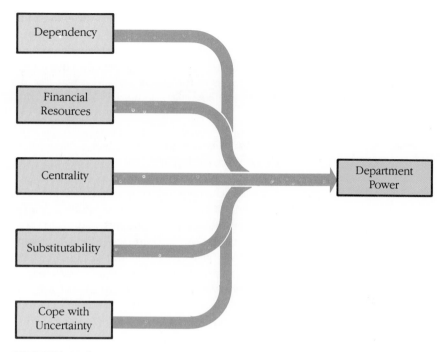

EXHIBIT 10.5. Strategic Contingencies That Influence Horizontal
Power Relationships among Departments.

Dependency   Interdepartmental dependency is a key element underlying
relative power. Power is derived from having something someone else wants.
The power of department A over department B is greater when department
B depends upon A.[33]

There are many dependencies in organizations. Materials, information,
and resources may flow between departments in one direction, such as in
the case of sequential task interdependence (chapter 4). The department
receiving resources is in a lower power position than the department providing them. The number and strength of dependencies are also important.
When seven or eight departments must come for help or service to the
engineering department, engineering is in a strong power position. Likewise,
a department that depends upon many other departments is in a very low
power position.

In a cigarette factory we might expect that the production department
would be more powerful than the maintenance department. This was not
the case in a government-owned cigarette plant near Paris.[34] The production
of cigarettes was a routine process. The machinery was automated and production jobs were small in scope. Production workers were not highly skilled,
and were paid on a piece-rate basis to encourage high production.

The maintenance department required skilled workers. They repaired
the automated machinery, which was complex. Maintenance workers had
many years of experience, which was needed to do their jobs well. Maintenance was a craft, and vital knowledge to fix machines was stored in the
minds of maintenance personnel.

The dependency between the two groups was caused by unpredictable
assembly-line breakdowns. Everything about the assembly process was rou-

tine and well-controlled except for machine failures. Managers could not remove the breakdown problem; consequently maintenance was the vital cog in a production process. Maintenance workers had the knowledge and ability to fix the machines, so production managers became dependent upon them. The reason for this dependence was that maintenance managers had control over a strategic contingency—they had the knowledge and ability to prevent work stoppages.

Financial Resources   There is a new golden rule becoming popular, which goes something like: "He who has the gold makes the rules." [35] Control over financial resources is an important source of power. Money can be converted into other kinds of resources that are needed by other departments. Money generates dependency; departments that provide financial resources have something other departments want. Departments that generate income for the organization have greater power. The survey of industrial firms reported in Exhibit 10.4 showed sales as the most powerful unit in those firms. Sales had power because salespeople find customers and sell the product, thereby removing an important problem for the organization. The sales department ensures the inflow of money. Financial resources also explain power relationships in other organizations, such as universities.

IN PRACTICE 10.3

University of Illinois

You might expect budget allocation in a state university to be a straightforward process. The need for financial resources can be determined by such things as the number of undergraduate students, the number of graduate students, and the number of faculty in each department. In some logical manner, central administration should be able to calculate the appropriate amount of resources to be allocated to each department.

In fact, resource allocation at the University of Illinois is not clear-cut. Some departments have more power because of their resource contribution to the university. Departments that generate large research grants are more powerful because research grants contain a sizable overhead payment to university administration. The size of the graduate student body and the national prestige of the department also add to power. Graduate students and national prestige are nonfinancial resources that add to the reputation and effectiveness of the university. The University of Illinois has a relatively fixed resource inflow from state government. Beyond that, important resources come from research grants and quality of students and faculty. Overhead money from grants pays for a sizable share of the universities' personnel and facilities. University departments that provide the most resources to the university have the most power.[36]

How do they use their power? Generally, to obtain even more resources from the rest of the university. Very powerful departments receive university resources, such as graduate-student fellowships, internal research support, and summer faculty salaries, far in excess of their needs based upon number of students and faculty.

Power accrues to those departments that bring in or provide resources that are highly valued by the organization. Power enables these departments to obtain more of the scarce resources allocated within the organization. "Power derived from acquiring resources is used to obtain more resources, which in turn can be employed to produce more power—the rich get richer." [37]

Centrality Centrality reflects the department's role in the primary activity of the organization.[38] One measure of **centrality** is the extent to which the work of the department affects the final output of the organization. The production department is more central and usually has more power than staff groups (assuming no other critical contingencies). Centrality is associated with power because it reflects the contribution made to the organization. In the departmental power relationships described in Exhibit 10.4, finance tended to be low in power. Finance is also less central. It has the task of recording money and expenditures, but it is not responsible for obtaining critical resources or for producing the products of the organization. As a result, finance is less powerful than marketing or production.

Substitutability Power is also determined by substitutability, which means that a department's function can be performed by other readily available resources. Substitutability decreases power.[39] If an employee can be easily replaced, his or her power is less. If the organization has alternative sources of skill and information, the department's power will be less. This can happen when staff groups are assigned routine duties and management uses outside consultants when unexpected problems arise.[40] Availability of consultants as substitutes for staff people reduces the power of staff groups.

The impact of substitutability on power was studied for programmers in computer departments.[41] When computers were first introduced, programming was a rare and specialized occupation. People had to be highly qualified to enter the profession. Programmers controlled the use of organizational computers because they alone possessed the knowledge to program them. Over a period of about ten years, computer programming became a more common activity. People could be substituted easily. The power of programming departments dropped:

> Twenty years ago there were only a few dozen programmers in the world. They were all very competent professional mathematicians. . . . Today there are hundreds of thousands of them, but most of them are not even graduates. A few inspired mathematicians have invented some astonishing techniques which make it possible for ordinary men to communicate with computers and explore them. Today a schoolboy can use a computer to solve problems that would have baffled experienced mathematicians only fifteen years ago.[42]

Coping with Uncertainty The chapters on environment and decision-making described how elements in the environment can change swiftly; they can be unpredictable and complex. In the face of uncertainty, little information is available to managers on appropriate courses of action. Departments that cope with this uncertainty will increase their power.[43] The presence of uncertainty does not provide power, but "reducing" the uncertainty on behalf of other departments will. When market research personnel accurately predict changes in demand for new products, they gain power and prestige because they have reduced a critical uncertainty. Forecasting is only one technique for coping with uncertainty. Sometimes uncertainty can be reduced by taking quick and appropriate action after the unpredictable event occurs.

Three techniques departments can use to cope with critical uncertainties are: (1) obtaining prior information, (2) absorption, or (3) prevention.[44] **Obtaining prior information** means the department can reduce the organization's uncertainty by forecasting the event. **Absorption** occurs when a department takes action after an event to reduce its negative consequences. Departments increase their power through **prevention** by predicting and forestalling negative events. In the following case, the industrial relations department increased its power by absorbing a critical uncertainty. They took action after the event to reduce uncertainty for the organization.

IN PRACTICE 10.4
Crystal Manufacturing

A new union is a crucial source of uncertainty for many manufacturing firms. The union can be a countervailing power to management in decisions concerning wages and working conditions. The workers in Crystal Manufacturing Company voted in 1980 to become part of the Glassmakers Craft Union. Management had been aware of union-organizing activities, but it had not taken the threat seriously. No one had acted to forecast or prevent the formation of a union in the company.

The presence of the union had serious consequences for Crystal. Glassmaking is a delicate and expensive manufacturing process. The float-glass process cannot be shut down even temporarily except at great expense. A strike or walkout would mean financial disaster. Top management decided that establishing a good working relationship with the union was critically important.

The industrial relations department was assigned to deal with the union. This department was responsible for coping with the uncertainties created by the new union. The industrial relations group quickly developed expertise in union relationships. They became the contact point for managers throughout the organization on industrial relations matters. Industrial relations members developed a network throughout the organization and could bypass the normal chains of command on issues they considered important. Industrial relations had nearly absolute knowledge and control over union relations.

In Crystal Manufacturing Company, the industrial relations unit was coping with the critical uncertainty by absorption. They took action to reduce the uncertainty after it appeared. This action gave them increased power. Other departments became dependent upon them for information and knowledge pertaining to union affairs. An example of their new-found power was displayed during the 1985 budget cycle. The industrial relations department obtained resources to add new personnel and office space, although the total company budget declined slightly. Less powerful departments lost out.

POLITICAL PROCESSES
IN ORGANIZATIONS

Politics, like power, is intangible and difficult to measure. Politics is hidden from view and is hard to observe in a systematic way. Two recent surveys uncovered interesting reactions by managers toward political behavior.[45]

1. Most managers have a negative view toward politics, and believe that politics will more often hurt than help the organization achieve its goals.
2. Managers believe that political behavior is common to practically all organizations.
3. Most managers think that political behavior occurs more often at upper rather than lower levels in organizations.
4. Political behavior arises in certain types of decisions, such as structural change, but is absent from other types of decisions, such as handling employee grievances.

Based upon these surveys, politics seems more likely to occur at the top levels of the organization and around certain issues and decisions. Moreover, managers do not approve of political behavior. In the remainder of this chapter we explore more fully what political behavior is, when it should be used, the type of issues and decisions most likely to be associated with politics, and some political tactics that may be effective.

Definition We have described power as the available force or potential for achieving desired outcomes. Politics is the actual behavior used to influence decisions in order to achieve those outcomes. The exercise of power and influence has led to two ways to define politics: as self-serving behavior or as a natural organizational decision process. (1) The first definition emphasizes that politics is self-serving and involves activities that are not sanctioned by the organization.[46] In this view, politics involves deception and dishonesty for purposes of individual self-interest. This view of politics is widely held by laypeople, and explains why managers described in the survey above did not approve of political behavior. (2) The second view sees politics as a natural organizational process for resolving differences among organizational interest groups.[47] Politics is the process of bargaining and negotiation that is used to overcome conflicts and differences of opinion. Politics in this view is very similar to the coalition-building decision processes defined in the previous chapter. For certain issues, a political rather than a rational decision process is needed to muster support for organizational actions.

The organization theory perspective views politics as a normal decision-making process. Politics is simply the activity through which power is exercised in the resolution of conflicts and uncertainty. Politics is neutral, and is not harmful to the organization. The formal definition of organizational politics is: **Organizational politics** involves those activities to acquire, develop, and use power and other resources to obtain one's preferred outcome when there is uncertainty or disagreement about choices.[48] The important point about this definition is that political behavior can be a positive force.

Politics is the use of power to get things accomplished, good as well as bad. Uncertainty and conflict are natural and inevitable, and politics is the mechanism for reaching agreement. Politics enables participants to arrive at a consensus and make decisions that otherwise might be stalemated or unsolvable.

One reason for the negative view of politics is that political behavior is compared to more rational procedures in organizations. Rational procedures are considered by many managers to be more objective and reliable, and to lead to better decisions than political behavior. Rational approaches are effective, but only in certain situations. Both rational and political processes are normally used in organizations.

RATIONAL CHOICE VERSUS POLITICAL BEHAVIOR

Rational Model   The rational model is an outgrowth of the rational approach to decision-making described in the previous chapter. The rational model of organization is summarized in Exhibit 10.6, and describes a number of activities beyond decision-making. Behavior in the rational organization is not random or accidental. Goals are clear and choices are made in a logical way. When a decision is needed, the goal is defined, alternatives are identified, and the choice with the highest probability of achieving the desired outcome

EXHIBIT 10.6. Rational versus Political Models of Organization.

Organizational Characteristic	Rational Model	Political Model
Goals, preferences:	Consistent across participants	Inconsistent, pluralistic within the organization
Power and control:	Centralized	Decentralized; shifting coalitions and interest groups
Decision process:	Orderly, logical, rational	Disorderly, characterized by push and pull of interests
Rules and norms:	Norm of optimization	Free play of market forces; conflict is legitimate and expected
Information:	Extensive, systematic, accurate	Ambiguous, information used and withheld strategically
Beliefs about cause-effect relationships:	Known, at least to a probability estimate	Disagreements about causes and effects
Decisions:	Based on outcome-maximizing choice	Result of bargaining and interplay among interests
Ideology:	Efficiency and effectiveness	Struggle, conflict, winners and losers

Source: Adapted from Jeffrey Pfeffer, *Power in Organizations* (Marshfield, MA: Pitman, 1981), p. 31.

is selected. The rational model of organization is also characterized by extensive, reliable information systems, central power, a norm of optimization, uniform values across groups, little conflict, and an efficiency orientation.[49]

Political Model The opposite view of organizational processes within organizations is the political model in Exhibit 10.6. This model assumes that organizations are made up of coalitions that disagree about goals and do not have good information about alternatives.[50] The political model defines the organization as made up of groups that have separate interests, goals, and values. Disagreement and conflict are normal, so power and influence are needed to reach decisions. Groups will engage in the push and pull of debate to decide goals and to reach decisions. Decisions are disorderly. Information is ambiguous and incomplete. Bargaining and conflict are the norm.

Mixed Model Neither the rational model nor the political model characterizes an organization fully, but each will be observed some of the time. Organizations can be placed on a continuum, as shown in Exhibit 10.7. One model may dominate, depending on organizational environment and context. The important thing is that both models apply to organizational processes. Managers may strive to adopt rational processes, but it is an illusion to assume that an organization can be run without politics. Bargaining and negotiation should not be avoided for fear that it is improper. The political model is an important mechanism for reaching decisions under conditions of uncertainty and disagreement.

The rational model applies best to organizations in stable environments with well-understood technologies. The rational model, however, is inade-

EXHIBIT 10.7. Continuum of Rational versus Political Models of Organizations.

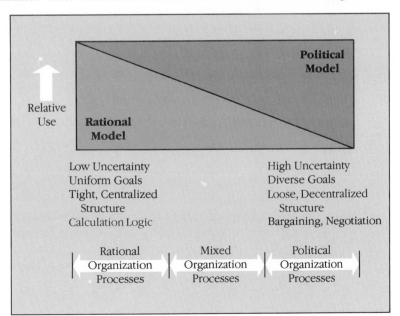

quate when there is uncertainty and conflict, as illustrated in the following case.

IN PRACTICE 10.5

Britt Technologies, Inc.

Britt Technologies was a new manufacturer of computer peripheral equipment, including tape and disc drives. The company's target was to sell equipment to manufacturers of complete computer systems. The strategy was working and the company was initially quite successful, but a problem emerged.

The problem pertained to the extent to which products should be custom-designed for customers. A manufacturer might be interested in a tape or disc product, but only if it could be reengineered to change some operating characteristics. This was expensive and time-consuming, and some managers felt it would be better to sell only what had already been designed. Indeed, almost every manufacturer would ask for some modifications rather than accept the standard models that were available.

The design problem led to disagreement among executives. The marketing vice-president believed that engineering and production should produce whatever the market demanded. The vice-president of production disagreed, saying that efficiencies would never be achieved unless the company developed a standardized product line. The controller agreed with the production vice-president, because profit margins would be reduced if redesigned units were continually produced. The engineering vice-president was willing to redesign products so long as it didn't result in engineering overload.

Rather than hammer out this problem among themselves, Britt's executives decided to retain an outside consultant. They believed an outside consultant with experience in these matters would know how to rationally arrive at the correct answer, which each manager would accept. The consultant did some market research, competitive analysis, and strategic planning. Another consultant was hired to examine manufacturing operations.

Unfortunately, the company was left in a state of drift while the consultants did their research. Without a clear strategy, Britt Technologies was not excelling at either standard products or custom-designed peripherals. Marketing would sometimes accept custom orders, but manufacturing would refuse to produce them. The consultants' reports arrived in due course, and were very logical, but Britt executives still disagreed among themselves. A clear strategy was delayed. In this highly competitive industry, once the company fell behind the competition, bankruptcy was inevitable.[51]

Britt Technologies was searching for a logical, correct answer to an orderly decision process that would use accurate information. Executives tried to apply the rational model to a situation that required a political model. The managers had to bargain and negotiate, use whatever information was available, and build a coalition among themselves. The search for rational answers was a time-consuming process that did not substitute for bargaining and compromise.

Domains of Political Activity

The definition of politics emphasizes the role of uncertainty and disagreement. Uncertainty is a key variable because political behavior is a response to uncertainty. Politics is a mechanism for arriving at a consensus when rules and past experience are not available. Managers at the top of the organization face greater uncertainty than those at lower levels, so more political activity will appear. Moreover, some issues are associated with inherent disagreement. Resources, for example, are critical for the survival and effectiveness of departments, so resource allocation often becomes a political issue. "Rational" methods of allocation do not satisfy participants. Four areas in which politics play a role in most organizations are structural change, interdepartment coordination, personnel changes, and resource allocation.

Structural Change Structural reorganizations strike at the heart of power and authority relationships. Structural change reallocates legitimate authority on the organization chart. Reorganizations such as those discussed in chapter 6 change responsibilities and tasks, which affects the underlying power base from strategic contingencies. For these reasons, a major reorganization can lead to an explosion of political activity.[52] Managers want to learn the implications of reorganization for themselves, and will actively bargain and negotiate to maintain the responsibilities and power base they have. Major reorganizations cause increases and decreases in power, hence a great deal of political activity is required to initiate and implement the change. Top management commitment is important for structural changes. Without their involvement, the implementation of a new structure would be difficult because of resistance and political disagreements. The effective use of top manager power was demonstrated by Don Keith at Phillips Electrical.

IN PRACTICE 10.6

Phillips Electrical, Ltd.

Phillips Electrical is a huge Canadian electronics manufacturer based in Toronto. The president of the radio group, Don Keith, wanted to reorganize from a functional structure to a product structure. His group had 4,200 employees and manufactured four types of sophisticated radio equipment for airlines and air forces around the world. Keith knew the proposed reorganization would generate resistance because the functional managers (e.g., Manager of Engineering) would lose power and stature. The functions would become service groups to the major product lines rather than being the dominant managers in the organization.

Keith's first step was to persuade headquarters' management that the reorganization was needed. Many of them believed that a functional structure was satisfactory. They did not understand the benefits of reorganization. A few of headquarters' managers said that a product structure overemphasized coordination and deemphasized the required competence in functional areas. Keith met with headquarters' managers many times, often one at a time, and finally achieved the whole-hearted support of top management for the concept.

The next step was to sell it within his radio group. He knew that he could impose reorganization unilaterally without explanation, but the cost would be great. He would lose the cooperation of some managers, especially those in the functional areas that stood to lose stature. Keith introduced a series of meetings to explain the problems being faced by the organization and the potential benefits of reorganization. He spent time teaching what product management was all about, especially to the functional managers. He also spent time talking to individual managers, thereby building a coalition in favor of the reorganization. Keith kept the allegiance of one key functional manager by agreeing to reassign him as a product manager to maintain his power base in the organization. For two other managers, Keith had to rely heavily on his formal authority to impose the new structure despite resistance.

The entire process of persuasion and reorganization took fourteen months. Once the organization structure was in place, eight additional months were required to change various systems, such as budgeting and accounting, to reflect the new lines of authority. Weekly meetings of functional and product managers were continued, chaired by Don Keith, so that managers could see each other's problems and gain confidence in the new structure.

The effective use of politics by Don Keith early in the development of the product structure at Phillips made the ultimate outcome successful. Obtaining headquarters' support and building a coalition in his radio group were critical. After the functional managers adapted to the changes, they became more cooperative and played an important support role to the product lines. Keith's use of politics was important, and the new structure enabled Phillips to attain a higher level of performance.

Interdepartmental Coordination*[53]   Relationships between major organizational departments typically are not well-defined. When joint issues arise, managers have to meet and work out solutions on an ad hoc basis. These ongoing coordination activities are often political in nature. The ability of one group to achieve its goal often involves the cooperation of other departments. Interdepartmental coordination lacks rules and precedents to guide it. Uncertainty and conflict are common, especially when the issue is departmental territory and responsibility. Political processes help define respective authority and task boundaries. The following is an example of one such border clash.

IN PRACTICE 10.7
MIS Department

A management information systems (MIS) group was established to handle the company's data-processing needs. The director of this group allocated resources to projects on the basis of financial payoff. A marketing administration group found that although they had many worthy projects for the MIS group, their projects would not get done because of other, better justified, projects from other areas.

The marketing administration manager used his political power to rally marketing executives together. His strategy was to show the poor service of the MIS group and thus justify his solution, which was to hire his own people for MIS work. He convinced his own management of the benefits of better service and got his own MIS group within marketing.

The MIS head then rallied the rest of the organization against the successful marketing administration group. Since the administration group was getting service that others weren't, the MIS head argued that this was done at the expense of the other department heads.

The result was that the marketing administration group's data-processing people were transferred to the MIS group.[54]

In this case, MIS preserved its boundaries by using political influence. Rules and past experience did not prescribe how to handle the disagreement, which was unique, so political negotiation resolved the problem.

Personnel Change Personnel change involves hiring new executives, promotions, transfers, and career development.[55] These changes have great political significance at top organization levels where uncertainty is high, and networks of trust, cooperation, and communication among executives are important. A new manager with a new set of alliances or values can upset stable working relationships and previous agreements. Hiring decisions can generate uncertainty, discussion, and disagreement. Hiring and promotion can be used to strengthen network alliances and coalitions by putting one's own people in prominent positions. Subordinates often feel obligated and will go along with their benefactor in critical decisions. This strategy was used by Fred Donner to consolidate the power of the finance group at General Motors:

> From him [Donner] developed what I call "promotion of the unobvious choice." This means promoting someone who was not regarded as a contender for the post. Doing so not only puts "your man" in position, but it earns for you his undying loyalty because he owes his corporate life to you. . . . A study of the past ten years of General Motors' top executives and an examination of their business biographies make it obvious that some men with undistinguished business careers moved to the top and in many cases occupy positions of power within the corporation today. An understanding of their benefactors makes their ascension more explicable.[56]

Resource Allocation Resource allocation decisions encompass all resources required for organizational performance, including salaries, operating budgets, number of employees, office facilities, equipment, use of the company airplane, and so forth. Resource allocation is something of a puzzle, because these decisions can be accomplished by either the rational or political models. The value of resources is easy to compute, so when managers are in agreement about goals and priorities the calculations should be straightforward. Allocation of the travel budget could be based upon number of employees in a department, for example. But the political model is often used. Resources are so vital that disagreement about priorities exists, and political processes help resolve the dilemmas.[57] Even something so simple as the opening of a new building can cause problems in the allocation of offices. When offices vary in size and location, discussion and bargaining may ensue as to who gets which office. Power and influence determine the outcome.

Naive managers sometimes lose out in the resource allocation process because they see only the rational side of decision-making. The dean of an engineering department knew that the tuition received by the university was determined by the number of student credit hours. He calculated the number of students in his department and submitted it to the vice-president for academic affairs, assuming that proportional resources would be given to each department. Little did he realize that allocations to departments were not calculated in a routine manner. There were many precedents, alliances, and special considerations. The dean of engineering learned the realities too late, when his department's share was reduced in order to benefit the powerful arts and science departments. In that university, the reputation of arts and science was responsible for student enrollment and the university's reputation. They dominated the resource allocation process. The dean of engineering, in order to counter that influence, must work to increase the stature of his own department and use political means to obtain what he sees as a fair share of resources. The following strategy, from another university, was more successful.

> In a budget presentation of all departments in a local community college, one head made a very pious and long presentation outlining the very deep cuts to be made in his area. The rest were moved by his presentation and a portion of his funds were restored.
> Following the meeting, the head asked for feedback on his "performance" from a small group of his staff who were also at the meeting. All were unanimous in awarding full marks for presentation, piety, . . . and success of the game plan.[58]

Process Framework   The framework in Exhibit 10.8 summarizes the political processes described so far. The amounts of uncertainty and disagreement are the antecedent conditions that influence whether the rational model or political model is the correct management approach. The political approach will typically be used in specific areas, such as structural change, interdepartmental coordination, personnel changes, and resource allocation. Political behavior is a mechanism for reaching decisions and achieving outcomes for decisions in these areas because they are uncertain and are associated with conflict. Managers who ignore political processes in these situations will have little influence over final outcomes. The other topic in Exhibit 10.8 is the specific tactics to be used when the political model is the correct approach. We will now examine specific tactics that can be used for either increasing power or for using power to achieve desired outcomes.

POWER AND POLITICAL TACTICS

One of the themes in this chapter has been that power in organizations is not primarily a phenomenon of the individual. Power in organizations is related to the resources that departments command, the role departments play in the organization, and the environmental contingencies with which departments cope. Position and responsibility more than personality and style determine a manager's influence on outcomes in the organization.

Power is used through individuals, however. Individual managers seek agreement about the strategy to achieve their department's desired outcomes. Individual managers negotiate decisions and adopt tactics that enable them to acquire and use power. The source of power comes from larger organi-

EXHIBIT 10.8. A Process Framework of Organizational Politics.

ANTECEDENT CONDITIONS	MANAGEMENT APPROACH	DESIRED OUTCOMES
● Uncertainty	● Rational Model ● Political Model	● Structural Change
● Disagreement	Tactics for Increasing Power Political Tactics for Using Power	● Interdepartmental Coordination
		● Personnel Changes
		● Resource Allocation

Source: Adapted from Donald J. Vredenburgh and John G. Maurer, "A Process Framework of Organizational Politics," *Human Relations,* 37 (1984):47–66.

zation processes, but the use of power involves individual-level activities. Based upon the material covered in this chapter, this section briefly summarizes tactics that managers can use to increase the power of their departments and achieve desired outcomes. These tactics are summarized in Exhibit 10.9.

Tactics for Increasing Power

1. *Enter Areas of High Uncertainty.* An important source of departmental power is to cope with critical uncertainties.[59] If department managers can identify key uncertainties and take steps to remove those uncertainties, the department's power position will be enhanced. Key uncertainties depend upon the situation. Uncertainties could arise from stoppages on the assembly line, from the needed quality of a new product, or from the inability to predict the demand for new services. Once identified, the department can take action to cope with the uncertainty. By their very nature, uncertain tasks will not be solved immediately. Trial and error will be needed, which is to the advantage of the department. The trial and error provides experience and expertise that cannot easily be duplicated by other departments.

2. *Create Dependencies.* Dependencies are an important source of power.[60] When another department or the entire organization depends upon a department for information, materials, knowledge or skills, this department will hold power over them. This power can be increased by incurring obligations. Doing additional work that helps out other departments will obligate them to respond at a future date.[61] The power accumulated by creating a dependency can be used to resolve future disagreements in the department's favor. An equally important and related strategy is to reduce dependency on other departments by acquiring the necessary information or skills.

3. *Provide Resources.* Resources are always important to organizational survival. Those departments that accumulate resources and provide them to the organization in the form of money, human resources, or facilities will be powerful. For example, university departments with the greatest power are

EXHIBIT 10.9. Power and Political Tactics in Organizations.

Tactics for increasing power	*Political Tactics for Using Power*
1. Enter areas of high uncertainty	1. Build coalitions
2. Create dependencies	2. Coopt key dissenters
3. Provide resources	3. Control decision premises
4. Satisfy strategic contingencies	4. Enhance legitimacy and expertise
	5. Make preferences explicit, but keep power implicit

those that obtain external research funds for contributions to university over-head.[62] Likewise, marketing departments are powerful in industrial firms because they bring in financial resources.[63] As mentioned earlier, "He who has the gold, makes the rules." [64]

4. *Satisfy Strategic Contingencies.* The theory of strategic contingencies says that some elements in the external environment and within the organization are especially important for organizational success. A contingency could be a critical event, a task for which there are no substitutes, or a central task that is interdependent with many others in the organization.[65] An analysis of the organization and its external environment will reveal strategic contingencies. To the extent that those contingencies are not being satisfied and that there is room for a department to move into those critical areas, the department can increase its importance and power.

Summary   The allocation of power in an organization is not random. Power is the result of organizational processes that can be understood and predicted. The ability to reduce uncertainty, increase dependency on one's own department, obtain resources, and cope with strategic contingencies will all enhance a department's power. Once power is available, the next challenge is to use it to attain helpful outcomes.

Political Tactics for Using Power

The use of power in organizations requires both skill and willingness. Many decisions are made through political processes because rational decision processes do not fit. Uncertainty or disagreement is too high. Political behaviors that influence decision outcomes are as follows.

1. *Build Coalitions.* Coalition-building means taking the time to talk with other managers to persuade them to your point of view.[66] Most important decisions are made outside formal meetings. Managers discuss issues with each other and reach agreements on a one-to-one basis. Effective managers are those who huddle, meeting in groups of twos and threes to resolve key issues.[67] An important aspect of coalition building is to build good relationships. Good interpersonal relationships mean creating a relationship built on liking, trust, and respect. Reliability and motivation to work with others rather than to exploit others are a part of coalition building.[68]

2. *Expand Networks.* Networks can be expanded by reaching out to establish contact with additional managers and by co-opting dissenters. One approach is to build new alliances through the hiring, transfer, and promotion process. Placing people in key positions who are sympathetic to the outcomes of the department can help achieve departmental goals.[69] On the other hand, coop-

tation is the act of bringing a dissenter into one's network.[70] A dissenter can be asked to join a group for the accomplishment of a specific activity. An example of cooptation in a university was the makeup of the university committee on promotion and tenure. Several women professors who were critical of the tenure and promotion process were appointed to the committee. Once a part of the administrative process, they discovered new information, could see the administrative point of view, and learned that administrators were not as evil as suspected. Cooptation effectively reduced divisiveness so that the administration had sufficient cooperation to achieve its goals.[71]

3. *Control Decision Premises.* The control of decision premises means to constrain the boundaries of a decision. One technique is to choose or limit information provided to other managers. A common method is simply to put your department's best foot forward, such as selectively using favorable criteria. A variety of statistics can be assembled to support the departmental point of view. A university department that is growing rapidly and has a large number of students can make claims for additional resources by emphasizing its growth and large size. Of course, objective criteria do not always work, but they are an important step.

Decision premises can be further influenced by limiting the decision process. Decisions can be influenced by the items put on the agenda for an important meeting, or even by the sequence in which items are discussed.[72] Items discussed last, when time is short and people want to leave, will receive less attention than those discussed early. Calling attention to specific problems, and the suggestion of alternatives, also will affect outcomes. Stressing a specific problem to get it, rather than problems not relevant to your department, on the agenda is an example of agenda setting.

4. *Enhance Legitimacy and Expertise.* Managers can exert the greatest influence in areas in which they have recognized legitimacy and expertise. If a request is within the task domain of the department, and consistent with the department's vested interest, other departments will tend to comply. Members can also identify external consultants or other experts within the organization to support their cause.[73] They can also appeal to people in positions of legitimate authority to cooperate with the desired outcome.

5. *Make Preferences Explicit, But Keep Power Implicit.* If managers do not ask, they seldom receive. Political activity is only effective when goals and needs are made explicit so the organization can respond. Managers should bargain aggressively, and be persuasive. An assertive proposal may be accepted because other managers have no better alternatives. Moreover, an explicit proposal will often receive favorable treatment because other alternatives are ambiguous and less well-defined. Effective political behavior requires sufficient forcefulness and risk-taking to at least try to achieve desired outcomes.

The use of power, however, should not be obvious.[74] If one formally draws upon his or her power base in a meeting by saying, "My department has more power, so the rest of you have to do it my way," the power will be diminished. Power works best when it is used quietly. To call attention to power is to lose it. Explicit claims for power are made by the powerless, not by the powerful.[75] People know who has power. There is substantial agreement on which departments are more powerful. Explicit claims to power are not necessary, and can even harm the department's cause.

When using any of the above tactics, managers should recall the survey described earlier that found most managers have a negative attitude toward self-serving political behavior. Many managers feel that self-serving behavior hurts rather than helps the organization. If managers are perceived to be throwing their weight around, or are perceived to be after things that are self-serving rather than beneficial to the organization, they will lose respect. Their power base will be eroded. The appropriate role of politics is to resolve conflicts and achieve ends that benefit the organization. Politics is a means to resolve disagreements. When political behaviors are perceived as illegitimate, as going too far, or as serving personal ends, they are dysfunctional. A recent example of where the perceived illegitimate use of power caused a problem was the relationship between Mary Cunningham and William Agee at Bendix Corporation.

IN PRACTICE 10.8

Bendix Corporation

Bill Agee had the world by the tail. He was president of Bendix Corporation, a major conglomerate, by age forty. His reign at Bendix produced record sales and earnings.

In 1979, he hired Mary Cunningham to be his executive assistant after a three-hour interview. A new graduate of the Harvard Business School, she was considered intelligent and ambitious. A year later, Agee promoted her to Vice-President for Corporate and Public Affairs. Three months later, she was promoted to Vice-President for Strategic Planning. The move created an uproar within Bendix. There was gossip about the relationship between Cunningham and Agee. Both had recently separated from their spouses. Here were two young, attractive, unattached people working together, traveling together, both staying in the Waldorf Towers. Other executives began to talk of a lack of trust and confidence in Agee. Tensions were heightened because of rumors that Agee intended to implement a significant structural reorganization at Bendix. The board of directors received anonymous letters questioning Agee's business judgment and his relationship with Cunningham. Conflicts with board members and executives ensued. One board member stated that Agee had provided "convincing evidence of a lack of the solid, hard headed, no-nonsense leadership that Bendix needs . . . I am concerned about the future of the company." Agee reacted quickly and arranged meetings with the board's executive committee and other top managers. Through these meetings Agee was able to reestablish control of the board and other managers.

Agee went public with the statement that Cunningham's advancement had nothing to do with a personal relationship. "It is true that we are very, very close friends, and she's a very close friend of my family," he said. "Her rise in this company is unusual because she is a very unusual and very talented individual."

The gossip, rumors, and insinuations continued, and Mary Cunningham resigned on October 9, 1980, just sixteen months after she was hired at Bendix. William Agee never fully reestablished himself either. About two years later one of the executives Agee alienated was responsible for the acquisition of Bendix, and Agee was let go.[76]

SUMMARY AND INTERPRETATION

This chapter presented two views of organization. One view, covered only briefly, is the rational model of organization. This view assumes that organizations have specific goals, and that problems can be logically solved. The other view, discussed throughout most of the chapter, is based upon a power and political model of organization. The goals of an organization are not specific or agreed upon. Organizational departments have different values and interests, so managers come into conflict. Decisions are made on the basis of power and political influence. Bargaining, negotiation, persuasion, and coalition-building decide outcomes.

The single most important idea from this chapter is the reality of power and political processes in organizations. Differences in departmental tasks and responsibilities inevitably lead to differences in power and influence. Power differences determine decision outcomes. Uncertainty and disagreement lead to political behavior. Understanding sources of power and how to use politics to achieve outcomes for the organization is a requirement for effective management.

Many managers prefer the rational model of decision-making. The rational model is clean and objective. Rational processes are effective when decision factors are sharply specified because of certainty, agreement, and good information. Political processes, however, should not be ignored. Political decision processes are used in situations of uncertainty, disagreement, and poor information. Decisions are reached through the clash of values and preferences, and by the influence of dominant departments.

Other important ideas in this chapter pertain to the analysis of power differences and political tactics. Research into power processes has uncovered characteristics that make some departments more powerful than others. Factors such as dependency, resources, and the removal of strategic contingencies determine the influence of departments. Political strategies such as coalition-building, expanded networks, and control of decision premises help departments achieve desired outcomes. Organizations can be more effective when managers appreciate the realities of power and politics.

Finally, despite its widespread use in organizations, many people distrust political behavior. They fear that political behavior may be used for selfish ends that benefit the individual but not the organization. If politics is used for personal gain, other managers will become suspicious and withdraw their support. Politics will be accepted when it is used to achieve the legitimate goal of the department or organization.

KEY CONCEPTS

authority
coping with uncertainty
decision premises
domains of political activity
mixed model
network centrality
organizational politics
political model

power
power sources
protection against tyranny
rational model
strategic contingencies
tactics for increasing power
tactics for using power
whistle-blowing

DISCUSSION QUESTIONS

1. One form of management tyranny occurs when male senior managers try to exploit sexual favors from female subordinates. These women experience extreme pressure because their jobs depend upon the recommendations of the manager, and they often need the job to support their family. Based upon the discussion in this chapter, what advice would you give to a woman to help her block the abuse of power by her manager?

2. Explain how control over decision premises gives power to a person.

3. In Exhibit 10.4, Research and Development has greater power in firms A, B, L, and N than in the other firms. Discuss possible strategic contingencies that give R&D greater power in those four firms.

4. If you are a lower-level employee in an organization, how might you increase your power base?

5. Some positions are practically powerless in an organization. Why should this be? How could those positions be redesigned to have greater power?

6. If a university department were suddenly to have its travel budget doubled so that members could present papers at other schools and attend professional meetings, would the power of the department be increased? Explain.

7. State University X receives 90% of its financial resources from the state, and is overcrowded with students. It is currently trying to pass regulations to limit student enrollment. Private University Y receives 90% of its income from student tuition, and has barely enough students to make ends meet. It is actively recruiting students for next year. In which university will students have greater power? What implications will this have for professors and administrators? Discuss.

8. Define politics. How does politics differ from power?

9. If a position has power, does it also have authority? Does it need authority?

10. Why do you think most managers have a negative view of politics?

11. The engineering college at a major university brings in three times as many government research dollars as the rest of the university combined. Engineering appears wealthy, and has many professors on full-time research status. Yet when internal research funds are allocated, engineering gets a larger share of the money, even though they already have external research funds. Why would this happen?

12. Discuss the differences between the rational model and political model

of organization decision-making. Would you expect both types of processes to appear in an organization?

13. Would the rational model, political model, or mixed model be used in the following decision situations: quality control-testing in the production department; resource allocation in the executive suite; deciding which division will be in charge of a recently built plant?

GUIDES TO ACTION

As an organization manager:

1. Do not leave lower organization levels powerless. If vertical power is too heavy in favor of top management, increase the power of lower levels by reducing rules, providing rewards for innovation, increasing visibility and outside contacts, and encouraging participation in important problem-solving task forces. Increase power of employees in order to increase performance.

2. Be aware of the less visible, but equally important, horizontal power relationships that come from the ability of a department to deal with strategic contingencies that confront the organization. Increase the horizontal power of a department by increasing involvement in strategic contingencies.

3. Expect and allow for political behavior in organizations. Politics provides the discussion and clash of interests needed to crystallize points of view and to reach a decision. Build coalitions, expand networks, control decision premises, enhance legitimacy, and make preferences explicit to attain desired outcomes.

4. Use the rational model of organization when alternatives are clear, when goals are defined, and when managers can estimate the outcomes accurately. In these circumstances coalition-building, cooptation, or other political tactics are not needed and will not lead to effective decisions.

Consider these Guides when analyzing the following cases.

CASES FOR ANALYSIS

DIAMY CORPORATION (CANADA)

Diamy Corporation is the second largest producer of household appliances in Canada. Three-quarters of Diamy's production is sold wholesale to retail chains who put their own brand on the product. Diamy also exports to the United States and Europe.

Len Sullivan became transportation director seven years ago. He has spent his entire career with Diamy. In the early days, his job was to trace shipments and check freight rates in huge catalogs. Sometimes he did other transportation jobs, such as chauffeuring VIPs or giving bus tours to groups of foreign visitors.

Times have changed in the transportation department. The director is a senior executive and his staff spends time negotiating with hundreds of carriers to reduce freight rates and improve service.

Freight rates have gradually increased to almost 10% of the wholesale price of appliances. Getting a good deal can make a real difference to Diamy's profit margin. Canada, like other countries, has also been hit with sharply higher fuel, labor, and raw material costs. Provincial regulations have been reduced in response to deregulation in the United States and to the federal government in Ottawa. Freight haulers used to set their rates by gentlemen's agreement, and they were all but identical. Now both truck and rail carriers are in head-to-head price competition to win the business of Diamy and other manufacturers.

The transportation department uses a computer to calculate the best freight rates. The cost of shipping a truckload of washing machines from Ottawa to Toronto could vary from $400 to $800. The computer keeps track of the dizzying array of changing freight rates and helps calculate the most economical mode of transportation.

Mr. Sullivan recently met with Elizabeth Dee from InterCanada Lines, Inc. Ms. Dee explained that several trucks were returning from the Maritimes half empty. She proposed that if Diamy would rent space on the half empty trailers, InterCanada would give them full truck load rates. This would save Diamy 10%–15% on hauls from their plant in New Brunswick.

Mr. Sullivan was noncommittal, and offered to have his team look over the details and calculate competitive rates.

Mr. Sullivan then casually mentioned that he hoped InterCanada would consider a proposal to be one of Diamy's major carriers. Diamy was considering giving increased business to carriers for discounts of up to 20%. He mentioned that InterCanada had not been enthusiastic when first approached by a Diamy representative. He also mentioned that Diamy did $150,000 business with InterCanada in the first eight months of 1982. Furthermore, he said, "Montreal Freight, a competitor of yours, has been signed on as one of our major carriers."

Elizabeth Dee wanted to know who at InterCanada sounded cool to the proposal. She would see what she could do. She promised to push for approval of Diamy's major carrier discount program.

Questions

1. Why has the stature and influence of the transportation department increased at Diamy over the last few years? Would this happen in other companies for which transportation makes up a sizable percentage of sales cost? Explain.

2. Does Mr. Sullivan use a rational or political model, or both? Does the decision model fit the type of decision? Does he seem willing to use his influence to achieve desired outcomes? Discuss.

3. Is Diamy a strategic contingency for other organizations? Would it be in Mr. Sullivan's interest to use just a few trucking lines and have them dependent upon Diamy for the majority of their business? Discuss.

THE AIR FORCE A-7D BRAKE PROBLEM*

From the hearing before the Subcommittee on Economy in Government of the Joint Economic Committee of the Congress of the United States, 91st Congress, August 13, 1969.

* From the Hearing before the Subcommittee on Economy in Government of the Joint Economic Committee of the Congress of the United States, 91st Congress, August 13, 1969.

Mr. Vandivier: In the early part of 1967, the B. F. Goodrich Wheel & Brake Plant at Troy, Ohio, received an order from the Ling-Temco-Vought Co. of Dallas, Texas, to supply wheels and brakes for the A-7D aircraft, built by LTV for the Air Force.

The tests on the wheels and brakes were to be conducted in accordance with the requirements of military specification Mil-W-5013G as prepared and issued by the U.S. Air Force and to the requirements set forth by LTV Specification Document 204-16-37D.

The wheels were successfully tested to the specified requirements, but the brake, manufactured by Goodrich under BEG part No. 2-1162-3, was unable to meet the required tests.

The laboratory tests specified for the brake were divided into two categories: dynamic brake tests and static brake tests.

The dynamic brake tests basically consisted of forty-five simulated normal energy stops, five overload energy stops, and one worn-brake maximum energy stop, sometimes called a rejected take-off, or RTO. These simulated stops were to be conducted on one brake assembly with no change in brake lining to be allowed during the test. In addition, a maximum energy brake stop (or RTO) was to be conducted on a brake containing new linings, and still another series of tests called a turnaround capability test was to be performed.

The turnaround capability test consisted of a series of taxis, simulated take-offs, flight periods, and landings, and time schedule for the turn-around test was supplied by LTV to coincide with conditions under which the A-7D brake might operate on a typical mission.

Generally speaking, the brake passed all the static brakes tests, but the brake could not and did not pass any of the dynamic tests I have just described with the exception of the new brake maximum energy stop.

During the first few attempts to qualify the brake to the dynamic tests, the brake ran out of lining material after a few stops had been completed and the tests were terminated. Attempts were made to secure a lining material that would hold up during the grueling fifty-one-stop test, but to no avail. Although I had been aware for several months that great difficulty was being experienced with the A-7D brake, it was not until April 11, 1968, almost a full year after qualification testing had begun, that I became aware of how these tests were being conducted.

The thirteenth attempt at qualification was being conducted under B. F. Goodrich Internal Test No. T-1867.

On the morning of April 11, Richard Gloor, who was the test engineer assigned to the A-7D project, came to me and told me he had discovered that some time during the previous twenty-four hours, instrumentation used to record brake pressure had been miscalibrated deliberately so that while the instrumentation showed that a pressure of 1,000 pounds per square inch had been used to conduct brake stop numbers 46 and 47 (two overload energy stops) 1,100 p.s.i. had actually been applied to the brakes. Maximum pressure available on the A-7D is 1,000 p.s.i.

Mr. Gloor further told me he had questioned instrumentation personnel about the miscalibration and had been told they were asked to do so by Searle Lawson, a design engineer on the A-7D.

Chairman Proxmire: Is this the gentleman who is with you now, Mr. Vandivier?

Mr. Vandivier: That is correct. I subsequently questioned Lawson who admitted he had ordered the instruments miscalibrated at the direction of a superior.

Upon examining the log sheets kept by laboratory personnel I found that other violations of the test specifications had occurred.

For example, after some of the overload stops, the brake had been disassembled and the three stators or stationary members of the brake had been taken to the plant toolroom for rework and, during an earlier part of the test, the position of elements within the brake had been reversed to distribute the lining wear more evenly.

Additionally, instead of braking the dynamometer to a complete stop as required by military specifications, pressure was released when the wheel and brake speed had decelerated to 10 miles per hour.

The reason for this, I was later told, was that the brakes were experiencing severe vibrations near the end of the stops, causing excessive lining wear and general deterioration of the brake.

All these incidents were in clear violation of military specifications and general industry practice.

I reported these violations to the test lab supervisor, Mr. Ralph Gretzinger, who reprimanded instrumentation personnel and stated that under no circumstance would intentional miscalibration of instruments be tolerated.

As for the other discrepancies noted in test procedures, he said that he was aware that they were happening but that as far as he was concerned the tests could not, in view of the way they were being conducted, be classified as qualification tests.

Later that same day, the worn-brake, maximum energy stop was conducted on the brake. The brake was landed at a speed of 161 m.p.h. and the pressure was applied. The dynamometer rolled a distance of 16,800 feet before coming to rest. The elapsed stopping time was 141 seconds. By computation, this stop time shows the aircraft would have traveled over 3 miles before stopping.

Within a few days, a typewritten copy of the test logs of test T-1867 was sent to LTV to assure LTV that a qualified brake was almost ready for delivery.

Virtually every entry in this so-called copy of the test logs was drastically altered. As an example, the stop time for the worn-brake maximum energy stop was changed from 141 seconds to a mere 46.8 seconds.

On May 2, 1968, the fourteenth attempt to qualify the brakes was begun, and Mr. Lawson told me that he had been informed by both Mr. Robert Sink, project manager at Goodrich—I am sorry, Mr. Sink is project manager—and Mr. Russell Van Horn, projects manager at Goodrich, that "Regardless of what the brake does on test, we're going to qualify it."

Chairman Proxmire: What was that?

Mr. Vandivier: The statement was, "Regardless of what the brake does on test, we're going to qualify it."

He also said that the latest instructions he had received were to the effect that, if the data from this latest test turned out worse than did test T-1867, then we would write our report based on T-1867.

Chairman Proxmire: The statement was made by whom?

Mr. Vandivier: Mr. Lawson told me this statement was made to him by Mr. Robert Sink, project manager, and Mr. Russell Van Horn, project manager.

During this latest and final attempt to qualify the four-rotor brake, the same illegal procedures were used as had been used on attempt No. 13. Again after thirty stops had been completed, the positions of the friction members of the brake were reversed to distribute wear more evenly. After each stop, the wheel was removed from the brake and the accumulated dust was blown out. During each stop, pressure was released when the deceleration had reached 10 miles per hour.

By these and other irregular procedures the brake was nursed along until the forty-five normal energy stops had been completed, but by this time the friction surfaces of the brakes were almost bare; that is, there was virtually no lining left on the brake. This lack of lining material introduced another problem.

The pistons that actuate the brake by forcing the friction surfaces together were almost at the end of their allowable travel, and it was feared that during the overload stops the pistons might actually pop out of their sockets within the brake, allowing brake fluid to spray the hot surfaces, resulting in fire.

Therefore, a metal spacer was inserted in the brake between the pressure plate and the piston housing.

This spacer served to make up for the lack of friction material and to keep the pistons in place. To provide room for the spacer, the adjuster assemblies were removed from the brake.

The five overload stops were conducted without the adjuster assemblies and with the spacer in place.

After stop number 48—the third overload stop—temperatures in the brake were so high that the fuse plug, a safety device that allows air to escape from the tire to prevent blowout, melted and allowed the tire to deflate.

The same thing happened after stop number 49—the fourth overload stop. Both these occurrences were highly irregular and in direct conflict with the performance criteria of the military requirements.

Chairman Proxmire: I understand you have a picture of this that might help us see it.

Mr. Vandivier: Yes.

Mr. Proxmire: Do you want to show that to us now?

Mr. Vandivier: I was going to show it here just a little bit later.

Chairman Proxmire: Go ahead. . . .

Mr. Vandivier: All right.

In addition to these highly questionable practices, a turnaround capability test, or simulated mission test, was conducted incorrectly due to a human error. When the error was later discovered, no corrections were made.

While these tests were being conducted, I was asked by Mr. Lawson to begin writing a qualification report for the brake. I flatly refused and told Mr. Gretzinger, the lab supervisor, who was my superior, that I could not write such a report because the brake had not been qualified.

He agreed and he said that no one in the laboratory was going to issue such a report unless a brake was actually qualified in accordance with the specification and using standard operating procedures.

He said that he would speak to his own supervisor, the manager of the technical services section, Mr. Russell Line, and get the matter settled at once.

He consulted Mr. Line and assured me that both had concurred in the decision not to write a qualification report.

I explained to Lawson that I had been told not to write the report and that the only way such a report could be written was to falsify test data.

Mr. Lawson said that he was well aware of what was required but that he had been ordered to get a report written, regardless of how or what had to be done.

He stated that, if I would not write the report, he would have to, and he asked if I would help him gather the test data and draw up the various engineering curves and graphic displays that are normally included in a report.

I asked Mr. Gretzinger, my superior, if this was all right and he agreed. As long as I was only assisting in the preparation of the data, it would be permissible.

Both Lawson and I worked on the elaborate curves and logs in the report for nearly a month. During this time we both frankly discussed the moral aspects of what we were doing, and we agreed that our actions were unethical and probably illegal.

Several times during that month I discussed the A-7D testing with Mr. Line and asked him to consult his superiors in Akron to prevent a false qualification report from being issued. Mr. Line declined to do so and advised me that it would be wise to just do my work and keep quiet.

I told him of the extensive irregularities during testing and suggested that the brake was actually dangerous and, if allowed to be installed on an aircraft, might cause an accident.

Mr. Line said he thought I was worrying too much about things that did not really concern me and advised me to just "do what you're told."

About the first of June. . . .

Chairman Proxmire: You skipped one line here.

Mr. Vandivier: Yes.

Chairman Proxmire: You said "I asked him" . . . .

Mr. Vandivier: Yes. I asked Mr. Line if his conscience would hurt him if such a thing caused the death of a pilot and this is when he replied that I was worrying about too many things that did not concern me and advised me to "do what you're told."

About the first of June 1968, Mr. Gretzinger asked if I was finished with the graphic data and said he had been advised by the chief engineer, Mr. H. C. Sunderman, that when the data were finished they were to be delivered to him—Sunderman—and he would instruct someone in the engineering department to actually write the report. Accordingly, when I had finished with the data, I gave it to Mr. Gretzinger who immediately took it from the room. Within a few minutes, he was back and was obviously angry.

He said that Mr. Sunderman had told him no one in the engineering department had time to write the report and that we would have to do it ourselves.

At this point, Mr. Line came into the room demanding to know "What the hell is going on." Mr. Gretzinger explained the situation again and said he would not allow such a report to be issued by the lab.

Mr. Line then turned to me and said he was "sick of hearing about this damned report. Write the ------ thing and shut up about it." . . .

Many, many of the elaborate engineering curves attached to the report were complete and total fabrications, based not on what had actually occurred, but on information that would fool both LTV and the Air Force.

I have mentioned already that the turnaround capability test that was supposed to determine what temperatures might be experienced by the brake during a typical flight mission had been misconducted through a human error on the part of the test lab operator.

Rather than rerun this very important test, which would have taken only some six hours to complete, it was decided to manufacture the data.

This we did, and the result was some very convincing graphic curves. These curves were supposed to demonstrate to LTV and the Air Force exactly what the temperatures in the brakes had been during each minute of the simulated mission.

They were completely false and based only on data that would be acceptable to the customers.

I could spend the entire day here discussing the various elaborate falsifications that went into this report but I feel that, by now, the picture is clear.

The report was finally issued on June 5, 1968, and almost immediately, flight tests on the brake were begun at Edwards Air Force Base in California.

Mr. Lawson was sent by Goodrich to witness these tests, and when he returned, he described various mishaps that had occurred during the flight tests and he expressed the opinion to me that the brake was dangerous.

That same afternoon, I contacted my attorney and after describing the situation to him, asked for his advice.

He advised me that, while I was technically not guilty of committing a fraud, I was certainly part of a conspiracy to defraud. He further suggested a meeting with U.S. Attorney Roger Makely in Dayton, Ohio.

I agreed to this and my attorney said that he would arrange an appointment with the federal attorney.

I discussed my attorney's appraisal of our situation with Mr. Lawson, but I did not, at this time, tell him of the forthcoming visit with Mr. Makely. Mr. Lawson said he would like to consult with my attorney and I agreed to arrange this.

Shortly thereafter, Mr. Lawson went to the Dallas offices of LTV, and, while he was gone, my attorney called and said that, upon advice of the U.S. attorney, he had arranged an interview with the Dayton office of the FBI. . . .

About this time the Air Force demanded that Goodrich produce its raw data from the tests. This Goodrich refused to do, claiming that the raw data was proprietary information.

Goodrich management decided that, since pressure was being applied by the Air Force, a conference should be arranged with LTV management and engineering staff. A preconference meeting was set for Goodrich personnel to go over the questionable points in the report.

On Saturday, July 27, 1968, Mr. Robert Sink, Mr. Lawson, Mr. John Warren—A-7D project engineer—and I met and went over the discrepant items contained in the qualification report. Each point was discussed at great length and a list of approximately forty separate discrepancies was compiled. These, we were told by Mr. Sink, would be revealed to LTV personnel the following week.

However, by the time of the meeting with LTV, only a few days later, the list of discrepancies had been cut by Mr. Sink from forty-three items to a mere three.

Mr. Chairman, during this meeting Mr. Lawson took from the blackboard at the Goodrich conference room word for word listing of all these discrepancies. This contains the forty-three items I have just mentioned. I would like to enter this into the record and also enter the subsequent list of three major discrepancies that later came out of this meeting.

Chairman Proxmire: Do you have copies of those documents?

Mr. Vandivier: Yes, I do have.

Mr. Vandivier: The following two-month period was one of a constant running battle with LTV and the Air Force, during which time the Air Force refused final approval of the qualification report and demanded a confrontation with Goodrich about supplying raw data.

On October 8, another meeting was held, again with Mr. Sink, Mr. Lawson, Mr. Warren, and myself present.

This was only one day prior to a meeting with Air Force personnel, and Mr. Sink said that he had called the meeting "so that we are all coordinated and tell the same story." Mr. Sink said that LTV personnel would be present at the meeting with the Air Force and our policy would be to "Let LTV carry the ball." Mr. Sink appeared to be especially concerned because Mr. Bruce Tremblay, the Air Force engineer most intimate with A-7D brake, would be present at the meeting, and it was felt at B. F. Goodrich that Mr. Tremblay was already suspicious.

Mr. Sink warned us that "Mr. Tremblay will probably be at his antagonistic best." He added that the Air Force had wanted to meet at the Goodrich plant, but that we—Goodrich—couldn't risk having them that close to the raw data. "We don't want those guys in the plant," Mr. Sink said.

What happened at the meeting with the Air Force, I do not know. I did not attend.

On October 18, I submitted my resignation to Goodrich effective November 1.

Chairman Proxmire: Thank you, Mr. Vandivier.

Mr. Lawson, you have heard the statement as read and I take it you have had a chance to see the full statement?

Mr. Lawson: No, I have not.

Chairman Proxmire: The statement you have just heard read by Mr. Vandivier, do you agree with it fully or in part or do you disagree and can you tell us your reaction to it?

Mr. Lawson: The factual data that Mr. Vandivier has presented is correct, to the best of my knowledge.

Chairman Proxmire: Let me ask you this [Mr. Vandivier]. You say you worked for Goodrich for six years?

Mr. Vandivier: That is correct.

Chairman Proxmire: How long did you work as a technical writer?

Mr. Vandivier: Approximately three years.

Chairman Proxmire: Three years. How many reports did you prepare for B. F. Goodrich?

Mr. Vandivier: At least 100, possibly 150.

Chairman Proxmire: Were any of these reports questioned in any way?

Mr. Vandivier: No, they were not.

Chairman Proxmire: Were they accepted? Did you get any reaction at all favorable or unfavorable in these reports that you wrote?

Mr. Vandivier: Occasionally we would get a question from the manufacturer about a wording or a clarification, and these would be supplied.

Chairman Proxmire: Was there any question as to the accuracy or competence of the report?

Mr. Vandivier: No, none whatsoever.

Chairman Proxmire: Were you criticized at any time that the reports were not adequate?

Mr. Vandivier: No, I was not.

Chairman Proxmire: In your statement, you say "Accordingly I wrote the report but in the conclusion I stated that the brake had 'not' met either the intent or the requirement of the specification and therefore was 'not' qualified." Then you add "When the final report was typewritten and ready for publication the two 'nots' in the conclusion had been eliminated, thereby changing the entire meaning of the conclusion." . . .

Was this the only time in the three years you worked as a technical writer with Goodrich; the only time that you made false entries into a report of manufacture?

Mr. Vandivier: Yes it was.

Chairman Proxmire: I cannot understand what was going through the minds of Goodrich's management the way you have told the story. I cannot see what they have to gain by passing on a brake that would not meet qualifications. Somewhere along the line this is going to be shown as an unqualified brake. As you pointed out, it might be under disastrous circumstances, but in any event Goodrich would suffer and suffer badly by passing on a brake to LTV or the Air Force that was not going to work. What is their motivation?

Mr. Vandivier: I cannot tell you what their motivation is. I can tell you what I feel was behind this.

Chairman Proxmire: All right.

Mr. Vandivier: I feel in the beginning stages of this program someone made a mistake and refused to admit that mistake, and to hide his stupidity or his ignorance, or his pride, or whatever it was, he simply covered up, you know, with more false statements, false information, and at the time it came time to deliver this brake, Goodrich was so far down the road that there was nothing else to do.

They had no time to start over; I think it was a matter not of company policy but of company politics. I think that probably three or four persons within the Goodrich organization at Troy were responsible for this. I do not believe for a moment that the corporate officials in Akron knew that this was going on.

Questions

1. Analyze the sources of vertical and horizontal power within the B. F. Goodrich Wheel & Brake Plant. Compare the power of project managers versus the power of technical specialists. Is this the type of situation in which politics can be expected to appear? Discuss.

2. Why do you think the company got to the point of needing to falsify data? Why did employees yield to pressures to falsify data? What were the costs to B. F. Goodrich? To the whistle-blower?

NOTES

1. Harlan S. Byrne, "New Chairman Passes Early Test with Ease at McDonnell Douglas," *Wall Street Journal,* August 25, 1983, pp. 1, 12; William M. Carley and David P. Garino, "Big Changes Lie Ahead in Management, Board of McDonnell," *Wall Street Journal,* September 8, 1980, pp. 1, 18; Lee Smith, "They've Turned Off the Seat-Belt Sign at McDonnell Douglas," *Fortune,* December 17, 1979, pp. 60–64; "Where Management Style Sets the Strategy," *Business Week,* October 23, 1978, pp. 88–99; Dale Dobbins, Greg Owens, and Scott Wilder, "McDonnell Douglas Corporation," unpublished manuscript, Texas A&M University, 1981.

2. Examples are Michael Korda, *Power: How to Get It, How to Use It* (New York: Random House, 1975) and Robert J. Ringer, *Winning Through Intimidation* (Los Angeles: Los Angeles Book Publishing Co., 1973).

3. Robert A. Dahl, "The Concept of Power," *Behavioral Science* 2 (1957):201–215.

4. W. Graham Astley and Paramjit S. Sachdeva, "Structural Sources of Intraorganizational Power: A Theoretical Synthesis," *Academy of Management Review,* 9 (1984): 104–113; Abraham Kaplan, "Power in Perspective," in Robert L. Kahn and Elise Boulding, eds., *Power and Conflict in Organizations* (London: Tavistock, 1964), pp. 11–32.

5. Gerald R. Salancik and Jeffrey Pfeffer, "The Bases and Use of Power in Organizational Decision-Making: The Case of the University," *Administrative Science Quarterly* 19 (1974):453–473.

6. R. M. Emerson, "Power-Dependence Relations," *American Sociological Review* 27 (1962):31–40.

7. Rosabeth Moss Kanter, "Power Failure in Management Circuits," *Harvard Business Review* (July-August, 1979):65–75.

8. A. J. Grimes, "Authority, Power, Influence and Social Control: A Theoretical Synthesis," *Academy of Management Review* 3 (1978):724–735.

9. Astley and Sachdeva, "Structural Sources of Intraorganizational Power."

10. Jeffrey Pfeffer, "The Micropolitics of Organizations," in Marshall W. Meyer et al., *Environments and Organizations* (San Francisco: Jossey-Bass, 1978), pp. 29–50.

11. Peabody, "Perceptions of Organizational Authority," p. 479.

12. John R. P. French, Jr., and Bertrand Raven, "The Basis of Social Power," in Dorwin Cartwright and Alvin Zander, eds., *Group Dynamics,* 3rd ed. (New York: Harper & Row, 1968), pp. 259–269.

13. Pfeffer, *Power in Organizations.*

14. Andrew M. Pettigrew, *The Politics of Organizational Decision-Making* (London: Tavistock, 1973).

15. Andrew M. Pettigrew, "Information Control as a Power Resource," *Sociology* 6 (1972):187–204.

16. Astley and Sachdeva, "Structural Sources of Intraorganizational Power" in Noel M. Tichy and Charles Fombrun, "Network Analysis in Organizational Settings," *Human Relations,* 32 (1979):923–965.

17. Laura Landro, "Gulf & Western Chief Moves Quickly to Cast Company in His Image," *The Wall Street Journal,* March 16, 1983, pp. 1, 14.

18. Kanter, "Power Failure in Management Circuits."

19. Ibid.

20. Ibid., p. 70.

21. David Mechanic, "Sources of Power in Lower Participants in Complex Organizations," *Administrative Science Quarterly* 7 (1962):349–364.

22. Richard T. Mowday, "The Exercise of Upward Influence in Organizations," *Administrative Science Quarterly* 23 (1978):137–156.

23. Warren K. Schilit and Edwin A. Locke, "A Study of Upward Influence in Organizations," *Administrative Science Quarterly,* 27 (1982):304–316.

24. Richard S. Blackburn, "Lower Participant Power: Toward a Conceptual Integration," *Academy of Management Review,* 6 (1981):127–131.

25. Doris Kearns, "Lyndon Johnson and the American Dream," *The Atlantic Monthly,* May 1976, p. 41. Specified material from *Lyndon Johnson* by Doris Kearns. Copyright © 1976 by Doris Kearns. Reprinted by permission of Harper & Row, Publishers, Inc.

26. Stanley Milgram, "Some Conditions of Obedience and Disobedience to Authority," *Human Relations* 18 (1965):57–75.

27. Marcia Parmerlee Miceli and Janet P. Near, "The Relationship among Beliefs, Organizational Positions, and Whistle-Blowing Status: A Discriminant Analysis," *Academy of Management Journal,* 27 (1984):687–705; Marcia A. Parmerlee, Janet P. Near, and Tamila C. Jensen, "Correlates of Whistle-Blowers' Perceptions of Organizational Retaliation," *Administrative Science Quarterly,* 27 (1982):17–34.

28. Claire Safran, "Women Who Blew the Whistle," *Good Housekeeping,* April 1985, pp. 25, 216–219.

29. Charles Perrow, "Departmental Power and Perspective in Industrial Firms," in Mayer N. Zald, ed., *Power in Organizations* (Nashville, TN: Vanderbilt University Press, 1970), pp. 59–89.

30. D. J. Hickson, C. R. Hinings, C. A. Lee, R. E. Schneck, and J. M. Pennings, "A Strategic Contingencies Theory of Intraorganizational Power," *Administrative Science Quarterly* 16 (1971):216–229; Gerald R. Salancik and Jeffrey Pfeffer, "Who Gets Power—And How They Hold Onto It: A Strategic-Contingency Model of Power," *Organizational Dynamics* (Winter 1977):3–21.

31. Salancik and Pfeffer, "Who Gets Power."

32. Ibid.; Pfeffer, *Power in Organizations;* C. R. Hinings, D. J. Hickson, J. M. Pennings, and R. E. Schneck, "Structural Conditions of Intraorganizational Power," *Administrative Science Quarterly* 19 (1974):22–44.

33. Richard M. Emerson, "Power-Dependence Relations," *American Sociological Review* 27 (1962):31–41.

34. Michel Crozier, *The Bureaucratic Phenomenon* (Chicago: University of Chicago Press, 1964).

35. Pfeffer, *Power in Organizations,* p. 101.

36. Jeffrey Pfeffer and Gerald Salancik, "Organizational Decision-Making As a Political Process: The Case of a University Budget," *Administrative Science Quarterly* (1974): 135–151.

37. Salancik and Pfeffer, "Basis and Use of Power in Organizational Decision-Making," p. 470.

38. Hickson et al., "Strategic Contingencies Theory."

39. Ibid.

40. Kanter, "Power Failure in Management Circuits."

41. Pettigrew, *Politics of Organizational Decision-Making.*

42. B. Bowden, "The Language of Computers," *American Scientist* 58 (1970):43.

43. Hickson et al., "Strategic Contingencies Theory."

44. Ibid.

45. Jeffrey Gantz and Victor V. Murray, "Experience of Workplace Politics," *Academy of Management Journal* 23 (1980):237–251; Dan L. Madison, Robert W. Allen, Lyman W. Porter, Patricia A. Renwick, and Bronston T. Mayes, "Organizational Politics: An Exploration of Managers' Perception," *Human Relations* 33 (1980):79–100.

46. Donald J. Vredenburgh and John G. Maurer, "A Process Framework of Organizational Politics," *Human Relations,* 37 (1984):47–66; Bronston T. Mayes and Robert W. Allen, "Toward a Definition of Organizational Politics," *Academy of Management Review* 2 (1977):675; Gantz and Murray, "Experience of Workplace Politics," p. 428.

47. Vredenburgh and Maurer, "A Process Framework of Organizational Politics."

48. Pfeffer, *Power in Organizations,* p. 70.

49. Pfeffer, *Power in Organizations.*

50. Ibid.

51. Adapted from Don Hellriegel, John W. Slocum, Jr., and Richard W. Woodman, *Organizational Behavior* (St. Paul: West, 1983), and Pfeffer, *Power in Organizations,* pp. 339–341.

52. Madison et al., "Organizational Politics"; Jay R. Galbraith, *Organization Design* (Reading, MA: Addison-Wesley, 1977).

53. Gantz and Murray, "Experience of Workplace Politics," p. 248.

54. Victor Murray and Jeffrey Gantz, "Games Executives Play: Politics at Work," *Business Horizons,* December 1980, p. 14.

55. Gantz and Murray, "Experience of Workplace Politics"; Pfeffer, *Power in Organizations.*

56. J. Patrick Wright, *On a Clear Day You Can See General Motors: John D. DeLorean's Look Inside the Automotive Giant* (Grosse Point, MI: Wright Enterprises, 1979), p. 41.

57. Pfeffer, *Power in Organizations.*

58. Murray and Gantz, "Games Executives Play," p. 14.

59. Hickson et al., "A Strategic Contingencies Theory."

60. Pfeffer, *Power in Organizations.*

61. Vredenburgh and Maurer, "A Process Framework of Organizational Politics"; Kotter, "Power, Dependence, and Effective Management."

62. Pfeffer and Salancik, "Organizational Decision-Making as a Political Process"; Jeffrey Pfeffer and William L. Moore, "Power in University Budgeting: A Replication and Extension," *Administrative Science Quarterly* 25 (1980):637–653; Vredenburgh and Maurer, "A Process Framework of Organizational Politics."

63. Perrow, "Departmental Power and Perspectives."

64. Pfeffer, *Power in Organizations,* p. 101.

65. Hickson et al., "A Strategic Contingencies Theory."

66. Pfeffer, *Power in Organizations.*

67. V. Dallas Merrell, *Huddling: The Informal Way to Management Success* (New York: AMACON, 1979).

68. Vredenburgh and Maurer, "A Process Framework of Organizational Politics."

69. Ibid.

70. Pfeffer, *Power in Organizations.*

71. Ibid.

72. Ibid.

73. Ibid.

74. Kanter, "Power Failure in Management Circuits"; Pfeffer, *Power in Organizations.*

75. Kanter, "Power Failure in Management Circuits."

76. Adapted from Hugh D. Menzies, "The Boardroom Battle at Bendix," *Fortune,* January 11, 1982, pp. 54–64; "Things the B-School Never Taught," *Fortune,* November 3, 1980, pp. 53–56; Manuel Velasquez, Dennis J. Moberg, and Gerald F. Cavanaugh, "Organizational Statemanship and Dirty Politics: Ethical Guidelines for the Organizational Politician," *Organizational Dynamics* (Autumn 1983):65–80.

Intergroup Relations and Conflict

IRON & STEEL TRADES CONFEDERATION

> Bill Sirs:
> You are scum. Every worker is ashamed of you. You let the miners down big. How can anyone trust you? All you want is to keep your precious steel works blasting away. I wonder how much you get for doing that from Maggie? Going to retire soon? You come from the Northeast and we are disgusted. You should help us smash Maggie now. Traitor.
>
> A. Redwell

> Dear Mr. Sirs:
> Just a note to let you know that many of us in the coalfields do understand your position. You said on the telly the other night that miners don't understand the steelmen's problems. But we do. And we just wanted to say you're quite right of course, you have to save what plants you have got. We are not stupid and most of us still see you as a brother trade unionist. Good wishes to you and your men.
>
> For four miners, South Yorkshire[1]

Bill Sirs is boss of Britain's biggest steel union, the Iron & Steel Confederation. For months, the mine workers' union has pressured him to order steel workers to stop production to support the coal miners' strike. Arthur Scargill, president of the National Union of Mine Workers, has been locked in a long battle with Prime Minister Margaret Thatcher about closing profitable mines. Scargill has the mine workers out on strike, and Thatcher refuses to compromise. If the steel workers would join the mine workers' strike, sufficient pressure would be brought to bear on the government to force a compromise.

Bill Sirs is solid union. He supports the miners, but cannot condone an additional strike. He is considered a moderate, who believes unions should improve wages and working conditions. But he also understands the bigger picture, and doesn't feel unions should use strikes to kill off the industry that creates the wealth. Indeed, he led a thirteen-week national steel strike in 1980, and won a 15% pay raise for his people. But he also allowed structural change, and the union is smaller now than when he took over in 1975.

Feelings are intense. The mine workers have sent protestors to disrupt Bill Sirs' day. But Sirs will not join this strike. "If you kill off the goose . . . you're left with nothing." Even if the mine workers' strike fails, he's not going to let the new-found profits and prosperity in the steel industry go down with the mine workers.[2]

Bill Sirs is caught in the middle of a dramatic conflict. The original conflict did not even involve his union, yet he was drawn into it because of his union affiliation. The clash between the National Union of Mine Workers and the British government is an example of intergroup conflict. The mine workers are employees who work for the government, and the workers and government officials are groups with different goals. The achievement of one side's goals was blocked by the opposing group.

426

Purpose of This Chapter

The purpose of this chapter is to explore the nature of conflict among groups in organizations. The topic of conflict has appeared in previous chapters. In chapter 6 on structure, integration mechanisms were described to enable coordination among departments. In chapter 9 on decision-making, coalition-building was proposed to overcome disagreements among departmental managers. In chapter 10, political processes were used to resolve disagreements about the allocation of scarce resources and power. The very nature of organizations invites conflict, because organizations are composed of many groups that have diverse and conflicting interests.

In this chapter we are going to examine the nature and resolution of conflict more closely. Organizational conflict comes in many forms. The type of conflict we are concerned with in this chapter occurs between major groups or departments, not between individuals. Departments differ in goals, work activities, and prestige, and their members differ in age, education, and experience. The seeds of conflict are sown in these differences. Conflict has to be effectively managed for the organization to perform effectively and achieve its goals.

In the next section, intergroup conflict is defined, and the consequences of conflict are identified. Then the causes of horizontal conflict in organizations are analyzed, followed by a detailed discussion of techniques for preventing and reducing horizontal conflict. The final section of the chapter turns to vertical conflict, such as between management and unions, and considers techniques for controlling and resolving this conflict.

NATURE OF INTERGROUP CONFLICT

Intergroup conflict requires three ingredients: group identification, observable group differences, and frustration. First, employees have to perceive themselves as part of an identifiable group or department.[3] Second, there has to be observable group difference of some form. Groups may be located in different parts of the building, members may have gone to different schools, or work in different departments. The ability to identify oneself as a part of one group and to observe differences in comparison with other groups is necessary.[4]

The third ingredient is frustration. Frustration means that if one group achieves its goal the other will not, and hence will be blocked. Frustration does not have to be severe, and only needs to be anticipated to set off intergroup conflict. Intergroup conflict will appear when one group tries to advance its position in relation to other groups. We can define **intergroup conflict** as the behavior that occurs between organizational groups when participants identify with one group and perceive that other groups may block their group's goal achievement or expectations.[5] Conflict is similar to competition but more severe. **Competition** means rivalry between groups in the pursuit of their goals, while conflict presumes perceived interference with goal achievement. Intergroup conflict within organizations can occur in both horizontal and vertical directions.

Horizontal Conflict As shown in Exhibit 11.1, horizontal conflict occurs between groups or departments at the same level in the hierarchy, such as

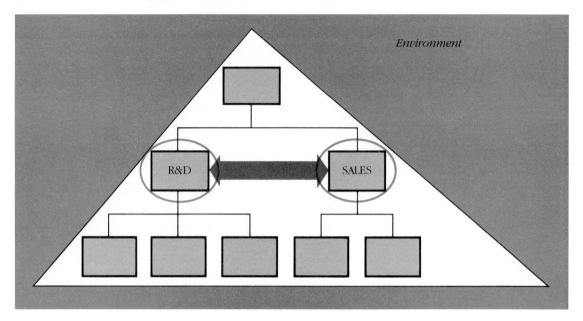

Horizontal Conflict

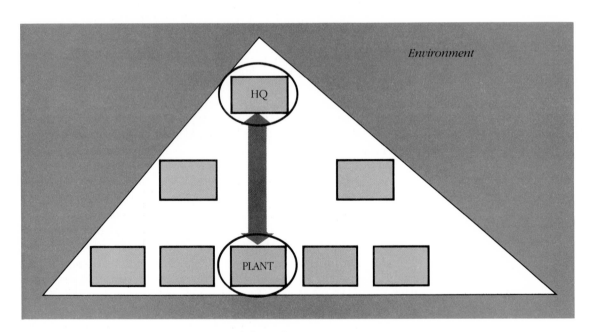

Vertical Conflict

EXHIBIT 11.1. Types of Intergroup Conflict.

between line and staff.[6] Production may have a dispute with quality control because new quality procedures reduce production efficiency. Purchasing may disagree with personnel about the qualifications or salaries of new purchasing agents. R&D and sales may fight over the design for a new product. Horizontal conflict is related to the process of differentiation described in chapter 2. Horizontal integration is needed to reduce conflict and achieve collaboration.

Vertical Conflict Conflict also arises vertically between hierarchical levels.[7] Vertical conflict arises over issues of control, power, goals, and wages and benefits. A typical source of vertical conflict is between headquarters' executives and regional plants or franchises. For example, one study found extensive conflict between a local television station and its New York headquarters.[8] Vertical conflict can occur among any level of the hierarchy, such as between supervisors and their superiors. The most visible form of vertical conflict occurs between management and workers, and is often formalized by union-management relations. The strike between the mine workers union and the British government described at the beginning of this chapter is an example of vertical conflict.

BEHAVIORAL CHANGES FROM INTERGROUP CONFLICT

Intergroup conflict in both vertical and horizontal directions has been studied in a variety of settings. Experimenters and consultants have been able to observe conflict and to test methods for reducing or resolving conflict. This research has provided several insights into the behavioral dynamics that occur within and between groups. Consider, for example, the conflict that occurred between Patco and the Federal Aviation Administration.

IN PRACTICE 11.1

PATCO

In early August 1981, 12,000 of the United States' air traffic controllers joined together in a strike against the federal government. The controllers were supremely confident, dedicated to their cause, and certain they would win.

One month later, the controller's strike seemed to symbolize a suicide march rather than a courageous mission. The controllers' self-confidence was badly eroded. The reaction of the FAA had been seriously miscalculated. The Professional Air Traffic Controllers Organization (PATCO) was frantically seeking a salvage operation that would save the jobs of the controllers and the dignity of the union.

One year later the union was dead. Most of its members were fired from their government jobs. The union was found by the courts to have broken the law by striking against the government. It was decertified.

What happened to bring about such a dramatic shift in the prospects of PATCO union members? Why did PATCO leaders miscalculate so badly?

Union members badly overestimated their importance to air travel and their worth to the government. Members genuinely believed the government could not operate the nation's air transport system without the controllers. They also believed their enormous demands were justified. While controllers probably do endure more stress than ordinary government workers, they are more highly paid than other workers and also have job security. An average salary of $33,000 didn't seem that low to outsiders.

Several other reasons for PATCO's failure also surfaced. One was internal cohesiveness. When the government issued an ultimatum with the backing of the full power of the presidency and the federal government, PATCO didn't flinch. Instead of compromising, PATCO members pulled together to stick it out. The emotional commitment to union solidarity became more important than the logical rationale for the strike.

Moreover, PATCO didn't listen. They refused to believe President Reagan, who insisted that federal strikes are illegal and would be broken regardless of cost. Drew Lewis, Secretary of Transportation, said that if a strike were called, the strikers would be dismissed, and there would be no amnesty. PATCO also didn't gain the support of other unions, such as the Airline Pilots Association or the Machinist's Union. They were overconfident to the point of believing they could shut down the airline system by themselves. Also, they went on strike in the fall, when air transportation is easy to manage. They should have waited until mid-winter when control problems are more severe.

The professional Air Traffic Controllers Organization made several blunders and miscalculations, which had high human and financial costs. The union members are no longer air traffic controllers, and the union itself is dead at the tender age of thirteen.[9]

The behavioral changes that took place among PATCO officials and union members during the strike are similar to changes that take place in most conflict situations. The types of changes frequently observed during inter-group conflict are as follows:[10]

1. People identify with a group very quickly when members have a common goal or activity. Members think of their group as separate and distinct from other groups. They develop pride and they show signs of "we feelings" that characterize an in-group. This in-group identification was very visible among members of PATCO.

2. The presence of another group invites comparison between "we" and "they." Members prefer the in-group to the out-group. The "they" for PATCO members was the Federal Aviation Administration.

3. If a group perceives itself in conflict with another group, it will become more closely knit and cohesive. Members pull together to present a solid front to defeat the other group. A group in conflict tends to become more formal and accepting of autocratic leader behavior. This strong internal cohesiveness was clearly visible among members of PATCO.

4. Group members tend to see other groups as the enemy rather than as a neutral object. PATCO perceived the FAA and the Department of Transportation as adversaries, and members displayed negative sentiments toward them.

5. Group members tend to experience a "superiority complex." They overestimate their own strengths and achievements and underestimate the strength and achievements of other groups. This certainly took place in PATCO. Overconfidence in their ability and strengths was the biggest mistake PATCO made.

6. Communication between competing groups will decrease. If it does take place, it tends to be characterized by negative statements and hostility. Members of one group do not listen or give credibility to statements by the other group. PATCO, for example, did not fully assimilate the statements made by President Reagan and Transportation Secretary Drew Lewis.

7. When one group loses in a conflict, members lose cohesion. Group members experience increased tension and conflict among themselves, and look for a scapegoat to blame for the group's failure. PATCO members at one point blamed one another and their leaders for the strike's failure and their loss of jobs.

8. Intergroup conflict and the associated changes in perception and hostility are not the result of neurotic tendencies on the part of group members. These processes are natural and occur when group members are normal, healthy, and well-adjusted.

These behavioral outcomes of intergroup conflict research were vividly displayed in PATCO. These outcomes can be observed in other organizations. Members of one high school or college often believe their school is superior to a rival school. Employees in one plant perceive themselves as making a greater contribution to the organization than people in other plants. Once these perceptions are understood, they can be accepted as a natural part of intergroup dynamics.

Model of Intergroup Conflict   The model in Exhibit 11.2 illustrates the process of intergroup conflict. The contextual and organizational factors determine the potential for conflict. Attributes of the relationship between specific departments may trigger intergroup conflict, and managers are responsible for managing the interface between groups. The intergroup relationship may not lead to conflict unless a specific incident or frustration triggers a dispute. Then management within the conflicting groups will attempt to change these attributes to resolve the conflict. If the conflict hurts organizational effectiveness, higher level executives may respond by changing contextual and organizational factors. The model in Exhibit 11.2 will serve as an organizing device for the material in the remainder of the chapter. The next section will examine the contextual and organizational attributes associated with horizontal conflict. Then we will turn to a description of techniques managers can use to cope with conflict.

HORIZONTAL CONFLICT

Contextual and Organizational Factors

The potential for horizontal conflict exists in any situation in which separate departments are created, members have an opportunity to compare themselves to other groups, and the goals and values of respective groups appear mutually exclusive. Several of the topics covered in previous chapters explain why organizational groups are in conflict with one another. Let's review five of these.

Environment   Departments are established to interact with major domains in the external environment. As uncertainty and complexity of the environ-

EXHIBIT 11.2. A Model of Intergroup Conflict in Organizations.

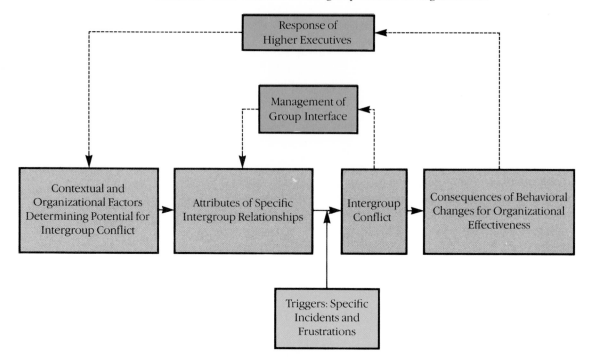

Source: Adapted from Richard E. Walton and John E. Dutton, "The Management of Interdepartmental Conflict," *Administrative Science Quarterly,* 14 (1969):73–84; and Louis R. Pondy, "Organizational Conflict: Concepts and Models," *Administrative Science Quarterly,* 12 (1967):296–320.

ment increases, greater differences among departments in skills, attitudes, power, and operative goals are required. Each department is tailored to "fit" its environmental domain, and thus is differentiated from other organizational groups.

Size   As organizations increase in size, subdivision into a larger number of departments takes place. Rules and regulations evolve to control behavior, but are not always effective. Relationships across departments are often ill-defined and prone to disagreement. The lengthening hierarchy also heightens power and resource differences among departments.

Technology   Technology determines task allocation among departments, as well as the interdependence among departments. Groups that have interdependent tasks interact more often and must share resources. Interdependence creates frequent contacts and situations that lead to conflict.

Goals   The overall goals of the organization are broken down into operative goals that guide each department. Operative goals pursued by marketing, accounting, legal, and personnel departments often seem mutually exclusive. The accomplishment of operative goals by one department may block goal accomplishment by other departments, and hence cause conflict.

Structure   Organization structure reflects the division of labor as well as the systems to facilitate coordination and control. Organization structure also influences the allocation of scarce resources. The choice of a functional versus product structure, for example, means that some groups will be located close together and share similar goals and resources, while other groups will have separate resources and goals.

Attributes of Interdepartmental Relationships

Environment, size, technology, goals, and structure are elements of the organizational context that lead to more or less horizontal conflict between departments. These contextual dimensions determine the specific organizational characteristics that generate conflict, as illustrated in Exhibit 11.3. The organizational context translates into seven attributes of interdepartmental relationships that influence the frequency, extent, and intensity of conflict between departments. These seven characteristics are: (1) operative goal incompatibility, (2) differentiation, (3) task interdependency, (4) resource scarcity, (5) power distribution, (6) uncertainty, and (7) reward systems.

Operative Goal Incompatibility   Goal incompatibility is probably the greatest single cause of intergroup conflict in organizations.[11] The operative goals of each department reflect the specific objectives that members are trying to achieve. The achievement of one department's goal often interferes with another department's goals. University police, for example, have a goal of providing a safe and secure campus. They can achieve their goal by locking all buildings on evenings and weekends and not distributing keys. Without easy access to buildings, however, progress toward the science department's research goals will proceed slowly. On the other hand, if scientists come

EXHIBIT 11.3. Sources of Horizontal Conflict between Departments.

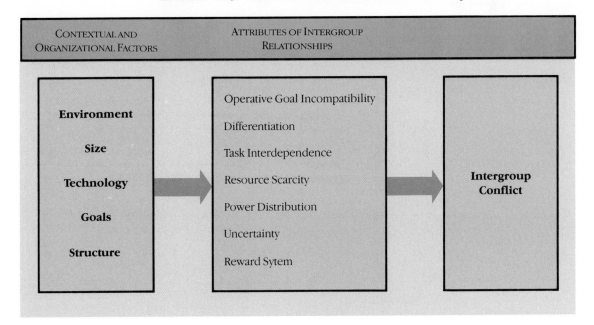

and go at all hours and security is ignored, police goals for security will not be met. Goal incompatibility throws the departments into conflict with each other.

Exhibit 11.4 provides examples of goal conflict between marketing and manufacturing departments. Marketing strives to increase the breadth of the product line to meet customer tastes for variety. A broad product line means short production runs so that manufacturing has to bear higher costs.[12] Other areas of goal conflict are quality, cost control, capacity planning, and new products. Goal incompatibility exists among many departments in most organizations.

Differentiation Differentiation was defined in chapter 2 as "the differences in cognitive and emotional orientations among managers in different functional departments." Organizational tasks require people with specific education, skills, attitudes, and time horizons. People may join a sales department because they have ability and aptitude consistent with sales work. After becoming a member of the sales department, they are influenced by departmental norms and values. The underlying attitudes and traits of per-

EXHIBIT 11.4. Marketing/Manufacturing Areas of Potential Goal Conflict.

Conflict Area	**MARKETING** Operative goal is customer satisfaction **Typical Comment**	**MANUFACTURING** Operative goal is production efficiency **Typical Comment**
1. Breadth of product line	"Our customers demand variety."	"The product line is too broad—all we get are short, uneconomical runs."
2. New product introduction	"New products are our life blood."	"Unnecessary design changes are prohibitively expensive."
3. Production scheduling	"We need faster response. Our lead times are too long."	"We need realistic customer commitments and sales forecasts that don't change like wind direction."
4. Physical distribution	"Why don't we ever have the right merchandise in inventory?"	"We can't keep everything in inventory."
5. Quality	"Why can't we have reasonable quality at reasonable cost?"	"Why must we always offer options that are too hard to manufacture and that offer little customer utility?"

Source: Adapted from Benson S. Shapiro, "Can Marketing and Manufacturing Coexist?" *Harvard Business Review,* 55 (September-October, 1977):104–114.

sonnel differ across departments, and these differences lead to horizontal conflicts.[13] Consider an encounter between a sales manager and an R&D scientist about a new product.

> The sales manager may be outgoing and concerned with maintaining a warm, friendly relationship with the scientist. He may be put off because the scientist seems withdrawn and disinclined to talk about anything other than the problems in which he is interested. He may also be annoyed that the scientist seems to have such freedom in choosing what he will work on. Furthermore, the scientist is probably often late for appointments, which, from the salesman's point of view, is no way to run a business. Our scientist, for his part, may feel uncomfortable because the salesman seems to be pressing for immediate answers to technical questions that will take a long time to investigate. All the discomforts are concrete manifestations of the relatively wide differences between these two men in respect to their working and thinking styles. . . .[14]

An area of frequent difference in personal style and background is between "line" and "staff." Employees that work in line management, especially near the shop floor, often have worked their way up from the bottom, are not college-educated, and have learned the manufacturing values of cost efficiency and short-run deadlines. Members of staff departments often are highly educated in a narrow specialty, are young, new to the organization, and are concerned with long-range projects. These lead to negative sentiments toward one another, as illustrated in the following statement by a staff specialist:

> We're always in hot water with those old guys on the line. You can't tell them a damned thing. They're bullheaded as hell! Most of the time we offer a suggestion it's either laughed at or not considered at all. The same idea in the mouth of some old codger on the line'd get a round of applause. They treat us like kids.[15]

Task Interdependence   Task interdependence refers to the dependence of one unit on another for materials, resources, or information. As described in chapter 4 on technology, pooled interdependence occurs when departments have little interaction with each other. Sequential interdependence means that the output of one department goes to the next department, as on an assembly line. Reciprocal interdependence is the highest form, and means that departments mutually exchange materials and information.[16]

Generally, as interdependence increases, the potential for conflict increases.[17] In the case of pooled interdependence, units have little need to interact. Conflict is at a minimum. Sequential and reciprocal interdependence require employees to spend time coordinating and sharing information. They must interact frequently, and differences in goals or attitudes will surface. Conflict is especially likely to occur when agreement is not reached about the coordination of services to each other. Greater interdependence means that departments often exert pressure for a fast response because departmental work activities have to wait on other departments.[18]

The following example of a purchasing department illustrates how the need to work together and depend upon each other provides the setting for intergroup conflict.

IN PRACTICE 11.2

Purchasing Department

The [Purchasing Department] had two primary functions: (1) to negotiate and place orders at the best possible terms—but only in accordance with specifications set by others—and (2) to expedite orders, that is, to check with suppliers to make sure that deliveries are made on time.

The purchasing agent would also like to suggest (1) alternative materials or parts to use, (2) changes in specifications or redesign of components that will save money or result in higher quality or quicker delivery, (3) more economical lot sizes, and (4) ways to influence "make or buy" decisions. The agent calls these functions "value analysis."

Normally orders flow in one direction only, from engineering through scheduling to purchasing. But the agent is dissatisfied with being at the end of the line and seeks to reverse the flow. Value analysis permits him to initiate for others. Such behavior may, however, result in ill feeling on the part of other departments, particularly engineering and production scheduling.

Engineers write up the specifications for the products that the agents buy. If the specifications are too tight, or what is worse, if they call for one brand only, agents have little or no freedom to choose among suppliers. Yet engineers find it much easier to write down a well-known brand name than to draw up a lengthy functional specification which lists all the characteristics of the desired item. . . .

The size of the order and the date on which it is to be delivered are typically determined by production scheduling. The agent's chief complaint against scheduling is that delivery is often requested on excessively short notice—that schedulers engage in sloppy planning or "cry wolf" by claiming they need orders earlier than they really do—and thus force the agent to choose from a limited number of suppliers, to pay premium prices, and to ask favors of salespeople (thus creating obligations that the agent must later repay). Schedulers, on the other hand, claim that "short lead times" are not their fault, but the fault of the departments further up the line, such as engineering (which delays its blueprints) or sales (which accepts rush orders).[19]

Engineering and production scheduling both depend upon purchasing to acquire products at favorable terms. Purchasing depends upon engineering for specification and production scheduling for delivery dates. These interdependencies cause frequent conflict.

Resource Scarcity Another major source of conflict involves competition between groups for what members perceive as limited resources.[20] Organizations have only a limited amount of money, physical facilities, staff resources, and human resources to share among departments. In their desire to achieve goals, groups want to increase their resources. This throws them into conflict. Managers may develop strategies, such as inflating budget requirements or working behind the scenes, to obtain the desired level of resources. Resources also symbolize power and influence within the organization. The ability to obtain resources enhances prestige. Departments typically believe they have a legitimate claim on additional resources, but exercising that claim results in conflict.

Conflict over resources tends to be minimized in a growing organization. If the organization is prospering and new resources are flowing in, departments can increase resources without taking away from other groups. In the case of organizational decline (chapter 5), the size of the resource pool is shrinking and intergroup conflict is at its greatest intensity. The very survival of subgroups is at stake, and pressure to maintain resources will be great.

Power Distribution   As we saw in the previous chapter, power differences evolve even when departments are at the same level on the organization chart. Some departments provide a more valuable service, or reduce critical uncertainties for the organization. Power differences provide a basis for conflict, especially when actual working relationships do not correspond to perceived power.[21] In the following case, a department with less power tried to tell a more powerful department what to do.

IN PRACTICE 11.3

Engineering Department

The engineering department took research designs and translated them into parts lists, production drawings, and fabrication and assembly specifications, and in addition processed engineering change orders (ECOs). Much of production's work—both its content and its timing—depended on production engineering's efforts, since product designs were constantly changing.

Engineering was seen by production as telling production what to do and when to do it. On the other hand, engineering was composed of people with skills no greater than—in fact, quite similar to—those possessed by production members. Production felt itself capable of performing not only engineering's tasks but the more important tasks of job design and methods work that were within production's jurisdiction but outside engineering's.

Production managers spent an inordinate amount of time checking for consistency among the various items produced by production engineering. When errors were discovered (as they seldom were), a cry of victory would ring out across the production office. A messenger would quickly be dispatched to carry the offending material back to engineering, amply armed with a message elaborately outlining the stupidity that had produced such an error. The most common topic of production conversation centered about "those goddam ECOs," in spite of the fact that production originated as many ECOs (making changes for its own convenience) as did any other department.[22]

In this case, energies were focused on the impropriety of a low-prestige department like engineering calling the tune for an equally prestigious or even superior department like production. Production devoted its energies to rebalancing power between the two departments. In other words, production's prestige could be maintained only by calling more tunes than it danced. This rebalancing process had little to do with accomplishing any work. Yet it consumed vast amounts of production management time.

Uncertainty   Another important factor for predicting intergroup conflict is the uncertainty experienced by organizational departments. When activities are predictable, departments know where they stand. They can rely on rules or previous decisions to resolve disputes that arise. When factors in the environment are rapidly changing or when problems arise that are poorly understood, departments may have to renegotiate their respective tasks.[23] Managers have to sort out how new problems should be handled. The boundaries of a department's territory or jurisdiction become indistinct. Members may reach out to take on more responsibility only to find other groups feel invaded. In a study of hospital purchasing decisions, managers reported significantly higher levels of conflict when purchases were nonroutine than when purchases were routine.[24] Generally, as uncertainty about departmental relationships increases, conflict can be expected to increase.

Reward System The reward system governs the degree to which subgroups cooperate or conflict with one another.[25] An experiment with student groups illustrated how incentives influence conflict.[26] In one-half of the groups, called cooperative groups, each student's grade was the grade given for the group's project. All students in each group, regardless of individual contribution, received the same grade. In the remaining groups, called competitive groups, students were rewarded on the basis of their personal contribution to the group project. Each student was graded individually, and could receive a high or low grade regardless of the overall group score.

The outcome of these incentives on conflict was significant. When the incentive system rewarded members for accomplishing the group goal (cooperative groups), coordination among members was better, communication among members was better, productivity was greater, and the quality of the group product was better. When individuals were graded according to their personal contributions to the group (competitive groups), they communicated less with each other and were more frequently in conflict. Members tried to protect themselves and to succeed at the expense of others in the group. Quality of the group project and productivity were lower.

Incentives and rewards have similar impact on conflict between organizational departments. When department managers are rewarded for achieving the goal of the organization, cooperation among departments is greater. Bechtel, for example, provides a bonus system to division managers based upon the achievement of Bechtel profit goals. Regardless of how well a manager's division does, the manager isn't rewarded unless the corporation performs well. This incentive system motivates division managers to cooperate with each other. If departments are rewarded only for departmental performance, managers are motivated to excel at the expense of the rest of the organization.

SHOULD HORIZONTAL
CONFLICT BE SUPPRESSED?

In the above section, we looked at several causes and examples of horizontal conflict. In this section, we want to consider whether conflict is healthy for organizations, that is, to what extent conflict should be reduced or suppressed. Then we will explore several techniques for managing the level of horizontal conflict in organizations.

Two Views

Traditional View[27] Is conflict bad for the organization? Early writings on management said that it was. Members of the "human relations" school saw conflict as unhealthy, and said it should be eliminated from organizations.[28] Conflict was perceived as an unfortunate event that should be reduced as much as possible. An effective organization should be cooperative and peaceful.

Pluralistic View More recent views argue that conflict is inevitable in organizations and, indeed, is beneficial.[29] An organization without conflict is not sufficiently differentiated in goals, skills, and attitudes to be successful. Conflict is a sign of health and energy, and should be controlled only so that it does not get out of hand. This view has been called the pluralistic view of conflict.[30] Exhibit 11.5 summarizes the two views.

Interdepartmental conflict can have both positive and negative outcomes. If an organization achieves the ideal of no conflict, the organization is probably in trouble. Conflict is a sign of an active, ongoing, forceful organization. Conflict becomes a problem only when there is too much of it. Too much conflict leads to the waste of valuable human and material resources. Some of the benefits and wastes associated with horizontal conflict, summarized in Exhibit 11.6, are as follows.

Benefits from Conflict

1. *Productive Task Focus.* When a group is experiencing moderate levels of conflict, within-group differences are submerged, and members focus on the task at hand. The natural differences that evolve between groups, such as in dress, age, education, and attitudes suit the task at hand. Engineering people can be successful at engineering tasks when they have a long-time horizon, are college educated, young, and project-oriented. Manufacturing personnel, on the other hand, can perform their task effectively when they have a short-time horizon, are oriented toward production goals, and are somewhat older

EXHIBIT 11.5. Underlying Beliefs about Conflict.

Traditional Approach	Pluralistic Approach
1. Conflict, by and large, is "bad" and should be eliminated or resolved.	1. Conflict is good and should be encouraged; conflict must be regulated, however, so that it does not get out of hand.
2. Conflict need not occur.	2. Conflict is inevitable.
3. Conflict results from breakdowns in communication and lack of understanding, trust, and openness between groups.	3. Conflict results from a struggle for limited rewards, competition, and potential frustration of goals—conditions that are natural in organizations.
4. People are essentially good; trust, cooperation, and goodness are givens in human nature.	4. People are not essentially bad, but are nevertheless driven by achievement, self-seeking, and competitive interests.

Source: Adapted from Donald Nightingale, "Conflict and Conflict Resolution," in George Strauss, Raymond Miles, Charles Snow, and Arnold Tannenbaum, eds., *Organizational Behavior: Research and Issues* (Belmont, Calif.: Wadsworth Publishing Company, 1976).

EXHIBIT 11.6. Benefits and Losses from Interdepartmental Conflict.

Benefits	Losses
1. Productive Task Focus	1. Diversion of Energy
2. Cohesion and Satisfaction	2. Altered Judgment
3. Power Equalization and Feedback	3. Loser Effects
4. Goal Attainment	4. Poor Coordination

and experienced. The characteristics that lead to conflict are the same characteristics that enable departments to excel at their respective tasks.[31]

2. *Cohesion and Satisfaction.* "We-feelings" and in-group identification add to group cohesion. Members are attracted to the group, and receive satisfaction from their membership. Members cooperate with each other and suspend the achievement of personal goals in order to achieve departmental goals. Group membership under conditions of mild intergroup conflict can be very satisfying to employees.[32]

3. *Power and Feedback.* The occasional flare-up of intergroup conflict serves both to balance power relationships across departments and to provide feedback to managers about the department's standing in the organization. Employees often have distorted perceptions about their roles and importance. They may expect and demand undue amounts of organization resources. Conflict with other groups will blunt these excesses.[33] Conflict calls attention to problems within the organization and balances disparities among groups. The feedback from conflict enables groups to correct their perceptions. Feedback acts as a regulatory mechanism. If power or resources are skewed out of balance toward certain groups, conflict will help correct the balance.

4. *Goal Attainment.* The organization's ability to achieve overall goals is related to the energy directed toward operational goals at the departmental level. Moderate competition and conflict serve to stimulate participants to work hard.[34] Cohesion results in an enjoyable work atmosphere. The intensity of an athletic team achieving its goal is an example of the benefits of competition. Complacency can be as great a problem as too much conflict.[35] The organization can prosper and achieve its overall goals only when subgroups are actively doing their tasks well.

Losses from Conflict

When conflict is carried too far, several negative consequences for the organization may occur.

1. *Diversion of Energy.* One of the most serious consequences is the diversion of a department's time and effort toward winning the conflict rather than toward achieving organization goals.[36] When the most important outcome becomes defeating other departments, no holds barred, resources are wasted. In extreme cases, sabotage, secrecy, and even illegal activities occur.

2. *Altered Judgment.* One of the findings from intergroup research is that judgment and perceptions become less accurate when conflict becomes more intense. The overconfidence and unrealistic expectations of PATCO members in IN PRACTICE 11.1 was an example. Groups may mistakenly blame opponents within the organization rather than acknowledge their own short-

comings. People involved in conflict also have a poor understanding of ideas offered by competitors.[37]

3. *Loser Effects.* Another unfortunate aspect of intense organizational conflict is that someone normally loses. The losing department undergoes substantial change. Losers tend to deny or distort the reality of losing. They often seek scapegoats, perhaps even members or leaders in their own department. Dissension replaces cohesion. Losers generally tend toward low cooperation and low concern for the needs and interests of other department members.[38]

4. *Poor Coordination.* The final problem with conflict is the emphasis given to achieving departmental goals. Departmental goals serve to energize employees, but these goals should not become an all-consuming priority. Departmental goals must be integrated with the goals of the organization. Under intense conflict, integration does not happen. Collaboration across groups decreases. Groups have less contact, and they are not sympathetic to other points of view. Under intense conflict, departmental goals and defeating the enemy take priority. There is no room for compromise. This rigid point of view is not in the interest of the organization.[39]

Managed Conflict

The benefits and wastes of conflict are related to amount of conflict. With too little conflict, the benefits of stimulation, cohesion, and task focus are lost. With too much conflict, the organization suffers negative outcomes. Managers should try to maintain a balance between too much and too little conflict.

Managed conflict is an intermediate level of intergroup conflict.[40] Managed conflict recognizes that conflict can be both beneficial and harmful. Managers strive for the benefits, while avoiding harmful effects. Managed conflict recognizes that organizational conflict is inevitable, even necessary. Executives should actively manage conflict toward an appropriate level rather than ignore or suppress it.

A continuum of conflict in organizations and the outcomes at each level is shown in Exhibit 11.7. The zones of too much or too little conflict should be avoided. The ideal conflict strategy is to maintain the organization in the intermediate zone. In the zone of managed conflict, group members identify

EXHIBIT 11.7. Levels of Interdepartmental Conflict and Organization Outcomes.

Zone of Complacency	Zone of Managed Conflict	Zone of Intense Conflict
Very Low Conflict ⟵⟶ Very High Conflict		
Poor Task Focus	Productive Task Focus	Diverted Energy
No Goal Orientation	High Cohesion	Distorted Judgment and Perceptions
Little Cohesion	Balance between Unit and Organization Goals	Loser Effects
No Competitive Stimulation	Stimulation	Organizational Goals Suffer
No Feedback about Intergroup Relations	Feedback about Intergroup Relationships	Distorted Feedback

with their group, are cohesive, and strive toward group goals. They also will compromise their goals for organizational benefit, and cooperate with other groups. Managed conflict means that moderate conflict should be encouraged, but conflict should not get out of control.

TECHNIQUES FOR MANAGING
CONFLICT BETWEEN GROUPS

Organizations are a collection of interest groups vying to achieve goals with limited resources. The ideal situation for most organizations is to have moderate inter-unit competition and conflict. But in many organizations, the problem is too much conflict rather than complacency. Conflict often gets out of hand. The purchasing department simply will not cooperate with the engineering department; the finance clerks won't talk to the accounting clerks. In these situations, departments adopt the goal of fighting each other. Most of the techniques developed for managing conflict between groups are designed to manage conflict that is too intense. We briefly cover a few ways to prevent or stimulate conflict. Then we will discuss several current techniques for managing conflict that is too high.

Preventing Conflict

Techniques for preventing conflict are used to keep conflict from increasing. Managers are often satisfied with the level of conflict, but wish to prevent it from getting out of control. Preventing conflict is often easier than undoing conflicts that have reached an intense level.

1. *Structural Separation or Combination.* Disaggregating or decoupling conflicting departments so they are physically separated is perhaps the surest way to prevent conflict. Groups are simply prevented from interacting with each other.[41] Separation is feasible when groups are not needed to work on a joint task. Combining or merging departments is another structural solution. Groups then share common resources, a common goal, and common supervision. Merging departments is similar to the self-contained unit structure described in chapter 6.

2. *Provide Stable, Independent Tasks.* When activities are well-understood, clearly defined, and independent, conflict is less likely to occur. If tasks can be designed so that each department works independently, employees will not have to interact to coordinate work activities. Conflict is likely to occur when activities and responsibilities are not well defined so that groups have to negotiate their respective positions.[42] When tasks are well defined, employees know the limits of their authority and their place in the organization.

3. *Expand Resources.* Insufficient resources to enable departments to achieve goals are a major source of conflict. If the amount of resources to conflicting departments can be increased, each can achieve its goal without blocking the other. If the organization has sufficient resources, each department can be a winner, and this reduces the potential for future conflict. If resources are scarce, managers should avoid putting departments in a position of intense competition for resources. Managers should pool resources to achieve maximum organizational contributions.[43]

4. *Joint Problem-Solving.* Engaging groups to work directly with one another to solve joint problems is an effective way to prevent conflict.[44] Mutual problem-solving means that departments collaborate rather than compete. Differences of opinion and goals can be surfaced and discussed. Frequent meetings can be used to solve problems and increase communication. Joint problem-solving often enables the groups to achieve a workable compromise or to integrate needs so that both goals can be attained. Joint problem-solving needs to be a continuous activity between groups in order to prevent and forestall conflict.

Stimulating Conflict

In a few organizational situations, departments are complacent. Employees are not energized, nor do they display cohesion or a productive task focus. In these cases managers may wish to induce moderate amounts of conflict using the following techniques.

1. *Increase Competition.* Conflict can be stimulated by creating competitive situations between departments. University academic departments can be encouraged to compete for teaching awards, and police department precincts can compete against each other to win the "Best Precinct" award. Competition enhances the identification with one's work group, but the competition should be temporary and constructive. Long-term competition that results in a loser with respect to major organizational resources would not be productive. New awards can be created to acknowledge winners in the competition, and to prevent other departments from becoming major losers.

2. *Increase Uncertainty.* Increasing uncertainty simply means to break up the traditional, patterned ways of doing things. This could mean bringing outsiders into key management posts who have new ideas and fresh energy. Another device is to create or assign new tasks to departments. Traditional procedures can be changed to create uncertainty that enables moderate amounts of conflict to flourish. Managers can also install the "devil's advocate" method to encourage conflict during decision-making. The devil's advocate method assigns different points of view to departments who are to champion these views during meetings.[45] In this way diverse perspectives from across departments are surfaced. Moderate conflict is thus engendered and departments are able to advocate their own opinions and positions.

3. *Redesign Rewards and Task Interdependencies.* If the organization has become stagnant and stale, the reward system and joint tasks can be redesigned. The reward system can encourage competition. Managers can give greater emphasis to departmental success. Increasing task interdependencies force groups to interact on a continuous basis and thus to strive for improved performance. Increasing interdependence means departments must cooperate, but also perform their own task successfully. Redesign of rewards and joint tasks provide an opportunity for moderate competition and conflict to take hold.

Managing Conflict

Managing extant conflict is often a greater challenge than stimulating or preventing conflict. When conflict is too great, participants may actively dislike each other, and may not want to change. The target of conflict management techniques is either the **behavior** or the **attitude** of group members.[46] By changing behavior, open conflict is reduced or eliminated, but department members will still dislike people in the other departments. A change in behavior makes the conflict less visible, or keeps the groups separated. A change in attitude is deeper and takes longer. A new attitude is difficult to achieve and requires a reduction in the negative perceptions and feelings of department members. A change in attitude also includes a change in behavior.

The techniques available for managing conflict are arranged along a scale in Exhibit 11.8. Techniques near the top of the scale, such as physically separating groups, will change behavior but not attitudes.[47] The techniques near the bottom of the scale, such as rotating group members or intergroup training, are designed to bring about change in basic understanding between groups.

Bureaucratic Authority Bureaucratic authority means that top management invokes rules, regulations, and formal authority to resolve the conflict issue or to suppress the conflict. For example, the advertising and sales departments may disagree about advertising strategy. The salesforce may want a strategy based on direct mail, while advertising prefers to use radio and television. This type of conflict can be resolved by passing it to the next level of the hierarchy, the marketing vice-president, who uses legitimate authority to resolve a conflict. The disadvantage is that it does not change attitudes and may treat only the immediate problem. The bureaucratic method is effective in the short run when members cannot agree on a solution to a specific conflict.[48]

Limited Interaction Limited communication between departments prevents the development of misperceptions about the abilities, skills, and traits

EXHIBIT 11.8. Strategies for Reducing Conflict Between Groups.

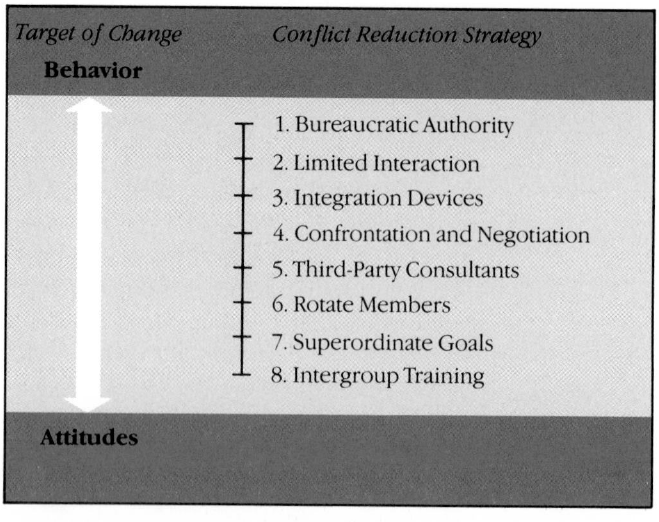

Target of Change
Behavior

Conflict Reduction Strategy

1. Bureaucratic Authority
2. Limited Interaction
3. Integration Devices
4. Confrontation and Negotiation
5. Third-Party Consultants
6. Rotate Members
7. Superordinate Goals
8. Intergroup Training

Attitudes

Source: Adapted from Eric H. Neilson, "Understanding and Managing Conflict," in Jay W. Lorsch and Paul R. Lawrence, eds., *Managing Group and Intergroup Relations* (Homewood, IL: Irwin and Dorsey, 1972), pp. 329–343.

of other departments. When departments are in conflict, controlled interaction can be used to resolve the conflict. Often the interaction can be limited to issues about which the departments are in conflict, yet have a common goal. A common goal means that the departments must talk and cooperate, at least for the achievement of that goal. For example, Datapoint Corporation experiences frequent conflict between the research and development and manufacturing divisions. Since senior managers in these divisions are located in the same city, a forum was devised for them to resolve differences. "Summit meetings" were created where managers could bring their cases for discussion and resolution. A dispute about R&D security in a new building was resolved in this fashion.[49] Limited interaction is most effective when rules of decision-making and intereaction are well-defined. This technique may make a small impact on attitude change.[50]

Integration Devices   Integration devices were described in chapter 6 as people or task forces who span the boundary between departments. Integration devices must have legitimacy and expertise in the eyes of both groups, otherwise they will not be trusted or used. Sometimes a full-time integrator is assigned to achieve cooperation and collaboration by meeting with members of the respective departments and exchanging information. The integrator has to understand each group's problems and be able to move both groups toward a solution that is mutually acceptable. The integrator may work continuously to keep conflicts between key departments at modest levels.[51] An example of the use of a committee to achieve integration and reduce conflict was the TQA at Whirlpool.

IN PRACTICE 11.4

Whirlpool Corporation

"Historically, we have worked pretty much in a vacuum," confesses Jeryl I. Schornhorst, director of automatic washer engineering at Whirlpool Corp., a major U.S. maker of home appliances. For years, he and his colleagues involved in Whirlpool's product planning worked on new designs without much contact with their colleagues in manufacturing engineering. "We would design the parts and send prints out to manufacturing," explains Schornhorst. "Whatever it took to make things, it was their business."

In 1979, Whirlpool senior management established procedures aimed squarely at boosting productivity and quality by forcing the two disciplines to work together. They gave it its own acronym, TQA, for total quality assurance.

Unlike earlier practices in which manufacturing engineering did not start work until the product design was virtually finished, the two review processes now start off almost simultaneously and continue in parallel. "You don't just throw the design over the wall any more," says Alvin J. Elders, general manager of laundry engineering for Whirlpool. "This is a management system that brings people together to design for quality."

The product planners first develop the general concept. But as soon as they have the basic idea down, the process changes. Manufacturing, as well as other disciplines, now become involved. First, the design itself faces a committee made up of people selected from every function that has a stake in it—from manufacturing to purchasing to home economics. Second, once over this hurdle, a manufacturing team starts working on the production process for it. And to further integrate functions, a separate, multifunctional review committee is established to go over manufacturing plans. The total number of formal reviews varies, but major projects go through at least six full reviews, three of the project and three of the manufacturing process.

Despite some early hitches, Whirlpool's TQA program is breaking down barriers between functions. "It has been slow—it has taken more time to adapt to the parallel approach than we expected," admits Koch, adding: "As more and more people have been involved, it's running along more smoothly." Product designer Schornhorst agrees: "American industry has tended to compartmentalize engineering. Now we're systematizing integration." [52]

Confrontation and Negotiation   **Confrontation** occurs when parties in conflict directly engage one another and try to work out their differences. **Negotiation** is the bargaining process that often occurs during confrontation that enables the parties to systematically reach a solution. These techniques bring appointed members of the departments together to work out a serious dispute. Confrontation and negotiation involve some risk. There is no guarantee that discussions will focus on the conflict or that emotions will not get out of hand. However, if members are able to resolve the conflict on the basis of face-to-face discussions, they will find new respect for each other and future collaboration becomes easier. The beginnings of relatively permanent attitude change are possible through direct negotiation.

Confrontation is successful when managers engage in a "win-win" strategy. Win-win means that both departments adopt a positive attitude and strive to resolve the conflict in a way that will benefit each other.[53] If the negotiations deteriorate into a strictly win-lose strategy (each group wants to defeat the other), the confrontation will be ineffective. Top management can urge group members to work toward mutually acceptable outcomes. The differences between win-win and win-lose strategies of negotiation are shown in Exhibit 11.9. With a win-win strategy—which includes defining the problem as mutual, communicating openly, and avoiding threats—understanding can be changed while resolving the dispute.

Third-Party Consultants   When conflict is intense, enduring, and department members are suspicious and uncooperative, a third-party consultant can be brought in from outside the organization to meet with representatives from both departments. These consultants should be experts on human behavior, and their advice and actions must be valued by both groups. Third-party consultants can make great progress toward changing attitudes and reducing conflict. Typical activities of third-party consultants are as follows.

■ Reestablish broken communication lines between groups.
■ Act as interpreter so that messages between groups are correctly understood and are not distorted by preconceived biases.
■ Challenge and bring out into the open the stereotyping done by one group or the other. Exposing stereotypes often leads to their dissolution.
■ Bring into awareness the positive acts and intentions of the other group.

EXHIBIT 11.9. Negotiating Strategies.

Win-Win Strategy	Win-Lose Strategy
1. Define the conflict as a mutual problem.	1. Define the conflict as a win-lose situation.
2. Pursue joint outcomes.	2. Pursue own group's outcomes.
3. Find creative agreements that satisfy both groups.	3. Force the other group into submission.
4. Use open, honest, and accurate communication of group's needs, goals, and proposals.	4. Use deceitful, inaccurate, and misleading communication of group's needs, goals, and proposals.
5. Avoid threats (to reduce the other's defensiveness).	5. Use threats (to force submission).
6. Communicate flexibility of position.	6. Communicate high commitment (rigidity) regarding one's position.

Source: Adapted from David W. Johnson and Frank P. Johnson, *Joining Together: Group Theory and Group Skills* (Englewood Cliffs, NJ: Prentice-Hall, 1975), pp. 182–183.

This forces a cognitive reassessment of their stance toward the other group.

■ The specific source of conflict must be defined and focused, and the surrounding emotions removed. Extraneous issues have to be ignored while the group is brought back into concentration on the key cause of conflict.[54]

Member Rotation　　Rotation means that individuals from one department can be asked to work in another department on a temporary or permanent basis. The advantage is that individuals become submerged in the values, attitudes, problems, and goals of the other department. In addition, the individuals can explain the problems and goals of their original departments to their new colleagues. This enables a frank, accurate exchange of views and information. Rotation works slowly to reduce conflict, and requires a long period of time, but it is very effective for changing the underlying attitudes and perceptions that promote conflict.[55] The following case illustrates the successful use of member rotation in one company.

IN PRACTICE 11.5
Canadian-Atlantic

Canadian-Atlantic, a transportation conglomerate headquartered in Vancouver, British Columbia, experienced intense conflict between research managers and operating managers at the home office. Research managers were responsible for developing operational innovations, such as for loading railroad cars, to increase operational efficiency. Operations managers were responsible for scheduling and running trains.

Operations management had absolutely no use for research personnel. They claimed that research personnel took far too long to do projects. One manager said, "A 50% solution when we need it is much better than a 100%

solution ten years from now when the crisis is over." Operating managers were also offended by the complicated terminology and jargon used by research personnel. Research personnel had developed several useful innovations, such as automated loading platforms and training simulators, but resistance to the innovations was great. Research personnel wanted to cooperate with operations managers, but they could not go along with certain requests. Researchers refused to release half-completed innovations, or to water down their ideas for less well-educated personnel in operations. One manager commented that the extent of communication between research and operations "was just about zero, and both groups are beginning to like it that way."

The vice-president of research and development was worried. He believed that intergroup hostility was dramatically reducing the effectiveness of R&D. Morale in R&D was low and operations managers had little interest in new developments. The vice-president persuaded the president to try rotating managers between operations and research. Initially, one manager from each department was exchanged. Later, two and three were exchanged simultaneously. Each rotation lasted about six months. After two and one-half years, the relationship between the departments was vastly improved. Key individuals now understood both points of view and could work to integrate the differences that existed. One operations manager enjoyed the work in research so much that he asked to stay on. The operations vice-president tried to hire two of the R&D managers to work permanently in his division.

Superordinate Goals   Another strategy is for top management to establish superordinate goals that require cooperation between departments.[56] Conflicting departments now share the same goal and must depend upon one another to achieve it. A superordinate goal, to be effective, must be significant and must consume a substantial amount of each group's time and energy. The reward system can also be redesigned to encourage the pursuit of the superordinate goal rather than departmental subgoals. One powerful goal is company survival. If the organization is about to fail and jobs will be lost, groups forget their differences and try to save the organization. The goal of survival has dramatically improved relationships between groups in meat packing plants and auto supply firms that have been about to go out of business.

Intergroup Training   The strongest intervention to reduce conflict is intergroup training. This technique has been developed by psychologists such as Blake, Mouton, and Walton.[57] When other techniques fail to reduce conflict to an appropriate level, or when other techniques do not fit the organization in question, extensive group training may be required. This training requires that department members attend an outside workshop away from day-to-day work problems. The training workshop may last several days, and various activities take place. This technique is expensive, but has great impact on attitude change. Intergroup training is similar to the OD approach described in chapter 7 on innovation and change. The steps typically associated with an intergroup training session are as follows:

1. The competing groups are both brought into a training setting and the common goals are stated to be an exploration of mutual perceptions and mutual relations.

2. The two groups are then separated and each group is invited to discuss and make a list of its perceptions of itself and the other group.

3. In the presence of both groups, representatives publicly share the perceptions of self and other that the groups have generated, while the groups are obligated to remain silent. The objective is simply to report to the other group as accurately as possible the images that each group has developed in private.

4. Before any exchange takes place, the groups return to private sessions to digest and analyze what they have heard; there is great likelihood that the representatives' reports have revealed discrepancies to each group between its self-image and the image that the other group holds of it. The private session is partly devoted to an analysis of the reasons for these discrepancies, which forces each group to review its actual behavior toward the other group and the possible consequences of that behavior, regardless of its intentions.

5. In public session, again working through representatives, each group shares with the other what discrepancies it has uncovered and the possible reasons for them, focusing on actual, observable behavior.

6. Following this mutual exposure, a more open exploration is permitted between the two groups on the now-shared goal of identifying further reasons for perceptual distortions.

7. A joint exploration is then conducted of how to manage future relations in such a way as to minimize a recurrence of the conflict.[58]

After this training experience, department employees understand each other much better. The improved attitudes lead to better working relationships for a long time.

VERTICAL CONFLICT

The discussion so far in this chapter has dealt with horizontal conflict between departments. Vertical conflict occurs between groups at different levels along the vertical hierarchy. Some of the same concepts apply to vertical conflict, but the groups and issues tend to be different.

Vertical conflict can take various forms. Student groups may find themselves in conflict with faculty or administration about the teaching versus research goals of the university. Individual employees may have conflicts with their bosses. Managers of geographic or product divisions often experience conflict with senior executives located at headquarters.

One visible and sometimes troublesome area of conflict within organizations is between management and workers, who are often represented by a union. All too often we see union or management representatives on television explaining why the other side is wrong and why a strike or lockout is necessary. These conflicts often occur in major industries such as transportation and steel, and in specialized areas such as sports or air traffic controllers.

Status and power differences between groups are greater for vertical conflict than for horizontal conflict. Part of the reason vertical conflict occurs is to equalize power differences. Unions try to give workers more power over wages or working conditions. Moreover, the ground rules for conflict between workers and management are formalized by laws and regulations. Formal negotiation procedures are available in which appointed representatives work to resolve differences. The conflict between union and management is thus different from conflict that occurs horizontally across departments. In this section, we explore some of the reasons for union-management conflicts, and techniques for its reduction.

SOURCES OF UNION-MANAGEMENT CONFLICT

Vertical conflict can exist with or without a union, but conflict is more visible when workers join a union. The union formalizes vertical differences, and provides a mechanism for resolving these differences. Workers form into unions for a variety of reasons:

1. *Psychological Distance.* Workers do not feel involved in the organization. They perceive that their needs are not being met. A union is a way of giving voice to these needs. The union provides workers with a clear group identity. Once the union is formed, members identify with the union, not the company, and try to achieve gains through the union. This often throws union and management into a win-lose conflict situation.

2. *Power and Status.* Workers are at the bottom of the hierarchy, and often feel powerless and alienated. They have little say in decisions that directly affect their lives, such as wages and benefits. Standing together in a union gives them strength that equalizes their power with management's. This power is restricted to areas directly affecting workers, but it is still more power than workers have alone.[59]

3. *Ideology.* One of the most basic differences between management and workers pertains to values and ideology. These differences represent basic beliefs about the purpose and goals of organizations and unions.[60] Major

EXHIBIT 11.10. Differences in Union-Management Beliefs.

	Strength of Belief	
Ideological Belief	Union Members	Management
1. Seniority	High	Low
2. Right to engage in a legal strike/ boycott	High	Low
3. Union security	High	Low
4. Free enterprise system	Low	High
5. Right to continue work during a legal strike/boycott	Low	High
6. Management rights	Low	High
7. Use of work quotas to measure performance	Low	High

Source: Adapted from Roger S. Wolters, "Union-Management Ideological Frames of Reference," *Journal of Management,* 8 (1982):21–33.

ideological differences were identified in a survey of managers and union members, and are listed in Exhibit 11.10. Union members strongly believe in seniority, the right to engage in a strike, and union security. Managers believe more strongly in the free enterprise system, the right to work during a strike, management rights, and the use of quotas to measure performance. These basic value differences represent a major conflict that has to be overcome in order for union and management to cooperate successfully.

4. *Scarce Resources.* Another important issue between unions and management is financial resources. Salary, fringe benefits, and working conditions are dominant bargaining issues. Workers look to the union to obtain financial benefits. Unions may strike if necessary to get the pay and benefits they want.

5. *Environmental Factors.* Other factors sometimes influence unionization or the amount of conflict that occurs between union and management. These include the technology of the organization, which can vary from white-collar jobs to assembly-line work. Other settlements in the same industry may determine worker expectations. State and local laws and public opinion are also important. Unions are less powerful in states with right-to-work laws. The personalities of the representatives may influence the goals and conflicts between workers and management.

The example at the beginning of this chapter of Bill Sirs, chief of the Iron & Steel Trades Confederation in Britain, illustrates how pressure was put on him from another union in the area because the other union needed help to gain government concessions.

STRENGTH OF UNION-MANAGEMENT CONFLICT

One of the most interesting studies to explore the underlying dynamics in union-management relationships was conducted by Blake and Mouton.[61] The study involved managers who were placed in competing roles similar to those experienced in union-management conflict.

The managers from a large company were brought together in a laboratory training session. They were divided into groups of from nine to twelve persons. Participants worked intensively with their own groups and developed a strong in-group identification. They worked as a group throughout the training period of from ten days to two weeks.

Each group was placed in conflict with another group. The groups were given a problem that would measure problem-solving effectiveness. The problem was presented so that both groups realized that one group would be a winner and one group a loser. This forced the groups into an intensive win-lose situation. Each group was given thirteen hours (overnight) to develop a solution.

Under this form of conflict, several behaviors were observed.

1. *Increased Group Cohesion.* Differences among managers within each group disappeared as group members closed ranks and concentrated on winning.

2. *Distorted Perceptions.* Each group developed a superiority complex. Virtually all groups saw themselves as "above average."

3. *Distorted Judgment.* After all solutions were presented, each group evaluated its own solution as best. Members were not fairminded or rational in making judgments. They believed in their own group's solutions and downgraded solutions of other groups.

4. *Unequal Knowledge.* Experimenters worked with each group to ensure a full understanding of their own and their competitors' solutions. When group members indicated full understanding of the other group's solution, an examination was given. All those surveyed had much greater knowledge of their own group's solution, despite the systematic effort made to ensure complete understanding of both solutions.

To simulate the negotiation strategies of unions and management, each group was asked to elect a representative who would meet with a representative from the competing group. The two representatives were asked to select one solution as the winner. An interesting thing happened.

5. *Representatives Stayed Loyal to Their Own Group's Solution.* The two representatives were asked to analyze and discuss each solution and to agree on a winner. After thirty-three such incidences, only two representatives agreed that the other group's solution was superior. Thirty-one representatives remained loyal to their own group, regardless of solution quality. Most representatives supported their own group's proposal, and they never did agree on a winner.[62]

These findings are striking because they emphasize just how difficult it can be for elected representatives to reach a solution when conflict is severe. The first priority for representatives is loyalty to their group. Conflict between management and unions is often intense because of differences in attitudes, values, and power. One resolution mechanism is to use negotiators, yet negotiators are committed to their own group's proposal, regardless of the quality of competing proposals. In an intensive union-management conflict, the fair resolution of conflict may seem impossible.

RESOLUTION OF UNION-MANAGEMENT CONFLICT

The primary approach to resolving union-management conflict is collective bargaining. In recent years, collective bargaining has expanded to include new types of issues of concern to both sides.

Collective Bargaining

Collective bargaining is the negotiation of an agreement between management and workers. The bargaining process is usually accomplished through a union, and it follows a prescribed format. Collective bargaining involves at least two parties that have a defined interest. The collective bargaining activity usually begins with the presentation of demands or proposals by one party that are evaluated by the other parties. This is followed by counter-proposals and concessions.

The approach taken in collective bargaining is determined by the compatibility of the goals of the respective parties. Three types of bargaining approaches are common: [63]

Distributive Bargaining Distributive bargaining refers to the attainment of one party's goals when they are in basic conflict with those of the other party. This is bargaining in the traditional union-management sense. Conflicts can relate to any issue, but they are typically economic, such as wage rates and working conditions. This type of bargaining usually takes place in a "fixed-sum" situation in which management's gain is the union's loss, and vice-versa. Both parties perceive a win-lose situation. This was the situation in the negotiations leading to the PATCO strike as well as the coal miners strike in Britain described earlier in this chapter.

Integrative Bargaining Integrative bargaining refers to the attainment of objectives that are not in conflict with those of the other party. Rather than union and management trying to win gains from one another, the two parties define a common concern or problem. Integrative bargaining exists when the problem is such that solutions can be developed that benefit both parties rather than benefit one party to the exclusion of the other. Integrative bargaining is a more enlightened approach that attempts to meet the needs of both union and management. Integrative bargaining characterized the UAW negotiations with Ford and General Motors in 1982. Each side was willing to help the other attain common objectives, such as lowering the price of cars to increase both sales and jobs.

Attitudinal Structuring Attitudinal structuring represents a newer approach to union-management relationships. Distributive and integrative bargaining pertain to economic issues. A new function of negotiation is to influence attitudes such as friendliness, trust, and respect. Attitudinal structuring occurs when negotiators take advantage of bargaining to develop a more positive attitude between parties. An important aspect of attitude change is that it reaches beyond formal negotiations. Trust and respect must become part of the day-to-day working relationships within the organization. Managers and union leaders must take the lead toward establishing a positive relationship that extends beyond economic issues. Companies that have had a history of labor-management trouble have sought to realign themselves toward a more positive working relationship.

The concept of a positive attitude has led to collaborative approaches to reduce union-management conflict. The economic recession during the early 1980s led many organizations to reevaluate these relationships. Frequently management and union leaders would adopt a win-win attitude in negotiations to help both the company and employees.[64] A win-win approach similar to that used in horizontal conflict reduction and summarized in Exhibit 11.9 has been adopted. The win-win approach can be used when union officials and management have had training in conflict-reduction, and believe that traditional attempts to win their goals at the expense of the other party will not be effective. Outside consultants often help the union-management relationship overcome the history of tension and strife. In other situations, such as at Packard Electric, workers and employees develop the approach on their own because of pressure to keep the organization alive.

IN PRACTICE 11.6
Packard Electric Division

Labor-management warfare made life miserable for both workers and managers at General Motors Corporation's Packard Electric Division in Warren, Ohio. Packard executives declared they would never hire employees in Warren again, and would even move jobs out of the area. Employees were represented by Local 717 of the International Union of Electronic Workers (IUE). During the 1970s, there were many slowdowns, wildcat strikes, and attempts by union officials to intimidate foremen on the shop floor. Management did their part by running the plant in a traditional adversary style. "It was miserable," says A. Lee Crawford, who was a foreman in the 1960s. "We were adversaries, screaming and yelling at one another. We didn't hire people to get involved."

With jobs leaving the community, both union officials and management became increasingly concerned. Fighting tradition and custom, a few managers and union leaders in 1977 started to change the negative climate. Packard's new general manager, James R. Rinehart, also wanted a good union relationship. With his approval, personnel executives began meeting weekly with top union officials. They began to share information and to cooperate on "low risk" programs such as collections for needy children.

A Jobs Committee of eight managers and eight union officials was created in June 1978. These people did not engage in collective bargaining. They simply studied ways to increase employment in Warren, and made recommendations to higher authorities. The talks were kept confidential, but were creative and fruitful.

Over the next five years, the Jobs Committee developed ideas for changing work practices to reduce costs. Continued progress led to an advanced model of union-management collaboration. The teamwork developed a dramatic innovation in the pay system. New workers will receive a lower pay rate, but all employees will have job security and new employees will have the opportunity to grow into the full salary other employees earn.

The collaboration at Packard works because trust has developed between labor and management on the shop floor and in top-level decision-making councils. *Business Week* interviews with managers, union officials, and workers discovered a commitment to worker involvement in decision-making. About sixty-five problem-solving committees have been created to encourage employees to use their ideas in improving productivity. Workers are also free to suggest improvements in the work environment.

The Warren, Ohio, plant and Local 717 have benefited from the special relationship. Packard Electric has rescinded its previous decision about not expanding in Warren. Collaboration did not mean the end of adversary bargaining, which is used when there are conflicting interests. Formal negotiations provide a conflict resolution mechanism on some issues, and outright collaboration works on others. One union official was proud that, "We collectively planned a way to keep union jobs." **65**

Teams that include both workers and managers reflect the belief that cooperation benefits both the company and employees. Companies in the steel industry have adopted participation teams so workers can contribute ideas to problems such as production bottlenecks, safety and health issues, the efficient use of tools, absenteeism, incentive pay, and other matters. Robinson Nugent Inc., an electronic-parts maker, has dramatically increased productivity by overcoming traditional labor-management hostility.[66] In the auto industry, GM and Ford agreed with the United Auto Workers to set up "new venture" funds with which union and management will launch new businesses to keep workers employed. Unions are becoming more proactive, and managers in manufacturing, mining, and transportation companies are seeking their unions' help. As the traditional barriers between union and management are broken down through collaboration, companies get increased productivity, and workers receive a better quality of work life. The win-win collaborative approach can be applied to union-management relationships more than people would have believed a few years ago.

SUMMARY AND INTERPRETATION

This chapter contains several ideas that complement the topics of power and decision-making in the two previous chapters. Probably the most important idea in this chapter is that intergroup conflict is a natural and useful outcome of organizing. At a personal level, most of us dislike conflict. But the dislike for conflict should not be applied to intergroup relations in organizations. Differences in goals, backgrounds, and tasks are necessary for departmental excellence. These differences throw groups into conflict. Intergroup conflict is healthy and should be directed toward successful outcomes for everyone. Conflict should not be suppressed or avoided. Understanding the role of organizational conflict and the importance of achieving appropriate levels of conflict are important lessons from this chapter.

Conflict between groups represents a dilemma for the organization. Intergroup conflict has clear advantages *within* each group. The increased focus on achieving group goals, increased cohesion, satisfaction, and stimulation represent the type of group atmosphere organizations strive for. Intergroup conflict is a powerful device for achieving a positive group atmosphere within departments. The atmosphere within departments does not translate into relationships *between* departments. The improved identification with one's own group leads to disregard and dislike for external groups. Members begin to see other departments as inferior, as the enemy, and cooperation with them may decrease. The dilemma for managers is to obtain the advantages of in-group feelings without the advantages of intense intergroup conflict. This is accomplished in the zone of managed conflict. A strategic level of conflict allows organizations to balance the within-group and between-group forces at a satisfactory level.

The research on intergroup conflict began over twenty years ago. Pioneering work in boys' camps and with managers in the laboratory provided rich insights into the causes of conflict. Recent research has focused on techniques for managing conflict. At this point in the development of organization theory, we now have an understanding of the causes of conflict, and a repertoire of techniques for managing conflict when it occurs.

Much of the work in organization theory has been concerned with horizontal rather than vertical conflict. Horizontal conflict is the day-to-day preoccupation of most managers. Horizontal relations across departments are less predictable than vertical relations, and there are fewer rules and regulations to prescribe conflict resolution. The concern for horizontal conflict in organization theory reflects its frequency in organizations. Vertical conflict is reflected in union-management relationships and is also important. Indeed, some of the most exciting developments taking place in the organizational world are techniques for improving union-management relationships. Problem-solving teams, employee ownership of company stock, and even union membership on the board of directors are steps to achieve collaboration between management and workers. As these developments become the focus of organizational research, new techniques and models for managing vertical conflict will become part of the organization theory literature.

KEY CONCEPTS

attitudinal structuring
behavior changes during
    conflict
benefits from conflict
competition
confrontation
collective bargaining
distributive bargaining
horizontal conflict
integrative bargaining
intergroup conflict

losses from conflict
managed conflict
model of intergroup conflict
negotiation
pluralistic view
sources of interdepartmental
    conflict
sources of vertical conflict
traditional view
vertical conflict

DISCUSSION QUESTIONS

1. Define intergroup conflict. How does this definition compare to that of competition? What impact does conflict have on groups?
2. What is vertical as opposed to horizontal conflict? What issues or topics would tend to characterize one type of conflict as opposed to the other?
3. Briefly describe how differences in tasks, personal background, and training lead to conflict between groups. How does task interdependence lead to conflict between groups?
4. What is meant by "managed" conflict?
5. Discuss the benefits and wastes of interdepartmental conflict. At what level of conflict do these benefits and wastes appear.

6. Intergroup training is located at a higher level on the scale of conflict-resolution techniques than is member rotation. What does this mean in terms of the amount of impact the two techniques have on behavior vs. attitudes? Can you think of situations in which rotation might have greater impact on understanding than would intergroup training?

7. What techniques can be used to overcome conflict between workers and management? Are there similarities in the techniques used to deal with vertical and horizontal conflict? Discuss.

8. What is meant by the organizational dilemma involving within-group and between-group relations? Discuss.

GUIDES TO ACTION

As a manager:

1. Do not eliminate or suppress conflict. Recognize that some interdepartmental conflict is natural and even necessary. Obtain the benefits of conflict without the waste by maintaining conflict at an appropriate level.

2. Associate the organizational design characteristics of goal incompatibility, differentiation, task interdependence, resource scarcity, power distribution, and reward systems with greater conflict between groups. Expect to devote more time and energy to resolving conflict in these situations.

3. Reduce conflict by diagnosing underlying causes, and then changing them. This approach may not be successful because some causes, such as environmental uncertainty or task interdependence, cannot be adjusted on a short-run basis.

4. Do not allow intense conflict to persist. Intense conflict is harmful to the organization because departments direct their resources toward sabotaging or defeating other groups rather than working with other departments to achieve firm goals. Intervene forcefully with conflict-resolution techniques.

5. Stimulate or reduce conflict as needed to "manage" conflict between departments. Conflict can be stimulated through competition, increased uncertainty, and changes in reward systems and tasks. Conflict can be reduced with bureaucratic authority, limited interaction, integration devices, confrontation, third-party consultants, member rotation, superordinate goals, and intergroup training. Select the techniques that fit the organization and the conflict.

6. Avoid placing groups in direct win-lose situations when managing either horizontal or vertical conflict. Direct the conflict toward enabling both groups to be partial winners. When negotiating, do not place representatives in the dilemma of choosing between loyalty to their group or loyalty to the best interest of the company as a whole. Representatives will usually be loyal to their group, even if their proposals are not the best solutions for the entire company.

Consider these Guides when analyzing the following case and when answering the questions listed after the case.

CASE FOR ANALYSIS

VALENA SCIENTIFIC CORPORATION*

PART I

Valena Scientific Corporation is one of the largest manufacturers of health-care products in the world. The health-care market includes hospitals, clinical laboratories, universities, and industry. Clinical laboratories represent 52% of VSC's sales. The laboratories are located in hospitals and diagnostic centers where blood tests and urine analyses are performed for physicians. Equipment sold to laboratories can range from a five-cent test tube to a blood analyzer that performs eighteen blood tests simultaneously for $195,000.

During the 1970s, many large energy and industrial corporations began to move into the clinical market. Eli Lilly, Dow Chemical, Revlon, and E. I. DuPont shifted more research dollars to medical products. Fifty percent of the nation's health-care bill goes into testing, and the medical profession is demanding more accurate tests as well as tests for a variety of new diseases.

By 1980, the industry experienced a new twist: genetic engineering. New companies such as Genentech Corp. and Cetus Scientific Laboratories were created as venture capital companies and were staffed with a handful of university microbiologists. These companies were designed to exploit the commercial potential for gene splicing.

Senior executives at VSC saw the trend developing, and late in 1979 decided to create the Biotech Research Department. Skilled microbiologists were scarce, so the department was created with only nine scientists, who had experience in the fields of biology and engineering. Twenty technicians, who helped with research at the scientists' direction, were also assigned. The department was divided into three groups—gene splicing, recombination, and fermentation. The organization chart for the Biotech Research Department is shown in Exhibit 11.11. It is the smallest of three research departments at VSC. An important characteristic of the new department was that the employees from each group were expected to work closely together. The most competent personnel had been selected to serve as part of the new department. They would be doing leading edge research compared to other departments at VSC. Each group was located on a separate floor in the research building, although they would be located together after a new research wing was constructed sometime in the future.

For the first eighteen months of operation, the work in the Biotech Department was moderately routine. The biotech department concentrated on applying principles established elsewhere. One example was the production of human insulin by gene splicing. The basic research was performed by a scientist at Harvard. The work required by private companies was to

---

* This case is based on "Genetic Engineering's Manpower Problem," *Dun's Business Month,* January, 1982, pp. 92–95; "Reid Scientific" case, distributed by the Intercollegiate Case Clearing House, Soldiers Field, Boston, MA 02163; "Daniels Computer Company," in Robert E. Coffey, Anthony G. Athos, and Peter A. Reynolds, *Behavior in Organizations: A Multidimensional View,* 2nd ed. (Englewood Cliffs, NJ: Prentice-Hall, 1975), pp. 416–420; "Biotech Comes of Age," *Business Week,* January 23, 1984, pp. 84–94; and "Biotech Firms Offer 'Interim' Products," *Dun's Business Month,* May 1984, pp. 103–105.

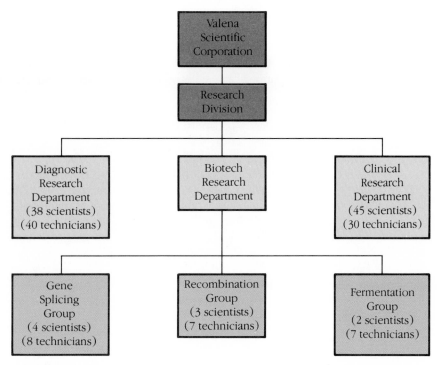

EXHIBIT 11.11. Organization Chart of VSC's Biotech Research Department.

produce insulin in large amounts. Other work included the refinement of blood tests, such as for diabetes and for the identification of hereditary diseases (e.g., sickle-cell anemia). The initial projects all followed a similar pattern. The work was started in the gene-splicing group, followed by work in recombination, and then to fermentation. Fermentation is used to breed the bacteria created by the other two groups in sufficient numbers to enable mass production.

The senior scientist in each group was appointed group leader and the three leaders reported to the director of the biotech department, who did not have a scientific background. The structure within each group was very informal and collegial.

Questions

1. Would the scientists and technicians be enthusiastic or unenthusiastic about becoming part of the new department? Would they identify more strongly with the department as a whole or with their subgroup? Explain.

2. Would conflict among group leaders be high or low during the initial eighteen months? Explain.

3. Would social relationships among technical personnel tend to be department-wide or limited to subgroups? Explain.

PART II

The scientists and technicians were enthusiastic about the new department. They felt proud to be selected and quickly identified with the new department. They were happy with the division of labor, but lunch and coffee gatherings included members from all three groups. Group leader meetings were cooperative, quickly resolved any coordination problems, and were conflict free.

During the summer of 1982, the Biotech Department received a special project. Hoffman-LaRoche was developing leukocyte interferon to use as a treatment against cancer. The company was unable to clone the bacteria in its own lab and hired other companies to do the job. VSC contracted with Hoffman-LaRoche to develop a technique for interferon production. The company had only six months to come up with a production technology. Because of the intense time pressure, the research could not be done in the sequence of gene splicing, recombination, and fermentation. Each group remained in its own geographic confines, and began immediately to test ideas relevant to its own work. Each group also examined the current research literature and contacted university colleagues in their own areas of specialization. The groups were aware that if findings from another group were strong enough to dictate the entire production sequence, the work undertaken by their own group would be lost.

Questions

1. Would department employees be enthusiastic or unenthusiastic as the interferon project developed? Would they identify more strongly with the department as a whole or with their own subgroup? Explain.

2. Would conflict among group leaders be high or low during this period? Explain.

3. Would social relationships tend to be department-wide or subgroup-oriented? Explain.

PART III

In September 1982, the group leaders met for the first time to explore the technical progress and discoveries made by each group. The goal of this meeting was to exchange information and to establish parameters for each group's subsequent research activities. It quickly became apparent that each group had taken a different research direction and had discovered concepts that the group considered paramount. The position of any one group required considerable extra work by the other two groups. The group leaders argued vehemently for their positions, and the meeting was concluded without compromise of original positions.

During the following six weeks, each worked desperately to complete its research before complementary segments were completed in the other groups. Haste was necessary because the late groups would have to reformulate their research based on what was found by the group that finished first. Future meetings among group leaders were conflict-laden and did not resolve the issues. No research approach was proven to be superior for cloning and manufacturing interferon. All three avenues looked promising, but mutually exclusive. A number of personal frictions developed between the groups. Enthusiasm for the project was initially high, but gradually dropped off as conflict increased. Social activities were limited to members in each subgroup and were dominated by talk of research and the need to beat the other groups.

On November 15, a Stanford professor with extensive research experience in recombinant DNA technology was hired. His first assignment was to be project leader for the interferon project. His title was Chief Biologist, and all scientists, engineers, and technicians working on the interferon project were to report to him. The group leaders in each area discussed their work with him. After one week, the chief biologist selected the basic approach that would be taken in future research. The new approach was a technique developed at Stanford, and in many ways was similar to the line taken in the fermentation group. Technical objections from the other groups were dismissed. The new approach was to be followed by everyone. Each group was assigned a set of research instructions within the overall research plan. Firm deadlines were established based upon group interdependence. Weekly progress reports were required from each group leader.

Questions

1. Would members of the three groups be enthusiastic or unenthusiastic after these developments? Would the scientists and technicians identify with the overall department or with their respective subgroups? Explain.

2. Would conflict among group leaders be high or low as work progressed on the project?

3. Would social relationships tend to be department-wide or subgroup-oriented? Explain.

PART IV

For several weeks after the chief biologist decided the direction of the interferon project, the group leaders from gene splicing and recombination disagreed with him. Considerable time was spent trying to find a weakness in the new plan and to prove that their previous research was superior. Few problems in the new plan could be found. The chief biologist defended his position and demanded that deadlines be met.

Schedules were met, and the three groups simultaneously developed the approach in their respective areas. Communication with the chief biologist became more frequent. Communication between groups become common. Problems discovered by one group were communicated to other groups so that effort was not expended needlessly. Group leaders coordinated many problems among themselves.

Cohesion within each group became less pronounced. Lunch and coffee groups comprising several members of each group began to appear. Group leaders had daily discussions and cooperated on research requirements. Enthusiasm for the department and for the interferon project was expressed by department members.

Questions

1. What intraorganizational changes in Valena Scientific Corporation led to heightened intergroup conflict? Explain. Why couldn't the group leaders resolve the conflict by themselves?

2. What factors account for the reduction of conflict after the chief biologist took over?

3. Should intergroup conflict be completely removed from the biotech department? Will these employees produce better if some competition or conflict is present? Discuss.

NOTES

1. Rosemary Brady, "Standing Up to the Rent-a-Gobs," *Forbes,* October 8, 1984, p. 187.
2. Adapted from Rosemary Brady, "Standing Up to the Rent-a-Gobs," pp. 187–192.

3. Clayton T. Alderfer and Ken K. Smith, "Studying Intergroup Relations Imbedded in Organizations," *Administrative Science Quarterly,* 27 (1982):35–65.

4. Muzafer Sherif, "Experiments in Group Conflict," *Scientific American* 195 (1956):54–58; Edgar H. Schein, *Organizational Psychology,* 3rd ed. (Englewood Cliffs, NJ: Prentice-Hall, 1980).

5. Kenneth Thomas, "Conflict and Conflict Management," in M. D. Dunnette, ed., *Handbook of Industrial and Organizational Psychology* (Chicago: Rand McNally, 1976); Joseph A. Litterer, "Conflict in Organizations: A Re-Examination," *Academy of Management Journal* 9 (1966):178–186; Stuart M. Schmidt and Thomas A. Kochan, "Conflict: Toward Conceptual Clarity," *Administrative Science Quarterly* 13 (1972): 359–370.

6. L. David Brown, "Managing Conflict among Groups," in David A. Kolb, Irwin M. Rubin, and James M. McIntyre, eds., *Organizational Psychology: A Book of Readings* (Englewood Cliffs, NJ: Prentice-Hall, 1979), pp. 377–389.

7. Ibid.

8. Susan V. Lourenco and John C. Glidewell, "A Dialectical Analysis of Organizational Conflict," *Administrative Science Quarterly,* 20 (1975):489–508.

9. Harry Bernstein, "Union Misjudged Government," *Houston Chronicle,* September 4, 1981, copyright © Los Angeles Times-Washington Post News Service: Paul Galloway, "Negotiating Consultant Says Air Controllers Can't Win Strike," *Houston Chronicle,* August 25, 1981, copyright © Chicago Sun-Times.

10. These conclusions are summarized from Sherif, "Experiments in Group Conflict"; M. Sherif, O. J. Harvey, B. J. White, W. R. Hood, and C. W. Sherif, *Intergroup Conflict and Cooperation* (Norman, OK: University of Oklahoma Books Exchange, 1961); M. Sherif and C. W. Sherif, *Social Psychology* (New York: Harper & Row, 1969); and Schein, *Organizational Psychology.*

11. Thomas A. Kochan, George P. Huber, and L. L. Cummings, "Determinants of Intraorganizational Conflict in Collective Bargaining in the Public Sector," *Administrative Science Quarterly* 20 (1975):10–23.

12. Benson S. Shapiro, "Can Marketing and Manufacturing Coexist?" *Harvard Business Review* 55 (September-October, 1977):104–114.

13. Eric H. Neilsen, "Understanding and Managing Intergroup Conflict," in Jay W. Lorsch and Paul R. Lawrence, *Managing Group and Intergroup Relations* (Homewood, IL: Irwin and Dorsey Press, 1972), pp. 329–343; Richard E. Walton and John M. Dutton, "The Management of Interdepartmental Conflict: A Model and Review," *Administrative Science Quarterly* 14 (1969):73–84.

14. Jay W. Lorsch, "Introduction to the Structural Design of Organizations," in Gene W. Dalton, Paul R. Lawrence, and Jay W. Lorsch, eds., *Organization Structure and Design* (Homewood, IL: Irwin and Dorsey, 1970), p. 5.

15. Melville Dalton, *Men Who Manage* (New York: John Wiley, 1959), p. 75.

16. James D. Thompson, *Organizations in Action* (New York: McGraw-Hill, 1967), pp. 54–56.

17. Walton and Dutton, "Management of Interdepartmental Conflict."

18. Joseph McCann and Jay R. Galbraith, "Interdepartmental Relationships," in Paul C. Nystrom and William H. Starbuck, eds., *Handbook of Organizational Design,* vol. 2 (New York: Oxford University Press, 1981), pp. 60–84.

19. George Strauss, "Tactics of Lateral Relationship: The Purchasing Agent," *Administrative Science Quarterly* 7 (1962):161–186. Quoted by permission.

20. Neilsen, "Understanding and Managing Intergroup Conflict"; Louis R. Pondy, "Organizational Conflict: Concepts and Models," *Administrative Science Quarterly* 12 (1968):296–320.

21. John A. Seiler, "Diagnosing Interdepartmental Conflict," *Harvard Business Review* 41 (September-October, 1963):121–132.

22. Ibid, pp. 126–127.

23. Walton and Dutton, "Management of Interdepartmental Conflict"; Pondy, "Organizational Conflicts"; Kochan, Huber, and Cummings, "Determinants of Intraorganizational Conflict"; Kenneth W. Thomas and Louis R. Pondy, "Toward an 'Intent' Model of Conflict Management among Principal Parties," *Human Relations* 30 (1977):1089–1102.

24. Daniel S. Cochran and Donald D. White, "Intraorganizational Conflict in the Hospital Purchasing Decision Making Process," *Academy of Management Journal,* 24 (1981):324–332.

25. Walton and Dutton, "Management of Interdepartmental Conflict."

26. Morton Deutsch, "The Effects of Cooperation and Competition upon Group Process," in Dorwin Cartwright and Alvin Zander, *Group Dynamics* (New York: Harper & Row, 1968), pp. 461–482.

27. Stephen P. Robbins, *Managing Organizational Conflict: A Nontraditional Approach* (Englewood Cliffs, NJ: Prentice-Hall, 1974).

28. Donald Nightingale, "Conflict and Conflict Resolution," in George Strauss, Raymond E. Miles, Charles C. Snow, and Arnold S. Tannenbaum, *Organizational Behavior: Research and Issues* (Belmont, CA: Wadsworth, 1976), pp. 141–164.

29. Robbins, *Managing Organizational Conflict.*

30. Nightingale, "Conflict in Conflict Resolution."

31. Paul R. Lawrence and Jay W. Lorsch, *Organization and Environment* (Homewood, IL: Irwin, 1969); Pondy, "Organizational Conflict"; Thomas and Pondy, "Toward an 'Intent' Model of Conflict Management."

32. Robert R. Blake and Jane S. Mouton, "Reactions to Intergroup Competition Under Win-Lose Conditions," *Management Science* 7 (1961):420–435; Sherif, et al., *Intergroup Conflict and Cooperation.*

33. Thomas and Pondy, "Toward an 'Intent' Model of Conflict Management"; Joe Kelly, "Make Conflict Work For You, *Harvard Business Review* 48 (July-August, 1970):103–113.

34. Kelly, ibid.

35. Robbins, *Managing Organizational Conflict.*

36. Seiler, "Diagnosing Interdepartmental Conflicts."

37. Blake and Mouton, "Reactions to Intragroup Competition."

38. Schein, *Organizational Psychology;* Blake and Mouton, "Reactions to Intergroup Competition," pp. 174–175.

39. Pondy, "Organizational Conflict."

40. This discussion is drawn from J. Victor Baldridge, *Power and Conflict in the University* (New York: John Wiley, 1971) and Mary Zey Ferrell, *Dimensions of Organizations* (Santa Monica, CA: Goodyear, 1979).

41. Neilsen, "Understanding and Managing Intergroup Conflict."

42. Pondy, "Organizational Conflict."

43. Robert R. Blake, Herbert A. Shepard, and Jane S. Mouton, *Managing Intergroup Conflict in Industry* (Houston: Gulf Publishing Company, 1964).

44. Robert R. Blake and Jane S. Mouton, "Overcoming Group Warfare," *Harvard Business Review* (November-December, 1984):98–108.

45. Charles R. Schwenk, "Devil's Advocacy in Managerial Decision-Making," *Journal of Management Studies,* 21 (1984):153–168.

46. Neilsen, "Understanding and Managing Intergroup Conflict."

47. Ibid.

48. Pondy, "Organizational Conflict."

49. Richard Cone, Bruce Snow, and Ricky Waclawcayk, "Datapoint Corporation," unpublished manuscript, Texas A&M University, 1981.

50. Neilsen, "Understanding and Managing Intergroup Conflict."

51. Ibid.; Paul R. Lawrence and Jay W. Lorsch, "New Management Job: The Integrator," *Harvard Business Review* 45 (November-December, 1967):142–151.

52. "When Engineers Talk to Each Other—The Slow But Sure Payoff," *International Management,* July 1984:26–27. Used with permission.

53. Blake, Shepard, and Mouton, *Managing Intergroup Conflict in Industry.*

54. Thomas, "Conflict and Conflict Management."

55. Neilsen, "Understanding and Managing Intergroup Conflict"; Joseph McCann and Jay R. Galbraith, "Interdepartmental Relations," in Paul C. Nystrom and William H. Starbuck, eds., *Handbook of Organizational Design,* vol. 2 (London: Oxford University Press, 1981), pp. 60–84.

56. Ibid.; Sherif et al., *Intergroup Conflict and Cooperation.*

57. Robert R. Blake and Jane S. Mouton, "Overcoming Group Warfare"; Schein, *Organizational Psychology;* Blake, Shepard, and Mouton, *Managing Intergroup Conflict in Industry;* Richard E. Walton, *Interpersonal Peacemaking: Confrontation and Third-Party Consultations* (Reading, MA: Addison-Wesley, 1969).

58. Edgar H. Schein, *Organizational Psychology,* 3rd ed., (Englewood Cliffs, NJ: Prentice-Hall, 1980, pp. 177–178. Reprinted by permission of Prentice-Hall, Inc.

59. Leon C. Megginson, *Personal and Human Resources Administration* (Homewood, IL: Irwin, 1977), pp. 519–520.

60. Roger S. Wolters, "Union-Management Ideological Frames of Reference," *Journal of Management,* 8 (1982):21–33.

61. Blake and Mouton, "Reactions to Intergroup Competition."

62. Ibid.

63. These bargaining approaches were developed by Richard Walton and Richard McKersie, *A Behavioral Theory of Labor Negotiations: An Analysis of the Social Interaction System* (New York: McGraw-Hill, 1965), ch. 1.

64. Blake and Mouton, "Reactions to Intergroup Competition."

65. "The Revolutionary Wage Deal at GM's Packard Electric," *Business Week,* August 29, 1983, pp. 54–56; "Now Unions Are Helping to Run the Business," *Business Week,* December 24, 1984, pp. 69–70.

66. Bruce G. Posner, "Toward a More Perfect Union," *Inc.,* January 1984, pp. 84–89.

Integrating the Total System

The Top Management Domain

A LOOK INSIDE

HARTMAN LUGGAGE COMPANY

The last time I was in Chicago, I was making a speech before the Executives Club. I don't know if you're familiar with that organization, but it's impressive for a couple of reasons. First, they have over 3,000 paid-up members. Second, they get anywhere from five hundred to one thousand of the members to come to a luncheon every Friday. The week before my speech, they'd had Senator Charles Percy. The week after me, they had Nelson Rockefeller. I felt good about the company I was in until I was introduced with the polite explanation to the audience by the club's president that a "change of pace" was desirable.

Anyway, the point of my telling you about this organization is that before each luncheon, they ask the speaker to meet with a half-dozen high school kids whom they've invited as guests. When I met with them, they took one look at me, looked at each other, and almost in one voice wanted to know what kind of education you needed to be in management. Was there a major course of study, a *degree* in management that they could pursue in college?

Naturally, I refused to answer a stupid question like that.

But if you know kids, you know they don't let go, especially if they smell a phony. They'd been told I had been president of the Plaza Hotel and had had no previous hotel experience, and no hotel schooling, and they seemed skeptical about what the BS degree I'd gotten in college really stood for.

"Mr. Lavenson," one particularly obnoxious little smart alec asked me, "If you had no experience running a hotel and you started at the top, how did you know what to do? Just what did you do?"

"I ran the place, that's what! Next question?" I snapped back and figured I'd won. I hadn't.

"Come now, Mr. Lavenson, these students won't accept that answer." It was their teacher who interrupted this time, a guy with a beard and a pipe and very high forehead. I hated him on sight. "What about an MBA degree? Wouldn't you say that a master's degree in business from a school like Harvard or The Wharton School would qualify a man or woman for management?"

I didn't have an MBA degree and it was painfully obvious this teacher did. If I let him win that point, I knew I was lost, so I resorted to a trick I'd learned through years of experience: I lied.

"Not an MBA degree," I said very calmly. "It takes an MBWA degree to qualify as a manager." With that one, I'd stopped the beard and pipe dead in his tracks. But he recovered and just before someone came in and announced lunch was starting, he growled a last question. "Just exactly what is an MBWA degree?"

I gave him my most generous smile, and gave him a pearl of wisdom in one sentence that I'm going to stretch out into a full speech today. You see, I'd never really thought about it before and my glib answer to that poor teacher and group of kids was the lucky, accidental, off-the-cuff, wise-guy response of a cornered rat. On my way home from Chicago, I thought a lot more about the questions the kids were asking and my answer. The longer I thought about it, the more I realized that MBWA is the qualification for management, and it's one I'd unwittingly been using in every job I've been in. And when I'd started each of the management jobs I've had over the past twenty years—in advertising, in toy products, in luggage, in publishing, in food processing, in sunglasses, T-shirts, dresses, and, yes, if you'll excuse the expression, in women's pants, there's one thing you can say about me without fear of contradiction from anyone with whom I ever worked. I didn't know from beans about any of these businesses. I don't really mean I didn't know *anything*. Naturally, since I was over thirty, I did know a thing or two about ladies' pants. But what I didn't know about any of the businesses when I started in them was how to *run* them. And I certainly didn't have any of the technical experience necessary to mold a doll, sew leather into a suitcase that would come out the other end of the production line as Hartman luggage, or dig clams out of the Atlantic Ocean, clean them, and vacuum pack them into cans labeled Doxsee. And what I knew about ladies' sportswear was confined to whistling—mostly at my wife's bills from Saks Fifth Avenue and Bergdorf Goodman. . . .

Oh my, that's right! I still haven't told you what MBWA stands for, have I? MBWA stands for *Management by Walking Around*. Just walking around with your eyes and ears open, asking questions like crazy, and trying to understand what the [people] working for you are doing. A good place to start is to see if *they* understand what they're doing. . . .

One day about ten years ago, I suddenly found myself chairman of the Hartman Luggage Company. Like you, I'd known the name for years and before I'd seen the figures, I would have guessed that Hartman was at least a ten- or twenty-million-dollar company. I was shocked to learn that its sales volume was under two million, so I started by walking around the territory with a couple of salespeople to see why they weren't selling more. They all told me the same thing—Hartman was a prestige name without a truly prestige product, a real top-of-the-line, expensive piece of luggage which by its very price had the snob appeal to get it into stores like Saks Fifth Avenue and Neiman Marcus. I brought that story back to the president, who pooh-poohed the idea but reached into a secret compartment in his office safe and produced the loveliest, richest-looking attache case made of belted leather and brass trim that I'd ever dreamed of. "Why isn't that in the line?" I wanted to know.

"Too expensive. It would never sell. We'd have to retail this thing for close to two hundred bucks."

I walked around again, taking the sample attache case with me and asking the salespeople if this was the kind of thing they had in mind. "Yeah, man!" was their reaction.

"How much should it sell for?" I wanted to know from the guys who had to sell it. The consensus was three hundred bucks. That MBWA attache case went into the Hartman line along with overnighters and two-suiters all made of belted leather with price tags that would shock the Shah of Iran. Today, Hartman is stocked by Saks and Neiman Marcus and doing one helluva lot more than two million dollars in sales.

Probably the most important principle of MBWA is really a philosophy— a philosophy that says that the boss's job is to make sure of three things: first, *that his staff understands what they are doing; second, that his staff has the tools they think they need to do the job; and last, that the boss lets the staff know he has an appreciation of what the employee is doing.*

You hear a lot of management types talk sanctimoniously about their "open door" policy. Their door is "always open to the staff," they tell you. In my book, the best reason for a boss's open door is so he can go out the door and walk around. . . . [1]

James Lavenson has definite ideas about how to manage an organization. His experience suggests that skillful top managers must spend time taking the pulse of the organization—talking to people, asking questions, and developing an accurate mental picture of the organization. The top manager also works to establish linkages between departments to make sure they work well together. Lavenson got sales and product design together at Hartman Luggage. The top manager also has to make strategic decisions. Lavenson decided to launch a new line of luggage to tap a new market. Top managers also symbolize values that influence the internal culture of the organization. In the above case, Lavenson valued a walking-around, problem-solving culture that led to increased sales and market share for Hartman. Finally, Lavenson's speech provides a clue to management succession. Turnover in the chief executive's position was a good thing for Hartman Luggage. Replacing the previous top manager led to a new line of briefcases that increased Hartman's sales and profits.

Purpose of This Chapter

In this chapter, we explore the domain of top management. The purpose of this chapter is to bring together findings about the top management domain that go beyond the material covered in previous chapters. The next section describes the responsibilities and activities of top managers to provide a flavor of how executives govern organizations. Then we examine the types of choices top managers make, with special emphasis on strategy formulation and implementation. We discuss strategy formulation only briefly because it is covered in courses on policy and strategy. Strategy implementation, however, uses the concepts and models from organization theory to help the organization achieve results. The importance of organization theory for top managers is the implementation of strategy. The concept of organizational culture will be discussed in detail because culture is a tool of strategy implementation that has not been discussed previously in this book. The final section of the chapter explores the issue of managerial succession. Here we answer the questions: Why does turnover occur, and does the top executive make any difference to organizational effectiveness? By the end of this chapter, students should understand the role of top management and how top managers steer the organization through an uncertain environment.

TOP MANAGEMENT RESPONSIBILITIES AND ACTIVITIES

One of the frustrations of management scientists has been the inability to develop a concise description of the chief executive's job; it is so complex and contains so many elements that complete documentation is nearly impossible. Some insight into the top manager's job has been obtained by following managers around and observing everything they do.[2] These studies indicate that top managers are responsible for governing the organization.

Governance

The term "governance" implies the notion of "government" without implications of elections, political processes, or sovereignty.[3] **Governance** is the means through which the organization is directed, controlled, and regulated. The formal hierarchy in organizations focuses the responsibility for governance on executives at the top of the hierarchy. They are responsible for governance decisions that define the goals, strategy, and well-being of the corporation.

Exhibit 12.1 identifies the domain of components executives use to control and regulate the organization. Organization structure is the arrangement of positions, responsibility, and authority needed to achieve the organization's

EXHIBIT 12.1. Domain of Top Management Governance.

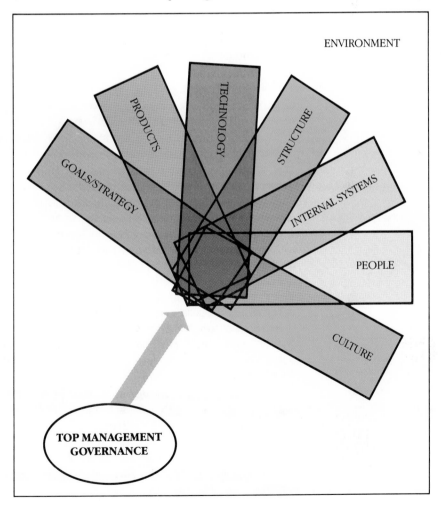

goals. Structure also includes horizontal linkage mechanisms to encourage coordination. Internal systems include the management information and control systems that assist executives in the regulation of organizational behavior. Technology represents the production process, and products are the organization's outputs. Technology and products are relatively fixed in the short run, but a major responsibility of top management is to make decisions about changes in technology and new products to facilitate organizational growth and development. Goals and strategy define the organization's mission and direction. People are the human resources available to the organization. Culture represents the beliefs and values within the organization. When cultural values are in alignment with structure, systems, goals, and technology, they represent an important element for accomplishing organizational outcomes.

The major components of governance all exist within the larger external environment. Executives are responsible for interpreting the external environment and defining responses to the environment. Top executives must learn about industry and market conditions, economic climate, government, and other sectors in its environment as described in chapter 2. The center square in Exhibit 12.1 indicates that top management is the place where all of the organizational components and the environment converge. The components are mechanisms through which the organization responds to the environment.

| Governance Process | The governance process is concerned with how the organization is governed. Governance processes include the tone and style of the organization. Processes include the extent to which the organization centralizes or decentralizes decision-making, and the extent to which rational and political processes are emphasized in decision-making. Process also includes the mechanisms for encouraging innovation, dealing with power, and for confronting and resolving conflict. Top managers use their behavior and official statements to define internal activities and dynamics that are valued by the organization. Organizational governance defines the type of due process within the organization. Based upon top-management governance, organizations can be characterized by the extent to which they are an autocratic, democratic, oligarchic, or federal system.[4] In this way, organizations can institutionalize participation or top-down decision processes. Governance also includes the extent to which political coalitions are important. The governance "process" means that the top management role in organizations is more than simply defining structure, products, technology, and internal systems. Top managers define the way in which these activities are carried out. |

| Interpretation and Enactment | Top management is located at the interface between the environment and the organization, and one critical activity is interpretation of the environment. The external environment is characterized by complexity and uncertainty. From this complexity and uncertainty top management must interpret, assess, and evaluate, and then make decisions about future strategies and courses of action.[5] **Interpretation** is the process through which managers learn about the environment; it enables them to make strategic choices about |

appropriate size, technology, structure, and strategy.[6] Top managers sit between their organization and a network of contacts, as illustrated in Exhibit 12.2. The manager is surrounded by a "diverse and complex web of contacts."[7] These contacts include associates, suppliers, staff experts, top managers of other organizations, trade organizations, government officials, clients, independent people, and boards of directors. Eighty percent of the manager's time is spent communicating with other people. Top management thereby absorbs and reduces uncertainty and provides a stable decision environment for lower-level managers and personnel.

Top management plays another interpretation and choice role also. The external environment must be enacted by the organization. **Enactment** is the process of defining which environmental elements are important enough to be attended to by the organization.[8] Since the environment is theoretically infinite, those subsets of the environment that are of primary importance have to be identified. Enactment is the process of defining the external environment into a manageable subset of elements that the organization can cope with effectively. The enacted environment is the limited set of external organizations and factors that the organization deals with on a continuous basis. Other elements in the environment may exist, and may even influence the organization. But if these elements are not enacted, management will not pay attention or respond to them.

The interesting aspect of enactment is that the environment is not assumed to be fixed.[9] Top management defines what the environment is. Top managers select the environmental elements that are imposed upon the organization. The process of top management governance thus includes those decisions

EXHIBIT 12.2. The Top Manager as Information-Processing System.

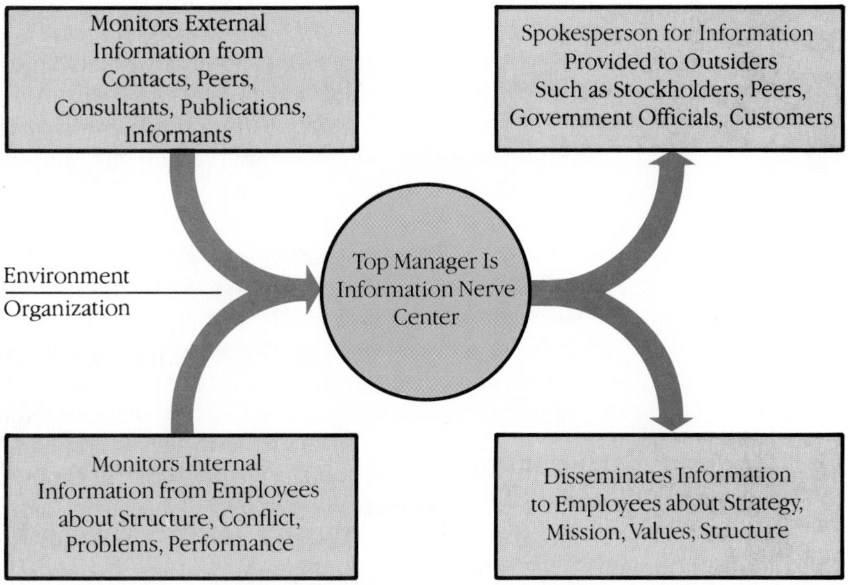

Source: Adapted from Henry Mintzberg, *The Nature of Managerial Work* (New York: Harper & Row: 1973), pp. 65–77.

that define the environment as well as those decisions about how the organization will respond to the environment.

The enactment process often has a fuzzy beginning, and leads to the identification of a new environmental domain with which the organization must cope, as illustrated in the following case.

IN PRACTICE 12.1
Consumer Products Company

The president of a large consumer products company was troubled by what seemed to be increasing government regulation. Managers from several functions within the organization commented on increasing paperwork and time being consumed in government-related activities. Government also influenced the company indirectly through its impact on customers. Gradually, from talking to his managers, he began to build up an image of how important government regulation was for the company. He began to define the government as a critical environmental contingency for his organization. He asked for advice of people within the company about how to deal with government regulation, and at the same time he identified the government as an important element to other managers. "I have started conversations with anyone inside or outside the company who can help. . . . I collect articles and talk to people about how things get done in Washington in this particular [industry]. I collect data from any reasonable source. I begin wide-ranging discussions with people inside and outside the corporation. From these a pattern eventually emerges. It is like fitting together a jigsaw puzzle. At first a vague outline of an approach appears like the sail of a ship. Then suddenly the rest of the puzzle becomes quite clear. You wonder why you didn't see it all along. And once it's crystallized, it's not difficult to explain to others." [10]

In this company, government activities in Washington became part of the enacted environment. The manager defined this external element and then communicated this perception to others in the organization. In the future, the organization will concentrate on the governmental sector.

Implications   What do these findings about governance and activities mean for top level managers? *The primary responsibility of the top leader is to determine the organization's goals and strategy, and therein adapt the organization to a changing environment.*[11] Top managers must use major organizational components, such as structure, systems, culture, and technology to carry out that responsibility. The challenge for top management is that they must determine strategy and use organizational components despite great uncertainty. Moreover, they must get things done through a large and diverse group of people, many of whom they have little direct control over.[12] Thus the managers' time is used to establish networks, build alliances, establish coalitions, define values, and in other ways set the tone and premises needed to move the organization toward its goals.[13] Through diverse activities and relationships, managers are able to gain agreement about goals, formulate strategy, and persuade the organization to take action through strategy implementation.

STRATEGIC MANAGEMENT

Strategic management is part of the governance process, and is probably the single most important responsibility of top managers. A corporation's **strategy** is the current set of plans, decisions, and objectives that have been adopted to achieve the organization's goals. The process of formulating and implementing strategy is illustrated in Exhibit 12.3. **Strategy formulation** includes the activities that lead to establishment of a firm's overall goals and mission and the development of a specific strategic plan.[14] Strategy formulation typically begins with an assessment of the opportunities and threats in the external environment. Managers interpret external information and decide which issues are critical. Assessment of strengths and weaknesses within the organization also occurs, and leads to a definition of distinctive competence.[15] Internal assessment includes an evaluation of each department (marketing, finance, production) as well as technology, products, and other characteristics. The next step is to define overall goal and mission based upon the correct fit between external opportunities and internal strengths. Within the overall mission, a specific strategy can then be formulated that defines how the organization is to accomplish its goals.

Strategy implementation is the use of managerial and organizational tools to direct and allocate resources to accomplish strategic results.[16] Strategy implementation is the administration and execution of the strategic plan. The concepts of organization theory are especially relevant for implementation. As illustrated in Exhibit 12.3, the direction and allocation of resources are accomplished with the tools of organization structure, control systems, culture, technology, and human resources. Changes in structure, control, technology, and human resources have been discussed in previous chapters, and from a top management perspective these are tools of implementation. Organizational culture and leader symbolism have not been described previously in this book and will be explored in this chapter.

Organizations facing a similar environment often formulate and implement different strategies because of different interpretation and enactment processes. One classic example of differing strategies was that of Sears Roebuck and Montgomery Ward in the retailing industry.[17] Immediately after World War II, both companies were similar in size and reputation. The top management at Sears assessed the business environment at the end of the war as having two characteristics—economic prosperity and population migration to the suburbs. Prosperity meant that immediate expansion was necessary to cash in on the spending habits of American families. The move toward the suburbs meant that the location of stores should shift from urban to suburban locations. In response to these perceived environmental conditions, Sears launched a strategy of expansion into suburban areas. The strategy was implemented by borrowing heavily and building large stores in major shopping centers throughout the country.

Montgomery Ward also interpreted the environment. Sewell Avery, the chief executive, saw a different trend. He believed that the war would precipitate a severe depression. Costs would be depressed, so affluent companies could make purchases at bargain rates. The strategy formulated by Wards was to not build new stores. They adopted a strategy of retrenchment and

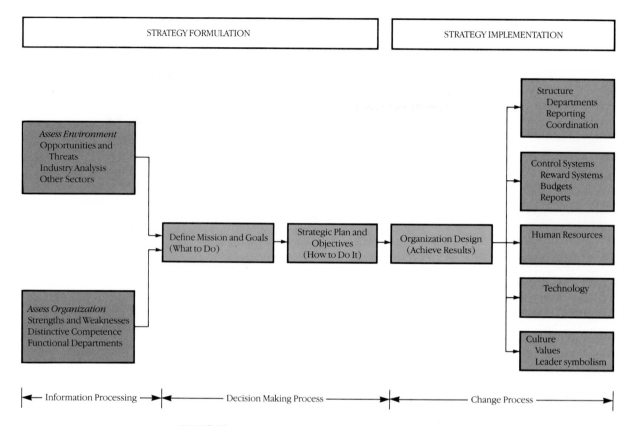

EXHIBIT 12.3. Strategic Management Process.

cost-cutting to save cash for expenditures during the coming business down-turn. The strategy adopted by Montgomery Wards was the opposite of Sears', and much less effective. They misdiagnosed the external environment. The strategy of retrenchment meant they would always be smaller than Sears. After realizing the inappropriateness of Ward's strategy, the Board of Directors voted to have Avery removed as Chief Executive. He did not go willingly, and had to be physically carried out of his office. Meanwhile, Sears grew by leaps and bounds. Wards was never again a well-matched competitor. By 1973, when Sears moved into their new office building—the tallest in the world—Sears had grown to almost four times the size of Wards, with sales of $12.3 billion compared to $3.2 billion for Wards.

STRATEGY FORMULATION

The issues involved in strategy formulation depend upon the size and scope of the organization. Strategy formulation differs according to corporate and business levels.

Corporate versus Business Strategy

Corporate strategy applies to large corporations and is concerned with the combination of business units and product lines that make a coherent business portfolio.[18] Strategic decisions at this level pertain to the acquisition of new businesses, divestments, joint ventures, and reorganizations. Strategies determine how much to grow by acquisition, and which type of businesses complement current lines. Corporate strategy also includes statements about the corporation's creed, values, and responsibility to society.

Business strategy is concerned with a single business or product line.[19] The question addressed by business strategy is: How do we compete? Strategic decisions at the business level pertain to marketing and advertising strategies, investments in new production facilities, product changes, and R&D planning. The difference between corporate and business strategy is illustrated in Exhibit 12.4.

In large, diversified corporations, corporate and business strategies are easily distinguished. Corporate strategies originate with the chief executive at the corporate level, and business strategies are developed within each business unit or product line. When the corporation is small and has only a few products that are similar, corporate and business levels are the same. R. R. Donnelley and Sons Co., for example, is in the business of printing catalogues, magazines, books, and directories. These products are all included within the printing business. Corporate and business levels are the same in a single-line business, and the strategic issues parallel business-level strategy in Exhibit 12.4.

EXHIBIT 12.4. Hierarchy of Corporate and Business Level Strategies.

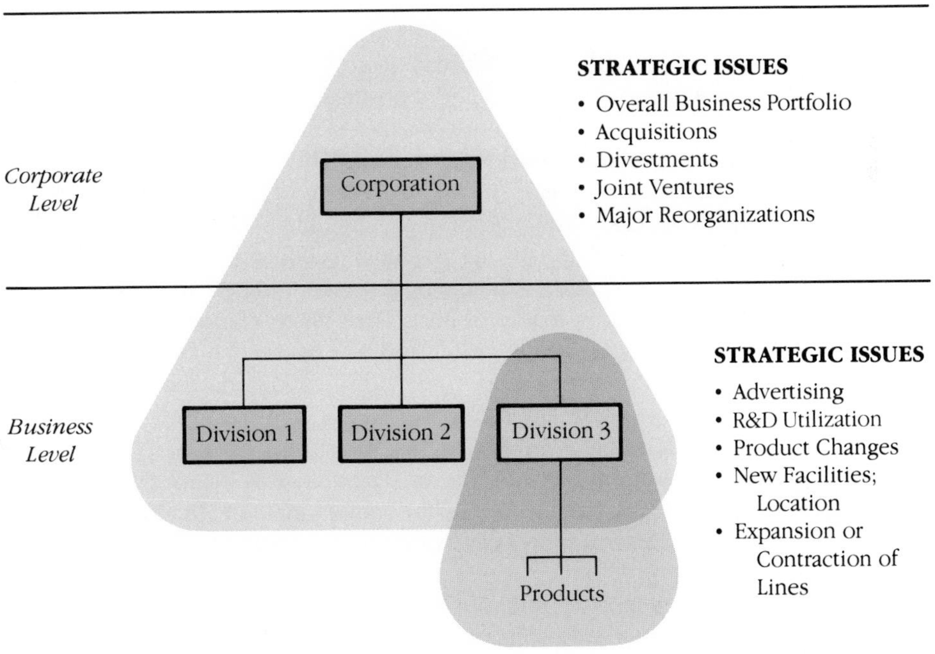

Corporate Level

Corporation

STRATEGIC ISSUES
- Overall Business Portfolio
- Acquisitions
- Divestments
- Joint Ventures
- Major Reorganizations

Business Level

Division 1   Division 2   Division 3

Products

STRATEGIC ISSUES
- Advertising
- R&D Utilization
- Product Changes
- New Facilities; Location
- Expansion or Contraction of Lines

Source: Adapted from Milton Leontiades, *Strategies for Diversification and Change*, (Little, Brown and Company, 1980).

Corporate-Level Strategy

The field of strategic management has developed several models of strategy formulation at the corporate level. One approach to successful corporate strategy is to acquire businesses that complement each other to achieve market and profit goals. Each business represents a different investment in the corporation portfolio.

One framework to analyze corporate-level businesses and product lines was developed by the Boston Consulting Group. The two dimensions in the framework are overall **market growth** and the **share of the market** held by the business. Market growth refers to the product stage in the life cycle.[20] Some products are in a stage of rapid growth, which typically occurs early in the product's life. After products have been widely consumed, growth levels off. The product becomes mature, so increases in company sales come only from increased market share rather than from total market growth. Market share is the percentage of the market held by the business. Regardless of total market size, those products that have a low percentage are considered low market share products. Attaining a high market share requires greater investment, but provides the opportunity for greater cash flow if it can be held.

The dimensions of market growth and market share combine to form four cells in Exhibit 12.5. Each cell describes a business in a different stage of development, each stage having unique implications for corporate cash flow and profits.

1. The star has both high market share and a rapidly growing market. The star has additional growth potential. The star provides increasing sales for the corporation, and the profits are plowed back into the business in the form of investment for future growth. The star is highly visible and attractive, and will generate profits and a positive cash flow as the product matures.

2. The cash cow is a mature business. This business has a large market share but the market is no longer growing. Investment in advertising and plant expansion is no longer required, so the corporation receives a huge positive inflow of cash. The corporation can milk the cash cow to invest in new product lines that have the potential to become stars.

3. The new venture is a new business with high market growth potential. In the initial stages, market share is low. When market share increases rapidly, the business is a prize heifer and will become a star. If market share stays low, it is a problem child. Under ideal conditions, the prize heifer becomes a star, and eventually a cash cow. Under poor conditions, a problem child becomes a dog.

4. The dog is a poor performer. The market is stagnant and mature, and the dog has only a small share of the limited market. The dog typically adds little profit to the corporation and is often identified for sale to other corporations.

The Boston Consulting Group model of corporate strategy seeks to maintain a balanced portfolio of business and product lines. Cash cows are needed to provide the cash for new ventures. Stars are needed to provide rapid growth. Prize heifers are needed to become stars of the future. If dogs provide a small positive cash flow, they may be kept. If dogs are a money loser, they will be divested or abandoned. One company that made effective use of the portfolio strategy for several years was Chesebrough-Ponds.

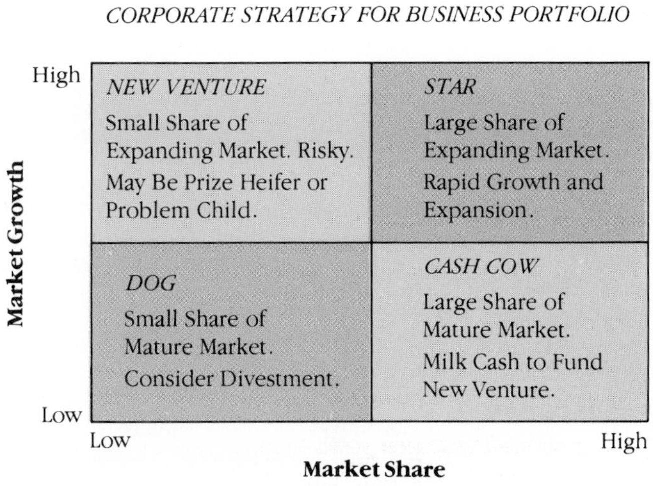

CORPORATE STRATEGY FOR BUSINESS PORTFOLIO

	Low ← Market Share → High

High

NEW VENTURE Small Share of Expanding Market. Risky. May Be Prize Heifer or Problem Child.	*STAR* Large Share of Expanding Market. Rapid Growth and Expansion.
DOG Small Share of Mature Market. Consider Divestment.	*CASH COW* Large Share of Mature Market. Milk Cash to Fund New Venture.

Low

Low   High

Market Share

(Y-axis label: **Market Growth**)

EXHIBIT 12.5. Boston Consulting Group Framework for Corporate Portfolio of Integrated Businesses.

IN PRACTICE 12.2

Chesebrough-Ponds

Ralph Ward took over as chief executive officer of Chesebrough-Ponds in 1968. Corporate strategy was his responsibility. Ralph Ward is a thoughtful, careful decision-maker, but he is also willing to take risks. The transformation he brought about in Chesebrough-Ponds is considered by some to be little short of a miracle.

When Ward took the helm in 1968, Chesebrough-Ponds consisted of two cash cows. Ponds Cold Cream and Vaseline Petroleum Jelly were profitable products that provided a steady inflow of cash. In 1969, Ward purchased Ragu Spaghetti Sauce. This seemed like an unusual business for a health-care products company. Ragu was a regional brand, but it was the market leader in the regions where it was sold. Ward immediately opened up the national market with extensive advertising and dealer promotion. By 1972, Ragu had over 60% of the national market. In three years, Ragu sales increased from $25 million to $350 million a year.

In 1973, Health-Tex, a manufacturer of children's clothing, was acquired. This also seemed like an unusual business for Chesebrough-Ponds, but it was the next star in the corporate portfolio. Health-Tex was a successful regional manufacturer that had great potential on the national level, which Ward exploited over the next few years. Shortly thereafter, he purchased G. H. Bass shoe manufacturing company. Once again, a regional manufacturer made a big kick on the national level. In three years, revenues soared and profits rose over 50%. An additional bonus was that Weejuns Loafers and Sunjuns Sandals were included in the preppy craze that boosted sales beyond expectations.

Other new products followed. Chesebrough-Ponds launched Rave home permanent to take on Toni in what had been a sleepy market for several years. Then came Prince Matchabelli men's fragrance, Chimere perfume for women, and hospital-care products such as Filac electronic thermometers. Vaseline Intensive Care lotion and Pond's Cream and Cocoa Butter lotion were introduced to complement the old cold cream and petroleum jelly products.

Chesebrough-Ponds has been transformed from a mature business into a highly diversified corporation in which no business has more than 14% of sales. The corporation has grown rapidly, and has been consistently profitable. What is most astonishing is that it has market leaders in five different product lines.[21]

Ward's corporate strategy was extraordinarily successful. He used cash from traditional products to invest in new ventures in growth markets. Many of these new ventures matured to become stars in their markets. However, by 1984, corporate growth tapered off as product lines matured. Now Chesebrough-Ponds is in search of more new products, and one candidate, described in In Practice 7.7, is its new "polishing pen," called Aziza, a marking pen through which nail polish can be cleanly put on fingernails.[22]

Business-Level Strategy

Within a given business or product line, what strategy should be adopted? Business strategy depends on demand for the product from the environment, internal structure, and resource allocation. Depending on how the external environment is interpreted, strategy may range from rapid expansion to retrenchment.

A typology of business strategies was proposed by Ray Miles and Charles Snow.[23] They proposed that individual businesses can be classified as defenders, analyzers, or prospectors, depending on how managers interpret the external environment and the product's stage in its life cycle. Exhibit 12.6 summarizes the three strategies.

The **defender** is characterized by stability and retrenchment. Top management perceives that environmental demand is not growing. The product market is mature and stable. The primary strategy is to protect the market share the product now has. Managers strive for efficient internal production and tight control of the organization. This type of business would be organized along the lines of a classic bureaucracy.

The **prospector** is at the other extreme. Managers interpret a dynamic, growing demand from the environment. The market is young and increasing in size. The strategy is to seek new market opportunities. Internal structure will be diverse in order to scan the environment and provide latitude for new ventures. Internal structure will be flexible and loosely controlled to encourage growth and change. The primary structural concern is to facilitate operations and coordinate activities so that growth is achieved.

The **analyzer** adopts an intermediate strategy. The environment is perceived as experiencing moderate change. The strategy of top management is to maintain the stable business while also innovating moderately. Top management wants to protect what they have and also to devote attention to locating new opportunities. Internal production is oriented toward efficiency of current methods, but with some flexibility for new product variations. The structure will provide tight control over existing activities but looser control for growing lines and new activities.

The key element in choosing either the defender, analyzer, or prospector strategy is interpretation of the external environment and assessment of internal characteristics. The top managers determine whether the organization will retrench and defend what they have, or expand into new markets.

EXHIBIT 12.6. Three Business-Level Strategies.

Characteristics	Strategic Types		
	Defender	Analyzer	Prospector
Environment:	Stable	Moderately changing.	Dynamic, growing.
Strategy:	Seal off share of market. Protect turf. Advertise to hold customers.	Maintain market but innovate at edges. Locate opportunities for expansion while protecting current position.	Find and exploit new market opportunities. Scan environment, take risks.
Internal Characteristics:	Efficient production. Retrench. Tight control. Centralized, mechanistic.	Efficient production, yet flexibility for new lines. Tight control over current activities, looser for new lines.	Flexible production. Innovation and coordination. Expansion. Decentralized, organic.

Source: Adapted from Raymond E. Miles, Charles C. Snow, Alan D. Meyer, Henry J. Coleman, Jr., "Organizational Strategy, Structure, and Process," *Academy of Management Review* 3 (1978): 546–562, with permission.

In 1981, Goodyear Tire & Rubber Co. adopted a prospector strategy by increasing plants and getting ready for increased demand for tires. Goodyear executives read the environment optimistically. Firestone, by contrast, perceived that tire demand would fall during the 1980s because of increased gasoline prices. Firestone closed several plants, and retrenched to become more efficient.[24] Companies may have to reevaluate business-level strategy, and occasionally change direction. One company that changed from a defender to prospector strategy was Church's Fired Chicken.

IN PRACTICE 12.3

Church's Fried Chicken Inc.

In 1978, the fast-food industry fad was rapid expansion by creating new menu items and spending heavily on advertising campaigns. But Church's Fried Chicken Inc. became highly profitable by going in the opposite direction. Instead of investing in promotion and new products, Church's stressed internal efficiency. Church's used only fresh chickens, and kept tight controls on franchise restaurants. It also offered large bonuses to managers of profitable restaurants. Efficiency enabled Church's to offer quality meals at low prices, and profitability was way ahead of Kentucky Fried Chicken. Church's designed and made its own kitchen equipment to reduce costs, and had successful training programs that stressed aggressiveness and proficiency.

By 1984, Church's strategy had changed. Profits started falling in about 1980. J. David Bamberger took over the company and started it moving. "We have not been marketing-oriented enough," said Bamberger. The advertising budget shot up from $6 million to $12 million in one year. He also ordered the real estate department to start buying land for new stores. He plans to add 120 stores a year beginning in 1985. One innovation is a newly designed, small, 400-square foot unit that can be operated by one person during slow periods. Bamberger now wants to broaden Church's product line by acquiring restaurant chains that sell foods other than chicken. He also wants to make Church's more upscale without changing its basic clientele. Time will tell whether rapid expansion is the right answer. Some companies are contracting, or moving more strongly into the upscale restaurant market.[25]

STRATEGY IMPLEMENTATION

As described earlier in this chapter, strategy implementation is the use of management and organizational tools to direct the use of organizational resources toward the pursuit of the chosen strategy. Implementation tools can be divided into five broad categories, including structure, control systems, human resources, technology, and culture. For example, in the Church's Fried Chicken case described above, implementation was accomplished through the allocation of resources to real estate to buy land, creating a group to design their own equipment, and paying bonuses to managers who achieved profit goals. A valuable way to think about implementation is for management to design an internal configuration that is congruent with organizational environment and goals. The notion of "configuration" suggests how these organizational components fit together to pursue strategy and enhance organizational performance.

A framework that includes five organizational configurations was proposed by Henry Mintzberg.[26] Each organization has five parts, as illustrated in Exhibit 12.7. Top management is located at the top of the organization. Middle management is at the intermediate levels, and the technical core includes the people who do the basic work of the organization. The technical support staff are the engineers, researchers, and analysts who are responsible for the formal planning and control of the technical core. The administrative support staff provide indirect services, and include clerical, maintenance, and the mailroom. The five parts of the organization may vary in size and importance depending upon the overall environment, strategy, and technology.

Mintzberg proposed that organizational parts could fit together in five basic configurations, which are illustrated in Exhibit 12.8. In addition to the distinct shapes of each organizational configuration, variables such as environment, goals, power, structure, formalization, technology, and size also vary with each configuration. Mintzberg's analysis suggested that these variables hang together in identifiable clusters. This framework is important because it defines key organization theory variables and tells managers the appropriate configuration for specific environments and goals.

The five organization configurations proposed by Mintzberg are simple structure, machine bureaucracy, professional bureaucracy, divisionalized form, and adhocracy.[27] A brief description of each configuration is below. Specific organizational characteristics associated with the appropriate configuration for strategy implementation are summarized in Exhibit 12.9.

EXHIBIT 12.7. The Five Basic Parts of the Organization.

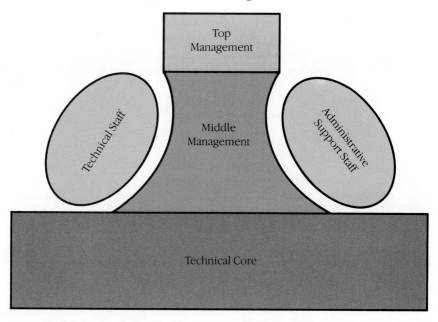

Source: Based on Henry Mintzberg, *The Structuring of Organizations* (Englewood Cliffs, NJ: Prentice-Hall, 1979), pp. 215–297; and Henry Mintzberg, "Organization Design: Fashion or Fit?" *Harvard Business Review*, 59 (January–February, 1981):103–116.

Simple Structure The simple organization is typically a new, small entrepreneurial company. The organization consists of a top manager and workers in the technical core. Only a few support staff are required. There is little specialization or formalization. Coordination and control is from the top, where power and influence are located. Employees have little discretion, although work procedures are typically informal. This organization is suited to a dynamic environment. It can maneuver quickly and competes successfully with larger, less adaptable organizations. Adaptability is required to establish its market. The organization is not powerful and is vulnerable to sudden changes. Unless adaptable, it will fail.

Machine Bureaucracy Machine bureaucracy describes the bureaucratic organizations discussed in chapter 5. This organization is very large, and the technology is routine, often oriented to mass production. Extensive specialization and formalization are present, and key decisions are made at the top. The environment is simple and stable because this organization is not adaptable. The machine bureaucracy is distinguished by large technical and administrative support staffs. Technical support staffs, including engineers, market researchers, financial analysts, and systems analysts, are used to scrutinize, routinize, and formalize work in other parts of the organization. The technical support staff is the dominant group in the organization. Machine bureaucracies are often criticized for lack of control by lower employees, lack of innovation, and an alienated workforce, but they are suited to large size, a stable environment, and the goal of efficiency.

EXHIBIT 12.8. Five Organizational Configurations.

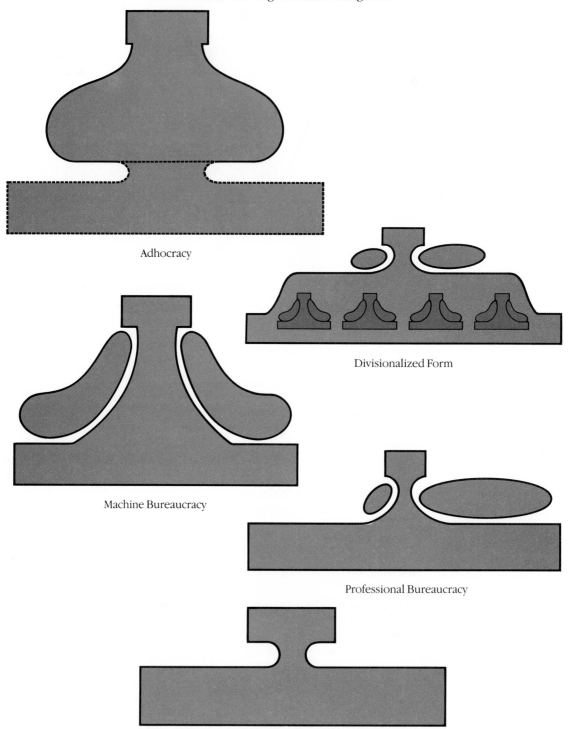

Adhocracy

Divisionalized Form

Machine Bureaucracy

Professional Bureaucracy

Simple Structure

Source: Based on Henry Mintzberg, *The Structuring of Organizations* (Englewood Cliffs, NJ: Prentice-Hall, 1979), pp. 215–297; and Henry Mintzberg, "Organization Design: Fashion or Fit?" *Harvard Business Review,* 59 (January–February, 1981):103–116.

EXHIBIT 12.9. Dimensions of Five Organizational Types.

	Simple Structure	Machine Bureaucracy	Professional Bureaucracy	Divisionalized Form	Adhocracy
Goals/strategy:	Growth survival	Efficiency	Effectiveness, quality	Efficiency, profit	Innovation, adaptation
Age and size:	Typically young and small	Typically old and large	Varies	Typically old and very large	Typically young
Technology:	Simple	Machines but not automated	Service	Divisible, like machine bureaucracy	Very sophisticated, often automated
Environment:	Simple and dynamic; sometimes hostile	Simple and stable	Complex and stable	Relatively simple and stable; diversified markets	Complex and dynamic
Formalization:	Little	Much	Little	Within divisions	Little
Structure:	Functional	Functional	Functional or product	Product, hybrid	Functional and product (matrix)
Coordination:	Direct supervision	Vertical linkage	Horizontal linkage	Headquarters staff	mutual adjustment
Control:	Clan	Bureaucratic	Clan/bureaucratic	Market/bureaucratic	Clan
Technical support staff:	None	Many	Few	Many at HQ for performance control	Small and within project work
Administrative support staff:	Small	Many	Many to support professionals	Split between HQ and divisions	Many but within project work
Key part of organization:	Top management	Technical support staff	Production core	Middle management	Support staff and technical core

Source: Adapted and modified from Henry Mintzberg, *The Structuring of Organizations: A Synthesis of the Research* (Englewood Cliffs, NJ: Prentice-Hall, Inc.: 1979), pp. 466–471.

Professional Bureaucracy   The distinguishing feature of professional bureaucracy is that the production core is composed of professionals, as in hospitals, universities, and consulting firms. While the organization is bureaucratized, people within the production core have autonomy. Long training and experience encourage clan control, and reduce the need for bureaucratic control structures. These organizations often provide services rather than tangible products, and they exist in complex environments. Most of the power rests with the professionals in the production core. Technical support groups are small or nonexistent, but a large administrative support staff is needed to handle the organization's routine administrative affairs.

Divisionalized Form   Divisionalized organizations are extremely large, and are subdivided into product or market groups. There are few liaison devices for coordination between divisions, and there is emphasis on market control using profit and loss statements. The divisionalized form can be quite formalized within divisions because technologies are often routine. The environment for any division will tend to be simple and stable, although the total organization will serve diverse markets. Many large corporations, such as General Motors, Procter & Gamble, Ford, and Westinghouse, are divisionalized organizations. Centralization exists within divisions, and a headquarters staff may retain some functions, such as planning and research.

Adhocracy   Adhocracy develops to survive in complex, dynamic environments. The technology is sophisticated, as in the aerospace and electronic industries. Adhocracies are typically young or middle-aged and quite large, but need to be adaptable. A matrix form of structure typically emerges with horizontal linkage mechanisms and a dual authority structure. Both technical support staff and the production core are important because both have authority over key production elements. The organization has an elaborate division of labor, but is not formalized. Employee professionalism is high, and clan control is stressed. There is selective decentralization, so people at any level may be involved in decision-making. The adhocracy is almost the opposite of the machine bureaucracy in terms of structure, power relationships, and environment.

The point of the five configurations is that strategy implementation should lead to harmony and fit among the elements of structure, control, technology, environment, and strategy. The machine bureaucracy is appropriate for strategy of efficiency in a stable environment. But to impose a machine bureaucracy in a hostile and dynamic environment is a mistake. Managers can implement strategy by designing the correct structural configuration.

ORGANIZATIONAL CULTURE AND SYMBOLS

Strategy implementation through the correct organizational configuration as described above is the responsibility of top management. The final implementation tool available to top managers is organizational culture. New research has discovered how culture fits together with other organizational elements. The reason culture is important is because top management can directly influence culture through activities and symbols.

What is Culture?

Culture is the set of key values, beliefs, and understandings that are shared by members of an organization.[28] Culture defines basic organizational values, and communicates to new members the correct way to think and act, and how things ought to be done.[29] Culture represents the unwritten, feeling part of the organization. The purpose of culture is to provide members with a sense of identity, and to generate a commitment to beliefs and values that are larger than themselves. Culture also enhances the stability of the organization and provides members with understanding that can help them make sense of organizational events and activities.[30]

Culture can be a positive force when used to reinforce the goals and strategy of the organization. Chief executives can influence internal culture to be consistent with corporate strategy. Culture indicates the values employees should adopt to behave in a way consistent with organizational goals. Hewlett-Packard, for example, has adopted an internal culture consistent with the "H-P way." The H-P way is to insist on product quality, recognize achievement, and respect individual employees. McDonald's trains all of its new employees in the dominant values of "quality, service, cleanliness, and value." Each organization has a distinct culture. Two such cultures exist within J. C. Penney and PepsiCo.

IN PRACTICE 12.4

J. C. Penney and PepsiCo.

J. C. Penney Co. cares about its employees and customers. J. C. Penney is a great place to work, and its customers will always receive satisfaction. These are the dominant values in Penney's corporate culture. Management actions have reinforced these values since founder James Cash Penney laid down the seven guiding principles, called "the Penney idea." These principles have brought forth tremendous loyalty from staff and customers. One store manager was reprimanded by the President for making too much profit, which was unfair to customers. Customers can return merchandise with no questions asked. Everyone is treated as an individual. Employees are encouraged to participate in the decision-making process. Layoffs are avoided at all costs. Unsuccessful employees are transferred to new jobs instead of being fired. Long-term employee loyalty is especially valued.

PepsiCo has a completely different value system. Pepsi is in hot competition with Coke for a larger share of the soft drink market. Pepsi's values reflect the desire to overtake Coke. Managers engage in fierce competition against each other to acquire market share, to squeeze more profits out of their business, and to work harder. Employees who do not succeed are terminated. They must win to get ahead. A career can be made or broken on one-tenth of a point of market share. Everyone knows the corporate culture and thrives on the creative tension thus generated. The internal structure is lean and adaptable. The company picnic is characterized by intensely competitive team sports. Managers change jobs frequently and are motivated to excel. The culture is characterized by a go-go atmosphere and success at all costs.

One tangible indicator of the difference in culture between J. C. Penney and PepsiCo is the length of employee tenure. Penney's executives have been with the company thirty-three years on average, while Pepsi's executives have averaged only ten years.[31]

Implementation of Culture

Top executives do not drive trucks or run machines. They deal in symbols, ceremonies, and images.[32] Managers signal values, beliefs, and goals to employees. Top executives are watched by employees just as professors are watched by students. Students look for signs about which topics are important for the exam, what the professor likes, and how to get a good grade. In the world of business and government, the ceremonial and symbolic activities of top executives are used to reach large numbers of people.

The underlying value system of the organization cannot be managed in the traditional way. Techniques top managers use to convey the appropriate values and beliefs are rites and ceremonies, stories, symbols, and slogans.[33] Executives often need to learn ceremonial skills, and how to use speech, writing, and gestures to influence company values. Symbols, stories, and ceremonies are techniques to manage organizational culture, which is hard to shape by conventional means.[34] These activities provide information about what counts in the organization, and where people fit into the organization. Issuing a written rule or policy, for example, would have almost no impact on the organization's value system. As one writer in organization theory, Karl Weick, expressed it, "managerial work can be viewed as managing myth, symbols, and labels ... because managers traffic so often in images, the appropriate role for the manager may be the evangelist rather than the accountant."[35] Ceremonies, stories, symbols, and slogans can all be used to directly influence internal corporate culture.

Ceremonies and Rites **Ceremonies and rites** are the elaborate, planned activities that make up a special event, and often are conducted for the benefit of an audience. Managers can hold ceremonies and rites in order to provide dramatic examples of what the company values. Ceremonies are a special occasion that reinforces specific values, creates a bond among people for sharing an important understanding, and can anoint and celebrate heroes and heroines who symbolize important beliefs and activities.[36]

The following examples illustrate how ceremonies are used by top managers to reinforce dominant values throughout the organization.

■ In a major midwestern firm, every Christmas the chairman of the board would come down from his office on the top floor to walk through every department, shaking hands with each employee. This was the only time he would be seen by many, and his appearance served as a ceremony to communicate concern for the organizational "family."[37]

■ In a major bank, election as an officer was seen as the key event in a successful career. A series of rites accompanied every promotion to bank officer, including a special method of notification, the new officer being taken to the officers' dining room for the first time, and the new officer buying drinks on Friday after his notification.[38]

■ An important annual event at McDonald's is the nationwide contest to determine the best hamburger cooking team in the country. Competition takes place among teams at the local level, and gradually progresses to where the best teams from the company compete at the national level. The cooking teams are judged on minute details that determine whether the hamburger is cooked to perfection. The ceremony is highly visible and communicates to all employees the McDonald's value of hamburger quality.[39]

■ Tupperware saleswomen hold a weekly Rally at which saleswomen are recognized in reverse order of sales volume. The event is associated with celebration and hoopla. Almost every employee receives some form of recognition. The ceremony reinforces the goal of sales volume held by the company.[40]

Stories   **Stories** are narratives based on true events that are frequently shared among organizational employees and told to new employees to inform them about the organization. Some stories are considered **legends** because the events are historic and may have been embellished with fictional details. Other stories are **myths,** which are consistent with the values and beliefs of the organization but are not supported by facts.[41] Stories are important because they keep alive the primary values of the organization and provide a shared understanding among all employees.

■ At Robinson Jewelers, a division of W. R. Grace & Co., stories are told during training programs for new employees. One story describes a store representative who delivered a wedding ring directly to the church because the ring had been ordered late. Another story is about Lou Schwartz, who once delivered an engagement ring in the midst of a blizzard. These stories stress the values of Robinson Jewelers, which are customer service and fair value.[42]

■ At Minnesota Mining and Manufacturing, top managers keep stories alive that describe development projects that were killed by top management. The hero of the stories worked on the project in secret, and eventually proved management wrong by developing a successful new product. These stories are even repeated by top managers to keep the entrepreneurial spirit at 3M, and to let employees know that if they feel frustrated and discouraged that they are not the first ones to overcome considerable odds in the process of innovation.[43]

▪ Two stories that symbolize the "H-P way" at Hewlett-Packard involved the founders, David Packard and Bill Hewlett. After work hours one evening, Packard was wandering around the Palo Alto lab. He discovered a prototype constructed of inferior materials. Packard destroyed the model and left a note saying, "That's not the H-P way. Dave." Similarly, Bill Hewlett is said to have gone to a plant on Saturday and found the lab stock room door locked. He cut the padlock, and left a note saying, "Don't ever lock this door again. Thanks, Bill." Bill wanted the engineers to have free access to components, and even take them home, in order to stimulate creativity that is part of the "H-P way." [44]

The importance of stories is that they provide a medium through which basic values and images can be communicated among employees. Managers can keep these stories going by repeating them at public gatherings. Stories also meet the needs of employees by giving them something to identify with and by clarifying organizational goals. Many organizations have stories about the founders and important events. Stories in different organizations often resemble one another in the way they reduce uncertainty for employees and clarify organizational values.[45]

Symbols   A **symbol** means that one thing represents another thing. In one sense, ceremonies, stories, slogans, and rites are symbols. They symbolize deeper values of the organization. Another important symbol is a physical artifact of the organization. Physical symbols are powerful because they focus attention on a specific item.

▪ Eastern Airlines made paperweights that included metal from each aircraft it had flown during its history. This paperweight was distributed to key employees and was never again to be duplicated. It took on almost spiritual value among employees who received it. Employees would not trade or sell them. Employees identified with the symbol and felt they were an integral part of the company.[46]

▪ At Mary Kay Cosmetics, Mary Kay gives Cadillacs to each year's top sales-people. The Cadillac is painted in a distinctive shade, called "Mary Kay pink," to symbolize a successful sales year. Another symbol at Mary Kay is the Golden Rule marble. The marble is a physical representation of the company credo. At luncheons that are part of training sessions, the Golden Rule marble is placed on each plate as a special memento. During speeches, the significance of the Golden Rule as a guiding value at Mary Kay Cosmetics is described.[47]

▪ At Chick-fil-A, a chicken franchise chain, franchise managers receive a white Continental Mark VII if they increase sales by 40%. They get to drive the car for a year, but if they increase sales again the following year, they get to keep the car. The company also has "Chick-fil-A" emblazoned in red and black on the Continental, which serves as an advertising symbol as well as a symbol of high sales productivity.[48]

The value of physical symbols is that they communicate important cultural values. If the physical symbols are consistent with the ceremonies, stories, values, and slogans, they are a powerful facilitator of culture.

Language   Many companies use a specific saying, slogan, metaphor, or other form of language to convey special meaning to employees. Slogans can be readily picked up and repeated by employees as well as customers of the company.

■ T. J. Watson, Jr., son of the founder of International Business Machines, used the metaphor "wild ducks" to describe the type of employees needed by IBM. The metaphor originated from a story about ducks flying south for the winter that found food set out on a lake. Some ducks continued to fly south while others stopped to eat and stayed for the winter. After a time, the ducks that stayed had difficulty flying at all. The moral was, "You can make wild ducks tame, but you can never make tame ducks wild again." [49] "Wild ducks" symbolized the freedom and opportunity that must be available to keep from taming creative employees at IBM.

■ H. R. "Bum" Bright, a Texas tycoon and new owner of the Dallas Cowboys, coined the phrase "Bring back the book" to symbolize the philosophy of success in his business enterprises. The philosophy began when Bright was a student at Texas A&M. He was assigned by a professor to get a book from the library. He came back with the information that the book had been checked out. The professor chewed him out, and said the world doesn't pay off on anything but results. Bright was embarrassed, so he went back to the library, contacted the person who had the book, and went through all necessary procedures to acquire it. Bright learned that persistence pays off, that only results count, and that if he failed to do a job he wouldn't get ahead. Employees within the company often wear buttons emblazoned, "Bring back the book," to foster the persistence-gets-results philosophy.[50]

Slogans are effective ways of communicating culture because they can be used in a variety of public statements by chief executives. Slogans enable the chief executive's philosophy to be disseminated widely. "IBM means service," "The 11th commandment is never kill a new product idea" (3M), and "Everybody at Northrup is in marketing" illustrate slogans that are used in organizations. They symbolize what the company stands for both for employees and for people outside the organization.

Summary   Organizational culture is an important new tool of strategy implementation. Managers can design ceremonies and slogans, devise symbols, and repeat stories to disseminate the underlying values and philosophy that are consistent with organizational strategy. These devices are means through which organizational members can reach a shared understanding about these values. Exhibit 12.10 illustrates the relationship between culture and the means of communicating culture. On the left side of Exhibit 12.10,

EXHIBIT 12.10. Examples of Cultural Values and Beliefs, and Means for Implementation.

Culture	Implementing Culture
Shared Values Customer service at any cost Employees are part of family Attain sales targets	*Shared Ceremonies* Annual awards for meritorious customer service Monthly meetings to acknowledge people who attain 100% of sales targets
Shared Beliefs Customers deserve special treatment We like this company The company cares about us	*Shared Stories* Founder's difficulty establishing company over many obstacles, but never laid off anyone Heroic efforts to please customers by legendary salespeople
	Shared Symbols and Slogans "Build bridges" (to be in touch with customers) "We don't stand on rank." (Equality of family) Open offices for easy communication Special plaques for customer service and sales leaders

Source: Adapted and modified from Vijay Sathe, "Implications of Corporate Culture: A Manager's Guide to Action," *Organizational Dynamics,* (Autumn, 1983):5–23.

specific cultural values and beliefs for a company are identified. On the right side, ceremonies, stories, symbols, and slogans that would be consistent with cultural values and beliefs are identified. Managers and employees thus share a common belief system that reinforces organizational strategy.

One example of a manager who takes advantage of his top leader position to influence strategy and culture is Jim Treybig of Tandem Computers. Through a variety of ceremonies and symbols, he helped the company define a culture that is just right for the strategy of Tandem.

IN PRACTICE 12.5

Tandem Computers

Tandem Computers is one of the biggest success stories ever, and one reason is the unusual management style. At 4:00 every Friday afternoon, the employee beer bust is in full swing at Tandem Computers' offices around the country. Every week 60% of the company drops in at the beer bust for an hour, joined by visiting customers and suppliers. President Jim Treybig does not confine the fun to Fridays. Last year they had a Halloween costume party. Another big event was the "incredible hunk" contest sponsored by the company's female employees. Employees have neither time clocks nor name tags, but they do have flexible hours, a swimming pool, a volleyball court with locker room and showers. To keep employees refreshed, they are required to take a six-week paid sabbatical every four years.

Is this company for real? After only seven and a half years, Tandem is selling over $300 million a year and is on *Fortune's* second 500 list. Despite all the fun, success has not been an accident. Treybig picked the right strategy, and developed an internal culture to enhance it. The strategy is to build foolproof computers for a precise market niche: on-line computer operations, like bank transactions or hotel bookings, where a system must not fail or garble the data. Tandem accomplishes this by providing two computers, working in Tandem, that split the work load evenly. If one half has a problem, the entire burden shifts to the other half to guard the data from contamination. Treybig reinforces his strategy by giving stock options to *every* employee in the company. He also makes sure employees understand the consequence of mistakes. He explains the business and the five-year plan, and shows them how a little oversight, such as shipping several computers late, can drop profits, which leaves less money for research and employee incentives.

Treybig is even more serious about his five cardinal points for running a company, which define the Tandem culture.

1. All people are good.
2. People, workers, management, and company are all the same thing.
3. Every single person in a company must understand the essence of the business.
4. Every employee must benefit from the company's success.
5. You must create an environment where all of the above can happen.

Employees are soaked in an endless stream of company information urging loyalty, hard work, and respect for co-workers. New employees go to orientation lectures and breakfasts, receive newsletters and glossy magazines, and study the mandatory volume entitled, *Understanding Our Philosophy,* which is the core of a two-day course.

Everyone learns that employee welfare is taken very, very seriously at Tandem. For example, *Understanding Our Philosophy* says, "You never have the right at Tandem to screw a person or to mistreat them. It's not allowed . . . ." A group of assemblers complained about their manager, and he was let go in a matter of days. "He didn't look on people as people," Treybig said.

One reason the culture works is that Tandem hires exceptional people. One stock clerk came for four interviews, taking about four hours. A potential middle manager can expect twenty grueling hours of interviews, both with top-level managers and prospective peers. Prospective employees have to want to work at Tandem for reasons other than money.

Treybig is a symbol, almost a hero. He symbolizes single-minded hard work and concern for people. Without question the system works. Tandem's productivity figures are among the highest in the industry. And the employees love it. They say the culture helps them grow. The rich opportunities for promotion, learning, and initiative are great for the self-image of employees, and lets them move toward achieving their goals of self realization.

The morale is fantastic and Treybig believes continued growth is crucial to success in this industry. Tandem must be large enough to play with the big boys like IBM and Digital Equipment. More management controls will be needed as size increases, but Treybig plans to stay involved in Tandem's culture.[51]

MANAGEMENT SUCCESSION

So far in this chapter we have described how top managers are responsible for assessing the external environment, evaluating internal strengths and weaknesses, formulating strategy, and implementing strategy through structure, people, systems, and culture. This final section of the chapter briefly explores top executive succession. Executive turnover has been studied as a way to determine the extent to which an executive can have positive or negative impact on organizational performance. An example of a top manager who had negative consequences is John DeLorean, whose extravagant and unrealistic decisions caused the downfall of DeLorean's motor company.[52] On the other hand, the decisions of Donald Burr, chairman of People Express, have been instrumental in creating the kind of internal culture and structure responsible for the overwhelming success of the new airline.[53] The research on executive succession indicates whether organizations should develop procedures to periodically replace top managers, and whether chief executives typically make a difference to corporate performance.

Succession and Adaptation

One finding from succession research is that for the organization as a whole, periodic management turnover is an important form of organizational adaptation. In organizations characterized by turbulent environments, rapid change, and uncertainty, the turnover of organizational leaders is greater.[54] Organizations in a turbulent environment are more difficult to manage, so new energy and vitality are needed on a frequent basis.

Top manager turnover also allows the organization to cope with specific contingencies. The selection of a new chief executive may reflect the need for a specific skill or specialization.[55] If the dominant issue confronting the organization is financing mergers, choosing a finance person as chief executive gives priority to financial activities. In a hospital, the background of the chief administrator often indicates that one medical specialty or environmental domain is important. A background in business is helpful if the hospital must raise funds from private corporations.[56] The selection of a new top manager enables the organization to adapt to specific environmental needs.

Large organizations tend to experience greater rates of succession than small organizations.[57] Large corporations often have specific turnover policies. Managers are promoted into the chief executive slot at the age of fifty-five or sixty, so they will not occupy the position for more than ten years. Turnover every few years can have a positive effect on the organization. If a corporation chief executive and top management team serve for a very long period of time, say twenty years or more, organizational stagnation is inevitable. New executives are not coming in to provide fresh energy, new goals, or expertise for new environmental situations.

One example of how management succession is used for adaptation is Coca-Cola Co. In recent years, Coca-Cola became a tradition-bound, stagnating corporation. Coke was not adapting to its turbulent international environment. Coca-Cola was also losing ground to PepsiCo in the U.S. market. That has all changed with the appointment of new top executives who provided new blood and an international perspective. The new chief executive of Coca-Cola was born in Havana, Cuba. The chief financial officer is Egyptian. The president of Coke USA is an Argentine. The marketing vice-president is a Mexican. These changes in top management have revitalized Coke in both the U.S. and foreign markets. The most visible changes were to create "Diet Coke," which immediately became the best-selling diet soft drink, and to change the secret formula for regular Coke.[58] Another example of top management turnover was the removal of President Donald N. Smith as president of Godfather's Pizza Inc. His skills did not meet the need for careful internal operations and cost control demanded by Godfather's competitive situation. His replacement, Charles Boppell, is helping improve Godfather's pressing internal problems.[59]

Succession and Performance

Another fundamental question is whether the chief executive can influence organizational performance. For example, in 1983 companies such as Continental Airlines, Celanese, Tiger International, Baldwin-United, and Northwest Energy had turnover at the top.[60] Does the replacement of the top executive make a difference to performance?

Ritual Scapegoating   One type of organization that can help answer the question of whether manager turnover influences performance is athletic teams. The coach is the top manager of the team, and coaches are regularly replaced in both college and professional sports. Several studies have analyzed coaching changes to see whether an improvement in performance occurs. The general finding is that manager turnover does *not* lead to improved performance.[61] Teams that are extremely bad tend to get better, whether or not the coach is replaced.

An interesting finding from these studies is that performance leads to turnover.[62] Teams with poor records experienced greater succession. The relationship between turnover and performance is the opposite of what we might expect. Rather than a new manager leading to a better record, the poor record leads to the firing of the old manager. The new manager does not make the team better, but firing the previous manager serves as a symbol for what the team is trying to achieve. Thus the term "ritual scapegoating" describes how turnover signals to fans and others associated with the team that efforts are being made to improve the team's performance record.[63] The firing of the manager is more of a ceremonial symbol than a strategy for improvement.

Corporate Performance   A corporation is much larger and more diverse than an athletic team. Can the chief executive make a difference in a corporate setting? Top managers in large corporations function under many constraints. Corporations have a huge number of employees, many of whom are unionized. Demand for a company's output is influenced by industry and economic conditions that seem outside anyone's control. Chief executives work within many restrictions. Can they influence the corporation to perform well, even within these constraints?

An important study of chief executives surveyed 167 corporations over a twenty-year period.[64] Each time a chief executive was replaced, the changes in sales, net earnings, and profits were recorded for the next three years. Analysis of these data indicated that sales and net earning levels were the result of general economic conditions and industry circumstances. When conditions were good and the industry was successful, all corporations had high sales and net earnings regardless of chief executive succession.

However, leader succession was associated with net profits. Top managers seemed to influence the factors that translated into profits. Chief executives influenced profits by changing the goals of the organization, by selling off unprofitable subsidiaries, or by adopting new strategies. Chief executives also had more impact in industries where advertising was important and consumers formed a sizable percentage of the market. Follow-up studies have also suggested that chief executives have impact on performance in certain organizational settings. A survey of 193 manufacturing companies found that chief executive turnover and financial strategies were associated with corporate profitability and improved stock prices. Stock prices indicate the evaluation of company performance by investors.[65] A study of ministers in Methodist churches found a significant impact by certain ministers.[66] Ministers were transferred on the average of every five and one-half years. Some ministers were able to improve church attendance, membership, and giving in every church they served, thus showing that some leaders regularly had positive impact on organizational performance.

On the other hand, importance of chief executives means that turnover in some situations may lead to poorer performance. A study of managerial succession in local newspapers found that when the founder who created and developed the organization left, performance dropped. In the early stages of the organizational life cycle, or when the organization depends heavily on a single individual, the importance of top managers is seen by a reduction rather than an improvement in performance after succession.[67]

A realistic interpretation of these findings is the conclusion that corporate performance is the result of many factors. General economic and industry conditions outside the control of the chief executive do affect sales and net earnings. However, outcomes under the control of executive strategy—such as net profit—are influenced by the chief executive because net profit is an outcome of strategic choices. The impact of chief executives on performance is also greater in smaller organizations and in organizations that serve ultimate consumers directly. In these situations chief executives can formulate and implement strategy, and use symbolic action to affect the direction and the performance of the company. An example of how a chief executive affected performance after a turnover is the Arkla Utility Company.

IN PRACTICE 12.6

Arkla Utility Co.

Arkla has been a household word in Arkansas for twenty-five years. Now the word is spreading to Wall Street, where the stock price has doubled in the last year to $40 a share. The price-earnings ratio recently was 12 to 1, one of the highest in the industry. In just three years Standard & Poor's and Moody's have upgraded the company's bond rating four times; both now give it a double-A. Security analysts expect earnings to increase by at least 20% annually for the next five years. Net income was $73 million last year on sales of $975 million.

Arkla is in an extraordinarily powerful position. With the help of an aggressive gas exploration and acquisition team, the company has cornered supplies to last fourteen years . . . and it's just now gearing up to penetrate the huge Louisiana industrial market. Many customers there will be petrochemical plants that use gas not only for fuel but also as a raw material.

Arkla is firmly in the grip of a brash young chairman, president, and chief executive, Sheffield Nelson, 40, who has proved to be a tangible asset in his own right. "Nelson has performed a staggering feat by turning Arkla from a humdrum utility into the best-positioned company in the industry," says Richard Lilly, an analyst who specializes in up-and-coming southern companies for Raymond James & Associates of St. Petersburg, Florida. Nelson has managed the company well and bargained the Arkansas Public Service Commission into some remarkably liberal rates. And he did this while waging a protracted struggle with his own mentor: Arkla's former boss and a big stockholder, William R. "Witt" Stephens, 74, patriarch of one of the South's wealthiest families.

By the early 1970s, Arkla executives now say, the company was turning into "junk." Talent was leaving, and half the company's cars were so old and ill-maintained that they had to be jump-started every morning. Stephens was earning, by choice, only $100,000 when he retired in January 1973. He had refused increases offered by the board, saying he didn't need the money and the government would only tax it away. Unfortunately, he was paying comparably low wages to employees who didn't own investment banks to supplement their paychecks. At the end of Stephens' tenure, some full-time Arkla employees qualified for and collected food stamps.

Nelson's flair for sales and public relations has been vital in Arkla's success. Like Stephens, Nelson projects a down-home image; he listens to country music and serves black-eyed peas and cornbread at board meetings. ("They don't eat that kind of cookin' anywhere else," he says.)

Nelson nurtures his and Arkla's image by raising funds and speaking for such causes as the United Way and a home for battered women. Four years ago, Arkla cut its lines of credit to New York banks and replaced them with a web of credit lines to 350 local banks in the five states where Arkla has operations. Three Arkla board members are active in politics: a woman who sits on the Little Rock city council, a state senator, and the former chairman of the state Democratic party.

Nelson's popularity seems to have helped him with the regulators. In 1975, he persuaded the Arkansas Public Service Commission to allow the company to charge large industrial customers prices based on the replacement cost of gas. Most state commissions apply a rate formula based on the average cost, which is almost always lower than replacement cost. Arkansas laws also permit Nelson to bill customers for anticipated rate increases before they're approved. This permits Arkla to move rates up gradually, avoiding sudden jumps that attract attention, and brings in cash without the usual delay. Nelson avoids the appearance of greed; he'll take a good rate without dickering for extra pennies. Says Mac Norton, head of the Arkansas utility commission, "Nelson knows if the hog gets too fat, it'll be slaughtered."[68]

Nelson's success with Arkla illustrates many of the themes in this chapter. Nelson interprets and builds linkages to key elements in the external environment, such as the public service commission and area banks. He nurtures Arkla's public image because it is good for business. He established an improved corporate culture. He implemented a strategy of supplying gas to petrochemical plants in Louisiana, and it paid off. Management turnover, with Nelson succeeding Stephens, led to dramatically increased profits and stock prices (Exhibit 12.11), thanks to a new internal culture and an effective corporate strategy.

SUMMARY AND INTERPRETATION

The purpose of this chapter has been to look at the role of top management in organizations. Top managers interpret and enact the external environment, set goals, formulate strategy, and implement strategy to ensure action to reach the goals. The task of top management involves information-processing, decision-making, influencing culture, and designing the correct structural configuration.

Within the array of managerial activities, one of the most important is strategy formulation. At the corporate level, top managers seek a balanced portfolio. Each business under the corporate umbrella can provide a different benefit. Some may be risky new ventures, but with the possibility of becoming a fast-growing star of the future. Other businesses represent stable sources of cash that can be used to finance other activities. At the level of individual businesses, strategy formulation is concerned with advertising campaigns, product changes, and whether to retrench or expand. Success at both the

EXHIBIT 12.11. Arkla's Earnings per Share.

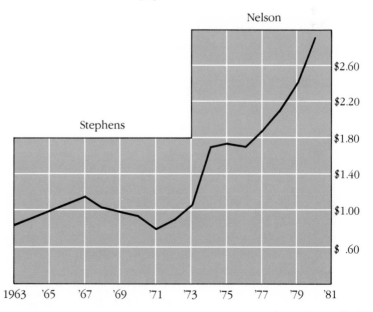

Source: Peter Nulty, "Little Rock's Hot-Cookin' Gas Company," *Fortune,* October 5, 1981, pp. 148–153, with permission. Copyright © Time, Inc. All rights reserved.

business and corporate level is related to the selection of correct strategies that integrate the needs of the external environment with the abilities of the organization.

An equally important responsibility of top management is strategy implementation. Implementation is the use of organization design to achieve results. The field of organization theory pertains to the administrative tools used in strategy implementation. Top managers use organization structure, control systems, human resources, technology, and internal culture to move the organization toward its strategic objectives. Strategy implementation requires that the top managers make things happen. One important goal of strategy implementation is to seek congruence among factors in the environment, technology, strategy, and structure of the organization. When these factors are in harmony, the organization is able to attain better performance.

Finally, recent research has discovered the impact of top managers on corporate culture, and has described the importance of succession procedures for organizational health. Top managers make a difference. Top managers stand for and symbolize cultural values and images they consider important. Symbols reinforce management strategy. Top manager turnover provides new energy and perspectives for organizational leadership. Succession also provides new skills to cope with changing environmental conditions, and may symbolize a new organizational direction. Enforced succession on a periodic basis enables the organization to adapt to the environment.

KEY CONCEPTS

adhocracy
analyzer
business-level strategy
cash cow
corporate-level strategy
ceremonies and rites
culture
defender
divisionalized form
dog
enactment
governance
interpretation
machine bureaucracy

new venture
professional bureaucracy
prospector
ritual
scapegoating
simple structure
star
stories
strategy
strategy formulation
strategy implementation
succession and performance
symbol

DISCUSSION QUESTIONS

1. Define the strategic management process. How does it link the internal and external domains of top managers?

2. Strategic choice means that the top managers interpret the environment and make decisions about size and technology. How does that differ from the concept of "enactment"?

3. Pitney-Bows Corporation recently decided to change strategy in the copier business. They closed down their research and development facility. They will rely on Japanese suppliers for their new technological developments. Would their strategic decision be considered a corporate- or business-level strategy? Discuss.

4. What is the difference between a prize heifer and a problem child? What role do cash cows play in the corporate portfolio?

5. How does internal organization structure and emphasis differ between organizations adopting prospector versus defender strategies?

6. What are the five organizational types proposed by Mintzberg? What are key similarities and differences among these types?

7. Is strategy formulation or implementation more important to organizational success? Which do you think is more difficult to do?

8. What is organizational culture? Describe the tools managers can use to influence internal culture.

9. Top management succession is one technique organizations use to adapt to the external environment. Describe how this happens and give an example.

10. What is ritual scapegoating? Do corporations ever do this?

11. A consultant said, "The individual who occupies the chief executive position can have substantial impact on profits, but not on sales." Explain why you agree or disagree with that statement.

GUIDES TO ACTION

As an organization top manager:

1. Pay attention to the environment. Interpret the external environment and enact measures that will allow the organization to be successful over the long run.

2. Evaluate internal strengths and weaknesses as well as environmental threats and opportunities. Combine these factors to define goals and select strategy that takes advantage of the fit between organization and environment. Use this information to formulate and implement the strategy best suited to the organization.

3. Take control of the organization's strategy-making machinery. Formulate either a corporate- or business-level strategy that determines which product to produce, growth rate, advertising budget, and acquisition or divestment of product lines. Implement strategy with the tools of structure, control systems, human resources, technology, and culture. Improve corporate profits and stock prices through the selection and implementation of appropriate strategies.

4. Act as a symbol for the internal culture and values that are important to the organization. Influence the value system of the organization through the use of ceremonies, slogans, symbols, and stories. Communicate important values to employees to enhance organizational effectiveness.

5. Encourage periodic top management succession. Use built-in succession procedures to ensure a continuous flow of fresh energy and ideas into the upper ranks. Adapt to specific environmental conditions by bringing needed

skills and experience into the chief executive positions through this periodic succession.

Consider these Guides when analyzing the following cases and when answering the questions listed after each case.

CASES FOR ANALYSIS

TIME, INC.*

J. Richard Munro, chief executive of Time, has been repeating a simple message for several years now: "Manage better, plan better, get your returns up." This advice has been needed because Time's performance has been mixed. Several new ventures have not turned out well. Time is now re-evaluating its strategy and culture, and preparing for change in its two primary product groups—publishing and video.

In the publishing business, Time's magazines are established and profitable. Its leading magazines—*Time, Fortune, People,* and *Sports Illustrated*—account for a sizable percentage of the market. The magazine unit also successfully relaunched *Life,* and has steadily improved *Money* magazine.

In contrast, Time's book-publishing business is not doing well. Time-Life books have broken even, but have never been highly profitable. A new magazine called *TV-Cable Week* was a failure. The magazine was to contain TV listings for each cable system in the country. Time misjudged the market, because cable-system operators would not give Time their subscription lists. Moreover, *TV Guide* responded with a better product. Coordinating programming for hundreds of cable systems also was overwhelmingly complicated.

The mixed results in the publishing business have been offset by successes in the video business. Time's stellar performer is HBO. In 1976, it was a small, struggling, money-losing business. Now HBO has two highly profitable networks, HBO and Cinemax, that accounted for over half of the video group's profits. HBO controls over 60% of the pay-television market. Future growth will probably slow, however. More pay-TV channels may become available, and the home-video cassette players are taking away part of the business.

The only cloud in the video group was Time's withdrawal from subscription TV and teletext. Teletext was a project that would deliver 4,000 pages of text, information, and games to home television sets via cable. Home terminals for using the text were not available, and there was little customer demand for the service. Subscription television was designed for use in areas not wired for cable. Distributed over normal TV, the signal was scrambled, and had to be unscrambled by a decoder. Again, the demand was not sufficient to offset high costs.

As Time overcomes past mistakes, top management is stressing change

* Laura Landro, "A Proposed Spinoff, Cancelled Projects Mark New Era at Time Inc.," *The Wall Street Journal,* December 6, 1983, pp. 1, 22; "Developing Ten Magazine Ideas, Expects Two Prototypes by End 1984," *The Wall Street Journal,* April 20, 1984, p. 14.

in the internal culture. Traditionally it's been known as a "country-club culture." Individual businesses could go pretty much at their own speed and do what they wanted. More centralized management is also expected. Top management will provide more direction from the top, and a centralized focus will characterize long-range planning. The strong top-management culture exists now at HBO, and Time hopes to see it spread through the publishing division.

One new move by Time is to have HBO make its own movies. Other new ventures under consideration are to develop cable and pay-television businesses in Europe. Executives plan to double the basic pay-television business in five years. But they also see the need to build other businesses as well. In the publishing division, ten new magazine ideas have been launched. Time is pushing several of these into prototype, which indicates a new willingness to take risks.

Questions

1. Analyze the products at Time Inc. using the Boston Consulting Group's framework for corporate-level strategy formulation.
2. Do the product groups differ with respect to business-level strategy? Is culture used to implement new strategy? Is the success of past strategies consistent with the internal culture of the two product groups? Discuss.

UNITED PRODUCTS, INC.*

Having just returned from lunch, Mr. George Brown, president of United Products, Inc., was sitting in his office thinking about his upcoming winter vacation where he and his family would be spending three weeks skiing on Europe's finest slopes. His daydreaming was interrupted by a telephone call from Mr. Hank Stevens, UPI's General Manager. Mr. Stevens wanted to know if their two o'clock meeting was still on. The meeting had been scheduled to review actions UPI could take in light of the currently depressed national economy. In addition, Mr. Brown was concerned about his accountant's report detailing results for the company's recently completed fiscal year. Although 1974 hadn't been a bad year, results were not as good as expected. This report, along with the economic situation, was forcing Mr. Brown to reevaluate alternative actions being considered for the future.

COMPANY HISTORY

United Products, Inc., established in 1941, was engaged in the sales and service of basic supply items for shipping and receiving, production and packaging, research and development, and office and warehouse departments. Mr. Brown's father, the founder of the company, recognized the tax advantages in establishing separate businesses rather than trying to operate the business through one large organization. Accordingly, over the years companies were either closed or sold off. By the mid-1960s, he had succeeded in structuring a chain of four related companies covering the geographic area from Chicago eastward.

* This case was prepared by Professor Jeffrey C. Shuman of Babson College. Copyright 1980, Babson College, Babson Park, Massachusetts. All rights reserved. Reproduced by permission.

In 1967, feeling it was time to step aside and turn over active control of the business to his sons, the elder Mr. Brown recapitalized the company and merged or sold off the separate companies. When the restructuring process was completed, he had set up two major companies. United Products, Inc. was to be run by his youngest son, George Brown, with its headquarters in Massachusetts, while his other son, Richard, was to operate United Products Southeast, Inc., headquartered in Florida.

Although the Brown brothers occasionally work together and are on each other's Board of Directors, the two companies operate on their own. As Mr. George Brown explained, "Since we are brothers, we often get together and discuss business, but the two are separate companies and each files its own tax return." This case considers only United Products, Inc. and the activities of Mr. George Brown.

During 1972, United Products moved into its new offices in Woburn, Massachusetts. From this location, it is believed the company is able to effectively serve its entire New England market area. "Our abilities and our desires to expand and improve our overall operation will be enhanced in the new specially designed structure containing our offices, repair facilities, and warehouse," is the way George Brown spoke about the new facilities. Concurrent with the recent move, the company segmented its over 3,500 different items carried into eight major product categories:

1. *Stapling Machines* includes Wire Stitchers, Carton Stitchers, Nailers, Hammers, Tackers, Manual—Foot—Air—Electric.
2. *Staples* to fit almost all makes of equipment—all sizes—types—steel, bronze, monel, stainless steel, aluminum, brass, etc.
3. *Stenciling Equipment* and supplies, featuring Marsh Hand and Electric Machines, Stencil Brushes, Boards, Inks.
4. *Gummed Tape Machines,* Hand and Electric featuring Marsh, Derby, Counterboy equipment.
5. *Industrial Tapes* by 3M, Mystick, Behr Manning, Dymo-specializing in strapping, masking, cellophane, electrical, cloth, nylon, waterproof tapes.
6. *Gluing Machines*—hand and electric.
7. *Work Gloves*—cotton, leather, neoprene, nylon, rubber, asbestos, etc.
8. *Marking and Labeling Equipment.*

In a flyer mailed at the time of the move to the United Products' 6,000 accounts, the company talked about its growth in this fashion:

> Here we grow again—thanks to you—our many long-time valued customers. . . .
> Time and Circumstances have decreed another United Products transPLANT— this time, to an unpolluted garden-type industrial area, ideally located for an ever-increasing list of our customers.
> Now, in the new 28,000-sq. ft. plant with enlarged offices and warehouse, we at United Products reach the peak of efficiency in offering our customers the combined benefits of maximum inventories, accelerated deliveries, and better repair services.

By 1974, the company had grown to a point where sales were $3.5 million (double that of four years earlier) and it employed thirty-four people. Results for 1973 compared to 1972 showed a sales increase of 22% and a 40% increase in profits. Exhibit 12.12 contains selected financial figures for 1971, 1972, and 1973, in addition to the fiscal 1973 balance sheet.

COMPETITION

Mr. George Brown believes that UPI does not have clearly defined competition for its business. It is felt that since UPI carries over 3,500 different items they have competition on parts of their business, but no one competes against their whole business:

> It is hard to get figures on competition since we compete with no one company directly. Different companies compete with various product lines but there is no one who competes across our full range of products.

On a regular basis, Mr. Brown receives Dun & Bradstreet Business Information Reports on specific firms with which he competes. Mr. Brown feels that since the competing firms are, like his own firm, privately held, the financial figures reported are easily manipulated and, therefore, are not sound enough to base plans on. Exhibit 12.13 contains comparative financial figures for two competing companies, and Exhibit 12.14 contains D&B's description of their operations along with two other firms operating in UPI's prime New England market areas.

MANAGEMENT PHILOSOPHY

When Mr. Brown took over UPI in 1967 at the age of twenty-four, he set a personal goal of becoming financially secure and developing a highly profitable business. With the rapid growth of the company, he soon realized his goal of financial independence and in so doing began to lose interest in the company. "I became a rich person at age twenty-eight and had few friends

EXHIBIT 12.12 United Products, Inc. Selected Financial Figures for UPI 1971–1973

	11-30-1971	*11-30-1972*	*11-30-1973*
Curr. Assets	$862,783	$689,024	$ 937,793
Curr. Liabilities	381,465	223,004	342,939
Other Assets	204,566	774,571	705,646
Worth	685,884	750,446	873,954
Sales			3,450,000

Following statement dated Nov. 30, 1973:

Cash	$ 46,963	Accts. Pay.	$ 320,795
Accts. Rec.	535,714	Notes. Pay.	20,993
Mdse.	352,136		
Ppd. Ins., Int., Texas	2,980		
Current	937,793	Current	342,939
Fixt. & Equip.	42,891	R.E.	471,655
Motor Vehicles	49,037	CAPITAL STOCK	519,800
Real Estate	685,768	Surplus	354,154
Total Assets	$1,688,486	Total	$1,688,486

EXHIBIT 12.13 United Products, Inc. Financial Information
on Selected Competitors

East Coast Supply Co., Inc.—Sales $1m.

	Fiscal Dec. 31, 1971	*Fiscal Dec. 31, 1972*	*Fiscal Dec. 31, 1973*
Curr. Assets	88,555	132,354	166,426
Curr. Liabilities	44,543	47,606	77,055
Other Assets	16,082	18,045	27,422
Worth	63,165	102,793	116,793

Statement dated Dec. 31, 1973:

Cash	$ 42,948	Accts. Pay.	$41,668
Accts. Rec.	86,123	Notes Pay.	27,588
Mdse.	34,882	Taxes	7,799
Prepaid	2,473		
Current	166,426	Current	77,055
Fixt. & Equip.	15,211	CAPITAL STOCK	10,000
Deposits	12,211	RETAINED EARNINGS	106,793
Total Assets	193,848	Total	193,848

Atlantic Paper Products, Inc.—Sales $6m.

	June 30, 1970	*June 30, 1971*	*June 30, 1972*
Curr. Assets	$101,241	$1,243,259	$1,484,450
Curr. Liabilities	574,855	502,572	1,120,036
Other Assets	93,755	101,974	107,001
Worth	403,646	439,677	471,415
Long-Term Debt		402,094	

with equal wealth that were my age. The business no longer presented a challenge, and I was unhappy with the way things were going."

After taking a ten-month "mental vacation" from the business, George Brown felt he was ready to return to work. He had concluded that one way of proving himself to himself and satisfying his ego would be to make the company as profitable as possible. However, the amount of growth that UPI is able to realize is limited by the level of energy exerted by Mr. Brown. "The company can only grow at approximately 20% per year, since this is the amount of energy I am willing to commit to the business."

Although Mr. Brown is only thirty-one, he feels that his philosophical outlook is very conservative and he tends to operate the same as his sixty-five-year-old father would. He has established several operating policies consistent with his philosophy that are constraining on the business.

> I am very concerned about making UPI a nice place to work. I have to enjoy what I'm doing and have fun at it at the same time. I cannot make any more money since I'm putting away as much money as I can. The government won't allow me to make more money since I already take the maximum amount.
>
> I like to feel comfortable, and if we grew too quickly it could get out of hand. I realize the business doesn't grow to its potential, but why should I put more into it? I have all the money I need. The company could grow, but why grow?

EXHIBIT 12.14 United Products Inc. Descriptive Information on Selective Competitors

East Coast Supply Co., Inc.

Manufactures and distributes pressure-sensitive tapes to industrial users throughout the New England area on 1/10 net 30-day terms. Thirty-four employed including the officers, thirty-three here. LOCATION: Rents 15,000 square feet on first floor of two-story brick building in good repair. Premises are orderly. Non-seasonal business. Branches are located at 80 Olife Street, New Haven, Connecticut and 86 Weybossett Street, Providence, Rhode Island.

Atlantic Paper Products Inc.

Wholesale paper products, pressure-sensitive tapes, paper specialties, twines, and other merchandise of this type. Sales to industrial accounts and commercial users on 1/10 net 30-day terms. There are about 1,000 accounts in Eastern Massachusetts and sales are fairly steady throughout the year. Employs sixty including officers. LOCATION: Rents 130,000 square feet of floor space in a six-story brick mill type building in a commercial area on a principal street. Premises orderly.

The Johnson Sales Co.

Wholesales shipping room supplies including staplings and packing devices, markers, and stencil equipment. Sells to industrial and commercial accounts throughout the New England area. Seasons are steady. Terms are 1/10 net 30 days. Number of accounts not learned, fifteen are employed including the owner. LOCATION: Rents the first floor of a two-story yellow brick building in good condition. Housekeeping is good.

Big City Staple Corp.

Wholesales industrial staples, with sales to 2,000 industrial and commercial firms, sold on 1/10 net 30-day terms. Territory mainly New Jersey. Employs ten including the officers. Seasons steady and competition active. LOCATION: Rents 5,000 square feet in one-story cinder block and brick structure in good condition, premises in neat order. Located on well-traveled street in a commercial area.

Why is progress good? You have to pay for everything in life, and I'm not willing to work harder since I don't need the money.

Another thing, I am a scrupulously honest businessman and it is very hard to grow large if you're honest. There are many deals that I could get into that would make UPI a lot of money, but I'm too moral of a person to get involved and besides, I don't need the money.

To me, happiness is being satisfied with what you have. I've got my wife, children, and health; why risk these for something I don't need. I don't have the desire to make money because I didn't come from a poor family; I'm not hungry.

Another thing—I have never liked the feeling of owing anything to anyone. If you can't afford to buy something, then don't. I don't like to borrow any money, and I don't like the company to borrow any. All of our bills are paid within fifteen days. I suppose I've constrained the business as a result of this feeling; but it's my business. The company can only afford to pay for a 20% growth rate, so that's all we will grow.

ORGANIZATIONAL STRUCTURE

Upon his return to the company, George Brown realigned UPI's organizational structure as shown in Exhibit 12.15 (company does not have an organizational chart; this one is drawn from the researcher's notes).

We have to have it on a functional basis now. We are also trying something new for us by moving to the general manager concept. In the past when I was away, there was no one with complete authority; now my general manager is in charge in my absence.

In discussing the new structuring of the organization, Mr. Brown was quick to point out that the company has not established formalized job descriptions. "Job descriptions are not worth anything. My people wear too many hats, and, besides, we're too small to put it in writing." At present the company employs thirty-four people including Mr. Brown.

Mr. Brown is quick to point out that he has never had a personnel problem. "All my people enjoy working here." He believes that "nobody should work for nothing" and has, therefore, established a personal goal of seeing to it that no one employed by UPI makes less than $10,000 per year. Mr. Brown commented on his attitude toward his employees:

> The men might complain about the amount of responsibility placed on them, but I think it's good for them. It helps them develop to their potential. I'm a nice guy who is interested in all of my people. I feel a strong social obligation to my employees and have developed very close relationships with all of them. My door is always open to them no matter what the problem may be.
>
> I make it a policy never to yell at anyone in public, it's not good for morale. Maybe it's part of my conservative philosophy, but I want everyone to call me Mr. Brown, not George. I think it's good for people to have a Mr. Brown. Although I want to run a nice friendly business, I have learned that it's hard to be real friends with an employee. You can only go so far. Employers and employees cannot mix socially, it just doesn't work out over the long run.

EXHIBIT 12.15 United Products, Inc. Organization Chart—December, 1974

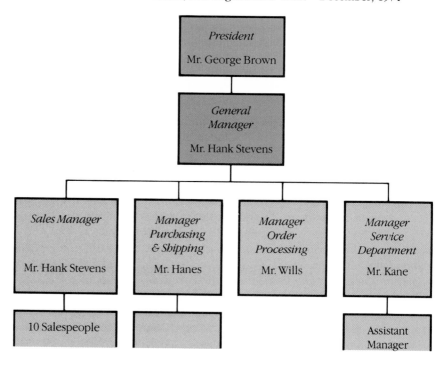

This is not your normal business. I am very approachable, I don't demand much, and I allow an easy open dialogue with my employees. Seldom do I take any punitive action. I'm just not a hard-driving tough guy.... I'm an easy-going guy.

It would take much of the enjoyment out of the business for me to come in here and run this place like a machine. [Researcher's note: When the researcher arrived at the plant one afternoon, he observed Mr. Brown running around the office deeply involved in a water fight with one of his office girls. By the way— he lost.]

I find it hard to motivate the company's salesmen. Since we have so much trouble finding good capable men, I'm not likely to fire any that I have. This situation makes it hard for me to put pressure on them to produce.

The bonus system, if you want to call it that, is I guess what you'd call very arbitrary. I have not set up specific sales quotas, or targeted goals for my inside people, so as a result, I base my bonus decisions on my assessment of how well I feel an employee performed during the past year.

Recently, I've given some thought to selling the company. I could probably get around $3 to $4 million for it. If I did that, I'm not sure what I would do with my time. Besides my family and UPI, there is not much that I am interested in. A couple of years ago, when I took my extended vacation, I got bored and couldn't wait to get back to the company.

UPI'S PLANNING PROCESS

George Brown claims to be a firm believer in planning. "I find myself spending more and more time planning for the company. Currently, I'm averaging about 50% of my time and I see this increasing." As he described it, the planning process at United Products is really a very loose system. "We have no planned way as to how we do the planning."

> Basically, the process is directed at ways of increasing the profitability of the company. I look at the salesmen's performance on a weekly and monthly basis, and use this information in the development of the plans.
>
> Since we have a very informal planning process, we only forecast out one year at most. The company's plans are reevaluated each month, and, if necessary, new plans are set. Only on rare occasions have we ever planned beyond one year.
>
> However, I think the current economic and political situation may force us into developing plans that cover a two-year period.

Although goals are not formally developed and written down, Mr. Brown had identified objectives in three areas: sales, profits, and organizational climate.

Specifically, they are:

1. Increase sales volume of business by 20% per year;
2. Increase gross profit margin ½ to 1% per year; and,
3. Make UPI a friendly place to work.

Mr. Brown feels that the company has been able to grow at about 20% a year in the past and, therefore, should have no problems realizing that level in the future. In addition, he believes that sales growth is a necessary evil. "Those companies that don't grow are swallowed up by the competition, and besides given the level of energy I'm willing to exert, I think 20% is a reasonable level of growth."

In the area of profits, the company actually sets no specific targeted figures other than saying they simply want an increase in the percentage of profits. Mr. Brown commented that:

> We do not set a goal because we would not have a way of measuring it. I have no way of knowing how much money I am making until the end of the year without considerable time and effort.

With respect to the third goal, Mr. Brown is concerned about the workplace environment and wants UPI to be a big happy family—and everyone employed to be happy.

In describing the planning process used at UPI, Mr. Brown emphasized the unstructured informal nature of the process.

> I am familiar with commonly accepted theory about planning systems, but I do not feel it is necessary for UPI to institute, in a formal manner, any of these I've read about. We perform many of the activities advocated in the planning models, but we do them in a relaxed, casual fashion. For example, I am a member of many organizations connected with my business and receive industry newsletters on a regular basis. In addition, I receive input from friends and business associates both inside and outside my line of business. Since we do not have a formal process, planning tends to be a continuous process at UPI.

When asked about UPI's strengths and weaknesses, Mr. Brown indicated that the company has four areas of strength and one major weakness:

Strengths
1. The number of different products carried;
2. The quality of its employees, particularly salesmen;
3. No debt; and,
4. Purchasing capabilities.

Weaknesses
1. An inability to get and train new personnel—primarily in the sales function of the business.

The salesmen are not assigned a sales quota for the year but rather are evaluated based on Mr. Brown's assessment of the particular salesman's territory and initiative. He feels his salesmen make more than competitive salesmen. Several of the ten salesmen have earned as much as $40,000 in a single year. All salesmen are compensated on a straight commission basis—as shown below:

8% for first $180,000 sales
7% for next $60,000 sales
6% for next $60,000 and
5% for everything over $300,000.

Mr. Brown is pleased with the sales success of his company and feels that UPI's greatest strength is its ability to "sell anything to anybody." However, the problem for UPI has been in finding good salesmen. "There just aren't any good salesmen around, and this is a problem because the salesmen are the lifeblood of our business."

INTERPERSONAL RELATIONSHIPS

Since Mr. Brown is concerned about the climate of the company, he has paid particular attention to the nature of the relationships within UPI. At the time of the company's reorganization, Hank Stevens was brought into the organization as general manager and assistant to the president. Over the past several years, Mr. Stevens' areas of responsibility have grown to the extent that they now comprise approximately 80% of the activities that were formerly done by Mr. Brown. As a result of this, George Brown sometimes finds himself with little to do and oftentimes works only five hours per day. As he describes it:

> Hank's management discretionary power has increased steadily since he has been here; partly as a result of the extent of responsibility I've placed on him and partly due to his aggressiveness. As it now stands, he makes almost all of the daily operating decisions for the company, leaving me with only the top-management decisions. Let's be realistic, there just aren't that many top-management decisions that have to be made here in the course of a day. A lot of the time, I walk around the plant checking on what other people are doing and, I guess, acting as a morale booster.

When asked about the management capabilities of Hank Stevens, Mr. Brown responded by saying, "Hank probably feels that he is working at a very fast pace, but when you evaluate the effectiveness of his actions, he is actually moving forward at what I would consider to be a very slow pace. However, everything else considered, Hank is the best of what is around. I guess if I could find a really good sales manager, I would add him to the company and relieve Hank of that area of responsibility."

MR. HANK STEVENS

Mr. Hank Stevens, 32, joined UPI at the time of the reorganization in 1970 after having graduated from a local university with a B.S. in Economics. As general manager, Mr. Stevens' responsibilities include planning, purchasing, sales management as well as involvement in other decisions that affect UPI policy. Mr. Stevens feels that he has been fortunate in that "ever since I came to UPI, I've reported to the president and in essence have had everyone else reporting to me."

When asked about the goals of UPI, Mr. Stevens responded that, "As I see it, we have goals in three major areas: profitability, sales level, and personal relationships." In discussing his own personal goals, Hank explained that he hoped that the organization would grow and as a result he would be able to grow along with it.

Since Mr. Steven works so closely with Mr. Brown, he has given considerable thought to his boss's business philosophy:

> I feel that George's business philosophy is unique. I guess the best way to describe it is to say that above all he is a businessman. Also, he has very high moral values and as a result of that he is extremely honest and would never cheat anybody.

Actually, the company would probably look better financially if it was run by someone who didn't operate with the same values as George.

When asked about the salesforce at UPI, Mr. Stevens commented that "when a new salesman starts with the company, he does so with full salary. After a period of about two years we change him over to a commission basis." As has always been the case, UPI concentrates its sales efforts on large customers. Mr. Stevens noted that "on the average the company processes approximately 105 orders per day, with an average dollar value per order of roughly $132. It's not that we won't write small orders, we just don't solicit business from small accounts. It just makes more sense to concentrate on the larger accounts."

MR. JIM HANES

Jim Hanes, age 24, has been with UPI for over six years and during that time has worked his way up from assistant service manager to his current position as the number-three man in the company functioning as the manager of purchasing and shipping. Jim is responsible for the front office, repair work and the warehouse. He feels that his reporting responsibility is approximately 60% to Mr. Stevens and 40% to Mr. Brown. "Since I have responsibility for all merchandise entering and leaving the company, I get involved with both Hank and George, and, therefore, I guess I report to both of them."

In talking about where he would go from his present position, he explained that:

> I guess the next step is for me to become a salesman so that I can broaden my background and move up in the company. However, I am a little worried; I don't think the salesmen in our company are given the right sales training. As the system works, a new man is assigned to work with an experienced salesman for about six weeks, after which time he is given his own territory. Perhaps if our sales manager had more experience as a salesman, he would handle the training differently.

In commenting on his understanding of Mr. Brown's philosophy, Jim summed up his position by noting that, "George is a very open person. I think he is too honest for a businessman. He certainly gives his people responsibility. He gives you the ball and lets you run with it. I don't think enough planning is done at UPI. At most, it appears that we look ahead one year and even then, what plans are developed are kept very flexible."

UPI STRATEGY

When asked about the current strategy at UPI, Mr. Brown responded that "the company is presently a distributor in the industrial packaging equipment, shipping supplies, and heavy-duty stapling equipment business. In the past when we've wanted to grow, we have done one or both of the following, either add new lines of merchandise or additional salesmen. For example, this past year I got the idea of what I call a contract sales department. It is a simple concept. I took one man, put him in an office with a telephone and a listing of the *Fortune* top 1,000 companies and told him to call and get new business. You would be surprised at how easy it was to pick up new accounts."

Mr. Stevens looks at UPI as being in the distribution and shipping of packaging supplies business. "In order for UPI to reach the goals that have been set, we have to see more products. That is, we can grow by doing the following:

1. Adding new salesmen;
2. Adding additional product lines;
3. Purchasing more effectively; and,
4. Undertaking more aggressive sales promotions."

Mr. Brown believes that UPI should try to maximize the profit on every item sold. To do this, the company tries to set its prices at a level that is approximately 10% above the competition. Mr. Brown explained his pricing philosophy:

> I don't understand why people are afraid to raise prices. If you increase the price, you will pick up more business and make more money. That allows you to keep the volume low and still make more money. In addition, although the customer may pay more, he gets more. The higher price allows me to provide top notch service to all my customers.

Mr. Brown feels that UPI is an innovative company. "Until very recently we were always innovating with new products and new applications. Now, I think it's again time that we started to look for additional new and exciting products."

As a result of the stated strategy of UPI and Mr. Brown's conservative philosophy, it is widely recognized that the organization is larger than it has to be given the level of business. Mr. Brown explained the reasoning behind this condition, "I know the organization is bigger than it has to be. We could probably handle three times the present volume of business with our present staff and facility. I think it's because of my conservative attitude; I've always wanted the organization to stay a step ahead of what is really needed. I feel comfortable with a built-in backup system and, therefore, I am willing to pay for it."

In December, 1973, Mr. Brown had talked optimistically about the future. He felt that sales should reach the $6–7 million range by 1978. "Looked at in another way, we should be able to grow at 20–25% per year without any particular effort."

> I want to grow and, therefore, I am making a concerted effort. I am constantly looking for possible merger avenues or expansion possibilities. I do not want to expand geographically. I would rather control that market area we are in now. I recently sent a letter to all competitors in New England offering to buy them out. Believe it or not no one responded. I don't see any problems in the future. The history has been good, therefore, why won't it continue to happen? Growth is easy. All I have to do is pick up a new line, and I've automatically increased sales and profits. Basically, we are distributors, and we operate as middlemen between the manufacturers and users, as shown:

| Manufacturer | → | United Products | → | Users |

In light of what has been happening in the environment, I feel that supply and demand will continue to be a problem. Therefore, I am giving serious thought to integrating vertically, i.e., become a manufacturer. This will guarantee our supply.*

Actually, I don't want to do the manufacturing. I think it would be better if I bought the manufacturing equipment and then had someone else use it to make my products.

THE FUTURE

After reviewing with his accountant the results for the just-completed fiscal year, Mr. Brown was concerned about the nature of changes that should be made with respect to the actions taken by UPI in the future. "I know changes have to be made for next year as a result of this year, but I'm not sure what they should be." Mr. Brown continued:

> I think next year is going to be a real bad year. Prices will probably fall like a rock from the levels they reached during 1974 and as a result those items that would have been profitable for the company aren't going to be, and we have much too large of an inventory as it is. It isn't easy to take away customers from the competition. As a result of this, I feel we have to step up our efforts to get new lines and new accounts. Recently, I've given some thought to laying off one or two people for economic reasons, but I'm not sure. I will probably give raises to all employees even though it's not a good business decision, but it's an ingrained part of my business philosophy.

When asked if he had informed his employees of his concern about the future, Mr. Brown referred to the minutes of a sales meeting that had been held in November 1974:

> ... Mr. Brown then presided at the meeting, and announced that Al King had won the coveted award of "Salesman of the Month." This was a "first" for our Al, and well deserved for his outstanding sales results in October. Congratulations and applauses were extended him by all present. The balance of the meeting was then spent in a lengthy, detailed discussion, led by Mr. George Brown of the general, overall picture of what the future portends in the sales area as a result of the current inflationary, recessionary, and complex competitive conditions prevailing in the economy.

The gist of the entire discussion can be best summarized as follows:

1. Everyone present must recognize the very real difficulties that lie ahead in these precarious economic times.
2. The only steps available to the salesmen and to the company for survival during the rough period ahead are as follows:
   a. Minimize contacts with existing accounts;
   b. Spend the majority of time developing new accounts on the less competitive products; and selling new products to established accounts.
3. Concentrate on and promote our new items.
4. Mr. Brown and inside management are making and will continue to make

---

* Refer to the Appendix which contains minutes of a United Products sales meeting held at the end of 1973.

every concentrated effort to find new products and new lines for the coming year.

In preparation for his meeting with Hank Stevens, Mr. Brown had prepared a list of activities to which Hank should address himself while running UPI during George's upcoming vacation. Mr. Brown believed that upon his return from Europe his activities at UPI would be increasing as a result of the problems caused by the uncertain economic conditions. The first item on the list was a possible redefinition of UPI marketing strategy. Mr. Brown now believed that UPI would have to be much more liberal with respect to new products considered for sale. "I'm not saying we are going to get into the consumer goods business, but I think he will give consideration to the inclusion of consumerable products requiring no service and at the same time capable of being sold with a high-profit-margin factor for the company."

As he sat at his desk thinking about possible changes which he could make in UPI's planning process, Mr. Brown was convinced that if he hadn't done some planning in the past, the situation would be more drastic than it was. Yet at the same time, he wasn't sure that if he had a more structured and formalized planning process, UPI might be in a better position with which to face the troubled times that lay ahead.

APPENDIX: UNITED PRODUCTS, INC.
SALES MEETING DECEMBER 5, 1973

Mr. Brown presided at the meeting. His opening remarks highlighted the extraordinary times our country and our company are going through as far as the general economy and the energy crisis are concerned, and the extraordinary effects of these unusual crises on people and businesses, including our company and our sources of supply.

He thanked all present for the many thoughtful, considered and excellent suggestions which they had offered in writing as to how best the salesmen and their company might handle the gasoline crisis without incurring an undue loss of sales and profits, and still maintain the high standards of service to which UNITED PRODUCTS' thousands of satisfied customers are accustomed.

The whole situation, according to Mr. Brown, boils down to a question of supply and prices. Mr. Brown reported that on his recent trip to the Orient, there were very few companies who wanted to sell their merchandise to us—rather, THEY WANTED TO BUY FROM US MANY OF THE ITEMS WE NORMALLY BUY FROM FOREIGN COMPANIES, i.e., carton-closing staples, tape, gloves, etc. . . . and at inflated prices!!! The Tokyo, Japan, market is so great that they are using up everything they can produce—and the steel companies would rather make flat steel than the steel rods which are used for making staples. A very serious problem exists, as a result, in the carton-closing staple field not only in Japan, but also in Europe and America.

Mr. Brown advised that every year the company's costs of operating increase just as each individual's cost of living goes up and up yearly. Additional personnel, increased group and auto insurance premiums, increased Social Security payments, new office equipment and supplies, new catalogues, "Beeper system" for more salesmen—and all of these costs accumulate and result in large expenditures of money. Manufacturers cover their increased operating costs by pricing their products higher—but to date, UNITED PRODUCTS has never put into their prices the increased costs resulting from increased operating expenses. Last year, the 3% increase which the company needed then was put into effect by many of you. HOWEVER, in order for the company to realize that additional profit, this 3% price increase had to be put into effect ACROSS THE BOARD . . . all customers . . . all items!

Mr. Brown advised that UNITED PRODUCTS got LAMBASTED when all of the sources of supply started to increase their prices. When SPOTNAILS, for example, went up 10%, the salesmen only increased their prices 7%, etc. We did not get the 3% price increase ABOVE the manufacturers' price increase—and we needed it then, and need it even more NOW.

Eliminating the possibility of cutting commissions, there are three possible solutions for the problem of how to get this much needed and ABSOLUTELY IMPERATIVE additional 3% PRICE INCREASE ACROSS THE BOARD to cover the constantly growing operating costs for running a successful, progressive-minded and growing business whose high standards of service and performance are highly regarded by customers and sources of supply alike, namely:

    a. a 3% increase on all items to all customers across the board.
    b. a surcharge on all invoices or decrease in discounts allowed off LIST.
    c. a G.C.I. charge (Government Cost Increase) on all invoices.

Considerable discussion regarding these three possibilities resulted in the following conclusions concerning the best method for obtaining this special 3% ACROSS THE BOARD PRICE INCREASE, as follows:

    a. A new PRICE BOOK should be issued with all new prices to reflect not only the manufacturers' new increased prices, but in addition the 3% UNITED PRODUCTS PRICE INCREASE. All of the salesmen agreed that it would be easier to affect the additional 3% price increase if the 3% was "built in" on their price book sheets.
    b. This new PRICE BOOK will be set up in such a way that prices will be stipulated according to quantity of item purchased. . .with no variances allowed. WITH NO EXCEPTIONS, the price of any item will depend on the quantity a customer buys.
    c. Some items will continue to be handled on a discount basis—but lower discounts in order to ascertain that UNITED PRODUCTS is getting its 3% price increase.
    d. Until these new PRICE BOOKS are issued, all salesmen were instructed to proceed IMMEDIATELY to effect these 3% price increases.

Ten New Accounts Contest

Seven of our ten salesmen won a calculator as a result of opening up ten new accounts each . . . a total of 70 NEW ACCOUNTS for our company!!! However, both Mr. Brown and Mr. Stevens confessed that the dollar volume amount stipulated in the contest had been set ridiculously low, as a "feeler" to determine the success and effectiveness of such a contest. All the salesmen voiced their approval of all of the contests offered to them—and agreed that they had enjoyed many excellent opportunities of increasing their personal exchequers.

New Customer Letters

Mr. Brown again reminded all present that we have an excellent printed letter, which is available for sending to every new customer—and urged all to take advantage of this service by the office personnel by clearly indicating on their sales and order slips "NEW CUSTOMER." This procedure is but another step towards our goal of becoming more and more professional in our approach with our customers.

New Catalogues

Mr. Brown advised that by the first of the new year, hopefully, all our hard-cover catalogues with their new divider breakdowns will be ready for hand-delivering to large accounts. These catalogues cost the company over $5.00 and should only be distributed by hand to those customers who can and will make intelligent and effective use of them.

Excessive Issuance of Credits

As a result of a detailed study made by Mr. Brown of the nature and reasons for the ever-increasing number of credits being issued, he instructed all of the salesmen to follow these procedures when requesting the issuing of CREDITS:

> a. Issue the CREDIT at the right time.
> b. Do not sell an item where is is not needed.
> c. NEVER PUT "NO COMMENT" for the reason why merchandise is being returned. EVERY CREDIT MUST HAVE A REASON FOR ITS ISSUANCE.

The ever-increasing number of credits being issued is extremely costly to the company: (1) new merchandise comes back 90 plus days after it has been billed, and frequently, if not always, is returned by the customer Freight College: (2) Credit 9-part forms, postage for mailing, extra work for both the bookkeeping and billing and order processing departments. More intelligent, considered and selective selling, plus greater care on the part of the order processing personnel, according to Mr. Brown, could easily eliminate a large percentage of these credits.

Questions

1. Evaluate George Brown's role and performance as president of United Products. To what extent is he responsible for UPI's performance?

2. What is UPI's strategy? Is the strategy appropriate for the external environment and internal strengths and weaknesses?

3. Do Mr. Brown's management style and personal values influence internal culture? UPI's growth? Does his style favor one of the three stated company goals of sales, profits, and climate? Discuss.

4. If you were running UPI, what tools and techniques would you use to govern the organization and implement a strategy for increased performance?

NOTES

1. James H. Lavenson, "How to Earn an MBWA Degree," *Vital Speeches of the Day* 42 (April 15, 1976):410–412.

2. Henry Mintzberg, *The Nature of Managerial Work* (New York: Harper & Row, 1973); John P. Kotter, "What Effective General Managers Really Do," *Harvard Business Review* (November–December, 1982):156–167.

3. Karen M. Hult and Charles Walcott, "Organizations as Polities: A Governance Approach to Complex Organizations," paper presented at the TIMS/ORSA Meetings, Boston, Massachusetts, April 29, 1985.

4. Charles J. Fombrun, "Structures of Organizational Governance," *Human Relations,* 37 (1984):207–223.

5. John Child, "Organization Structure, Environment and Performance: The Role of Strategic Choice," *Sociology* 6 (1972):1–22; H. Randolph Bobbitt and Jeffrey D. Ford, "Decision-Maker Choice As a Determinant of Organizational Structure," *Academy of Management Review* 5 (1980):13–23.

6. Richard L. Daft and Karl E. Weick, "Organizations As Interpretation Systems," *Academy of Management Review,* 9 (1984):284–295.

7. Henry Mintzberg, "Managerial Work: Analysis from Observation," *Management Science* 18 (1971):B97–B110.

8. Karl E. Weick, *The Social Psychology of Organizing* (Reading, MA: Addison-Wesley, 1979), pp. 130–131.

9. Ibid., p. 130.

10. James Brian Quinn, "Strategic Change: 'Logical Incrementalism,'" *Sloan Management Review,* 20 (1978):14.

11. Kotter, "What Effective General Managers Really Do"; Mintzberg, *The Nature of Managerial Work.*

12. Kotter, ibid.

13. Robert E. Kaplan, "Trade Routes: The Manager's Network of Relationships," *Organizational Dynamics* (Spring 1984):37–52.

14. Milton Leontiades, "The Confusing Words of Business Policy," *Academy of Management Review,* 7 (1982):45–48.

15. Charles C. Snow and Lawrence G. Hrebiniak, "Strategy, Distinctive Competence, and Organizational Performance," *Administrative Science Quarterly,* 25 (1980):317–335.

16. Lawrence G. Hrebiniak and William F. Joyce, *Implementing Strategy* (New York: Macmillan, 1984).

17. Milton Leontiades, *Strategies for Diversification and Change* (Boston: Little Brown, 1980), p. 63.

18. Ibid., pp. 102–105.

19. Ibid.

20. William L. Shanklin and John K. Ryans, Jr., "Is the International Cash Cow Really a Prize Heifer?" *Business Horizon* 24 (1981):10–16.

21. Howard Rudnitsky with Jay Gissen, "Chesebrough-Ponds: The Unsung Miracle," *Forbes,* September 28, 1981, pp. 105–109; "A Shoe-In?" *Forbes,* November 13, 1978, p. 218.

22. "How Chesebrough-Ponds Put Nail Polish in a Pen," *Business Week,* October 8, 1984:196–200.

23. Raymond E. Miles and Charles C. Snow, *Organizational Strategy, Structure, and Process* (New York: McGraw-Hill, 1978).

24. Ralph E. Winter, "Goodyear, Firestone Split on Future Demand for Tires," *Wall Street Journal,* February 23, 1981, p. 21; Subratan Chakravaty, "Firestone: 'It Worked,'" *Forbes,* August 17, 1981, pp. 56–58.

25. "Church's: A Fast-Food Recipe That Is Light on Marketing," *Business Week,* February 20, 1978, pp. 110–112; "Church's Fried Chicken: Cutting Loose from Its Penny-Pinching Past," *Business Week,* February 27, 1984, pp. 72–74.

26. Henry Mintzberg, *The Structuring of Organizations* (Englewood Cliffs, NJ: Prentice-

Hall, 1979), pp. 215–297; and Henry Mintzberg, "Organization Design: Fashion or Fit?" *Harvard Business Review,* 59 (January–February, 1981):103–116.

27. Ibid.

28. Linda Smircich, "Concepts of Culture and Organizational Analysis," *Administrative Science Quarterly,* 28 (1983):339–358; Vijay Sathe, "Implications of Corporate Culture: A Manager's Guide to Action," *Organizational Dynamics* (Autumn 1983):5–23.

29. Edgar H. Schein, "Coming to a New Awareness of Organizational Culture," *Sloan Management Review* (Winter 1984):3–15.

30. Smircich, "Concepts of Culture and Organizational Analysis"; Thomas J. Peters and Robert H. Waterman, Jr., *In Search of Excellence* (New York: Harper & Row, 1982).

31. "Corporate Culture," *Business Week,* October 27, 1980, pp. 148–160.

32. Thomas J. Peters, "Symbols, Patterns, and Settings: An Optimistic Case for Getting Things Done," *Organizational Dynamics* (1978):2–23; Harrison M. Trice and Janice M. Beyer, "Studying Organizational Cultures through Rites and Ceremonials," *Academy of Management Review,* 9 (1984):653–669.

33. Terrence E. Deal and Allan A. Kennedy, *Corporate Cultures* (Reading, MA: Addison-Wesley, 1982); Trice and Beyer, "Studying Organizational Cultures through Rites and Ceremonials."

34. Jeffrey Pfeffer, "Management as Symbolic Action: The Creation and Maintenance of Organizational Paradigms," in L. L. Cummings and Barry M. Staw, eds., *Research in Organizational Behavior,* vol. 3 (Greenwich, CT: JAI Press, 1981), pp. 1–52; Thomas C. Dandridge, Ian I. Mitroff, and William F. Joyce, "Organizational Symbolism: A Topic to Expand Organizational Analysis," *Academy of Management Review* 5 (1980):77–82.

35. Karl E. Weick, "Cognitive Processes in Organizations," in B. M. Staw, ed., *Research in Organizations,* vol. 1 (Greenwich, CT: JAI Press, 1979), p. 42.

36. Charlotte B. Sutton, "Richness Hierarchy of the Cultural Network: The Communication of Corporate Values," unpublished manuscript, Texas A&M University, 1985; Terrence E. Deal and Allan A. Kennedy, "Culture: A New Look through Old Lenses," *The Journal of Applied Behavioral Science,* 19 (1983):498–505.

37. Thomas C. Dandridge, "Symbols at Work," working paper, School of Business, State University of New York at Albany, 1978, p. 1.

38. Ibid.

39. Peters and Waterman, *In Search of Excellence.*

40. Ibid.

41. Trice and Beyer, "Studying Organizational Cultures through Rites and Ceremonials."

42. Robert C. Wood, "Rituals and Stories, Heroes and Priests," *Inc.,* December, 1982, pp. 105–106.

43. Sutton, "The Communication of Corporate Values"; L. W. Lehr, "How 3M Develops Entrepreneurial Spirit throughout the Organization," *Management Review,* 69, no. 10 (1980):31.

44. Sutton, "The Communication of Corporate Values"; Deal and Kennedy, *Corporate Cultures.*

45. Joanne Martin, Martha S. Feldman, Mary Jo Hatch, and Sim B. Sitkin, "The Uniqueness Paradox in Organizational Stories," *Administrative Science Quarterly,* 28 (1980):438–453.

46. Personal communication from Thomas Dandridge.

47. Mary Kay Ash, *Mary Kay on People Management* (New York: Warner Books, 1984).

48. "Off Beat Company Customs," *Dun's Business Month,* November 1984, pp. 65–75.

49. Richard Ott, "Are Wild Ducks Really Wild: Symbolism and Behavior in the Corporate Environment," paper presented at the Northeastern Anthropological Association, March, 1979.

50. Jeff Hampton, "One-on-One with H. R. 'Bum' Bright," *Dallas,* October 1984, pp. 23–25.

51. Myron Magnet, "Managing by Mystique at Tandem Computers," *Fortune,* June 28, 1982, pp. 84–91; T. E. Deal and A. A. Kennedy, *Corporate Cultures: The Rites and Rituals of Corporate Life* (Reading, MA: Addison-Wesley, 1982), pp. 3–19; "An Acid Test for Tandem's Growth," *Business Week,* February 28, 1983, pp. 63–64; "What Makes Tandem Run," *Business Week,* July 14, 1980, pp. 73–74.

52. Craig R. Waters, "John DeLorean and the Icarus Factor," *Inc.,* April 1983, pp. 35–42.

53. Lucien Rhodes, "That Daring Young Man and His Flying Machines," *Inc.,* January 1984, pp. 42–52.

54. Gerald R. Salancik, Barry M. Staw, and Louis R. Pondy, "Administrative Turnover as a Response to Unmanaged Organizational Interdependence," *Academy of Management Journal* 23 (1980):422–437; Jeffrey Pfeffer and William L. Moore, "Average Tenure of Academic Department Heads: The Effects of Paradigm, Size, and Departmental Philosophy," *Administrative Science Quarterly* 25 (1980):387–406.

55. Jeffrey Pfeffer and Gerald R. Salancik, "Organizational Context and the Characteristics and Tenure of Hospital Administrators," *Academy of Management Journal* 20 (1977):74–88.

56. Ibid.

57. Oscar Grusky, "Corporate Size, Bureaucratization, and Managerial Succession," *American Journal of Sociology* 69 (1961):261–269.

58. John Huey, "New Top Executives Shake up Old Order at Soft-Drink Giant," *Wall Street Journal,* November 6, 1981, pp. 1, 17.

59. "How Donald Smith Got Tossed Out by Diversifoods," *Business Week,* January 21, 1985, pp. 82–84.

60. "Turnover at the Top," *Business Week,* December 19, 1983, pp. 104–110.

61. Michael Patrick Allen, Sharon K. Panian, and Roy E. Lotz, "Managerial Succession and Organizational Performance: A Recalcitrant Problem Revisited," *Administrative Science Quarterly* 24 (1979):167–180; M. Craig Brown, "Administrative Succession and Organizational Performance: The Succession Effect," *Administrative Science Quarterly,* 27 (1982):1–16.

62. David R. James and Michael Soref, "Profit Constraints on Managerial Autonomy: Managerial Theory and the Unmaking of the Corporation President," *American Sociological Review,* 46 (1981):1–18; Oscar Grusky, "Managerial Succession and Organizational Effectiveness," *American Journal of Sociology* 69 (1963):21–31.

63. M. Craig Brown, "Administrative Succession and Organizational Performance: The Succession Effect," *Administrative Science Quarterly* 27 (1982):1–16; William Gamson and Norman Scotch, "Scapegoating in Baseball," *American Journal of Sociology* 70 (1964):69–72.

64. Stanley Lieberson and James F. O'Connor, "Leadership and Organizational Performance: A Study of Large Corporations," *American Sociological Review* 37 (1972):119.

65. Nan Weiner and Thomas A. Mahoney, "A Model of Corporate Performance As a Function of Environmental, Organizational, and Leadership Influences," *Academy of Management Journal* 24 (1981):453–470.

66. Jonathan E. Smith, Kenneth P. Carson, and Ralph A. Alexander, "Leadership: It Can Make a Difference," *Academy of Management Journal,* 27 (1984):765–776.

67. Glenn E. Carroll, "Dynamics of Publishers Succession in Newspaper Organizations," *Administrative Science Quarterly,* 29 (1984):93–113.

68. Peter Nulty, "Little Rock's Hot-Cookin' Gas Company," *Fortune,* October 5, 1981, pp. 148–153, with permission. Copyright © Time, Inc. All rights reserved.

Organizational Learning and Renewal

BRUNSWICK CORPORATION

In 1982, Brunswick Corp. was a mature company, and investment bankers were pessimistic about its future. They recommended that Brunswick sell off its recreation businesses (bowling, billiards, outboard motors), and concentrate instead on defense and technical products. The new chief executive, Jack S. Reichert, was angered by the negative assessment of Brunswick. He was determined to prove the analysts wrong.

Reichert's goal was to pump new life into the slow-moving, bureaucratic company. He decided to keep the recreation businesses because Brunswick needed a clear focus and should not try to become something it wasn't. A medical equipment business was sold, and Reichert restructured the remaining organization to make it lean and quick footed. He consolidated eleven divisions into eight. Two corporate planes were sold, the executive dining room was closed, and the $20 million of administrative overhead was eliminated. The headquarters' staff was reduced from 560 to 230 people. The vertical hierarchy was shrunk so that only five layers of management were between Reichert and the lowest employee.

The bureaucracy and big corporate staffs were remnants from the previous CEO, who liked reams of analysis. Now managers are expected to run their business hands on, and not develop twenty pages of financial data to back up every proposal. Divisional general managers can now get decisions back from headquarters in a few hours or a couple of days, where it used to take weeks or months.

Reichert wants to instill a new culture of risk-taking. He supports the notion, "Go ahead and try it," even if it means occasional failures. To help implement the new culture, he established venture capital groups within each division. Small groups of managers are dedicated to nurturing new products.

Reichert has also improved morale and performance through the use of compensation. All employees have been awarded company stock. The bonus plan for senior management has been expanded to include 500 managers. Bonus size is tied directly to the financial performance of the manager's division. Nonfinancial goals such as personal development are also taken into account in performance ratings.

Performance has also been enhanced through improved forecasts and greater contact with dealers and sales representatives. Mercury Marine dealers, who distribute outboard motors, stern drives, and boating parts, are now courted by Brunswick's marketing department. Dealers receive discounts, and are given bonuses if they meet sales forecasts.

The trimmed-down Brunswick has proven the investment bankers wrong. By 1984, performance was up. Stock value jumped 30% in one year, and reflected the efficiencies gained from decentralization and staff reduction. Debt has fallen and profits are near record levels.[1]

Jack Reichert revitalized Brunswick Corporation. A stagnating, bureaucratic company was transformed into an adaptive, risk-taking, efficient organization. The company was out of step with the environment but now is in close touch with customers and dealers. By making selected changes in both structure and culture, Brunswick Corporation learned and changed, and performance rebounded.

Purpose of This Chapter

Companies in the United States and Canada face many problems. In many industries, pressures on business conduct and investment decisions have increased. In industries such as airlines and banking, decreased regulation has changed the competitive ground rules. Inflationary pressure has decreased in North America, but remains rampant in other parts of the world. Financial pressure continues through high interest rates. Perhaps the most serious threat has been the tough competition from other countries. North America has lost its leadership in radios, television, home appliances, motorcycles, watches, and machine tools. Automobiles are also threatened.

The competitive problem is not severe in newly emerging industries such as personal computers. The problem strikes mature companies that often seem unable to sustain innovation and competitive efficiency. The companies lose their vitality, and fail to learn and adapt to new environmental pressures.

The purpose of this chapter is to explore from an organization theory perspective how organizations can revitalize themselves. Brunswick Corporation illustrates that a mature company can catch new fire through a combination of structural and human resource changes. Executives in many companies are concerned with how large, mature organizations can develop a culture of innovation and entrepreneurship. They are also concerned about how organizations can learn to be efficient, while at the same time maintaining the effective cooperation needed for learning and adaptation.[2]

The field of organization theory has responded to the need for organizational learning and renewal with best-selling books that propose techniques based on Japanese management *(Theory Z, The Art of Japanese Management),* a management style to influence internal culture and the motivation of human resources *(In Search of Excellence),* and structural change to fit a potentially hostile environment *(Renewing American Industry).*[3] The ideas conveyed in these publications are important because they help managers renew organizations.

In the next section we will define organizational learning. Then we will draw from recent publications to suggest how organizational structure and management practices can be used to revitalize and renew organizations.

LEARNING AND READAPTATION

Organizational learning typically involves three steps: (1) data collection about the environment via formal or informal scanning; (2) interpretation and agreement among managers about the state of the environment based on the data; (3) a new organizational response or action.[4] **Organizational learning** thus is defined as the process by which organizations develop knowledge about organizational actions and environmental outcomes.[5] Organizational learning includes the process through which management ideas are put into action.[6] Organizational learning is analogous to acquiring a new skill by an individual. Trial and error is involved so that each action provides new data to facilitate learning. Feedback from organizational action provides understanding about the action-outcome relationship with the environment.

Organizational learning can work at two levels. Single-loop learning occurs when errors are corrected by changing organizational strategies (products, advertising), but within the same framework of norms, performance expectations, and manager beliefs.[7] Double-loop learning cuts deeper and involves the restructuring of organizational norms, assumptions, and culture to be congruent with a radical change in organizational strategy. Double-loop learning involves fundamental change in the direction, climate, and values within the organization. Brunswick underwent double-loop learning because Jack Reichert forced changes in fundamental structure and values.

Readaptation

A somewhat different approach to organizational learning was proposed by Lawrence and Dyer.[8] They introduced the concept of **readaptation,** which is the organizational state of being simultaneously efficient and innovative. This is an interesting approach to organizational renewal because efficiency and innovation are in conflict with one another. Efficiency requires the careful use of resources and often leads to a highly specialized and bureaucratic structure. Innovation is concerned with being on the leading edge of new products and services desired by the environment. Efficiency and innovation are difficult to reconcile in the same organization because they require different skills. Cost-cutting may inhibit innovation. Innovation may require a loosening of internal control.

The point of the readaptation idea is that successful organizations manage to reconcile these two forces. Brunswick Corporation, for example, erred by being too efficiency oriented. The new CEO was able to shift Brunswick back toward a better balance between efficiency and innovation. In order to sustain readaptation, the organization must learn. It must learn to be efficient, and it must learn to be innovative. Maintaining an influx of fresh ideas while being efficient requires continuous trial and error, interpretation of the environment, and learning and adjustment by organizational members. Striving for both innovation and efficiency energizes the organization into a learning mode that enables it to avoid the pitfalls of too much internal control as well as the pitfalls of not enough efficiency and control.

The readaptation concept has received support from industry research. A study of companies in eight basic industries in the United States, including steel, tire and rubber, construction equipment, home appliances, beer, and cigarettes, found variations in the firms' emphasis on efficiency versus innovation.[9] Firms could survive by emphasizing either efficiency or innovation, but the most successful firms were able to excel at both. Caterpillar was the most efficient manufacturer of construction equipment but also the most innovative, and its results were spectacular. Philip Morris had the lowest cost, fully automated cigarette manufacturing operation, but also provided innovative product and promotion strategies and was the industry profit leader. Striving for both efficiency and innovation is a mechanism through which firms can be activated toward learning. Learning keeps the organization healthy, adaptive, and vital.

During the mid-1980s, companies in the agricultural industry have faced a hostile environment. Despite almost overwhelming difficulties, John Deere has prospered as part of a mature and even declining industry.

IN PRACTICE 13.1

Deere & Company

Deere & Company is something of a contrarian. Its managers see opportunities in what some would call the wasteland of the agricultural implement industry. Farmers have been bearing the burden of ending inflation. Production costs for farmers have risen and prices have fallen. Many farmers are going bankrupt. They can't afford new machinery. Deere's two biggest competitors—International Harvester and Massey-Ferguson—have been practically destroyed by the agricultural recession.

John Deere, in contrast, is fighting hard and coming on strong despite the obstacles. Deere completed a $1.8 billion capital program that added 30% capacity to its factories in Waterloo, Iowa. The manufacturing facilities are the most advanced in the world. The plants contain huge, flexible manufacturing systems that are directed by computerized machining centers. The enormous cost pays off in efficiency. As one example, an automated press makes battery-box covers 43% cheaper than the old way.

The developments have made Deere the lowest cost producer in the industry. Breakeven is at 50% of capacity. Deere is ready for the price wars that occur in a depressed industry. Perhaps more important, Deere has the best customer base of any farm equipment maker. Its innovations in production are equaled by innovations in customer satisfaction. In an unexciting industry, Deere spends over 5% of sales on research, nearly as much as IBM. When it comes up with an improved product, it gives it free to customers to experiment with as a way to build customer loyalty.

All Deere needs now is an upswing in the fortunes of farmers. It is positioned as both the low cost producer and innovator in the industry. Once demand moves above 50% of capacity, the profits will begin to roll in.[10]

Managers at John Deere understand the importance of learning and readaptation. They haven't allowed the company to stagnate. This vitality has put them in the position of industry leader.

ENVIRONMENT FOR READAPTATION

The readaptation approach of Lawrence and Dyer proposes that the environment provides both the opportunity and need for readaptation. Two key characteristics of the relationship between the organization and environment are: (1) the organization must obtain information from its environment to interpret and make sense out of external events and (2) the organization must obtain resources from its environment in order to survive. As mentioned in chapter 2, elements in the environment are associated with the organization's need for either resources or information. Organizations can experience difficulty or uncertainty with respect to the acquisition of information, resources, or both.

The two dimensions of an organization's environment are illustrated in Exhibit 13.1. The vertical axis describes variations in information complexity. The amount of information the organization must process to understand the

EXHIBIT 13.1. Environmental Characteristics Associated with Organizational Readaptation.

INFORMATION DOMAIN		AREA 1	AREA 2	AREA 3
	High	High IC Low RS	High IC Intermediate RS	High IC High RS
COMPETITIVE VARIATIONS				
TECHNICAL VARIATIONS	Intermediate	AREA 4 Intermediate IC Low RS	AREA 5 Intermediate IC Intermediate RS	AREA 6 Intermediate IC High RS
CUSTOMER VARIATIONS				
PRODUCT VARIATIONS				
GOVERNMENT REGULATORY VARIATIONS	Low	AREA 7 Low IC Low RS	AREA 8 Low IC Intermediate RS	AREA 9 Low IC High RS
		Low	Intermediate	High

INFORMATION COMPLEXITY (IC) (vertical axis)

RESOURCE SCARCITY (RS) (horizontal axis)

RESOURCE DOMAIN

AVAILABILITY OF RAW MATERIALS, HUMAN RESOURCES, CAPITAL
CUSTOMER IMPACT ON RESOURCE AVAILABILITY
COMPETITOR IMPACT ON RESOURCE AVAILABILITY
GOVERNMENT IMPACT ON RESOURCE AVAILABILITY
ORGANIZED LABOR IMPACT ON RESOURCE AVAILABILITY

Source: Paul R. Lawrence and Davis Dyer, *Renewing American Industry* (New York: The Free Press, 1983), p. 6. Used by permission of the publisher.

environment increases with variations in external technology, customers, products, government regulations, and competitors. The knowledge explosion associated with technology and the increasing pace of events means that many organizations have complex environments and hence face uncertainty with respect to the amount of information to be processed.[11]

The horizontal axis in Exhibit 13.1 represents low, intermediate, and high resource scarcity. Resource scarcity measures the difficulty facing an organization in obtaining the resources it needs to survive and operate successfully. The intensity of competition, the munificence of the environment, the availability of employees, raw materials, and capital all determine the amount of resources available to the organization. Low environmental scarcity would mean a large customer demand for goods and service, available labor and raw materials, and a benign government. High resource scarcity would mean that the organization has difficulty selling its products and obtaining necessary resource inputs.

Lawrence and Dyer propose that the ideal environment to foster organizational learning and readaptation consists of intermediate levels of both information complexity and resource scarcity. A small amount of information complexity does not provide sufficient diversity to stimulate creative thinking. Too much information complexity means the organization membership cannot scan and interpret the environment effectively. Confusion results. In a similar way, low resource scarcity (abundant resources) reduces the motivation of management and employees to be efficient. Too much resource scarcity means the organization has to focus exclusively on efficiency, and resources needed for innovation are not available. Intermediate levels of both information complexity and resource scarcity foster internal striving and learning as well as the resource capacity to be both efficient and innovative.

Design for Readaptation

How do managers encourage both efficiency and innovation within their organizations? There is no easy answer. Environments change over time, and so do organizations. For example, Exhibit 13.2 illustrates historical changes associated with three industries. In the case of steel and autos, the industry started out with resource abundance, but increasing foreign competition and consumer dissatisfaction led to severe resource scarcity. Information complexity for these industries also increased somewhat as new technologies evolved for both product innovation and internal efficiency. Hospitals, by contrast, have been characterized by high information complexity from the beginning. The latest technologies for medical specialties are housed in hospitals. The major change has been in resource scarcity. In the past, the medical industry was able to acquire needed resources without difficulty. Insurance companies, the government, and consumers would pay whatever was asked. Now resources are becoming scarce because governments and insurance companies are paying a fixed fee for each service. Hospitals are in competition for customers. Efficiency is becoming more important.

What does this mean for managers? They may adopt two approaches: restructure the organization to find an environmental niche that has intermediate levels of information complexity and resource scarcity, or redesign the organization to make the best of the current environmental niche in which the company exists. Many organizations adopt a combination of both strategies, and Lawrence and Dyer specifically recommended a number of internal changes that could make organizations readaptive.[12]

1. Design the organization to fit an environment of intermediate information complexity. This means if the organization faces too complex an environment, it can simplify itself by dropping technologies or product lines until the information complexity problem is manageable. A firm with a single technology and a single type of customer has a simple information problem.

EXHIBIT 13.2. Example of Environmental Changes for Three Industries.

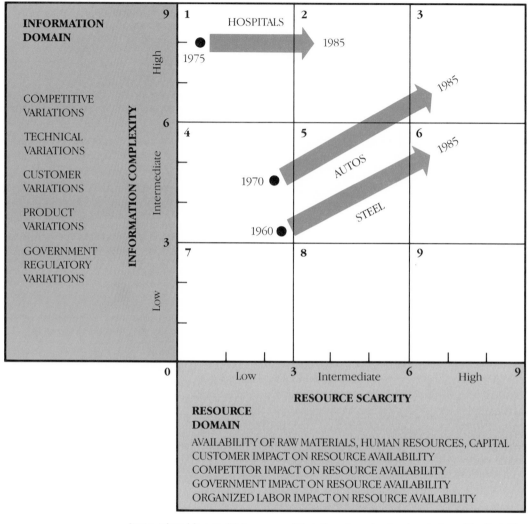

Source: Adapted from Paul R. Lawrence and Davis Dyer, *Renewing American Industry* (New York: The Free Press, 1983), p. 334. Used by permission of the publisher.

Managers can design the organization toward an intermediate level of information complexity to make readaptation possible.

2. Design the organization to fit an environment of intermediate resource scarcity. This means trying to find products, services, and an environmental domain where adequate resources are available. An organization may drop products that are not profitable, and encourage innovations in areas with high potential. The overall organizational strategy should be to maintain the balance of businesses and products that provide adequate resources to foster the readaptation process. Moderate resources foster innovation, but also foster a value for efficiency.

The strategy of Brunswick Corporation described at the beginning of this chapter reflected the desire to achieve intermediate levels of both information complexity and resource scarcity. Brunswick simplified the organization structure into a manageable number of products, and focused on products that had a good resource potential with respect to the environment. In some organizations, major surgery or reconstruction to mold a new environmental niche is not possible. There are, however, strategies suggested by Lawrence and Dyer that can make organizations readaptive without changing the environment.

3. The organizations' entire membership must be made aware of the broad purpose, ethical standards, and operating principles of the firm with emphasis given to the value of both efficiency and innovation. Membership cannot help the organization learn if they are not aware of what the organization is trying to accomplish. Communicating central values throughout the organization is similar to the top manager role in defining organizational culture described in chapter 12. Managers can use any number of devices including ceremonies, public statements, and slogans to communicate to the entire membership the importance of both efficiency and innovation.

4. As information complexity from the environment increases, organizations should employ new kinds of specialists to help the organization learn and innovate with respect to the new, incoming information. This simply means that the organization will become more specialized as external complexity increases. Boundary roles were described in chapter 2 as a way to make contact with and to cope with complex external environments. As environmental complexity increases, the organization can be designed to be more specialized and differentiated.

5. As resource scarcity in the environment increases, the organization must increase the mechanisms available for coordinating internal activities. In order to achieve both efficiency and innovation, departments must cooperate with one another. Organizational innovation does not occur alone—it is a collective achievement.[13] A variety of specialists are required before an innovation is appropriate for adoption and utilization. Internal efficiency also requires coordination. The organization that is readaptive must find mechanisms to effectively coordinate the organizational parts into a coherent whole.

6. The organization's structure should reflect a relatively balanced distribution of power, including a reasonable balance along the vertical hierarchy as well as among the operating departments. Of course power is never perfectly equal throughout an organization, but too much imbalance seriously impedes cooperation, participation, and communication. If one department has too much clout, its ideas may dominate and fail to take advantage of the information and ideas from other groups. Likewise, too much power centralized at the top of the organization impedes participation and learning at the lower levels.

7. Human resource and control practices should encourage the involvement of employees. Lawrence and Dyer recommend that employee involvement be increased through the balanced use of the control mechanisms described in chapter 7. Market mechanisms offer tangible financial rewards, bureaucratic mechanisms encourage stability, and clan mechanisms encourage a sense of belonging. For example, Brunswick Corporation revitalized itself partly by providing greater financial rewards to high performing people, and

by encouraging a stronger sense of membership. Brunswick previously had been tilted too far toward bureaucratic control. Balance is the key. An organization dominated by market control and financial incentives might become too competitive. Domination by clan mechanisms would be very satisfying, but people may not be oriented toward efficiency.

The model of readaptation proposed by Lawrence and Dyer is illustrated in Exhibit 13.3. The ideal environment has intermediate levels of both resource scarcity and information complexity. Internal design reflects specialization and coordination, power balance, and the balanced use of human resource and control practices. Arrows are shown in both directions between the environment and the organization in Exhibit 13.3 because the design of internal elements may partly reflect the organization's location in the environment. Likewise internal design problems may influence the type of domain the organization seeks. Both the environment and internal elements influence member involvement and their emphasis on learning and striving. These processes enable the organization to seek both efficiency and innovation simultaneously. One company that redesigned itself to be readaptive is Texas Instruments.

IN PRACTICE 13.2

Texas Instruments Inc.

Texas Instruments was so successful for so many years that it gained a reputation as an arrogant company. TI was a worldwide leader in the semiconductor industry, and was doing well in two new businesses—computers and consumer electronics. TI beat the Japanese at the low-cost manufacture of calculators and electronic watches, and compiled a record of 15% compounded annual growth for fifteen years. The bubble burst in June 1983 when TI's stock dropped fifty points in two days.

What happened? Management and investors alike woke up to the fact that TI was no longer innovating in a way that met customer needs. The biggest shock was the failure of its home computer business. The business was disbanded and accounted for $660 million write-down in 1983. The failure of the home computer was a dramatic problem, but further analysis indicated that TI was losing its competitive edge.

For one thing, management systems were overly complex and overly bureaucratic. Systems emphasized strict financial controls and top-down strategic planning. Complex internal reporting structures and financial systems smothered innovation. New products like large-scale computer memory chips were long delayed.

Another problem was power centralization to top management. In the beginning, TI was decentralized, and encouraged bottom-up innovation. But the domineering styles of chairman Mark Shepherd and president Fred Bucy often intimidated product managers. People were telling the bosses what they wanted to hear rather than what was needed to keep the company innovative.

The other major problem was being out of touch with customers. TI was technology driven, a successful strategy in industrial markets. But consumer markets for home computers and digital watches require more effective scan-

EXHIBIT 13.3. The Readaptive Process: Interaction Between
The Environment and Readaptive Form.

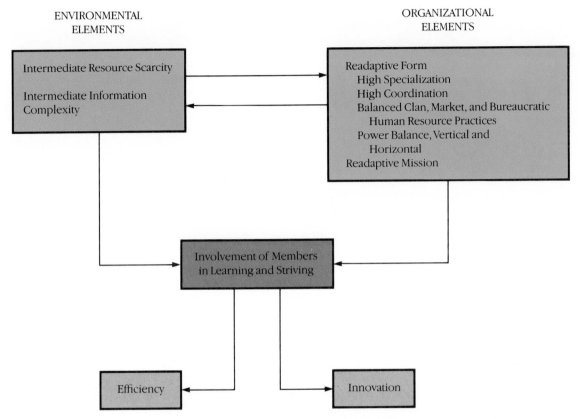

Source: Adapted from Paul R. Lawrence and Davis Dyer, *Renewing American Industry* (New York: The Free Press, 1983), p. 13. Used by permission of the publisher.

ning and interpretation systems. The company was remote from consumers and was bureaucratic and unyielding to their needs.

Now that TI is awake, what is being done? For one thing, the product lines are being pared down to a manageable scope. The home computer line was dropped. Unprofitable product lines such as digital watches and some electronic components were eliminated. A project to develop magnetic-bubble memory was also dropped as too expensive. TI has given up on multichip microprocessors, and has redirected its effort toward chips that contain all elements needed by computers. Refocusing on selected product lines has made the organization more manageable.

Another important move was to decentralize to recreate an innovative culture. Decentralization has been facilitated by reorganizing into a product structure, with each product line having all the resources needed to run the business. Each independent business unit can cope with its own environment and make its own decisions. The bureaucratic structure is also being simplified. Red tape has been slashed. Managers can move ahead on a project without specifying minor details such as the square feet of floor space that an eventual product might require. The new culture also stresses marketing. Employees are encouraged to be in touch with customers and to learn what they want.

Decentralization, a renewed innovative culture, simplified management systems, and autonomous business units are good moves. They should help revitalize the company, and make it both more efficient and more innovative. TI can implement a new product much faster now, and fewer resources are squandered on management overkill.[14]

The model in Exhibit 13.3 and the TI case illustrate how organizations can learn, and how they can renew themselves. When organizations are able to obtain high levels of both efficiency and innovation, they will be successful, perhaps even industry leaders. The value of this approach is that it indicates the organization must design itself to fit the environment as well as to provide mechanisms for membership involvement and learning. Managing the organization to involve the entire membership in organizational learning and development has been a somewhat neglected area in organization theory. Primary emphasis had been given to organizational structure and design in response to technology, size, and environment. Human resources are now being perceived as an equally important variable. Some of this work evolved from the discovery of Japanese management practices that seemed more effective than our own. We will now turn to a brief examination of these ideas.

MANAGING HUMAN RESOURCES

The concern for control and use of human resources in the Lawrence and Dyer model are part of a trend in organization theory. Ideas about participative leadership and worker motivation have been in the management literature for a long time. But organization theorists have rediscovered the importance of people in organizations. It is not just structure, technology, and control systems that make organizations successful. The involvement and commitment of the organizational membership has taken on new importance.

The new trend is different from work on motivation because it pertains to the organization as a whole. The question is not how managers can motivate individual subordinates, but how the total organization including culture and values can be designed to fully use all employees. This new approach changes the basic assumptions that have characterized American corporations for years. The rediscovery of human resources was fueled by the industrial miracle that occurred in Japan. Japan adopted Western technologies and then beat American corporate performance. Organization scholars began studying and writing about Japanese methods. The perspective on human resource management has been influenced by William Ouchi's *Theory Z,* and Richard Pascale and Anthony Athos's *The Art of Japanese Management.*[15] The Japanese seem to have developed a system wherein the individual is given more trust. Employees are treated as adults, as partners. Employees are involved in making Japanese companies both efficient and innovative.

The findings from Japan are sometimes controversial, especially when they are applied directly to North American culture. However, many firms in the United States seem to have adopted a hybrid management system that reflects techniques from both Japan and the United States. Successful organizations in the United States and Canada have not adopted the Japanese method in total, but have used methods in combination with traditional North American practices. William Ouchi and Alfred Jaeger identified seven dimensions along which Japanese and American firms differed. These seven characteristics are listed in Exhibit 13.4 and provide the basis for characterizing type A (American) and type J (Japanese) organizations.[16]

Length of employment refers to the average tenure of employees. Long tenure means that employees will be familiar with organizational workings and co-workers. Anticipation of a long career with a single organization encourages an employee to become integrated into the organization. The modes of **decision-making** and **responsibility** refer to whether the organization culture values individual action or a collective approach to decision-making and responsibility. **Speed of evaluation and promotion** refers to the frequency of employee review. When evaluations and promotions are slow, employees have an opportunity to become fully integrated into the organizational culture. They also adopt a longer term perspective. **Control** refers to whether employees are controlled with explicit standards, rules, and measurement, or whether less explicit social values and norms are used to control behavior. **Career path** pertains to whether employees are highly specialized within a single functional area or whether they are exposed to several functions. Lateral transfers enable employees to become more committed and involved in the entire organization. Finally, **concern** refers to how the organization views the employee. Segmented concern means the employee is valued only during time involved on the job. Holistic concern is oriented toward the total personal life circumstance of the employee.

The differences between traditional American and Japanese firms on these seven dimensions are summarized in Exhibit 13.4. The American organization values individual mobility, personal independence and self reliance, rapid promotion, explicit forms of control, and is concerned with only the work behavior of employees. This type of organization is oriented toward the short-run and toward getting measurable benefits from the employee in exchange for quick promotion opportunities.

EXHIBIT 13.4. Characteristics of Type A and Type Z Organizations.

	Type A (American)	Type J (Japanese)
Employment	Short-term	Lifetime
Decision-Making	Individual	Consensual
Responsibility	Individual	Collective
Evaluation	Rapid evaluation and promotion	Slow evaluation and promotion
Control	Explicit, formalized	Implicit, informal
Career Path	Specialized	Nonspecialized
Concern for Employees	Segmented	Holistic

Source: William G. Ouchi and Alfred M. Jaeger, "Type Z Organizations: Stability in the Midst of Mobility," *Academy of Management Review* 3 (1978):308, with permission.

Japanese organizations reflect a culture in which individual mobility is low. Employees are expected to be with a firm for a lifetime, and social norms rather than rules and regulations control behavior. Employee involvement and commitment to the organization enable a consensual decision-making process to emerge. Employees will be with the organization for a longer time. They are able to invest time working in diverse functions learning the organization. The Japanese firm is concerned with the total needs of employees since they are to be with the organization for a lifetime.

It is not logical to transplant the Japanese system intact into American culture. It wouldn't fit. But the type Z organization proposed by Ouchi and Jaeger integrates key Japanese ideas with management styles from American firms.[17] The type Z characteristics are listed in Exhibit 13.5. The type Z organization combines the best characteristics of traditional Japanese and American management to meet current needs of American organizations.

The type Z organization retains the American cultural value of individualism, but combines it with a collective approach to decision-making. Employment is for a longer term, which slows down the evaluation and promotion process and enables employees to become integrated into the organization. Explicit, formal control procedures are retained, but are combined with implicit, social control. Career paths in the type Z organization are moderately specialized. Paths may include only a few diverse activities but are no longer limited to a single specialized function. Slow evaluation and stability of membership is associated with greater concern for employees, including their families. The combination of these processes embodies the type Z philosophy.

When firms successfully achieve the theory Z management structure, distinct characteristics emerge. Employees experience a sense of equality and involvement, as if they were full partners in the enterprise. Employees have greater understanding of each other's point of view, so shared norms and values begin to emerge. Nissan, Japan's number two automaker, opened a plant in Tennessee, and adopted a hybrid management system. The workers all feel involved. If a machine breaks down, they help fix it rather than wait for maintenance. Indeed, managers and workers help each other on the line. Gary Bagett, a technician, enjoys working in the Nissan plant compared to his previous employment.

> Right now I work on the metal line. We mig weld, braze brass and then we grind. We have four work positions, and we swap, and on the ninth day you get

EXHIBIT 13.5. Characteristics of Type Z Organizations.

Type Z (Modified American)
Employment: Long-term
Decision Making: Consensual
Responsibility: Individual
Evaluation: Slow evaluation and promotion
Control: Implicit, informal control with explicit, formalized measures
Career Path: Moderately specialized
Concern for Employees: Holistic concern, including family

Source: William G. Ouchi and Alfred M. Jaeger, "Type Z Organization: Stability in the Midst of Mobility," *Academy of Management Review* 3 (1978): 311, with permission.

a rest, you become a relief person. If a person's out, the relief man has to take that person's place.

I worked almost seven years for Western Electric in Nashville. My wife is still there. But they're laying off now. So next time she's gone. Next time I would've been gone. That would have been both incomes out the window. That would have been terrible.

The people who work in this place—really, they screen them out. I work on a line with ten people, and there isn't a lazy bone in anyone's body. Used to be pretty easy to get lazy when you were working for Ma Bell. You had a lot of slack time. I never missed a day's work in seven years. I think that helped me here.

What's really wild here is seeing the supervisor work. The supervisors get right in there beside you. I just count on him as one of the work crew. He'll do it. Miss a weld, he'll catch a weld. Everybody helps everybody.[18]

Firms using a hybrid form of Japanese management are also very efficient. Time is spent identifying production problems. In a type Z firm, seventy or eighty people may be included in a discussion because they may be affected by decisions. But while problems are discussed at length, implementation is a snap. Traditional American firms have great difficulty with implementation, which is overcome by theory Z management processes. The sense of collective responsibility increases productivity. For example, workers on a type A assembly line have clearly prescribed individual jobs, and they follow specific instructions. When an incomplete component comes down the line, no one reports it because it is not their responsibility. In a type Z firm, each worker is part of the organization and is collectively responsible with other employees. An incomplete component will be called to the attention of others by the first person to spot it, so that it will not proceed any farther down the assembly process.

An example of the efficiency and quality that can arise from employees who feel involved was illustrated at the Nissan plant in Tennessee. Lead technician Beverly Bogle, who works in the trim and chassis department, describes how things are for her.

We get the cab when it first comes out of the drop lift or after paint. We put in the main harness, the master vac, which is the brake booster.

There are twenty-four people, including myself, in Zone 1. There's a supervisor over me, but I'm with the technicians all the time. There are quite a few ladies on the line. Everybody does real good, and they are always looking out for each other, or if they can't, they always holler for me, 'Hon, Beverly, Beverly!' No, they don't mind hollering. I'm just one of the guys.

The mistakes we have are usually on small things. Really small things. Like we left a rubber plug out of a hole, usually something like that. I walk back and forth through the zone quite a bit, up, back and forth, up and down the line a lot, and I see something that's not right and I'll fix it. Like we've had a new guy training, and he's been putting on vents instead of a.c. plates on air-conditioned trucks. But you catch it. And it never gets all the way over to where they put in the dash.[19]

Many companies have adopted a management philosophy that reflects the values of hybrid Japanese management. Dana Corporation, Hewlett-Packard, Wal-mart, and Delta Airlines have both explicit company policies and deep cultural values that stress the importance of employees.[20] At People's Express, the philosophy from its inception has stressed people values. Every employee is called a manager. Every employee is given stock in the company. Every employee is involved in decision-making. Other companies did not begin with strong human resource values, and are now trying to adopt them. One such company is Westinghouse.

IN PRACTICE 13.3
Westinghouse

Westinghouse Electric Corporation decided to experiment with Japanese management techniques. The guinea pig was the company's construction group, which was a bastion of traditional American-style management. It had a strong chain of command and many tradition-minded engineers. Westinghouse's goal in this experiment was to overturn traditional boss-employee relationships to enhance performance. In a period of difficult economic conditions, top management felt they must make better use of human resources. Bosses are no longer expected to issue orders. Instead they seek consensus. Rather than chew out workers, they ask for suggestions. New committees and councils are involved in both major and minor decisions.

The Westinghouse Construction Group will not suspend performance measurement. They will measure productivity improvement, and are going to test whether Japanese management ideas allow them to increase productivity faster than the 2%–3% increases of the last three years. Senior executives made several trips to Japanese plants, and were deeply impressed. "When you visit Japanese factories and see everyone, but everyone, working like tigers to make that product more reliable at a lower cost, it's awesome. . . . They even come back early from their breaks." [21]

Implementation of theory Z-type management has not been easy. Top management expected it to be implemented at lower levels so they could see how it would work. Consultants insisted that this approach wouldn't do. Either top executives made their own decisions by consensus or theory Z would never work on the shop floor.

Once top management agreed to be involved, the construction group was blitzed with training programs. Managers at all levels in the construction group were exposed to theory Z ideas and began to practice the techniques in five-day seminars. Once lower-level managers realized that top management was serious, the rumor mill helped diffuse the program. People at all levels began to look forward to attending the training programs and trying the new techniques.

Committees and decision groups have been set up at all management levels in the construction group. At the top, general managers meet monthly to discuss common interests. Councils under them bring together counterparts with common problems from several departments. Sixty quality circles were formed at lower levels, which brought together workers and supervisors to discuss production problems. A new cafeteria was designed to replace the vending machine area by a committee of workers and managers. Even a problem of restroom vandalism was tackled by a committee. The most difficult decision of all—the allocation of budget resources—has been handled by a committee. Instead of fighting with each other for the resources, managers moved quickly to a consensus once all problems were laid on the table. Some divisions gave up expected budget increases to help divisions that had more severe needs. The open decision process led to a much better allocation of resources than the group president could have accomplished alone.

Westinghouse is now working to spread the gospel to other divisions. A Productivity and Quality Center has been established and staffed with 300 employees to teach managers throughout the company how to improve productivity. About 2,000 quality circles have been created. More study teams have been sent to Japan. So far the results seem promising. Productivity in the construction group was up 8%, more than any previous increase. Productivity for the entire corporation climbed 6%. One executive commented, "We are doing to the Japanese what they have done to us for twenty or thirty years." [22]

CHARACTERISTICS OF SUCCESSFUL COMPANIES

The work on Japanese management techniques has been followed by new research in American corporations. The human resource ideas that characterize American-Japanese hybrid management have been reinforced by studies in North America of successful and unsuccessful companies. Human resource management is a vital part of company success. Other factors have also been uncovered, many of which are congruent with the organization theory ideas described in this book. The most notable publication was *In Search of Excellence* by Peters and Waterman.[23] This book helped expand the perspective on human resource management to include new ideas for running the corporation. Other research has also been undertaken to understand why companies succeed or fail.[24] Findings have been drawn from major American corporations, small business, and high tech companies. This research provides additional guidelines for organizations that want to renew themselves. The ideas are summarized below and in Exhibit 13.6 under the four categories of environment, management, structure, and human resources.

Environment

Three characteristics identified in corporate research pertain to the organization's relationship with the environment. These characteristics pertain to the customer, adaptation, and business focus.

Close to the Customer   Successful companies are customer driven. New-product innovations arise from customer needs. Managers act as boundary spanners to stay in communication with customers. Successful companies thrive on sales and service overkill. Top managers interact directly with customers when necessary. If management begins to take customers for granted, and grows out of touch with customer needs, the organization will find itself in difficulty. J. Willard Marriott, Sr, stayed informed by reading every single customer complaint card—raw and unsummarized. Satisfied customers was the dominant value at Marriott, and managers around the

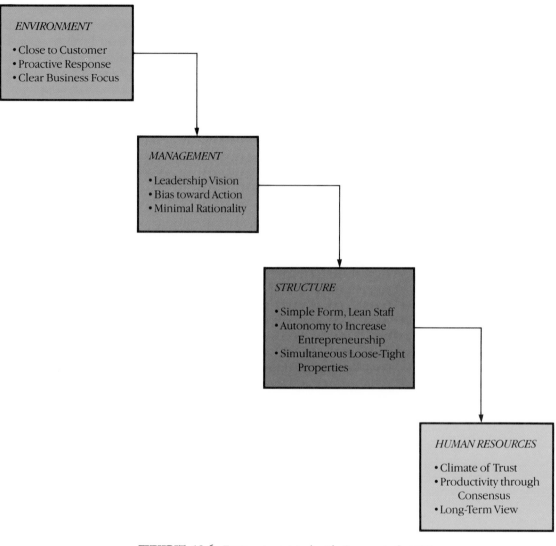

EXHIBIT 13.6. Factors Associated with Corporate Success.

country worked long hours to make sure the boss had a very light reading load.

Proactive, Adaptive Response Companies get in trouble when their products become obsolete or noncompetitive. New technologies, products, and administrative structures are needed to stay abreast of environmental changes. Organizations must develop mechanisms to encourage change and innovation. Major shifts in products require agility and daring. Investing in separate departments or venture groups to create and implement technological change is important.

Clear Business Focus Successful firms are highly focused. They stay in their area of expertise. They define their internal strengths and product line, and realize the bulk of their sales from closely related products. A clear business focus reduces the information complexity from the environment to a manageable level. Moreover, the company can focus on research and development and customers that are consistent with its focus. Peters and Waterman call this "stick to the knitting." Business priorities must be identified, and implemented in a consistent fashion, and a priority given to quality, innovation, marketing, or manufacturing efficiency.

Management

Management techniques and processes are another dimension of successful corporations. Three factors unique to managers are part of the readaptive firm.

Leadership Vision   The readaptive organization requires a special kind of leadership, which is leadership of the organization, not leadership within the organization. The leader must provide a vision of what can be accomplished, and give a sense of purpose and meaning to employees. The leader's vision can build commitment and excitement. It can create the belief that both efficiency and innovation are possible and do-able. Leadership is often "hands-on." Managers are involved in important company issues, not because they fail to delegate, but to communicate and facilitate critical behaviors. They also learn how the organization works and can do something about problems. They lead by example. They push the dominant value with a single-minded focus. At Texas Instruments, top management stresses both innovation and marketing. At McDonald's, the norms of quality, cleanliness, value, and service are stressed repeatedly to all employees. Employees in successful organizations do not receive mixed signals or suffer doubts about what the organizational leadership is trying to accomplish.

Bias toward Action   Successful companies are oriented toward doing, toward implementation. They don't talk problems to death, or spend all their time creating exotic solutions. These companies "do it, fix it, try it." These companies are goal-directed, but they also tolerate failure. Trial and error experimentation is an effective learning device. Managers are encouraged to take risks, and need courage to succeed. Johnson & Johnson's founder said, "If I wasn't making mistakes, I wasn't making decisions." The CEO of a computer peripherals company put it this way, "We tell our people to make at least ten mistakes a day. If you are not making ten mistakes a day, you're not trying hard enough." [25]

Minimal Rationality   Research into self-designing, adaptive organizations indicates that they do not rely heavily on objective, quantitative decision rules.[26] This is especially important under crisis conditions. Rational methods may not be fast enough, accurate enough, or be able to handle ambiguity. During a crisis at Hugh Russell Inc. in Canada, the organization had to transform itself from a "hard box" to a "soft bubble" decision process. Instead of top management analyzing the data and providing the answer, a multitude of task forces were spontaneously formed to address urgent issues. The passion, warmth, and trust arising from these groups lacked analytical rationality, but saved the company.[27] Too much rationality can hurt rather than help, especially when the company must readapt instantly. A readaptive organization minimizes rationality in the sense that overlapping, unplanned, and intuitive processes become the source of wisdom.

Structure

Structure pertains to internal design for control and coordination. Successful corporations are characterized by three structural attributes.

Simple Form and Lean Staff   Successful organizations are sufficiently formalized to meet the needs for standardization and control, but they don't overdo it. Upper levels are not loaded with staff personnel. Large companies are subdivided into product divisions, so each division can act like a small corporation. Adaptive companies sometimes give up economies of scale to subdivide into product groups for simplicity and adaptability. At McDonald's, the stores have procedures to keep the work simple and to ensure good food, but other management levels are more organic. Decisions are pushed downward whenever possible.

Autonomy to Encourage Entrepreneurship   Organization structure is designed to encourage innovation and change in adaptive organizations. A product form of structure is used where possible to give each unit a product focus so that creativity and innovation will be rewarded. Technical people are located near marketing people so they can have lunch together and socialize outside working hours. Organizational units may be kept small to create a sense of belonging and adaptability. Idea champions are encouraged, and risk-taking is rewarded. People can also be given autonomy through the establishment of new venture groups or separate R&D staff.

Simultaneous Loose-Tight Properties   This may seem like a paradox, but adaptive companies use tight controls in some areas and loose control in others. For example, Lawrence and Dyer described the need for both market and clan control in organizations. Market control is used to evaluate the performance of divisions, but clan control is used to encourage commitment and involvement. Moreover, employees are not allowed to deviate from the basic business values, which are controlled tightly. They are, however, encouraged to be flexible, to innovate, and to take risks in ways that will help the organization accomplish its goals. Readaptive companies successfully manage the loose-tight paradox.

Human Resources

The organization's membership is recognized as an underutilized resource. Successful companies manage to harness enormous employee energy and enthusiasm. One of the lessons from research on Japanese companies is that employee commitment is a vital component of organization success.

Climate of Trust   A climate of trust is needed in successful companies so that employees can deal honestly and openly with one another. Collaboration across departments requires trust. Involvement of employees and managers in joint problem-solving requires trust on both sides. Overcoming conflict requires trust. Managers must treat employees as adults with dignity. Even General Motors has learned that it cannot build high quality, inexpensive cars with an antagonistic workforce. Employee commitment and involvement are required to maintain innovation and efficiency. Successful companies have respect for the individual. At IBM, managers spend a major portion of their time on the idea that the company respects the individual. And employees respond with commitment, good will, and quality work.

Productivity through People and Consensus   Readaptation requires cooperation. The translation of an idea into a new product or service cannot be done without the help of several departments. People must be encouraged to participate. Production, marketing, and manufacturing must collaborate in a common cause. Good communication is essential. Successful organizations find excuses to bring people together to exchange ideas. Conflicting ideas are encouraged rather than suppressed. Job rotation enables employees to see one another's perspective. Some organizations use shop floor teams and cross-functional groups to feed ideas into goal-setting and decision-making processes. The ability to move ahead by consensus preserves trust and a sense of family, and enables innovation and efficiency that unsuccessful companies lack.

Long-Term View   One of the important lessons learned from the Japanese is that organizational success is not built in a day. They invest time training employees and do not encourage short-term evaluation and promotion. Career paths are designed to give employees broad backgrounds rather than rapid upward mobility. A long-term view also reduces the pressure for immediate profits. The appropriate internal culture and relationships can thus be built. Investment in technology and human resources needed for the future can be made. Readaptive and successful organizations are not trying to maximize returns in the short run.

Summary

The most recent findings on the management of successful companies and on organizational readaptation are consistent with the topics discussed in this book. The most relevant organization theory topics seem to be innovation and change, the environment, top management domain, decision-making, and information and control systems. Organization theory topics are relevant to current management philosophy, with one exception. One reason for excellence in corporations is the productivity through human resources, which has only recently been stressed in organization theory. Human behavior has normally been in the domain of organizational psychology because it was treated as an individual-level phenomenon. The aggregate membership is an issue for top management, however, and is an important topic for organization theory. The important point is to use the concepts and models from organization theory to manage organizations effectively. One well-known example of a successful corporation that uses the techniques described above is Delta Air Lines Inc.

IN PRACTICE 13.4

Delta Air Lines Inc.

Through the years, Delta has been one of the world's most profitable airlines. Delta's secret is a massive effort to motivate employees that makes it the most efficient airline in the industry. Delta is also innovative, having pioneered the hub and spoke scheduling system, and quickly adopts new technologies and employee suggestions for more efficient work procedures.

Delta's management orientation began years ago when the CEO suffered a long illness. The burdens of management were delegated to lower levels, and when the CEO died in 1966, the team was already functioning as a unit.

The basis of Delta's management philosophy is that employees are to be treated like members of a family. Delta went twenty-five years without laying off a full-time employee. The president's open door policy also sets the family tone. His rug has to be cleaned once a month because mechanics, pilots, flight attendants—everyone—goes to see him. When there is a problem, such as when a mechanic did not get paid overtime for coming in at 2:00 A.M. to repair an engine, the president takes immediate action. The quick response is an important signal to employees that they count. During an economic downturn, excess pilots and flight attendants will be put to work elsewhere rather than be laid off.

Delta's benefit plan is also one of the most generous in the U.S. Employees and their families are provided for in any emergency. This is part of the philosophy—you protect the family.

The monthly employee publication, *Delta Digest*, reports citations for employees who were especially compassionate toward passengers. Special procedures have been adopted to identify and reward these employees, which reinforces the customer service philosophy at Delta.

Beyond the open door policy, top management makes it a point to meet all employees at least once every eighteen months. Groups of twenty-five to thirty people are brought together with one of the top executives. The executive provides a formal briefing, and then throws the discussion open to questions and complaints. At one meeting it became clear that the group's supervisor was the problem. Managers took him aside later and helped transform him into one of the best supervisors in the system.

The management structure is unusually lean. The concept of interchangeable parts has been applied to top management. The nine senior officers—the president, vice-chairman and secretary, and seven senior vice-presidents—are almost interchangeable because lines of communication are so short. Everyone is constantly being updated. There are no large support staffs writing reports. Top managers handle things themselves.

If a difficult decision comes up, whoever is present can make it, and make it quickly. Managers have been working together for a long time, so they know what others are thinking. The interchangeability of senior managers, with anyone able to make a decision, allows a quick response to any problem that develops.

Delta is the least unionized of U.S. airlines. The pilots belong to a union but they are promanagement compared to pilots from other airlines. The vast majority of workers prefer not to have a union. The last union vote was in 1955. A lead mechanic described it this way, "Listen, if we needed a union here at Delta we'd have a union. But the way they treat you, we don't need one."

The lack of union procedures makes Delta flexible and efficient. Rigid union work rules are absent. Supervisors can pull people out of one part of the shop and put them in another when things get jammed up. Employees are expected to pitch in wherever they are needed, and this is a key reason why Delta is consistently profitable.

Delta further increases efficiency with its fleet improvement program. New airplanes and new capital equipment are purchased on a regular basis.

Success at Delta comes down to the underlying philosophy of treating customers well and taking care of employees. Up to 25% of management's time is spent listening to people problems. Management knows what's going on with the people, and the people are regularly informed about what's going on in the company.[28]

EPILOGUE: TWENTY YEARS OF PROGRESS

Organization theory is a new field of study. It is not a mature discipline, with a large, well-defined body of knowledge. Organization theory is still in the formative stages, and is now being recognized as a separate discipline in universities, where courses are being established. Because of its newness, the last twenty years have seen remarkable progress. The field got its start when significant ideas on the topics of organization technology and structure were published in the late 1960s. Since then a vast amount of new research has been reported. Not all organization theory topics have been studied equally or have developed at the same pace. In some topic areas, organization theory can be quite specific about how an organization should be designed. In other areas, knowledge and frameworks are scarce. Many contingencies have yet to be discovered.

The topics that are part of organization theory are reflected in the chapter content of this book. These topics are also consistent with a survey of organization theorists that asked their opinions about the field's boundaries.[29] Each topic can be classified according to whether the level of development is high, moderate, or low compared with other topics within the discipline. This classification indicates where significant progress has been made in the last twenty years and, conversely, where we can expect the most rapid development in the future. The classification of organization theory topics by level of development is given in Exhibit 13.7.

High Development Three topics that have a high level of development in organization theory concern organization structure and design. Research into (1) size and bureaucracy, (2) technology and structure, and (3) functional versus product structural processes has been reported since the 1960s. A substantial amount of information has accumulated. Relationships among variables such as bureaucracy, size, formalization, complexity, administrative ratio, and clerical ratio are well understood. Organization theorists can say with some certainty when a bureaucratic structure is appropriate or is not appropriate. We know that small-batch technology should be associated with a quite different organization structure than assembly-line technology. At the department level, nonroutine departments require a different structure than routine departments. Similarly, organization theorists can suggest when a product form of structure is preferable to a functional structure for an organization.

Recall from chapter 1 that organizations are social systems, and are not characterized by the same level of precision and prediction that occurs in the physical and biological sciences. The amount of bureaucracy or extent of functional structure cannot be calculated with mathematical precision. Even in this well-developed area of organization theory precise formulas do not exist. But definite patterns do exist, and organization theorists can say with some certainty that large deviations from these patterns will lead to serious problems.

Moderate Development   Several of the topics in organization theory have experienced moderate development. These include (1) the environment, (2) goals and effectiveness, (3) innovation and change, (4) decision-making, and (5) intergroup relationships. These topics are moderately developed because a few models have been developed for analyzing organizations. For instance, organizations can be analyzed by the amount of change and complexity in the external environment. Techniques for managing the environment have also been reported. Another example is the dual-core and ambidextrous models that apply to innovation and change. Organizational decision-making can be understood with reference to the rational model, the Carnegie model, and the garbage can model.

These topics are considered moderately developed because while there are specific frameworks in each area, unexplored contingencies still exist. Moreover, the application of these models requires substantial training and experience within the specific organization. The models are not sufficiently developed or comprehensive to fit every organizational setting. Also, there has not been research that has confirmed or replicated patterns and relationships. As that kind of research is reported, the body of knowledge will become more well-developed and the models will become more precise. Models in these areas are relatively conceptual and abstract, and do not translate into managerial applications as easily as findings from the highly developed topics.

Low Development   Four topic areas are classified as low development: (1) information and control, (2) power and politics, (3) top management domain, including culture, and (4) human resource management, including how organizations learn. These areas are considered low in development because the body of knowledge is new and relatively small. Ten years ago, chapters on these topics could not have been written. Sufficient research did not exist. Even five years ago, the amount of research was small. The work in information-processing, for example, has been dominated by research on communication and data. But information is the interpretation of meaning, which has been studied only recently in the form of information amount and richness. Likewise, only in the last few years have theories of control moved beyond the simple feedback mechanisms used in machine systems. New theories concerned with market control, clan control, and bureaucratic control have been developed. Power and politics has been an especially difficult area of study because managers are reluctant to report their perceptions of power and

EXHIBIT 13.7. Areas of High, Moderate, and Low Development in Organization Theory.

High	Moderate	Low
1. Bureaucracy and size	1. Environment	1. Power and politics
2. Technology and structure	2. Goals and effectiveness	2. Information and control
3. Functional versus product structure	3. Innovation and change	3. Top management domain/culture
	4. Decision-making	4. Human resources/ organization learning
	5. Intergroup relations	

politics. The top management domain is also difficult because strategy formulation, symbolism, and culture are difficult to define, and top managers are extremely busy and reluctant to be interviewed. The work on human resource management and organizational learning has gotten a start from research on Japanese firms. New ideas have been reported from research into excellent American companies, but additional research is needed to refine and generalize from this beginning.

Future Research One explanation why topics have developed at different rates is the difficulty of research for organization theorists.[30] The greatest development in research methods over the past twenty years has been the use of questionnaires and statistical analysis. These techniques are very effective for measuring well-defined characteristics of organizations. With a questionnaire, the researcher can ask about the organization's size, formalization, structure, technology, and administrative ratio, and these data can be analyzed with statistics.

But the topics in the low and moderate developed categories are more complicated. They pertain to behavioral processes that are elusive and ambiguous. Organization scholars are now beginning to attack these more complex topics, and they are doing so with new methods. Richer forms of research, such as intensive case analyses, observation, and open-ended interviews are able to reveal insights about complex organizational processes. These methods are able to provide more exhaustive descriptions of organization.[31] The new methodologies are less precise, but they can capture and communicate ideas and emotions that cannot be quantified. They are able to capture some of the complexity and variety inherent in complex social systems.

Organization theory is rich and exciting. It seems to be changing almost daily. Future research can be expected to reveal new knowledge about information processes, power, culture, and human resources. In information-processing, future studies may explore the use of organizational languages and jargon for interpreting activities. Power and politics will be more closely linked to the process of decision-making as well as to goals, innovation, and conflict. New ideas will be forthcoming about organizational cultures, and about how to motivate and involve the entire employee membership as an integral part of the organization. Additional developments can also be expected in the areas of organization environment, innovation and change, and other topics that are moderately developed. Models that describe new variables and that give more elaborate frameworks for manager application will be forthcoming. New research is accumulating at a rapid rate.

SUMMARY AND INTERPRETATION

The material in this chapter addresses an important problem: the competitiveness of organizations in North America. As organizations have matured, they have in many cases become less adaptive and efficient than foreign competitors. The concept of readaptation was introduced to understand how organizations could renew and revitalize themselves. Organizations can be readaptive by striving to be both efficient and innovative. Readaptation can be accomplished by finding the right environmental domain, and by communicating a common goal to the organizational membership, specializing to cope with the environment, coordinating across departments, and using appropriate human resource management techniques. This approach to the management of organizations enables organizations to learn, which means they constantly change and improve themselves.

Another major idea in this chapter is the notion of human resource management. One answer to the declining competitiveness of firms in North America is to make better use of human resources. The success of Japanese firms, which take a different approach to employees, has generated new research in this area. While Japanese techniques cannot be employed wholesale in the United States or Canada, they do suggest approaches that may have some value in our own culture. Longer term employment, consensual decision-making, slower evaluation, and greater concern and trust for employees all represent techniques that improve both the productivity and innovativeness of organizations.

Recent studies of excellent American corporations suggest that human resources are an important part of excellent organizations. These studies also suggest that successful firms are able to respond to the environment by being close to the customer and having a clear business focus. Management techniques include a vision for the organization, bias toward action, and minimal rationality. Structural techniques have also been proposed, which include simple form and lean staff, autonomy, and simultaneous loose-tight properties. All these ideas in combination with the emphasis on human resources are associated with excellent performance and readaptation.

A final point made within the chapter is that the field of organization theory is new and research findings have been available only in the last twenty years. Also, within the field different topics reflect different stages of development. The highly developed topics of technology, structure, and bureaucracy have larger bodies of knowledge and well defined frameworks. Less-developed areas, such as power and politics, culture, and organizational learning will receive greater research attention in the future. The less-developed topics tend to be more complex and ambiguous so new research techniques are being used to study them. These areas have the greatest potential for new knowledge.

KEY CONCEPTS

autonomy to encourage
    entrepreneurship
bias toward action
clear business focus
close to the customer
design for readaptation
high development topics
information complexity
leadership vision
low development topics
minimal rationality

moderate development topics
organizational learning
productivity through people
readaptation
resource scarcity
simple form and lean staff
simultaneous loose-tight
    properties
type A
type J
type Z

DISCUSSION QUESTIONS

1. What is readaptation? Why is it important to organizational survival and success?
2. What environmental characteristics are associated with readaptation? Can managers influence the environment their firms face? Discuss.
3. What internal control mechanisms are typically associated with readaptive firms?
4. Briefly describe the seven characteristics of type Z organizations. How does a type Z firm differ from a traditional type A firm?
5. Two management characteristics of successful firms are "bias toward action" and "minimal rationality." What do these concepts mean? Are they related to each other?
6. What topics in organization theory are classified as low in development? What does low in development mean? How do topics in this category differ from those in the high development category?
7. Are research methods related to the extent of development of organization theory topics? Explain.

GUIDES TO ACTION

As an organization designer:

1. To renew and revitalize your organization, strive toward both efficiency and innovation. Simultaneous efficiency and innovation can best be accomplished in external environments characterized by intermediate information complexity and intermediate resource scarcity.
2. Facilitate readaptation within the organization by communicating the purpose to the entire membership, adopting specialized units to cope with information complexity, increasing mechanisms for coordination to facilitate

innovation, and encouraging balanced power and control processes. Through these mechanisms encourage member involvement in learning and striving to accomplish both efficiency and innovation.

3. Use modified Japanese management techniques, such as theory Z, to increase productivity through human participation. The modified management techniques encourage long-term relationships and provide more stability and involvement of employees.

4. Make your organization successful by emphasizing closeness to the customer, proactive response, clear business focus, leadership vision, bias toward action, minimal rationality, simple form and lean staff, autonomy, simultaneous loose-tight properties, climate of trust, productivity through consensus, and a long-term view.

5. Use organization theory concepts to provide explicit tools that can assist and guide managers and future managers. The topics of environment, innovation, top management domain, decision-making, information and control system, organization structure, goals and effectiveness, and organizational learning are all things that need to be understood when supplying guidance for managers.

Consider these Guides when analyzing the following case and when answering the questions listed after the case.

CASE FOR ANALYSIS

KOLLMORGEN CORPORATION*

In 1974, Skip Griggs interviewed for a job as manufacturing manager at the Inland Motor Division of Kollmorgen in Radford, Virginia. Corwin Matthews, the personnel manager, explained to Griggs that Kollmorgen—a $79 million-a-year electronics company—was not like other corporations. There was a new philosophy at work there, Matthews said, which disagreed strongly with the precepts of traditional authoritarian management. People came first at Kollmorgen, he said, and they were seen as basically good, well-intentioned, willing to work, responsible, and creative. Everyone was treated as an equal in an environment grounded on mutual trust and respect. Here people felt secure and could talk openly about their opinions and problems.

Griggs listened politely to this description of what seemed like a mythical kingdom, and took the job, reasoning: "I looked at it as one of two things— a gold mine or a disaster. Either way, I felt I'd know soon enough."

A year passed, and even after Griggs listened to Robert L. Swiggett, Kollmorgen's chairman of the board, chief executive officer, and leading evangelist, describe the company's new corporate vision at a meeting in Hartford, he was still uncertain. Maybe the vision was only that, he thought, fun for a sunny day but quick to evaporate when business got tough. "Maybe then they'd say, 'Let's go back to the old way and tell those dumb bunnies what to do,'" he recalls thinking. "I thought it was working in our division, but what about the others? You know you go so far, but you sometimes tread

* Lucien Rhodes, "The Passion of Robert Swiggett," *Inc.,* April 1984, pp. 121–140. Used with permission.

lightly. I still had some vague reservations. Let's face it, freedom and respect for the individual are just different."

Four more years passed. Storm clouds came and went and, if anything, the "bunnies" were given more freedom. Meanwhile, Griggs' division also witnessed extraordinary growth. From 1974 to 1979, the company's sales nearly doubled, from $79.1 million to $154.5 million, while earnings almost tripled, from $3.3 million to $9.8 million. Yet Griggs still had some doubts.

Then, in 1980, Swiggett published the company's philosophy in a seven-page brochure that was widely distributed. Griggs was ecstatic. "I knew he had to mean it because he put it in black and white for the world," he says. "He was putting his reputation and all his experience on the line. I said to myself: 'I'm in this for the rest of my life.' "

*   *   *

"Freedom and respect for the individual," [Swiggett] wrote, "are the best motivators of man, especially when innovation and growth are the objectives." To avoid misunderstanding, "innovation" was quickly defined as "techno-logical leadership" and "first to market with the best" in the company's three business segments: printed circuitry and associated technology, special direct current motors and controls, and electro-optical instruments. And "growth" was identified as doubling sales and earnings every four years while exceeding a 20% return on shareholders' average equity.

Traditional forms of management cannot sustain these goals, Swiggett went on, particularly in larger companies. In order to achieve innovation and growth, a company must maintain "a free-market environment for every individual in the company," wherein "each employee is exposed to the risk and rewards of the market ... [and is] primarily responsible for using his abilities and for his own success or failure." The best way to encourage such entrepreneurial commitment is to break a company into small, autonomous "profit center" teams.

"Within each small, close-to-its-market business unit," Swiggett wrote, "each person can accurately assess the contributions of the other team members. Each can feel like a partner. Each can feel he contributes, and feel confident that his contribution will be recognized. . . . Each feels responsible. Each individual is every other's judge."

*   *   *

Swiggett traces the origins of his faith back to a day in 1967 when he stood on the edge of the production floor and watched some of his company's 500 employees moving through the complex patterns of their individual enterprise. The company's name was Photocircuits Corp.—it later merged with Kollmorgen—and it was a model of traditional, rational management. Indeed, there were more than 1,000 open orders out there on the floor, each one with a different set of manufacturing requirements, often fifty process steps long, and each one passing through ten or fifteen different departments. "It was a classic case of confusion," Swiggett recalls. "Later, when we began to analyze what it took to get an order through the shop, [we realized] we were lucky ever to ship anything."

Photocircuit's primary business was the manufacture of printed circuit boards. The company had, in fact, pioneered the field, which in turn had revolutionized electronics-assembly technology.

From 1957 to 1967, Photocircuits nourished an intense effort to diversify the business and overwhelm the competition. "We couldn't deal with competition," Swiggett says. "We wanted to have something the other guys didn't have." Routinely spending 10% of sales on research and development, the company accelerated its chemical-engineering research and established a product-development operation. By 1967, it had come up with a number of new technologies that promised substantial additions to the company's $10-million sales base.

Perhaps it was this flurry of activity that obscured the subterranean rumblings of approaching disaster. In any case, when Swiggett finally heard them on that day in 1967, it was nearly too late. Somehow Photocircuits had trapped itself in a paradox of self-defeating success. "Rarely did we meet promised deliveries," Swiggett recalls. "Quality problems were enormous, profit performance was erratic; morale was poor. Production managers burned out quickly. Functional departments fought with one another. Only the rapid growth of the market and the even more disorganized condition of our large competitors sustained us."

Such difficulties, typically dismissed as "growing pains," are not uncommon in young companies. Swiggett sensed, however, that Photocircuits's problem was at once small and prosaic, yet cosmic and mystifying, with implications far larger than the company's size. He was like a man who in simply asking for the correct time had, in turn, been posed a question that involved determining the correct relationships between the earth, the sun, and all the planets.

The prevailing Ptolemaic view of management theory saw its universe as quantitative, analytical, coolly objective, and unerringly precise. It held that systems could be devised that, once fueled with enough numbers and hard facts, could transform any given company to harmony and order. The system, flawlessly rational and detached, was even immune to the unpredictable and irksome frailties of the employees who served it. People, in the celestial mechanics of this view, revolved around the system.

Jim Swiggett (Bob's brother), then vice-president of manufacturing and production, was put in charge of development System 70, a customized method of scheduling and management that was to produce daily departmental scheduling by 1970. The project was successfully completed in late 1969 at a cost of around $500,000. Then it bombed. "Statistically, we got everything we wanted," Bob Swiggett says. "We could spit out printouts that would cover the wall in about fifteen minutes. The computer worked beautifully, but company performance, if anything, got worse. Foremen were preoccupied with printouts instead of people. Managers spent time worrying about internal systems instead of our customers. People couldn't relate to those printouts, and they resented the control."

The failure of System 70 triggered Jim Swiggett's survival instinct. Time after time, Jim traced back over his experiences, searching for a solution to the company's dilemma, and time after time, he paused at the idea of small, dedicated teams, an idea he called "team manufacturing." He began to see it as something more than a temporary expediency. Meanwhile, the recession of 1970 had made cost-cutting imperative, and that meant either eliminating crucial R&D projects or junking System 70, the shibboleth of modern management. But if System 70 died violently, what would take its place?

These were weighty matters indeed, so Jim packed his bags and went to Harvard University's Graduate School of Business Administration to consult "the world's leading guy on production control," whose name is now shrouded in the mists of time. "I must have talked for quite a while," Jim says, "but he was very patient. Then he said, "Here you are in the modern age, with computers, control theory, and you've just spent two hours telling me how you want to abdicate your responsibilities. Forget this team manufacturing you've got lurking in the back of your mind and go with what you're doing. You're doing it absolutely right.""

* * *

While Jim was off to see the guru, Bob was home signing the final papers on the merger of Photocircuits and Kollmorgen. As if the crash of System 70 and a recession weren't enough to worry about, Photocircuits needed outside capital to support its growth. Bob had consulted with investment bankers who told him that Photocircuits would be worth $9 million in a public offering. Shortly thereafter, his old friend Dick Rachals, the president of Kollmorgen, telephoned him with an offer. . . . In February 1970, the merger was completed.

"There we were," Bob Swiggett says, "newly merged at a great price, and naturally we wanted to look good. So you can imagine the chaos when Jim came back from Harvard saying, 'The hell with it. We're going to throw out System 70. We're going to throw out the whole thing.' "

To Bob and many of his colleagues, especially those who had worked on System 70, Jim's intuitive leap to team manufacturing was actually a stunning setback. "To give up modern management technology for something simpler," Bob says, "to throw that out meant to all of us at that time that we were giving up on another pioneering effort, and we didn't want to ever give up." But within six months, Photocircuits doubled its output per employee, and its on-time delivery rate rose from 60% to more than 90%. "In the middle of a depression," Bob says, "what could've been a disaster turned into a real good money-maker. So we really had it burned into our souls that small teams can be terribly effective."

As soon as the decision was made, Jim Swiggett went to work on what Bob describes as "a chaos of empire shattering." Using the Proto department as a model, Jim and his wrecking crew first broke up the company into some half dozen teams, each with an average of seventy-five people, and differentiated them by product line, market segment, or customer group. A manager was chosen to lead each team and was given responsibility for the team's profits, losses, and balance sheet. Then they threw out the standard cost system and eliminated most functional manufacturing and overhead departments, including customer service, order processing, production control, and quality control, all of which were turned over to the teams. Every manager was expected to deal directly with customers or field salespeople, set prices, bargain with other product managers for machine time and overhead allocation, and take monthly physical inventories in person.

"In spite of the yelling, almost magically everything improved," Bob Swiggett once said in a speech. "Customers were happier, pricing was better, profits rose, inventories turned faster, troublesome book-to-physical-inventory variance surprises disappeared. Morale rose with the evidence of success."

Today, this grand process is known throughout the company by the unfortunate term "productization." It is regarded as a powerful, but generally neglected, elixir that can make sick companies well and dullards into champions of innovation and growth.

The discovery of productization's curative powers occurred none too soon: Shortly after the Photocircuits merger and resurrection, Kollmorgen itself took sick. In 1971, the company recorded an operating loss, as its eight divisions went about reenacting the confusion Swiggett had observed once before from the edge of the production floor at Photocircuits. These problems were exacerbated by conflicting management styles among the three men who occupied the "president's office." "Dick Rachals was an intellectual," says Swiggett, "a solid engineer, not a great people-motivator, but very logical; Norman Macbeth, the flamboyant sales deal maker; and John Maxwell, a quiet man with a great sense of justice and order. I loved them all, but they really didn't get along so well, and they were all so polite that they really didn't work their problems out." The three group vice-presidents, of which Swiggett was one, were also squabbling over style. He himself stood for "team manufacturing, openness, small profit-centers, and bonus-sharing," while the others fought for "strong line control and no communication other than by the chain of command. [Their attitude was] don't come to see my divisions unless I'm there."

"We had more guys in management then than we do now, and we were only doing $40 million in business," says Allan Doyle, Kollmorgen's vice-chairman and chief financial officer. "It all had to get sorted out."

"The time had come," Swiggett adds, "for Kollmorgen to achieve some type of corporate consciousness. We had to answer basic questions like, What do we want to do? What do we want to become? and How do we relate to the divisions?"

In late spring of 1972, all of Kollmorgen's corporate officers convened for a weekend of deliberation at The Old Tavern, in Grafton, Vermont. The discussions were, to say the least, vigorous. After the Saturday dinner meeting, Bob Swiggett was fired in a fit of pique for disloyalty. "I simply said that I felt Dick, Norman, and John weren't clear on what they were trying to do," he says, "that they were thrashing around and were frequently counterproductive." Later that day, Swiggett was rehired when the principals reviewed his presumed transgression and found it more an expression of vital concern than disloyalty. He was invited to try his luck with Kollmorgen's difficulties, a move soon seen by the two other group vice-presidents as adequate grounds for their resignations. "By 1973," Swiggett says, "we had a clean slate. I'd read the literature, and I was telling a pretty good story. It fit together theoretically and pragmatically because it worked."

Swiggett was no longer a neophyte; he was by now a seasoned practitioner, as well as a serious student of a new, essentially self-taught management art. He set about reorganizing Kollmorgen's eight divisions as if each were a small Photocircuits in need of productization. Henceforth, they would stand free, with no centralized manufacturing and overhead departments to rely on. Every division, he said, must be an "autonomous profit-center," and he meant "autonomous" in the sense of being strong enough to go public. Next, Swiggett pushed the same responsibility as far down into the divisions as he could by creating small profit-center teams arranged by product, process, market, customer, contract, or whatever logical method presented itself.

Swiggett had created the teams, now he needed the game itself. At Kollmorgen today, that game is known as "vision," which, by definition, refers to something extraordinary. . . . In a series of meetings, the corporate officers committed themselves to superior performance in three areas: innovation, growth, and profitability.

There was also a commitment to freedom and respect for the individual at work, a commitment that was later given form in the so-called partners statement, built word-by-word by twenty corporate officers and division presidents huddled for three days in a hotel in Stamford, Connecticut. That statement reads: "The purpose of the partnership is to fulfill its responsibility to Kollmorgen shareholders and employees by creating and supporting an organization of strong and vital business divisions where a spirit of freedom, equality, mutual trust, respect, and even love prevails, and whose members strive together toward an exciting vision of economic, technical, and social greatness."

Together, the technological goals, the financial goals, and the partners' statement constitute the Kollmorgen "vision." Having thus defined the game and set up the teams, Swiggett and his colleagues went on to find a way of keeping score, a ballpark, and some rules of good sportsmanship—or, respectively, a bonus plan, an organizational structure, and a corporate culture.

Swiggett wanted each division to struggle in the free-market arena. he also needed a method for making sure that the financial goals of the divisions conformed to those of Kollmorgen as a whole, without sacrificing divisional autonomy and a vigorous spirit of individual self-interest. What he came up with was "RONA," for "return on net assets," in which "net assets" are defined as the sum of receivables, inventories, and net fixed assets, minus payables.

As the basis for a new bonus plan, RONA also gave individuals a handy way of keeping score. If a division has a good year, even its least skilled workers can gain an additional 15% to 20% of their gross annual salaries. And indeed, the RONA plan quickly proved to be a powerful motivator. It was introduced throughout the company in the first quarter of 1975; six months later, receivables and inventories had been reduced by $11 million. "When people started thinking about an asset," Swiggett says, "they found they had five years worth of drills, five years worth of sheet metal, five years worth of everything. We practically didn't buy a thing for six months after putting in the bonus plan, and we ran the business beautifully."

Kollmorgen also needed an organizational structure that would ensure divisional autonomy, yet allow for coordination at the corporate level. After some experimentation, Swiggett and his colleagues hit on an ingenious solution: Every division president would communicate quarterly with his own board of directors. Each board of directors would generally be composed of three corporate officers, two other division presidents, and a senior technical person from another division. The boards would offer guidance and suggestions but never commands. "After all, what's the role of a leader?" Swiggett asks rhetorically. "It's to create a vision, not to kick somebody in the ass. The role of a leader is the servant's role. It's supporting his people, running interference for them. It's coming out with an atmosphere of understanding and trust and love. You want people to feel they have complete control over their own destiny at every level. Tyranny is not tolerated here. People who want to manage in the traditional sense are cast off by their peers like dandruff."

In addition to the divisional boards of directors, Swiggett and friends also designed a forum, similar in spirit, to review each division's actual operating results and projections. Now, once a month, every profit-center team gives its division president a financial statement detailing its operating results for the past several quarters and projecting results twelve months out. These are then sent to corporate headquarters for consolidation, along with a statement from the division president reflecting the operating results of the division as a whole.

*   *   *

At some final and irreducible level, culture appears to rest on an act of faith in which individuals experience the company's vision in very personal terms. They are not "sold" on the vision; they commit themselves to it voluntarily because they perceive it as essential in shaping the meaning and significance of their own lives. Culture, then, is created every day as employees give life to the values of their shared belief. Management cannot control, nor even ensure, the moment of its flowering, but it can prepare the soil.

Swiggett himself goes to extraordinary lengths to foster the Kollmorgen culture. Twelve times a year, he leads so-called Kolture Workshops, designed to "keep the fires burning and spread them broadly." These workshops are either one or three days long and include from 35 to 100 people. At the three-day session, Swiggett reviews the history of Kollmorgen and, using a relaxed, Socratic method, examines the philosophical issues that inform the company's culture. "Do you think this philosophy can work in a corporation?" he asks. "Do you think it can work at Kollmorgen? Is it working now? How can we improve it?"

Through the Kolture Workshops, the company articulates its vision, over and over and over. At the least, the process bears witness to the potential of that vision; at best, it becomes part of a self-fulfilling prophecy. "Actually, it's very simple," Swiggett says. "We preach trust and the Golden Rule, and we're very careful that what we do is the same thing as what we say."

Accordingly, there are no time clocks at Kollmorgen, no policy or operations manuals, no information monopolies, no cafeterias closed during breaks. All such things, according to Swiggett, are "signals" that belie lofty rhetoric, and employees read them unerringly. "Once we had a rule book," Skip Griggs says, "that said you get three days off if your mommy or daddy dies, but if your neighbor, whom you've known for thirty-five years, dies, you get no time off. We threw it out."

If you want openness and trust, Swiggett urges, then you have to act openly and with trust, every day. Thus, every division president sees the monthly financial statements prepared by every other division president. And the employees are similarly kept informed at monthly meetings that cover the company's progress, as well as the division's specific performance and its effect on the RONA bonus.

Fred Paris, 45, a maintenance man at Industrial Drives, describes his feelings this way: "This is the best job I've ever had. A lot of people won't realize how good it is unless they've had a chance to work somewhere else. We're like a family here. In December, when our people were laid off, we all pitched in and promised ourselves that we would get all those people back as soon as possible. And we did it." Indeed, recalls began as soon as business turned around during the second quarter of 1983. By July, everyone who had been laid off was back at work.

"There's a lot of sin out there in the world," Swiggett says. "People lie, they cheat, they steal, they rip off your car radio. You don't have to set up your business like it is in the outside world. You want people to feel as free from threat as they do in their own bedrooms. We just assume that everybody's honest, and we run the business that way. And people rise to this. But the devil's out there, and he's always whispering in the ear of some manager, 'Hey, you've got to control these suckers or they'll run away from you.' So we can't even give away the secret of our success, because most people think it's crap."

But not everybody thinks so, as Skip Griggs can attest. On that day in 1980 when he finished reading the Kollmorgen Philosophy, he went straight home and asked his wife, Sue, to read it. He waited impatiently as she turned the pages. "What do you think?" he asked.

"It's okay," Sue said.

"Just 'okay'?" Griggs demanded.

"Well," Sue asked, "aren't all companies run this way?"

Questions

1. Which management concepts described in this chapter are used at Kollmorgen? Would Kollmorgen be considered an example of an excellent firm? Of a firm that uses enlightened human resource practices? Discuss.

2. Do characteristics of the technology, environment, or top leaders at Kollmorgen facilitate the adoption of its management style? Do you think this approach to management could be applied to every organization? Discuss why or why not.

NOTES

1. J. Vettner, "Bowling for Dollars," *Forbes,* September 12, 1983, p. 138; "A Slimmed-Down Brunswick Is Proving Wall Street Wrong," *Business Week,* May 28, 1984, pp. 90–98.

2. Paul R. Lawrence and Davis Dyer, *Renewing American Industry* (New York: The Free Press, 1983).

3. William G. Ouchi, *Theory Z: How American Business Can Meet the Japanese Challenge* (Reading, Ma: Addison-Wesley, 1981); Richard Pascale and Anthony Athos, *The Art of Japanese Management* (New York: Warner Books, 1981); Thomas J. Peters and Robert H. Waterman, Jr., *In Search of Excellence* (New York: Harper & Row,

1982); Andrew H. Van de Ven, "Central Problems in the Management of Innovation," *Management Science,* 32, (1986): in press.

4. Richard L. Daft and Karl E. Weick, "Toward a Model of Organizations As Interpretation Systems," *Academy of Management Review,* 9 (1984):284–295.

5. Robert B. Duncan and A. Weiss, "Organizational Learning: Implications for Organizational Design," in Barry Staw, ed., *Research in Organizational Behavior,* vol. 1 (Greenwich, CT: JAI Press, 1979), pp. 75–123.

6. Chris Argyris and Donald A. Schon, *Organizational Learning: A Theory of Action Perspective* (Reading, MA: Addison-Wesley, 1978); Bo Hedberg, "How Organizations Learn and Unlearn," in Paul Nystrom and William Starbuck, eds., *Handbook of Organizational Design,* vol. 1 (New York: Oxford University Press, 1981), pp. 1–27.

7. Argyris and Schon, *Organizational Learning;* Paul Shrivastava, "A Typology of Organizational Learning Systems," *Journal of Management Studies,* 20 (1983):7–28.

8. Lawrence and Dyer, *Renewing American Industry.*

9. William K. Hall, "Survival Strategies in a Hostile Environment," *Harvard Business Review* (September–October, 1980): 75–85.

10. Adapted from Jill Bettner with Lisa Gross, "Planting Deep and Wide at John Deere," *Forbes,* March 14, 1983, pp. 119–122.

11. George P. Huber, "The Nature and Design of Post-Industrial Organizations," *Management Science,* 30 (1984):928–951.

12. This discussion is based on Lawrence and Dyer, *Renewing American Industry.*

13. Van de Ven, "Central Problems in the Management of Innovations."

14. "TI: Shot Full of Holes and Trying to Recover," *Business Week,* November 5, 1984, pp. 82–83; "Texas Instruments Cleans up Its Act," *Business Week,* September 19, 1983; pp. 56–64; "An About-Face in TI's Culture," *Business Week,* July 5, 1982, p. 77.

15. Ouchi, *Theory Z,* Pascale and Athos, *The Art of Japanese Management.*

16. William G. Ouchi and Alfred M. Jaeger, "Type Z Organizations: Stability in the Midst of Mobility," *Academy of Management Review,* 3 (1978):305–314.

17. Ibid.

18. James Cook, "We Started From Ground Zero," *Forbes,* March 12, 1984, pp. 98–106.

19. Ibid., 104.

20. Ouchi and Jaeger, "Type Z Organizations."

21. Jeremy Main, "Westinghouse's Cultural Revolution," *Fortune,* June 15, 1981, p. 76.

22. This case was drawn from Main, "Westinghouse's Cultural Revolution," pp. 74–93; "Operation Turnaround," *Business Week,* December 5, 1983, pp. 124–133; and Bruce A. Jacobs, "Does Westinghouse Have the Productivity Answer," *Industry Week,* 208 (1981), pp. 95–98.

23. Peters and Waterman, *In Search of Excellence.*

24. Modesto A. Maidique and Robert H. Hayes, "The Art of High-Technology Management," *Sloan Management Review,* 25 (1984):17–31; Bo L. T. Hedberg, Paul C. Nystrom, and William H. Starbuck, "Camping on Seesaws: Prescriptions for a Self-Designing Organization," *Administrative Science Quarterly,* 21 (1976):41–65; John Banaszewski, "Thirteen Ways to Get a Company in Trouble," *Inc.,* September 1981, pp. 97–100.

25. Tom Peters, "An Excellent Question," *Inc.,* December 1984, pp. 155–162.

26. Hedberg, et al., "Camping on Seesaws."

27. David K. Hurst, "Of Boxes, Bubbles, and Effective Management," *Harvard Business Review* (May–June 1984):78–88.

28. "Delta: The World's Most Profitable Airline," *Business Week,* August 31, 1981, pp. 68–71; Peters and Waterman, *In Search of Excellence;* Don Aldrich and Mary Filpus-Luyckx, "Delta Airlines: A Company Analysis," unpublished manuscript, Texas A&M University, 1983.

29. Allen C. Bluedorn, "The Teaching of Organization Theory: A Report on the Survey of the Management/Organization Theory Division of the Academy of Management," paper presented at the National Academy of Management Meetings, San Diego, CA, August, 1981.

30. Richard L. Daft, "The Evolution of Organizational Analysis in *ASQ:* 1959–1979," *Administrative Science Quarterly,* 25 (1980):623–636.

31. Ibid.

Name Index

Subject Index